Library of America, a nonprofit organization,
champions our nation's cultural heritage
by publishing America's greatest writing in
authoritative new editions and providing resources
for readers to explore this rich, living legacy.

JIM CROW

Jim Crow

VOICES FROM A CENTURY OF STRUGGLE

Part One: 1876–1919
Reconstruction to the Red Summer

Tyina L. Steptoe, *editor*

THE LIBRARY OF AMERICA

JIM CROW: VOICES FROM A CENTURY OF STRUGGLE
PART ONE: 1876–1919
Volume compilation, introduction, and backmatter copyright © 2024 by
Literary Classics of the United States, Inc., New York, N.Y.
All rights reserved.
No part of this book may be reproduced in any manner whatsoever without
the permission of the publisher, except in the case of brief
quotations embodied in critical articles and reviews.

Published in the United States by Library of America.
Visit our website at www.loa.org.

Some of the material in this volume is reprinted by permission of the
holders of copyright and publication rights. Every effort has been made to
contact the copyright holders. If an owner has been unintentionally omitted,
acknowledgment will gladly be made in future printings.
See the Note on the Texts for further information.

This paper exceeds the requirements of
ANSI/NISO Z39.48–1992 (Permanence of Paper).

Distributed to the trade in the United States
by Penguin Random House Inc.
and in Canada by Penguin Random House Canada Ltd.

Library of Congress Control Number: 2023938933
ISBN 978–1–59853–766–6

First Printing
The Library of America—376

Manufactured in the United States of America

Jim Crow:
Voices from a Century of Struggle
is published and kept in print with support from

THE BERKLEY FAMILY FOUNDATION

and

ELIZABETH W. SMITH

Contents

Introduction by Tyina L. Steptoe xix

1876–1896

Frederick Douglass: Speech to the Republican National
Convention, June 14, 1876
Protecting the Black Vote in the South. 3

Denver Daily Tribune: "A Threatening Power,"
January 12, 1877
A Republican Newspaper Mocks Democratic Fears 6

St. Louis Globe Democrat: The Future of the Negro,
April 27, 1877
"The new order of things" 8

National Colored Colonization Society: Address to
Rutherford B. Hayes, September 15, 1877
"A worse state of slavery" 11

Hester Hickman: The Land That Gives Birth to Freedom,
1877; Extending Our Voices to Heaven
A Song of the Black Exodus 14

The New York Times: New Homes for Freedmen,
January 23, 1879
"A territory for colored men" 16

The Chicago Tribune: The Debtor South, May 13, 1879
Sharecropping in Louisiana and Mississippi 19

Benjamin Singleton: from Testimony to the Senate Select
Committee, April 17, 1880
"The father of the exodus" 28

Stephen Field: Opinion in *Pace v. Alabama*,
January 29, 1883
Upholding Anti-Miscegenation Laws 40

John Marshall Harlan: Dissenting Opinion in *Civil Rights
Cases*, October 15, 1883
"Universal freedom in this country". 43

New York Globe: The Civil Rights Decision,
  October 20, 1883
  "Aliens in our native land"   78

Nathaniel S. Shaler: The Negro Problem, November 1884
  "The real dangers that this African blood brings"   80

George Washington Cable: The Freedman's Case in Equity,
  January 1885
  "The outrageousness of these tyrannies". 101

Thomas Miller: Speech in Congress on the Elections Bill,
  January 12, 1891
  The Need for a Federal Elections Law 124

Ida B. Wells: *Southern Horrors: Lynch Law in All Its Phases*,
  1892
  A Crusade for Justice Begins 128

Frederick Douglass: from *The Reason Why the Colored
  American is not in the World's Columbian Exposition*, 1893
  The Enduring Impact of Slavery 154

Ida B. Wells: from *The Reason Why the Colored
  American is not in the World's Columbian Exposition*, 1893
  Class Legislation and the Convict Lease System 164

Richard T. Greener: The White Problem, May 1894
  "The so-called 'Caucasian' intellect" 175

Ida B. Wells: from *A Red Record*, 1895
  Examining Excuses for Lynching 188

Booker T. Washington: Address at the Atlanta Exposition,
  September 18, 1895
  "As separate as the fingers" 197

Clark Howell: To the Editor of *The World*,
  September 19, 1895
  A Southern Newspaper Editor Praises Washington 202

Republican Members of the South Carolina Convention:
  To the Editor of *The World*, September 30, 1895
  Defending Black Suffrage 204

Grover Cleveland: To Booker T. Washington,
  October 6, 1895
  Praise from the President. 207

Robert Smalls: from Speech in the South Carolina
   Convention, October 26, 1895
Arguing Against Disenfranchisement 208

Albion W. Tourgée: Brief for the Plaintiff in *Plessy v.
   Ferguson*, c. 1895
The Unconstitutionality of Railroad Segregation 214

Henry B. Brown: Opinion in *Plessy v. Ferguson*,
   May 18, 1896
Upholding "equal but separate" Accommodations 250

John Marshall Harlan: Dissenting Opinion in
   Plessy v. Ferguson, May 18, 1896
"The wrong this day done" 262

1897–1909

The Washington Evening Star: Negro Emigration,
   October 21, 1897
An Interview with Bishop Henry McNeal Turner 277

The Wilmington Morning Star: Mrs. Felton Speaks,
   August 18, 1898
A White Southern Woman Defends Lynching 280

The Wilmington Morning Star: A Horrid Slander,
   August 30, 1898
A Black Editor Responds to Rebecca Felton 282

The Raleigh News and Observer: Defamer Must Go,
   November 10, 1898
Inciting the Wilmington Insurrection 286

W. H. Councill: The Future of the Negro, July 1899
"The terrible, stern reality of the situation" 290

The New Orleans Daily Picayune: To Protect the City;
   End of a Desperado, July 28, 1900
The Deadly Manhunt for Robert Charles 299

The Richmond Planet: The Butchery at New Orleans;
   With a Rifle in His Hand, August 4, 1900
Praising Robert Charles: "Bold and defiant to the last" 302

The Navasota Daily Examiner: Campaign Oratory,
   September 29, 1900
The White Man's Union Holds a Rally 306

George H. White: Speech in Congress in Defense of the
    Negro Race, January 29, 1901
A Black Congressman's Valedictory Address 309

The Independent: The Negro Problem: How It Appeals
    to a Southern Colored Woman, September 18, 1902
"Why are we forgotten?" 328

Benjamin R. Tillman: from Speech in the Senate on the
    Race Problem, February 24, 1903
Advocating White Supremacy 336

The Joplin Daily Globe: Murderer of Leslie Lynched by
    Angry Mob, April 16, 1903
The Lynching of Thomas Gilyard 380

W.E.B. Du Bois: Of Mr. Booker T. Washington and Others,
    1903
Criticizing Washington's Leadership 391

Charles W. Chesnutt: The Disfranchisement of the Negro,
    1903
The Nullification of the Fifteenth Amendment 404

Charles Brantley Aycock: from Speech to the North Carolina
    Society, December 18, 1903
A Southern Governor Celebrates Disfranchisement 424

William Monroe Trotter to W.E.B. Du Bois, March 26, 1905
Challenging Washington's Leadership. 426

Aida Overton Walker: Colored Men and Women on the
    Stage, October 1905
A Black Vaudeville Star Speaks 428

Mary Church Terrell: What It Means to Be Colored in the
    Capital of the United States, October 10, 1906
Segregation in Washington, D.C. 433

The New York Times: Negro Pastors Assail Roosevelt's Army
    Order, November 19, 1906
Protesting the Brownsville Dismissals 443

Mary Church Terrell: Peonage in the United States:
    The Convict Lease System and the Chain Gangs,
    August 1907
"Violation of the thirteenth amendment" 446

Sally Nash: Interview about Life in Rentiesville, Oklahoma,
1903–08, June 22, 1937
Remembering a Black Town in the Southwest 468

San Pedro Daily News: The Candidates and the Negro,
October 14, 1908
Rallying the Black Vote for the Republicans 470

The New York Evening Post: Conference on Negroes,
February 13, 1909
"The renewal of the struggle for civil and political liberty". . . . 472

Platform Adopted by the National Negro Committee,
June 1, 1909
Founding the NAACP 476

1909–1919

Hanford Daily Journal: Lynching Bees in Present Year
Numerous, December 17, 1909
Seventy Victims of Mob Violence 481

Los Angeles Times: The Fight and Its Consequences,
July 6, 1910
The Johnson-Jeffries Fight. 485

William Pickens: Talladega College Professor Speaks on
Reno Fight, July 30, 1910
Celebrating Jack Johnson's Victory 488

Lester A. Walton: Concert at Carnegie Hall, May 9, 1912
James Reese Europe and the Clef Club 492

The Austin Daily Statesman: Negroes to Gather Here by
Thousands, May 20, 1912
Celebrating Juneteenth 496

Moorfield Storey, W.E.B. Du Bois, Oswald Garrison Villard
to Woodrow Wilson, August 15, 1913
Protesting the Segregation of Federal Workers 498

William Monroe Trotter: Address to Woodrow Wilson,
November 12, 1914
"A gratuitous blow against ever-loyal citizens" 501

Woodrow Wilson and William Monroe Trotter:
An Exchange, November 12, 1914
A White House Confrontation 505

Provisional Directorate of the Revolutionary Plan: The Plan
   of San Diego, January 6, 1915
   Plotting the Overthrow of "Yankee tyranny" 514

Francis Hackett: Brotherly Love, March 20, 1915
   Reviewing The Birth of a Nation: *"vicious and
   defamatory"* 518

Outlook: The Birth of a Nation, April 14, 1915
   "An exaltation of race war" 522

W.E.B. Du Bois: "We Should Worry," June 1917
   Wartime Opportunities. 524

The New York Times: Mob of 3,000 Rules in East St. Louis,
   May 29, 1917
   Mob Attacks on Black Workers 526

Carlos F. Hurd: Post-Dispatch Man, An Eye-Witness,
   Describes Massacre of Negroes, July 3, 1917
   A Deadly Riot in East St. Louis. 527

John Pero: from Testimony to the House Select Committee,
   October 24, 1917
   Racial Tensions in East St. Louis 535

James Weldon Johnson: An Army with Banners,
   August 2, 1917
   A Silent March in New York City 541

Ralph Van Deman: Army Intelligence Memorandum on
   William Monroe Trotter, October 2, 1917
   Watching a "Radical colored man" 543

Martha Gruening: Houston: An N.A.A.C.P. Investigation,
   November 1917
   A Rebellion by Black Soldiers. 544

The Chicago Defender: Migration and Its Effect,
   April 20, 1918
   The Great Migration North 555

Leonidas C. Dyer: Speech in Congress on the
   Anti-Lynching Bill, May 7, 1918
   The Constitutionality of a Federal Law 557

W.E.B. Du Bois: Close Ranks, July 1918
   "The crisis of the world". 568

Cyril Briggs: The American Race Problem,
  September–December 1918
  "Hatred of the unlike" 569

The Right-About: Hell-Fighters Cheered on Homecoming,
  February 19, 1919
  A Black Regiment Returns from France. 579

W.E.B. Du Bois: Returning Soldiers, May 1919
  "This country . . . is yet a shameful land" 582

Jeannette Carter: Negroes of Washington Were Forced to
  Protect Themselves, August 2, 1919
  "Striking terror into . . . the white mob" 584

James E. Scott: Statement on Attack by Rioters in
  Washington, D.C., August 4, 1919
  "Lynch him" 587

Martina Simms: Washington Riot, August 15, 1919
  "They will fight" 588

The Chicago Daily Tribune: Report Two Killed, Fifty Hurt,
  in Race Riots, July 28, 1919
  A City Erupts. 589

The Chicago Daily Tribune: Negroes Call on Mayor,
  Lowden, to Stop Riots, July 31, 1919
  "The Causes and Cure" for the Riot 595

A. Philip Randolph: Our Reason for Being, August 1919
  A Program for "Negro labor radicalism" 599

Marcus Garvey: Speech in New York City, August 25, 1919
  "For a free and independent race"..................... 604

W. A. Domingo and Claude McKay: If We Must Die,
  September 1919
  "The New Negro has arrived" 616

Chronology.. 621
Note on the Texts 632
Notes.. 641
Index.. 701

Introduction

BY TYINA L. STEPTOE

FREDERICK DOUGLASS first encountered Jim Crow at the age of twenty-three. The young agent for the Massachusetts Anti-Slavery Society was traveling for business when he boarded a car on the Eastern Railroad in Massachusetts on a late summer day. On September 8, 1841, Douglass and John Collins, a white abolitionist, were on their way to an antislavery meeting in New Hampshire, but the train conductor interrupted their plans.

Spying the interracial pair seated together, the conductor ordered the men to separate. After Douglass refused to leave the first-class car, half a dozen white men dragged him to the second-class car set aside for Black passengers. His encounters with the color line convinced Douglass, who had escaped enslavement in Maryland only three years earlier, that racism was not merely a southern phenomenon. "Prejudice against color is stronger north than south; it hangs around my neck like a heavy weight," he told a Massachusetts audience the next month.[1]

The experiences of Frederick Douglass and John Collins in antebellum New England defy most temporal and spatial understandings of the history of segregation in the United States. In the popular imagination, "Jim Crow" began in the post–Civil War South when white Democrats passed laws to segregate and disenfranchise Black southerners. But the origins of Jim Crow reveal a more complicated history, one that begins in the antebellum North, not the postbellum South. In the earliest days of train travel, many railroad lines in the Northeast relegated Black passengers to separate cars as a matter of company policy. In parts of Massachusetts, locals already referred to those segregated public accommodations as "Jim Crow cars" by the late 1830s.

By that point, New Englanders—like many other Americans—had encountered the character called "Jim Crow" through blackface minstrelsy, an increasingly popular form of entertainment. Credited as the "originator" of the form, Thomas

Dartmouth "Daddy" Rice performed in blackface for the first time in Pittsburgh around 1830. Writer Robert P. Nevin reported in *The Atlantic Monthly* that Rice's inspiration came from a "negro stage-driver" singing on the streets of Cincinnati. Nevin transcribed the song that caught Rice's attention:

"Turn about an' wheel about an' do jis so,
 An' ebery time I turn about I jump Jim Crow."²

The encounter reportedly inspired Rice to create the minstrel character Jim Crow. His routines depicted Jim Crow as happy and content in the plantation South, which implied that the institution of slavery was "amusing, right, and natural."³

The origin story of Jim Crow demonstrates how the intertwined cultural, social, and political understandings of race helped produce a segregated nation. Because of the popularity of minstrelsy, white Americans associated the phrase "Jim Crow" with the most debased stereotypes of blackness. They applied those ideas to the practice of racial segregation, first in the North before the Civil War and then the South and West in the late nineteenth century.

This volume chronicles the history of "the color line" through contemporary writing by participants and observers. Those written artifacts include evidence from politicians who drafted or supported the myriad federal, state, and local laws and policies that segregated public spaces and disenfranchised Black voters, as well as the courts that upheld the constitutionality of those laws. Primary documents also demonstrate the ways white supremacists enforced racial hierarchies of white over Black without the use of state-sanctioned laws, through tactics like racial violence and cultural representations that denigrated people of African descent. Contemporary writing in this volume depicts the dynamic ways diverse Americans challenged segregation and racial terror in every part of the United States—North, South, East, and West. Spanning the end of Reconstruction through the Great Migration, this volume offers representations of the political, economic, social, and cultural realities of life in Jim Crow America from 1877 to 1919.

On a Saturday afternoon in September 1883, a twenty-one-year-old schoolteacher stepped onto a train in Tennessee clutching a first-class ticket. Originally from Holly Springs, Mississippi, Ida B. Wells had moved to Memphis in 1881 when she was nineteen years old. She was traveling on the Chesapeake, Ohio & Southwestern Railroad between Memphis and Woodstock, a town ten miles away in Shelby County where she taught school. Wells purchased a ticket and took a seat in the rear first-class car, the so-called ladies' coach, because smoking and the use of "vulgar" language were prohibited there. After the train left the station, the conductor ordered her to move to the forward coach because the ladies' coach was reserved for white passengers.

The Tennessee legislature had passed a law in 1875 allowing railroad companies to racially segregate passengers. In 1881 the four Black members of the state assembly tried unsuccessfully to repeal the law. Instead, the legislature passed a new law requiring railroads to provide Black first-class passengers with accommodations equal to those reserved for whites. That fall, activists in Nashville boarded ladies' cars during three days of protests, but the railroad companies avoided taking actions that could have led to a court challenge. Opponents of segregated rail travel argued that it violated one of the last statutes passed by Republicans during Reconstruction, the Civil Rights Act of 1875, which entitled "citizens of every race and color, regardless of any previous condition of servitude," to access public transportation and accommodations.[4] In October 1883 the Supreme Court declared the law to be unconstitutional, ruling that the Fourteenth Amendment to the Constitution did not forbid racial discrimination by private businesses.

When the train conductor demanded that Ida B. Wells move to the coach designated for Black passengers in 1883, she ignored him. But the conductor tried to remove her by force. "He tried to drag me out of the seat," Wells later wrote in her autobiography, "but the moment he caught hold of my arm I fastened my teeth in the back of his hand."[5] Two white passengers rushed to help the conductor carry Wells from the rear coach. She refused to move, choosing instead to leave the train at the next stop. The white passengers cheered as the young schoolteacher departed the train. Wells took action, hiring a lawyer and suing the railroad company while writing about the incident in *Living Way*, a Black church weekly.

Wells fought against segregation as the nation moved toward what the historian Rayford W. Logan called "the nadir of the Negro's status in American society," which he framed as the "last decade of the nineteenth century and the opening of the twentieth century."[6] Worn down by violent resistance by former Confederates to Reconstruction policies, disillusioned by continuing political turmoil in the South, and alarmed by the Democratic resurgence in the North, many northern Republicans who had previously supported Black citizenship rights turned away from the struggle for racial equality even before the 1876 election. The withdrawal of federal troops protecting Republican state governments in Louisiana and South Carolina in 1877 followed several years of redeployment in which soldiers left the South and headed west to help expand white settlement in the western territories. Without the threat of federal intervention, white southern Democrats—"Redeemers"—worked to institute a postwar version of white supremacy, one that extolled pastoral visions of the antebellum South while pushing for industrialization and economic development. Their attention to business interests and white supremacy aligned as they first targeted railroads with statutes that required "separate but equal" accommodations for Black and white passengers.

Southern Democrats designed these laws to enforce a hierarchy of white over Black in the spaces that both groups used, like public transportation. Segregation was more profitable than outright exclusion. Black southerners paid first-class prices for second-class accommodations. The relegation of Black customers to inferior spaces reminded them of their inferior status. "Segregation did not provide physical distance," writes the historian Blair L. M. Kelley, "rather, it reaffirmed social distance."[7] The sight of Black passengers in a smoking car provided a visual reminder of white supremacy.

The business of segregating the South and relegating Black Americans to second-class status was neither swift nor uncontested, as demonstrated by Ida B. Wells's lawsuit against the Chesapeake, Ohio & Southwestern Railroad. In December 1884 a circuit court judge in Memphis awarded her $500 in damages, ruling that because the railroad had failed to curtail smoking and drunkenness in the forward car (where white male passengers often rode along with Black men and women), it had failed to provide Wells with the accommodations required under the state's "separate but equal" law. The railroad appealed, and in 1887 the state supreme court reversed the lower court's ruling.

Other southern states soon went beyond the Tennessee legislation that permitted railroads to segregate their passengers. In 1888 the Mississippi legislature passed a law requiring railroads to provide "equal, but separate, accommodation for the white and colored races."[8] The Louisville, New Orleans and Texas Railway Company sued, arguing that the statute interfered with interstate commerce. In 1890 the U.S. Supreme Court upheld the law, ruling that it applied only to travel within the state. Encouraged by the court's decision, Louisiana enacted a Separate Car Act in July 1890.

In New Orleans, a group of prominent Creoles of Color organized a Comité des Citoyens (Citizens' Committee) to protest the law and arrange for a court case to test its constitutionality. In their first attempt to test the law, a Creole man named Daniel Desdunes was arrested on February 24, 1892, while traveling from New Orleans to Mobile, Alabama, in a first-class car. The New Orleans criminal court dismissed the case, however, because the Louisiana Supreme Court decided in a different case that the Separate Car Act only applied to intrastate travel. The committee then focused on a racially ambiguous twenty-nine-year-old shoemaker named Homer Plessy. On June 7, 1892, Plessy boarded an intrastate train in New Orleans and was arrested after he refused to move from the car reserved for whites. After the Louisiana Supreme Court upheld Plessy's conviction in December 1892, the Citizens' Committee's legal advisor, the former Union officer and civil rights activist Albion Tourgée, joined an appeal to the U.S. Supreme Court on the basis that the Separate Car Act violated the Fourteenth Amendment. The Supreme Court finally heard the case in the spring of 1896, deciding 7–1 to uphold the Louisiana law. The ruling established that "separate but equal" accommodations were constitutional. By permitting each state to decide "the proportion of colored blood necessary to constitute a colored person," the court also gave legal sanction to the so-called one drop rule that any degree of

African ancestry was sufficient to legally classify a person as Black.[9] In the aftermath of *Plessy*, Black southerners continued to mobilize against segregation on public transportation. A grassroots boycott movement against segregation on streetcars rippled throughout towns and cities in the South in the first decade of the twentieth century.

Black Republicans formed interracial coalitions that kept Black politicians in public offices across the South. In Virginia they joined the Readjuster Party, which dominated state politics from 1879 to 1883 by winning support from both Black and white voters, including many white farmers from the western part of the state who opposed the planter aristocracy of eastern Virginia. Black Republicans running on the Readjuster ticket were elected to local offices and the general assembly, where they helped eliminate the poll tax as a prerequisite for voting and abolish public whipping as a punishment for petty larceny. In North Carolina Black and white Republicans formed a successful electoral alliance with the white Populist Party in 1894. Although the two parties differed on many economic issues, the so-called Fusion was united by its opposition to the corrupt Democratic control of the state's election machinery. The Fusionists won a legislative majority in 1894 and elected a Republican governor two years later. Once in power, they reformed election laws, increased funding for education, helped debt-burdened farmers, and decentralized local government, giving Black men the opportunity to hold elective office in majority Black counties. And in rural Grimes County, located in eastern Texas, a coalition of Black and white Populists dominated local elections in 1896 and 1898.

These interracial coalitions had largely died by fire by the turn of the twentieth century, as white Democrats used racial terror to quell Black southerners' political, economic, and social aspirations. In the majority Black city of Danville, Virginia, a street altercation near a Democratic election rally in November 1883 led to a group of white men firing into a crowd, killing one white and four Black men. The Democrats then repossessed the city from its interracial government and defeated the Readjusters in the state legislative elections. Similar coups overthrew democratically elected local governments in other parts of the South. Articles in the white-owned press incited violence by depicting Black Americans in ways that sought to reinforce their subordinate status. In 1898 a Democratic newspaper in Wilmington, North Carolina, printed an inflammatory diatribe by Rebecca Felton, a prominent white reformer in Georgia, in which she marked Black men as rapists who deserved the wrath of white mobs. When Alexander Manly, the Black editor of the *Wilmington Daily Record*, challenged her portrayals of violent Black men in his newspaper, his defiant stance became fuel for the white supremacist election campaign against the state's Fusionist movement. In November 1898 the Democrats regained control of the legislature, and within days a white supremacist militia staged a deadly insurrection that ousted the elected government of Wilmington and forced Manly to flee for his life. And in Grimes County, Texas, the White Man's Union defeated the Populists in 1900 in an election campaign marked by murder and intimidation. They then held the county seat of Anderson under siege, killing political rivals and forcing the sheriff into exile.

As they fought interracial coalitions, white Democrats across the South ensured their continued domination by writing Black exclusion into law. In addition to legislation that segregated railroad travel, other statutes targeted social relations, such as restrictions on cohabitation between Black and white people. Of special importance were measures taken to permanently disenfranchise Black voters. To avoid violating the Fifteenth Amendment's prohibition against denying the vote on account of race, disenfranchisement laws erected barriers that ostensibly applied to both Black and white voters. From 1877 to 1902 all eleven former Confederate states made the payment of poll taxes a prerequisite for voting, and from 1890 to 1908 eight southern states made disenfranchisement part of their new or amended constitutions. Most of these states adopted literacy requirements along with loopholes designed to keep white voters from being disqualified. One provision, first used in the Mississippi constitution of 1890, was a clause permitting officials to register illiterate men if they understood passages from the state constitution when they were read aloud. Another loophole, first used in the Louisiana constitution of 1898, was the grandfather clause allowing men who were eligible voters on January 1, 1867, as well as their sons and grandsons, to register even if they failed the new literacy test. Eight southern states also adopted white primary laws from 1896 to 1906 that excluded Black voters from voting in Democratic Party primary elections. Together these measures drastically reduced the number of Black voters and eventually ensured the disappearance of Black elected officials for a generation. After George White departed the House of Representatives in March 1901, no Black elected official served in the U.S. Congress again until 1929.

The spread of legal segregation was a national phenomenon, reaching nearly every corner of the United States. In parts of the West, local ordinances barred Black and ethnic Mexican residents from parks and other public spaces. Black Americans even faced exclusion from many parts of the nation's capital. In 1913 President Woodrow Wilson condoned the segregation of Black and white federal employees in Washington, D.C., where they used separate government offices, restrooms, and cafeterias.

Segregation laws were only one way that white supremacists promoted a hierarchy of "white over Black." Labor exploitation left millions of Black southerners in a state of debt servitude, also known as peonage. Sharecroppers could claim only a fraction of the crops they cultivated, and even with a solid harvest, they still found themselves indebted to white landowners. Black women workers, largely confined to domestic labor, battled low wages, long hours, and the ever-present threat of sexual violence. Convict leasing further allowed white southerners to assert control over Black labor after the Civil War. Throughout the South, "People accused of property crime stood a greater chance of a conviction than those accused of other kinds of crimes and blacks and property crime were virtually synonymous in Southern courts from Reconstruction on."[10] The leasing of Black inmates became profitable for southern state governments and private companies, while creating an exploitative labor system that some deemed "worse than slavery."[11]

At the same time, violence fostered a climate of racial terror in the postbellum South. Riots, individual acts of aggression, brutality by law enforcement, and lynching targeted Black Americans who challenged white supremacy. The number of lynchings spiked after 1890, when white mobs created public spectacles often attended by thousands of people who gathered without fear of government intervention. The Tuskegee Institute in Alabama defined lynching as an illegal killing committed by a group of three or more persons "acting under the pretext of service to justice, race, or tradition." According to the institute, lynch mobs killed approximately three thousand Black Americans, almost all of them in the South, from 1882 to 1919—an average of three persons every two weeks.

The spectacle of public lynching became one of the most visible demonstrations of white supremacy in the United States. In Memphis an act of mob violence targeted three of Ida B. Wells's friends. Thomas Moss, a postman and one of the first Black men in Memphis to hold a federal position, opened a business called the People's Grocery with two of his friends, Will Stewart and Calvin McDowell. White owners of a competing store instigated a raid on the People's Grocery one Saturday night, but a group of Black men fired at the intruders, wounding three white men in the process. Moss, Stewart, and McDowell were arrested, but a mob abducted them from their jail cell, took them outside the city, and lynched them. Following the killings, Wells, by then the editor of the *Memphis Free Speech*, bought a pistol and began investigating the lynching sprees that had gripped the South for the past decade. When she wrote an outspoken anti-lynching editorial in May 1892, a mob destroyed her newspaper office, and she was forced into exile in the North. Wells continued her anti-lynching crusade in the pages of the *New York Age* and published the pamphlets *Southern Horrors* (1892) and *A Red Record* (1895), in which she detailed the causes of lynching and debunked the myth that lynch mobs primarily targeted Black men who had sexually assaulted white women. She also lectured extensively in the United States and Great Britain and helped form an international anti-lynching society. Her work, as the historian Mia Bay writes, "helped transform the understanding of lynching into a powerful symbol of the racial terror that was Jim Crow."[12] As the Black literacy rate passed 50 percent in the first decades of the twentieth century, journalists like Wells used writing to advance civil rights issues to a growing public.

Meanwhile, Booker Taliaferro Washington urged Black southerners to focus on pursuing education and economic opportunity rather than organizing to fight segregation and disenfranchisement. Born in Virginia in 1856 and freed during the Civil War, Washington became the first president of Tuskegee Normal and Industrial Institute in Alabama in 1881. His speech at the Cotton States and International Exposition in Atlanta in September 1895, seven months after the death of Frederick Douglass, launched him into the national spotlight, making him the most well-known Black man in the United States. Washington assured his mostly white audience: "In all things that are purely social we can be as separate as the fingers, yet one as the hand in all things essential to mutual progress."[13]

While Washington implored Black southerners to "cast down your buckets where you are," thousands of them responded to the climate of violence, cultural degradation, and legal restrictions by "voting with their feet." Black southerners looking for respite in a new region often faced west. When the Memphis lynch mob that abducted Thomas Moss in 1892 asked if he had any final words, Moss used his last breath to utter, "tell my people to go west—there is no justice for them here."[14] By then, Black settlements in the West had garnered widespread attention. The first mass movement out of the South began in 1877 when Black homesteaders built a town called Nicodemus on the Kansas prairie. "Exodusters" soon established other autonomous Black towns in the state. A new wave of Black migration to Oklahoma began in 1889 and resulted in the founding of twenty-seven Black towns by the time of statehood in 1907.

Some Black Americans championed armed self-defense in response to racial terror. Robert Charles shook the city of New Orleans on July 23, 1900, when he wounded a white police officer during an altercation, then shot and killed two other white officers who came to arrest him at his rooming house. He fled the scene and evaded a citywide manhunt for days as New Orleans descended into chaos. White mobs terrorized Black residents and killed at least six of them, causing the mayor to deputize an emergency "citizen police" in an attempt to restore order in the city. When authorities stumbled upon Charles's hiding place on July 27, he used a Winchester rifle and homemade ammunition to kill two white police officers and three white onlookers. As a crowd of several thousand watched, his hideout was set on fire and Charles was fatally shot by a police volunteer as he fled from the flames. Newspapers across the nation covered the shootings, manhunt, and riots, and Ida B. Wells and other Black journalists praised Charles for defending himself.

During the hunt for Robert Charles, investigators discovered that he distributed publications from the International Migration Society, an organization in Alabama that helped hundreds of Black southerners emigrate to Liberia. He also sold copies of *Voice of Missions*, a newspaper edited by Bishop Henry McNeal Turner of the African Methodist Episcopal (AME) Church, an advocate of armed self-defense who extolled the benefits of emigration and the potential for trade between West Africa and the southern United States. In an era of segregation, disenfranchisement, and public racial violence, the answer for some Black Americans was "Negro independence" in the form of self-government.

Religious organizations also helped to foster a sense of Black autonomy. Following Reconstruction, churches provided space for education, leadership, community self-help, and activism. Black Baptists marshalled that legacy, drawing the largest number of Black devotees. Created in 1895, the National Baptist Convention emerged as a different denomination from the white Northern Baptist Convention and Southern Baptist Convention. By 1906 it accounted for 61 percent of Black church members, and by 1916 constituted the third largest denomination in the nation.

Black women organizers cast an eye toward national politics and local concerns. As the historian Evelyn Brooks Higginbotham notes, Black women were largely responsible for the National Baptist Convention's self-help efforts that targeted education and social welfare. The National Association of Colored Women, a federation of Black women's clubs, emerged in 1896 with Mary Church Terrell serving as its first president. Encapsulated by its motto "Lifting as We Climb," the NACW focused on improving the lives of those less fortunate. The organization also lobbied for voting rights for Black women and men, protested the system of convict leasing, and championed a host of reforms. The writing and speeches of members such as Terrell helped establish the "race woman" as an intellectual tradition, an effort designed to shift public discourse on Black women in U.S. society.

Culture producers such as vaudeville performer Aida Overton Walker and bandleader James Reese Europe also worked to counter stereotypical images of Black Americans. A singer and dancer, Walker fused art and political protest. She viewed Black stage performers as exemplars of racial uplift, since they brought Black cultural expressions to international audiences. Europe established the Clef Club, a labor union and booking agency for Black musicians in New York as part of his efforts to heighten the cultural and professional value of Black music. During World War I, Europe served as lieutenant in the 369th Regiment, known as the Harlem Hellfighters, and he directed a regimental band that toured and made recordings.

The annual holiday on June 19, first celebrated in Reconstruction-era Texas to commemorate the end of chattel slavery in 1865, also existed at the intersection of labor and culture. Although caricatured by white-owned newspapers, "Juneteenth" celebrations reveled in Black cultural expressions—from local foodways to emerging musical styles like the blues—while providing domestic laborers a needed day off from work, a practice reported in Houston and Austin newspapers.

Some of the most esteemed and enduringly influential civil rights organizations formed early in the twentieth century to challenge segregation, disenfranchisement, and violence. In 1905, William Monroe Trotter, founder of the *Boston Guardian*, and W.E.B. Du Bois, at the time a professor at Atlanta University, invited other Black activists to join them for a conference in Fort Erie, Ontario. The "Niagara Movement," formed by twenty-nine men from at least fourteen different states, adopted an uncompromising stance on Black political rights in contrast to Washington's gradual accommodationist approach. A lack of funds and internal conflicts caused the group to disband in 1911, by which time a far stronger organization had emerged. In August 1908 white mobs lynched two Black men during a race riot in Springfield, Illinois, Abraham Lincoln's hometown. In the aftermath of the riot, an interracial group of more than fifty activists, including Ida B. Wells-Barnett, Jane Addams, Mary Church Terrell, Mary Ovington, and W.E.B.

Du Bois, issued a call on February 12, 1909, the centennial of Lincoln's birth, for a national conference "to discuss the present state" of Black Americans. The conference eventually led to the founding of the National Association for the Advancement of Colored People in 1910. Du Bois would edit the NAACP's official journal, *The Crisis: A Record of the Darker Races*, until 1934. As the Great Migration from the South was getting under way, a group of New Yorkers founded another enduring organization, the National Urban League, in 1910 to improve employment, housing, and educational opportunities for the growing Black population in northern cities.

On August 19, 1917, Private Richard Griggs boarded a Houston streetcar. Griggs served in the 24th Infantry of the U.S. Army, one of the post–Civil War Black regiments historically known as "Buffalo Soldiers." The Third Battalion of the 24th Infantry had arrived in Houston in late July to guard the construction of Camp Logan, a new military training center. Earlier that spring, President Woodrow Wilson stood before Congress and asked for a declaration of war against Germany, proclaiming: "the world must be made safe for democracy." Thousands of Black men responded to that call. More than 380,000 Black men served in the army during World War I and about 200,000 were sent to Europe, where approximately 40,000 of them fought in combat units.

Soldiers like Private Griggs realized they had their own war to fight at home. On that particular summer day, Private Griggs found the Black section of the streetcar full, so he chose a seat next to a white boy in the front section. The child's father was not pleased by the soldier's decision and reached for Griggs, who allegedly drew a knife. Summoned by the conductor, a deputy sheriff boarded the car, drew his pistol, and told Griggs he was "violating the law." Griggs allegedly replied: "I don't give a god damn about no law or anything else." The deputy arrested the soldier, who was jailed and charged with violation of the city's segregation laws.

Racial violence characterized the U.S. home front in the World War I era. In January 1915, authorities uncovered the "Plan de San Diego" (named after the town in South Texas), a manifesto outlining a plot by a small group of Mexican and Mexican American revolutionaries to unite ethnic Mexicans,

Black Americans, and Indigenous peoples into a "liberating army" that would free Texas and the Southwest from Anglo domination. Although the general uprising called for in the manifesto never took place, the Plan de San Diego helped inspire a series of raids in the summer and fall of 1915 that targeted ranches, farms, railroads, and rural settlements in the lower Rio Grande valley, resulting in the deaths of around twenty soldiers and civilians. Anglo vigilantes, local sheriffs, and the Texas Rangers lynched approximately three hundred ethnic Mexicans in retaliation.

News of race riots and massacres filled U.S. newspapers during the war. White mobs in East St. Louis, angry over the influx of Black laborers, attacked Black workers in May 1917 and in July unleashed a two-day reign of terror. At least thirty-nine Black men died during the massacre. And in Houston tensions between white law enforcement officials and the 24th Infantry reached a boiling point four days after the arrest of Private Griggs. On August 23, white police officers publicly assaulted a Black woman and pistol-whipped two Black soldiers in separate, but related, incidents. That night approximately one hundred soldiers marched on the city, killing fifteen white people, including five police officers and two soldiers, as well as an ethnic Mexican laborer who was hit by a stray bullet. Four Black soldiers died that night, making the Houston rebellion one of the few instances of racial violence in any era when more whites died than Blacks. The army convened three different courts-martial in 1917 and 1918. The first condemned thirteen soldiers to death for mutiny and murder, and the men were hanged in December 1917 before President Wilson had a chance to review their sentences. The executions sparked widespread protest from Black Americans. Ida B. Wells-Barnett distributed buttons memorializing the "Martyred Negro Soldiers," and W.E.B. Du Bois protested the executions in *The Crisis*. When another sixteen soldiers were sentenced to death for their part in the mutiny, pressure from James Weldon Johnson and other Black leaders persuaded Wilson to commute the sentences of ten of the condemned men.

The Houston rebellion reverberated throughout Black communities during the first Great Migration.[15] Droves of Black southerners relocated to cities in search of jobs in a war-stimulated economy. Natural disaster had made cotton farming increasingly difficult in the South. The boll weevil, a beetle that feeds on cotton buds, entered Texas from Mexico in 1892, reached Alabama in 1909, and had covered all of Mississippi by 1915. Meanwhile, the United States supplied the Allied Powers, especially Britain and France, with food, raw materials, and manufactured goods, increasing industrial labor opportunities. The need for labor in industrializing southern cities enticed some migrants to relocate to places such as Louisville, Houston, and Atlanta.

While most rural Black southerners who left the countryside chose to remain in the region, more than one million would leave the South entirely from 1917 to 1930. The war and the 1917 Immigration Act reduced the flow of immigrants from southern and eastern Europe, causing labor shortages in industrial cities and towns in the Northeast and Midwest. Following the previous generation that had established Black towns in the West, a new wave of southerners set their sights on different parts of the country.

The first Great Migration reshaped the demographics of the urban North, as cities with previously small Black populations swelled with migrants. Black southerners increasingly made contact with migrants from the Caribbean in some cities. For example, Caribbean migrants made up 25 percent of the 160,340 Black people living in Harlem in 1930. Daily interactions between diverse people of African descent spurred a rise in Pan-Africanism. Jamaican-born Marcus Garvey moved to Harlem in 1916 and made it the headquarters for his Universal Negro Improvement Association, an organization that aimed to unite African-descended people throughout the world through the promotion of Black self-government. Born on the island of Nevis in the West Indies, Cyril Briggs immigrated to New York City in 1905 and became a writer for the *Amsterdam News*. In 1917 Briggs called for a "colored autonomous State" to be established in the western part of the country. He launched his own publication, *The Crusader*, in 1918 and the following year founded the African Blood Brotherhood to foster class solidarity within the African diaspora and fight racial discrimination. While centered in Harlem, both the UNIA and the ABB had local chapters across the United States.

The ABB was part of a growing number of Socialist-influenced organizations and journals created during and after World War I, inspired in part by the Russian Revolution of 1917. Briggs focused on collective control of resources and production, reflecting rising interest in Marxist ideology within the Black diaspora. Meanwhile, Asa Philip Randolph moved from Florida to New York City, where in 1917 he co-founded with his friend Chandler Owen a Socialist journal, *The Messenger*, that was critical of both the NAACP and the UNIA. Before launching the Brotherhood of Sleeping Car Porters in 1925, Randolph championed Black labor and unionization in the pages of *The Messenger*.

The murderous rampage in East St. Louis in 1917 was one sign of how many white Americans would respond to Black migration and political organizing. Most acts of anti-Black violence in the World War I era were not the work of the Ku Klux Klan or any organized white supremacist group. From April to November 1919 twenty-six race riots erupted across the United States along with more than a dozen lynchings in a wave of mob violence the writer and NAACP leader James Weldon Johnson called the "Red Summer."

As deadly racial strife erupted across the nation, from Washington, D.C., and Chicago to Bisbee, Arizona, and Longview, Texas, repeated instances of Black armed self-defense demonstrated that World War I had set the tone for a "new mood of militancy." A native of Jamaica, poet Claude McKay penned "If We Must Die" in response to the white violence and Black self-defense: "If we must die, oh, let us nobly die." As the historian David Levering Lewis writes, "Washington D.C. and Chicago had shown how little fear of white men there was among demobilized Afro-American soldiers or peasants who had braved the unknowns of migration."[16] Whether they remained in the South, faced west, or headed north, the experiences of war, migration, and community-building signaled the dawn of a new era, the age of the self-proclaimed "New Negro."

Tyina L. Steptoe

¹Frederick Douglass, "I Have Come to Tell You Something About Slavery: An Address," *Frederick Douglass: Speeches & Writings*, ed. David W. Blight (New York: Library of America, 2022), 2.

²Robert P. Nevin, "Stephen C. Foster and Negro Minstrelsy," *The Atlantic Monthly*, November 1867, page 608.

³Eric Lott, *Love and Theft: Black Minstrelsy and the American Working Class* (New York: Oxford University Press, 1993), 4.

⁴An act to protect all citizens in their civil and legal rights, March 1, 1875. *The Statutes at Large, The United States, from December, 1873, to March, 1875, and Recent Treaties, Postal Conventions, and Executive Proclamations* (Washington, DC: Government Printing Office, 1875), 366.

⁵Ida B. Wells, *Crusade for Justice: The Autobiography of Ida B. Wells*, 2nd ed., ed. Alfreda Duster (Chicago: University of Chicago Press, 2020), 17.

⁶Rayford W. Logan, *The Negro in American Life and Thought: The Nadir, 1877–1901* (New York: Dial Press, 1954), 52.

⁷Blair L. M. Kelley, *Right to Ride: Streetcar Boycotts and African American Citizenship in the Era of Plessy v. Ferguson* (Chapel Hill: The University of North Carolina Press, 2010), 38.

⁸133 U.S. Reports 587.

⁹Henry B. Brown, Opinion in *Plessy v. Ferguson*, p. 260 in this volume.

¹⁰Edward L. Ayers, *Vengeance and Justice: Crime and Punishment in the Nineteenth Century American South* (New York: Oxford University Press, 1984), 176.

¹¹Lyda Gordon Shivers, "A History of the Mississippi Penitentiary" (1930), quoted in David M. Oshinsky, *Worse Than Slavery: Parchman Farm and the Ordeal of Jim Crow Justice* (New York: Free Press, 1997), vii.

¹²Mia Bay, "'If Iola Were a Man': Gender, Jim Crow and Public Protest in the Work of Ida B. Wells," *DQR Studies in Literature*, vol. 45 (2010), 106.

¹³Booker T. Washington, Address at the Atlanta Exposition, p. 197 in this volume.

¹⁴Wells, *Crusade for Justice*, 46. In her speech "Lynch Law in All Its Phases," delivered in Boston on February 13, 1893, Wells said that the Memphis newspapers had reported Thomas Moss's last words as "If you will kill us, turn our faces to the West."

¹⁵Historians often date the first Great Migration as 1910 to 1940, and the second from 1940 to 1970.

¹⁶David Levering Lewis, *When Harlem Was in Vogue* (New York: Alfred A. Knopf, 1981), 23–24.

1876–1896

PROTECTING THE BLACK VOTE IN THE SOUTH

FREDERICK DOUGLASS
Speech to the Republican National Convention
June 14, 1876

MR. CHAIRMAN AND GENTLEMEN OF THE NATIONAL CONVENTION: Allow me to express my deep, my heartfelt gratitude to you for the warm, cordial invitation you have extended to me to make my appearance on this platform at this time. The work to which you have called me is somewhat new; it is the first time in my life that I have ever had the pleasure of looking the Republican Party squarely in the face (applause and laughter), and I must say, and I hope you will acquit me of everything like a disposition to flatter, that you are pretty good looking men. (Laughter and applause.) But I will not detain you here by any attempt at a speech. You have had speeches, eloquent speeches, glorious speeches, wise speeches, patriotic speeches, speeches in respect of the importance of managing correctly your currency, speeches in defense of purity of administration, and speeches in respect of the great principles for which you struggled, and for which the race to which I belong struggled on the battle-field and poured out their blood. (Cheers.)

The thing, however, in which I feel the deepest interest, and the thing in which I believe this country feels the deepest interest is that the principles involved in the contest which carried your sons and brothers to the battle-field, which draped our Northern churches with the weeds of mourning and filled our towns and our cities with mere stumps of men, armless, legless, maimed, and mutilated—the thing for which you poured out your blood and piled a debt for after-coming generations higher than a mountain of gold to weigh down the necks of your children and your children's children—I say those principles involved in that tremendous contest are to be dearer to the American people in the great political struggle now upon them than any other principles we have. (Applause and cheers.)

FURTHER PROTECTION DEMANDED.

You have emancipated us. I thank you for it. You have enfranchised us, and I thank you for it. But what is your emancipation—what is your enfranchisement? What does it all amount to, if the black man, after having been made free by the letter of your law, is unable to exercise that freedom; and after having been freed from the slaveholders' lash he is to be subject to the slaveholder's shotgun? (Cheers.) Oh, you freed us; you emancipated us; I thank you for it; but under what circumstances did you emancipate us? Under what circumstances have we obtained our freedom? Sir, our case is the most extraordinary case of any people ever emancipated on the globe. I sometimes wonder that we still exist as a people in this country; that we have not all been swept out of existence, and nothing left to show that we had ever existed. Look at it! When the Israelites were emancipated, they were told to go and borrow of their neighbors—borrow their corn, borrow their jewels—load themselves down with the means of subsistence after they should go free in the land which the Lord God gave them. When the Russian serfs had their chains broken and were given their liberty, the Government of Russia—aye, the despotic Government of Russia—gave to these poor emancipated serfs a few acres of land on which they could live and earn their bread; but when you turned us loose, you gave us none. You turned us loose to the sky, to the storm, to the whirlwind, and, worst of all, you turned us loose to the wrath of our infuriated masters. (Applause.)

The question now is, do you mean to make good the promises in your Constitution? Talk not to me of finance. Talk not of mere reform in your administration. (Applause.) I believe there is honesty in the American people—honesty in the men whom you elect—wisdom in the men to manage those affairs; but tell me, if your hearts be as my heart, that the liberty which you have asserted for the black man in this country shall be maintained! (Applause.) You say, some of you, that you can get along without the vote of the black man of the South. Yes, that may be possible, but I doubt it. At any rate we, in order to secure our protection hereafter, feel the need, in the candidate whom you will place before the country, of the assurance that the black man shall walk to the ballot-box in safety, even if we have to bring a bayonet behind us. (Applause.) And I have these feelings—without bringing forth either of the gentlemen named here—that the Government of the United States and the moral feeling of this country will surround the black voter as by a wall of fire, and instead of electing your President without the black vote you may count in the number of your victorious Republican States, five or six at least of the old master States of the South. (Cheers.) But I have no voice to address you any longer, and you may now move down there for an adjournment. (Laughter and applause.)

A REPUBLICAN NEWSPAPER MOCKS DEMOCRATIC FEARS

DENVER DAILY TRIBUNE
"A Threatening Power"
January 12, 1877

THE House Committee at New Orleans have discovered a new peril to the Republic, and one that arouses all the indignant patriotism of the Democracy. The negro women have become a threatening power in politics. They order their husbands, brothers and fathers to vote the Republican ticket. For the purpose of enforcing their commands and punishing disobedience to them, they are not content with those pleasing little devices so naturally resorted to by sisters, wives and mothers in-law, when they would make the lives of brothers, husbands and sons-in-law a burden and a torture. The exasperating remark, the refusal to build fires cold mornings, atrocious cooking, the reference to father's ways, the abuse of the brother's sweetheart, the lecture, the hints of neglect and the rolling pin, are not the only means resorted to by them. To these they add the club, the shot gun and the revolver. To vote against their order is as great a peril as to refuse to drink in a crowd of Nevada miners. But these African Amazons are not satisfied with compelling their male relatives to vote the Republican ticket. They attire themselves in the habiliments of the other, but hardly the sterner sex, and proceed to the polls, and in defiance of all law, all authority, and all resistance by the legal guardians of the ballot boxes, proceed to cast as many votes as they desire or as may be necessary to elect their candidates. They, in fact, drive the White Leaguers from the polling places, take possession and conduct the elections to suit themselves. In other words, they completely bulldoze the Democratic voters. Now, something should certainly be done about this. These arrogant defiers of the laws, these rampaging revolutionists should be put down. Every patriotic instinct must move the Democratic warriors to organize for the suppression of this rebellion against the laws. Sam. Randall, Fernando Wood, Bill Springer, General Banning, Henry Watterson, Abe

Hewitt, John Morrissey and the others must feel an irresistible impulse to call together their legions and lead them against these law defying Amazonians. And this Amazonian outbreak affords these men and others of the same sort the great opportunity of the year for working off their warlike feelings.

"THE NEW ORDER OF THINGS"
ST. LOUIS GLOBE DEMOCRAT
The Future of the Negro
April 27, 1877

THE FUTURE OF THE NEGRO

Among the early acts of the Florida Legislature has been the passage of an amendment to the jury law, providing that in cases where a knowledge of reading and writing is essential to forming a judgment, jurors who do not possess such knowledge shall not be allowed to sit. The law is apparently a most reasonable and harmless one; it would be impossible to argue against the exclusion of ignorance and stupidity from the jury-box; but it is, on the other hand, impossible not to regard this innocent-looking law as the first step in a long course of legislation, which, under different pretexts and by different degrees, will end in reducing the negro to a position in which he will not interfere with the most extreme views of the most extreme White League fanatics.

The negro's political power is gone. Politically, he has as little influence or strength as if he were a Pole in Warsaw or a Christian in Turkey. The fate from which the Republican party has vainly tried for twelve years to save him has overtaken him at last, and it is merely a question of a little while and of a few forms before the last vestige of his political rights shall disappear. He is still free to vote, but he is free to vote only on condition that his vote shall not elect anybody. If there were any danger of his electing an obnoxious candidate he would very soon find how deceptive was his fancied right. He may still give witness, serve as juror, bring suit, attend school, ride in the cars and stop at the hotels, but Florida has entered upon the congenial task of expelling him from the jury-box, and we need not indulge in any false or foolish hopes about his retention of his other rights. He has no rights except such as the white people of the South choose to allow him, and it is impossible to overestimate the importance of the negro question in the new light thrown on it by the new situation. What rights will the negro be allowed to retain? Under what conditions will he be allowed to retain them? What will be the end of the new order of things?

We have spoken on this question before; we are compelled to speak of it again, and will be compelled to recur to it more often than we should like, for it is the overpowering national question of the future, a question more pregnant with vital consequences and changes than any which can occupy the political arena, a real question about which opinion may be divided, a vital question which may determine the form of our national existence, and a question which common prudence compels us to take charge of in time. Merely to show how vast are its dimensions, and how portentous its consequences, let us look at the educational interest involved. We do not hestitate to say that if the cause of negro education shall be neglected by the Southerners for ten years to come as it has been opposed by them for ten years past, the better and sterner conscience of the North will force it on them, and we shall have the public schools of South Carolina and of Mississippi, of Richmond, Savannah, Mobile and New Orleans, taught, managed and maintained by a central bureau at Washington. This is not prophecy; it is cause and effect, absolute fate, irresistible destiny, and yet the mind can hardly grasp the immense far-reaching changes involved in this transfer of power from the local to the central Government.

Every instinct of freedom protests against such centralization of power, yet it will be the inevitable penalty for the abuse or misuse of local power. Destiny, which was too strong for the Republican party, and which foiled it in the high undertaking in which noble motive was marred by shameful performance, will be too strong for the white man's party if it misuses the form of a free government to maintain and perpetuate by law a vassalage only one step higher than slavery. It will foil them and baffle them more disastrously than it has baffled the Republicans, and the instrument it will use will be the Federal power; it will use it even at the risk of converting it into a despotism stronger than the Czar's, and old men may yet live to see school boards, justices of the peace, policemen, assessors, and all other local officials receiving their commissions from

Washington and recognizing the authority of a central magistrate or cabal as omnipotent, as omnipresent and as despotic as the Council of the Ten in Venice.

Our only hope of escape from this fate lies in the good sense of those who have never shown any good sense thus far, in the tolerance of those who have shown nothing but intolerance, in the political sagacity of those whose most conspicuous contribution to our political history has been the act of a party of maniacs. The outlook is not promising; it is impossible to contemplate it without apprehension, yet there is no other remedy. The attempt to place political equality securely within the power of the negro was strongest at the start, and in its twelve years' struggle merely grew weaker from day to day. Its failure leaves us helpless, and the best we can hope for is that some unforeseen circumstance may avert a fate which so many of our citizens are inviting. Fortunately, there is reason to believe that a great deal of the Southern intolerance, bitterness and bigotry will pass away in the flush of triumph, and it is even possible that the solemn promises of Hampton and Nicholls may be remembered in a twelvemonth from now. This may give us a little time, and with time may come wisdom, and, through wisdom, justice; but we shall be very agreeably disappointed if the people of the South shall, of their own accord, act so fairly and generously to the negro as to prevent the Federal Government from compelling them to do it against their will.

"A WORSE STATE OF SLAVERY"
NATIONAL COLORED COLONIZATION SOCIETY
Address to Rutherford B. Hayes

SHREVEPORT, CADDO PARISH, LA.,
September 15, 1877.

To his Excellency R. B. HAYES,
President of the United States:

At a meeting of the National Colored Colonization Society, held in Shreveport, Caddo Parish, State of Louisiana, held on September 15, 1877, there being at said meeting representatives representing 29,000 colored people of the South, the following preambles and resolutions were unanimously adopted:

Whereas the Constitution of the United States guarantees to us equal civil and political rights and protection in the exercise of those rights, and as we the colored people of the South have been debarred from exercising those rights, the right to vote, hold office, and the privilege of education without molestation, and it being a well-established fact that we have been oppressed, murdered, and disfranchised on account of our race and color, and have not received that protection in the exercise of our rights guaranteed to us by the Constitution; and

Whereas we feel that the blood of the martyrs of freedom —John Brown and Abraham Lincoln—and the thousands that fell upon the battle-field have been shed in vain, having failed to awaken that interest as to demand in unmistaken language the enforcement of the Constitution relative to the amendments that guarantees protection to our race and color in the exercise of our rights, and after twelve years we find the colored race of the South in a worse condition than they were before those constitutional guarantees were extended, and we find our race in a worse state of slavery than before, being denied those rights that belong to us, and we feel that that passage in Lamentations, chapter 5th, of the Holy Scriptures, fully cover our grievances, and we cry out with a full heart that we have suffered all that and even more in the maintenance of our rights, and we feel and know that unless some protection is guaranteed to our race that we will cease to be a race or people and that we cannot live in the South in peace, harmony, and happiness, and we feel that our only hope and preservation of our race is the exodus of our people to some country where they can make themselves a name and nation and be happy and prosperous; and

Whereas we, the down-trodden race of Ham residing in the South, feeling that we can no longer dwell in the South in peace, harmony, and happiness, call on you as the President, and Congress of the United States, to assist us in our exodus by using your power and influence to aid us either by appropriating some Territory in which we may colonize our race, or, if that cannot be done, appropriate means whereby we can colonize in Liberia or some other country, as we feel that for us to remain in the South will be the destruction of our race. We therefore ask the Government of the United States, with full confidence that the same will be granted, an appropriation to enable us to colonize, knowing full well that we are more worthy than the Indians who return the favors of the government by murder, war, and rapine, while we return neglect by cotton and sugar. We as a race can point back to the robberies perpetrated on us by the Freedman's Bank, whereby thousands of our race were plunged from affluence to poverty; we also look back to the battle-field where thousands of our race shed their blood in defense of that government who guaranteed rights to us and have failed to perform them. We look at our soldiers faithfully fighting in defense of that government who neglects them. We look back to those lost victories gained at the ballot-box, lost lives in vain. We look to the future where in case of war we would feel compelled to fight for that government that looks coolly on our sufferings and see our rights one by one taken away from us, and we cry out with a full heart, the cup is full and running over, and with a loud voice cry to God, O, how long?

Therefore be it resolved, That we, the colored race of the South, do call upon the President and Congress of the United States to look back upon the blood shed on the battle-field by our race in defense of the government; to look back on the cotton and sugar raised by our labor; and we, in view of those facts that the rights guaranteed to us by the Constitution be restored to us, and ample protection be given to us in the maintenance of those rights. If that protection cannot be given and our lost rights restored, we would respectfully ask that some Territory be assigned to us in which we can colonize our race; and if that cannot be done, to appropriate means so that we can colonize in Liberia or some other country, for we feel and know that unless full and ample protection is guaranteed to us we cannot live in the South, and will and must colonize under some other government, and we put our full trust in God that our prayers and petition will be speedily answered.

Be it further resolved, That we respectfully and earnestly call upon Congress to restore back to us the savings of years that our race was robbed of by the failure of the Freedman's Bank, feeling that it is only an act of justice due us.

Be it further resolved, That we as a race will abstain from voting on all national questions and at the elections for national officers unless we have full protection and our own officers to guard our interests and rights.

A SONG OF THE BLACK EXODUS

HESTER HICKMAN
The Land That Gives Birth to Freedom;
Extending Our Voices to Heaven

1877

THE LAND THAT GIVES BIRTH TO FREEDOM.

1. We have held a meeting to ourselves, to see if we can't Plan some way to live. (Repeat.)
   CHORUS.—Marching along, yes we are marching along,
   To Kansas City we are bound. (Repeat.)
2. We have Mr. Singleton for our President, he will go on before us, and lead us through. (Repeat.)
   CHORUS—
3. Surely this must be the Lord that has gone before him, and opened the way. (Repeat.)
   CHORUS—
4. For Tennessee is a hard slavery State, and we find no Friends in this country. (Repeat.)
   CHORUS—
5. Truly it is hard, but we all have to part, and flee into a Strange land unknown. (Repeat.)
   CHORUS—
6. We want peaceful homes and quiet firesides; no one to Disturb us or turn us out. (Repeat.)
   CHORUS—

EXTENDING OUR VOICES TO HEAVEN.

Farewell, dear friends, farewell.
1. We are on our rapid march to Kansas, the land that gives Birth to freedom. May God Almighty bless you all.
   Farewell, dear friends, farewell.

2. Many dear mothers who are sleeping in the tomb of clay
   Have spent all their days in slavery in old Tennessee.
   >   Farewell, dear friends, farewell.
3. The time has come, we all must part, and take the parting hand.
   >   Farewell, dear friends, farewell.
4. It seems to me like the year of jubilee has come; surely this is the time that is spoken of in history.
   >   Farewell, dear friends, farewell.

"A TERRITORY FOR COLORED MEN"

THE NEW YORK TIMES
New Homes for Freedmen
January 23, 1879

NEW HOMES FOR FREEDMEN
SENATOR WINDOM'S
EMIGRATION PROJECT.

VIEWS OF A DELEGATION OF COLORED MEN REPRESENTING SIX STATES—REST AND FREEDOM FROM POLITICAL TURMOIL DESIRED—DISCONTENT AND UNHAPPINESS IN THE SOUTH—EMIGRATION TO THE WESTERN TERRITORIES PROPOSED.

Special Dispatch to the New-York Times.

WASHINGTON, Jan. 22.—At the request of Senator Windom, a number of prominent colored men, representing six of the Southern States, to-day held a long consultation with him regarding his resolution, which proposes a migration of the freedmen from the South to the West. Prof. Greener, of the Law Department of Howard University, was selected to speak for the delegation. He alluded to the wide-spread discontent at present existing among the colored people at the South, resulting, naturally, from their changed political condition. Deprived of rights guaranteed by the Constitution, there was no alternative except migration to some place where, in a measure, they might enjoy that freedom which a great party had pledged itself to maintain for them. Many had gone to Africa, he said, and others were still looking to that land as a refuge. He said the colored people asked no gratuity, no more guardianship, but only judicious and constitutional assistance in reaching the Territories best adapted to their methods of living. One thing was certain, the present anomalous condition of the colored people of the South could not long continue. Men accustomed to liberty and the enjoyment of their rights would not always submit to the outrages which were systematically perpetrated upon them with impunity. It was idle, unstatesmanlike, and contrary to the American theory of suffrage, to talk of taking away the right of voting from the colored man. No such dangerous principle could be tolerated. Better save the credit of Northern foresight and philanthropy by helping the colored people to emigrate to places where laws are equally and fairly administered, and where prejudice engendered by slavery and Confederate service are unknown. There were leading colored men now at the South who had proved their capacity, men who had filled creditably high offices. Such men might be appointed to official positions in some of the Territories, and the people thus encouraged would naturally follow their leaders. He knew the objection likely to be urged against any plan to help the colored people in a movement of this kind. Paternal government, no subsidies, no special legislation, were the specious cries when anything was suggested which could really benefit the colored people, unconnected with politics. The black man was tired of being a mere political buffet. If the advice of leading colored men had been listened to 10 years ago, many of the mistakes of reconstruction might have been prevented, and the black man would not have been left, as now, naked and helpless in the hands of his enemies.

In conclusion, Prof. Greener showed that societies were already in process of formation in several Southern States and in the District of Columbia and in Virginia. The colored people needed information as to the character of the soil, the temperature, and prospects held out to them, and he thought the Government had as much right to be at pains to furnish this data to the colored people as to send documents and agents abroad to disseminate knowledge of the resources of our country to foreigners. In some States and Territories the colored people would be just such a population as was desired. He ridiculed the idea that the black man was seeking political supremacy. In States where the negro had enjoyed the widest political scope he had elevated native whites and Democrats often to the highest judicial and political offices. The colored man did not seek the West or Southwest now for political power. He looked forward to a period of rest from political turmoil, where he might enjoy that freedom of political and civil privileges which very evidently and conclusively the present Administration was utterly powerless, however much it may be inclined, to secure for him at the South.

Congressmen Rainey, Cain, and Smalls spoke briefly to the same effect, the latter drawing particular attention to the fact that on some of the islands off the coast of South Carolina, where all the inhabitants were negroes, they prospered and lived at peace. He and all the other speakers were warmly in favor of setting apart a territory for colored men, to be governed by them.

SHARECROPPING IN LOUISIANA AND MISSISSIPPI

THE CHICAGO TRIBUNE
The Debtor South
May 13, 1879

THE DEBTOR SOUTH.

Effect of the Credit System in Driving the Labor Away.

The Planters in the Clutches of Their Factors—
Anticipating the Crop.

Consuming More than Is Produced, and
Eating What Is Not Earned.

Consequent Oppression of the Negroes,
Who Imitate Their Betters.

The Contracts and Liens in Common Use—Trust-Deeds for Supplies—
The Chivalry Dealing in "Chats."

State and County Indebtedness—Heavy Taxes—
No Place for Capital or Enterprise.

From Our Own Correspondent.

NATCHEZ, Miss., May 8.—The extent to which the credit system of the South is responsible for the present disaffection among the negroes is not fully understood. The extortions of the merchants and the high rents charged by the planters have been alluded to, but it has not been perceived that the root of the whole difficulty is back of that. In the days before the War, it is well known, many of the planters were in the clutches of their cotton-brokers. The proceeds of the crop were anticipated. Frequently, at the end of the season, the planter found that he had consumed more than he had produced. In this case part of his account was carried over, and he would be under obligations to patronize the same broker the following year. Mortgages followed, as a matter of course. The interest of the broker in the plantation grew year by year, until he foreclosed.

In this way some of the finest plantations in the South passed into the hands of money-lenders.

THE SYSTEM HAS NOT CHANGED SINCE THE WAR,
so far as the relations of the planter to his factor are concerned. I am told that nine-tenths of all the planters ask and receive advances on the crop. This is probably a large estimate, but three-fifths would not be an overstatement. The practice of taking advances is ruinously expensive. The factor charges first 8 per cent on all the money loaned, and holds a lien on the crop and the plantation. He furnishes the rations to keep the laborers alive, and charges a profit to cover risks and interest on them. Then he charges 2½ per cent "for making advances," and 2½ per cent more for "commissions" when the crop is sold. The planter rarely gets away from his factor on less than 15 per cent of his whole crop; and one excellent planter in Concordia Parish, who has adopted a strictly cash system for his own part, informs me that, on looking carefully into the matter, he estimated that it would cost him one-third of the crop to do business with a factor's credit.

THE ARRANGEMENT
must in the long run be ruinous to the planter who adopts it. That of itself may not be a matter of consequence. But precisely here arises the peculiar effect of it upon the laborers of the country. In the old days the planter went to ruin proudly on his own account. His slaves were sold, and they found another master as good as or better than the old one. But now the planter does not bear his burdens alone. He tries to shift them upon his laborers. Being pressed for money, he presses others. He insists upon the last cent that can be wrung out of the laborers. He sells his supplies, already charged at extortionate price by his factors, at an advance of 60 per cent; he allows nothing for repairs or improvements. He seizes and sells chattels and stock on the least failure of his tenants. I have been amazed at finding these Southern planters, once the chivalry of the land, engaged so largely in the chattel-mortgage business. At the North the man who deals in "chats" is considered a land-shark, but here the very salt of the earth are in that business.

IMPROVIDENCE

is not chargeable solely upon the negroes, it is evident. There is a good deal of it in the South. It is a very common charge against the negroes, but when white men pay 15 per cent for money advanced, and eat every year more than they earn, it must be confessed the negroes have shining examples. The curse of the thing is in the whole country, and it needs to be changed if the South is to have any lasting prosperity. Business principles must prevail in business transactions. There is no remedy in trying to throw the penalties of their system exclusively on the negroes, for the negroes have just shown that they will not stand it any longer. The white men, who are patrons and landlords of the negroes, ought to teach them better.

CREDITS AT THE STORES.

There are two kinds of stores that furnish the negroes, and two kinds of credits. First, there is the plantation-store, kept and owned by the planter. It deals principally in staples, and if the planter is any way a decent man or a man of means he endeavors to keep the expenses of negroes down to the lowest possible point. Sensible planters understand that it is for their interest to have the negroes come out ahead at the end of the year. Advances made by planters at their stores are covered by the general Vendors' Lien law, which gives the planter and laborer the right to mortgage, the one to the other, the crop not in existence. The Lien law differs in no essential respect from any mortgage law, except that it relates to property not in existence, and it provides that the crop referred to in its stipulations must be raised within fifteen months of the signing of the contract. One of these contracts, which secures to the planter at once the rent-cotton and the supplies, I give below. This is a genuine document, copied from the records, with the exception of the names:

> THIS AGREEMENT, made and entered into this 18th day of January, 1879, between Solid South, of the first part, and John Dawson, of the second part, *Witnesseth*: That the said party of the first part for and in consideration of eighty-eight pounds of lint cotton to be paid to the said Solid South, as hereinafter expressed, hereby leases to said Dawson, for the year A. D.

1879, a certain tract of land, the boundaries of which are well understood by the parties hereto, and the area of which the said parties hereby agree to be fifteen acres, being a portion of the Waterford Plantation, in Madison Parish, Louisiana.

The said Dawson is to cultivate said land in a proper manner, under the general superintendence of the said Solid South, or his agent or manager, and is to surrender to said lessor peaceable possession of said leased premises at the expiration of this lease without notice to quit. All ditches, turn-rows, bridges, fences, etc., on said land shall be kept in proper condition by said Dawson, or at his expense. All cotton-seed raised on said land shall be held for the exclusive use of said plantation, and no goods of any kind shall be kept for sale on said land unless by consent of said lessor. If said Solid South shall furnish to said lessee money, or necessary supplies, or stock, or material, or either or all of them during this lease, to enable him to make a crop, the amount of said advances, not to exceed $475 (of which $315 has been furnished in two mules, plows, etc.), the said Dawson agrees to pay for the supplies and advances so furnished, out of the first cotton picked and saved on said land from the crop of said year, and to deliver said cotton of the first picking to said Solid South in the gin on said plantation, to be by him bought or shipped at his option, the proceeds to be applied to payment of said supply bill, which is to be fully paid on or before the 1st day of January, 1880. After payment of said supply bill, the said lessee is to pay to said lessor, in the gin on said plantation, the rent-cotton hereinbefore stipulated, said rent to be fully paid on or before the 1st day of January, 1880. All cotton raised on said land is to be ginned on the gin of said lessor, on said plantation, and said lessee is to pay $4 per bale for ginning same. To secure payment of said rent and supply bill, the said Dawson grants unto said Solid South a special privilege and right of pledge on all the products raised on said land, and on all his stock, farming implements, and personal property, and hereby waives in favor of said Solid South the benefit of any and all homestead laws and exemption laws now in force, or which may be in force, in Louisiana, and agrees that all his property shall be seized and sold to pay said rent and supply bill in default of payment thereof as herein agreed. Any violation of this contract shall render the lease void.

Solid South,
his
John X Dawson.
mark.

Planters usually charge an advance of 60 per cent on the first cost of their supplies to cover risks. I have an instance of the kind in mind, the planter having a large place in Concordia Parish, and being accounted the most liberal in the parish. He informs me that there is no money in the business at this rate; that the losses are enormous, and that he engages in it only to protect his laborers. He is every way a strictly honorable and truthful man, and entitled to the fullest belief.

THE OUTSIDE STOREKEEPERS

come in after the planters, and they have to protect themselves by separate trust-deeds, a specimen of which is appended:

State of Louisiana, Parish of Madison, May 13, 1878.— Whereas, McClellan & Calthorp, merchants in Miliken's Bend, Parish and State aforesaid, at the special instance and request of William Hinton, whose name is hereunto signed, have agreed and undertaken to furnish him supplies and other things necessary to be used in producing a crop of cotton, corn, and other products during the current year. Now, to secure unto the said McClellan & Calthorp the prompt and certain payment for any and all advances they may make the said William Hinton during the current year, he hereby waives in favor of said McClellan & Calthorp the benefit of any stay law, homestead law, and exemption law that may now be or hereafter be in force in the State, and by these presents do give and grant unto the said McClellan & Calthorp, as furnishers of supplies, a prior lien and claim, preference and privilege on the entire crop of cotton, corn, etc., that he may raise or cause to be raised during the current year. Also, on all farming implements and the following described personal property, to-wit: One two-horse iron axle wagon and one bluish cow.

Attest:
R. C. McCay,
H. C. White.

His
William X Hinton.
mark.

These outside storekeepers are for the most part Israelites. They are horribly spoken of by many, but I am unable to find any special instance of extortion on their part. There is not any choice between them and their Gentile neighbors. All alike have two prices,—a credit price and a cash price. The credit price is 100 per cent higher than the cash prices.

SOME OF THE BILLS THE NEGROES HAVE BEEN PAYING, specimens of which are herewith given, throw a flood of light on the whole question of their dissatisfaction:

Ebitt Green to account with Samuel Cahn. Delta, La., June 25, 1877. Ebitt Green to Samuel Cahn, debtor:

Date.	Article.	Price.
1877—March 31,	To 1 gallon molasses	$1.00
April 14,	To cash $1, coffee 50¢	1.50
April 21,	To sugar and coffee 50¢, 1 hat $1	1.50
April 25,	To 1 barrel meal	4.50
April 25,	To 38 lbs bacon at 18¢, $6.84; 1 gal sirup $1.24	8.09
May 5,	To 1 molasses barrel	3.00
May 5,	To 1 suit clothes	5.50
May 11,	To 6 yards Nansook at 60¢	3.60
May 19,	To 32 lbs bacon	5.76
May 19,	To 1 gallon molasses	1.25
May 19,	To 1 pair shoes	3.00
May 30,	To paying for labor on order 50¢	50
June 2,	To cash 25¢, labor paid 50¢	75
	Total	$39.95

State of Louisiana, Parish of Madison—Samuel Cahn, being sworn, deposes and says that the annexed and above account is unpaid and correct, and that the supplies mentioned in the account to the sum of $39.95 were furnished at their dates by affiant to enable Ebitt Green to make a crop of corn and cotton on the Groves Plantation during this year, and that affiant is entitled to and has a first privilege as furnisher of necessary plantation supplies on all the crops raised this year, 1877.

SAMUEL CAHN.

Accounts must be settled every thirty days—*Interest charged after that date.*

F. L. MAXWELL.   JAMES H. GOODMAN.

DELTA, La., Feb. 25, 1875.—Mr. Ransom Frost, bought of Maxwell & Goodman, wholesale dealers in plantation supplies and merchandise generally (cash paid for cotton):

Feb. 24—2 hose		$ 2.00
Feb. 25—1 brl meat		23.00
Feb. 25—1 brl meal		4.50
Total		$29.50

The negroes are invariably

CHARGED FOR RECORDING THE TRUST-DEED.

In Hinds County, the cost is $2.50, which, as the bills do not average $100 per annum, is a considerable item. It has been said that the negroes are extravagant and thoughtless, and will buy all they can get on credit. Within limits this is true; but it is also true that they never have any trouble in buying when they have the prospect of a good crop. The outside storekeepers keep them down strictly until there is some indication of the character of the crop. Then, if the indications are favorable, the storekeepers urge them to carry away all they want. They are plied with whisky, which is sold at all country stores for 50 cents a pint. They are encouraged to invest in sardines, canned fruits, and potted salmon, for all which condiments they have a special weakness. The amount of the sales of some of these country stores is surprising. Harris & Lewis, at Edwards Station, Hinds County, Miss., are reported to be worth $200,000 to $300,000 a year, and have annual sales of over $100,000. A store at Newelltown, Tensas Parish, has sales of $30,000 per annum, and it is situated only at a cross-roads. The store of Mr. Murdoch, at St. Joseph, must have sales approaching $50,000 per annum. The number of the stores is not less surprising. Nearly every plantation has one, and there are half-a-dozen to a dozen in the town, many of which are composed of stores alone. There are ten or twelve, for instance, at Waterproof, Tensas Parish, and there is nothing else in the town besides saloons and a Post-Office. The business has been marvelously profitable in the past, and, though it is so no longer on the same scale, there is money in it, or the storekeepers would quit. Sympathy would be thrown away if bestowed upon them as a class, for they made nearly all their money here, and made it for the most part by practicing extortion and oppression upon the ignorant negroes.

THERE ARE SOME HONORABLE EXCEPTIONS

among the store-keepers. Harris & Lewis, of Edwards, carried over accounts amounting to $60,000 this year, and the principal storekeeper in Vidalia, just opposite here in Concordia Parish, made an even more generous proposition. In a town-meeting, called to consider the best means of pacifying the negroes, one of the bullies of the town, who had been a bulldozer himself, arose and said it was idle to ascribe this movement in any degree to bulldozing. He knew there was nothing of that sort in it, because the negroes had moved in large numbers from parishes where there had been no bulldozing. Thereupon the storekeeper I have referred to, not having the fear of anybody's revolver before his eyes, said that the statements of the previous speaker were not true; that whatever might be the causes of the emigration in other places, the cause in Concordia and Tensas was principally bulldozing; and that he hoped to see a Committee of Safety formed in the town to protect the negroes, and reassure them. The speaker closed by offering to sponge out the debts of all the negroes in the camp at the landing who owed them money if they would return to their plantations. At last accounts they held out even against this unparalleled offer, so determined were they to flee the land of the bulldozers. It is

A FORTUNATE THING FOR THE NEGROES

that the laws do not permit their creditors to restrain their movements when they intend to leave the State. If it were otherwise, they might be in effect re-enslaved, and in some instances would be. It would be an easy thing to keep them in debt, and easier still to swear that they were about to leave the State for the purpose of evading their just debts; many of them unquestionably are going for that purpose. It is understood that the Constitutional Convention now in session at New Orleans will make some important changes in this respect, and if so it will be time for the negroes to go. If the work of the Convention is to be approved, as many Bourbons say it should be, without being submitted to the negroes,—who are to be excluded from the suffrage by an educational qualification and a poll-tax,—there will probably be few provisions left in the law of the State to protect the personal liberty of the negroes in their contracts on the credit system with planters and storekeepers.

The credit system of the South makes and

KEEPS THE COUNTRY POOR.

Capital is shy wherever such a system prevails. The only banking-firm in Natchez—Britton & Koontz, who have been established for many years—say that there is no opportunity for the investment of money in Mississippi or Louisiana. The only securities offered are plantations, and, under the present system, they are not safe. They may rent for $8 an acre this year, and for nothing next year. Everything depends upon the crop and the supply of laborers.

The credit system was carried on very extensively both before and since the War by the State and County Governments. It is customary to charge the bad financial condition of the South to the negroes and the carpet-baggers; but we know that Mississippi was a bankrupt and repudiating State when the negroes were still slaves. The improvident way of doing business then prevailed at the South, as it does still. Mississippi is financially dead now. Money cannot be obtained on any terms for any public works. Natchez, a city of 10,000 to 12,000 inhabitants, has no communication by rail with the outside world, and cannot get it. Only forty miles of road are needed to make a connection, but that is esteemed more of an undertaking here than 400 miles would be at the North. The taxes are appalling,—in some cases 2 to 3 per cent on the value of property. And what is true of Mississippi is true in a less degree of Louisiana. All the region affected by the exodus has been for years stricken with a financial blight, and to this fact and the consequent oppression of labor I attribute a large part of the dissatisfaction among the negroes,—a large part, but not all.

ONE OF THREE GREAT CAUSES.

The credit system of the South is one of the three main causes of the negro exodus. Another cause is the system of land-tenures, and a third is bulldozing. These latter I will consider separately, reviewing the practices of the widely-different parts of the country I have been through. With reference to the credit system, it is sufficient to say, in conclusion, that it has been injurious to all classes alike, but especially to the laborers. In good years it stripped them of all they made; in bad years it left them in debt. No agricultural system can stand up under it and prosper. It must be reformed altogether, or the South be periodically subject to labor-disturbances of this kind.

R. W. P.

"THE FATHER OF THE EXODUS"
BENJAMIN SINGLETON
from *Testimony to the Senate Select Committee*
April 17, 1880

TESTIMONY OF BENJAMIN SINGLETON.

WASHINGTON, D. C., *April* 17, 1880.
BENJAMIN SINGLETON (colored) sworn and examined.

By Mr. WINDOM:
Question. Where were you born, Mr. Singleton?—Answer. I was born in the State of Tennessee, sir.

Q. Where do you now live?—A. In Kansas.

Q. What part of Kansas?—A. I have a colony sixty miles from Topeka, sir.

Q. Which way from Topeka—west?—A. Yes, sir; sixty miles from Topeka west.

Q. What is your colony called?—A. Singleton colony is the name of it, sir.

Q. How long has it been since you have formed that colony? —A. I have two colonies in Kansas—one in Cherokee County, and one in Lyon, Morris County.

Q. When did you commence the formation of that colony—the first one?—A. It was in 1875, perhaps.

Q. That is, you first began this colonizing business in 1875?—A. No; when I first commenced working at this it was in 1869.

Q. You commenced your colony, then, in 1869?—A. No, I commenced getting the emigration up in 1875; I think it was in 1875.

Q. When did you leave Tennessee, Mr. Singleton?—A. This last time; do you mean?

Q. No; when you moved from there to Kansas?—A. It has been a year this month just about now.

Q. You misunderstand me; you say you were born in Tennessee?—A. Yes, sir.

Q. And you now live in Kansas?—A. Yes, sir.

Q. When did you change your home from Tennessee to Kansas?—A. I have been going there for the last six or seven years, sir.

Q. Going between Tennessee and Kansas, at different times?—A. Yes, sir; several times.

Q. Well, tell us about it?—A. I have been fetching out people; I believe I fetched out 7,432 people.

Q. You have brought out 7,432 people from the South to Kansas?—A. Yes, sir; brought and sent.

Q. That is, they came out to Kansas under your influence?—A. Yes, sir; I was the cause of it.

Q. How long have you been doing that—ever since 1869?—A. Yes, sir; ever since 1869.

Q. Did you go out there yourself in 1869, before you commenced sending them out?—A. No, sir.

Q. How did you happen to send them out?—A. The first cause, do you mean, of them going?

Q. Yes; What was the cause of your going out, and in the first place how did you happen to go there, or to send these people there?—A. Well, my people, for the want of land—we needed land for our children—and their disadvantages—that caused my heart to grieve and sorrow; pity for my race, sir, that was coming down, instead of going up—that caused me to go to work for them. I sent out there perhaps in '66—perhaps so; or in '65, any way—my memory don't recollect which; and they brought back tolerable favorable reports; then I jacked up three or four hundred, and went into Southern Kansas, and found it was a good country, and I thought Southern Kansas was congenial to our nature, sir; and I formed a colony there, and bought about a thousand acres of ground—the colony did—my people.

Q. And they went upon it and settled there?—A. Yes, sir; they went and settled there.

Q. Were they men with some means or without means?—A. I never carried none there without means.

Q. They had some means to start with?—A. Yes; I prohibited my people leaving their country and going there without they had money—some money to start with and go on with a while.

Q. You were in favor of their going there if they had some means?—A. Yes, and not staying at home.

Q. Tell us how these people are getting on in Kansas?—A. I am glad to tell you, sir.

Q. Have they any property now?—A. Yes; I have carried some people in there that when they got there they didn't have fifty cents left, and now they have got in my colony—Singleton colony—a house, nice cabins, their milch cows, and pigs, and sheep, perhaps a span of horses, and trees before their yards, and some three or four or ten acres broken up, and all of them has got little houses that I carried there. They didn't go under no relief assistance; they went on their own resources; and when they went in there first the country was not overrun with them; you see they could get good wages; the country was not overstocked with people; they went to work, and I never helped them as soon as I put them on the land.

Q. Well, they have been coming continually, and adding from time to time to your colony these few years past, have they?—A. Yes, sir; I have spent, perhaps, nearly six hundred dollars flooding the country with circulars.

Q. You have sent the circulars yourself, have you?—A. Yes, sir; all over these United States.

Q. Did you send them into other Southern States besides Tennessee?—A. O, yes, sir.

Q. Did you do that at the instance of Governor St. John and others in Kansas?—A. O, no, sir; no white men. This was gotten up by colored men in purity and confidence; not a political negro was in it; they would want to pilfer and rob at the cents before they got the dollars. O, no, it was the muscle of the arm, the men that worked that we wanted.

Q. Well, tell us all about it.—A. These men would tell all their grievances to me in Tennessee—the sorrows of their heart. You know I was an undertaker there in Nashville, and worked in the shop. Well, actually, I would have to go and bury their fathers and mothers. You see we have the same heart and feelings as any other race and nation. (The land is free, and it is nobody's business, if there is land enough, where the people go. *I* put that in my people's heads.) Well, that man would die, and I would bury him; and the next morning maybe a woman would go to that man (meaning the landlord), and she would have six or seven children, and he would say to her, "Well, your husband owed me before he died;" and they would say that to every last one of them, "You owe me." Suppose he would? Then he would say, "You must go to some other place; I cannot take care of you." Now, you see, that is something I would take notice of. That woman had to go out, and these little children was left running through the streets, and the next place you would find them in a disorderly house, and their children in the State's prison.

Well, now, sir, you will find that I have a charter here. You will find that I called on the white people in Tennessee about that time. I called conventions about it, and they sat with me in my conventions, and "Old man," they said, "you are right." The white people said, "You are right; take your people away." And let me tell you, it was the white people—the ex-governor of the State, felt like I did. And they said to me, "You have taken a great deal on to yourself, but if these negroes, instead of deceiving one an other and running for office, would take the same idea that you have in your head, you will be a people."

I then went out to Kansas, and advised them all to go to Kansas; and, sir, they are going to leave the Southern country. The Southern country is out of joint. The blood of a white man runs through my veins. That is congenial, you know, to my nature. That is my choice. Right emphatically, I tell you to-day, I woke up the millions right through me! The great God of glory has worked in me. I have had open air interviews with the living spirit of God for my people; and we are going to leave the South. We are going to leave it if there ain't an alteration and signs of a change. I am going to advise the people who left that country (Kansas) to go back.

Q. What do you mean by a change?—A. Well, I am not going to stand bulldozing and half pay and all those things. Gentlemen, allow me to tell you the truth; it seems to me that they have picked out the negroes from the Southern country to come here and testify who are in good circumstances and own their homes, and not the poor ones who don't study their own interests. Let them go and pick up the men that has to walk when they goes, and not those who have money.

There is good white men in the Southern country, but it ain't the minority (majority); they can't do nothing; the bulldozers has got possession of the country, and they have got to go in there and stop them; if they don't the last colored man will leave them. I see colored men testifying to a positive lie, for they told me out there all their interests were in Louisiana and Mississippi. Said I, "You are right to protect your own country;" and they would tell me "I am obliged to do what I am doing." Of course I have done the same, but I am clear footed.

Q. Now you say that during these years you have been getting up this colony you have spent, yourself, some six hundred dollars in circulars, and in sending them out; where did you send them, Mr. Singleton?—A. Into Mississippi, Alabama, South Carolina, Georgia, Kentucky, Virginia, North Carolina, Texas, Tennessee, and all those countries.

Q. To whom did you send them; how were they circulated?—A. Every man that would come into my country, and I could get a chance, I would put one in his hand, and the boys that started from my country on the boats, and the porters on the cars. That is the way I circulated them.

Q. Did you send any out by mail?—A. I think I sent some perhaps to North Carolina by mail—I think I did. I sent them out by people, you see.

Q. Yes; by colored people, generally?—A. Some white people, too. There was Mrs. Governor Brown, the first Governor Brown of Tennessee—Mrs. Sanders, she was a widow, and she married the governor. He had thirty on his place. I went to him, and he has given me advice. And Ex-Governor Brown, he is there too.

Q. You say your circulars were sent all over these States?—A. Yes, sir; to all of 'em.

Q. Did you ever hear from them; did anybody ever write to you about them?—A. O, yes.

Q. And you attribute this movement to the information you gave in your circulars?—A. Yes, sir; *I am the whole cause of the Kansas immigration!*

Q. You take all that responsibility on yourself?—A. I do, and I can prove it; and I think I have done a good deal of good, and I feel relieved!

Q. You are proud of your work?—A. Yes, sir; I am! (Uttered emphatically.)

Q. Well, now, some of those people that go there suffer a great deal; what have you to say about that?—A. I tell you how it is. I speak plainly. It is "root hog, or die." I tell the truth. Kansas is not a warm climate.

Q. Do you think that your people suffer more from the climate there than they do at home?—A. No, sir.

Q. Have you talked with the people that have gone there lately as to the reason for their going?—A. Yes.

Q. What reasons did they give?—A. They say they have been badly treated in their countries. I speak for my country—Tennessee.

Q. In what way did they say they were badly treated?—A. Bulldozed, you call it; bulldozed, I suppose.

Q. In what way?—A. Well, they say they have been cheated and defrauded, and I know for myself, in my county—I better talk about what I know, when there is so much hearsay—our people in times of their little social gatherings at nights—quilting, perhaps, and weddings, throughout the country, you will see a dirty, low-lived, trashy man out in the town, and he will send some weak-minded one there to tell some colored man's daughter or wife he loves to come out, he wants a word with them. He will stop along the road and have some talk with them, and then that poor black man daren't say nothing; or there will go to his house, a lot of them scoundrels—I am not talking of Democrats only—a lot of scoundrels will go in there and take that negro out and kill him. I know lots of folks they took out. Julia Haven; I made the outside box and her coffin, in Smith County, Tennessee. And another young colored lady I knew, about my color, they committed an outrage on her and then shot her, and I helped myself to make the outside box. And other cases I could tell you. I did see a white man tied down and drowned in the river by these scoundrels, and he was carried to Dick Somers' shop in Cherry street, Nashville. But I have a thousand hearsays, that I don't care to talk about—not much.

Q. Well, have any of your people got employment that came in large crowds from Tennessee, Mississippi, and Louisiana?—A. The greater part of them have.

Q. Are they disposed to work?—A. Yes, sir. Let me tell you somethink about that, and you will agree with me. Now listen; these people that comes from these large farms have been used to—and I am sorry for that habit—living where there was a hundred or two hundred of them, where they can sing and go on, you know, and amuse themselves after the day's labor. Now when a gentleman comes in Kansas and says "I want a good man or woman,"—I have heard them testify that they came in and told these miraculous tales, when it was not so—they went out there and got lonesome. They are just like a hog that is used to a drove, take him out and he is a crazy hog; and they became just lonely, that is all; the people treated them well, and they got good prices, and they slept in the same house and the same room that these white people slept in, but they got lonely and wanted to be where their own people were, and I know that to be the facts; but they came rushing in very fast. Now I see where some of them said from eighty to a hundred thousand was coming. I am the very man that predicted that. It was me published it. I thought in eighteen months there would be from eighty thousand to one hundred thousand leaving the South. It was me done it; I published it; they say other folks did it. No, Governor St. John or other folks, they did not do it, it was me; *I* did it.

Q. Well, what do you think of it now?—A. I think it will come; it is sure to come.

Q. Is there any way to stop it?—A. No way, sir, on God's earth to stop it.

Q. Suppose the white people where they come from were to treat them well, give them their rights as American citizens, and give them what they earn, would not that stop the exodus?—A. Allow me to say to you that confidence is perished and faded away; they have been lied to every year. Every year when they have been going to work the crops, they have said, "I will do what is right to you," and just as soon as that man sees everything blooming and flourishing in the flowers and cotton blooms, he will look at that negro who has been his slave, and when he sees him walk up to take his half of the crop it is too much for him to stand, and he just denies his word, he denies his contract; and we will leave that country, and they will leave, till these people actually refrains from this way of treatment, and gives the negro the right hand of fellowship and acknowledges their wrongs, and then we have got no wrongs to acknowledge. My plan is for them to leave the country, and learn the South a lesson; and the whole of

America—this Union—will have a lesson when cotton is from forty to fifty cents a pound, and you can't get it at that.

We don't want to leave the South, and just as soon as we have confidence in the South I am going to be an instrument in the hands of God to persuade every man to go back, because that is the best country; that is genial to our nature; we love that country, and it is the best country in the world for us; but we are going to learn the South a lesson. I have talked about this, and called a convention, and tried to harmonize things and promote the spirit of conciliation, and to do everything that could be done in the name of God. Why, I have prayed to the Almighty when it appeared to me an imposition before heaven to pray for them. I have taken my people out in the roads and in the dark places, and looked to the stars of heaven and prayed for the Southern man to turn his heart.

Q. You believe, then, there is no way to stop the exodus except by stopping the abuse of these people, and by treating them fairly, and that it will take some time to get their confidence, even then?—A. They will then go back. I have heard some say they will never go back; but they will go back.

Q. Has there been anything political in this move of yours? —A. I never had any political men in it, white or black.

Q. Have leading men in Kansas had any talk with you about your movement as a political one?—A. No, sir; this thing was got up by an ignorant class of men, and I will prove it to you. I am the leader of it, and have been at for thirteen years, and I am the smartest man in it, and I am only an ignorant man.

Q. What is your age?—A. Seventy years past.

Q. Do you know anything that Governor St. John has done to encourage your people to leave their homes in the Southern country?—A. I have talked with him on the subject; his view is like mine about it.

Q. Has he sent any circulars out, as you have done, encouraging them to come?—A. No, sir; I have heard false tales told on him.

Q. In what respect?—A. Why, that he persuaded people to come there without money or price. Not so. He welcomed them all in there, but his advice was to bring something to sustain them. I wish you could read this, and see my sentiment about that (referring to one of the earlier circulars sent out by witness). I have never asked a man to come without money; I have told him not to come without money, but to stay there; and I am the man that has done this, and I can prove it that I have never asked one of them to go to Kansas if he was without money, but I have told him to stay there.

Q. Well, can you tell us anything more on this subject of the exodus?—A. Why, my dear friends, I am full now.

Q. Well, if you can think of anything more that will give us any light on it, do so.—A. I think you have got all you want. I will tell you, now, that I do not want to hurt anybody; I love the South, and I want every one of my people to come out, to teach the South a lesson, that she may know if she thinks more of bulldozing than she does of the colored man's muscle; the colored man's muscle is her interest; and these dare devils that ride around in the night and abuse the people, when the country ought to be harmonized, then I say to them go, and whenever they change from that, then I want them to go back.

Mr. WINDOM. You consider yourself the father of the exodus, then, Mr. Singleton?

The WITNESS. Yes, sir; I am the father of it!

The CHAIRMAN. You are called "Pap Singleton," I believe?

The WITNESS. I am sir; I love everybody!

The CHAIRMAN. They call you "Pap" Singleton, because you are father of the exodus, is that it?

The WITNESS. I reckon they honor me with that name for my old age, sir.

By the CHAIRMAN:

Q. Whereabouts is this colony of yours in Kansas?—A. It is sixty miles rather southwest of Topeka.

Q. And you say there are a thousand acres in your colony? —A. Not that; that is in the Cherokee County. There was one hundred and sixty thousand acres, I think, of the old Indian reservation—Indian lands; at first it was appraised too high; well, then, the government could not sell it; then it was reappraised at a dollar and a quarter an acre; so that I think it is now pretty well all taken up.

Q. Yes; and you have encouraged nobody to come unless they have had some means?—A. O, no; I have never encouraged or advised nobody to come to a prairie country without means. I am bitterly opposed to it. I am not that man.

Q. I am requested to ask if you allude to the half-breed lands?—A. Well, sir, I really don't know whether they are half-breed or not, because when I went there there was none there but a few only.

Q. Your home was in Tennessee?—A. O, yes, sir; my home was in Tennessee.

Q. Until how long ago?—A. Well—(hesitating)——

Q. How long since you moved from Tennessee, I mean?—A. April a year ago; I think I got to Topeka this last time perhaps on the 16th of March, or the latter part of March it was.

Q. In what county did you live?—A. In Morris and Lyon Counties my colony is.

Q. I am speaking of the county in Tennessee where you lived.—A. O! in Davidson County.

Q. How long did you live there?—A. Well, I don't know long, but I know I was raised up there.

Q. Were you born in Tennessee?—A. I was, sir.

Q. And raised there?—A. Yes, sir; and raised there.

Q. And spent all your life in Davidson County?—A. No, sir; I spent part of my life running through Indiana and going to Canada.

Q. Did you acquire some property in Tennessee; had you something to go on?—A. I did not; no, sir.

Q. You had nothing when you went to Kansas?—A. Nothing; I only worked there in the cabinet business.

Q. You lived there until about a year ago, but you had been going there for some time before that; do I so understand you?—A. Yes, sir; that is it.

Q. And you want us to understand that there is trouble between the white and the black races in Tennessee at this time, do you?—A. I do, sir; and I will prove it to you. Wherever there is people that has got no homes, and the State prisons enlarging every day—I am not talking about bulldozing and all that sort of thing—I am talking about a community; yes, there is trouble there between the white and the black races.

Q. How old a man did you say you were?—A. Seventy years past the 15th day of last August, sir.

Q. Do you think that the negroes have anything to complain of in Nashville, Tenn.?—A. Well, not really now in the city.

Q. Nashville is in Davidson County, is it not?—A. Yes, sir; that is the county.

Q. Well, is there any complaint in the city?—A. No; I think they do very well in the city.

Q. They are treated well?—A. Yes; in the city.

Q. Well, what have they to complain of out in the country in Davidson County?—A. They say they are cheated. They get $8 a month; in fact, the lands, in Middle Tennessee particularly, is worn-out, and I do not really believe they are able to pay as much money for labor there as they can in the lower cotton States.

Q. You think that the farm lands in Davidson County are pretty well worn-out?—A. I do.

Q. How much do they pay the colored people there?—A. Eight to ten dollars a month.

Q. Don't they pay as high as twelve and sometimes fifteen dollars a month?—A. I don't know it, sir; no, sir.

Q. You have not heard of any troubles between the whites and blacks at elections in Tennessee of late years, have you?—A. Well, no; I saw a great many of them around the city, who told me they was turned out of their places on account of their political sentiments.

Q. You always voted in Tennessee, didn't you?—A. Yes; I voted there very often.

Q. What ticket did you vote?—A. I voted for both parties, whichever one I liked, Democrat or Republican.

Q. Nobody tried to get you to vote one way or the other, any more than in the usual and proper methods of electioneering, did they?—A. Running for office, do you mean?

Q. No; I do not allude to that—but to your freedom to vote what ticket you please?—A. They sometimes would ask you if you wouldn't vote this ticket or that.

Q. But they never threatened you to induce you to vote any one ticket?—A. No, sir.

Q. And you never saw any one molested for voting either the Democratic or Republican ticket?—A. Right in the city?

Q. Yes; in Nashville?—A. No; I have not.

Q. Well, out of the city?—A. I have not been out of the city at these elections.

Q. That is what I supposed. Did you ever hear anybody tell of any difficulties they ever saw at the polls in Davidson County between the whites and the blacks?—A. O, yes, sir.

Q. When?—A. At nearly every election, pretty much all the governor's elections.

Q. What governor's—Brownlow's?—A. Any of them.

Q. But that won't quite do?—A. Well, any of the governor's elections, I mean.

Q. Do you mean that they always have trouble whenever they have an election for governor?—A. It appears so, from what they say.

Q. Who say?—A. The colored people of the county; they are turned off for voting against their interests.

Q. Did you ever know of any one who was turned off for voting as they pleased?—A. They say so.

Q. But did you ever *know* of such a case of your own knowledge?—A. Never.

Q. Well, you have become perfectly wrapped up in your colony of colored people?—A. Yes, sir.

Q. I do not blame you for it, not the slightest in the world.—A. No.

Q. And you state that you are the whole cause of the movement to Kansas?—A. I am, sir.

UPHOLDING ANTI-MISCEGENATION LAWS

STEPHEN FIELD
Opinion in Pace v. Alabama
January 29, 1883

ERROR to the Supreme Court of the State of Alabama.

Section 4184 of the Code of Alabama provides that "if any man and woman live together in adultery or fornication, each of them must, on the first conviction of the offence, be fined not less than one hundred dollars, and may also be imprisoned in the county jail or sentenced to hard labor for the county for not more than six months. On the second conviction for the offence, with the same person, the offender must be fined not less than three hundred dollars, and may be imprisoned in the county jail, or sentenced to hard labor for the county for not more than twelve months; and for a third or any subsequent conviction with the same person, must be imprisoned in the penitentiary, or sentenced to hard labor for the county for two years."

Section 4189 of the same code declares that "if any white person and any negro, or the descendant of any negro to the third generation, inclusive, though one ancestor of each generation was a white person, intermarry or live in adultery or fornication with each other, each of them must, on conviction, be imprisoned in the penitentiary or sentenced to hard labor for the county for not less than two nor more than seven years."

In November, 1881, Tony Pace, a negro man, and Mary J. Cox, a white woman, were indicted, under sect. 4189, in a Circuit Court of Alabama, for living together in a state of adultery or fornication, and were tried, convicted, and sentenced, each to two years' imprisonment in the State penitentiary. On appeal to the Supreme Court of the State the judgment was affirmed, and he brought the case here on writ of error, insisting that the act under which he was indicted and convicted is in conflict with the concluding clause of the first section of the Fourteenth Amendment of the Constitution, which declares that no State shall "deny to any person the equal protection of the laws."

Mr. John R. Tompkins for the plaintiff in error.
Mr. Henry C. Tompkins, Attorney-General of Alabama, *contra*.

MR. JUSTICE FIELD delivered the opinion of the court, and after stating the case as above, proceeded as follows:—

The counsel of the plaintiff in error compares sects. 4184 and 4189 of the Code of Alabama, and assuming that the latter relates to the same offence as the former, and prescribes a greater punishment for it, because one of the parties is a negro, or of negro descent, claims that a discrimination is made against the colored person in the punishment designated, which conflicts with the clause of the Fourteenth Amendment prohibiting a State from denying to any person within its jurisdiction the equal protection of the laws.

The counsel is undoubtedly correct in his view of the purpose of the clause of the amendment in question, that it was to prevent hostile and discriminating State legislation against any person or class of persons. Equality of protection under the laws implies not only accessibility by each one, whatever his race, on the same terms with others to the courts of the country for the security of his person and property, but that in the administration of criminal justice he shall not be subjected, for the same offence, to any greater or different punishment. Such was the view of Congress in the enactment of the Civil Rights Act of May 31, 1870, c. 114, after the adoption of the amendment. That act, after providing that all persons within the jurisdiction of the United States shall have the same right, in every State and Territory, to make and enforce contracts, to sue, be parties, give evidence, and to the full and equal benefit of all laws and proceedings for the security of person and property as is enjoyed by white citizens, declares, in sect. 16, that they "shall be subject to like punishment, pains, penalties, taxes, licenses, and exactions of every kind and none other, any law, statute, ordinance, regulation, or custom to the contrary notwithstanding."

The defect in the argument of counsel consists in his assumption that any discrimination is made by the laws of Alabama in the punishment provided for the offence for which the plaintiff in error was indicted when committed by a person of the African race and when committed by a white person. The two sections of the code cited are entirely consistent. The one prescribes, generally, a punishment for an offence committed between persons of different sexes; the other prescribes a punishment for an offence which can only be committed where the two sexes are of different races. There is in neither section any discrimination against either race. Sect. 4184 equally includes the offence when the persons of the two sexes are both white and when they are both black. Sect. 4189 applies the same punishment to both offenders, the white and the black. Indeed, the offence against which this latter section is aimed cannot be committed without involving the persons of both races in the same punishment. Whatever discrimination is made in the punishment prescribed in the two sections is directed against the offence designated and not against the person of any particular color or race. The punishment of each offending person, whether white or black, is the same.

Judgment affirmed.

"UNIVERSAL FREEDOM IN THIS COUNTRY"

JOHN MARSHALL HARLAN
Dissenting Opinion in Civil Rights Cases

October 15, 1883

MR. JUSTICE HARLAN dissenting.

The opinion in these cases proceeds, it seems to me, upon grounds entirely too narrow and artificial. I cannot resist the conclusion that the substance and spirit of the recent amendments of the Constitution have been sacrificed by a subtle and ingenious verbal criticism. "It is not the words of the law but the internal sense of it that makes the law: the letter of the law is the body; the sense and reason of the law is the soul." Constitutional provisions, adopted in the interest of liberty, and for the purpose of securing, through national legislation, if need be, rights inhering in a state of freedom, and belonging to American citizenship, have been so construed as to defeat the ends the people desired to accomplish, which they attempted to accomplish, and which they supposed they had accomplished by changes in their fundamental law. By this I do not mean that the determination of these cases should have been materially controlled by considerations of mere expediency or policy. I mean only, in this form, to express an earnest conviction that the court has departed from the familiar rule requiring, in the interpretation of constitutional provisions, that full effect be given to the intent with which they were adopted.

The purpose of the first section of the act of Congress of March 1, 1875, was to prevent *race* discrimination in respect of the accommodations and facilities of inns, public conveyances, and places of public amusement. It does not assume to define the general conditions and limitations under which inns, public conveyances, and places of public amusement may be conducted, but only declares that such conditions and limitations, whatever they may be, shall not be applied so as to work a discrimination solely because of race, color, or previous condition of servitude. The second section provides a penalty against any one denying, or aiding or inciting the denial, to any citizen, of that equality of right given by the first section, except for reasons by law applicable to citizens of every race or color and regardless of any previous condition of servitude.

There seems to be no substantial difference between my brethren and myself as to the purpose of Congress; for, they say that the essence of the law is, not to declare broadly that all persons shall be entitled to the full and equal enjoyment of the accommodations, advantages, facilities, and privileges of inns, public conveyances, and theatres; but that such enjoyment shall not be subject to conditions applicable only to citizens of a particular race or color, or who had been in a previous condition of servitude. The effect of the statute, the court says, is, that colored citizens, whether formerly slaves or not, and citizens of other races, shall have the same accommodations and privileges in all inns, public conveyances, and places of amusement as are enjoyed by white persons; and *vice versa.*

The court adjudges, I think erroneously, that Congress is without power, under either the Thirteenth or Fourteenth Amendment, to establish such regulations, and that the first and second sections of the statute are, in all their parts, unconstitutional and void.

Whether the legislative department of the government has transcended the limits of its constitutional powers, "is at all times," said this court in *Fletcher* v. *Peck*, 6 Cr. 128, "a question of much delicacy, which ought seldom, if ever, to be decided in the affirmative, in a doubtful case. . . . The opposition between the Constitution and the law should be such that the judge feels a clear and strong conviction of their incompatibility with each other." More recently in *Sinking Fund Cases*, 99 U. S., 718, we said: "It is our duty when required in the regular course of judicial proceedings, to declare an act of Congress void if not within the legislative power of the United States, but this declaration should never be made except in a clear case. Every possible presumption is in favor of the validity of a statute, and this continues until the contrary is shown beyond a rational doubt. One branch of the government cannot encroach on the domain of another without danger. The safety of our institutions depends in no small degree on a strict observance of this salutary rule."

Before considering the language and scope of these amendments it will be proper to recall the relations subsisting, prior to their adoption, between the national government and the institution of slavery, as indicated by the provisions of the Constitution, the legislation of Congress, and the decisions of this court. In this mode we may obtain keys with which to open the mind of the people, and discover the thought intended to be expressed.

In section 2 of article IV. of the Constitution it was provided that "no person held to service or labor in one State, under the laws thereof, escaping into another, shall, in consequence of any law or regulation therein, be discharged from such service or labor, but shall be delivered up on claim of the party to whom such service or labor may be due." Under the authority of this clause Congress passed the Fugitive Slave Law of 1793, establishing a mode for the recovery of fugitive slaves, and prescribing a penalty against any person who should knowingly and willingly obstruct or hinder the master, his agent, or attorney, in seizing, arresting, and recovering the fugitive, or who should rescue the fugitive from him, or who should harbor or conceal the slave after notice that he was a fugitive.

In *Prigg* v. *Commonwealth of Pennsylvania*, 16 Pet. 539, this court had occasion to define the powers and duties of Congress in reference to fugitives from labor. Speaking by MR. JUSTICE STORY it laid down these propositions:

That a clause of the Constitution conferring a right should not be so construed as to make it shadowy, or unsubstantial, or leave the citizen without a remedial power adequate for its protection, when another construction equally accordant with the words and the sense in which they were used, would enforce and protect the right granted;

That Congress is not restricted to legislation for the execution of its expressly granted. powers; but, for the protection of rights guaranteed by the Constitution, may employ such means, not prohibited, as are necessary and proper, or such as are appropriate, to attain the ends proposed;

That the Constitution recognized the master's right of property in his fugitive slave, and, as incidental thereto, the right of seizing and recovering him, regardless of any State law, or regulation, or local custom whatsoever; and,

That the right of the master to have his slave, thus escaping, delivered up on claim, being guaranteed by the Constitution, the fair implication was that the national government was clothed with appropriate authority and functions to enforce it.

The court said: "The fundamental principle, applicable to all cases of this sort, would seem to be that when the end is required the means are given, and when the duty is enjoined the ability to perform it is contemplated to exist on the part of the functionary to whom it is entrusted." Again: "It would be a strange anomaly and forced construction to suppose that the national government meant to rely for the due fulfilment of its own proper duties, and the rights which it intended to secure, upon State legislation, and not upon that of the Union. *A fortiori*, it would be more objectionable to suppose that a power which was to be the same throughout the Union, should be confided to State sovereignty which could not rightfully act beyond its own territorial limits."

The act of 1793 was, upon these grounds, adjudged to be a constitutional exercise of the powers of Congress.

It is to be observed from the report of Priggs' case that Pennsylvania, by her attorney-general, pressed the argument that the obligation to surrender fugitive slaves was on the States and for the States, subject to the restriction that they should not pass laws or establish regulations liberating such fugitives; that the Constitution did not take from the States the right to determine the status of all persons within their respective jurisdictions; that it was for the State in which the alleged fugitive was found to determine, through her courts or in such modes as she prescribed, whether the person arrested was, in fact, a freeman or a fugitive slave; that the sole power of the general government in the premises was, by judicial instrumentality, to restrain and correct, not to forbid and prevent in the absence of hostile State action; and that, for the general government to assume primary authority to legislate on the subject of fugitive slaves, to the exclusion of the States, would be a dangerous encroachment on State sovereignty. But to such suggestions this court turned a deaf ear, and adjudged that primary legislation by Congress to enforce the master's right was authorized by the Constitution.

We next come to the Fugitive Slave Act of 1850, the constitutionality of which rested, as did that of 1793, solely upon the implied power of Congress to enforce the master's rights. The provisions of that act were far in advance of previous legislation. They placed at the disposal of the master seeking to recover his fugitive slave, substantially the whole power of the nation. It invested commissioners, appointed under the act, with power to summon the *posse comitatus* for the enforcement of its provisions, and commanded all good citizens to assist in its prompt and efficient execution whenever their services were required as part of the *posse comitatus*. Without going into the details of that act, it is sufficient to say that Congress omitted from it nothing which the utmost ingenuity could suggest as essential to the successful enforcement of the master's claim to recover his fugitive slave. And this court, in *Ableman* v. *Booth*, 21 How. 506, adjudged it to be "in all of its provisions fully authorized by the Constitution of the United States."

The only other case, prior to the adoption of the recent amendments, to which reference will be made, is that of *Dred Scott* v. *Sandford*, 19 How. 399. That case was instituted in a circuit court of the United States by Dred Scott, claiming to be a citizen of Missouri, the defendant being a citizen of another State. Its object was to assert the title of himself and family to freedom. The defendant pleaded in abatement that Scott—being of African descent, whose ancestors, of pure African blood, were brought into this country and sold as slaves —was not a *citizen*. The only matter in issue, said the court, was whether the descendants of slaves thus imported and sold, when they should be emancipated, or who were born of parents who had become free before their birth, are citizens of a State in the sense in which the word "citizen" is used in the Constitution of the United States.

In determining that question the court instituted an inquiry as to who were citizens of the several States at the adoption of the Constitution, and who, at that time, were recognized as the people whose rights and liberties had been violated by the British government. The result was a declaration, by this court, speaking by Chief Justice Taney, that the legislation and histories of the times, and the language used in the Declaration of Independence, showed "that neither the class of persons who had been imported as slaves, nor their descendants, whether they had become free or not, were then acknowledged as a part of the people, nor intended to be included in the general words used in that instrument;" that "they had for more than a century before been regarded as beings of an inferior race, and altogether unfit to associate with the white race, either in social or political relations, and so far inferior that they had no rights which the white man was bound to respect, and that the negro might justly and lawfully be reduced to slavery for his benefit;" that he was "bought and sold, and treated as an ordinary article of merchandise and traffic, whenever a profit could be made by it;" and, that "this opinion was at that time fixed and universal in the civilized portion of the white race. It was regarded as an axiom in morals as well as in politics, which no one thought of disputing, or supposed to be open to dispute; and men in every grade and position in society daily and habitually acted upon it in their private pursuits, as well as in matters of public concern, without for a moment doubting the correctness of this opinion."

The judgment of the court was that the words "people of the United States" and "citizens" meant the same thing, both describing "the political body who, according to our republican institutions, form the sovereignty and hold the power and conduct the government through their representatives;" that "they are what we familiarly call the 'sovereign people,' and every citizen is one of this people and a constituent member of this sovereignty;" but, that the class of persons described in the plea in abatement did not compose a portion of this people, were not "included, and were not intended to be included, under the word 'citizens' in the Constitution;" that, therefore, they could "claim none of the rights and privileges which that instrument provides for and secures to citizens of the United States;" that, "on the contrary, they were at that time considered as a subordinate and inferior class of beings, who had been subjugated by the dominant race, and, whether emancipated or not, yet remained subject to their authority, and had no rights or privileges but such as those who held the power and the government might choose to grant them."

Such were the relations which formerly existed between the government, whether national or state, and the descendants, whether free or in bondage, of those of African blood, who had been imported into this country and sold as slaves.

The first section of the Thirteenth Amendment provides that "neither slavery nor involuntary servitude, except as a punishment for crime, whereof the party shall have been duly convicted, shall exist within the United States, or any place subject to their jurisdiction." Its second section declares that "Congress shall have power to enforce this article by appropriate legislation." This amendment was followed by the Civil Rights Act of April 9, 1866, which, among other things, provided that "all persons born in the United States, and not subject to any foreign power, excluding Indians not taxed, are hereby declared to be citizens of the United States." 14 Stat. 27. The power of Congress, in this mode, to elevate the enfranchised race to national citizenship, was maintained by the supporters of the act of 1866 to be as full and complete as its power, by general statute, to make the children, being of full age, of persons naturalized in this country, citizens of the United States without going through the process of naturalization. The act of 1866, in this respect, was also likened to that of 1843, in which Congress declared "that the Stockbridge tribe of Indians, and each and every one of them, shall be deemed to be and are hereby declared to be, citizens of the United States to all intents and purposes, and shall be entitled to all the rights, privileges, and immunities of such citizens, and shall in all respects be subject to the laws of the United States." If the act of 1866 was valid in conferring national citizenship upon all embraced by its terms, then the colored race, enfranchised by the Thirteenth Amendment, became citizens of the United States prior to the adoption of the Fourteenth Amendment. But, in the view which I take of the present case, it is not necessary to examine this question.

The terms of the Thirteenth Amendment are absolute and universal. They embrace every race which then was, or might thereafter be, within the United States. No race, as such, can be excluded from the benefits or rights thereby conferred. Yet, it is historically true that that amendment was suggested by the condition, in this country, of that race which had been declared, by this court, to have had—according to the opinion entertained by the most civilized portion of the white race, at the time of the adoption of the Constitution—"no rights which the white man was bound to respect," none of the privileges or immunities secured by that instrument to citizens of the United States. It had reference, in a peculiar sense, to a people which (although the larger part of them were in slavery) had been invited by an act of Congress to aid in saving from overthrow a government which, theretofore, by all of its departments, had treated them as an inferior race, with no legal rights or privileges except such as the white race might choose to grant them.

These are the circumstances under which the Thirteenth Amendment was proposed for adoption. They are now recalled only that we may better understand what was in the minds of the people when that amendment was considered, and what were the mischiefs to be remedied and the grievances to be redressed by its adoption.

We have seen that the power of Congress, by legislation, to enforce the master's right to have his slave delivered up on claim was *implied* from the recognition of that right in the national Constitution. But the power conferred by the Thirteenth Amendment does not rest upon implication or inference. Those who framed it were not ignorant of the discussion, covering many years of our country's history, as to the constitutional power of Congress to enact the Fugitive Slave Laws of 1793 and 1850. When, therefore, it was determined, by a change in the fundamental law, to uproot the institution of slavery wherever it existed in the land, and to establish universal freedom, there was a fixed purpose to place the authority of Congress in the premises beyond the possibility of a doubt. Therefore, *ex industria*, power to enforce the Thirteenth Amendment, by appropriate legislation, was expressly granted. Legislation for that purpose, my brethren concede, may be direct and primary. But to what specific ends may it be directed? This court has uniformly held that the national government has the power, whether expressly given or not, to secure and protect rights conferred or guaranteed by the Constitution. *United States* v. *Reese*, 92 U. S. 214; *Strauder* v. *West Virginia*, 100 U. S. 303. That doctrine ought not now to be abandoned when the inquiry is not as to an implied power to protect the master's rights, but what may Congress, under powers expressly granted, do for the protection of freedom and the rights necessarily inhering in a state of freedom.

The Thirteenth Amendment, it is conceded, did something more than to prohibit slavery as an *institution*, resting upon distinctions of race, and upheld by positive law. My brethren admit that it established and decreed universal *civil freedom* throughout the United States. But did the freedom thus established involve nothing more than exemption from actual slavery? Was nothing more intended than to forbid one man from owning another as property? Was it the purpose of the nation simply to destroy the institution, and then remit the race, theretofore held in bondage, to the several States for such protection, in their civil rights, necessarily growing out of freedom, as those States, in their discretion, might choose to provide? Were the States against whose protest the institution was destroyed, to be left free, so far as national interference was concerned, to make or allow discriminations against that race, as such, in the enjoyment of those fundamental rights which by universal concession, inhere in a state of freedom? Had the Thirteenth Amendment stopped with the sweeping declaration, in its first section, against the existence of slavery and involuntary servitude, except for crime, Congress would have had the power, by implication, according to the doctrines of *Prigg* v. *Commonwealth of Pennsylvania*, repeated in *Strauder* v. *West Virginia*, to protect the freedom established, and consequently, to secure the enjoyment of such civil rights as were fundamental in freedom. That it can exert its authority to that extent is made clear, and was intended to be made clear, by the express grant of power contained in the second section of the Amendment.

That there are burdens and disabilities which constitute badges of slavery and servitude, and that the power to enforce by appropriate legislation the Thirteenth Amendment may be exerted by legislation of a direct and primary character, for the eradication, not simply of the institution, but of its badges and incidents, are propositions which ought to be deemed indisputable. They lie at the foundation of the Civil Rights Act of 1866. Whether that act was authorized by the Thirteenth

Amendment alone, without the support which it subsequently received from the Fourteenth Amendment, after the adoption of which it was re-enacted with some additions, my brethren do not consider it necessary to inquire. But I submit, with all respect to them, that its constitutionality is conclusively shown by their opinion. They admit, as I have said, that the Thirteenth Amendment established freedom; that there are burdens and disabilities, the necessary incidents of slavery, which constitute its substance and visible form; that Congress, by the act of 1866, passed in view of the Thirteenth Amendment, before the Fourteenth was adopted, undertook to remove certain burdens and disabilities, the necessary incidents of slavery, and to secure to all citizens of every race and color, and without regard to previous servitude, those fundamental rights which are the essence of civil freedom, namely, the same right to make and enforce contracts, to sue, be parties, give evidence, and to inherit, purchase, lease, sell, and convey property as is enjoyed by white citizens; that under the Thirteenth Amendment, Congress has to do with slavery and its incidents; and that legislation, so far as necessary or proper to eradicate all forms and incidents of slavery and involuntary servitude, may be direct and primary, operating upon the acts of individuals, whether sanctioned by State legislation or not. These propositions being conceded, it is impossible, as it seems to me, to question the constitutional validity of the Civil Rights Act of 1866. I do not contend that the Thirteenth Amendment invests Congress with authority, by legislation, to define and regulate the entire body of the civil rights which citizens enjoy, or may enjoy, in the several States. But I hold that since slavery, as the court has repeatedly declared, *Slaughter-house Cases*, 16 Wall. 36; *Strauder* v. *West Virginia*, 100 U. S. 303, was the moving or principal cause of the adoption of that amendment, and since that institution rested wholly upon the inferiority, as a race, of those held in bondage, their freedom necessarily involved immunity from, and protection against, all discrimination against them, because of their race, in respect of such civil rights as belong to freemen of other races. Congress, therefore, under its express power to enforce that amendment, by appropriate legislation, may enact laws to protect that people against the deprivation, *because of their race*, of any civil rights granted to other freemen in the same State; and such legislation may be of a direct and primary character, operating upon States, their officers and agents, and, also, upon, at least, such individuals and corporations as exercise public functions and wield power and authority under the State.

To test the correctness of this position, let us suppose that, prior to the adoption of the Fourteenth Amendment, a State had passed a statute denying to freemen of African descent, resident within its limits, the same right which was accorded to white persons, of making and enforcing contracts, and of inheriting, purchasing, leasing, selling and conveying property; or a statute subjecting colored people to severer punishment for particular offences than was prescribed for white persons, or excluding that race from the benefit of the laws exempting homesteads from execution. Recall the legislation of 1865–6 in some of the States, of which this court, in the *Slaughter-House Cases*, said, that it imposed upon the colored race onerous disabilities and burdens; curtailed their rights in the pursuit of life, liberty and property to such an extent that their freedom was of little value; forbade them to appear in the towns in any other character than menial servants; required them to reside on and cultivate the soil, without the right to purchase or own it; excluded them from many occupations of gain; and denied them the privilege of giving testimony in the courts where a white man was a party. 16 Wall. 57. Can there be any doubt that all such enactments might have been reached by direct legislation upon the part of Congress under its express power to enforce the Thirteenth Amendment? Would any court have hesitated to declare that such legislation imposed badges of servitude in conflict with the civil freedom ordained by that amendment? That it would have been also in conflict with the Fourteenth Amendment, because inconsistent with the fundamental rights of American citizenship, does not prove that it would have been consistent with the Thirteenth Amendment.

What has been said is sufficient to show that the power of Congress under the Thirteenth Amendment is not necessarily restricted to legislation against slavery as an institution upheld by positive law, but may be exerted to the extent, at least, of protecting the liberated race against discrimination, in respect of legal rights belonging to freemen, where such discrimination is based upon race.

It remains now to inquire what are the legal rights of colored persons in respect of the accommodations, privileges and facilities of public conveyances, inns and places of public amusement?

First, as to public conveyances on land and water. In *New Jersey Steam Navigation Co.* v. *Merchants' Bank*, 6 How. 344, this court, speaking by Mr. Justice Nelson, said that a common carrier is "in the exercise of a sort of public office, and has public duties to perform, from which he should not be permitted to exonerate himself without the assent of the parties concerned." To the same effect is *Munn* v. *Illinois*, 94 U. S. 113. In *Olcott* v. *Supervisors*, 16 Wall. 678, it was ruled that railroads are public highways, established by authority of the State for the public use; that they are none the less public highways, because controlled and owned by private corporations; that it is a part of the function of government to make and maintain highways for the convenience of the public; that no matter who is the agent, or what is the agency, the function performed is *that of the State*; that although the owners may be private companies, they may be compelled to permit the public to use these works in the manner in which they can be used; that, upon these grounds alone, have the courts sustained the investiture of railroad corporations with the State's right of eminent domain, or the right of municipal corporations, under legislative authority, to assess, levy and collect taxes to aid in the construction of railroads. So in *Township of Queensbury* v. *Culver*, 19 Wall. 83, it was said that a municipal subscription of railroad stock was in aid of the construction and maintenance of a public highway, and for the promotion of a public use. Again, in *Township of Pine Grove* v. *Talcott*, 19 Wall. 666: "Though the corporation [railroad] was private, its work was public, as much so as if it were to be constructed by the State." To the like effect are numerous adjudications in this and the State courts with which the profession is familiar. The Supreme Judicial Court of Massachusetts in *Inhabitants of Worcester* v. *The Western R. R. Corporation*, 4 Met. 564, said in reference to a railroad:

"The establishment of that great thoroughfare is regarded as a public work, established by public authority, intended for the public use and benefit, the use of which is secured to the whole community, and constitutes, therefore, like a canal, turnpike, or highway, a public easement. . . . It is true that the real and personal property, necessary to the establishment and management of the railroad, is vested in the corporation; but it is in trust for the public." In *Erie, Etc., R. R. Co.* v. *Casey*, 26 Penn. St. 287, the court, referring to an act repealing the character of a railroad, and under which the State took possession of the road, said: "It is a public highway, solemnly devoted to public use. When the lands were taken it was for such use, or they could not have been taken at all. . . . Railroads established upon land taken by the right of eminent domain by authority of the commonwealth, created by her laws as thoroughfares for commerce, are her highways. No corporation has property in them, though it may have franchises annexed to and exercisable within them."

In many courts it has been held that because of the public interest in such a corporation the land of a railroad company cannot be levied on and sold under execution by a creditor. The sum of the adjudged cases is that a railroad corporation is a governmental agency, created primarily for public purposes, and subject to be controlled for the public benefit. Upon this ground the State, when unfettered by contract, may regulate, in its discretion, the rates of fares of passengers and freight. And upon this ground, too, the State may regulate the entire management of railroads in all matters affecting the convenience and safety of the public; as, for example, by regulating speed, compelling stops of prescribed length at stations, and prohibiting discriminations and favoritism. If the corporation neglect or refuse to discharge its duties to the public, it may be coerced to do so by appropriate proceedings in the name or in behalf of the State.

Such being the relations these corporations hold to the public, it would seem that the right of a colored person to use an improved public highway, upon the terms accorded to freemen of other races, is as fundamental, in the state of freedom established in this country, as are any of the rights which my brethren concede to be so far fundamental as to be deemed the essence of civil freedom. "Personal liberty consists," says Blackstone, "in the power of locomotion, of changing situation, or removing one's person to whatever places one's own inclination may direct, without restraint, unless by due course of law." But of what value is this right of locomotion, if it may be clogged by such burdens as Congress intended by the act of 1875 to remove? They are burdens which lay at the very foundation of the institution of slavery as it once existed. They are not to be sustained, except upon the assumption that there is, in this land of universal liberty, a class which may still be discriminated against, even in respect of rights of a character so necessary and supreme, that, deprived of their enjoyment in common with others, a freeman is not only branded as one inferior and infected, but, in the competitions of life, is robbed of some of the most essential means of existence; and all this solely because they belong to a particular race which the nation has liberated. The Thirteenth Amendment alone obliterated the race line, so far as all rights fundamental in a state of freedom are concerned.

Second, as to inns. The same general observations which have been made as to railroads are applicable to inns. The word 'inn' has a technical legal signification. It means, in the act of 1875, just what it meant at common law. A mere private boarding-house is not an inn, nor is its keeper subject to the responsibilities, or entitled to the privileges of a common innkeeper. "To constitute one an innkeeper, within the legal force of that term, he must keep a house of entertainment or lodging for all travellers or wayfarers who might choose to accept the same, being of good character or conduct." Redfield on Carriers, etc., § 575. Says Judge Story:

> "An innkeeper may be defined to be the keeper of a common inn for the lodging and entertainment of travellers and passengers, their horses and attendants. An innkeeper is bound to take in all travellers and wayfaring persons, and to entertain them, if he can accommodate them, for a reasonable compensation; and he must guard their goods with proper diligence. . . . If an innkeeper improperly refuses to receive or provide for a guest, he is liable to be indicted therefor. . . . They (carriers of passengers) are no more at liberty to refuse a passenger, if they have sufficient room and accommodations, than an innkeeper is to refuse suitable room and accommodations to a guest." Story on Bailments, §§ 475–6.

In *Rex* v. *Ivens*, 7 Carrington & Payne, 213, 32 E. C. L. 495, the court, speaking by Mr. Justice Coleridge, said:

> "An indictment lies against an innkeeper who refuses to receive a guest, he having at the time room in his house; and either the price of the guest's entertainment being tendered to him, or such circumstances occurring as will dispense with that tender. This law is founded in good sense. The innkeeper is not to select his guests. He has no right to say to one, you shall come to my inn, and to another you shall not, as every one coming and conducting himself in a proper manner has a right to be received; and for this purpose innkeepers are a sort of public servants, they having in return a kind of privilege of entertaining travellers and supplying them with what they want."

These authorities are sufficient to show that a keeper of an inn is in the exercise of a quasi public employment. The law gives him special privileges and he is charged with certain duties and responsibilities to the public. The public nature of his employment forbids him from discriminating against any person asking admission as a guest on account of the race or color of that person.

Third. As to places of public amusement. It may be argued that the managers of such places have no duties to perform with which the public are, in any legal sense, concerned, or with which the public have any right to interfere; and, that the exclusion of a black man from a place of public amusement, on account of his race, or the denial to him, on that ground, of equal accommodations at such places, violates no legal right for the vindication of which he may invoke the aid of the courts. My answer is, that places of public amusement, within the meaning of the act of 1875, are such as are established and maintained under direct license of the law. The authority to establish and maintain them comes from the public. The colored race is a part of that public. The local government granting the license represents them as well as all other races within its jurisdiction. A license from the public to establish a place of public amusement, imports, in law, equality of right, at such places, among all the members of that public. This must be so, unless it be—which I deny—that the common municipal government of all the people may, in the exertion of its powers, conferred for the benefit of all, discriminate or authorize discrimination against a particular race, solely because of its former condition of servitude.

I also submit, whether it can be said—in view of the doctrines of this court as announced in *Munn* v. *State of Illinois*, 94 U. S. 113, and reaffirmed in *Peik* v. *Chicago & N. W. Railway Co.*, 94 U. S. 164—that the management of places of public amusement is a purely private matter, with which government has no rightful concern? In the Munn case the question was whether the State of Illinois could fix, by law, the maximum of charges for the storage of grain in certain warehouses in that State—the *private property of individual citizens*. After quoting a remark attributed to Lord Chief Justice Hale, to the effect that when private property is "affected with a public interest it ceases to be *juris privati* only," the court says:

> "Property does become clothed with a public interest when used in a manner to make it of public consequence and affect the community at large. When, therefore, one devotes his property to a use in which the public has an interest, he, in effect, grants to the public an interest in that use, and must submit to be controlled by the public for the common good, to the extent of the interest he has thus created. He may withdraw his grant by discontinuing the use, but, so long as he maintains the use, he must submit to the control."

The doctrines of *Munn* v. *Illinois* have never been modified by this court, and I am justified, upon the authority of that case, in saying that places of public amusement, conducted under the authority of the law, are clothed with a public interest, because used in a manner to make them of public consequence and to affect the community at large. The law may therefore regulate, to some extent, the mode in which they shall be conducted, and, consequently, the public have rights in respect of such places, which may be vindicated by the law. It is consequently not a matter purely of private concern.

Congress has not, in these matters, entered the domain of State control and supervision. It does not, as I have said, assume to prescribe the general conditions and limitations under which inns, public conveyances, and places of public amusement, shall be conducted or managed. It simply declares, in effect, that since the nation has established universal freedom in this country, for all time, there shall be no discrimination, based merely upon race or color, in respect of the accommodations and advantages of public conveyances, inns, and places of public amusement.

I am of the opinion that such discrimination practised by corporations and individuals in the exercise of their public or quasi-public functions is a badge of servitude the imposition of which Congress may prevent under its power, by appropriate legislation, to enforce the Thirteenth Amendment; and, consequently, without reference to its enlarged power under the Fourteenth Amendment, the act of March 1, 1875, is not, in my judgment, repugnant to the Constitution.

It remains now to consider these cases with reference to the power Congress has possessed since the adoption of the Fourteenth Amendment. Much that has been said as to the power of Congress under the Thirteenth Amendment is applicable to this branch of the discussion, and will not be repeated.

Before the adoption of the recent amendments, it had become, as we have seen, the established doctrine of this court that negroes, whose ancestors had been imported and sold as slaves, could not become citizens of a State, or even of the United States, with the rights and privileges guaranteed to citizens by the national Constitution; further, that one might have all the rights and privileges of a citizen of a State without being a citizen in the sense in which that word was used in the national Constitution, and without being entitled to the privileges and immunities of citizens of the several States. Still, further, between the adoption of the Thirteenth Amendment and the proposal by Congress of the Fourteenth Amendment, on June 16, 1866, the statute books of several of the States, as we have seen, had become loaded down with enactments which, under the guise of Apprentice, Vagrant, and Contract regulations, sought to keep the colored race in a condition, practically, of servitude. It was openly announced that whatever might be the rights which persons of that race had, as freemen, under the guarantees of the national Constitution, they could not become citizens of a State, with the privileges belonging to citizens, except by the consent of such State; consequently, that their civil rights, as citizens of the State, depended entirely upon State legislation. To meet this new peril to the black race, that the purposes of the nation might not be doubted or defeated, and by way of further enlargement of the power of Congress, the Fourteenth Amendment was proposed for adoption.

Remembering that this court, in the *Slaughter-House Cases*, declared that the one pervading purpose found in all the recent amendments, lying at the foundation of each, and without which none of them would have been suggested—was "the freedom of the slave race, the security and firm establishment of that freedom, and the protection of the newly-made freeman and citizen from the oppression of those who had formerly exercised unlimited dominion over him"—that each amendment was addressed primarily to the grievances of that race—let us proceed to consider the language of the Fourteenth Amendment.

Its first and fifth sections are in these words:

> "SEC. 1. All persons born or naturalized in the United States, and subject to the jurisdiction thereof, are citizens of the United States and of the State wherein they reside. No State shall make or enforce any law which shall abridge the privileges or immunities of citizens of the United States; nor shall any State deprive any person of life, liberty, or property, without due process of law; nor deny to any person within its jurisdiction the equal protection of the laws.
>
> * * * * * *
>
> "SEC. 5. That Congress shall have power to enforce, by appropriate legislation, the provisions of this article."

It was adjudged in *Strauder* v. *West Virginia*, 100 U. S. 303, and *Ex parte Virginia*, 100 U. S. 339, and my brethren concede, that positive rights and privileges were intended to be secured, and are in fact secured, by the Fourteenth Amendment.

But when, under what circumstances, and to what extent, may Congress, by means of legislation, exert its power to enforce the provisions of this amendment? The theory of the opinion of the majority of the court—the foundation upon which their reasoning seems to rest—is, that the general government cannot, in advance of hostile State laws or hostile State proceedings, actively interfere for the protection of any of the rights, privileges, and immunities secured by the Fourteenth Amendment. It is said that such rights, privileges, and immunities are secured by way of *prohibition* against State laws and State proceedings affecting such rights and privileges, and by power given to Congress to legislate for the purpose of carrying *such prohibition* into effect; also, that congressional legislation must necessarily be predicated upon such supposed State laws or State proceedings, and be directed to the correction of their operation and effect.

In illustration of its position, the court refers to the clause of the Constitution forbidding the passage by a State of any law impairing the obligation of contracts. That clause does not, I submit, furnish a proper illustration of the scope and effect of the fifth section of the Fourteenth Amendment. No express power is given Congress to enforce, by primary direct legislation, the prohibition upon State laws impairing the obligation of contracts. Authority is, indeed, conferred to enact all necessary and proper laws for carrying into execution the enumerated powers of Congress and all other powers vested by the Constitution in the government of the United States or in any department or officer thereof. And, as heretofore shown, there is also, by necessary implication, power in Congress, by legislation, to protect a right derived from the national Constitution. But a prohibition upon a State is not a *power* in *Congress* or *in the national government.* It is simply a *denial* of *power* to the *State.* And the only mode in which the inhibition upon State laws impairing the obligation of contracts can be enforced, is, indirectly, through the courts, in suits where the parties raise some question as to the constitutional validity of such laws. The judicial power of the United States extends to such suits for the reason that they are suits arising under the Constitution. The Fourteenth Amendment presents the first instance in our history of the investiture of Congress with affirmative power, by *legislation*, to *enforce* an express prohibition upon the States. It is not said that the *judicial* power of the nation may be exerted for the enforcement of that amendment. No enlargement of the judicial power was required, for it is clear that had the fifth section of the Fourteenth Amendment been entirely omitted, the judiciary could have stricken down all State laws and nullified all State proceedings in hostility to rights and privileges secured or recognized by that amendment. The power given is, in terms, by congressional *legislation*, to enforce the provisions of the amendment.

The assumption that this amendment consists wholly of prohibitions upon State laws and State proceedings in hostility to its provisions, is unauthorized by its language. The first clause of the first section—"All persons born or naturalized in the United States, and subject to the jurisdiction thereof, are citizens of the United States, and of the State wherein they reside" —is of a distinctly affirmative character. In its application to the colored race, previously liberated, it created and granted, as well citizenship of the United States, as citizenship of the State in which they respectively resided. It introduced all of that race, whose ancestors had been imported and sold as slaves, at once, into the political community known as the "People of the United States." They became, instantly, citizens of the United States, *and* of their respective States. Further, they were brought, by this supreme act of the nation, within the direct operation of that provision of the Constitution which declares that "the citizens of each State shall be entitled to all privileges and immunities of citizens in the several States." Art. 4, § 2.

The citizenship thus acquired, by that race, in virtue of an affirmative grant from the nation, may be protected, not alone by the judicial branch of the government, but by congressional legislation of a primary direct character; this, because the power of Congress is not restricted to the enforcement of prohibitions upon State laws or State action. It is, in terms distinct and positive, to enforce "the *provisions* of *this article*" of amendment; not simply those of a prohibitive character, but the provisions—*all* of the provisions—affirmative and prohibitive, of the amendment. It is, therefore, a grave misconception to suppose that the fifth section of the amendment has reference exclusively to express prohibitions upon State laws or State action. If any right was created by that amendment, the grant of power, through appropriate legislation, to enforce its provisions, authorizes Congress, by means of legislation, operating throughout the entire Union, to guard, secure, and protect that right.

It is, therefore, an essential inquiry what, if any, right, privilege or immunity was given, by the nation, to colored persons, when they were made citizens of the State in which they reside? Did the constitutional grant of State citizenship to that race, of its own force, invest them with any rights, privileges and immunities whatever? That they became entitled, upon the adoption of the Fourteenth Amendment, "to all privileges and immunities of citizens in the several States," within the meaning of section 2 of article 4 of the Constitution, no one, I suppose, will for a moment question. What are the privileges and immunities to which, by that clause of the Constitution, they became entitled? To this it may be answered, generally, upon the authority of the adjudged cases, that they are those which are fundamental in citizenship in a free republican government, such as are "common to the citizens in the latter States under their constitutions and laws by virtue of their being citizens." Of that provision it has been said, with the approval of this court, that no other one in the Constitution has tended so strongly to constitute the citizens of the United States one people. *Ward* v. *Maryland*, 12 Wall. 418; *Corfield* v. *Coryell*, 4 Wash. C. C. 371; *Paul* v. *Virginia*, 8 Wall. 168; *Slaughter-house Cases*, 16 id. 36.

Although this court has wisely forborne any attempt, by a comprehensive definition, to indicate all of the privileges and immunities to which the citizen of a State is entitled, of right, when within the jurisdiction of other States, I hazard nothing, in view of former ajudications, in saying that no State can sustain her denial to colored citizens of other States, while within her limits, of privileges or immunities, fundamental in republican citizenship, upon the ground that she accords such privileges and immunities only to her white citizens and withholds them from her colored citizens. The colored citizens of other States, within the jurisdiction of that State, could claim, in virtue of section 2 of article 4 of the Constitution, every privilege and immunity which that State secures to her white citizens. Otherwise, it would be in the power of any State, by discriminating class legislation against its own citizens of a particular race or color, to withhold from citizens of other States, belonging to that proscribed race, when within her limits, privileges and immunities of the character regarded by all courts as fundamental in citizenship; and that, too, when the constitutional guaranty is that the citizens of each State shall be entitled to "all privileges and immunities of citizens of the several States." No State may, by discrimination against a portion of its own citizens of a particular race, in respect of privileges and immunities fundamental in citizenship, impair the constitutional right of citizens of other States, of whatever race, to enjoy in that State all such privileges and immunities as are there accorded to her most favored citizens. A colored citizen of Ohio or Indiana, while in the jurisdiction of Tennessee, is entitled to enjoy any privilege or immunity, fundamental in citizenship, which is given to citizens of the white race in the latter State. It is not to be supposed that any one will controvert this proposition.

But what was secured to colored citizens of the United States —as between them and their respective States—by the national grant to them of State citizenship? With what rights, privileges, or immunities did this grant invest them? There is one, if there be no other—exemption from race discrimination in respect of any civil right belonging to citizens of the white race in the same State. That, surely, is their constitutional privilege when within the jurisdiction of other States. And such must be their constitutional right, in their own State, unless the recent amendments be splendid baubles, thrown out to delude those who deserved fair and generous treatment at the hands of the nation. Citizenship in this country necessarily imports at least equality of civil rights among citizens of every race in the same State. It is fundamental in American citizenship that, in respect of such rights, there shall be no discrimination by the State, or its officers, or by individuals or corporations exercising public functions or authority, against any citizen because of his race or previous condition of servitude. In *United States* v. *Cruikshank*, 92 U. S. 542, it was said at page 555, that the rights of life and personal liberty are natural rights of man, and that "the equality of the rights of citizens is a principle of republicanism." And in *Ex parte Virginia*, 100 U. S. 334, the emphatic language of this court is that "one great purpose of these amendments was to raise the colored race from that condition of inferiority and servitude in which most of them had previously stood, into perfect equality of civil rights with all other persons within the jurisdiction of the States." So, in *Strauder* v. *West Virginia*, 100 U. S. 306, the court, alluding to the Fourteenth Amendment, said: "This is one of a series of constitutional provisions having a common purpose, namely, securing to a race recently emancipated, a race that through many generations had been held in slavery, all the civil rights that the superior race enjoy." Again, in *Neal* v. *Delaware*, 103 U. S. 386, it was ruled that this amendment was designed, primarily, "to secure to the colored race, thereby invested with the rights, privileges, and responsibilities of citizenship, the enjoyment of all the civil rights that, under the law, are enjoyed by white persons."

The language of this court with reference to the Fifteenth Amendment, adds to the force of this view. In *United States* v. *Cruikshank*, it was said: "In *United States* v. *Reese*, 92 U. S. 214, we held that the Fifteenth Amendment has invested the citizens of the United States with a new constitutional right, which is exemption from discrimination in the exercise of the elective franchise, on account of race, color, or previous condition of servitude. From this it appears that the right of suffrage is not a necessary attribute of national citizenship, but that exemption from discrimination in the exercise of that right on account of race, &c., is. The right to vote in the States comes from the States; but the right of exemption from the prohibited discrimination comes from the United States. The first has not been granted or secured by the Constitution of the United States, but the last has been."

Here, in language at once clear and forcible, is stated the principle for which I contend. It can scarcely be claimed that exemption from race discrimination, in respect of civil rights, against those to whom State citizenship was granted by the nation, is any less, for the colored race, a new constitutional right, derived from and secured by the national Constitution, than is exemption from such discrimination in the exercise of the elective franchise. It cannot be that the latter is an attribute of national citizenship, while the other is not essential in national citizenship, or fundamental in State citizenship.

If, then, exemption from discrimination, in respect of civil rights, is a new constitutional right, secured by the grant of State citizenship to colored citizens of the United States—and I do not see how this can now be questioned—why may not the nation, by means of its own legislation of a primary direct character, guard, protect and enforce that right? It is a right and privilege which the nation conferred. It did not come from the States in which those colored citizens reside. It has been the established doctrine of this court during all its history, accepted as essential to the national supremacy, that Congress, in the absence of a positive delegation of power to the State legislatures, may, by its own legislation, enforce and protect any right derived from or created by the national Constitution. It was so declared in *Prigg* v. *Commonwealth of Pennsylvania*. It was reiterated in *United States* v. *Reese*, 92 U. S. 214, where the court said that "rights and immunities created by and dependent upon the Constitution of the United States can be protected by Congress. The form and manner of the protection may be such as Congress, in the legitimate exercise of its discretion, shall provide. These may be varied to meet the necessities of the particular right to be protected." It was distinctly reaffirmed in *Strauder* v. *West Virginia*, 100 U. S. 310, where we said that "a right or immunity created by the Constitution or only guaranteed by it, even without any express delegation of power, may be protected by Congress." How then can it be claimed in view of the declarations of this court in former cases, that exemption of colored citizens, within their States, from race discrimination, in respect of the civil rights of citizens, is not an immunity created or derived from the national Constitution?

This court has always given a broad and liberal construction to the Constitution, so as to enable Congress, by legislation, to enforce rights secured by that instrument. The legislation which Congress may enact, in execution of its power to enforce the provisions of this amendment, is such as may be appropriate to protect the right granted. The word appropriate was undoubtedly used with reference to its meaning, as established by repeated decisions of this court. Under given circumstances, that which the court characterizes as corrective legislation might be deemed by Congress appropriate and entirely sufficient. Under other circumstances primary direct legislation may be required. But it is for Congress, not the judiciary, to say that legislation is appropriate—that is—best adapted to the end to be attained. The judiciary may not, with safety to our institutions, enter the domain of legislative discretion, and dictate the means which Congress shall employ in the exercise of its granted powers. That would be sheer usurpation of the functions of a co-ordinate department, which, if often repeated, and permanently acquiesced in, would work a radical change in our system of government. In *United States* v. *Fisher*, 2 Cr. 358, the court said that "Congress must possess the choice of means, and must be empowered to use any means which are in fact conducive to the exercise of a power granted by the Constitution." "The sound construction of the Constitution," said Chief Justice Marshall, "must allow to the national legislature that discretion, with respect to the means by which the powers it confers are to be carried into execution, which will enable that body to perform the high duties assigned to it in the manner most beneficial to the people. Let the end be legitimate, let it be within the scope of the Constitution, and all means which are appropriate, which are plainly adapted to that end, which are not prohibited, but consist with the letter and spirit of the Constitution, are constitutional." *McCulloch* v. *Maryland*, 4 Wh. 421.

Must these rules of construction be now abandoned? Are the powers of the national legislature to be restrained in proportion as the rights and privileges, derived from the nation, are valuable? Are constitutional provisions, enacted to secure the dearest rights of freemen and citizens, to be subjected to that rule of construction, applicable to private instruments, which requires that the words to be interpreted must be taken most strongly against those who employ them? Or, shall it be remembered that "a constitution of government, founded by the people for themselves and their posterity, and for objects of the most momentous nature—for perpetual union, for the establishment of justice, for the general welfare, and for a perpetuation of the blessings of liberty—necessarily requires that every interpretation of its powers should have a constant reference to these objects? No interpretation of the words in which those powers are granted can be a sound one, which narrows down their ordinary import so as to defeat those objects." 1 Story Const. § 422.

The opinion of the court, as I have said, proceeds upon the ground that the power of Congress to legislate for the protection of the rights and privileges secured by the Fourteenth Amendment cannot be brought into activity except with the view, and as it may become necessary, to correct and annul State laws and State proceedings in hostility to such rights and privileges. In the absence of State laws or State action adverse to such rights and privileges, the nation may not actively interfere for their protection and security, even against corporations and individuals exercising public or quasi public functions. Such I understand to be the position of my brethren. If the grant to colored citizens of the United States of citizenship in their respective States, imports exemption from race discrimination, in their States, in respect of such civil rights as belong to citizenship, then, to hold that the amendment remits that right to the States for their protection, primarily, and stays the hands of the nation, until it is assailed by State laws or State proceedings, is to adjudge that the amendment, so far from enlarging the powers of Congress—as we have heretofore said it did—not only curtails them, but reverses the policy which the general government has pursued from its very organization. Such an interpretation of the amendment is a denial to Congress of the power, by appropriate legislation, to enforce one of its provisions. In view of the circumstances under which the recent amendments were incorporated into the Constitution, and especially in view of the peculiar character of the new rights they created and secured, it ought not to be presumed that the general government has abdicated its authority, by national legislation, direct and primary in its character, to guard and protect privileges and immunities secured by that instrument. Such an interpretation of the Constitution ought not to be accepted if it be possible to avoid it. Its acceptance would lead to this anomalous result: that whereas, prior to the amendments, Congress, with the sanction of this court, passed the most stringent laws—operating directly and primarily upon States and their officers and agents, as well as upon individuals—in vindication of slavery and the right of the master, it may not now, by legislation of a like primary and direct character, guard, protect, and secure the freedom established, and the most essential right of the citizenship granted, by the constitutional amendments. With all respect for the opinion of others, I insist that the national legislature may, without transcending the limits of the Constitution, do for human liberty and the fundamental rights of American citizenship, what it did, with the sanction of this court, for the protection of slavery and the rights of the masters of fugitive slaves. If fugitive slave laws, providing modes and prescribing penalties, whereby the master could seize and recover his fugitive slave, were legitimate exercises of an implied power to protect and enforce a right recognized by the Constitution, why shall the hands of Congress be tied, so that—under an express power, by appropriate legislation, to enforce a constitutional provision granting citizenship—it may not, by means of direct legislation, bring the whole power of this nation to bear upon States and their officers, and upon such individuals and corporations exercising public functions as assume to abridge, impair, or deny rights confessedly secured by the supreme law of the land?

It does not seem to me that the fact that, by the second clause of the first section of the Fourteenth Amendment, the States are expressly prohibited from making or enforcing laws abridging the privileges and immunities of citizens of the United States, furnishes any sufficient reason for holding or maintaining that the amendment was intended to deny Congress the power, by general, primary, and direct legislation, of protecting citizens of the several States, being also citizens of the United States, against all discrimination, in respect of their rights as citizens, which is founded on race, color, or previous condition of servitude.

Such an interpretation of the amendment is plainly repugnant to its fifth section, conferring upon Congress power, by appropriate legislation, to enforce not merely the provisions containing prohibitions upon the States, but all of the provisions of the amendment, including the provisions, express and implied, in the first clause of the first section of the article granting citizenship. This alone is sufficient for holding that Congress is not restricted to the enactment of laws adapted to counteract and redress the operation of State legislation, or the action of State officers, of the character prohibited by the amendment. It was perfectly well known that the great danger to the equal enjoyment by citizens of their rights, as citizens, was to be apprehended not altogether from unfriendly

State legislation, but from the hostile action of corporations and individuals in the States. And it is to be presumed that it was intended, by that section, to clothe Congress with power and authority to meet that danger. If the rights intended to be secured by the act of 1875 are such as belong to the citizen, in common or equally with other citizens in the same State, then it is not to be denied that such legislation is peculiarly appropriate to the end which Congress is authorized to accomplish, viz., to protect the citizen, in respect of such rights, against discrimination on account of his race. Recurring to the specific prohibition in the Fourteenth Amendment upon the making or enforcing of State laws abridging the privileges of citizens of the United States, I remark that if, as held in the *Slaughter-House Cases*, the privileges here referred to were those which belonged to citizenship of the United States, as distinguished from those belonging to State citizenship, it was impossible for any State prior to the adoption of that amendment to have enforced laws of that character. The judiciary could have annulled all such legislation under the provision that the Constitution shall be the supreme law of the land, anything in the constitution or laws of any State to the contrary notwithstanding. The States were already under an implied prohibition not to abridge any privilege or immunity belonging to citizens of the United States as such. Consequently, the prohibition upon State laws in hostility to rights belonging to citizens of the United States, was intended—in view of the introduction into the body of citizens of a race formerly denied the essential rights of citizenship—only as an express limitation on the powers of the States, and was not intended to diminish, in the slightest degree, the authority which the nation has always exercised, of protecting, by means of its own direct legislation, rights created or secured by the Constitution. Any purpose to diminish the national authority in respect of privileges derived from the nation is distinctly negatived by the express grant of power, by legislation, to enforce every provision of the amendment, including that which, by the grant of citizenship in the State, secures exemption from race discrimination in respect of the civil rights of citizens.

It is said that any interpretation of the Fourteenth Amendment different from that adopted by the majority of the court, would imply that Congress had authority to enact a municipal code for all the States, covering every matter affecting the life, liberty, and property of the citizens of the several States. Not so. Prior to the adoption of that amendment the constitutions of the several States, without perhaps an exception, secured all *persons* against deprivation of life, liberty, or property, otherwise than by due process of law, and, in some form, recognized the right of all *persons* to the equal protection of the laws. Those rights, therefore, existed before that amendment was proposed or adopted, and were not created by it. If, by reason of that fact, it be assumed that protection in these rights of persons still rests primarily with the States, and that Congress may not interfere except to enforce, by means of corrective legislation, the prohibitions upon State laws or State proceedings inconsistent with those rights, it does not at all follow, that privileges which have been *granted by the nation*, may not be protected by primary legislation upon the part of Congress. The personal rights and immunities recognized in the prohibitive clauses of the amendment were, prior to its adoption, under the protection, primarily, of the States, while rights, created by or derived from the United States, have always been, and, in the nature of things, should always be, primarily, under the protection of the general government. Exemption from race discrimination in respect of the civil rights which are fundamental in *citizenship* in a republican government, is, as we have seen, a new right, created by the nation, with express power in Congress, by legislation, to enforce the constitutional provision from which it is derived. If, in some sense, such race discrimination is, within the letter of the last clause of the first section, a denial of that equal protection of the laws which is secured against State denial to all persons, whether citizens or not, it cannot be possible that a mere prohibition upon such State denial, or a prohibition upon State laws abridging the privileges and immunities of citizens of the United States, takes from the nation the power which it has uniformly exercised of protecting, by direct primary legislation, those privileges and immunities which existed under the Constitution before the adoption of the Fourteenth Amendment, or have been created by that amendment in behalf of those thereby made *citizens* of their respective States.

This construction does not in any degree intrench upon the just rights of the States in the control of their domestic affairs. It simply recognizes the enlarged powers conferred by the recent amendments upon the general government. In the view which I take of those amendments, the States possess the same authority which they have always had to define and regulate the civil rights which their own people, in virtue of State citizenship, may enjoy within their respective limits; except that its exercise is now subject to the expressly granted power of Congress, by legislation, to enforce the provisions of such amendments—a power which necessarily carries with it authority, by national legislation, to protect and secure the privileges and immunities which are created by or are derived from those amendments. That exemption of citizens from discrimination based on race or color, in respect of civil rights, is one of those privileges or immunities, can no longer be deemed an open question in this court.

It was said of the case of *Dred Scott* v. *Sandford*, that this court, there overruled the action of two generations, virtually inserted a new clause in the Constitution, changed its character, and made a new departure in the workings of the federal government. I may be permitted to say that if the recent amendments are so construed that Congress may not, in its own discretion, and independently of the action or non-action of the States, provide, by legislation of a direct character, for the security of rights created by the national Constitution; if it be adjudged that the obligation to protect the fundamental privileges and immunities granted by the Fourteenth Amendment to citizens residing in the several States, rests primarily, not on the nation, but on the States; if it be further adjudged that individuals and corporations, exercising public functions, or wielding power under public authority, may, without liability to direct primary legislation on the part of Congress, make the race of citizens the ground for denying them that equality of civil rights which the Constitution ordains as a principle of republican citizenship; then, not only the foundations upon which the national supremacy has always securely rested will be materially disturbed, but we shall enter upon an era of constitutional law, when the rights of freedom and American citizenship cannot receive from the nation that efficient protection which heretofore was unhesitatingly accorded to slavery and the rights of the master.

But if it were conceded that the power of Congress could not be brought into activity until the rights specified in the act of 1875 had been abridged or denied by some State law or State action, I maintain that the decision of the court is erroneous. There has been adverse State action within the Fourteenth Amendment as heretofore interpreted by this court. I allude to *Ex parte Virginia, supra*. It appears, in that case, that one Cole, judge of a county court, was charged with the duty, by the laws of Virginia, of selecting grand and petit jurors. The law of the State did not authorize or permit him, in making such selections, to discriminate against colored citizens because of their race. But he was indicted in the federal court, under the act of 1875, for making such discriminations. The attorney-general of Virginia contended before us, that the State had done its duty, and had not authorized or directed that county judge to do what he was charged with having done; that the State had not denied to the colored race the equal protection of the laws; and that consequently the act of Cole must be deemed his individual act, in contravention of the will of the State. Plausible as this argument was, it failed to convince this court, and after saying that the Fourteenth Amendment had reference to the political body denominated a State, "by whatever instruments or in whatever modes that action may be taken," and that a State acts by its legislative, executive, and judicial authorities, and can act in no other way, we proceeded:

> "The constitutional provision, therefore, must mean that no agency of the State, or of the officers or agents by whom its powers are exerted, shall deny to any person within its jurisdiction the equal protection of the laws. Whoever, by virtue of public position under a State government, deprives another of property, life, or liberty without due process of law, or denies or takes away the equal protection of the laws, violates the constitutional inhibition; and, as he acts under the name and for the State, and is clothed with the State's power, his act is that of the State. This must be so, or the constitutional prohibition has no meaning. Then the State has clothed one of its agents with power to annul or evade it. But the constitutional amendment was ordained for a purpose. It was to secure equal rights to all

persons, and, to insure to all persons the enjoyment of such rights, power was given to Congress to enforce its provisions by appropriate legislation. Such legislation must act upon persons, not upon the abstract thing denominated a State, but upon the persons who are the agents of the State, in the denial of the rights which were intended to be secured." *Ex parte Virginia*, 100 U. S. 346–7.

In every material sense applicable to the practical enforcement of the Fourteenth Amendment, railroad corporations, keepers of inns, and managers of places of public amusement are agents or instrumentalities of the State, because they are charged with duties to the public, and are amenable, in respect of their duties and functions, to governmental regulation. It seems to me that, within the principle settled in *Ex parte Virginia*, a denial, by these instrumentalities of the State, to the citizen, because of his race, of that equality of civil rights secured to him by law, is a denial by the State, within the meaning of the Fourteenth Amendment. If it be not, then that race is left, in respect of the civil rights in question, practically at the mercy of corporations and individuals wielding power under the States.

But the court says that Congress did not, in the act of 1866, assume, under the authority given by the Thirteenth Amendment, to adjust what may be called the social rights of men and races in the community. I agree that government has nothing to do with social, as distinguished from technically legal, rights of individuals. No government ever has brought, or ever can bring, its people into social intercourse against their wishes. Whether one person will permit or maintain social relations with another is a matter with which government has no concern. I agree that if one citizen chooses not to hold social intercourse with another, he is not and cannot be made amenable to the law for his conduct in that regard; for even upon grounds of race, no legal right of a citizen is violated by the refusal of others to maintain merely social relations with him. What I affirm is that no State, nor the officers of any State, nor any corporation or individual wielding power under State authority for the public benefit or the public convenience, can, consistently either with the freedom established by the fundamental law, or with that equality of civil rights which now belongs to every citizen, discriminate against freemen or citizens, in those rights, because of their race, or because they once labored under the disabilities of slavery imposed upon them as a race. The rights which Congress, by the act of 1875, endeavored to secure and protect are legal, not social rights. The right, for instance, of a colored citizen to use the accommodations of a public highway, upon the same terms as are permitted to white citizens, is no more a social right than his right, under the law, to use the public streets of a city or a town, or a turnpike road, or a public market, or a post office, or his right to sit in a public building with others, of whatever race, for the purpose of hearing the political questions of the day discussed. Scarcely a day passes without our seeing in this court-room citizens of the white and black races sitting side by side, watching the progress of our business. It would never occur to any one that the presence of a colored citizen in a court-house, or court-room, was an invasion of the social rights of white persons who may frequent such places. And yet, such a suggestion would be quite as sound in law—I say it with all respect—as is the suggestion that the claim of a colored citizen to use, upon the same terms as is permitted to white citizens, the accommodations of public highways, or public inns, or places of public amusement, established under the license of the law, is an invasion of the social rights of the white race.

The court, in its opinion, reserves the question whether Congress, in the exercise of its power to regulate commerce amongst the several States, might or might not pass a law regulating rights in public conveyances passing from one State to another. I beg to suggest that that precise question was substantially presented here in the only one of these cases relating to railroads—*Robinson and Wife* v. *Memphis & Charleston Railroad Company.* In that case it appears that Mrs. Robinson, a citizen of Mississippi, purchased a railroad ticket entitling her to be carried from Grand Junction, Tennessee, to Lynchburg, Virginia. Might not the act of 1875 be maintained in that case, as applicable at least to commerce between the States, notwithstanding it does not, upon its face, profess to have been passed in pursuance of the power of Congress to regulate commerce? Has it ever been held that the judiciary should overturn a statute, because the legislative department did not accurately recite therein the particular provision of the Constitution authorizing its enactment? We have often enforced municipal bonds in aid of railroad subscriptions, where they failed to recite the statute authorizing their issue, but recited one which did not sustain their validity. The inquiry in such cases has been, was there, in any statute, authority for the execution of the bonds? Upon this branch of the case, it may be remarked that the State of Louisiana, in 1869, passed a statute giving to passengers, without regard to race or color, equality of right in the accommodations of railroad and street cars, steamboats or other water crafts, stage coaches, omnibuses, or other vehicles. But in *Hall v. De Cuir*, 95 U. S. 487, that act was pronounced unconstitutional so far as it related to commerce between the States, this court saying that "if the public good requires such legislation it must come from Congress, and not from the States." I suggest, that it may become a pertinent inquiry whether Congress may, in the exertion of its power to regulate commerce among the States, enforce among passengers on public conveyances, equality of right, without regard to race, color or previous condition of servitude, if it be true—which I do not admit—that such legislation would be an interference by government with the social rights of the people.

My brethren say, that when a man has emerged from slavery, and by the aid of beneficent legislation has shaken off the inseparable concomitants of that state, there must be some stage in the progress of his elevation when he takes the rank of a mere citizen, and ceases to be the special favorite of the laws, and when his rights as a citizen, or a man, are to be protected in the ordinary modes by which other men's rights are protected. It is, I submit, scarcely just to say that the colored race has been the special favorite of the laws. The statute of 1875, now adjudged to be unconstitutional, is for the benefit of citizens of every race and color. What the nation, through Congress, has sought to accomplish in reference to that race, is—what had already been done in every State of the Union for the white race—to secure and protect rights belonging to them as freemen and citizens; nothing more. It was not deemed enough "to help the feeble up, but to support him after." The one underlying purpose of congressional legislation has been to enable the black race to take the rank of mere citizens. The difficulty has been to compel a recognition of the legal right of the black race to take the rank of citizens, and to secure the enjoyment of privileges belonging, under the law, to them as a component part of the people for whose welfare and happiness government is ordained. At every step, in this direction, the nation has been confronted with class tyranny, which a contemporary English historian says is, of all tyrannies, the most intolerable, "for it is ubiquitous in its operation, and weighs, perhaps, most heavily on those whose obscurity or distance would withdraw them from the notice of a single despot." To-day, it is the colored race which is denied, by corporations and individuals wielding public authority, rights fundamental in their freedom and citizenship. At some future time, it may be that some other race will fall under the ban of race discrimination. If the constitutional amendments be enforced, according to the intent with which, as I conceive, they were adopted, there cannot be, in this republic, any class of human beings in practical subjection to another class, with power in the latter to dole out to the former just such privileges as they may choose to grant. The supreme law of the land has decreed that no authority shall be exercised in this country upon the basis of discrimination, in respect of civil rights, against freemen and citizens because of their race, color, or previous condition of servitude. To that decree —for the due enforcement of which, by appropriate legislation, Congress has been invested with express power—every one must bow, whatever may have been, or whatever now are, his individual views as to the wisdom or policy, either of the recent changes in the fundamental law, or of the legislation which has been enacted to give them effect.

For the reasons stated I feel constrained to withhold my assent to the opinion of the court.

"ALIENS IN OUR NATIVE LAND"

NEW YORK GLOBE
The Civil Rights Decision
October 20, 1883

THE CIVIL RIGHTS DECISION.

THE COLORED PEOPLE of the United States feel to-day as if they had been baptized in ice water. From Maine to Florida they are earnestly discussing the decision of the Supreme Court declaring the Civil Rights law to be unconstitutional. Public meetings are being projected far and wide to give expression to the common feeling of disappointment and apprehension for the future.

The Republican party has carried the war into Africa, and Africa is accordingly stirred to its centre.

We need not at this time review the legal aspects of the law or the decision. In times past we have done so.

It was only a few months ago that the Supreme Court declared that the Ku Klux law was unconstitutional—that the United States was powerless to protect its citizens in the enjoyment of life, liberty and the pursuit of happiness. What sort of Government is that which openly declares it has no power to protect its citizens from ruffianism, intimidation and murder! Is such a Government worthy the respect and loyalty of honest men? It certainly does not enjoy our respect and our loyalty to it is the cheapest possession we have.

Having declared that colored men have no protection from the government in their political rights, the Supreme Court now declares that we have no civil rights—declares that railroad corporations are free to force us into smoking cars or cattle cars; that hotel keepers are free to make us walk the streets at night; that theatre managers can refuse us admittance to their exhibitions for the amusement of the public—it has reaffirmed the infamous decision of the infamous Chief Justice Taney that a "black man has no rights that a white man is bound to respect."

We look facts squarely in the face; we are not given to

dodging and hedging—we believe in striking squarely from the shoulder. Then, what is the position in which the Supreme Court has left us? Simply this—we have the ballot without any law to protect us in the enjoyment of it; we are declared to be created equal, and entitled to certain rights, among them life, liberty and the pursuit of happiness, but there is no law to protect us in the enjoyment of them. We are aliens in our native land; we are denied an equal measure of that protection which flows from citizenship, and which is denied to no other class of American citizens—denied to us because the position we hold to the American people is a decidedly new and peculiar one. The colored people have been told emphatically that they have the ballot, and if they cannot use it it can't be helped. We are placed at the mercy of every lawless ruffian; we are declared to be the victims of infamous injustice without redress; we are told that we can expect nothing from the United States government, which we have always regarded as the football of the States—an expensive thing that could just as well be lopped off as not.

The Republican party has certainly tried the faith of the colored man. It has gradually stripped him of all the rights which had been given to him for his valor in the field and his patriotism in time of peace. We maintain that the Republican party has made an infamous use of the power which our votes aided to bestow upon it; we maintain that it has betrayed us at every point, and that it stands to-day denuded of its successful hypocrisy, a mean, cunning, treacherous organization.

We should not misinterpret the signs of the times; we should not be deceived by men and parties; we should not hide it from ourselves that there are huge breakers ahead. The Democratic party is a fraud—a narrow-minded, corrupt, bloody fraud; the Republican party has grown to be but little better. We do not any longer know where to put our hands upon it; we are no longer able to say whether it is a friend or a foe.

We are disgusted with the Democratic party.

Our faith in the Republican party hangs upon the frailest thread.

The Government of the United States is the puppet of the States—a thing without power to protect the citizens of its own creation.

"THE REAL DANGERS THAT THIS
AFRICAN BLOOD BRINGS"

NATHANIEL S. SHALER
The Negro Problem

The Atlantic Monthly, November 1884

THE NEGRO PROBLEM.

WHEN the civil war determined by its result the political position of the black people in the Southern States, there was a general belief among their friends that the race had thereby received a complete enfranchisement as American citizens; that they were made free to all our national inheritances; that all the problems of their future involved only questions of a detached nature,—such slight matters as their rights in hotels and railways, in fields of labor, or at the polling booths. But those who by their eagerness to bid the negro welcome to his new place in the state did so much credit to the spirit of hope and friendship of our time could not see the gravity of this problem.[1] Never before in the history of peoples had so grave an experiment been tried as was then set about with a joyous confidence of success. Only their great military triumph could have given to our hard-minded, practical people such rash confidence. Here, on the one hand, was a people, whose written history shows that the way to the self-government on which alone a state can be founded is through slowly and toilfully gained lessons, handed from father to son,—lessons learned on

---

[1] This article was sent in advance of publication to several gentlemen whose position and experience especially qualify them to comment upon the assertions made and the suggestions offered. Among these correspondents were General S. C. Armstrong, at the head of the Normal and Agricultural Institute, Hampton, Va.; Colonel T. W. Higginson, author of *Army Life in a Black Regiment*; and Hon. D. H. Chamberlain, formerly governor of South Carolina: their comments appear as foot-notes. The editor regrets that, while Southern statesmen and others of distinction wrote with more or less freedom upon the subject of the article, their communications were confidential, and he is obliged to adopt their opinions as his own, when adding an occasional note.
—EDITOR ATLANTIC MONTHLY.

hard tilled and often hard fought fields. The least knowledge of the way in which their own position in the world had been won would have made it clear that such a national character as theirs could be formed only by marvelous toil of generations after generations, and an almost equally marvelous good fortune that brought fruit to their labor. There, on the other hand, was a folk, bred first in a savagery that had never been broken by the least effort towards a higher state, and then in a slavery that tended almost as little to fit them for a place in the structure of a self-controlling society. Surely, the effort to blend these two peoples by a proclamation and a constitutional amendment will sound strangely in the time to come, when men see that they are what their fathers have made them, and that resolutions cannot help this rooted nature of man.

But the evident novelty of this undertaking and the natural doubt of its success do not diminish the interest which it has as an experiment in human nature: far from it, for this trial of the African as an American citizen is the most wonderful social endeavor that has ever been made by our own or any other race. If it succeeds, even in the faintest approach to a fair measure; if these men, bred in immemorial savagery and slavery, can blossom out into self-upholding citizens, fit to stand alone in the battle with the world, then indeed we must confess that human nature is a thing apart from the laws of inheritance,—that man is more of a miracle in the world than we deemed him to be.

Although this experiment of making a citizen of the negro grew out of a civil war, and necessarily led to the awakening of much hatred among the people where it was undertaken, there is no reason to doubt that it is being very fairly tried, and that if ever such changes are possible they will be here. There was no deep antagonism between these two diverse peoples, such as would have existed if either had been the conqueror of the other; on the contrary, a century or two of close relations had served to develop a curious bond of mutual likings and dependencies between the two races.[2] It was only through slavery that it could have been possible to make the trial at all.

---

[2] The planters and people of the South never feared their household servants, but they did fear their field hands. Insurrection with them was the standing bugaboo, the mere suspicion of which would throw a whole community into

American slavery, though it had the faults inherent in any system of subjugation and mastery among men, was infinitely the mildest and most decent system of slavery that ever existed. When the bonds of the slave were broken, master and servant stayed beside each other, without much sign of fear or any very wide sundering of the old relations of service and support.[3] As soon as the old order of relations was at an end, the two races settled into a new accord, not differing in most regards from the old. External force during the period of disturbance prevented this natural social order from asserting itself in all the South; but in the States that were not "reconstructed," as in Kentucky, it might have been possible for any one who had known the conditions of 1860 to live in 1870 for weeks, in sight of the contact of whites and blacks, without seeing anything to show that a great revolution had been effected.[4]

The important relations between men are not matters that can be managed by legislative enactments, so the black soon found his way back to the plantations as a freeman, and hoed the rows of corn or cotton in the same fields with as much sweat of brow and far more care than awaited him of old. In place of the old lash, his master had the crueller whip of wages and account books. He could not be sold, but he could be turned off; his family could not be severed at the auction block, but they were more often parted by the death that came from the want of the watchful eye of a foresightful master, or by

---

terror, during which the masters often perpetrated cruelties, honestly supposing them preventives. The civil war drew into the Southern army first only such whites as could be spared, yet when the exigency drove almost every available man into the army there was no insurrection. On the contrary, I have yet to learn of a single instance where a family servant or a field hand abused his opportunity.—ED.

[3] There were two kinds of American slavery before the war, domestic and agricultural. The former was probably the most gentle slavery practiced on earth; the latter was the reverse. No punishment was more dreaded by the house-servant than to be sent to the negro quarters.—ED.

[4] This is true because freedom was a change in relations rather than in the practical realities of life. The destruction of the buffalo is a more serious fact to the Indian than emancipation was to the negro. In the altered relations of the whites and negroes there was little visible change, because in six generations the two races had become adjusted to each other.—S. C. A.

poverty. He was no longer crushed, but he was left without help to rise.[5]

To the mass of those born in slavery the change was one of no profit. When the excitement of the change was over they seemed to feel like children lost in a wood, needing the old protection of the stronger mastering hand. It was clear to even the best wishers of the newly freed slaves that the generation that first saw the dawn of freedom must pass away before it would be known just how the race would meet the new life.

The forecast of the unprejudiced observer was exceedingly unfavorable. Every experiment of freeing blacks on this continent has in the end resulted in even worse conditions than slavery brought to them. The trial in Hayti, where freemen of the third generation from slaves possess the land to the exclusion of all whites, has been utterly disastrous to the best interests of the negro. In that island, one of the most fertile lands of the world, where Africans in the relatively mild slavery of resident proprietors had created great industries in sugar and coffee culture, the black race has fallen through its freedom to a state that is but savagery with a little veneer of European customs. There is now in Hayti a government that is but a succession of petty plundering despotisms, a tillage that cannot make headway against the constant encroachments of the tropical forests, a people that is without a single trace of promise except that of extinction through the diseases of sloth and vice.

In Jamaica the history, though briefer, is almost equally ominous. The emancipation of the negro was peaceable, and was not attended, as in Hayti, by the murder or expulsion of the whites. Yet that garden land of the tropics, that land which our ancestors hoped to see the Britain of the South, has been settling down toward barbarism, and there is nothing left but the grip of the British rule to keep it from falling to the state of the sister isle. Nor is the case much better where, as in the Spanish and Portuguese settlements, the negro blood has to a great

---

[5] Does not this rather mean that after two hundred years or more of labor drill he was thrown on himself? And was he not better off *plus* this labor drill than was his whilom master who had succeeded in evading it? Consider the increase of wealth in the South; count the negro paupers; ask who is caring for the majority of the negro blind and infirm.—S. C. A.

extent blended with that of the whites. There the white blood has served for a little leaven, but the mingling of the races has brought with it a fatal degradation of the whole population that puts those peoples almost out of the sphere of hope.

Such are the facts of experience in the effort to bring together the races of Africa and of Europe on American ground. They may be summed up in brief words,—uniform hopeless failure, a sinking towards the moral conditions of the Congo and the Guinea coast.[6] I am not criticising the policy that enfranchised the blacks when their freedom came. I am not deploring the freeing of these Africans of America: that was the least of evils. These people were here in such numbers that any effort for their deportation was futile. It was their presence here that was the evil, and for this none of the men of our century are responsible. Whatever the dangers they might give rise to, they would be less if the Africans were freemen than if they were slaves. The burden lies on the souls of our dull, greedy ancestors of the seventeenth and eighteenth centuries, who were too stupid to see or too careless to consider anything but immediate gains. There can be no sort of doubt that, judged by the light of all experience, these people are a danger to America greater and more insuperable than any of those that menace the other great civilized states of the world. The armies of the Old World, the inheritances of mediævalism in its governments, the chance evils of Ireland and Sicily, are all light burdens when compared with this load of African negro blood that an evil past has imposed upon us. The European evils are indigenous; this African life is an exotic, and on that account infinitely hard to grapple with.[7]

---

[6]The cases cited are hardly parallel. The conditions of climate and surrounding civilization were very different in Hayti, Jamaica, and elsewhere. American slavery was a great educator of its chattels, and their gain by emancipation was the loss of the whites. The experience of our Southern States has no analogue. —ED.

[7]I have always felt, as the result of my contact with and observation of the negro, that he did suffer from the want of support afforded by ancestral virtue and experience in the ways of freedom. This will probably make his progress less sure and rapid than that of the white race; but that the tendency stated by Professor Shaler exists in the case of the negro in any different sense from what is true of other races, even our own, I do not believe.—D. H. C.

The twenty years that have passed since the Emancipation Proclamation gave the name of freedmen to this folk have removed the freedmen into the past and put their children in their place. More than half the blacks who are living—certainly the larger part of those who are now of vigorous body—have never felt the influence of actual bondage; though perhaps the greater part of them were born during the days of slavery, they were but children when the war came, and never were sensible of the old system.

The economic history of these years since the war, though still too brief for any very sound opinions, seems to point to the conclusion that we may for the present, at least, escape the sloth which fell upon Jamaica and Hayti with the overthrow of slavery. The South has advanced in every branch of material wealth, though without much immigration to swell its activities. All its important staples except rice, especially those which are the result of negro labor, have increased in quantity much beyond the measure of the days of slavery. Even if we allow that the increase in the number of blacks has been as great as appears from the comparison of the census of 1870 with that of 1880, it is clear that the negro laborer is doing as much work as a freeman as he did when a slave, and is probably doing more.[8] That he is doing it contentedly is clear from the general absence of disorder, even throughout the regions where the blacks are the most numerous. This is as far as it goes a matter of great encouragement and hope. It should not, however, blind our eyes to the danger which still lies before us. At present the negro population still feels the strong stimulus of the greatest inspiration that can be given to human beings. The very novel experience of a passage from slavery to freedom affected this sensitive people as by an electric shock. The ideas of advance in life, of education, of property, have yet something of the keenness that novelty brings. Let us hope that they will wear until the habits of thrift and labor are firmly bred in them.

---

[8] This statement appears to me to refute the special conclusion as to the negro's tendency to revert to his ancestral conditions. The race is industrious, and if it is, it seems to me there can be no tendency to reversion to lower states, but rather an impetus toward higher.—D. H. C.

The real dangers that this African blood brings to our state lie deeper than the labor problem; they can be appreciated only by those who know the negro folk by long and large experience, —such as comes to none who have not lived among them in youth, and afterwards had a chance to compare them with the laboring classes of our own race in other regions. Those who study this people after their tests of human kind are all made up and fixed by habit easily overlook the peculiarities of nature which belong to the negroes as a race. They are confounded by the essential manhood of the colored man; they are charmed by his admirable and appealing qualities, and so make haste to assume that he is in all respects like themselves. But if they have the patience and the opportunity to search closely into the nature of this race they will perceive that the inner man is really as singular, as different in motives from themselves, as his outward aspect indicates.

The important characteristics of the negro nature are not those that mark themselves in any of the features which appear in casual intercourse. Human relations are so stereotyped that we never see the deeper and more important qualities of any men through such means. The negro nature, charming in many respects, is most favorably seen in what we may call the phenomena of human contact: quick sensibilities and a mind that takes a firm hold of the present is characteristic of the race. Even if we watch them for a long time we find that the essential structure of their minds is very like our own.[9] I believe that one feels closer akin to them than to the Indians of this country or to the peasants of Southern Italy. The fundamental, or at least the most important, differences between them and our own race are in the proportions of the hereditary motives and the balance of native impulses within their minds.

This sense of close kinship felt with the negro may be due to the fact that for many generations his mind has been externally moulded in those of our own race. I fancy there would be none of it with native Africans; indeed, I have found little trace of it

---

[9] True. "Intensely human" was General Saxton's brief answer to a long list of inquiries.—T. W. H.

in intercourse with the blacks of the Sea Islands,[10] who represent a people nearer to Africa by several generations, and deprived of that close contact with the whites which would give their minds an external resemblance to those of our own race.

When we know the negro well, we recognize that he differs from our own race in the following respects:—

The passage from childhood to adult age brings in the negro a more marked and important change in the tone of the mind than it does in the white. In youth the black children are surprisingly quick,—their quickness can be appreciated only by those who have taught them; but in the pure blacks, with the maturing of the body the animal nature generally settles down like a cloud on that promise.[11] In our own race inheritance has brought about a correlation between the completion of development and the expansion of the mental powers; so that, unless one of our youth distinctly reverts towards some old savagery, the imagination and the reasoning faculties receive a stimulus from the change that this period brings. But, with rare exceptions, the reverse is the case with the negro: at this stage of life he becomes less intellectual than he was before; the

---

[10] I lived nearly two years on the Sea Islands, in the most intimate intercourse with the very subdivision of the negroes described, and felt a constant sense of mental kinship with them at the time.—T. W. H.

[11] My attention was first called to this fact by my late master, Louis Agassiz. He had excellent opportunities of observation upon this point during his residence in Charleston and his frequent visits to the South. Personal observations and many questionings of persons who had a right to an opinion have served only to corroborate it.—N. S. S.

In the main, I find Mr. Shaler's statements in regard to negro characteristics and distinctive features admirable, but from the above my own and my associates' experience leads me to differ. After careful study, each year for fifteen years, of three hundred negro children of from five to thirteen years of age in our primary department, and of four hundred adults of from fourteen to twenty-five in our Normal School, our deductions are not those of Mr. Shaler. We have not found a lack or a "clouding" of brain power to be the chief difficulty of the maturing negro, though we admit, of course, a decided race difference in intellectual development. I consider that where on an average from twelve to fifteen out of every hundred boys of our own race are able to receive a college education, not more than two or three negroes would be similarly capable. As to the differences between mulattoes and pure blacks, we find the former usually quicker, the latter simpler, stronger, with more definite characteristics; and this is also the case among our Indians.—S. C. A.

passions cloud and do not irradiate the mind. The inspirational power of the sexual impulses is the greatest gain our race has made out of all its past. We can hardly hope to impose this feature upon a people; such treasures cannot be given, however good the will to give them.

Next we notice that the negro has little power of associated action,—that subordination of individual impulse to conjoint action which is the basis of all modern labor of a high grade. I have never seen among them anything approaching a partnership in their business affairs. They are so little capable of a consensus that they never act together, even in a mob, except for some momentary deed.[12] This ability to coöperate with their fellow men is a capacity which is probably only slowly to be acquired by any people; it is indeed one of the richest fruits of a civilization. In this point most negroes in Africa as well as in America are below the American Indian. They show us in their native lands as well as here no trace of large combining ability; they do not build any semblance of empires. Combining power seems to have been particularly low among the West Coast tribes that furnished the most of our American-African blood.

Along with these defects goes another, which is less clearly manifest in casual intercourse, but which is in fact a more radical want. It is the lack of a power of continuous will. Few of us can see how much we owe to this power, the most precious of our inheritances. It is the power of continuous will, of will that goes beyond the impulse of passion or excitement, that most distinctly separates the mind of man from that of the lower animals. The gradations of this power mark the limits between savage and civilized man. In the negro the ability to maintain the will power beyond the stimulus of excitement is on the whole much lower than in the lowest whites. They are as a class incapable of firm resolve.[13]

---

[12] What I should say is that their impulse of organization is very strong, but that through ignorance they cannot keep together, like whites.—T. W. H.

[13] The negro is certainly lacking in the capacity for associated action. From the debating society to the general convention, the assembled negro demonstrates this. But the individual negro has remarkable resource. I am tempted to say that in a tight place, under familiar conditions, I should prefer the instinct of the black to the thought of the white man. After all, the best product of civilization is what we call "common sense;" and as the chief want of the negro I should put "level heads" in place of "continuous will" or "firm resolve," in

At first sight it might be supposed that slavery has weakened this capacity, but it seems to me that the enforced consecutive labor which it gave must have accustomed the race to a continuity of effort that they knew nothing of in their lower state. So that they have gained rather than lost in consecutiveness, through slavery. Lastly, we may notice the relatively feeble nature of all the ties that bind the family together among these African people. The peculiar monogamic instinct which in our own race has been slowly, century by century, developing itself in the old tangle of passions has yet to be fixed in this people. In the negro this motive, more than any other the key to our society, is very weak, if indeed it exists at all as an indigenous impulse.[14] It is a well-known fact that we may find among them a high development of the religious impulse with a very low morality. Along with this and closely linked with it goes the love of children. This motive is fairly strong among the negroes; it gives reason to hope that out of it may come a better sense of the marital relation.

Although these defects may not at first sight seem in themselves very serious differences between the two races, yet they are really the most vital points that part the men who make states from those who cannot rise above savagery. The modern state is but a roof built to shelter the lesser associations of men. Chief of these is the family, which rests on a certain order of alliance of the sexual instincts with the higher and more human faculties. Next come the various degrees of human coöperation in various forms of business life; and then this power of will, that gives the continuity to effort which is the key to all profitable labor; and last, but not least, the impulse to sexual morality. If the black is weak in these things, he is in so far unfit for an independent place in a civilized state. Without them the framework of a state, however beautiful, is a mere empty shell that must soon fall to pieces. Like all other mechanisms, the state has only the strength of its weakest part.

---

which we do not find them lacking. Our labor system at Hampton furnishes a severe ordeal, and while many fail, many also endure it successfully, and the test seems a fair one.—S. C. A.

[14] Is it not too soon after slavery to justify this statement? Slavery necessarily discouraged monogamy; but the multitude of cases in which slaves after escaping from slavery have gone back into danger to bring away their wives indicates an indigenous impulse.—T. W. H.

It is my belief that the negro as a race is weak in the above mentioned qualities of mind. Conspicuous exceptions may be found, but *exceptio probat*. Here and there cases of higher-minded black men give us hope, but no security. The occurrence of Miltons and Shakespeares makes us hope that to those elevations of mind all men may in time attain, but it is a hope that is very near despair.

Let no one suppose that these opinions are born of a dislike for the black race; on the contrary, I am conscious of a great liking for this people. They seem to me full of charming traits, but unhappily they are not the hard-minded attributes that sustain a state. The negro has, on the whole, greater social sensibilities than any other uneducated man. He is singularly ready to respond to any confidence that may be placed in him. He acquires the motives and actions of social intercourse with noticeable readiness. He has within a certain range a quick constructive imagination and therefore reads character remarkably well. He has a very quick, instinctive sympathy, and is in a discontinuous way affectionate. When he neglects his wife or his children, the fault generally arises from the lack of consecutive will, and not from want of feeling. His emotions are easily aroused through the stimulus of music or motion, and the tide of life that then fills him is free and unrestrained. The religious sense, that capacity for a sense of awe before the great mystery of religion, is also fairly his, though its expression is often crude and its feelings are readily confounded with the lower passions.

I have now set forth the fear that must come upon any one who will see what a wonderful thing our modern Teutonic society is; how slowly it has won its treasures, and at what a price of vigilance and toil it must keep them; and therefore how dangerous it must be to have a large part of the state separated in motives from the people who have brought it into existence. I cannot expect to find many to share this fear with me, for there are very few who have had any chance to see the problem fairly. But to those who do feel with me that the African question is a very serious matter, I should like to propose the following statement of the prime nature of the dangers, and the means whereby they may be minimized, if not avoided.

First, I hold it to be clear that the inherited qualities of the negroes to a great degree unfit them to carry the burden of our own civilization; that their present Americanized shape is due in large part to the strong control to which they have been subjected since the enslavement of their blood; that there will naturally be a strong tendency, for many generations to come, for them to revert to their ancestral conditions. If their present comparative elevation had been due to self-culture in a state of freedom, we might confide in it; but as it is the result of an external compulsion issuing from the will of a dominant race, we cannot trust it.[15] Next, I hold it to be almost equally clear that they cannot as a race, for many generations, be brought to the level of our own people. There will always be a danger that by falling to the bottom of society they will form a proletariat class, separated by blood as well as by estate from the superior classes; thus bringing about a measure of the evils of the slavery system,—evils that would curse both the races that were brought together in a relation so unfit for modern society.

The great evil of slavery was not to be found in the fact that a certain number of people were compelled to labor for their masters and were sometimes beaten. It lay in the states of mind of the master and of the slave: in the essential evil to the master of this relation of absolute personal control over others untempered by the affection of parent for child; and to the slave in the subjugation of the will that destroyed the very basis of all spiritual growth. The mere smart of the lash was relatively of small account: if every slave had been beaten every day it would have been a small matter compared with this arrest of

---

[15] True, unless that external force shall be in some shape continued. There *is* serious danger of a proletariat class, especially in the Gulf States, where an Anglo-African population is massed together, but the outlook is *not hopeless*. Why may not these people continue to improve in the future, as they have improved in the past fifteen years, and from the same causes, namely, their own efforts, aided by the directly educative forces, by commercial activity, and by the general steady tendency towards an orderly social state? It cannot be too strongly urged that the most willing outside aid is the wise training of their best young men and women, who, as teachers and examples, mingle with and leaven the whole lump. So long as ignorant leaders, either religious or political, can keep control there is undoubtedly danger.—S. C. A.

all advancement in will power that his bonds put upon him. It is clear that the best interests of the negro require that these dangers should be recognized, and as far as may be provided against by the action of the governmental and private forces of the state. It seems to me that the following course of action may serve to minimize the dangers:—

In the first place, the gathering of the negroes into large unmixed settlements should be avoided in every way possible:[16] the result of such aggregations is the immediate degradation of this people. Where such aggregations exist, we see at once the risk of the return of this people to their old ancestral conditions, and it is from a study of these negroes, who are limited in their association to their own people, that I have become so fully satisfied that they tend to fall away from the position which their intercourse with the whites has given them. Of course this separation of the negro from his kind cannot be accomplished by any direct legislation. Such action is not in the possibilities of the situation nor in the system of our government. But where there are such aggregations, the force of public and private action should be brought to bear to diminish the evils that they entail, and as far as possible to break up the communities. The founding of public schools in such communities, with teachers of the best quality, affords the simplest and perhaps the only method by which these tendencies can be combated. To educate a people is to scatter them. There are now many devoted teachers in the South who are working to this end. These schools should give more than the elements of a literary education, for such teaching is of even less value to the black youth than it is to the children of our race: the schools should give the foundations of a technical education, in order that the life of the people be lifted above the dull

---

[16]Where these aggregations exist in the South, the establishment of well-taught schools in their midst is immediately remedial. We can cite counties in Virginia, peopled mostly by blacks, where the influence of a single teacher has practically changed the social condition. Our graduates who go out into these neighborhoods show us results which are most encouraging; not only is there an increase of intelligence, but a decrease of vice. It is on the testimony of Southern whites that we rely, and they do not hesitate to tell us that the work of one strong man or woman can and does change the standard of a whole community.—S. C. A.

routine of Southern cotton-farming, and that the probability of migration may be increased.

When there is a chance to do it, the regions where the negroes have gathered in dense unmixed communities should be interspersed with settlements of whites. Fortunately, there is only a small part of the South where the negroes show much tendency to gather by themselves. These are mainly in the shore regions of the Atlantic and the Gulf States, where the climate is tolerable to the African, but difficult for those of European blood to endure. Any colonies of whites in these districts should be drawn from Southern Europe, from peoples accustomed to a hot climate and miasmatic conditions.[17] Elsewhere in the South the negroes show a commendable preference for association with their white fellow citizens. There is no trace of a tendency to seclusion. In the cities they are gathered into a quarter which becomes given up to them; but this is owing rather to their poverty and to the exclusiveness of the whites than to any desire of the blacks to escape from contact with the superior race; so that this people is still in very favorable conditions for benefiting by social intercourse with the whites.

There is clearly a tendency for the negro to fall into the position of an agricultural laborer, or a household servant.[18] Neither of these positions affords the best chance for development. It is very much to be desired that there should be a better chance for him to find his way into the mechanical employments. Negroes make good blacksmiths and joiners; they can be used to advantage in mill work of all kinds, provided they are mingled with white laborers, to which the prejudice of race now offers

---

[17] This has been curiously tested in Florida, and with results which contradict this view. About 1770 a large colony of Greeks, Italians, and Minorcans was brought to St. Augustine. Their descendants, known generally as Minorcans, are far inferior mentally, morally, and physically to the Florida negroes. I have seen many of them.—T. W. H.

[18] I think the destiny and the best hold of the large majority of blacks is to become cultivators of small farms, and their progress in this direction is rapid and hopeful. In the breaking up of the old estates, the negro and his almost equally emancipated brother, the poor white, get their full share. Their landed wealth to-day is surprising, and they are moving with the general movement about them.—S. C. A.

no material barrier.[19] The immediate need of the South is not for academies, high schools, or colleges which shall be open to the negro,—he is yet very far from being in a shape to need this form of education,—but for technical schools which will give a thorough training in craft work of varied kinds. Every well-trained craftsman would be a missionary in his field. As a race they are capable of taking pride in handiwork, that first condition of success in mechanical labor. Such occupations tend to breed forethought, independence, and will power. There is no better work for a benevolent society than to take up this task of improving the technical education of the negro as a means for his temporal and especially his political salvation. Technical schools are not costly to start compared with good literary colleges. Three or four teachers can do valuable work, in an establishment that need not be very costly, and might be partly self-sustaining. At present there are deplorably few opportunities for negroes to learn craft work in an effective way; a few schools have made some essay towards it, but none of them have proposed it as their main object.

The federal government would do well to found a number of technical schools, in the Southern States, under state control, but perhaps with federal supervision. These schools need not cost over twenty thousand dollars per annum, beyond the value of their products. They should train young men for trade work alone, requiring for admission the simplest elements of an education. The expense of teaching and feeding the students might be borne by the government. The pupils should be trained for the commoner departments of manual labor. I would suggest the following occupations as well fitted to give useful employment and as easily taught: smithing, turning, furniture making, carpentering, wheelwright work, management of steam engines, the art of the potter.

The desired results might be attained by a method of apprentice labor, the government paying competent masters for the instruction of youths by placing several of these together in large shops. The price of their indentures need not be more

---

[19] In my judgment, the persons who most influence the Southern blacks are not the whites, but the colored preachers,—a class whose ignorance forms a very great obstacle, and who particularly need "academies, high schools, and colleges."—T. W. H.

than one hundred dollars per annum. Of course this system would require supervision, but it seems clear that the cost of maintaining ten thousand such apprentices need not exceed about a million dollars per annum. While the effect of such education in lifting the negro would be immense, it would in time give one trained mechanic in about each fifty a good practical education.

One of the best results that would follow from this method of technical instruction would be the wider diffusion of the negro over the country. Under the present system it is not possible to scatter the six millions of negroes in the South throughout the country, though it is from a national point of view very important that it should be done. The risk of degeneration in the communities where they are now gathered together would then be much reduced. If, on the closing of the war, we had begun to educate ten thousand negroes each year in technical work, we should perhaps have spent somewhere near thirty million dollars on the work, and should have brought up near two hundred thousand black men to occupations that would have bettered their physical and moral conditions.[20]

I confess a dislike to seeing this work done by means of the federal government, for there are many risks of abuse attendant on it. But the difficulty is a vast one; it is indeed a form of war against a national danger, and requires national resources for effective action; and the need justifies the trespass upon the usual principles that should regulate governmental interference with the course of society.[21]

---

[20] The most manifest solution of this great negro problem is in the education of the race. The technical education on which Professor Shaler lays such stress is a part of it. Some negroes have very fair mechanical talents and take to the work naturally. They vary, like other people. Education must be effected by environment. A redistribution of the negro population must precede any high development. To this end technical training is of great value, since it loosens the negro's hold on a particular spot.—ED.

[21] I find myself heartily in accord with Professor Shaler in his practical considerations. Our duty and interest must lead us to aid the negro, and this aid will best come in the way of some special agencies such as Professor Shaler suggests, though I cannot favor the plan of putting this work or burden to any extent on the federal government instead of the States. Such a course is contrary to our scheme of division of duties and powers between the State and the nation, and will be attended by results likely to deprive such efforts of much of their usefulness.—D. H. C.

Even if all possible means be taken to keep the negro in the course of progress that his previous conditions have imposed upon him, success will depend on the rate of increase of the two races in the Southern States. The last census shows an apparent relative increase of the blacks. It is probable that this census was the first that gave a true account of the numerical relations of the races in the South; that the desire to avoid taxation during the slaveholding days led to a general understating of the numbers of slaves on most plantations. These numbers were not taken by actual count, but by questioning the owners. The census of 1870 was of the most viciously imperfect nature in some of the Southern States, its result being to underestimate the population in regions where the negroes were most abundant. The very high death-rate among the negroes in all the large cities where statistics are obtained, and the evident want of care of young children in negro families in the country districts, make it most probable that the increase of adults is not as rapid among the negroes as among the whites.

From extended observations among these people in almost every year since the war, I am inclined to believe that there are two important changes going on in the negro population. First, we have the very rapid reduction in the number of half-breed mulattoes.[22] It is now rare indeed to see a child under fifteen years that the practiced eye will recognize as from a white father. This is an immense gain. Once stop the constant

---

[22] There seems to be no doubt as to the decrease in the mulatto element, although, as a rule, the young blacks prefer the lighter shades; they do not like to "marry back into Africa." The color feeling, though quiet, is deep and strong, but the white man as a factor is less potent than formerly. To-day, in the more northerly of the Southern States, the pure-blooded negro is the exception rather than the rule.

The difference in the original strains of negro blood is marked, but, personally, I have not been able to make any trustworthy observations in regard to the superiority of one over another. I have often noticed the varied types among the eight hundred youth who are taught at Hampton: there are black skins with European features, blonde or even auburn coloring with African noses and lips, but neither color nor features seem to be decisive. Of averages one can speak with some certainty as to probable lines of development; of individuals it is not safe to dogmatize.

There appears to be no "dead line" of progress for the negro. The possibilities of some among them are not to be limited to the level of the majority of the race, and it is too soon to generalize as to distinctive types.—S. C. A.

infusion of white blood, and the weakly, mixed race will soon disappear, leaving the pure African blood, which is far better material for the uses of the state than any admixture of black and white. The half-breeds are more inclined to vice and much shorter-lived (I never saw one more than fifty years old), and are of weaker mental power, than the pure race.[23]

The other change consists in a rapid destruction by death, from want of care and from vice, of the poorer strains of negro blood. Any one who knows the negroes well has remarked that there was a much greater difference among them than we perceive among the whites of the same low position in England or elsewhere. It is clear from the history of the slave trade that this African blood was drawn from widely different tribes. Even the leveling influence of slavery has not served to efface these aboriginal differences. The most immediate result of the struggles which this race is now undergoing is the preservation of those households where there is an element of better blood or breeding, which secures the family from the diseases incident to thriftless and vicious lives. Thus we have some compensation for the evils that lead to this rapid death-rate.

Now and then, in studying a negro population, we find some man or woman, evidently of pure African blood, whose face and form have a nobility denied to the greater part of the race.[24] We often find the character of these individuals clear and strong, apparently affording the basis for the truest citizenship. Every such American-African is a blessing to the state, and a source of hope to all who see the dark side of the problem that his race has brought to this continent. It is to be hoped that all such strains of blood will live, and their inheritors come to be leaders among their people.

I believe that the heavy death-rate among the negroes is not altogether due to vice or neglect. This is really a tropical people; the greater part of the South is as foreign to their blood as the equatorial regions to our own. Their decline in the more northerly States of the South could be predicted by experience, for in no part of the world has a black skin been indigenous in

---

[23]The pure black in the former time always had a larger money value than a mulatto of the same age and general appearance.—ED.
[24]Very marked among the Florida blacks, men and women.—T. W. H.

such high latitudes. There is little doubt that the tide of immigration which is rapidly filling the open lands of the Northern States must soon turn to flow into the South. This will tend further to break up the negro population of that region, driving its weaker members to the wall.[25]

Still, though these influences may serve to minimize the danger arising from the presence of this alien blood, there can be no doubt that for centuries to come the task of weaving these African threads of life into our society will be the greatest of all American problems. Not only does it fix our attention by its difficulty and its utter novelty among national questions, but it moves us by the infinite pathos that lies within it. The insensate greed of our ancestors took this simple folk from their dark land and placed them in our fields and by our firesides. Here they have multiplied to millions, and have been forced without training into the duties of a citizenship that often puzzles the brains of those who were trained by their ancestry to a sense of its obligations. Our race has placed these burdens upon them, and we, as its representatives, owe a duty to these black-skinned folk a thousand times heavier than that which binds us to the voluntary immigrants to our land.[26] If they fall

---

[25] While they indubitably are of the tropics, they have a curious natural affiliation for the higher civilization into which they have been thrown, and in spite of ignorance, disease, and intemperance they multiply where the red man melts away. They cling to the skirts of our civilization; there is a black fringe on the edge of most towns in this country; the negroes are here to stay. Before the vigorous pressure of immigration it is possible that they may yield somewhat, fall back here and there, but nothing more.—S. C. A.

[26] All other foreign elements assimilate, and in the third generation are fully Americanized. The negro is the closest imitator of all: but in spite of the oceans of white blood which have been poured into his veins; in spite of the obliteration of the remembrance of his fatherland, its language and its traditions; in spite of the closest of contact with the race which enslaved him, he remains substantially the most foreign of all our foreign elements. The lines of his life are parallel with, and not convergent to, our own, and here lies the danger.

But what would the cotton mills of Christendom do without him? Who would fit into our industrial and household life as he does? We need him, the nation needs what he can do; but his training must be directed by ideas, and not by demagogues. The work of the old taskmasters is still telling tremendously, and the old "uncles" sometimes shake their wise gray heads over the rising generation. It is a many-sided education that they need, and the result of anything less seems to justify the reply of the colored school-girl, who, on

and perish without a trial of every means that can lift and support them, then our iniquitous share in their unhappy fate will be as great as that of our forefathers who brought them here. If they pass away by natural laws, from inability to maintain themselves in a strange climate or utter unfitness to understand the ever-growing stress of our modern life, it may be accepted as the work of nature; perhaps, by some severe philosophers, as a beneficent end of the most wonderful ethnic experiment that the world has known. But they cannot be allowed to perish without the fullest effort in their behalf. So much we owe to ourselves, to our time, and to our place before the generations that are to be.

If the negro is thoughtfully cared for, if his training in civilization, begun in slavery, is continued in his state of freedom, we may hope to find abundant room for him in our society. He has a strong spring of life within him, though his life flows in channels foreign to our own. Once fix in him the motives that are necessary for citizenship in a republic, and we may gain rather than lose from his presence on our soil. The proper beginning is to give him a chance to receive the benefits of the education that comes from varied and skillful industry.

CONCLUDING NOTE.

I have read with great interest the notes of the gentlemen who have permitted their criticisms of this paper to be published with it, as well as many others which, to my regret, do not appear. The second note by the editor needs qualification. It is true that there was a wide difference between household slavery and that of the large Southern cotton, rice, and sugar plantations. But by far the larger part of the Southern slaves were held on places essentially like the Northern farms, in a bondage that was strongly affected by their near relation to the master's family. The sixth note denies the parallel between the

---

being criticised for careless sweeping, answered, "You can't git clean corners and algebra into the same nigger."

Technical training is important, wisely directed mental work is essential, better ideas must somehow be put into better men, but it is the spirit of the Sermon on the Mount that must permeate it all. Practical Christian education, without dogma and without cant, is the great need of the negro, as well as of most of his brethren, of whatever shade or type.—S. C. A.

experiment in the United States and in the West Indies. Undoubtedly there is a diversity in the conditions, for the results differ; but to lay this diversity on the climate "fetish" is to get out of the path of inquiry. The "surrounding civilization" in Jamaica did not differ essentially from that of South Carolina.

Note seventeen, concerning the Minorcan settlement of Florida, seems to me not to militate against the opinion that Southern Europeans, as a whole, will make the best colonists for the Gulf States. A discussion of the Minorcan settlements would probably show plenty of reasons for the decay of this people, if they have decayed.

I cannot agree with Colonel Higginson that the negro preacher has the influence which is so generally attributed to him over the laymen of the black race. The negro as by an instinct and insensibly strives to simulate the white. His religious advisers naturally have a very great hold upon him, and their education is of importance; but the two most important developing agents for this race in their present general state are free contacts with whites in the ordinary work of the world and a wide and long-continued technical training; of course not excluding the elements of what is ordinarily called education. I do not deny that now and then a negro appears who justifies the highest education,—men like Joseph Bannecker, for instance.

I am very glad to find that in most points I am so fortunate as to be of one mind with General Armstrong, who has done more than any one else to help the enfranchised blacks on their way towards a true citizenship. I regret to differ from him in my estimate of the value to the negro of a high purely literary education. The time may come when such a training will bear the same relation to their inheritances that it does to those of the literate class of our own race, but as a rule the little colored girl was right: "You can't get clean corners and algebra into the same nigger." That combination is with difficulty effected in our own blood. The world demands the *clean corners*; it is not so particular about the *algebra*.

"THE OUTRAGEOUSNESS OF THESE TYRANNIES"

GEORGE WASHINGTON CABLE
The Freedman's Case in Equity
The Century, January 1885

THE FREEDMAN'S CASE IN EQUITY.

THE greatest social problem before the American people to-day is, as it has been for a hundred years, the presence among us of the negro.

No comparable entanglement was ever drawn round itself by any other modern nation with so serene a disregard of its ultimate issue, or with a more distinct national responsibility. The African slave was brought here by cruel force, and with everybody's consent except his own. Everywhere the practice was favored as a measure of common aggrandizement. When a few men and women protested, they were mobbed in the public interest, with the public consent. There rests, therefore, a moral responsibility on the whole nation never to lose sight of the results of African-American slavery until they cease to work mischief and injustice.

It is true these responsibilities may not fall everywhere with the same weight; but they are nowhere entirely removed. The original seed of trouble was sown with the full knowledge and consent of the nation. The nation was to blame; and so long as evils spring from it, their correction must be the nation's duty.

The late Southern slave has within two decades risen from slavery to freedom, from freedom to citizenship, passed on into political ascendency, and fallen again from that eminence. The amended Constitution holds him up in his new political rights as well as a mere constitution can. On the other hand, certain enactments of Congress, trying to reach further, have lately been made void by the highest court of the nation. And another thing has happened. The popular mind in the old free States, weary of strife at arm's length, bewildered by its complications, vexed by many a blunder, eager to turn to the cure of other evils, and even tinctured by that race feeling whose grosser excesses it would so gladly see suppressed, has retreated from its uncomfortable dictational attitude and thrown the whole matter over to the States of the South. Here it rests, no longer a main party issue, but a group of questions which are to be settled by each of these States separately in the light of simple equity and morals, and which the genius of American government does not admit of being forced upon them from beyond their borders. Thus the whole question, become secondary in party contest, has yet reached a period of supreme importance.

Before slavery ever became a grave question in the nation's politics,—when it seemed each State's private affair, developing unmolested,—it had two different fates in two different parts of the country. In one, treated as a question of public equity, it withered away. In the other, overlooked in that aspect, it petrified and became the corner-stone of the whole social structure; and when men sought its overthrow as a national evil, it first brought war upon the land, and then grafted into the citizenship of one of the most intelligent nations in the world six millions of people from one of the most debased races on the globe.

And now this painful and wearisome question, sown in the African slave-trade, reaped in our civil war, and garnered in the national adoption of millions of an inferior race, is drawing near a second seed-time. For this is what the impatient proposal to make it a dead and buried issue really means. It means to recommit it to the silence and concealment of the covered furrow. Beyond that incubative retirement no suppressed moral question can be pushed; but all such questions, ignored in the domain of private morals, spring up and expand once more into questions of public equity; neglected as matters of public equity, they blossom into questions of national interest; and, despised in that guise, presently yield the red fruits of revolution.

This question must never again bear that fruit. There must arise, nay, there has arisen, in the South itself, a desire to see established the equities of the issue; to make it no longer a question of endurance between one group of States and another, but between the moral débris of an exploded evil and the duty, necessity, and value of planting society firmly upon universal justice and equity. This, and this only, can give the matter final burial. True, it is still a question between States; but only secondarily, as something formerly participated in, or as it concerns every house-holder to know that what is being built against his house is built by level and plummet. It is the interest of the Southern States first, and *consequently* of the whole land, to discover clearly these equities and the errors that are being committed against them.

If we take up this task, the difficulties of the situation are plain. We have, first, a revision of Southern State laws which has forced into them the recognition of certain human rights discordant with the sentiments of those who have always called themselves the community; second, the removal of the entire political machinery by which this forcing process was effected; and, third, these revisions left to be interpreted and applied under the domination of these antagonistic sentiments. These being the three terms of the problem, one of three things must result. There will arise a system of vicious evasions eventually ruinous to public and private morals and liberty, or there will be a candid reconsideration of the sentiments hostile to these enactments, or else there will be a division, some taking one course and some the other.

This is what we should look for from our knowledge of men and history; and this is what we find. The revised laws, only where they could not be evaded, have met that reluctant or simulated acceptance of their narrowest letter which might have been expected—a virtual suffocation of those principles of human equity which the unwelcome decrees do little more than shadow forth. But in different regions this attitude has been made in very different degrees of emphasis. In some the new principles have grown, or are growing, into the popular conviction, and the opposing sentiments are correspondingly dying out. There are even some limited districts where they have received much practical acceptance. While, again, other sections lean almost wholly toward the old sentiments; an easy choice, since it is the conservative, the unyielding attitude, whose strength is in the absence of intellectual and moral debate.

Now, what are the gains, what the losses of these diverse attitudes? Surely these are urgent questions to any one in our country who believes it is always a losing business to be in the wrong. Particularly in the South, where each step in this affair is an unprecedented experience, it will be folly if each region, small or large, does not study the experiences of all the rest. And yet this, alone, would be superficial; we would still need to do more. We need to go back to the roots of things and study closely, analytically, the origin, the present foundation, the rationality, the rightness, of those sentiments surviving in us which prompt an attitude qualifying in any way peculiarly the black man's liberty among us. Such a treatment will be less abundant in incident, less picturesque; but it will be more thorough.

First, then, what are these sentiments? Foremost among them stands the idea that he is of necessity an alien. He was brought to our shores a naked, brutish, unclean, captive, pagan savage, to be and remain a kind of connecting link between man and the beasts of burden. The great changes to result from his contact with a superb race of masters were not taken into account. As a social factor he was intended to be as purely zero as the brute at the other end of his plow-line. The occasional mingling of his blood with that of the white man worked no change in the sentiment; one, two, four, eight, multiplied upon or divided into zero, still gave zero for the result. Generations of American nativity made no difference; his children and children's children were born in sight of our door, yet the old notion held fast. He increased to vast numbers, but it never wavered. He accepted our dress, language, religion, all the fundamentals of our civilization, and became forever expatriated from his own land; still he remained, to us, an alien. Our sentiment went blind. It did not see that gradually, here by force and there by choice, he was fulfilling a host of conditions that earned at least a solemn moral right to that naturalization which no one at first had dreamed of giving him. Frequently he even bought back the freedom of which he had been robbed, became a tax-payer, and at times an educator of his children at his own expense; but the old idea of alienism passed laws to banish him, his wife, and children by thousands from the state, and threw him into loathsome jails as a common felon for returning to his native land.

It will be wise to remember that these were the acts of an enlightened, God-fearing people, the great mass of whom have passed beyond all earthly accountability. They were our fathers. I am the son and grandson of slave-holders. These were their faults; posterity will discover ours; but these things must be frankly, fearlessly taken into account if we are ever to understand the true interests of our peculiar state of society.

Why, then, did this notion that the man of color must always remain an alien stand so unshaken? We may readily recall how, under ancient systems, he rose not only to high privileges, but often to public station and power. Singularly, with us the trouble lay in a modern principle of liberty. The whole idea of American government rested on all men's equal, inalienable right to secure their life, liberty, and the pursuit of happiness by governments founded in their own consent. Hence, our Southern forefathers, shedding their blood, or ready to shed it, for this principle, yet proposing in equal good conscience to continue holding the American black man and mulatto and quadroon in slavery, had to anchor that conscience, their conduct, and their laws in the conviction that the man of African tincture was, not by his master's arbitrary assertion merely, but by nature and unalterably, an alien. If that hold should break, one single wave of irresistible inference would lift our whole Southern social fabric and dash it upon the rocks of negro emancipation and enfranchisement. How was it made secure? Not by books, though they were written among us from every possible point of view, but, with the mass of our slave-owners, by the calm hypothesis of a positive, intuitive knowledge. To them the statement was an axiom. They abandoned the methods of moral and intellectual reasoning, and fell back upon this assumption of a God-given instinct, nobler than reason, and which it was an insult to a freeman to ask him to prove on logical grounds.

Yet it was found not enough. The slave multiplied. Slavery was a dangerous institution. Few in the South to-day have any just idea how often the slave plotted for his freedom. Our Southern ancestors were a noble, manly people, springing from some of the most highly intelligent, aspiring, upright, and refined nations of the modern world; from the Huguenot, the French Chevalier, the Old Englander, the New Englander. Their acts were not always right; whose are? But for their peace of mind they had to believe them so. They therefore spoke much of the negro's contentment with that servile condition for which nature had designed him. Yet there was no escaping the knowledge that we dared not trust the slave caste with any power that could be withheld from them. So the perpetual alien was made also a perpetual menial, and the belief became fixed that this, too, was nature's decree, not ours.

Thus we stood at the close of the civil war. There were always a few Southerners who did not justify slavery, and many who cared nothing whether it was just or not. But what we have described was the general sentiment of good Southern people. There was one modifying sentiment. It related to the slave's spiritual interests. Thousands of pious masters and mistresses flatly broke the shameful laws that stood between their slaves and the Bible. Slavery was right; but religion, they held, was for the alien and menial as well as for the citizen and master. They could be alien and citizen, menial and master, in church as well as out; and they were.

Yet over against this lay another root of to-day's difficulties. This perpetuation of the alien, menial relation tended to perpetuate the vices that naturally cling to servility, dense ignorance and a hopeless separation from true liberty; and as we could not find it in our minds to blame slavery with this perpetuation, we could only assume as a further axiom that there was, by nature, a disqualifying moral taint in every drop of negro blood. The testimony of an Irish, German, Italian, French, or Spanish beggar in a court of justice was taken on its merits; but the colored man's was excluded by law wherever it weighed against a white man. The colored man was a prejudged culprit. The discipline of the plantation required that the difference between master and slave be never lost sight of by either. It made our master caste a solid mass, and fixed a common masterhood and subserviency between the ruling and the serving race.* Every one of us grew up in the idea that he had, by birth and race, certain broad powers of police over any and every person of color.

---

*The old Louisiana Black Code says, "That free people of color ought never to . . . presume to conceive themselves equal to the white; but, on the contrary, that they ought to yield to them in every occasion, and never speak or answer to them but with respect, under the penalty of imprisonment according to the nature of the offense." (Section 21, p. 164.)

All at once the tempest of war snapped off at the ground every one of these arbitrary relations, without removing a single one of the sentiments in which they stood rooted. Then, to fortify the freedman in the tenure of his new rights, he was given the ballot. Before this grim fact the notion of alienism, had it been standing alone, might have given way. The idea that slavery was right did begin to crumble almost at once. "As for slavery," said an old Creole sugar-planter and former slave-owner to me, "it was damnable." The revelation came like a sudden burst of light. It is one of the South's noblest poets who has but just said:

> I am a Southerner;
> I love the South; I dared for her
> To fight from Lookout to the sea,
> With her proud banner over me:
> But from my lips thanksgiving broke,
> As God in battle-thunder spoke,
> And that Black Idol, breeding drouth
> And dearth of human sympathy
> Throughout the sweet and sensuous South,
>   Was, with its chains and human yoke,
> Blown hellward from the cannon's mouth,
>   While Freedom cheered behind the smoke!*

With like readiness might the old alien relation have given way if we could only, while letting that pass, have held fast by the other old ideas. But they were all bound together. See our embarrassment. For more than a hundred years we had made these sentiments the absolute essentials to our self-respect. And yet if we clung to them, how could we meet the freedman on equal terms in the political field? Even to lead would not compensate us; for the fundamental profession of American politics is that the leader is servant to his followers. It was too much. The ex-master and ex-slave—the quarter-deck and the forecastle, as it were—could not come together. But neither could the American mind tolerate a continuance of martial law. The agonies of reconstruction followed.

---

*Maurice Thompson, in the "Independent."

The vote, after all, was a secondary point, and the robbery and bribery on one side, and whipping and killing on the other, were but huge accidents of the situation. The two main questions were really these: on the freedman's side, how to establish republican State government under the same recognition of his rights that the rest of Christendom accorded him; and on the former master's side, how to get back to the old semblance of republican State government, and—allowing that the freedman was *de facto* a voter—still to maintain a purely arbitrary superiority of all whites over all blacks, and a purely arbitrary equality of all blacks among themselves as an alien, menial, and dangerous class.

Exceptionally here and there some one in the master caste did throw off the old and accept the new ideas, and, if he would allow it, was instantly claimed as a leader by the newly liberated thousands around him. But just as promptly the old master race branded him also an alien reprobate, and in ninety-nine cases out of a hundred, if he had not already done so, he soon began to confirm by his actions the brand on his cheek. However, we need give no history here of the dreadful episode of reconstruction. Under an experimentative truce its issues rest to-day upon the pledge of the wiser leaders of the master class: Let us but remove the hireling demagogue, and we will see to it that the freedman is accorded a practical, complete, and cordial recognition of his equality with the white man before the law. As far as there has been any understanding at all, it is not that the originally desired ends of reconstruction have been abandoned, but that the men of North and South have agreed upon a new, gentle, and peaceable method for reaching them; that, without change as to the ends in view, compulsory reconstruction has been set aside and a voluntary reconstruction is on trial.

It is the fashion to say we paused to let the "feelings engendered by the war" pass away, and that they are passing. But let not these truths lead us into error. The sentiments we have been analyzing, and upon which we saw the old compulsory reconstruction go hard aground—these are not the "feelings engendered by the war." We must disentangle them from the "feelings engendered by the war," and by reconstruction. They are older than either. But for them slavery would have perished of itself, and emancipation and reconstruction been peaceful revolutions.

Indeed, as between master and slave, the "feelings engendered by the war" are too trivial, or at least were too short-lived, to demand our present notice. One relation and feeling the war destroyed: the patriarchal tie and its often really tender and benevolent sentiment of dependence and protection. When the slave became a freedman the sentiment of alienism became for the first time complete. The abandonment of this relation was not one-sided; the slave, even before the master, renounced it. Countless times, since reconstruction began, the master has tried, in what he believed to be everybody's interest, to play on that old sentiment. But he found it a harp without strings. The freedman could not formulate, but he could see, all our old ideas of autocracy and subserviency, of master and menial, of an arbitrarily fixed class to guide and rule, and another to be guided and ruled. He rejected the overture. The old master, his well-meant condescensions slighted, turned away estranged, and justified himself in passively withholding that simpler protection without patronage which any one American citizen, however exalted, owes to any other, however humble. Could the freedman in the bitterest of those days have consented to throw himself upon just that one old relation, he could have found a physical security for himself and his house such as could not, after years of effort, be given him by constitutional amendments, Congress, United States marshals, regiments of regulars, and ships of war. But he could not; the very nobility of the civilization that had held him in slavery had made him too much a man to go back to that shelter; and by his manly neglect to do so he has proved to us who once ruled over him that, be his relative standing among the races of men what it may, he is worthy to be free.

To be a free man is his still distant goal. Twice he has been a freedman. In the days of compulsory reconstruction he was freed in the presence of his master by that master's victorious foe. In these days of voluntary reconstruction he is virtually freed by the consent of his master, but the master retaining the exclusive right to define the bounds of his freedom. Many everywhere have taken up the idea that this state of affairs is the end to be desired and the end actually sought in reconstruction as handed over to the States. I do not charge such folly to the best intelligence of any American community; but I cannot ignore my own knowledge that the average thought of some regions rises to no better idea of the issue. The belief is all too common that the nation, having aimed at a wrong result and missed, has left us of the Southern States to get now such other result as we think best. I say this belief is not universal. There are those among us who see that America has no room for a state of society which makes its lower classes harmless by abridging their liberties, or, as one of the favored class lately said to me, has "got 'em so they don't give no trouble." There is a growing number who see that the one thing we cannot afford to tolerate at large is a class of people less than citizens; and that every interest in the land demands that the freedman be free to become in all things, as far as his own personal gifts will lift and sustain him, the same sort of American citizen he would be if, with the same intellectual and moral caliber, he were white.

Thus we reach the ultimate question of fact. Are the freedman's liberties suffering any real abridgment? The answer is easy. The letter of the laws, with but few exceptions, recognizes him as entitled to every right of an American citizen; and to some it may seem unimportant that there is scarcely one public relation of life in the South where he is not arbitrarily and unlawfully compelled to hold toward the white man the attitude of an alien, a menial, and a probable reprobate, by reason of his race and color. One of the marvels of future history will be that it was counted a small matter, by a majority of our nation, for six millions of people within it, made by its own decree a component part of it, to be subjected to a system of oppression so rank that nothing could make it seem small except the fact that they had already been ground under it for a century and a half.

Examine it. It proffers to the freedman a certain security of life and property, and then holds the respect of the community, that dearest of earthly boons, beyond his attainment. It gives him certain guarantees against thieves and robbers, and then holds him under the unearned contumely of the mass of good men and women. It acknowledges in constitutions and statutes his title to an American's freedom and aspirations, and then in daily practice heaps upon him in every public place the most odious distinctions, without giving ear to the humblest plea concerning mental or moral character. It spurns his ambition, tramples upon his languishing self-respect, and indignantly refuses to let him either buy with money, or earn by any excellence of inner life or outward behavior, the most momentary immunity from these public indignities even for his wife and daughters. Need we cram these pages with facts in evidence, as if these were charges denied and requiring to be proven? They are simply the present avowed and defended state of affairs peeled of its exteriors.

Nothing but the habit, generations old, of enduring it could make it endurable by men not in actual slavery. Were we whites of the South to remain every way as we are, and our six million blacks to give place to any sort of whites exactly their equals, man for man, in mind, morals, and wealth, provided only that they had tasted two years of American freedom, and were this same system of tyrannies attempted upon them, there would be as bloody an uprising as this continent has ever seen. We can say this quietly. There is not a scruple's weight of present danger. These six million freedmen are dominated by nine million whites immeasurably stronger than they, backed by the virtual consent of thirty-odd millions more. Indeed, nothing but the habit of oppression could make such oppression possible to a people of the intelligence and virtue of our Southern whites, and the invitation to practice it on millions of any other than the children of their former slaves would be spurned with a noble indignation.

Suppose, for a moment, the tables turned. Suppose the courts of our Southern States, while changing no laws requiring the impaneling of jurymen without distinction as to race, etc., should suddenly begin to draw their thousands of jurymen all black, and well-nigh every one of them counting not only himself, but all his race, better than any white man. Assuming that their average of intelligence and morals should be not below that of jurymen as now drawn, would a white man, for all that, choose to be tried in one of those courts? Would he suspect nothing? Could one persuade him that his chances of even justice were all they should be, or all they would be were the court not evading the law in order to sustain an outrageous distinction against him because of the accidents of his birth?

Yet only read white man for black man, and black man for white man, and that—I speak as an eye-witness—has been the practice for years, and is still so to-day; an actual emasculation, in the case of six million people both as plaintiff and defendant, of the right of trial by jury.

In this and other practices the outrage falls upon the freedman. Does it stop there? Far from it. It is the first premise of American principles that whatever elevates the lower stratum of the people lifts all the rest, and whatever holds it down holds all down. For twenty years, therefore, the nation has been working to elevate the freedman. It counts this one of the great necessities of the hour. It has poured out its wealth publicly and privately for this purpose. It is confidently expected that it will soon bestow a royal gift of millions for the reduction of the illiteracy so largely shared by the blacks. Our Southern States are, and for twenty years have been, taxing themselves for the same end. The private charities alone of the other States have given twenty millions in the same good cause. Their colored seminaries, colleges, and normal schools dot our whole Southern country, and furnish our public colored schools with a large part of their teachers. All this and much more has been or is being done in order that, for the good of himself and everybody else in the land, the colored man may be elevated as quickly as possible from all the debasements of slavery and semi-slavery to the full stature and integrity of citizenship. And it is in the face of all this that the adherent of the old régime stands in the way to every public privilege and place—steamer landing, railway platform, theater, concert-hall, art display, public library, public school, courthouse, church, everything—flourishing the hot branding-iron of ignominious distinctions. He forbids the freedman to go into the water until *he* is satisfied that he knows how to swim, and for fear he should learn hangs mill-stones about his neck. This is what we are told is a small matter that will settle itself. Yes, like a roosting curse, until the outraged intelligence of the South lifts its indignant protest against this stupid firing into our own ranks.

I say the outraged intelligence of the South; for there are thousands of Southern-born white men and women in the minority in all these places—in churches, courts, schools, libraries, theaters, concert-halls, and on steamers and railway carriages—who see the wrong and folly of these things, silently blush for them, and withhold their open protests only because their belief is unfortunately stronger in the futility of their counsel than in the power of a just cause. I do not justify their silence; but I affirm their sincerity and their goodly numbers. Of late years, when condemning these evils from the platform in Southern towns, I have repeatedly found that those who I had earlier been told were the men and women in whom the community placed most confidence and pride—they were the ones who, when I had spoken, came forward with warmest hand-grasps and expressions of thanks, and pointedly and cordially justified my every utterance. And were they the young South? Not by half! The gray-beards of the old times have always been among them, saying in effect, not by any means as converts, but as fellow-discoverers, "Whereas we were blind, now we see."

Another sort among our good Southern people make a similar but feebler admission, but with the time-worn proviso that expediency makes a more imperative demand than law, justice, or logic, and demands the preservation of the old order. Somebody must be outraged, it seems; and if not the freedman, then it must be a highly refined and enlightened race of people constantly offended and grossly discommoded, if not imposed upon, by a horde of tatterdemalions, male and female, crowding into a participation in their reserved privileges. Now, look at this plea. It is simply saying in another way that though the Southern whites far outnumber the blacks, and though we hold every element of power in greater degree than the blacks, and though the larger part of us claim to be sealed by nature as an exclusive upper class, and though we have the courts completely in our own hands, with the police on our right and the prisons on our left, and though we justly claim to be an intrepid people, and though we have a superb military experience, with ninety-nine hundredths of all the military equipment and no scarcity of all the accessories, yet with all the facts behind us we cannot make and enforce that intelligent and approximately just assortment of persons in public places and conveyances on the merits of exterior decency that is made in all other enlightened lands. On such a plea are made a distinction and separation that not only are crude, invidious, humiliating, and tyrannous, but which do not reach their ostensible end or come near it; and all that saves such a plea from being a confession of driveling imbecility is its utter speciousness. It is advanced sincerely; and yet nothing is easier to show than that these distinctions on the line of color are really made not from any necessity, but simply for their own sake—to preserve the old arbitrary supremacy of the master class over the menial without regard to the decency or indecency of appearance or manners in either the white individual or the colored.

See its every-day working. Any colored man gains unquestioned admission into innumerable places the moment he appears as the menial attendant of some white person, where he could not cross the threshold in his own right as a well-dressed and well-behaved master of himself. The contrast is even greater in the case of colored women. There could not be a system which when put into practice would more offensively condemn itself. It does more: it actually creates the confusion it pretends to prevent. It blunts the sensibilities of the ruling class themselves. It waives all strict demand for painstaking in either manners or dress of either master or menial, and, for one result, makes the average Southern railway coach more uncomfortable than the average of railway coaches elsewhere. It prompts the average Southern white passenger to find less offense in the presence of a profane, boisterous, or unclean white person than in that of a quiet, well-behaved colored man or woman attempting to travel on an equal footing with him without a white master or mistress. The holders of the old sentiments hold the opposite choice in scorn. It is only when we go on to say that there are regions where the riotous expulsion of a decent and peaceable colored person is preferred to his inoffensive company, that it may seem necessary to bring in evidence. And yet here again it is *prima facie* evidence; for the following extract was printed in the Selma (Alabama) "Times" not six months ago, and not as a complaint, but as a boast:

> "A few days since, a negro minister, of this city, boarded the east-bound passenger train on the E. T., V. & G. Railway and took a seat in the coach occupied by white passengers. Some of the passengers complained to the conductor and brakemen, and expressed considerable dissatisfaction that they were forced to ride alongside of a negro. The railroad officials informed the

complainants that they were not authorized to force the colored passenger into the coach set apart for the negroes, and they would lay themselves liable should they do so. The white passengers then took the matter in their own hands and ordered the ebony-hued minister to take a seat in the next coach. He positively refused to obey orders, whereupon the white men gave him a sound flogging and forced him to a seat among his own color and equals. We learned yesterday that the vanquished preacher was unable to fill his pulpit on account of the severe chastisement inflicted upon him. Now [says the delighted editor] the query that puzzles is, 'Who did the flogging?'"

And as good an answer as we can give is that likely enough they were some of the men for whom the whole South has come to a halt to let them get over the "feelings engendered by the war." Must such men, such acts, such sentiments, stand alone to represent us of the South before an enlightened world? No. I say, as a citizen of an extreme Southern State, a native of Louisiana, an ex-Confederate soldier, and a lover of my home, my city, and my State, as well as of my country, that this is not the best sentiment in the South, nor the sentiment of her best intelligence; and that it would not ride up and down that beautiful land dominating and domineering were it not for its tremendous power as the *traditional* sentiment of a conservative people. But is not silent endurance criminal? I cannot but repeat my own words, spoken near the scene and about the time of this event. Speech may be silvern and silence golden; but if a lump of gold is only big enough, it can drag us to the bottom of the sea and hold us there while all the world sails over us.

The laws passed in the days of compulsory reconstruction requiring "equal accommodations," etc., for colored and white persons were freedmen's follies. On their face they defeated their ends; for even in theory they at once reduced to half all opportunity for those more reasonable and mutually agreeable self-assortments which public assemblages and groups of passengers find it best to make in all other enlightened countries, making them on the score of conduct, dress, and price. They also led the whites to overlook what they would have seen instantly had these invidious distinctions been made against themselves: that their offense does not vanish at the guarantee against the loss of physical comforts. But we made, and are still making, a mistake beyond even this. For years many of us have carelessly taken for granted that these laws were being carried out in some shape that removed all just ground of complaint. It is common to say, "We allow the man of color to go and come at will, only let him sit apart in a place marked off for him." But marked off how? So as to mark him instantly as a menial. Not by railings and partitions merely, which, raised against any other class in the United States with the same invidious intent, would be kicked down as fast as put up, but by giving him besides, in every instance and without recourse, the most uncomfortable, uncleanest, and unsafest place; and the unsafety, uncleanness, and discomfort of most of these places are a shame to any community pretending to practice public justice. If any one can think the freedman does not feel the indignities thus heaped upon him, let him take up any paper printed for colored men's patronage, or ask any colored man of known courageous utterance. Hear them:

> "We ask not Congress, nor the Legislature, nor any other power, to remedy these evils, but we ask the people among whom we live. Those who *can* remedy them if they *will*. Those who have a high sense of honor and a deep moral feeling. Those who have one vestige of human sympathy left. . . . Those are the ones we ask to protect us in our weakness and ill-treatments. . . . As soon as the colored man is treated by the white man as a *man*, that harmony and pleasant feeling which should characterize all races which dwell together, shall be the bond of peace between them."

Surely their evidence is good enough to prove their own feelings. We need not lean upon it here for anything else. I shall not bring forward a single statement of fact from them or any of their white friends who, as teachers and missionaries, share many of their humiliations, though my desk is covered with them. But I beg to make the same citation from my own experience that I made last June in the far South. It was this: One hot night in September of last year I was traveling by rail in the State of Alabama. At rather late bed-time there came aboard the train a young mother and her little daughter of three or four years. They were neatly and tastefully dressed in cool, fresh muslins, and as the train went on its way they sat together very still and quiet. At the next station there came aboard a most melancholy and revolting company. In filthy rags, with vile odors and the clanking of shackles and chains, nine penitentiary convicts chained to one chain, and ten more chained to another, dragged laboriously into the compartment of the car where in one corner sat this mother and child, and packed it full, and the train moved on. The keeper of the convicts told me he should take them in that car two hundred miles that night. They were going to the mines. My seat was not in that car, and I staid in it but a moment. It stank insufferably. I returned to my own place in the coach behind, where there was, and had all the time been, plenty of room. But the mother and child sat on in silence in that foul hole, the conductor having distinctly refused them admission elsewhere because they were of African blood, and not because the mother was, but because she was *not*, engaged at the moment in menial service. Had the child been white, and the mother not its natural but its hired guardian, she could have sat anywhere in the train, and no one would have ventured to object, even had she been as black as the mouth of the coal-pit to which her loathsome fellow-passengers were being carried in chains.

Such is the incident as I saw it. But the illustration would be incomplete here were I not allowed to add the comments I made upon it when in June last I recounted it, and to state the two opposite tempers in which my words were received. I said: "These are the facts. And yet you know and I know we belong to communities that, after years of hoping for, are at last taking comfort in the assurance of the nation's highest courts that no law can reach and stop this shameful foul play until we choose to enact a law to that end ourselves. And now the east and north and west of our great and prosperous and happy country, and the rest of the civilized world, as far as it knows our case, are standing and waiting to see what we will write upon the white page of to-day's and to-morrow's history, now that we are simply on our honor and on the mettle of our far and peculiarly famed Southern instinct. How long, then, shall we stand off from such ringing moral questions as these on the flimsy plea that they have a political value, and, scrutinizing the Constitution, keep saying, 'Is it so nominated in the bond? I cannot find it; 'tis not in the bond.'"

With the temper that promptly resented these words through many newspapers of the neighboring regions there can be no propriety in wrangling. When regions so estranged from the world's thought carry their resentment no further than a little harmless invective, it is but fair to welcome it as a sign of progress. If communities nearer the great centers of thought grow impatient with them, how shall we resent the impatience of these remoter ones when their oldest traditions are, as it seems to them, ruthlessly assailed? There is but one right thing to do: it is to pour in upon them our reiterations of the truth without malice and without stint.

But I have a much better word to say. It is for those who, not voiced by the newspapers around them, showed, both then and constantly afterward in public and private during my two days' subsequent travel and sojourn in the region, by their cordial, frequent, specific approval of my words, that a better intelligence is longing to see the evils of the old régime supplanted by a wiser and more humane public sentiment and practice. And I must repeat my conviction that if the unconscious habit of oppression were not already there, a scheme so gross, irrational, unjust, and inefficient as our present caste distinctions could not find place among a people so generally intelligent and high-minded. I ask attention to their bad influence in a direction not often noticed.

In studying, about a year ago, the practice of letting out public convicts to private lessees to serve out their sentences under private management, I found that it does not belong to all our once slave States nor to all our once seceded States.* Only it is no longer in practice outside of them. Under our present condition in the South, it is beyond possibility that the individual black should behave mischievously without offensively rearousing the old sentiments of the still dominant white man. As we have seen, too, the white man virtually monopolizes the jury-box. Add another fact: the Southern States have entered upon a new era of material development. Now, if with these conditions in force the public mind has been captivated by glowing pictures of the remunerative economy of the

---

*See "The Convict Lease System in the Southern States," in THE CENTURY for February, 1884.—ED.

convict-lease system, and by the seductive spectacle of mines and railways, turnpikes and levees, that everybody wants and nobody wants to pay for, growing apace by convict labor that seems to cost nothing, we may almost assert beforehand that the popular mind will—not so maliciously as unreflectingly—yield to the tremendous temptation to hustle the misbehaving black man into the State prison under extravagant sentence, and sell his labor to the highest bidder who will use him in the construction of public works. For ignorance of the awful condition of these penitentiaries is extreme and general, and the hasty, half-conscious assumption naturally is, that the culprit will survive this term of sentence, and its fierce discipline "teach him to behave himself."

But we need not argue from cause to effect only. Nor need I repeat one of the many painful rumors that poured in upon me the moment I began to investigate this point. The official testimony of the prisons themselves is before the world to establish the conjectures that spring from our reasoning. After the erroneous takings of the census of 1880 in South Carolina had been corrected, the population was shown to consist of about twenty blacks to every thirteen whites. One would therefore look for a preponderance of blacks on the prison lists; and inasmuch as they are a people only twenty years ago released from servile captivity, one would not be surprised to see that preponderance large. Yet, when the actual numbers confront us, our speculations are stopped with a rude shock; for what is to account for the fact that in 1881 there were committed to the State prison at Columbia, South Carolina, 406 colored persons and but 25 whites? The proportion of blacks sentenced to the whole black population was one to every 1488; that of the whites to the white population was but one to every 15,644. In Georgia the white inhabitants decidedly outnumber the blacks; yet in the State penitentiary, October 20, 1880, there were 115 whites and 1071 colored; or if we reject the summary of its tables and refer to the tables themselves (for the one does not agree with the other), there were but 102 whites and 1083 colored. Yet of 52 pardons granted in the two years then closing, 22 were to whites and only 30 to blacks. If this be a dark record, what shall we say of the records of lynch law? But for them there is not room here.

A far pleasanter aspect of our subject shows itself when we turn from courts and prisons to the school-house. And the explanation is simple. Were our educational affairs in the hands of that not high average of the community commonly seen in jury-boxes, with their transient sense of accountability and their crude notions of public interests, there would most likely be no such pleasant contrast. But with us of the South, as elsewhere, there is a fairly honest effort to keep the public-school interests in the hands of the State's most highly trained intelligence. Hence our public educational work is a compromise between the unprogressive prejudices of the general mass of the whites and the progressive intelligence of their best minds. Practically, through the great majority of our higher educational officers, we are fairly converted to the imperative necessity of elevating the colored man intellectually, and are beginning to see very plainly that the whole community is sinned against in every act or attitude of oppression, however gross or however refined.

Yet one thing must be said. I believe it is wise that all have agreed not to handicap education with the race question, but to make a complete surrender of that issue, and let it find adjustment elsewhere first and in the schools last. And yet, in simple truth and justice and in the kindest spirit, we ought to file one exception for that inevitable hour when the whole question must be met. There can be no more real justice in pursuing the freedman's children with humiliating arbitrary distinctions and separations in the school-houses than in putting them upon him in other places. If, growing out of their peculiar mental structure, there are good and just reasons for their isolation, by all means let them be proved and known; but it is simply tyrannous to assume them without proof. I know that just here looms up the huge bugbear of Social Equality. Our eyes are filled with absurd visions of all Shantytown pouring its hordes of unwashed imps into the company and companionship of our own sunny-headed darlings. What utter nonsense! As if our public schools had no gauge of cleanliness, decorum, or moral character! Social Equality? What a godsend it would be if the advocates of the old Southern régime could only see that the color line points straight in the direction of social equality by tending toward the equalization of all whites on one side of the line and of all blacks on the other. We may reach the moon some day, not social equality; but the only class that really effects anything toward it are the makers and holders of arbitrary and artificial social distinctions interfering with society's natural self-distribution. Even the little children everywhere are taught, and begin to learn almost with their A B C, that they will find, and must be guided by, the same variations of the social scale in the public school as out of it; and it is no small mistake to put them or their parents off their guard by this cheap separation on the line of color.

But some will say this is not a purely artificial distinction. We hear much about race instinct. The most of it, I fear, is pure twaddle. It may be there is such a thing. We do not know. It is not proved. And even if it were established, it would not necessarily be a proper moral guide. We subordinate instinct to society's best interests as apprehended in the light of reason. If there is such a thing, it behaves with strange malignity toward the remnants of African blood in individuals principally of our own race, and with singular indulgence to the descendants of —for example—Pocahontas. Of mere race *feeling* we all know there is no scarcity. Who is stranger to it? And as another man's motive of private preference no one has a right to forbid it or require it. But as to its being an instinct, one thing is plain: if there is such an instinct, so far from excusing the malignant indignities practiced in its name, it furnishes their final condemnation; for it stands to reason that just in degree as it is a real thing it will take care of itself.

It has often been seen to do so; whether it is real or imaginary. I have seen in New Orleans a Sunday-school of white children every Sunday afternoon take possession of its two rooms immediately upon their being vacated by a black school of equal or somewhat larger numbers. The teachers of the colored school are both white and black, and among the white teachers are young ladies and gentlemen of the highest social standing. The pupils of the two schools are alike neatly attired, orderly, and in every respect inoffensive to each other. I have seen the two races sitting in the same public high-school and grammar-school rooms, reciting in the same classes and taking recess on the same ground at the same time, without one particle of detriment that any one ever pretended to discover, although the fiercest enemies of the system swarmed about it on every side. And when in the light of these observations I reflect upon the enormous educational task our Southern States have before them, the inadequacy of their own means for performing it, the hoped-for beneficence of the general Government, the sparseness with which so much of our Southern population is distributed over the land, the thousands of school districts where, consequently, the multiplication of schools must involve both increase of expense and reduction of efficiency, I must enter some demurrer to the enforcement of the tyrannous sentiments of the old régime until wise experiments have established better reasons than I have yet heard given.

What need to say more? The question is answered. Is the freedman a free man? No. We have considered his position in a land whence nothing can, and no man has a shadow of right to, drive him, and where he is multiplying as only oppression can multiply a people. We have carefully analyzed his relations to the finer and prouder race, with which he shares the ownership and citizenship of a region large enough for ten times the number of both. Without accepting one word of his testimony, we have shown that the laws made for his protection against the habits of suspicion and oppression in his late master are being constantly set aside, not for their defects, but for such merit as they possess. We have shown that the very natural source of these oppressions is the surviving sentiments of an extinct and now universally execrated institution; sentiments which no intelligent or moral people should harbor a moment after the admission that slavery was a moral mistake. We have shown the outrageousness of these tyrannies in some of their workings, and how distinctly they antagonize every State and national interest involved in the elevation of the colored race. Is it not well to have done so? For, I say again, the question has reached a moment of special importance. The South stands on her honor before the clean equities of the issue. It is no longer whether constitutional amendments, but whether the eternal principles of justice, are violated. And the answer must—it shall —come from the South. And it shall be practical. It will not cost much. We have had a strange experience: the withholding of simple rights has cost us much blood; such concessions of them as we have made have never yet cost a drop. The answer is coming. Is politics in the way? Then let it clear the track or get run over, just as it prefers. But, as I have said over and over to my brethren in the South, I take upon me to say again here, that there is a moral and intellectual intelligence there which is not going to be much longer beguiled out of its moral right of way by questions of political punctilio, but will seek that plane of universal justice and equity which it is every people's duty before God to seek, not along the line of politics,—God forbid!—but across it and across it and across it as many times as it may lie across the path, until the whole people of every once slave-holding State can stand up as one man, saying, "Is the freedman a free man?" and the whole world shall answer, "Yes."

THE NEED FOR A FEDERAL ELECTIONS LAW

THOMAS MILLER
Speech in Congress on the Elections Bill
January 12, 1891

Mr. MILLER. Mr. Chairman, it is late in the day and in the session, but some things are being said to which I should like to reply. To hold office is a precious gift, and the race to which I belong are desirous of it, but there are gifts superior to office. Gentlemen talk about the North and about its not giving negroes representation on their tickets. That is not the thing we are suffering most from in the South.

There are other things of more importance to us. First is the infernal lynch law. That is the thing we most complain of. It is a question whether when we go to work we will return or not. Second, they have little petty systems of justices who rob us of our daily toil, and we can not get redress before the higher tribunals. Third, we work for our task-masters, and they pay us if they please, for the courts are so constructed that negroes have no rights if those rights wind up in dollars and cents to be paid by the white task-masters.

They speak about pure elections and call the election law a force law. Do not gentlemen from the South boast here in their speeches that it is the white man's right to rule and to control elections, and if they can not control them by a majority vote they will control them by force or fraud? Take the speech delivered by my colleague from South Carolina [Mr. HEMPHILL], and you will see his brazen-faced boast that it is his right to remain here even without votes; and then when we have an appropriation bill the North is to be taunted with not giving negroes representation upon their tickets.

Yes, gentlemen, we want office; but the first and dearest rights the negro of the South wants are the right to pay for his labor, his right of trial by jury, his right to his home, his right to know that the man who lynches him will not the next day be elected by the State to a high and honorable trust; his right to know that murderers shall be convicted and not be elected to high office, and sent abroad in the land as grand representatives of the toiling and deserving people.

These are rights that we want; and we call upon you gentlemen of the North to speak for us and ask the Chamber over yonder to give us an election law—not a force law—a national law, Mr. Chairman, that will compel the people of the South to register the votes of the negro and the white man alike, and count them as they are cast, and let the wishes of those people in this American country be expressed here by duly elected Representatives of their States. [Applause on the Republican side.]

The sickly sentiment about not giving negroes positions in the North! The negroes of the North have their schoolhouses. Taxes are levied and schoolhouses supported. What do we find in South Carolina, where the Democrats rule? First, the newly elected governor, who claims to stand upon the platform of Jefferson's principles, denies that all men are born free and equal and endowed with equal rights by their Creator. In his annual message to the Legislature he asks for the annihilation of the public-school system which is bringing South Carolina out of the bog of ignorance that she is in to-day and fast placing her along in the phalanx of other States in prosperity.

The CHAIRMAN. The time of the gentleman has expired.

Mr. CUTCHEON. I yield the gentleman five minutes more of my time.

Mr. MILLER. Why, Mr. Chairman, the governor in his annual message, to re-establish ignorance, desires to close the schoolhouse door against the poor children by creating class schools. Yes; that is the way. What does he recommend? He recommends that the constitutional guaranty of a 2-mill tax be abolished; that communities be left to themselves to levy school taxes; and to the community shall also be left the right to say whether the education of the rich man's son or the education of the poor man's son shall be supported by the taxes levied. How do they seek to do it? The largest taxpayers are those people generally who have not many children; and as they are compelled by the State law to pay a tax, it is to be left to them whether it shall be used to educate the poor man's child or whether it shall be used to educate their children. It amounts to having no educational system at all and is the destruction of the school system down there. Then they come North and speak about the bitterness of sectionalism, while right there in our Southland country, for want of experience, the governor of South Carolina recommends the destruction of the school system, which has been erected upon the promise of universal education.

What else does he do? He recommends the abolishment of two colleges established, by my assistance, to educate the white young men that they may know how to lead the old State up out of poverty and ignorance. Ah, gentlemen, what we need in this land is not so many offices. Offices are only emblems of what we need and what we ought to have. We need protection at home in our rights, the chiefest of which is the right to live. First, the right to live, and next the right to own property and not have it taken from us by the trial justices. I will read you an illustrative chapter, if gentlemen will allow me the time. A Democratic lawyer from my State, Mr. Monteith, speaking about the trial-justice system as sustained by the Democratic party of that State, says that under it no man is secure in his rights, and he gives a picture like this.

I hope gentlemen will listen. A negro was employed to plow for a white man for $10 a month. This man had a game hen. The hen was lost, and simply because the negro was plowing there he was assumed to be guilty of stealing her, was tried and sentenced to imprisonment, and they chained him by his hands to the plow, but before the thirty days of his sentence expired the good old game hen, with fourteen chicks, came out from under the barn where she had been "setting." [Laughter and applause.] The same gentleman gives another illustration which will bring the blush of shame to the face of every white man. A negro woman, in the absence of her husband, got into a dispute with a white neighbor concerning a boundary line, a question which the trial justices have no right to settle; but they take such a question when it comes before them and whip it around and whip it around until they manage to work it into a criminal case. They put this woman on trial in his absence, and, although her attorney pleaded that she was in a condition in which women can not go to court, she was tried, convicted, and sentenced; and a white constable went to her house, two hours after she had become a mother, dragged her from a sick bed and carried her 15 long miles, to the very seat and center of the intelligence of our State, old Columbia. There, to the honor of the jailer and his white wife, they called together several women, white and black, and they ran that inhuman constable away from the jail and took the poor woman and made her an object of charity.

These are some of the outrages that are inflicted upon my people in the Southland which this "force" bill, as you call it, will protect them from; because, if we get it, instead of seeing South Carolina represented as she has been in this Congress by seven Democrats, you will find six or seven Republicans here. The offices will not go around among the Democrats, and then the spirit of fight that made them secede will make them break up the Democratic party and we shall have peace. [Applause on the Republican side.]

A CRUSADE FOR JUSTICE BEGINS

IDA B. WELLS
Southern Horrors: Lynch Law in All Its Phases
1892

PREFACE.

THE greater part of what is contained in these pages was published in the New York *Age* June 25, 1892, in explanation of the editorial which the Memphis whites considered sufficiently infamous to justify the destruction of my paper, *The Free Speech.*

Since the appearance of that statement, requests have come from all parts of the country that "Exiled," (the name under which it then appeared) be issued in pamphlet form. Some donations were made, but not enough for that purpose. The noble effort of the ladies of New York and Brooklyn Oct. 5 have enabled me to comply with this request and give the world a true, unvarnished account of the causes of lynch law in the South.

This statement is not a shield for the despoiler of virtue, nor altogether a defense for the poor blind Afro-American Sampsons who suffer themselves to be betrayed by white Delilahs. It is a contribution to truth, an array of facts, the perusal of which it is hoped will stimulate this great American Republic to demand that justice be done though the heavens fall.

It is with no pleasure I have dipped my hands in the corruption here exposed. Somebody must show that the Afro-American race is more sinned against than sinning, and it seems to have fallen upon me to do so. The awful death-toll that Judge Lynch is calling every week is appalling, not only because of the lives it takes, the rank cruelty and outrage to the victims, but because of the prejudice it fosters and the stain it places against the good name of a weak race.

The Afro-American is not a bestial race. If this work can contribute in any way toward proving this, and at the same time arouse the conscience of the American people to a demand for justice to every citizen, and punishment by law for the lawless, I shall feel I have done my race a service. Other considerations are of minor importance.

IDA B. WELLS.

New York City, Oct. 26, 1892.

> To the Afro-American women of New York and Brooklyn, whose race love, earnest zeal and unselfish effort at Lyric Hall, in the City of New York, on the night of October 5th, 1892,—made possible its publication, this pamphlet is gratefully dedicated by the author.

HON. FRED. DOUGLASS'S LETTER.

Dear Miss Wells:

Let me give you thanks for your faithful paper on the lynch abomination now generally practiced against colored people in the South. There has been no word equal to it in convincing power. I have spoken, but my word is feeble in comparison. You give us what you know and testify from actual knowledge. You have dealt with the facts with cool, painstaking fidelity and left those naked and uncontradicted facts to speak for themselves.

Brave woman! you have done your people and mine a service which can neither be weighed nor measured. If American conscience were only half alive, if the American church and clergy were only half christianized, if American moral sensibility were not hardened by persistent infliction of outrage and crime against colored people, a scream of horror, shame and indignation would rise to Heaven wherever your pamphlet shall be read.

But alas! even crime has power to reproduce itself and create conditions favorable to its own existence. It sometimes seems we are deserted by earth and Heaven—yet we must still think, speak and work, and trust in the power of a merciful God for final deliverance.

Very truly and gratefully yours,
FREDERICK DOUGLASS.

Cedar Hill, Anacostia, D. C., Oct. 25, 1892.

CHAPTER I.

THE OFFENSE.

Wednesday evening May 24th, 1892, the city of Memphis was filled with excitement. Editorials in the daily papers of that date caused a meeting to be held in the Cotton Exchange Building: a committee was sent for the editors of the "Free Speech" an Afro-American journal published in that city, and the only reason the open threats of lynching that were made were not carried out was because they could not be found. The cause of all this commotion was the following editorial published in the "Free Speech" May 21st, 1892, the Saturday previous.

"Eight negroes lynched since last issue of the 'Free Speech' one at Little Rock, Ark., last Saturday morning where the citizens broke (?) into the penitentiary and got their man; three near Anniston, Ala., one near New Orleans; and three at Clarksville, Ga., the last three for killing a white man, and five on the same old racket—the new alarm about raping white women. The same programme of hanging, then shooting bullets into the lifeless bodies was carried out to the letter.

Nobody in this section of the country believes the old thread-bare lie that Negro men rape white women. If Southern white men are not careful, they will over-reach themselves and public sentiment will have a reaction; a conclusion will then be reached which will be very damaging to the moral reputation of their women."

"The Daily Commercial" of Wednesday following, May 25th, contained the following leader:

"Those negroes who are attempting to make the lynching of individuals of their race a means for arousing the worst passions of their kind are playing with a dangerous sentiment. The negroes may as well understand that there is no mercy for the negro rapist and little patience with his defenders. A negro organ printed in this city, in a recent issue publishes the following atrocious paragraph: 'Nobody in this section of the country believes the old thread-bare lie that negro men rape white women. If Southern white men are not careful they will over-reach themselves, and public sentiment will have a reaction:

and a conclusion will be reached which will be very damaging to the moral reputation of their women.'

The fact that a black scoundrel is allowed to live and utter such loathsome and repulsive calumnies is a volume of evidence as to the wonderful patience of Southern whites. But we have had enough of it.

There are some things that the Southern white man will not tolerate, and the obscene intimations of the foregoing have brought the writer to the very outermost limit of public patience. We hope we have said enough."

The "Evening Scimitar" of same date, copied the "Commercial's" editorial with these words of comment: "Patience under such circumstances is not a virtue. If the negroes themselves do not apply the remedy without delay it will be the duty of those whom he has attacked to tie the wretch who utters these calumnies to a stake at the intersection of Main and Madison Sts., brand him in the forehead with a hot iron and perform upon him a surgical operation with a pair of tailor's shears."

Acting upon this advice, the leading citizens met in the Cotton Exchange Building the same evening, and threats of lynching were freely indulged, not by the lawless element upon which the deviltry of the South is usually saddled—but by the leading business men, in their leading business centre. Mr. Fleming, the business manager and owning a half interest the Free Speech, had to leave town to escape the mob, and was afterwards ordered not to return; letters and telegrams sent me in New York where I was spending my vacation advised me that bodily harm awaited my return. Creditors took possession of the office and sold the outfit, and the "Free Speech" was as if it had never been.

The editorial in question was prompted by the many inhuman and fiendish lynchings of Afro-Americans which have recently taken place and was meant as a warning. Eight lynched in one week and five of them charged with rape! The thinking public will not easily believe freedom and education more brutalizing than slavery, and the world knows that the crime of rape was unknown during four years of civil war, when the white women of the South were at the mercy of the race which is all at once charged with being a bestial one.

Since my business has been destroyed and I am an exile from home because of that editorial, the issue has been forced, and as the writer of it I feel that the race and the public generally should have a statement of the facts as they exist. They will serve at the same time as a defense for the Afro-Americans Sampsons who suffer themselves to be betrayed by white Delilahs.

The whites of Montgomery, Ala., knew J. C. Duke sounded the keynote of the situation—which they would gladly hide from the world, when he said in his paper, "The Herald," five years ago: "Why is it that white women attract negro men now more than in former days? There was a time when such a thing was unheard of. There is a secret to this thing, and we greatly suspect it is the growing appreciation of white Juliets for colored Romeos." Mr. Duke, like the "Free Speech" proprietors, was forced to leave the city for reflecting on the "honah" of white women and his paper suppressed; but the truth remains that Afro-American men do not always rape (?) white women without their consent.

Mr. Duke, before leaving Montgomery, signed a card disclaiming any intention of slandering Southern white women. The editor of the "Free Speech" has no disclaimer to enter, but asserts instead that there are many white women in the South who would marry colored men if such an act would not place them at once beyond the pale of society and within the clutches of the law. The miscegenation laws of the South only operate against the legitimate union of the races; they leave the white man free to seduce all the colored girls he can, but it is death to the colored man who yields to the force and advances of a similar attraction in white women. White men lynch the offending Afro-American, not because he is a despoiler of virtue, but because he succumbs to the smiles of white women.

CHAPTER II.

THE BLACK AND WHITE OF IT.

The "Cleveland Gazette" of January 16, 1892, publishes a case in point. Mrs. J. S. Underwood, the wife of a minister of Elyria, Ohio, accused an Afro-American of rape. She told her husband that during his absence in 1888, stumping the State for the Prohibition Party, the man came to the kitchen door, forced his way in the house and insulted her. She tried to drive him out with a heavy poker, but he overpowered and chloroformed her, and when she revived her clothing was torn and she was in a horrible condition. She did not know the man but could identify him. She pointed out William Offett, a married man, who was arrested and, being in Ohio, was granted a trial.

The prisoner vehemently denied the charge of rape, but confessed he went to Mrs. Underwood's residence at her invitation and was criminally intimate with her at her request. This availed him nothing against the sworn testimony of a minister's wife, a lady of the highest respectability. He was found guilty, and entered the penitentiary, December 14, 1888, for fifteen years. Some time afterwards the woman's remorse led her to confess to her husband that the man was innocent.

These are her words: "I met Offett at the Post Office. It was raining. He was polite to me, and as I had several bundles in my arms he offered to carry them home for me, which he did. He had a strange fascination for me, and I invited him to call on me. He called, bringing chestnuts and candy for the children. By this means we got them to leave us alone in the room. Then I sat on his lap. He made a proposal to me and I readily consented. Why I did so, I do not know, but that I did is true. He visited me several times after that and each time I was indiscreet. I did not care after the first time. In fact I could not have resisted, and had no desire to resist."

When asked by her husband why she told him she had been outraged, she said: "I had several reasons for telling you. One was the neighbors saw the fellows here, another was, I was afraid I had contracted a loathsome disease, and still another was that I feared I might give birth to a Negro baby. I hoped to save my reputation by telling you a deliberate lie." Her husband horrified by the confession had Offett, who had already served four years, released and secured a divorce.

There are thousands of such cases throughout the South, with the difference that the Southern white men in insatiate fury wreak their vengeance without intervention of law upon the Afro-Americans who consort with their women. A few instances to substantiate the assertion that some white women love the company of the Afro-American will not be out of place. Most of these cases were reported by the daily papers of the South.

In the winter of 1885–6 the wife of a practicing physician in Memphis, in good social standing whose name has escaped me, left home, husband and children, and ran away with her black coachman. She was with him a month before her husband found and brought her home. The coachman could not be found. The doctor moved his family away from Memphis, and is living in another city under an assumed name.

In the same city last year a white girl in the dusk of evening screamed at the approach of some parties that a Negro had assaulted her on the street. He was captured, tried by a white judge and jury, that acquitted him of the charge. It is needless to add if there had been a scrap of evidence on which to convict him of so grave a charge he would have been convicted.

Sarah Clark of Memphis loved a black man and lived openly with him. When she was indicted last spring for miscegenation, she swore in court that she was *not* a white woman. This she did to escape the penitentiary and continued her illicit relation undisturbed. That she is of the lower class of whites, does not disturb the fact that she is a white woman. "The leading citizens" of Memphis are defending the "honor" of *all* white women, *demi-monde* included.

Since the manager of the "Free Speech" has been run away from Memphis by the guardians of the honor of Southern white women, a young girl living on Poplar St., who was discovered in intimate relations with a handsome mulatto young colored man, Will Morgan by name, stole her father's money to send the young fellow away from that father's wrath. She has since joined him in Chicago.

The Memphis "Ledger" for June 8th has the following: "If Lillie Bailey, a rather pretty white girl seventeen years of age, who is now at the City Hospital, would be somewhat less reserved about her disgrace there would be some very nauseating details in the story of her life. She is the mother of a little coon. The truth might reveal fearful depravity or it might reveal the evidence of a rank outrage. She will not divulge the name of the man who has left such black evidence of her disgrace, and, in fact, says it is a matter in which there can be no interest to the outside world. She came to Memphis nearly three months ago and was taken in at the Woman's Refuge in the southern part of the city. She remained there until a few weeks ago, when the child was born. The ladies in charge of the Refuge were horrified. The girl was at once sent to the City Hospital, where she has been since May 30th. She is a country girl. She came to Memphis from her father's farm, a short distance from Hernando, Miss. Just when she left there she would not say. In fact she says she came to Memphis from Arkansas, and says her home is in that State. She is rather good looking, has blue eyes, a low forehead and dark red hair. The ladies at the Woman's Refuge do not know anything about the girl further than what they learned when she was an inmate of the institution; and she would not tell much. When the child was born an attempt was made to get the girl to reveal the name of the Negro who had disgraced her, she obstinately refused and it was impossible to elicit any information from her on the subject."

Note the wording. "The truth might reveal fearful depravity or rank outrage." If it had been a white child or Lillie Bailey had told a pitiful story of Negro outrage, it would have been a case of woman's weakness or assault and she could have remained at the Woman's Refuge. But a Negro child and to withhold its father's name and thus prevent the killing of another Negro "rapist." A case of "fearful depravity."

The very week the "leading citizens" of Memphis were making a spectacle of themselves in defense of all white women of every kind, an Afro-American, M. Stricklin, was found in a white woman's room in that city. Although she made no outcry of rape, he was jailed and would have been lynched, but the woman stated she bought curtains of him (he was a furniture dealer) and his business in her room that night was to put them up. A white woman's word was taken as absolutely in this case as when the cry of rape is made, and he was freed.

What is true of Memphis is true of the entire South. The daily papers last year reported a farmer's wife in Alabama had given birth to a Negro child. When the Negro farm hand who was plowing in the field heard it he took the mule from the plow and fled. The dispatches also told of a woman in South Carolina who gave birth to a Negro child and charged three men with being its father, *every one of whom has since disappeared*. In Tuscumbia, Ala., the colored boy who was lynched there last year for assaulting a white girl told her before his accusers that he had met her there in the woods often before.

Frank Weems of Chattanooga who was not lynched in May only because the prominent citizens became his body guard until the doors of the penitentiary closed on him, had letters in his pocket from the white woman in the case, making the appointment with him. Edward Coy who was burned alive in Texarkana, January 1, 1892, died protesting his innocence. Investigation since as given by the Bystander in the Chicago Inter-Ocean, October 1, proves:

"1. The woman who was paraded as a victim of violence was of bad character: her husband was a drunkard and a gambler.

2. She was publicly reported and generally known to have been criminally intimate with Coy for more than a year previous.

3. She was compelled by threats, if not by violence, to make the charge against the victim.

4. When she came to apply the match Coy asked her if she would burn him after they had 'been sweethearting' so long.

5. A large majority of the 'superior' white men prominent in the affair are the reputed fathers of mulatto children.

These are not pleasant facts, but they are illustrative of the vital phase of the so-called 'race question,' which should properly be designated an earnest inquiry as to the best methods by which religion, science, law and political power may be employed to excuse injustice, barbarity and crime done to a people because of race and color. There can be no possible belief that these people were inspired by any consuming zeal to vindicate God's law against miscegenationists of the most practical sort. The woman was a willing partner in the victim's guilt, and being of the 'superior' race must naturally have been more guilty."

In Natchez, Miss., Mrs. Marshall, one of the *creme de la creme* of the city, created a tremendous sensation several years ago. She has a black coachman who was married, and had been in her employ several years. During this time she gave birth to a child whose color was remarked, but traced to some brunette ancestor, and one of the fashionable dames of the city was its godmother. Mrs. Marshall's social position was unquestioned, and wealth showered every dainty on this child which was idolized with its brothers and sisters by its white papa. In course of time another child appeared on the scene, but it was unmistakably dark. All were alarmed, and "rush of blood, strangulation" were the conjectures, but the doctor, when asked the cause, grimly told them it was a Negro child. There was a family conclave, the coachman heard of it and leaving his own family went West, and has never returned. As soon as Mrs. Marshall was able to travel she was sent away in deep disgrace. Her husband died within the year of a broken heart.

Ebenzer Fowler, the wealthiest colored man in Issaquena County, Miss., was shot down on the street in Mayersville, January 30, 1885, just before dark by an armed body of white men who filled his body with bullets. They charged him with writing a note to a white woman of the place, which they intercepted and which proved there was an intimacy existing between them.

Hundreds of such cases might be cited, but enough have been given to prove the assertion that there are white women in the South who love the Afro-American's company even as there are white men notorious for their preference for Afro-American women.

There is hardly a town in the South which has not an instance of the kind which is well-known, and hence the assertion is reiterated that "nobody in the South believes the old thread-bare lie that negro men rape white women." Hence there is a growing demand among Afro-Americans that the guilt or innocence of parties accused of rape be fully established. They know the men of the section of the country who refuse this are not so desirous of punishing rapists as they pretend. The utterances of the leading white men show that with them it is not the crime but the *class*. Bishop Fitzgerald has become apologist for lynchers of the rapists of *white* women only. Governor Tillman, of South Carolina, in the month of June, standing under the tree in Barnwell, S. C., on which eight Afro-Americans were hung last year, declared that he would lead a mob to lynch "a *negro* who raped a *white* woman." So say the pulpits, officials and newspapers of the South. But when the victim is a colored woman it is different.

Last winter in Baltimore, Md., three white ruffians assaulted a Miss Camphor, a young Afro-American girl, while out walking with a young man of her own race. They held her escort and outraged the girl. It was a deed dastardly enough to arouse Southern blood, which gives its horror of rape as excuse for lawlessness, but she was an Afro-American. The case went to the courts, an Afro-American lawyer defended the men and they were acquitted.

In Nashville, Tenn., there is a white man, Pat Hanifin, who outraged a little Afro-American girl, and, from the physical injuries received, she has been ruined for life. He was jailed for six months, discharged, and is now a detective in that city. In the same city, last May, a white man outraged an Afro-American girl in a drug store. He was arrested, and released on bail at the trial. It was rumored that five hundred Afro-Americans had organized to lynch him. Two hundred and fifty white citizens armed themselves with Winchesters and guarded him. A cannon was placed in front of his home, and the Buchanan Rifles (State Militia) ordered to the scene for his protection. The Afro-American mob did not materialize. Only two weeks before Eph. Grizzard, who had only been *charged* with rape upon a white woman, had been taken from the jail, with Governor Buchanan and the police and militia standing by, dragged through the streets in broad daylight, knives plunged into him at every step, and with every fiendish cruelty a frenzied mob could devise, he was at last swung out on the bridge with hands cut to pieces as he tried to climb up the stanchions. A naked, bloody example of the blood-thirstiness of the nineteenth century civilization of the Athens of the South! No cannon or military was called out in his defense. He dared to visit a white woman.

At the very moment these civilized whites were announcing their determination "to protect their wives and daughters," by murdering Grizzard, a white man was in the same jail for raping eight-year-old Maggie Reese, an Afro-American girl. He was not harmed. The "honor" of grown women who were glad enough to be supported by the Grizzard boys and Ed Coy, as long as the liaison was not known, needed protection;

they were white. The outrage upon helpless childhood needed no avenging in this case; she was black.

A white man in Guthrie, Oklahoma Territory, two months ago inflicted such injuries upon another Afro-American child that she died. He was not punished, but an attempt was made in the same town in the month of June to lynch an Afro-American who visited a white woman.

In Memphis, Tenn., in the month of June, Ellerton L. Dorr, who is the husband of Russell Hancock's widow, was arrested for attempted rape on Mattie Cole, a neighbor's cook; he was only prevented from accomplishing his purpose, by the appearance of Mattie's employer. Dorr's friends say he was drunk and not responsible for his actions. The grand jury refused to indict him and he was discharged.

CHAPTER III.

THE NEW CRY.

The appeal of Southern whites to Northern sympathy and sanction, the adroit, insidious plea made by Bishop Fitzgerald for suspension of judgment because those "who condemn lynching express no sympathy for the *white* woman in the case," falls to the ground in the light of the foregoing.

From this exposition of the race issue in lynch law, the whole matter is explained by the well-known opposition growing out of slavery to the progress of the race. This is crystalized in the oft-repeated slogan: "This is a white man's country and the white man must rule." The South resented giving the Afro-American his freedom, the ballot box and the Civil Rights Law. The raids of the Ku-Klux and White Liners to subvert reconstruction government, the Hamburg and Ellenton, S. C., the Copiah County Miss., and the Lafayette Parish, La., massacres were excused as the natural resentment of intelligence against government by ignorance.

Honest white men practically conceded the necessity of intelligence murdering ignorance to correct the mistake of the general government, and the race was left to the tender mercies of the solid South. Thoughtful Afro-Americans with the strong arm of the government withdrawn and with the hope to stop such wholesale massacres urged the race to sacrifice its political rights for sake of peace. They honestly believed the race should fit itself for government, and when that should be done, the objection to race participation in politics would be removed.

But the sacrifice did not remove the trouble, nor move the South to justice. One by one the Southern States have legally (?) disfranchised the Afro-American, and since the repeal of the Civil Rights Bill nearly every Southern State has passed separate car laws with a penalty against their infringement. The race regardless of advancement is penned into filthy, stifling partitions cut off from smoking cars. All this while, although the political cause has been removed, the butcheries of black men at Barnwell, S. C., Carrollton, Miss., Waycross, Ga., and Memphis, Tenn., have gone on; also the flaying alive of a man in Kentucky, the burning of one in Arkansas, the hanging of a fifteen year old girl in Louisiana, a woman in Jackson, Tenn., and one in Hollendale, Miss., until the dark and bloody record of the South shows 728 Afro-Americans lynched during the past 8 years. Not 50 of these were for political causes; the rest were for all manner of accusations from that of rape of white women, to the case of the boy Will Lewis who was hanged at Tullahoma, Tenn., last year for being drunk and "sassy" to white folks.

These statistics compiled by the Chicago "Tribune" were given the first of this year (1892). Since then, not less than one hundred and fifty have been known to have met violent death at the hands of cruel bloodthirsty mobs during the past nine months.

To palliate this record (which grows worse as the Afro-American becomes intelligent) and excuse some of the most heinous crimes that ever stained the history of a country, the South is shielding itself behind the plausible screen of defending the honor of its women. This, too, in the face of the fact that only *one-third* of the 728 victims to mobs have been *charged* with rape, to say nothing of those of that one-third who were innocent of the charge. A white correspondent of the Baltimore Sun declares that the Afro-American who was lynched in Chestertown, Md., in May for assault on a white girl was innocent; that the deed was done by a white man who had since disappeared. The girl herself maintained that her assailant was a white man. When that poor Afro-American was murdered, the whites excused their refusal of a trial on the ground that they wished to spare the white girl the mortification of having to testify in court.

This cry has had its effect. It has closed the heart, stifled the conscience, warped the judgment and hushed the voice of press and pulpit on the subject of lynch law throughout this "land of liberty." Men who stand high in the esteem of the public for christian character, for moral and physical courage, for devotion to the principles of equal and exact justice to all, and for great sagacity, stand as cowards who fear to open their mouths before this great outrage. They do not see that by their tacit encouragement, their silent acquiescence, the black shadow of lawlessness in the form of lynch law is spreading its wings over the whole country.

Men who, like Governor Tillman, start the ball of lynch law rolling for a certain crime, are powerless to stop it when drunken or criminal white toughs feel like hanging an Afro-American on any pretext.

Even to the better class of Afro-Americans the crime of rape is so revolting they have too often taken the white man's word and given lynch law neither the investigation nor condemnation it deserved.

They forget that a concession of the right to lynch a man for a certain crime, not only concedes the right to lynch any person for any crime, but (so frequently is the cry of rape now raised) it is in a fair way to stamp us a race of rapists and desperadoes. They have gone on hoping and believing that general education and financial strength would solve the difficulty, and are devoting their energies to the accumulation of both.

The mob spirit has grown with the increasing intelligence of the Afro-American. It has left the out-of-the-way places where ignorance prevails, has thrown off the mask and with this new cry stalks in broad daylight in large cities, the centres of civilization, and is encouraged by the "leading citizens" and the press.

CHAPTER IV.

THE MALICIOUS AND UNTRUTHFUL WHITE PRESS.

The "Daily Commercial" and "Evening Scimitar" of Memphis, Tenn., are owned by leading business men of that city, and yet, in spite of the fact that there had been no white woman in Memphis outraged by an Afro-American, and that Memphis possessed a thrifty law-abiding, property owning class of Afro-Americans the "Commercial" of May 17th, under the head of "More Rapes, More Lynchings" gave utterance to the following:

"The lynching of three Negro scoundrels reported in our dispatches from Anniston, Ala., for a brutal outrage committed upon a white woman will be a text for much comment on 'Southern barbarism' by Northern newspapers; but we fancy it will hardly prove effective for campaign purposes among intelligent people. The frequency of these lynchings calls attention to the frequency of the crimes which causes lynching. The 'Southern barbarism' which deserves the serious attention of all people North and South, is the barbarism which preys upon weak and defenseless women. Nothing but the most prompt, speedy and extreme punishment can hold in check the horrible and bestial propensities of the Negro race. There is a strange similarity about a number of cases of this character which have lately occurred.

In each case the crime was deliberately planned and perpetrated by several Negroes. They watched for an opportunity when the women were left without a protector. It was not a sudden yielding to a fit of passion, but the consummation of a devilish purpose which has been seeking and waiting for the opportunity. This feature of the crime not only makes it the most fiendishly brutal, but it adds to the terror of the situation in the thinly settled country communities. No man can leave his family at night without the dread that some roving Negro ruffian is watching and waiting for this opportunity. The swift punishment which invariably follows these horrible crimes doubtless acts as a deterring effect upon the Negroes in that immediate neighborhood for a short time. But the lesson is not widely learned nor long remembered. Then such crimes, equally atrocious, have happened in quick succession, one in Tennessee, one in Arkansas, and one in Alabama. The facts of the crime appear to appeal more to the Negro's lustful imagination than the facts of the punishment do to his fears. He sets aside all fear of death in any form when opportunity is found for the gratification of his bestial desires.

There is small reason to hope for any change for the better. The commission of this crime grows more frequent every year. The generation of Negroes which have grown up since the war have lost in large measure the traditional and wholesome awe of the white race which kept the Negroes in subjection, even when their masters were in the army, and their families left unprotected except by the slaves themselves. There is no longer a restraint upon the brute passion of the Negro.

What is to be done? The crime of rape is always horrible, but for the Southern man there is nothing which so fills the soul with horror, loathing and fury as the outraging of a white woman by a Negro. It is the race question in the ugliest, vilest, most dangerous aspect. The Negro as a political factor can be controlled. But neither laws nor lynchings can subdue his lusts. Sooner or later it will force a crisis. We do not know in what form it will come."

In its issue of June 4th, the Memphis "Evening Scimitar" gives the following excuse for lynch law:

"Aside from the violation of white women by Negroes, which is the outcropping of a bestial perversion of instinct, the chief cause of trouble between the races in the South is the Negro's lack of manners. In the state of slavery he learned politeness from association with white people, who took pains to teach him. Since the emancipation came and the tie of mutual interest and regard between master and servant was broken, the Negro has drifted away into a state which is neither freedom nor bondage. Lacking the proper inspiration of the one and the restraining force of the other, he has taken up the idea that boorish insolence is independence, and the exercise of a decent degree of breeding toward white people is identical with servile submission. In consequence of the prevalence of this notion there are many Negroes who use every opportunity to make themselves offensive, particularly when they think it can be done with impunity.

We have had too many instances right here in Memphis to doubt this, and our experience is not exceptional. *The white people won't stand this sort of thing, and whether they be insulted as individuals are as a race, the response will be prompt and effectual.* The bloody riot of 1866, in which so many Negroes perished, was brought on principally by the outrageous conduct of the blacks toward the whites on the streets. It is also a remarkable and discouraging fact that the majority of such scoundrels are Negroes who have received educational advantages at the hands of the white taxpayers. They have got just enough of learning to make them realize how hopelessly their race is behind the other in everything that makes a great people, and they attempt to 'get even' by insolence, which is ever the resentment of inferiors. There are well-bred Negroes among us, and it is truly unfortunate that they should have to pay, even in part, the penalty of the offenses committed by the baser sort, but this is the way of the world. The innocent must suffer for the guilty. If the Negroes as a people possessed a hundredth part of the self-respect which is evidenced by the courteous bearing of some that the 'Scimitar' could name, the friction between the races would be reduced to a minimum. It will not do to beg the question by pleading that many white men are also stirring up strife. The Caucasian blackguard simply obeys the promptings of a depraved disposition, and he is seldom deliberately rough or offensive toward strangers or unprotected women.

The Negro tough, on the contrary, is given to just that kind of offending, and he almost invariably singles out white people as his victims."

On March 9th, 1892, there were lynched in this same city three of the best specimens of young since-the-war Afro-American manhood. They were peaceful, law-abiding citizens and energetic business men.

They believed the problem was to be solved by eschewing politics and putting money in the purse. They owned a flourishing grocery business in a thickly populated suburb of Memphis, and a white man named Barrett had one on the opposite corner. After a personal difficulty which Barrett sought by going into the "People's Grocery" drawing a pistol and was thrashed by Calvin McDowell, he (Barrett) threatened to "clean them out." These men were a mile beyond the city limits and police protection; hearing that Barrett's crowd was coming to attack them Saturday night, they mustered forces and prepared to defend themselves against the attack.

When Barrett came he led a *posse* of officers, twelve in number, who afterward claimed to be hunting a man for whom they had a warrant. That twelve men in citizen's clothes should think it necessary to go in the night to hunt one man who had never before been arrested, or made any record as a criminal has never been explained. When they entered the back door the young men thought the threatened attack was on, and fired into them. Three of the officers were wounded, and when the *defending* party found it was officers of the law upon whom they had fired, they ceased and got away.

Thirty-one men were arrested and thrown in jail as "conspirators," although they all declared more than once they did not know they were firing on officers. Excitement was at fever heat until the morning papers, two days after, announced that the wounded deputy sheriffs were out of danger. This hindered rather than helped the plans of the whites. There was no law on the statute books which would execute an Afro-American for wounding a white man, but the "unwritten law" did. Three of these men, the president, the manager and clerk of the grocery —"the leaders of the conspiracy"—were secretly taken from jail and lynched in a shockingly brutal manner. "The Negroes are getting too independent," they say, "we must teach them a lesson."

"What lesson?" The lesson of subordination. "Kill the leaders and it will cow the Negro who dares to shoot a white man, even in self-defense."

Although the race was wild over the outrage, the mockery of law and justice which disarmed men and locked them up in jails where they could be easily and safely reached by the mob—the Afro-American ministers, newspapers and leaders counselled obedience to the law which did not protect them.

Their counsel was heeded and not a hand was uplifted to resent the outrage; following the advice of the "Free Speech," people left the city in great numbers.

The dailies and associated press reports heralded these men to the country as "toughs," and "Negro desperadoes who kept a low dive." This same press service printed that the Negro who was lynched at Indianola, Miss., in May, had outraged the sheriff's eight-year-old daughter. The girl was more than eighteen years old, and was found by her father in this man's room, who was a servant on the place.

Not content with misrepresenting the race, the mob-spirit was not to be satisfied until the paper which was doing all it could to counteract this impression was silenced. The colored people were resenting their bad treatment in a way to make itself felt, yet gave the mob no excuse for further murder, until the appearance of the editorial which is construed as a reflection on the "honor" of the Southern white women. It is not half so libelous as that of the "Commercial" which appeared four days before, and which has been given in these pages. They would have lynched the manager of the "Free Speech" for exercising the right of free speech if they had found him as quickly as they would have hung a rapist, and glad of the excuse to do so. The owners were ordered not to return, "The Free Speech" was suspended with as little compunction as the business of the "People's Grocery" broken up and the proprietors murdered.

CHAPTER V.

THE SOUTH'S POSITION.

Henry W. Grady in his well-remembered speeches in New England and New York pictured the Afro-American as incapable of self-government. Through him and other leading men the cry of the South to the country has been "Hands off! Leave us to solve our problem." To the Afro-American the South says, "the white man must and will rule." There is little difference between the Ante-bellum South and the New South.

Her white citizens are wedded to any method however revolting, any measure however extreme, for the subjugation of the young manhood of the race. They have cheated him out of his ballot, deprived him of civil rights or redress therefor in the civil courts, robbed him of the fruits of his labor, and are still murdering, burning and lynching him.

The result is a growing disregard of human life. Lynch law has spread its insidious influence till men in New York State, Pennsylvania and on the free Western plains feel they can take the law in their own hands with impunity, especially where an Afro-American is concerned. The South is brutalized to a degree not realized by its own inhabitants, and the very foundation of government, law and order, are imperilled.

Public sentiment has had a slight "reaction" though not sufficient to stop the crusade of lawlessness and lynching. The spirit of christianity of the great M. E. Church was aroused to the frequent and revolting crimes against a weak people, enough to pass strong condemnatory resolutions at its General Conference in Omaha last May. The spirit of justice of the grand old party asserted itself sufficiently to secure a denunciation of the wrongs, and a feeble declaration of the belief in human rights in the Republican platform at Minneapolis, June 7th. Some of the great dailies and weeklies have swung into line declaring that lynch law must go. The President of the United States issued a proclamation that it be not tolerated in the territories over which he has jurisdiction. Governor Northern and Chief Justice Bleckley of Georgia have proclaimed against it. The citizens of Chattanooga, Tenn., have set a worthy example in that they not only condemn lynch law, but her public men demanded a trial for Weems, the accused rapist, and guarded him while the trial was in progress. The trial only lasted ten minutes, and Weems chose to plead guilty and accept twenty-one years sentence, than invite the certain death which awaited him outside that cordon of police if he had told the truth and shown the letters he had from the white woman in the case.

Col. A. S. Colyar, of Nashville, Tenn., is so overcome with the horrible state of affairs that he addressed the following earnest letter to the Nashville "American." "Nothing since I have been a reading man has so impressed me with the decay of manhood among the people of Tennessee as the dastardly submission to the mob reign. We have reached the unprecedented low level; the awful criminal depravity of substituting the mob for the court and jury, of giving up the jail keys to the mob whenever they are demanded. We do it in the largest cities and in the country towns; we do it in midday; we do it after full, not to say formal, notice, and so thoroughly and generally is it acquiesced in that the murderers have discarded the formula of masks. They go into the town where everybody knows them, sometimes under the gaze of the governor, in the presence of the courts, in the presence of the sheriff and his deputies, in the presence of the entire police force, take out the prisoner, take his life, often with fiendish glee, and often with acts of cruelty and barbarism which impress the reader with a degeneracy rapidly approaching savage life. That the State is disgraced but faintly expresses the humiliation which has settled upon the once proud people of Tennessee. The State, in its majesty, through its organized life, for which the people pay liberally, makes but one record, but one note, and that a criminal falsehood, 'was hung by persons to the jury unknown.' The murder at Shelbyville is only a verification of what every intelligent man knew would come, because with a mob a rumor is as good as a proof."

These efforts brought forth apologies and a short halt, but the lynching mania was raged again through the past three months with unabated fury.

The strong arm of the law must be brought to bear upon lynchers in severe punishment, but this cannot and will not be done unless a healthy public sentiment demands and sustains such action.

The men and women in the South who disapprove of lynching and remain silent on the perpetration of such outrages, are particeps criminis, accomplices, accessories before and after the fact, equally guilty with the actual law-breakers who would not persist if they did not know that neither the law nor militia would be employed against them.

CHAPTER VI.

SELF HELP.

In the creation of this healthier public sentiment, the Afro-American can do for himself what no one else can do for him. The world looks on with wonder that we have conceded so much and remain law abiding under such great outrage and provocation.

To Northern capital and Afro-American labor the South owes its rehabilitation. If labor is withdrawn capital will not remain. The Afro-American is thus the backbone of the South. A thorough knowledge and judicious exercise of this power in lynching localities could many times effect a bloodless revolution. The white man's dollar is his god, and to stop this will be to stop outrages in many localities.

The Afro-Americans of Memphis denounced the lynching of three of their best citizens, and urged and waited for the authorities to act in the matter and bring the lynchers to justice. No attempt was made to do so, and the black men left the city by thousands, bringing about great stagnation in every branch of business. Those who remained so injured the business of the street car company by staying off the cars, that the superintendent, manager and treasurer called personally on the editor of the "Free Speech," asked them to urge our people to give them their patronage again. Other business men became alarmed over the situation and the "Free Speech" was run away that the colored people might be more easily controlled. A meeting of white citizens in June, three months after the lynching, passed resolutions for the first time, condemning it. *But they did not punish the lynchers.* Every one of them was known by name, because they had been selected to do the dirty work, by some of the very citizens who passed these resolutions. Memphis is fast losing her black population, who proclaim as they go that there is no protection for the life and property of any Afro-American citizen in Memphis who is not a slave.

The Afro-American citizens of Kentucky, whose intellectual and financial improvement has been phenomenal, have never had a separate car law until now. Delegations and petitions poured into the Legislature against it, yet the bill passed and the Jim Crow Car of Kentucky is a legalized institution. Will the great mass of Negroes continue to patronize the railroad? A special from Covington, Ky., says:

Covington, June 13th.—The railroads of the State are beginning to feel very markedly, the effects of the separate coach bill recently passed by the Legislature. No class of people in the State have so many and so largely attended excursions as the blacks. All these have been abandoned, and regular travel is reduced to a minimum. A competent authority says the loss to the various roads will reach $1,000,000 this year.

A call to a State Conference in Lexington, Ky., last June had delegates from every county in the State. Those delegates, the ministers, teachers, heads of secret and other orders, and the head of every family should pass the word around for every member of the race in Kentucky to stay off railroads unless obliged to ride. If they did so, and their advice was followed persistently the convention would not need to petition the Legislature to repeal the law or raise money to file a suit. The railroad corporations would be so affected they would in self-defense lobby to have the separate car law repealed. On the other hand, as long as the railroads can get Afro-American excursions they will always have plenty of money to fight all the suits brought against them. They will be aided in so doing by the same partisan public sentiment which passed the law. White men passed the law, and white judges and juries would pass upon the suits against the law, and render judgment in line with their prejudices and in deference to the greater financial power.

The appeal to the white man's pocket has ever been more effectual than all the appeals ever made to his conscience. Nothing, absolutely nothing, is to be gained by a further sacrifice of manhood and self-respect. By the right exercise of his power as the industrial factor of the South, the Afro-American can demand and secure his rights, the punishment of lynchers, and a fair trial for accused rapists.

Of the many inhuman outrages of this present year, the only case where the proposed lynching did *not* occur, was where the men armed themselves in Jacksonville, Fla., and Paducah, Ky., and prevented it. The only times an Afro-American who was assaulted got away has been when he had a gun and used it in self-defense.

The lesson this teaches and which every Afro-American should ponder well, is that a Winchester rifle should have a place of honor in every black home and it should be used for that protection which the law refuses to give. When the white man who is always the aggressor knows he runs as great risk of biting the dust every time his Afro-American victim does, he will have greater respect for Afro-American life. The more the Afro-American yields and cringes and begs, the more he has to do so, the more he is insulted, outraged and lynched.

The assertion has been substantiated throughout these pages that the press contains unreliable and doctored reports of lynchings, and one of the most necessary things for the race to do is to get these facts before the public. The people must know before they can act, and there is no educator to compare with the press.

The Afro-American papers are the only ones which will print the truth, and they lack means to employ agents and detectives to get at the facts. The race must rally a mighty host to the support of their journals, and thus enable them to do much in the way of investigation.

A lynching occurred at Port Jervis, N. Y., the first week in June. A white and colored man were implicated in the assault upon a white girl. It was charged that the white man paid the colored boy to make the assault, which he did on the public highway in broad day time, and was lynched. This, too was done by "parties unknown." The white man in the case still lives. He was imprisoned and promises to fight the case on trial. At the preliminary examination, it developed that he had been a suitor of the girl's. She had repulsed and refused him, yet had given him money, and he had sent threatening letters demanding more.

The day before this examination she was so wrought up, she left home and wandered miles away. When found she said she did so because she was afraid of the man's testimony. Why should she be afraid of the prisoner? Why should she yield to his demands for money if not to prevent him exposing something he knew? It seems explainable only on the hypothesis that a *liaison* existed between the colored boy and the girl, and the white man knew of it. The press is singularly silent. Has it a motive? We owe it to ourselves to find out.

The story comes from Larned, Kansas, Oct. 1st, that a young white lady held at bay until daylight, without alarming any one in the house, "a burly Negro" who entered her room and bed. The "burly Negro" was promptly lynched without investigation or examination of inconsistent stories.

A house was found burned down near Montgomery, Ala., in Monroe County, Oct. 13th, a few weeks ago; also the burned bodies of the owners and melted piles of gold and silver.

These discoveries led to the conclusion that the awful crime was not prompted by motives of robbery. The suggestion of the whites was that "brutal lust was the incentive, and as there are nearly 200 Negroes living within a radius of five miles of the place the conclusion was inevitable that some of them were the perpetrators."

Upon this "suggestion" probably made by the real criminal, the mob acted upon the "conclusion" and arrested ten Afro-Americans, four of whom, they tell the world, confessed to the deed of murdering Richard L. Johnson and outraging his daughter, Jeanette. These four men, Berrell Jones, Moses Johnson, Jim and John Packer, none of them 25 years of age, upon this conclusion, were taken from jail, hanged, shot, and burned while yet alive the night of Oct. 12th. The same report says Mr. Johnson was on the best of terms with his Negro tenants.

The race thus outraged must find out the facts of this awful hurling of men into eternity on supposition, and give them to the indifferent and apathetic country. We feel this to be a garbled report, but how can we prove it?

Near Vicksburg, Miss., a murder was committed by a gang of burglars. Of course it must have been done by Negroes, and Negroes were arrested for it. It is believed that 2 men, Smith Tooley and John Adams belonged to a gang controlled by white men and, fearing exposure, on the night of July 4th, they were hanged in the Court House yard by those interested in silencing them. Robberies since committed in the same vicinity have been known to be by white men who had their faces blackened. We strongly believe in the innocence of these murdered men, but we have no proof. No other news goes out to the world save that which stamps us as a race of cut-throats, robbers and lustful wild beasts. So great is Southern hate and prejudice, they legally (?) hung poor little thirteen year old Mildrey Brown at Columbia, S. C., Oct. 7th, on the circumstantial evidence that she poisoned a white infant. If her guilt had been proven unmistakably, had she been white, Mildrey Brown would never have been hung.

The country would have been aroused and South Carolina disgraced forever for such a crime. The Afro-American himself did not know as he should have known as his journals should be in a position to have him know and act.

Nothing is more definitely settled than he must act for himself. I have shown how he may employ the boycott, emigration and the press, and I feel that by a combination of all these agencies can be effectually stamped out lynch law, that last relic of barbarism and slavery. "The gods help those who help themselves."

THE ENDURING IMPACT OF SLAVERY

FREDERICK DOUGLASS
from *The Reason Why the Colored American is not in the World's Columbian Exposition*
1893

CHAPTER I.

INTRODUCTION.

The colored people of America are not indifferent to the good opinion of the world, and we have made every effort to improve our first years of freedom and citizenship. We earnestly desired to show some results of our first thirty years of acknowledged manhood and womanhood. Wherein we have failed, it has been not our fault but our misfortune, and it is sincerely hoped that this brief story, not only of our successes, but of trials and failures, our hopes and disappointments will relieve us of the charge of indifference and indolence. We have deemed it only a duty to ourselves, to make plain what might otherwise be misunderstood and misconstrued concerning us. To do this we must begin with slavery. The duty undertaken is far from a welcome one.

It involves the necessity of plain speaking of wrongs and outrages endured, and of rights withheld, and withheld in flagrant contradiction to boasted American Republican liberty and civilization. It is always more agreeable to speak well of one's country and its institutions than to speak otherwise; to tell of their good qualities rather than of their evil ones.

There are many good things concerning our country and countrymen of which we would be glad to tell in this pamphlet, if we could do so, and at the same time tell the truth. We would like for instance to tell our visitors that the moral progress of the American people has kept even pace with their enterprise and their material civilization; that practice by the ruling class has gone on hand in hand with American professions; that two hundred and sixty years of progress and enlightenment have banished barbarism and race hate from the United States; that the old things of slavery have entirely passed away, and that all things pertaining to the colored people have become new; that American liberty is now the undisputed possession of all the American people; that American law is now the shield alike of black and white; that the spirit of slavery and class domination has no longer any lurking place in any part of this country; that the statement of human rights contained in its glorious Declaration of Independence, including the right to life, liberty and the pursuit of happiness is not an empty boast nor a mere rhetorical flourish, but a soberly and honestly accepted truth, to be carried out in good faith; that the American Church and clergy, as a whole, stand for the sentiment of universal human brotherhood and that its Christianity is without partiality and without hypocrisy; that the souls of Negroes are held to be as precious in the sight of God, as are the souls of white men: that duty to the heathen at home is as fully recognized and as sacredly discharged as is duty to the heathen abroad; that no man on account of his color, race or condition, is deprived of life, liberty or property without due process of law; that mobs are not allowed to supercede courts of law or usurp the place of government; that here Negroes are not tortured, shot, hanged or burned to death, merely on suspicion of crime and without ever seeing a judge, a jury or advocate; that the American Government is in reality a Government of the people, by the people and for the people, and for all the people; that the National Government is not a rope of sand, but has both the power and the disposition to protect the lives and liberties of American citizens of whatever color, at home, not less than abroad; that it will send its men-of-war to chastise the murder of its citizens in New Orleans or in any other part of the south, as readily as for the same purpose it will send them to Chili, Hayti or San Domingo; that our national sovereignty, in its rights to protect the lives of American citizens is ample and superior to any right or power possessed by the individual states; that the people of the United States are a nation in fact as well as in name; that in time of peace as in time of war, allegiance to the nation is held to be superior to any fancied allegiance to individual states; that allegiance and protection are here held to be reciprocal; that there is on the statute books of the nation no law for the protection of personal or political rights, which the nation may not or can not enforce, with or without the consent of individual states; that this World's Columbian Exposition, with its splendid display of wealth and power, its triumphs of art and its multitudinous architectural and other attractions, is a fair indication of the elevated and liberal sentiment of the American people, and that to the colored people of America, morally speaking, the World's Fair now in progress, is not a whited sepulcher.

All this, and more, we would gladly say of American laws, manners, customs and Christianity. But unhappily, nothing of all this can be said, without qualification and without flagrant disregard of the truth. The explanation is this: We have long had in this country, a system of iniquity which possessed the power of blinding the moral perception, stifling the voice of conscience, blunting all human sensibilities and perverting the plainest teaching of the religion we have here professed, a system which John Wesley truly characterized as the sum of all villainies, and one in view of which Thomas Jefferson, himself a slaveholder, said he "trembled for his country" when he reflected "that God is just and that His justice cannot sleep forever." That system was American slavery. Though it is now gone, its asserted spirit remains.

The writer of the initial chapter of this pamphlet, having himself been a slave, knows the slave system both on the inside and outside. Having studied its effects not only upon the slave and upon the master, but also upon the people and institutions by which it has been surrounded, he may therefore, without presumption, assume to bear witness to its baneful influence upon all concerned, and especially to its malign agency in explaining the present condition of the colored people of the United States, who were its victims; and to the sentiment held toward them both by the people who held them in slavery, and the people of the country who tolerated and permitted their enslavement, and the bearing it has upon the relation which we the colored people sustain to the World's Fair. What the legal and actual condition of the colored people was previous to emancipation is easily told.

It should be remembered by all who would entertain just views and arrive at a fair estimate of our character, our attainments and our worth in the scale of civilization, that prior to the slave-holder's rebellion thirty years ago, our legal condition was simply that of dumb brutes. We were classed as goods and chattels, and numbered on our master's ledgers with horses, sheep and swine. We were subject to barter and sale, and could be bequeathed and inherited by will, like real estate or any other property. In the language of the law: A slave was one in the power of his master to whom he belonged. He could acquire nothing, have nothing, own nothing that did not belong to his master. His time and talents, his mind and muscle, his body and soul, were the property of the master. He, with all that could be predicated of him as a human being, was simply the property of his master. He was a marketable commodity. His money value was regulated like any other article; it was increased or diminished according to his perfections or imperfections as a beast of burden.

Chief Justice Taney truly described the condition of our people when he said in the infamous Dred Scott decision, that they were supposed to have no rights which white men were bound to respect. White men could shoot, hang, burn, whip and starve them to death with impunity. They were made to feel themselves as outside the pale of all civil and political institutions. The master's power over them was complete and absolute. They could decide no question of pursuit or condition for themselves. Their children had no parents, their mothers had no husbands and there was no marriage in a legal sense.

But I need not elaborate the legal and practical definition of slavery. What I have aimed to do, has not only been to show the moral depths, darkness and destitution from which we are still emerging, but to explain the grounds of the prejudice, hate and contempt in which we are still held by the people, who for more than two hundred years doomed us to this cruel and degrading condition. So when it is asked why we are excluded from the World's Columbian Exposition, the answer is Slavery.

Outrages upon the Negro in this country will be narrated in these pages. They will seem too shocking for belief. This doubt is creditable to human nature, and yet in view of the education and training of those who inflict the wrongs complained of, and the past condition of those upon whom they were inflicted as already described, such outrages are not only credible but entirely consistent and logical. Why should not these outrages be inflicted?

The life of a Negro slave was never held sacred in the estimation of the people of that section of the country in the time of slavery, and the abolition of slavery against the will of the enslavers did not render a slave's life more sacred. Such a one could be branded with hot irons, loaded with chains, and whipped to death with impunity when a slave. It only needed be said that he or she was impudent or insolent to a white man, to excuse or justify the killing of him or her. The people of the south are with few exceptions but slightly improved in their sentiments towards those they once held as slaves. The mass of them are the same to-day that they were in the time of slavery, except perhaps that now they think they can murder with a decided advantage in point of economy. In the time of slavery if a Negro was killed, the owner sustained a loss of property. Now he is not restrained by any fear of such loss.

The crime of insolence for which the Negro was formerly killed and for which his killing was justified, is as easily pleaded in excuse now, as it was in the old time and what is worse, it is sufficient to make the charge of insolence to provoke the knife or bullet. This done, it is only necessary to say in the newspapers, that this dead Negro was impudent and about to raise an insurrection and kill all the white people, or that a white woman was insulted by a Negro, to lull the conscience of the north into indifference and reconcile its people to such murder. No proof of guilt is required. It is enough to accuse, to condemn and punish the accused with death. When he is dead and silent, and the murderer is alive and at large, he has it all his own way. He can tell any story he may please and will be believed. The popular ear is open to him, and his justification is sure. At the bar of public opinion in this country all presumptions are against the Negro accused of crime.

The crime to which the Negro is now said to be so generally and specially addicted, is one of which he has been heretofore, seldom accused or supposed to be guilty. The importance of this fact cannot be over estimated. He was formerly accused of petty thefts, called a chicken thief and the like, but seldom or never was he accused of the atrocious crime of feloniously assaulting white women. If we may believe his accusers this is a new development. In slaveholding times no one heard of any such crime by a Negro. During all the war, when there was the fullest and safest opportunity for such assaults, nobody ever heard of such being made by him. Thousands of white women were left for years in charge of Negroes, while their fathers, brothers and husbands were absent fighting the battles of the rebellion; yet there was no assault upon such women by Negroes, and no accusation of such assault. It is only since the Negro has become a citizen and a voter that this charge has been made. It has come along with the pretended and baseless fear of Negro supremacy. It is an effort to divest the Negro of his friends by giving him a revolting and hateful reputation. Those who do this would make the world believe that freedom has changed the whole character of the Negro, and made of him a moral monster.

This is a conclusion revolting alike to common sense and common experience. Besides there is good reason to suspect a political motive for the charge. A motive other than the one they would have the world believe. It comes in close connection with the effort now being made to disfranchise the colored man. It comes from men who regard it innocent to lie, and who are unworthy of belief where the Negro is concerned. It comes from men who count it no crime to falsify the returns of the ballot box and cheat the Negro of his lawful vote. It comes from those who would smooth the way for the Negro's disfranchisement in clear defiance of the constitution they have sworn to support—men who are perjured before God and man.

We do not deny that there are bad Negroes in this country capable of committing this, or any other crime that other men can or do commit. There are bad black men as there are bad white men, south, north and everywhere else, but when such criminals, or alleged criminals are found, we demand that their guilt shall be established by due course of law. When this will be done, the voice of the colored people everywhere will then be "Let no guilty man escape." The man in the South who says he is for Lynch Law because he honestly believes that the courts of that section are likely to be too merciful to the Negro charged with this crime, either does not know the South, or is fit for prison or an insane asylum.

Not less absurd is the pretense of these law breakers that the resort to Lynch Law is made because they do not wish the shocking details of the crime made known. Instead of a jury of twelve men to decently try the case, they assemble a mob of five hundred men and boys and circulate the story of the alleged outrage with all its concomitant, disgusting detail. If they desire to give such crimes the widest publicity they could adopt no course better calculated to secure that end than by a resort to lynch law. But this pretended delicacy is manifestly all a sham, and the members of the blood-thirsty mob bent upon murder know it to be such. It may deceive people outside of the sunny south, but not those who know as we do the bold and open defiance of every sentiment of modesty and chastity practiced for centuries on the slave plantations by this same old master class.

We know we shall be censured for the publication of this volume. The time for its publication will be thought to be ill chosen. America is just now, as never before, posing before the world as a highly liberal and civilized nation, and in many important respects she has a right to this reputation. She has brought to her shores and given welcome to a greater variety of mankind than were ever assembled in one place since the day of Penticost. Japanese, Javanese, Soudanese, Chinese, Cingalese, Syrians, Persians, Tunisians, Algerians, Egyptians, East Indians, Laplanders, Esquimoux, and as if to shame the Negro, the Dahomians are also here to exhibit the Negro as a repulsive savage.

It must be admitted that, to outward seeming, the colored people of the United States have lost ground and have met with increased and galling resistance since the war of the rebellion. It is well to understand this phase of the situation. Considering the important services rendered by them in suppressing the late rebellion and the saving of the Union, they were for a time generally regarded with a sentiment of gratitude by their loyal white fellow citizens. This sentiment however, very naturally became weaker as, in the course of events, those services were retired from view and the memory of them became dimmed by time and also by the restoration of friendship between the north and the south. Thus, what the colored people gained by the war they have partly lost by peace.

Military necessity had much to do with requiring their services during the war, and their ready and favorable response to that requirement was so simple, generous and patriotic, that the loyal states readily adopted important amendments to the constitution in their favor. They accorded them freedom and endowed them with citizenship and the right to vote and the right to be voted for. These rights are now a part of the organic law of the land, and as such, stand to-day on the national statute book. But the spirit and purpose of these have been in a measure defeated by state legislation and by judicial decisions. It has nevertheless been found impossible to defeat them entirely and to relegate colored citizens to their former condition. They are still free.

The ground held by them to-day is vastly in advance of that they occupied before the war, and it may be safely predicted that they will not only hold this ground, but that they will regain in the end much of that which they seem to have lost in the reaction. As to the increased resistance met with by them of late, let us use a little philosophy. It is easy to account in a hopeful way for this reaction and even to regard it as a favorable symptom. It is a proof that the Negro is not standing still. He is not dead, but alive and active. He is not drifting with the current, but manfully resisting it and fighting his way to better conditions than those of the past, and better than those which popular opinion prescribes for him. He is not contented with his surroundings, but nobly dares to break away from them and hew out a way of safety and happiness for himself in defiance of all opposing forces.

A ship rotting at anchor meets with no resistance, but when she sets sail on the sea, she has to buffet opposing billows. The enemies of the Negro see that he is making progress and they naturally wish to stop him and keep him in just what they consider his proper place.

They have said to him "you are a poor Negro, be poor still," and "you are an ignorant Negro, be ignorant still and we will not antagonize you or hurt you." But the Negro has said a decided no to all this, and is now by industry, economy and education wisely raising himself to conditions of civilization and comparative well being beyond anything formerly thought possible for him. Hence, a new determination is born to keep him down. There is nothing strange or alarming about this. Such aspirations as his when cherished by the lowly are always resented by those who have already reached the top. They who aspire to higher grades than those fixed for them by society are scouted and scorned as upstarts for their presumptions.

In their passage from an humble to a higher position, the white man in some measure, goes through the same ordeal. This is in accordance with the nature of things. It is simply an incident of a transitional condition. It is not the fault of the Negro, but the weakness, we might say the depravity, of human nature. Society resents the pretentions of those it considers upstarts. The new comers always have to go through with this sort of resistance. The old and established are ever adverse to the new and aspiring. But the upstarts of to-day are the elite of tomorrow. There is no stopping any people from earnestly endeavoring to rise. Resistance ceases when the prosperity of the rising class becomes pronounced and permanent.

The Negro is just now under the operation of this law of society. If he were white as the driven snow, and had been enslaved as we had been, he would have to submit to this same law in his progress upward. What the Negro has to do then, is to cultivate a courageous and cheerful spirit, use philosophy and exercise patience. He must embrace every avenue open to him for the acquisition of wealth. He must educate his children and build up a character for industry, economy, intelligence and virtue. Next to victory is the glory and happiness of manfully contending for it. Therefore, contend! contend!

That we should have to contend and strive for what is freely conceded to other citizens without effort or demand may indeed be a hardship, but there is compensation here as elsewhere. Contest is itself enobling. A life devoid of purpose and earnest effort, is a worthless life. Conflict is better than stagnation. It is bad to be a slave, but worse to be a willing and contented slave. We are men and our aim is perfect manhood, to be men among men. Our situation demands faith in ourselves, faith in the power of truth, faith in work and faith in the influence of manly character. Let the truth be told, let the light be turned on ignorance and prejudice, let lawless violence and murder be exposed.

The Americans are a great and magnanimous people and this great exposition adds greatly to their honor and renown, but in the pride of their success they have cause for repentance as well as complaisance, and for shame as well as for glory, and hence we send forth this volume to be read of all men.

CLASS LEGISLATION AND THE CONVICT LEASE SYSTEM

IDA B. WELLS
from *The Reason Why the Colored American is not in the World's Columbian Exposition*
1893

CHAPTER II.

CLASS LEGISLATION.

The Civil War of 1861–5 ended slavery. It left us free, but it also left us homeless, penniless, ignorant, nameless and friendless. Life is derived from the earth, and the American Government is thought to be more humane than the Russian. Russia's liberated serf was given three acres of land and agricultural implements with which to begin his career of liberty and independence. But to us no foot of land nor implement was given. We were turned loose to starvation, destitution and death. So desperate was our condition that some of our statesmen declared it useless to try to save us by legislation as we were doomed to extinction.

The original fourteen slaves which the Dutch ship landed at Jamestown, Virginia in 1619, had increased to four millions by 1865, and were mostly in the southern states. We were liberated not only empty-handed but left in the power of a people who resented our emancipation as an act of unjust punishment to them. They were therefore armed with a motive for doing everything in their power to render our freedom a curse rather than a blessing. In the halls of National legislation the Negro was made a free man and citizen. The southern states, which had seceded from the Union before the war, regained their autonomy by accepting these amendments and promising to support the constitution. Since "reconstruction" these amendments have been largely nullified in the south, and the Negro vote reduced from a majority to a cipher. This has been accomplished by political massacres, by midnight outrages of KuKlux Klans, and by state legislative enactment. That the legislation of the white south is hostile to the interests of our race is shown by the existence in most of the southern states of the convict lease system, the chain-gang, vagrant laws, election frauds, keeping back laborers wages, paying for work in worthless script instead of lawful money, refusing to sell land to Negroes and the many political massacres where hundreds of black men were murdered for the crime (?) of casting the ballot. These were some of the means resorted to during our first years of liberty to defeat the little beneficence comprehended in the act of our emancipation.

The South is enjoying to-day the results of this course pursued for the first fifteen years of our freedom. The Solid South means that the South is a unit for white supremacy, and that the Negro is practically disfranchised through intimidation. The large Negro population of that section gives the South thirty-nine more votes in the National Electoral College which elects the President of the United States, than she would otherwise have. These votes are cast by white men who represent the Democratic Party, while the Negro vote has heretofore represented the entire Republican Party of the South. Every National Congress has thirty-nine more white members from the South in the House of Representatives than there would be, were it not for the existence of her voiceless and unrepresented Negro vote and population. One Representative is allowed to every 150,000 persons. What other States have usurped, Mississippi made in 1892, a part of her organic law.

The net result of the registration under the educational and poll tax provision of the new Mississippi Constitution is as follows.

	Over 21 years.	Registered votes.
Whites	110, 100	68, 127
Negroes	147, 205	8, 615
Total	257, 305	76, 742

In 1880 there were 130, 278 colored voters a colored majority of 22, 024. Every county in Mississippi now has a white majority. Thirty-three counties have less than 100 Negro votes.

Yazoo county, with 6,000 Negroes of voting age, has only nine registered votes, or one to each 666. Noxubee has four colored voters or one to each 150 colored men. In Lowndes there is one colored voter to each 310 men. In the southern tier counties on the Gulf about one Negro man in eight or ten is registered, which is the best average.

Depriving the Negro of his vote leaves the entire political, legislative, executive and judicial machinery of the country in the hands of the white people. The religious, moral and financial forces of the country are also theirs. This power has been used to pass laws forbidding intermarriage between the races, thus fostering immorality. The union, which the law forbids, goes on without its sanction in dishonorable alliances.

Sec. 3291 M. & V. Code Tennessee, provides that: The intermarriage of white persons with Negroes, Mulattoes or persons of mixed blood descended from a Negro to the third generation inclusive, or their living together as man and wife in this State, is hereby forbidden.

Sec. 3292, M. & V. Code, Tenn., provides that: The persons knowingly violating the provisions in above Section shall be deemed guilty of a felony, and upon conviction thereof shall undergo imprisonment in the penitentiary not less than one nor more than five years; and the court may, in the event of conviction, on the recommendation of the jury, substitute in lieu of punishment in the penitentiary, fine and imprisonment in the county jail.

NOTES:—It need not charge the act to have been done knowingly. Such persons may be indicted for living together as man and wife, though married in another state where such marriages are lawful. 7 Bok. 9. This law is constitutional. 3 Hill's 287.

Out of 44 states only twenty-three states and territories allow whites and Negroes to marry if they see fit to contract such alliances, viz: Louisiana, Illinois, Kansas, Connecticut, Iowa, Maine, Massachusetts, Michigan, Minnesota, Montana, New Hampshire, New Jersey, New York, North Dakota, Ohio, Oklahoma, Pennsylvania, Rhode Island, South Dakota, Vermont, Washington, Wisconsin, and Wyoming. All of these are northern states and territories except one—Louisiana.

The others, especially Virginia, Maryland, W. Virginia, Delaware, North Carolina, South Carolina, Georgia, Florida, Alabama, Mississippi, Arkansas, Kentucky, Missouri, Indiana,

Tennessee, and Texas, have laws similar to the Tennessee Statute. Under these laws men and women are prosecuted and punished in the courts of these states for inter-marrying, but not for unholy alliances.

"The Thirteenth amendment to the Constitution making the race citizens, was virtually made null and void by the legislatures of the re-constructed states. So it became necessary to pass the Civil Rights Bill giving colored people the right to enter public places and ride on first-class railroad cars." —Johnson's History of the Negro race in America. This Bill passed Congress in 1875. For nearly ten years it was the Negro's only protection in the south. In 1883 the United States Supreme Court declared the Civil Rights Bill unconstitutional. With "state's rights" doctrine once more supreme and this last barrier removed, the southern states are enacting separate car laws. Mississippi, Louisiana, Texas, Arkansas, Tennessee, Alabama, Georgia and Kentucky have each passed a law making it punishable by fine and imprisonment for colored persons to ride in the same railway carriage with white persons unless as servants to white passengers. These laws have all been passed within the past 6 years. Kentucky passed this law last year (1892). The legislatures of Missouri, West Virginia and North Carolina had such bills under consideration at the sessions this year, but they were defeated.

Aside from the inconsistency of class legislation in this country, the cars for colored persons are rarely equal in point of accommodation. Usually one-half the smoking car is reserved for the "colored car." Many times only a cloth curtain or partition run half way up, divides this "colored car" from the smoke, obscene language and foul air of the smokers' end of the coach. Into this "separate but equal (?)" half-carriage are crowded all classes and conditions of Negro humanity, without regard to sex, standing, good breeding, or ability to pay for better accommodation. White men pass through these "colored cars" and ride in them whenever they feel inclined to do so, but no colored woman however refined, well educated or well dressed may ride in the ladies, or first-class coach, in any of these states unless she is a nurse-maid traveling with a white child. The railroad fare is exactly the same in all cases however. There is no redress at the hands of the law. The men who execute the law share the same prejudices as those who made these laws, and the courts rule in favor of the law. A colored young school teacher was dragged out of the only ladies coach on the train in Tennessee by the conductor and two trainmen. She entered suit in the state courts as directed by the United States Supreme Court. The Supreme Court of the State of Tennessee, although the lower courts had awarded damages to the plaintiff, reversed the decision of those courts and ruled that the smoking car into which the railway employees tried to force the plaintiff was a first-class car, equal in every respect to the one in which she was seated, and as she was violating the law, she was not entitled to damages.

The Tennessee law is as follows,
——Chapter 52——Page 135—An Act to promote the comfort of passengers on railroad trains by regulating separate accommodations for the white and colored races.

SECTION 1. Be it enacted by the General Assembly of the State of Tennessee—That all railroads carrying passengers in the State (other than street railroads) shall provide equal but separate accommodations for the white and colored races, by providing two or more passenger cars for each passenger train, or by dividing the passenger cars by a partition so as to secure separate accommodations; PROVIDED, that any person may be permitted to take a nurse in the car or compartment set aside for such persons; PROVIDED, that this Act shall not apply to mixed and freight trains which only carry one passenger or combination passenger and baggage; PROVIDED, always that in such cases the one passenger car so carried shall be partitioned into apartments, one apartment for the whites and one for the colored.

SEC. 2. Be it further enacted: That the conductors of such passenger trains shall have power and are hereby required to assign to the car or compartments of the car (when it is divided by a partition) used for the race to which such passengers belong, and should any passenger refuse to occupy the car to which he or she is assigned by such conductor, said conductor shall have power to refuse to carry such passenger on his train, and for such neither he nor the railroad company shall be liable for any damages in any court in this State.

SEC. 3. Be it further enacted: That all railroad companies that shall fail, refuse or neglect to comply with the requirements of section 1, of this Act shall be deemed guilty of a misdemeanor, and, upon conviction in a court of competent jurisdiction, be fined not less than one hundred, nor more than four hundred dollars, and any conductor that shall fail, neglect or refuse to carry out the provisions of this Act shall, upon conviction, be fined not less than twenty-five, nor more than fifty dollars for each offense.

SEC. 4. Be it further enacted: That this Act take effect ninety days from and after its passage, the public welfare requiring it.

Passed March 11, 1891.

THOMAS R. MYERS.
Speaker of the House of Representatives.
Approved March 27, 1891. W. C. DISMUKES,
Speaker of Senate.
JOHN P. BUCHANAN,
Governor.

CHAPTER III.

THE CONVICT LEASE SYSTEM.

The Convict Lease System and Lynch Law are twin infamies which flourish hand in hand in many of the United States. They are the two great outgrowths and results of the class legislation under which our people suffer to-day. Alabama, Arkansas, Florida, Georgia, Kentucky, Louisiana, Mississippi, Nebraska, North Carolina, South Carolina, Tennessee and Washington claim to be too poor to maintain state convicts within prison walls. Hence the convicts are leased out to work for railway contractors, mining companies and those who farm large plantations. These companies assume charge of the convicts, work them as cheap labor and pay the states a handsome revenue for their labor. Nine-tenths of these convicts are Negroes. There are two reasons for this.

(1) The religious, moral and philanthropic forces of the country—all the agencies which tend to uplift and reclaim the degraded and ignorant, are in the hands of the Anglo-Saxon.

Not only has very little effort been made by these forces to reclaim the Negro from the ignorance, immorality and shiftlessness with which he is charged, but he has always been and is now rigidly excluded from the enjoyment of those elevating influences toward which he felt voluntarily drawn. In communities where Negro population is largest and these counteracting influences most needed, the doors of churches, schools, concert halls, lecture rooms, Young men's Christian Associations, and Women's Christian Temperance Unions, have always been and are now closed to the Negro who enters on his own responsibility. Only as a servant or inferior being placed in one corner is he admitted. The white Christian and moral influences have not only done little to prevent the Negro becoming a criminal, but they have deliberately shut him out of everything which tends to make for good citizenship.

To have Negro blood in the veins makes one unworthy of consideration, a social outcast, a leper, even in the church. Two Negro Baptist Ministers, Rev. John Frank, the pastor of the largest colored church in Louisville, Ky., and Rev. C. H. Parrish, President of Eckstein Norton University at Cane Spring, Ky., were in the city of Nashville, Tennessee, in May when the Southern Baptist Convention was in session. They visited the meeting and took seats in the body of the church. At the request of the Association, a policeman was called and escorted these men out because they would not take the seats set apart for colored persons in the back part of the Tabernacle. Both these men are scholarly, of good moral character, and members of the Baptist denomination. But they were Negroes, and that eclipsed everything else. This spirit is even more rampant in the more remote, densely populated plantation districts. The Negro is shut out and ignored—left to grow up in ignorance and vice. Only in the gambling dens and saloons does he meet any sort of welcome. What wonder that he falls into crime?

(2) The second reason our race furnishes so large a share of the convicts is that the judges, juries and other officials of the courts are white men who share these prejudices. They also make the laws. It is wholly in their power to extend clemency to white criminals and mete severe punishment to black criminals for the same or lesser crimes. The Negro criminals are

mostly ignorant, poor and friendless. Possessing neither money to employ lawyers nor influential friends, they are sentenced in large numbers to long terms of imprisonment for petty crimes. The *People's Advocate*, a Negro journal, of Atlanta, Georgia, has the following observation on the prison showing of that state for 1892. "It is an astounding fact that 90 per cent. of the state's convicts are colored. 194 white males and 2 white females; 1,710 colored males and 44 colored females. Is it possible that Georgia is so color prejudiced that she won't convict her white law-breakers. Yes, it is just so, but we hope for a better day."

George W. Cable, author of *The Grandissimes, Dr. Sevier*, etc., in a paper on "The Convict Lease System," read before a Prison Congress in Kentucky says: "In the Georgia penitentiary in 1880, in a total of nearly 1200 convicts, only 22 prisoners were serving as low a term as one year, only 52 others as low as two years, only 76 others as low a term as three years; while those who were under sentences of ten years and *over* numbered 538, although ten years, as the rolls show, is the *utmost* length of time that a convict can be expected to remain alive in a Georgia penitentiary. Six men were under sentence for simple assault and battery—mere fisticuffing—one of two years, two of five years, one of six years, one of seven and one of eight. For larceny, three men were serving under sentence of twenty years, five were sentenced each for fifteen years; one for fourteen years, six for twelve years; thirty-five for ten years, and 172 from one year up to nine years. In other words, a large majority of these 1200 convicts had for simple stealing, without breaking in or violence, been virtually condemned to be worked and misused to death. One man was under a twenty years' sentence for hog-stealing. Twelve men were sentenced to the South Carolina penitentiary on no other finding but a misdemeanor commonly atoned for by a fine of a few dollars, and which thousands of the state's inhabitants (white) are constantly committing with impunity —the carrying of concealed weapons. Fifteen others were sentenced for mere assault and battery. In Louisiana a man was sentenced to the penitentiary for 12 months for stealing five dollars worth of gunnysacks! Out of 2378 convicts in the

Texas prison in 1882, only two were under sentence of less than two years length, and 509 of these were under twenty years of age. Mississippi's penitentiary roll for the same year showed 70 convicts between the ages of 12 and 18 years of age serving long terms. Tennessee showed 12 boys under 18 years of age, under sentences of more than a year; and the North Carolina penitentiary had 234 convicts under 20 years of age serving long terms."

Mr. Cable goes on to say in another part of his admirable paper: "In the Georgia convict force only 15 were whites among 215 who were under sentences of more than ten years." What is true of Georgia is true of the convict lease system everywhere. The details of vice, cruelty and death thus fostered by the states whose treasuries are enriched thereby, equals anything from Siberia. Men, women and children are herded together like cattle in the filthiest quarters and chained together while at work. The Chicago *Inter-Ocean* recently printed an interview with a young colored woman who was sentenced six months to the convict farm in Mississippi for fighting. The costs etc., lengthened the time to 18 months. During her imprisonment she gave birth to two children, but lost the first one from premature confinement, caused by being tied up by the thumbs and punished for failure to do a full day's work. She and other women testified that they were forced to criminal intimacy with the guards and cook to get food to eat.

Correspondence to the Washington D. C. *Evening Star* dated Sept. 27, 1892, on this same subject has the following:

> "The fact that the system puts a large number of criminals afloat in the community from the numerous escapes is not its worst feature. The same report shows that the mortality is fearful in the camps. In one camp it is stated that the mortality is 10 per cent per month, and in another even more than that. In these camps men and women are found chained together, and from twenty to twenty-five children have been born in captivity in the convicts camps.
>
> Some further facts are cited with reference to the system in use in Tennessee. The testimony of a guard at the Coal Creek prison in Tennessee shows that prisoners, black and dirty from their work in the mines, were put into their rooms in the stockades without an opportunity to change their clothing or

sufficient opportunity for cleanliness. Convicts were whipped, a man standing at the head and another at the feet, while a third applied the lash with both hands. Men who failed to perform their task of mining from two to four tons of coal per day were fastened to planks by the feet, then bent over a barrel and fastened by the hands on the other side, stripped and beaten with a strap. Out of the fifty convicts worked in the mines from one to eight were whipped per day in this manner. There was scarcely a day, according to the testimony of the witness, James Frazier, in which one or more were not flogged in this manner for failure to perform their day's task. The work in the mines was difficult and the air sometimes so bad that the men fell insensible and had to be hauled out. Their beds he describes as 'dirty, black and nasty looking.' One of the convicts, testifying as to the kind of food given them, said that the pea soup was made from peas containing weevils and added: 'I have got a spoonful of weevils off a cup of soup.' In many cases convicts were forced to work in water six inches deep for weeks at a time getting out coal with one-fourth of the air necessary for a healthy man to live in, forced to drink water from stagnant pools when mountain springs were just outside of the stockades, and the reports of the prison officials showing large numbers killed in attempting to escape.

The defense of this prison is based wholly upon its economy to the state. It is argued that it would cost large sums of money to build penitentiaries in which to confine and work the prisoners as is done in the Northern States, while the lease system brings the state a revenue and relieves it of the cost of building and maintaining prisons. The fact that the convicts labor is in this way brought into direct competition with free labor does not seem to be taken into account. The contractors, who get these laborers for 30 or 40 cents per day, can drive out of the market the man who employs free labor at $1 a day.

This condition of affairs briefly alluded to in detail in Tennessee and Georgia exists in other Southern States. In North Carolina the same system exists, except that only able-bodied convicts are farmed out. The death rates among the convicts is reported as greater than the death rate of New Orleans in the greatest yellow fever epidemic ever known. In Alabama a new warden with his natural instincts unblunted by familiarity with the situation wrote of it: 'The system is a better training school for criminals than any of the dens of iniquity in our large cities. The system is a disgrace to the state and the reproach of the civilization and Christian sentiment of the age.'"

Every Negro so sentenced not only means able-bodied men to swell the state's number of slaves, but every Negro so convicted is thereby *disfranchised*.

It has been shown that numbers of Negro youths are sentenced to these penitentiaries every year and there mingle with the hardened criminals of all ages and both sexes. The execution of law does not cease with the incarceration of those of tender years for petty crimes. In the state of South Carolina last year Mildred Brown, a little thirteen year old colored girl was found guilty of murder in the first degree on the charge of poisoning a little white infant that she nursed. She was sentenced to be hanged. The Governor refused to commute her sentence, and on October 7th, 1892, at Columbia, South Carolina, she was hanged on the gallows. This made the second colored female hanged in that state within one month. Although tried, and in rare cases convicted for murder and other crimes, no white girl in this country ever met the same fate. The state of Alabama in the same year hanged a ten year old Negro boy. He was charged with the murder of a peddler.

"THE SO-CALLED 'CAUCASIAN' INTELLECT"

RICHARD T. GREENER
The White Problem
Lend a Hand, May 1894

THE WHITE PROBLEM.

If one wishes to observe eccentricity, vagary, platitude, and idiosyncracy all combined, let him only read the literary effusions of the so-called "Caucasian" intellect from Thomas Jefferson's "Notes on Virginia," down to the recent contributions to the *Forum*, when discussing any phase of the "Negro Problem." Jefferson, fresh from Hume, uttered some platitudes about the two races living together in freedom, treading very cautiously, as is his custom, when not too sure of his premises. Imlay and Abbé Grégoire routed him at once, and, as if to complete the poetic irony, the negro almanac maker, Benjamin Banneker, who had, from 1792 until 1800, calculated alone the only almanacs printed for Maryland, Delaware, District of Columbia, and Virginia, sent him a copy, with an autograph letter, couched in as choice English as Jefferson ever penned, and of equal chirography. Nevertheless, the special negro-hate went on. Nott & Gliddon, DeLeon, DeBow, *alius, alii*, quoting, rehashing Jefferson, supplementing him with modern discoveries.

A phase of the white problem is seen in the determination, not only to treat the Negro as a member of a child-like race, but the grim determination to keep him a child or a ward. In every advance, since emancipation, it has, with true Caucasian gall, been assumed that everything must be done for him, and under no circumstances must he be allowed to do for himself. In religion, in politics, in civil and social life, he must be developed in a pen, staked off from the rest of mankind, and nursed, coddled, fed, and trained by aid of the longest spoons, forks, and rakes obtainable. All along there has been heard the solemn, low refrain of doubt, small hope, and feeble expectation as to the probable survival of this black infant. Indeed, nothing has so weighed upon the average American Christian heart as the precarious health of this infant, whom no one had the heart exactly to kill, were it possible, but whose noiseless and peaceful departure to a better world, would have been hailed with smothered sighs of intense relief.

This feeling obtains North as well as South; scalawag, native, carpet-bagger or sand-hiller, democrat, republican, or independent, seemed to think that for some occult reason this infant must not be allowed to grow in any one of the social, religious, or political ways, in which other American citizens grow and develop healthfully for the good of their country. All the traditions seemed against the negro, all the arguments surely were. He was rarely given a real chance, as here, to talk freely for himself, and when such opportunity was afforded, he generally took his cue from his audience, and talked to the jury, and usually with 'bated breath. When he spoke humbly, apologetically, deprecatingly, he was an intelligent, sensible fellow, a milder form of "good nigger," before the war. Among the *novi homines* of the Republic it is so self-satisfying to have some one to look down upon and despise, just perhaps, as you have emerged from the mire yourself, and before, indeed, the evidence of "previous condition" has been thoroughly obliterated.

> Wut *is* there lef' I'd like to know,
> Ef't ain't the difference o' color,
> To keep up self-respec' an' show
> The human natur' of a fullah?
> Wut good in bein' white, onless
> It's fixed by law, nut lef' to guess,
> That we are smarter, an' they duller.

Another difficulty of this white problem is the universal belief that somehow the Negro race began its career with President Lincoln's proclamation. All such novices would do well to look up their old histories, newspapers, and pamphlets. Next to the Indian, he is probably of the purest racial stock in the country, and as has been stated, whatever accession has come to him, has been from the "choicest" blood of the country. He has been thoroughly identified with it from the beginning. He was the agricultural laborer and the artisan at the South, the trusted servant and companion; at the North he took part in all mechanical pursuits, helped build the houses, worked on the first newspapers, made the first wood cuts, and was the best pressman at Charleston, Philadelphia, and Boston. In every industrial, social, and political movement, as well as in the different warlike struggles, he has borne an honorable part, which to profess ignorance of, is not creditable, or, if denied, shows wilful prejudice. He was on the heights of Abraham with Wolfe; in the French and Indian wars with Braddock; the first martyr of the Revolution; is seen in Trumbull's picture retreating with the patriots from Bunker Hill, musket in hand; Washington did not disdain to share a blanket with him on the cold ground at Valley Forge; at the South with Marion and Green; at the North with Washington and Gates, with Wayne and Allen. On account of the injury to the United States through him, the war of 1812 was begun, and his fertile brain suggested the defence of New Orleans, and, after the battle, led Andrew Jackson to say in public proclamation:

"I expected much: I knew well how you loved your native country. * * * You have done more than I expected. * * * The President of the United States shall hear how praiseworthy was your conduct in the hour of danger. * * * The American people, I doubt not, will give you the praise your exploits entitle you to." Do we not know how they fought with Lawrence in the Chesapeake, and formed more than half of the crew of Old Ironsides, were with Scott and Taylor in Mexico, as they were with Grant and Sherman, and Sheridan and Butler, with Farragut and Foote and Porter, at Port Hudson and Battery Wagner. He who doubts the record can read it from the pen of Negro historians, from Nell or Williams or Wilson, for "of those who perform the deeds, and those who write, many such are praised."

No sneer of race, no assumption of superiority, no incrusted prejudice will ever obscure this record, much less obliterate it, and while it stands, it is the Negro's passport to every right and privilege of every other American.

Not alone a soldier and a sailor, the Negro was a citizen, under colonial and proprietary governments, under the Articles of Confederation, and in most of the original thirteen states, was an honorable part of "we people," who ordained and established this constitution for the United States of America. Long before Calhoun and Taney, he fought, lived, voted, and acted like any other citizen; and if many of his race were enslaved, he was not alone. There were "free willers," "indentured servants," and "apprentices," many of them to bear him company. Not a few of these, as records show, white men, Irishmen, Scotchmen, Englishmen, Moors, Palatines, were ruthlessly sold into slavery as the exactions of the traffic became more pressing. At the earliest period there was always a class of black freemen, and they were found at the South as well as at the North,—at New Orleans, Mobile, Charleston, and Virginia, as well as at Washington, Baltimore, Philadelphia, New York, and Boston, where in business, in social life, in church and in politics, they were active, enterprising, and respected. In rare instances, with acquired wealth, like some "free willers," and "indentured servants," they went West or North, as the case might be, and mingled and blended into the new surroundings and developed civilization, where, but for names and traditions, all traces of them would be lost. There come to mind of such men, three United States senators of distinction, at least ten representatives in Congress before the war, five eminent officers of the United States Army, two cabinet officers, three eminent Catholic prelates, four prominent divines of the Episcopal Church, while in the other churches, in medicine and in law, the list is too long for enumeration.

But of those who were content to remain chafing under the indignities and ostracism, which increased from 1820 it is time it should be clearly, emphatically and proudly stated that instead of being a pauper pariah class as is supposed, there was no movement looking to the amelioration of their condition, from 1808 until John Brown raid in 1859,—nothing which tended to unshackle the slave or remove the clogs from the free colored man, in which he was not the foremost, active, intelligent participant, never a suppliant, never a mere recipient. On the contrary he was first to organize for his own emancipation; among the first to speak, and write, and print in his own behalf. From Benezet and Grégoire, Condorcet, Brissot de Warville, from Franklin, Rush and Rittenhouse, and more than all, from that "glorious communion of the saints," the Friends, he had early learned the value of his own manhood, was willing to fight for it, and acquired the art of putting his complaint into pretty choice English, at a time, too, when Abbé Raynal, 1779, thought it a matter of astonishment that America had not a good poet, an able mathematician, or a man of genius, in any single art or science, and "not one of them shows any decisive talent for one in particular."

When Fisher Ames was saying, 1807, "Except the authors of two able books on our politics, we have no authors; shall we match Joel Barlow against Homer or Hesiod? Can Tom Paine contend against Plato?" When Sydney Smith, 1818, wrote, "There does not seem to be in America, at this moment, one man of any considerable talents," a Negro astronomer was calculating logarithms, studying all alone, in the woods of Maryland, Ferguson's Astronomy, and making valuable observations, viewing the stars, and computing his almanacs. During this period, 1780–1810, the Negro had his churches, literary societies, abolition societies, and, later on, newspapers, with educated editors, and active agents for the assertion of their rights and privileges, before Lundy and Garrison.

Mr. Howells looks up the streets of "Nigger Hill," and sees only a few straggling negroes. They are of no interest, and of course have "no story, bless you, to tell." And yet there are many stories, many traditions, much history clustering about that hill, from Cambridge street to the Common, from Charles to Hancock. Big Dick, the boxer, the precursor of Jackson; the Blind Preacher, Raymond, Prince Hall, and Easton, Master Paul and his church and *school*, in which the first American Anti-slavery Society was organized, Jan. 6, 1832.

"On that dismal night, and in the face of public opinion, fiercer far than the tempest, or wind and hail that beat upon the windows of that 'nigger school-house,' were laid the foundations of an organized movement against American slavery that at last became too mighty to be resisted." Mr. Garrison might have told Mr. Howells, he certainly could have learned that among colored men of that dear old town, the first patrons of the *Liberator* were found, who supported it the first year, when it had not fifty white subscribers. Mr. Garrison, at Exeter Hall in London, sixty years ago said, "I am proud to say that the funds for my mission * * * were principally made up by the voluntary contributions of my free colored brethren at very short notice. * * * Many of their number are in the most affluent circumstances, and distinguished for their refinement, enterprise, and talents * * * they have flourishing churches, temperance and other societies. * * * Among them is taken a large number of daily and weekly papers, and of literary and scientific periodicals, from the popular monthlies up to the grave and erudite *North American* and *American Quarterly Reviews*. I have, at this moment, to my own paper, *'The Liberator,'* *one thousand subscribers among this people*; and from an occupancy of the editorial chair of more than seven years, I can testify that they are more punctual in their payments than any five hundred white subscribers whose names I ever placed indiscriminately in my subscription book."

Not alone Wm. Lloyd Garrison. Long before Frederick Douglass began "to pray with his legs" and look toward the "north star," the leading colored men of Washington, Cary, and Fleet, and Cook; of Philadelphia, Forten, Allen, Burr, and Purvis; of Baltimore, Grice, Greener, and Watkins; of Boston, Paul, Easton, Barbadoes, and Walker, corresponded with, aided, lodged and fed the apostle Lundy, in his mysterious journeyings through the southern states, and circulated his Genius of Universal Emancipation.

My account is from Isaac Cary, who knew "the little, pale, thin man," and he says Lundy never departed empty handed.

It was in Master Paul's Church, Belknap street, that the abolitionists, driven from Tremont Temple, in 1860, found refuge, and preserved there free speech for Boston and America. Master Paul himself was a college graduate, accompanied Mr. Garrison to England, and won praise from Daniel O'Connell for his scholarship and eloquence.

Before emancipation in New York state, *Freedom's Journal*, edited by Cornish and Russwurm, a graduate of Bowdoin, I am told, afterwards President of Liberia, demonstrated the public spirit, intelligence, and literary character of the American Negro. If David Walker's *Appeal*, issued in 1829, had been printed in 1765 or '70, and had been about the rights of the colonies, it would long since have attracted attention. But it was written by one of the "old clo' merchants" of Brattle street —an extinct guild—and is the voice of a black John the Baptist, crying in the wilderness. It attained the honor of legislative attention, and a reward set for the author's head; but it is an American classic, and forever answers all hints at Negro contentment under oppression. By law of heredity, thanks to Governor Butler, Walker's son became a lawyer and a municipal judge in Boston.

These facts taken at random would tend to show that the American Negro has traditions—far more, and more honorable than many of his traducers. They are of services, ancestry, interests in public affairs in his own future. Now traditions of blood and training and achievement can never be permanently repressed. Pile Etna upon them, they will break forth, no matter how long or persistently kept down. As a help to the solution of the White Problem, this article is to show that they exist, and if they have not hitherto asserted themselves, it is because they could afford to wait, not because they are not cherished and kept for inspiration. Some complacent critics of the Negro, who analyze, weigh, measure him with their little poles, discuss his removal to Africa, debate his admission to trades unions, into the ranks of business, into the literary circle, into social life, would save themselves much unrest if they knew his motto, *J'y suis reste.*

He is a reader of the Census. He calmly contemplates either horn of the politico economic problem—absorption, all he asks to be is an actual American citizen; repression and fifty years of race isolation,—one of the ruling forces of this Republic, the arbiter of the South. For, in fifty years, he will be nearly 100,000,000 strong, and, judging solely by the advance since 1863, in thrift, in education, in race development, in equipoise, in aspiration, all that tend to consolidate and strengthen, he will have no fear of the few white chips which will here and there attempt to stem the rush of this black Niagara. Truly he can afford to wait. One of the worst phases of the White Problem is the fatuous clinging to certain ideas, especially the good done to the Negro by bringing him to America. As well tell the descendants of Virginia convicts, the progeny of the kidnapped Irish, 1645–52; the proud descendants of Dutch, Scotch and English poor-houses, shambles and heaths, of the benefits which have accrued to them.

For the presence of all these, the negro included, America is the gainer, humanity the debtor. The value of his contribution far outweighs any benefit he may be supposed to have received. He has reaped down the fields, developed new ideas, preserved the ark of the Nation's inheritance, and if Fletcher of Saltoun, and Dr. Dvorak have any weight, he is to become greater than the lawgiver, he is to found the American music of the future.

"The future music of this country must be founded upon what are called negro melodies. * * * They are American. They are the folk songs of America, and your composers must turn to them. * * In the negro melodies of America, I discover all that is needed for a great and noble school of music. There is nothing in the whole range of composition that cannot find a themetic source here."—*Dvorak*.

The Negro has no tears to shed over that, "wonderful school of slavery, under Providence," so often quoted. He is no such hypocrite as to go through the pretence of believing that slavery is ever a good, a necessary, or beneficial school. Much less does he grant that any phase of that school, at any stage, affected him morally, socially, or physically, except adversely, while he does know from bitter experience, how utterly pharasaical, how absurdly hypocritical, and how thoroughly unchristian the entire system was in practice, example, and influence.

Whatever of intelligence, Christianity, or civilization the Negro possesses today, let it be remembered he retains in spite of slavery, and its relic, caste. Whatever of honesty or morality or thrift has survived the charnel-house, comes from that excellent stock—better than the Indian—which Galton says is now farther behind the best English brain of today than it is behind the brain of Athens! It is due to brain that slavery could not disintegrate, to a happy heart, an abiding faith.

I am at loss to observe how close the race maintains its hold on orthodox Christianity, when it is remembered how even the maxims of the common law were set aside, at its behests —*partus sequitur patiem*—how Virginia (Hening Vol. II., pp. 356–7) declared that those imported thither "except Turks and Moors in amity," shall be accounted slaves * * "notwithstanding a conversion to Christianity after their importation." How far from solution seems the white problem, when the Negro reflects how powerless is Christianity to repress race prejudice; how often indifferent to real brotherhood, while affecting deep denominational interest. Indeed, while an emasculated religion has been preached to the Negro, each denomination has seemed to shirk the question of, Who is my Neighbor? A premium has been offered every self-respecting Negro to repudiate Christianity as it is taught. Why speak of the Christian? Take the cultured editor, the moulder of public opinion. How despairing the "White Problem," when this is the high watermark of culture:—"Consider him at his best. I cite the case of a manly and accomplished gentleman of the race. His life has no background. What we mean by ancestry is lacking to him; and not only is it lacking but its lack is proclaimed by his color, and he is always reminded of it. Be who he may and do what he may, when the personal test comes he finds himself a man set apart, a marked man.

There is a difference between the discrimination against him in one part of the country (the South) and in another part (the North), but it is a difference in degree only. He is not any where in a fellowship in complete equipoise with men of the other race. Nor does this end it. The boundless sweep of opportunity which is the inheritance of every white citizen of the Republic, falls to him curtailed, hemmed in, a mere pathway to a few permissible endeavors. A sublime reliance on the ultimate coming of justice may give him the philosophic temper. But his life will bring chiefly opportunities to cultivate it. And for his children what better? To those that solve great social problems with professional ease, I commend this remark that Mr. Lowell is said to have made, "I am glad I was not born a Jew; but if I had been a Jew, I should be prouder of that fact than any other." You can find men who are glad that they were not born Negroes; but can you find a man, who, if he had been born a Negro, would be prouder of that fact, than of any other? When you have found many men of this mind, then this race problem will, owing to some change in human nature, have become less tough, but till then, patience and tolerance."

Here is a paragraph which most people would acquiesce in; which bears the air of hard sense, stern reality, deep philosophic insight, keen analysis and delicate humor. It is already winging its way, and will be quoted as a solid fact. If it were true then Schopenhauer reigns in America; religion and culture have failed to soften the manner but have hardened and intensified the small prejudices of two centuries ago. If the statements were true, acquiescence in such condition, would show the utmost callousness, a more than heathen indifference, a heartlessness, and inhumanity, unworthy of the century. If character, reputation, manly accomplishments, the heights reached, the palm won, still find any black hero a "marked man," because of no fault of his own, and church and society, home and club, united in thus ostracising him and his children, then is it not demonstrated that it is not the Black but the White Problem, which needs most serious attention in this country?

Mr. Lowell, as always, was wisely terse. No trace of the snob was in him; he was no panderer to caste. Of course he was not anxious to be born a Jew, for he knew unreasoning and unreasonable pride of race still pecked often at its superior; but Lowell, knowing the history of the race, and what its sons had accomplished in spite of persecution felt he "would be prouder of that fact if he were a Jew than any other." Nor is it true that every social avenue is closed to the aspiring and manly Negro of today. Professor Washington, of Tuskeegee, the leader in perhaps the greatest work of the race, is received among the best people of Boston, Philadelphia, and New York. The late Professor Price of North Carolina, was the recipient of exceptional attention at home and abroad, on account of his talents and rare eloquence. Professor Scarborough, the best Greek scholar of the race, meets the members of the American Philological Association, on terms of equality, and Mr. Dubois, who won a travelling scholarship at Harvard, read a paper before the American Historical Society, and has been offered a professorship in a white college. It is surely no unusual thing in New York city to see educated colored men, at various social functions, collegiate, theological, political, literary, professional. These are sporadic cases, of course; but so are the cases of the bright farmer boys from Vermont, North Carolina, Michigan, Connecticut, and New York State, who have, by virtue of study or talent, gained entree to the same salons. The fact springs from the new ozone of equality, or better liberality, which is in the air, and is prompted and encouraged by those who have a clear notion of the fitness of things. Here at least, it is not a race, nor color, nor creed line.

Against that flippancy which draws too hasty conclusions, which cannot conquer its early prejudices, or ignore its limitations, there looms up a quiet, unobtrusive but persistent force, which is determined not to give way to caste distinctions; but to see to it that there is a career open to all, despite sex, or creed, or race, in order that no atom of intellectual force shall be lost to our common country, and it is this which tends to the solution of our problem. Once in a while the great utterance of some broad-souled, warm-hearted American, determined to give his testimony comes to us. Bishop Potter, broader than his entire church, says tersely, "What the Negro needs more than anything else is, opportunity." Or, it is Cable: "I must repeat my conviction, that if the unconscious habit of oppression were not already a scheme so gross, irrational, unjust and inefficient as our present caste distinctions it could not find a place among a people so generally intelligent and high-minded. We hear much about race instinct. The most of it is pure twaddle. It may be there is such a thing. We do not know. It is not proved. And even if it were established, it could not necessarily be a proper moral guide."

Then, it is Bishop Dudley, bravely fighting his way through traditions: "The time may come and will, when the prejudices now apparently invincible, shall have been conquered. Society then as now organized upon the basis of community of interests, congeniality of tastes, and equality of position, will exclude the multitude, who cannot speak its shibboleth, but there will be no color line of separation.

* * Such a social revolution as will open wide the drawing-rooms of Washington to the black men who have been honored guests in the palaces of England and France. * * Capacity is not lacking, but help is needed, the help I repeat, which the intelligence of the superior race must give by careful selection and personal contact with the selected. Does not our mother Nature teach us that this is the only process, such being her method of procedure, working under the Creator's law."

Not on the Protestant side alone. Hear this clearer blast from the leader of the Catholic cause in the Northwest, Archbishop Ireland of Minnesota: "The right way. There is a work for us. Slavery has been abolished in America; the trail of the serpent, however, yet marks the ground. We do not accord to our black brother all the rights and privileges of freedom and of a common humanity. They are the victims of an unreasonable and unjustifiable ostracism. * * * It looks as if we had grudgingly granted to them emancipation, as if we fain still would be masters, and hold them in servitude.

What do I claim for the black men? That which I claim for the white men, neither more nor less. I would blot out the color line. White men have their estrangements. They separate on lines of wealth, of intelligence, of culture, of ancestry. Those differences and estrangements I do not now discuss, and will not complain if the barriers they erect are placed on the pathway of the black man. But let there be no barrier against mere color. Treat Negroes who are intellectually inferior to us as we treat inferior whites, and I shall not complain. The Negro problem is upon us, and there is no other solution to it, peaceful and permanent, than to grant to our colored citizens practical and effective equality with white citizens." Here are men, whose words shed some rays of light upon the solution of this terrible White Problem, which I may lay some slight claim to the distinction of having discovered, though it would be presumptuous for me to say the solution is clear to me. If it could properly be stated, perhaps, Edmund Burke's "*timid prudence with which a tame circumspection so frequently enervates the work of beneficence*," and of all things being "*afraid of being too much in the right*," might be found its salient point on the positive side, while, as I have hinted, the absolute ignorance about the Negro, presents the negative side.

> Slaves of Gold! whose sordid dealings
> Tarnish all your boasted powers,
> Prove that you have human feelings
> Ere you proudly question ours.

We learn from the *Forum* editor that there are members of this race who are, "accomplished" and "manly." He is mistaken in supposing they have "no back-ground;" some of them have several, three generations of education, sufficient, according to Emerson, to make a scholar. Some have proved their capacity, not in contests with Negroes alone, but with representatives of all races; some have, it is true, from training and heredity, the philosophic temperament. Like Hebrews, who look not back to Jerusalem, or await a Messiah; like Irishmen, who do not dream alone of a resuscitated Irish monarchy, or see visions of an Irish Parliament at Dublin, they are painfully aware what disadvantages still hedge the members of any proscribed race, in ordinary pursuits, and in daily life; but they see no reason because of this, why they should feel ashamed of the fact, seek to deny it, or attempt to ignore it. They feel that they are first of all American citizens, and secondarily Negroes. From their reading, observation, and reflection, they are not sure but that the very fact of their origin may have been the means, under God's guidance of the Universe, of saving them from illiberal prejudices, from over-weening race-pride, from utter disregard of other races' rights, feelings and privileges, and from intellectual narrowness and bigotry.

EXAMINING EXCUSES FOR LYNCHING

IDA B. WELLS
from *A Red Record*
1895

CHAPTER I.

THE CASE STATED.

THE student of American sociology will find the year 1894 marked by a pronounced awakening of the public conscience to a system of anarchy and outlawry which had grown during a series of ten years to be so common, that scenes of unusual brutality failed to have any visible effect upon the humane sentiments of the people of our land.

Beginning with the emancipation of the Negro, the inevitable result of unbridled power exercised for two and a half centuries, by the white man over the Negro, began to show itself in acts of conscienceless outlawry. During the slave regime, the Southern white man owned the Negro body and soul. It was to his interest to dwarf the soul and preserve the body. Vested with unlimited power over his slave, to subject him to any and all kinds of physical punishment, the white man was still restrained from such punishment as tended to injure the slave by abating his physical powers and thereby reducing his financial worth. While slaves were scourged mercilessly, and in countless cases inhumanly treated in other respects, still the white owner rarely permitted his anger to go so far as to take a life, which would entail upon him a loss of several hundred dollars. The slave was rarely killed, he was too valuable; it was easier and quite as effective, for discipline or revenge, to sell him "Down South."

But Emancipation came and the vested interests of the white man in the Negro's body were lost. The white man had no right to scourge the emancipated Negro, still less has he a right to kill him. But the Southern white people had been educated so long in that school of practice, in which might makes right, that they disdained to draw strict lines of action in dealing with the Negro. In slave times the Negro was kept subservient and submissive by the frequency and severity of the scourging, but, with freedom, a new system of intimidation came into vogue; the Negro was not only whipped and scourged; he was killed.

Not all nor nearly all of the murders done by white men, during the past thirty years in the South, have come to light, but the statistics as gathered and preserved by white men, and which have not been questioned, show that during these years more than ten thousand Negroes have been killed in cold blood, without the formality of judicial trial and legal execution. And yet, as evidence of the absolute impunity with which the white man dares to kill a Negro, the same record shows that during all these years, and for all these murders only three white men have been tried, convicted, and executed. As no white man has been lynched for the murder of colored people, these three executions are the only instances of the death penalty being visited upon white men for murdering Negroes.

Naturally enough the commission of these crimes began to tell upon the public conscience, and the Southern white man, as a tribute to the nineteenth century civilization, was in a manner compelled to give excuses for his barbarism. His excuses have adapted themselves to the emergency, and are aptly outlined by that greatest of all Negroes, Frederick Douglass, in an article of recent date, in which he shows that there have been three distinct eras of Southern barbarism, to account for which three distinct excuses have been made.

The first excuse given to the civilized world for the murder of unoffending Negroes was the necessity of the white man to repress and stamp out alleged "race riots." For years immediately succeeding the war there was an appalling slaughter of colored people, and the wires usually conveyed to northern people and the world the intelligence, first, that an insurrection was being planned by Negroes, which, a few hours later, would prove to have been vigorously resisted by white men, and controlled with a resulting loss of several killed and wounded. It was always a remarkable feature in these insurrections and riots that only Negroes were killed during the rioting, and that all the white men escaped unharmed.

From 1865 to 1872, hundreds of colored men and women were mercilessly murdered and the almost invariable reason assigned was that they met their death by being alleged participants in an insurrection or riot. But this story at last wore itself out. No insurrection ever materialized; no Negro rioter was ever apprehended and proven guilty, and no dynamite ever recorded the black man's protest against oppression and wrong. It was too much to ask thoughtful people to believe this transparent story, and the southern white people at last made up their minds that some other excuse must be had.

Then came the second excuse, which had its birth during the turbulent times of reconstruction. By an amendment to the Constitution the Negro was given the right of franchise, and, theoretically at least, his ballot became his invaluable emblem of citizenship. In a government "of the people, for the people, and by the people," the Negro's vote became an important factor in all matters of state and national politics. But this did not last long. The southern white man would not consider that the Negro had any right which a white man was bound to respect, and the idea of a republican form of government in the southern states grew into general contempt. It was maintained that "This is a white man's government," and regardless of numbers the white man should rule. "No Negro domination" became the new legend on the sanguinary banner of the sunny South, and under it rode the Ku Klux Klan, the Regulators, and the lawless mobs, which for any cause chose to murder one man or a dozen as suited their purpose best. It was a long, gory campaign; the blood chills and the heart almost loses faith in Christianity when one thinks of Yazoo, Hamburg, Edgefield, Copiah, and the countless massacres of defenseless Negroes, whose only crime was the attempt to exercise their right to vote.

But it was a bootless strife for colored people. The government which had made the Negro a citizen found itself unable to protect him. It gave him the right to vote, but denied him the protection which should have maintained that right. Scourged from his home; hunted through the swamps; hung by midnight raiders, and openly murdered in the light of day, the Negro clung to his right of franchise with a heroism which would have wrung admiration from the hearts of savages.

He believed that in that small white ballot there was a subtle something which stood for manhood as well as citizenship, and thousands of brave black men went to their graves, exemplifying the one by dying for the other.

The white man's victory soon became complete by fraud, violence, intimidation and murder. The franchise vouchsafed to the Negro grew to be a "barren ideality," and regardless of numbers, the colored people found themselves voiceless in the councils of those whose duty it was to rule. With no longer the fear of "Negro Domination" before their eyes, the white man's second excuse became valueless. With the Southern governments all subverted and the Negro actually eliminated from all participation in state and national elections, there could be no longer an excuse for killing Negroes to prevent "Negro Domination."

Brutality still continued; Negroes were whipped, scourged, exiled, shot and hung whenever and wherever it pleased the white man so to treat them, and as the civilized world with increasing persistency held the white people of the South to account for its outlawry, the murderers invented the third excuse—that Negroes had to be killed to avenge their assaults upon women. There could be framed no possible excuse more harmful to the Negro and more unanswerable if true in its sufficiency for the white man.

Humanity abhors the assailant of womanhood, and this charge upon the Negro at once placed him beyond the pale of human sympathy. With such unanimity, earnestness and apparent candor was this charge made and reiterated that the world has accepted the story that the Negro is a monster which the Southern white man has painted him. And to-day, the Christian world feels, that while lynching is a crime, and lawlessness and anarchy the certain precursors of a nation's fall, it can not by word or deed, extend sympathy or help to a race of outlaws, who might mistake their plea for justice and deem it an excuse for their continued wrongs.

The Negro has suffered much and is willing to suffer more. He recognizes that the wrongs of two centuries can not be righted in a day, and he tries to bear his burden with patience for to-day and be hopeful for to-morrow. But there comes a time when the veriest worm will turn, and the Negro feels to-day that after all the work he has done, all the sacrifices he has made, and all the suffering he has endured, if he did not, now, defend his name and manhood from this vile accusation, he would be unworthy even of the contempt of mankind. It is to this charge he now feels he must make answer.

If the Southern people in defense of their lawlessness, would tell the truth and admit that colored men and women are lynched for almost any offense, from murder to a misdemeanor, there would not now be the necessity for this defense. But when they intentionally, maliciously and constantly belie the record and bolster up these falsehoods by the words of legislators, preachers, governors and bishops, then the Negro must give to the world his side of the awful story.

A word as to the charge itself. In considering the third reason assigned by the Southern white people for the butchery of blacks, the question must be asked, what the white man means when he charges the black man with rape. Does he mean the crime which the statutes of the civilized states describe as such? Not by any means. With the Southern white man, any mesalliance existing between a white woman and a colored man is a sufficient foundation for the charge of rape. The Southern white man says that it is impossible for a voluntary alliance to exist between a white woman and a colored man, and therefore, the fact of an alliance is a proof of force. In numerous instances where colored men have been lynched on the charge of rape, it was positively known at the time of lynching, and indisputably proven after the victim's death, that the relationship sustained between the man and woman was voluntary and clandestine, and that in no court of law could even the charge of assault have been successfully maintained.

It was for the assertion of this fact, in the defense of her own race, that the writer hereof became an exile; her property destroyed and her return to her home forbidden under penalty of death, for writing the following editorial which was printed in her paper, the Free Speech, in Memphis, Tenn., May 21, 1892:

"Eight Negroes lynched since last issue of the 'Free Speech' one at Little Rock, Ark., last Saturday morning where the citizens broke (?) into the penitentiary and got their man; three near Anniston, Ala., one near New Orleans; and three at Clarksville, Ga., the last three for killing a white man, and five on the same old racket—the new alarm about raping white women. The same programme of hanging, then shooting bullets into the lifeless bodies was carried out to the letter. Nobody in this section of the country believes the old threadbare lie that Negro men rape white women. If Southern white men are not careful, they will over-reach themselves and public sentiment will have a reaction; a conclusion will then be reached which will be very damaging to the moral reputation of their women."

But threats cannot suppress the truth, and while the Negro suffers the soul deformity, resultant from two and a half centuries of slavery, he is no more guilty of this vilest of all vile charges than the white man who would blacken his name.

During all the years of slavery, no such charge was ever made, not even during the dark days of the rebellion, when the white man, following the fortunes of war went to do battle for the maintenance of slavery. While the master was away fighting to forge the fetters upon the slave, he left his wife and children with no protectors save the Negroes themselves. And yet during those years of trust and peril, no Negro proved recreant to his trust and no white man returned to a home that had been dispoiled.

Likewise during the period of alleged "insurrection," and alarming "race riots," it never occurred to the white man, that his wife and children were in danger of assault. Nor in the Reconstruction era, when the hue and cry was against "Negro Domination," was there ever a thought that the domination would ever contaminate a fireside or strike to death the virtue of womanhood. It must appear strange indeed, to every thoughtful and candid man, that more than a quarter of a century elapsed before the Negro began to show signs of such infamous degeneration.

In his remarkable apology for lynching, Bishop Haygood, of Georgia, says: "No race, not the most savage, tolerates the rape of woman, but it may be said without reflection upon any other people that the Southern people are now and always have been most sensitive concerning the honor of their women—their mothers, wives, sisters and daughters." It is not the purpose of this defense to say one word against the white women of the South. Such need not be said, but it is their misfortune that the chivalrous white men of that section, in order to escape the deserved execration of the civilized world, should shield themselves by their cowardly and infamously false excuse, and call into question that very honor about which their distinguished priestly apologist claims they are most sensitive. To justify their own barbarism they assume a chivalry which they do not possess. True chivalry respects all womanhood, and no one who reads the record, as it is written in the faces of the million mulattoes in the South, will for a minute conceive that the southern white man had a very chivalrous regard for the honor due the women of his own race or respect for the womanhood which circumstances placed in his power. That chivalry which is "most sensitive concerning the honor of women" can hope for but little respect from the civilized world, when it confines itself entirely to the women who happen to be white. Virtue knows no color line, and the chivalry which depends upon complexion of skin and texture of hair can command no honest respect.

When emancipation came to the Negroes, there arose in the northern part of the United States an almost divine sentiment among the noblest, purest and best white women of the North, who felt called to a mission to educate and Christianize the millions of southern ex-slaves. From every nook and corner of the North, brave young white women answered that call and left their cultured homes, their happy associations and their lives of ease, and with heroic determination went to the South to carry light and truth to the benighted blacks. It was a heroism no less than that which calls for volunteers for India, Africa and the Isles of the sea. To educate their unfortunate charges; to teach them the Christian virtues and to inspire in them the moral sentiments manifest in their own lives, these young women braved dangers whose record reads more like fiction than fact. They became social outlaws in the South. The peculiar sensitiveness of the southern white men for women, never shed its protecting influence about them. No friendly word from their own race cheered them in their work; no hospitable doors gave them the companionship like that from which they had come. No chivalrous white man doffed his hat in honor or respect. They were "Nigger teachers"—unpardonable offenders in the social ethics of the South, and were insulted, persecuted and ostracised, not by Negroes, but by the white manhood which boasts of its chivalry toward women.

And yet these northern women worked on, year after year, unselfishly, with a heroism which amounted almost to martyrdom. Threading their way through dense forests, working in schoolhouse, in the cabin and in the church, thrown at all times and in all places among the unfortunate and lowly Negroes, whom they had come to find and to serve, these northern women, thousands and thousands of them, have spent more than a quarter of a century in giving to the colored people their splendid lessons for home and heart and soul. Without protection, save that which innocence gives to every good woman, they went about their work, fearing no assault and suffering none. Their chivalrous protectors were hundreds of miles away in their northern homes, and yet they never feared any "great dark faced mobs," they dared night or day to "go beyond their own roof trees." They never complained of assaults, and no mob was ever called into existence to avenge crimes against them. Before the world adjudges the Negro a moral monster, a vicious assailant of womanhood and a menace to the sacred precincts of home, the colored people ask the consideration of the silent record of gratitude, respect, protection and devotion of the millions of the race in the South, to the thousands of northern white women who have served as teachers and missionaries since the war.

The Negro may not have known what chivalry was, but he knew enough to preserve inviolate the womanhood of the South which was entrusted to his hands during the war. The finer sensibilities of his soul may have been crushed out by years of slavery, but his heart was full of gratitude to the white women of the North, who blessed his home and inspired his soul in all these years of freedom. Faithful to his trust in both of these instances, he should now have the impartial ear of the civilized world, when he dares to speak for himself as against the infamy wherewith he stands charged.

It is his regret, that, in his own defense, he must disclose to the world that degree of dehumanizing brutality which fixes upon America the blot of a national crime. Whatever faults and failings other nations may have in their dealings with their own subjects or with other people, no other civilized nation stands condemned before the world with a series of crimes so peculiarly national. It becomes a painful duty of the Negro to reproduce a record which shows that a large portion of the American people avow anarchy, condone murder and defy the contempt of civilization.

These pages are written in no spirit of vindictiveness, for all who give the subject consideration must concede that far too serious is the condition of that civilized government in which the spirit of unrestrained outlawry constantly increases in violence, and casts its blight over a continually growing area of territory. We plead not for the colored people alone, but for all victims of the terrible injustice which puts men and women to death without form of law. During the year 1894, there were 132 persons executed in the United States by due form of law, while in the same year, 197 persons were put to death by mobs who gave the victims no opportunity to make a lawful defense. No comment need be made upon a condition of public sentiment responsible for such alarming results.

The purpose of the pages which follow shall be to give the record which has been made, not by colored men, but that which is the result of compilations made by white men, of reports sent over the civilized world by white men in the South. Out of their own mouths shall the murderers be condemned. For a number of years the Chicago Tribune, admittedly one of the leading journals of America, has made a specialty of the compilation of statistics touching upon lynching. The data compiled by that journal and published to the world January 1st, 1894, up to the present time has not been disputed. In order to be safe from the charge of exaggeration, the incidents hereinafter reported have been confined to those vouched for by the Tribune.

"AS SEPARATE AS THE FINGERS"
BOOKER T. WASHINGTON
Address at the Atlanta Exposition
September 18, 1895

Mr. President and Gentlemen of the Board of Directors and Citizens:

One third of the population of the South is of the Negro race. No enterprise seeking the material, civil, or moral welfare of this section can disregard this element of our population and reach the highest success. I but convey to you, Mr. President and Directors, the sentiment of the masses of my race when I say that in no way have the value and manhood of the American Negro been more fittingly and generously recognized than by the managers of this magnificent Exposition at every stage of its progress. It is a recognition that will do more to cement the friendship of the two races than any occurrence since the dawn of our freedom.

Not only this, but the opportunity here afforded will awaken among us a new era of industrial progress. Ignorant and inexperienced, it is not strange that in the first years of our new life we began at the top instead of at the bottom; that a seat in Congress or the State Legislature was more sought than real estate or industrial skill; that the political convention or stump speaking had more attractions than starting a dairy farm or truck garden.

A ship lost at sea for many days suddenly sighted a friendly vessel. From the mast of the unfortunate vessel was seen a signal: "Water, water; we die of thirst!" The answer from the friendly vessel at once came back: "Cast down your bucket where you are." A second time the signal, "Water, water; send us water!" ran up from the distressed vessel, and was answered: "Cast down your bucket where you are." And a third and fourth signal for water was answered: "Cast down your bucket where you are." The captain of the distressed vessel, at last heeding the injunction, cast down his bucket, and it came up full of fresh, sparkling water from the mouth of the

Amazon River. To those of my race who depend on bettering their condition in a foreign land, or who underestimate the importance of cultivating friendly relations with the Southern white man, who is their next door neighbor, I would say: "Cast down your bucket where you are"—cast it down in making friends in every manly way of the people of all races by whom we are surrounded.

Cast it down in agriculture, mechanics, in commerce, in domestic service, and in the professions. And in this connection it is well to bear in mind that whatever other sins the South may be called to bear, when it comes to business, pure and simple, it is in the South that the Negro is given a man's chance in the commercial world, and in nothing is this Exposition more eloquent than in emphasizing this chance. Our greatest danger is, that in the great leap from slavery to freedom we may overlook the fact that the masses of us are to live by the productions of our hands, and fail to keep in mind that we shall prosper in proportion as we learn to dignify and glorify common labor and put brains and skill into the common occupations of life; shall prosper in proportion as we learn to draw the line between the superficial and the substantial, the ornamental gewgaws of life and the useful. No race can prosper till it learns that there is as much dignity in tilling a field as in writing a poem. It is at the bottom of life we must begin, and not at the top. Nor should we permit our grievances to overshadow our opportunities.

To those of the white race who look to the incoming of those of foreign birth and strange tongue and habits for the prosperity of the South, were I permitted I would repeat what I say to my own race, "Cast down your bucket where you are." Cast it down among the 8,000,000 Negroes whose habits you know, whose fidelity and love you have tested in days when to have proved treacherous meant the ruin of your firesides. Cast down your bucket among these people who have, without strikes and labor wars, tilled your fields, cleared your forests, builded your railroads and cities, and brought forth treasures from the bowels of the earth, and helped make possible this magnificent representation of the progress of the South. Casting down your bucket among my people, helping and encouraging them as you are doing on these grounds, and to education of head, hand, and heart, you will find that they will buy your surplus land, make blossom the waste places in your fields, and run your factories. While doing this, you can be sure in the future, as in the past, that you and your families will be surrounded by the most patient, faithful, law-abiding, and unresentful people that the world has seen. As we have proved our loyalty to you in the past, in nursing your children, watching by the sick bed of your mothers and fathers, and often following them with tear-dimmed eyes to their graves, so in the future, in our humble way, we shall stand by you with a devotion that no foreigner can approach, ready to lay down our lives, if need be, in defense of yours, interlacing our industrial, commercial, civil, and religious life with yours in a way that shall make the interests of both races one. In all things that are purely social we can be as separate as the fingers, yet one as the hand in all things essential to mutual progress.

There is no defense or security for any of us except in the highest intelligence and development of all. If anywhere there are efforts tending to curtail the fullest growth of the Negro, let these efforts be turned into stimulating, encouraging, and making him the most useful and intelligent citizen. Effort or means so invested will pay a thousand per cent interest. These efforts will be twice blessed—"blessing him that gives and him that takes."

There is no escape through law of man or God from the inevitable:

> The laws of changeless justice bind
>   Oppressor with oppressed;
> And close as sin and suffering joined
>   We march to fate abreast.

Nearly sixteen millions of hands will aid you in pulling the load upwards, or they will pull against you the load downwards. We shall constitute one third and more of the ignorance and crime of the South, or one third its intelligence and progress; we shall contribute one third to the business and industrial prosperity of the South, or we shall prove a veritable body of death, stagnating, depressing, retarding every effort to advance the body politic.

Gentlemen of the Exposition, as we present to you our humble effort at an exhibition of our progress, you must not expect overmuch. Starting thirty years ago with ownership here and there in a few quilts and pumpkins and chickens (gathered from miscellaneous sources), remember the path that has led from these to the inventions and production of agricultural implements, buggies, steam engines, newspapers, books, statuary, carving, paintings, the management of drug stores and banks has not been trodden without contact with thorns and thistles. While we take pride in what we exhibit as a result of our independent efforts, we do not for a moment forget that our part in this exhibition would fall far short of your expectations but for the constant help that has come to our educational life, not only from the Southern States, but especially from Northern philanthropists, who have made their gifts a constant stream of blessing and encouragement.

The wisest among my race understand that the agitation of questions of social equality is the extremest folly, and that progress in the enjoyment of all the privileges that will come to us must be the result of severe and constant struggle rather than of artificial forcing. No race that has anything to contribute to the markets of the world is long in any degree ostracized. It is important and right that all privileges of the law be ours, but it is vastly more important that we be prepared for the exercises of these privileges. The opportunity to earn a dollar in a factory just now is worth infinitely more than the opportunity to spend a dollar in an opera house.

In conclusion, may I repeat that nothing in thirty years has given us more hope and encouragement, and drawn us so near to you of the white race, as this opportunity offered by the Exposition; and here bending, as it were, over the altar that represents the results of the struggles of your race and mine, both starting practically empty-handed three decades ago, I pledge that in your effort to work out the great and intricate problem which God has laid at the doors of the South you shall have at all times the patient, sympathetic help of my race; only let this be constantly in mind that, while from representations in these buildings of the product of field, of forest, of mine, of factory, letters, and art, much good will come, yet far above and beyond material benefits will be that higher good, that let us pray God will come, in a blotting out of sectional differences and racial animosities and suspicions, in a determination to administer absolute justice, in a willing obedience among all classes to the mandates of law. This, this, coupled with our material prosperity, will bring into our beloved South a new heaven and a new earth.

A SOUTHERN NEWSPAPER
EDITOR PRAISES WASHINGTON

CLARK HOWELL
To the Editor of The World
New York World, September 19, 1895

ATLANTA, GA., September 19.
TO THE EDITOR OF THE WORLD:

I do not exaggerate when I say that Prof. Booker T. Washington's address yesterday was one of the most notable speeches, both as to character and the warmth of its reception, ever delivered to a Southern audience. It was an epoch-making talk, and marks distinctly a turning point in the progress of the Negro race, and its effect in bringing about a perfect understanding between the whites and blacks of the South will be immediate. The address was a revelation. It was the first time that a Negro orator had appeared on a similar occasion before a Southern audience.

The propriety of inviting a representative of the Negro race to participate in the opening exercises was fully discussed a month ago, when the opening program was being arranged. Some opposition was manifested on account of the fear that public sentiment was not prepared for such an advanced step. The invitation, however, was extended by a vote of the Board of Directors, and the cordial greeting which the audience gave Washington's address shows that the board made no mistake. There was not a line in the address which would have been changed even by the most sensitive of those who thought the invitation to be imprudent. The whole speech is a platform on which the whites and blacks can stand with full justice to each race.

The speech is a full vindication from the mouth of a representative Negro of the doctrine so eloquently advanced by Grady and those who have agreed with him that it is to the South that the Negro must turn for his best friend, and that his welfare is so closely identified with the progress of the white people of the South that each race is mutually dependent upon the other, and that the so-called "race problem" must be solved in the development of the natural relations growing out of the association between the whites and blacks of the South.

The question of social equality is eliminated as a factor in the development of the problem, and the situation is aptly expressed by Washington in the statement that "in all things that are purely social we can be as separate as the fingers, yet one as the hand in all things essential to mutual progress."

The speech will do good, and the unanimous approval with which it has been received demonstrates the fact that it has already done good.

CLARK HOWELL,
Editor of the Atlanta Constitution.

DEFENDING BLACK SUFFRAGE

REPUBLICAN MEMBERS OF THE SOUTH CAROLINA CONVENTION
To the Editor of The World
New York World, September 30, 1895

SPECIAL TO THE WORLD.

COLUMBIA, S. C., Sept. 30.—Five of the six Negro delegates to the South Carolina Constitutional Convention, which proposes to disfranchise the blacks, have joined in the following address to the North, through The World:

To the Editor of the World:

The Seventh Constitutional Convention called in South Carolina is in session. It has been called for the purpose of dealing with the Negro problem. Those who have advocated its assembling have been explicit in their declaration of the purposes to be accomplished—the disfranchisement of the Negro and the elimination of him entirely, not from a participation in elections, for he has not since 1886 had any show at all in any of the elections held in the State, but of the possibility of the Negro uniting with the conservative Democratic faction and thus oust from place and power those now in control of the Government. The chief obstacle in the way of accomplishing what is desired is the Fourteenth and Fifteenth Amendments to the Federal Constitution. This difficulty removed, there will be plain sailing.

The Hon. Benjamin Ryan Tillman, who is the head and front of the movement, has not been at all politic or hypocritical as to his intentions. He has said that his object is to disfranchise as many Negroes as he possibly can without disfranchising a single white man, except for crime.

WHAT THE CENSUS SHOWS.

In the State, according to the census of the United States, taken in 1890, there were: Negroes over twenty-one years of age, 132,949; whites over twenty-one years of age, 102,567;

Negro majority, 30,292. Of these are illiterate, 58,086 Negroes and 13,242 whites. Now, it will plainly be seen that a purely educational qualification, honestly administered, would give the whites 89,415, and the Negroes 74,851 votes; white majority, 14,564 votes.

But the nut for Tillman to crack is how he can disfranchise the Negro without disfranchising the 13,242 illiterate whites, whose votes would be lost entirely to his faction should the conservative element nominate and vote an independent ticket. The highest vote his faction has ever been able to poll in round numbers is 60,000, and the Conservatives 35,000. If Tillman's faction, therefore, should lose 13,242 votes it would leave him only 46,758 votes, and the Conservatives 35,000 votes, and Tillman's majority over the Conservatives would be only 11,758 votes.

It will readily be seen that the 74,851 Negro votes or any considerable part of them uniting with the Conservatives would make that faction master of the situation, and that is what Tillman wants to prevent. He has thus far hypnotized the whites of both factions with the scarecrow, "White supremacy," which he has shaken in their faces on every occasion, and which he is shrewd enough to know has the same effect upon the whites as a red flag has upon an enraged bull.

TILLMAN'S SUFFRAGE PLAN.

The real truth is that "white supremacy" has never been endangered; for even in the days of Republican ascendancy all the great offices, and a large majority of all the offices, were held by white men, and no one ever thought of making it a Negro government. The suffrage plan, as we have been informed, as agreed upon by the committee, is as follows: Every male citizen twenty-one years of age who has not been convicted of crime, and is not an idiot or an inmate of a prison or a charitable institution, who can read a section of the Constitution to the satisfaction of the officers of election, or who can explain said section when read to him to the satisfaction of said officers, or who pays taxes on $500 worth of real property; or who can satisfy the election officers that he has paid all taxes due by him to the State, and who shall be duly registered according to law, shall be entitled to vote.

Every one of these provisions, as simple and just as they appear, when read by the uninitiated, are freighted with fraud, corruption and prostitution of the suffrage. For the officers of election are the sole judges of the qualification of the elector, and can at their will make the Negro vote or the white vote as large or as small as they choose.

INSTRUMENTS OF FRAUD.

Everyone of these innocent little "ors" is the instrument of and contains infinite possibilities of fraud, and in the hands of election officers, all of whom are members of one party and of the same faction, are construed to mean one thing to one set of voters and another thing to another set, when they offer to register.

As Mr. Creelman has explained in his dispatches, the registration officer and his board will have the sole power to make voters in South Carolina, as the Supreme Court of the State has decided that there is no appeal to any Court of law from the acts of election officers. In short, the Convention has been called to legalize the frauds which have been perpetrated upon the elective franchise in this State since 1876. No one can tell or estimate what the vote will be, and that question can be answered only by the election officers.

ROBERT SMALLS,
THOMAS E. MILLER,
JAMES E. WIGG,
R. B. ANDERSON,
ISAIAH REED,

Republican Members of the Constitutional Convention. Columbia, S. C. Sept. 30, 1895.

PRAISE FROM THE PRESIDENT

GROVER CLEVELAND
To Booker T. Washington
October 6, 1895

Gray Gables, Buzzard's Bay, Mass.,
October 6, 1895.

Booker T. Washington, Esq.

My Dear Sir: I thank you for sending me a copy of your address delivered at the Atlanta Exposition.

I thank you with much enthusiasm for making the address. I have read it with intense interest, and I think the Exposition would be fully justified if it did not do more than furnish the opportunity for its delivery. Your words cannot fail to delight and encourage all who wish well for your race; and if our colored fellow citizens do not from your utterances gather new hope and form new determinations to gain every valuable advantage offered them by their citizenship, it will be strange indeed.

Yours very truly,
Grover Cleveland.

ARGUING AGAINST DISENFRANCHISEMENT

ROBERT SMALLS
Speech in the South Carolina Convention
October 26, 1895

PLAN OF SUFFRAGE.

THE following plan of suffrage was introduced by Hon. Robert Smalls and referred to the suffrage committee, which reported it unfavorably, notwithstanding that he went before the committee and made a strong speech in advocacy of the said plan, and said report was adopted by the Convention:

SECTION 1. In all elections by the people the electors shall vote by ballot.

SEC. 2. Every male citizen of the United States of the age of twenty one years and upwards, not laboring under the disabilities named in this Constitution, without distinction of race, color or former condition, who shall be a resident of this State at the time of the adoption of this Constitution, or who shall thereafter reside in this State one year, and in the county in which he offers to vote sixty days next preceding any election, shall be entitled to vote for all officers that are now or hereafter may be elected by the people, and upon all questions submitted to the electors at any elections; provided, That no person shall be allowed to vote or hold office who is now, or hereafter may be, disqualified therefor by the Constitution of the United States, until such disqualification shall be removed by the Congress of the United States; provided, further, That no person while kept in any alms house or asylum, or any of unsound mind, or confined in any public prison, shall be allowed to vote or hold office.

SEC. 3. It shall be the duty of the General Assembly to provide from time to time for the registration of all electors.

SEC. 4. For the purpose of voting, no person shall be deemed to have lost his residence by reason of absence while employed in the service of the United States, nor while engaged upon the waters of this State, or the United States, or the high seas, nor while temporarily absent from the State, or removing from one house to another or from one place to another in the same precinct.

Sec. 5. No soldier, seaman or marine in the army or navy of the United States shall be deemed a resident of this State in consequence of having been stationed therein.

Sec. 6. Electors shall in all cases, except treason, felony, or breach of the peace, be privileged from arrest and civil process during attendance at elections and in going to and returning from the same.

Sec. 7. Every person entitled to vote at any election shall be eligible to any office, which now is, or hereafter shall be elective by the people in the county where he shall have resided sixty days previous to such election, except as otherwise provided in this Constitution or the Constitution and laws of the United States.

Sec. 8. The General Assembly shall never pass any law that will deprive any of the citizens of this State of the right of suffrage, except for treason, murder, robbery, or duelling, whereof the persons shall have been duly tried and convicted.

Sec. 9. Presidential electors shall be elected by the people.

Sec. 10. In all elections, State and Federal, there shall be but one ballot box, and one ticket for each party or faction thereof, with the names of all the candidates thereon. There shall be three commissioners of election for each county and three managers for each polling precinct, not more than two of whom shall be of the same political party.

Sec. 11. In all elections held by the people under this Constitution the person or persons who shall receive the highest number of votes shall be declared elected.

ON THE SUFFRAGE.

Mr. President: I have been asked whether I would speak on this important matter. I replied that it all depended on circumstances whether or not I would. The circumstances are such that I have made up my mind to make a short speech on the general bill, and content myself with the vote I will cast on the amendments and sections as they are brought up; inasmuch as I have been perfectly pleased with the speeches made last night, and the one just concluded by the representatives from my county, as I feel that they echo the sentiments not only of the county they represent, but the entire race in the State, and every one I could claim to represent. I endorse their utterances in the language of Mr. Cash when he said he endorsed "every syllable" and accepted it as his own in this letter. I want to hear some of the speeches on the other side, because I do not like this matter that is called Indian file, as it seems now we are to form a Negro file in this Convention. I will only say that this Convention has violated the principle laid down in the Constitution under which we are now living, it giving the right for any two members to call for an "aye" and "nay" vote, but the skillful chairman of the committee on rules, from Edgefield, I mean ex-governor No. 1, (laughter) has made a rule which requires 10, four above the number we have, to call for the "aye" and "nay" vote, hence we cannot put the members on record without the assistance of some of the white members of the Convention. They formed a "dark corner" over there by themselves.

I was born and raised in South Carolina, and to-day I live on the very spot on which I was born, and I expect to remain here as long as the great God allows me to live, and I will ask no one else to let me remain. I love the State as much as any member of this Convention, because it is the garden spot of the South.

Mr. President, this Convention has been called for no other purpose than the disfranchisement of the Negro. Be careful and bear in mind that the elections which are to take place early next month in very many of the States are watching the action of this Convention, especially on the suffrage question. Remember that the Negro was not brought here of his own accord. I found by reference to a history in the Congressional Library in Washington, written by Neil, that he says that in 1619, in the month of June, a Dutch man-of-war landed at Jamestown, Va., with 15 sons of Africa aboard, at the time Miles Kendall was deputy Governor of Virginia. He refused to allow the vessel to be anchored in any of her harbors. But he found out after his order had been sent out that the vessel was without provisions, and the crew was in a starving condition. He countermanded his order, and supplied the vessel with the needed provisions in exchange for 14 Negroes. It was then that the seed of slavery was planted in the land. So you see we did not come here of our own accord; we were brought here in a Dutch vessel, and we have been here ever since. The Dutch are here, and are controlling the business of Charleston to-day. They are not to blame, and are not being blamed.

We served our masters faithfully, and willingly, and as we were made to do for 244 years. In the last war you left them home. You went to the war, fought, and came back home, shattered to pieces, worn out, one-legged, and found your wife and family being properly cared for by the Negroes you left behind. Why should you now seek to disfranchise a race that has been so true to you?

This Convention has a good leader in the person of the distinguished gentleman from Edgefield. Mr. President, when men go out shooting and want to shoot straight, they are compelled to shut one eye, and this leader uses only one eye in this Convention, hence he is always striking the bull's eye; let him beware lest he strikes it one time too often. (Laughter.)

Since Reconstruction times 53,000 have been killed in the South, and not more than three white men have been convicted and hung for these crimes. I want you to be mindful of the fact that the good people of the North are watching this Convention upon this subject. I hope you will make a Constitution that will stand the test. I hope that we may be able to say when our work is done that we have made as good a Constitution as the one we are doing away with.

The Negroes are paying taxes in the South on $263,000,000 worth of property. In South Carolina, according to the census, the Negroes pay tax on $12,500,000 worth of property. That was in 1890. You voted down without discussion merely to lay on the table, a proposition for a simple property and educational qualification. What do you want? You tried the infamous eight-box and registration laws until they were worn to such a thinness that they could stand neither the test of the law nor of public opinion. In behalf of the 600,000 Negroes in the State and the 132,000 Negro voters all that I demand is that a fair and honest election law be passed. We care not what the qualifications imposed are; all that we ask is that they be fair and honest and honorable, and with these provisos we will stand or fall by it. You have 102,000 white men over 21 years of age; 13,000 of these cannot read nor write. You dare not disfranchise them; and you know that the man who proposes it will never be elected to another office in the State of South Carolina. But whatever Mr. Tillman can do, he can make nothing worse than the infamous eight-box law, and I have no praise for the Conservatives, for they gave the people that law. Fifty-eight thousand Negroes cannot read nor write. This leaves a majority of 14,000 white men who can read and write over the same class of Negroes in this State. We are willing to accept a scheme that provides that no man who cannot read nor write can vote, if you dare pass it. How can you expect an ordinary man to "understand and explain" any section of the Constitution, to correspond to the interpretation put upon it by the manager of election, when by a very recent decision of the Supreme Court, composed of the most learned men in the State, two of them put one construction upon a section, and the other Justice put an entirely different construction upon it. To embody such a provision in the election law would be to mean that every white man would interpret it aright and every Negro would interpret it wrong. I appeal to the gentleman from Edgefield to realize that he is not making a law for one set of men. Some morning you may wake up to find that the bone and sinew of your country is gone. The Negro is needed in the cotton fields and in the low country rice fields, and if you impose too hard conditions upon the Negro in this State there will be nothing else for him to do but to leave. What then will you do about your phosphate works? No one but a Negro can work them: the mines that pay the interest on your State debt. I tell you the Negro is the bone and sinew of your country and you cannot do without him. I do not believe you want to get rid of the Negro, else why did you impose a high tax on immigration agents who might come here to get him to leave?

Now, Mr. President, we should not talk one thing and mean another. We should not deceive ourselves. Let us make a Constitution that is fair, honest and just. Let us make a Constitution for all the people, one we will be proud of and our children will receive with delight. Don't let us act like a gentleman said he talked. The other day a gentleman told me that a prominent lawyer, a member of this Convention, made a very bitter speech against the Negro while he was a candidate for election to this Convention. After the lawyer had concluded his speech of bitterness against the Negro and in favor of white supremacy, some colored men waited on him and asked him why he had made such a bitter speech against them, saying they had regarded the gentleman as their friend, as he had often acted as their lawyer. This gentleman replied to them: "Don't mind my speech. I am a friend to the Negro, but I have got to make bitter speeches to fool the Crackers because I want their votes." Gentlemen, I warn you that you can fool the Crackers when you talk to them, but if you pass this ordinance that has been proposed by the committee on suffrage you will fool nobody, for every person in the nation has been informed of your speeches on the stump and you will not be able to explain it away as that lawyer did his words of bitterness to the colored men who waited on him.

Mr. President, strange things have happened and I have been shocked in my life, but the greatest surprise of my life was when the distinguished lawyer from Barnwell, Mr. Aldrich, introduced a Constitution in this Convention that was taken verbatim et literatim from the Constitution of '65 and the black code of '66, which deprived every Negro from holding an office in this State, notwithstanding that Constitution and black code were rejected by Congress. That Constitution caused the passage of the acts of reconstruction by Congress and made it necessary for the Constitutional Convention of 1868, which gave to you the best Constitution of any one of the Southern States. Let us make a Constitution, Mr. President, that will demand the respect of mankind everywhere, for we are not above public opinion. While in Washington a committee of capitalists came over from England hunting for timber land in which to invest. One of South Carolina's Representatives in Congress called upon those gentlemen and informed them that there were large tracts of land in Beaufort County, in the Township of Blufton, for sale. They inquired for the name of the State, and when they were informed that the timber lands were in South Carolina they answered: "You need not go any further, as our instructions were, before we left England, not to invest money in a State where life and property was not secure under the law." In God's name let us make a Constitution that will receive the approval of everybody—the outside world as well as those at home.

THE UNCONSTITUTIONALITY
OF RAILROAD SEGREGATION

ALBION W. TOURGÉE
Brief for the Plaintiff in Plessy v. Ferguson

c. 1895

QUESTIONS ARISING.

Some of the questions arising on this statement of facts and the decision of the court below, as we conceive, are as follows: Has the State the power under the provisions of the Constitution of the United States, to make a distinction based on color in the enjoyment of chartered privileges within the state?

Has it the power to require the officers of a railroad to assort its citizens by race, before permitting them to enjoy privileges dependent on public charter?

Is the officer of a railroad competent to decide the question of race?

Is it a question that *can* be determined in the absence of statutory definition and without evidence?

May not such decision reasonably result in serious pecuniary damage to a person compelled to ride in a car set apart for one particular race?

Has a State power to compel husband and wife, to ride in separate coaches, because they happen the one to be colored and the other white?

Has the State the power to exempt the railroad and its officers from an action for damages on the part of any person injured by the mistake of such officer?

Has the State the power under the Constitution to authorize any officer of a railroad to put a passenger off the train and refuse to carry him *because* he happens to differ with the officer as to the race to which he properly belongs?

Has the State the power under the Constitution, to declare a man guilty of misdemeanor and subject to fine and imprisonment, *because* he may differ with the officer of a railroad as to "the race to which he belongs?"

Has the State a right to declare a citizen of the United States guilty of a crime because he peacefully continues to occupy a seat in a car after being told by the conductor that it is not the one set apart for the race to which he belongs?

Is not the question of race, scientifically considered, very often impossible of determination?

Is not the question of race, legally considered, one impossible to be determined, in the absence of statutory definition?

Would any railway company venture to execute such a law unless secured against action for damage by having the courts of the state closed against such action?

Is not the provision exempting railway companies and their servants and officers, from action for damages in carrying into effect the provisions of this statute, of such importance as to be essential to the operation of the law in question?

Is not a statutory assortment of the people of a state on the line of race, such a perpetuation of the essential features of slavery as to come within the inhibition of the XIIIth Amendment?

Is it not the establishment of a statutory difference between the white and colored races in the enjoyment of chartered privileges, a badge of servitude which is prohibited by that amendment?

Is not *state* citizenship made an essential incident of *national* citizenship, by the XIVth Amendment, and if so are not the rights, privileges and immunities of the same within the scope of the national jurisdiction?

Can the rights of a citizen of the United States be protected and secured by the general government without securing his *personal* rights against invasion by the State?

Does not the exemption of nurses in attendance upon children, render this act obnoxious as class legislation and rebut the claim that it is *bona fide* a police regulation necessary to secure the health and morals of the community?

CONSTITUTIONAL PROVISIONS INVOLVED.

The Plaintiff in Error relies on the following provisions of the Constitution of the United States in support of his contention that the said statute No. 111, of the State of Louisiana, 1890, is null and void.

THE THIRTEENTH AMENDMENT.

Section 1.—Neither SLAVERY nor involuntary servitude except as a punishment for crime whereof the party shall have been duly convicted, shall exist within the United States or any place subject to its jurisdiction.

THE FOURTEENTH AMENDMENT.

Section 1—*Affirmative Provisions.*

"All persons born or naturalized in the United States and subject to the jurisdiction thereof, are—

    1—Citizens of the United States," and

    2—(Citizens) "of the state in which they shall reside."

Restrictive Provisions.

    1—"No State shall make or enforce any law which shall abridge the privileges and immunities of citizens of the United States."

    2—"Nor shall any State deprive any citizen of life, liberty or property, without due process of law."

    3—"Nor deny to any person within its jurisdiction, the equal protection of the laws."

This section has been separated into its constituent clauses, the more readily to show the construction for which the Plaintiff in Error contends.

POINTS OF PLAINTIFF'S CONTENTION.

I—The exemption of officers and railway companies from suits for damage by persons aggrieved by their action under this law.

The Court below held that the language of this section did not exempt from damage resulting from *bona fide* exercise of the power conferred upon them by its provisions. The language of the act is explicit: "should any passenger refuse to occupy"—not the coach used for the race to which he belongs but—"the coach or compartment *to which he or she is assigned by the officer of such railway*, said officer shall have power to refuse to carry such passenger on his train and *for such refusal*, neither he nor the railway company he represents, shall be liable for damage, *in any of the courts of this state.*" Is not this a clear denial to the person thus put off the train, of any right of action? Is it not that very denial of the "equal protection of the laws" which is clearly contemplated by the third restrictive provision of the Fourteenth Amendment?

If so, is this provision of such importance as to be essential to the validity of the law as a whole? Our contention is that no individual or corporation could be expected or induced to carry into effect this law, in a community where race admixture is a frequent thing and where the hazard of damage resulting from such assignment is very great, unless they were protected by such exemption. The State very clearly says to the railway, "You go forward and enforce this system of assorting the citizens of the United States on the line of race, and we will see that you suffer no loss through prosecution in OUR courts." Relying on this assurance, the company is willing to undertake the risk. Without it they might well shrink from such liability. The denial of the *right to prosecute*, then, becomes essential to the operation of the act, and if such "denial" is in derogation of the restriction of the Fourteenth Amendment, the whole act is null and void. It is a question for the Court to determine upon its knowledge of human nature and the conditions affecting human conduct, in regard to which it would be idle to cite authorities. If it is NOT a violation of this provision it would be difficult to imagine a statutory provision which could be violative of it.

II—We shall also contend that, in any mixed community, the reputation of belonging to the dominant race, in this instance the white race, is *property*, in the same sense that a right of action or of inheritance is *property*; and that the provisions of the act in question which authorize an officer of a railroad company to assign a person to a car set apart for a particular race, enables such officer to deprive him, to a certain extent at least, of this property—this reputation which has an actual pecuniary value—"without due process of law," and are, therefore, in violation of the Second restrictive clause of the first section of the XIVth Amendment of the Constitution of the United States.

This provision authorizing and requiring the officer in charge of the train to pass upon and decide the question of race, is the very essence of the statute. If this is repugnant to the Constitutional provision, all the rest must fall.

There is no question that the law which puts it in the power of a railway conductor, at his own discretion, to require a man to ride in a "Jim Crow" car, that is, in the car "set apart exclusively for persons of the colored race," confers upon such conductor the power to deprive one of the reputation of being a white man, or at least to impair that reputation. The man who rides in a car set apart for the colored race, will inevitably be regarded as a colored man or at least be suspected of being one. And the officer has undoubtedly the power to entail upon him such suspicion. To do so, is to deprive him of "property" if such reputation *is* "property." Whether it is or not, is for the court to determine from its knowledge of existing conditions. Perhaps it might not be inappropriate to suggest some questions which may aid in deciding this inquiry. How much would it be *worth* to a young man entering upon the practice of law, to be regarded as a *white* man rather than a colored one? Six-sevenths of the population are white. Nineteen-twentieths of the property of the country is owned by white people. Ninety-nine hundredths of the business opportunities are in the control of white people. These propositions are rendered even more startling by the intensity of feeling which excludes the colored man from the friendship and companionship of the white man. Probably most white persons if given a choice, would prefer death to life in the United States *as colored persons*. Under these conditions, is it possible to conclude that the *reputation of being white* is not property? Indeed, is it not the most valuable sort of property, being the master-key that unlocks the golden door of opportunity?

III—The Plaintiff in Error also contends that the provision of this act authorizing the conductor to "refuse to carry," *anglice* put off the train, any passenger who refuses to accept his decision as to "the race to which he belongs," is a deprivation of the *liberty* and *property* of the citizen "without due process of law," and as such is in conflict with the third restrictive clause of the XIVth Amendment.

The passenger is deprived of his liberty by being removed by the power with which the statute vests the conductor, from a place where he has a *right to be*; and of his property, by being refused and denied the enjoyment of that for which he has paid his money, to wit, the ticket purchased by him to the point of destination. This gave him the right to ride upon *that train* or any train, to the point designated. To take away that right, compel the passenger to go on foot or by other means to such point, is to seize, convert and destroy his property by pretended force of law. It is *pro tanto* an act of legalized spoliation,—an act of forcible confiscation —a taking of property and interference with liberty under legalized forms and statutory methods, but without "*due* process of law."

IV—The plaintiff also contends that the provisions authorizing the officers of a train to require parties to occupy the particular cars or compartments set apart for distinct races, is a statutory grant of authority to interfere with natural domestic rights of the most sacred character.

A man may be white and his wife colored; a wife may be white and her children colored. Has the State the right to compel the husband to ride in one car and the wife in another? Or to assign the mother to one car and the children to another? Yet this is what the statute in question requires. In our case, it does not appear that the plaintiff may not have had with him a wife belonging to the other race, or children differing with him in the color of their skins? Has a State the right to order the mother to ride in one car and her young daughter, because her cheek may have a darker tinge, to ride alone in another? Yet such things as these, the act in question not only permits, but actually requires and commands to be done under penalty of fine and imprisonment, for failure or neglect. Are the courts of the United States to hold such things to be within the purview of a State's right to impose on citizens of the United States?

V—The plaintiff also insists that a wholesale assortment of the citizens of the United States, resident in the state of Louisiana, on the line of race, is a thing wholly impossible to be made, equitably and justly by any tribunal, much less by the conductor of a train without evidence, investigation or responsibility.

The Court will take notice of the fact that, in all parts of the country, race-intermixture has proceeded to such an extent that there are great numbers of citizens in whom the preponderance of the blood of one race or another, is impossible of ascertainment, except by careful scrutiny of the pedigree. As slavery did not permit the marriage of the slave, in a majority of cases even an approximate determination of this preponderance is an actual impossibility, with the most careful and deliberate weighing of evidence, much less by the casual scrutiny of a busy conductor.

But even if it were possible to determine preponderance of blood and so determine racial character in certain cases, what should be said of those cases in which the race admixture is equal. Are they white or colored?

There is no law of the United States, or of the State of Louisiana defining the limits of race—who are white and who are "colored"? By what rule then shall any tribunal be guided in determining racial character? It may be said that all those should be classed as colored in whom appears a visible admixture of colored blood. By what law? With what justice? Why not count every one as white in whom is visible any trace of white blood? There is but one reason to wit, the domination of the white race. Slavery not only introduced the rule of caste but prescribed its conditions, in the interests of that institution. The trace of color raised the presumption of bondage and was a bar to citizenship. The law in question is an attempt to apply this rule to the establishment of legalized caste-distinction *among citizens.*

It is not consistent with reason that the United States, having granted and bestowed *one equal citizenship* of the United States and prescribed *one equal citizenship in each state*, for all, will permit a State to compel a railway conductor to assort them arbitrarily according to his ideas of race, in the enjoyment of chartered privileges.

VI—The Plaintiff in Error, also insists that, even if it be held that such an assortment of citizens by race in the enjoyment of public privileges, is not a deprivation of liberty or property without due process of law, it is still such an interference with the personal liberty of the individual as is impossible to be made consistently with his rights as an equal citizen of the United States and of the State in which he resides.

In construing the first section of the XIVth Amendment, there appears to have been, both on the part of the Courts and of textual writers, an inclination to overlook and neglect the force and effect of its affirmative provisions.

The evident effect of these provisions taken alone and construed according to the plain and universal meaning of the terms employed, is to confer upon every person born or naturalized in the United States, two things:

(1)—National Citizenship.

(2)—Statal Citizenship, as *an essential incident* of national citizenship.

This grant both of *national* and *statal* citizenship in the Constitution of the United States, is a guaranty not only of *equality* of right but of *all natural rights and the free enjoyment of all public privileges* attaching either to *state* or national citizenship. Its effect is (1) to make national citizenship expressly *paramount and universal*: (2) to make Statal citizenship *expressly subordinate and incidental* to national citizenship.

The State is thereby ousted of *all control over citizenship*. It cannot make any man a citizen nor deprive any one of the estate of citizenship or of any of its rights and privileges.

What are the rights, "privileges and immunities of a citizen of the United States?" Previous to the adoption of this section of the Constitution they were very vague and difficult of definition. Now they include all "the rights, privileges and immunities" of a citizen *of a State*, because that citizenship is made incidental to, and co-extensive with *national* citizenship in every State; and the United States guarantees the full enjoyment of both. It is evident that National citizenship *plus* State citizenship covers the whole field of individual relation, so far as the same is regulated or prescribed by law. All the rights, "privileges and immunities," which *can attach* to the individual as a part of the body-politic, are embraced either by the relation of "Citizen of the United States" or by the relation of *citizen* "of the *State* in which he may reside." The United States having granted *both* stands pledged to protect and defend both.

This provision of Section 1 of the Fourteenth Amendment, *creates* a *new* citizenship of the United States embracing new rights, privileges and immunities, derivable in a *new* manner, controlled by *new* authority, having a *new* scope and extent, dependent on national authority for its existence and looking to national power for its preservation.

VII—It may be urged against this construction that it ousts the exclusive control of the State over "its own citizens" by inference based on the effect of the grant of citizenship.

That this is the real force of this provision of the Constitution would seem to be the only conclusion that can be reached from any reasonable interpretation of the language employed. The language of the affirmative provisions of the section, certainly includes everything that can be embraced by citizenship *of the United States and* citizenship of *the State of residence*. This leaves no room for any *exclusive State jurisdiction* of the personal rights of the citizen. If this provision means anything, it means that the government of the United States will not permit any legislation by the State which invades the *rights* of such citizens. These are fully covered by the grant of citizenship of the United States AND citizenship of the State. This construction is strengthened by the negative provisions which are supplemental of the positive ones. These prohibit the making or enforcement of any law "abridging the privileges and immunities of citizens of the United States;" provide that "life, liberty or property shall not be taken without due process of law;" and forbid the denial to any person of the equal protection of the law. All these are express restrictions of statal power already made subordinate and incidental to the national jurisdiction by the positive provisions of the same section.

These restrictive provisions were not intended to be construed by themselves, but in connection with and as supplemental to the affirmative provisions—taken together they constitute this section, the *magna charta* of the American citizen's rights.

VIII—Taken by themselves, however, and read in the light of the construction put upon Section 3 Article II of the Constitution, these negative provisions would seem quite sufficient to oust the *exclusive* jurisdiction of the State and establish the appellate or supervisory jurisdiction of the United States in all matters touching the personal rights of citizens.

It has no doubt occurred to every member of the Court, though no allusion seems hitherto to have been made to it, that the construction and phraseology of this section is strikingly similar to that of Section 2 of the IVth Article of the Constitution: "No person held to service or labour in one State under the laws thereof, escaping into another shall, in consequence of any law or regulation therein, be discharged from such service or labour, but shall be delivered up on the claim of the party to whom such service or labour may be due."

The celebrated case of Prigg vs. Pennsylvania, 16 Peters, 539, which finally determined the force of this section decided two things; (1) That the Courts of the United States had jurisdiction to consider and pass upon the validity of the acts of a State touching the rendition of fugitives from labour—to undo or invalidate all that might be done or attempted by virtue of State authority, in regard to the estate or condition of one claimed as a fugitive from labour; (2) That whenever the United States legislated upon the question, such legislation *wholly ousted* the State jurisdiction. What this section was to the fugitive from slavery, the provisions of the first section of the XIVth Amendment are to the rights and liberties of the citizen. In the former case, the Federal jurisdiction is inferred from the declaration "No person held to service, * * * shall be discharged therefrom;" in the other case, the jurisdiction is much more clearly indicated by the unqualified grant of national *and* state citizenship in the constitution. As the former gave jurisdiction concerning every matter relating to persons escaping from service or labour, so the latter gives jurisdiction of *all* matters pertaining to the rights of a citizen of the United States and the essential incident of such citizenship, his status as a citizen of any state. As in that case, state legislation was to be judged by its effect upon the acquired right of the master over the slave, so in this case, the statute is to be judged by its effect upon the *natural and legal rights* of the citizen. The Plaintiff in Error only asks that the rule of construction adopted by this Court *to perpetuate the interests of Slavery*, be *now* applied *in promotion of liberty* and for the protection of *the rights of the citizen*.

IX—The prime essential of all citizenship is *equality* of personal right and the *free* and secure enjoyment of all public privileges. These are the very essence of citizenship in all free governments.

A law assorting the citizens of a State in the enjoyment of a public franchise on the basis of race, is obnoxious to the spirit of republican institutions, because it is a legalization of *caste*. Slavery was the very essence of caste; the climax of unequal conditions. The citizen held the highest political rank attainable in the republic: the slave was the lowest grade of existence. ALL rights and privileges attached to the one; the other had *no legal rights*, either of person or property. Between them stood that strange nondescript, the "free person of color," who had such rights only as the white people of the state where he resided saw fit to confer upon him, but he could neither become a citizen of the United States *nor of any State*. The effect of the words of the XIVth Amendment, was to put *all* these classes on *the same level of right*, as *citizens*; and to make this Court the final arbiter and custodian of these rights. The effect of a law distinguishing between citizens as to race, in the enjoyment of a public franchise, is to legalize caste and restore, in part at least, the inequality of right which was an essential incident of slavery.

X—The power of the State to establish "police regulations."

The theory that the State governments had exclusive jurisdiction of certain specific areas of individual relation, which prevailed under our government up to the adoption of the XIVth Amendment, was so unique as to become a sort of fetich in our legal and political thought. The idea that certain phases of personal right were *wholly excluded* from the jurisdiction of the general government, was entirely correct. There was no definition of national citizenship in the constitution except in regard to naturalization, and so no relation was established between the individual and the general government requiring the latter to define or secure his natural rights or equal privileges and immunities. All the general government could do was to exercise the special jurisdiction conferred by the constitution. All outside of that was the *exclusive* domain of the States. The State might extend or withhold citizenship at its pleasure, the only check upon its power in this respect being that imposed by the Court in Scott *vs.* Sandford, that the State could not make any colored person a citizen, so as to entitle him to any right as such, outside its own jurisdiction. Such exclusive jurisdiction still exists in regard to matters of political organization and control, and, indeed, in regard to all internal affairs, so long as the same do not conflict with the personal rights and privileges of the citizen. Of these, a final and corrective jurisdiction is reserved to the general government. It has the right, through its Courts, to inquire into and decide upon the force, tenor and justice of all provisions of State laws affecting the rights of the citizen. As in the case of fugitives from labor before the Congress had legislated upon the subject, the Federal Courts had jurisdiction to pass upon state laws and decide whether their purpose was to promote or to hinder such rendition, so now, the Court has jurisdiction to decide whether a State law is promotive of the citizen's right or intended to secure unjust restriction and limitation thereof.

It was natural that so great a change should prove a shock to established preconception. To avoid giving full and complete effect to the plain words of this amendment, the theory of exclusive state control over "police regulations" was formulated in what are known as the "Slaughter House Cases," 16 Wallace, 36.

In this case, an act of the legislature of Louisiana required all slaughter of food animals to be conducted at certain abattoirs to be erected by a company created by the act, during a period of twenty-five years. It was assailed on the ground that it deprived certain persons plying the trade of butcher, of the free exercise of their calling. The Court held that the law was a "police regulation" to promote the public health and that the state had the right to enact such legislation without being subject to the inhibition of the XIVth amendment unless it discriminated against the rights of colored citizens *as such*.

The demurring judges, Chief justice Chase, justices Field, Swayne and Bradley, concurring in the opinion of Mr. Justice Field, did not question the right of the State to make laws which should restrict individual right and privilege whenever the same were necessary for the promotion of public health and morals, but they contended that the XIVth Amendment conferred the jurisdiction to inquire whether this was the *real purpose* of the act, whether any discrimination against the colored citizen as such, was made by it or not. In other words, the Court held that the act was a police regulation intended to secure the public health and did not discriminate against *colored citizens* as such. The dissenting justices held that the promotion of the public health was a mere pretence for the grant of an exclusive privilege which impaired the rights of many for the benefit of the few, and that the XIVth Amendment by its express terms did embrace an assertion of the rights of *all citizens* without regard to race or color. Two things are noticeable in these opinions. (1) That the Court expressly refrains from asserting that cases may not arise which will be within the purview of this Amendment, which do not embrace any distinction against the colored citizen as such. (2) That so strong a dissenting portion of the Court concur in the construction of this Amendment given by Mr. Justice Field, found on pages 95 to 101, including these significant declarations:

"It recognizes, if it does not create, citizens of the United States, and makes their citizenship depend upon the place of birth and not upon the laws of any State or the condition of their ancestry. A citizen of a State is now only a citizen of the United States residing in that State. The fundamental rights, privileges and immunities which belong to him as a free man and a free citizen, now belong to him *as a citizen of the United States*."

Speaking of the "privileges and immunities" of the first restrictive clause, he says: "The privileges and immunities designated are those which of right belong to the citizens of all free governments."

The opinion of the Court, p. 72 et seq, treats the affirmative provisions of this Amendment as a "*definition* of citizenship, not only citizenship of the United States but citizenship of the States," and regards the negative ones as restrictive only of discrimination directed against colored citizens, *as such*.

The opinion in Strauder *vs.* West Virginia, 100 U. S., 303, clearly shows, however, that the Court had, in the interval, advanced from the position held in the "Slaughter House Cases" to an unhesitating avowal of the conclusion, that the Fourteenth Amendment was intended and would be effective, in preventing discrimination as to right. In this opinion *only* the prohibitive clauses of the Amendment are considered and the language of the Court is based upon the inference to be made from them without any regard for the positive endowing force of the affirmative provisions.

"It ordains," says the Court "that no state shall deprive any person of life, liberty or property, without due process of law, or to deny to any person within its jurisdiction, the equal protection of the laws. What is this but declaring that the law in the States shall be the same for the black as for the white; that all persons, whether colored or white, shall stand equal before the laws of the States, and, in regard to the colored race for whose protection the Amendment was primarily designed, that no discrimination shall be made against them by law because of their color? The words of the Amendment are prohibitive but they contain a necessary implication of a most positive immunity or right most valuable to the colored man—the right to exemption from unfriendly legislation against them as colored—exemption from legal discrimination *implying inferiority* in civil society, lessening the enjoyment of the rights which others enjoy, and *discriminations which are steps towards reducing them to the condition of a subject race.*"

In our case, the Plaintiff in Error contends that this is the precise purpose and intended and inevitable effect of the statute in question. It is a "step toward reducing the colored people and those allied with it, to the condition of a *subject race.*"

XI—What an exclusive jurisdiction in the State to make and enforce "Police regulations" imports.

It is needless to cite authorities as to what constitute police regulations. All attempts at definition agree that they are regulations necessary to secure the physical health and moral welfare of society. No one questions the necessity of such regulations in any community or that they must to some extent interfere with the enjoyment of personal right and privilege. Every man must surrender something of his liberty for the well-being of the community of which he is a part. Two questions are of importance in regard to the jurisdiction of such regulations accorded to the State in the Slaughter House Cases. The one is, "How are police regulations to be distinguished from other criminal or correctional legislation? Is there any distinctive form or character by which they may be distinguished?

The Court very properly declares that the term is "incapable of exact definition." It even adopts the words of the decision in Thorpe *vs.* Rutland and Burlington Railroad, 27 Vermont 149, as indicating its character.

"It extends to the protection of the lives, limbs, health, comfort and quiet of all persons and the protection of all property; and persons and property are subjected to all kinds of restraints and burdens in order to secure the general comfort, health and prosperity. Of the perfect right of the legislature to do this, no question ever was, or upon acknowledged general principles, ever can be made so far as natural persons are concerned."

No one pretends to contravene this right of the State to enact police regulations that shall to a limited extent affect personal liberty. The question is whether this is an unrestricted right; whether the State has the right under the claim of protecting public health or regulating public morals, to restrict the rights of the individual to *any extent* it may see fit? This seems to be the force of the decision in the Slaughter House Cases. I say seems because the Court very clearly intimates that if it had been a case of discrimination against *colored citizens* as such, it would have been within the jurisdiction of this Court to consider at least the intent and character of this discrimination. As near as I am able to state it, then, the Court's definition of the relation of the XIVth Amendment to the State's power to enact and enforce police regulations is, that it has the sole power and sovereignty to do so, as long as it does not distinguish against the rights of colored citizens *as such*. It may distinguish against white citizens or invade the rights of all to any extent and the general government has no right to intervene; but if it imposes a greater burden or any inequality of privilege, upon the colored citizen, the general government is thereby vested with power to prevent or correct this inequality. This position viewed analytically, is a strange one. As has already been indicated, it is difficult to see how this section can be held to protect a colored citizen's right and not secure the rights of white citizens. If it did, it would be obnoxious to the objection of being class legislation just as opprobrious and unjust as that by which slavery was established.

But if the State has exclusive and final jurisdiction to make and enforce police regulations without question or review by the Federal Courts, why has it not sole sovereignty and exclusive jurisdiction over all the personal rights of the citizen in the same manner and to the same extent, as before the adoption of this Amendment? If this section means anything, it would seem that it must give authority to review the "police regulations" of the State just the same as any other legislation, to determine whether they unduly or unnecessarily interfere with the individual rights of the citizen or make unjust discrimination against any class; that if it gives the right to annul legislation inimical to one class, it must of necessity, give the same power as regards legislation injurious to any class.

In order to come within the scope of a "police regulation," even as defined in the "Slaughter House Cases," the act prohibited must be of a character to affect the general health or public morals of a whole community, not merely to minister to the wishes of one class or another. What is the act prohibited in the statute in question in this case? The sitting of a white man or woman in the car in which a colored man or woman sits or the sitting of a colored man or woman in the car in which white men or women are sitting,—is this dangerous to the public health? Does this contaminate public morals? If it does from whence comes the contamination? Why does it contaminate any more than in the house or on the street? Is it the white who spreads the contagion or the black? And if color breeds contagion in a railway coach, why exempt nurses from the operation of the Act?

The title of an Act does not make it a "police provision" and a discrimination intended to humiliate or degrade one race in order to promote the pride of ascendency in another, is not made a "police regulation" by insisting that the one will not be entirely happy unless the other is shut out of their presence. Haman was troubled with the same sort of unhappiness because he saw Mordecai the Jew sitting at the Kings gate. He wanted a "police regulation" to prevent his being contaminated by the sight. He did not set out the real cause of his zeal for the public welfare: neither does this statute. He wanted to "down" the Jew: this act is intended to "keep the negro in his place." The exemption of nurses shows that the real evil lies not in the color of the skin but in the relation the colored person sustains to the white. If he is a dependent it may be endured: if he is not, his presence is insufferable. Instead of being intended to promote the *general* comfort and moral well-being, this act is plainly and evidently intended to promote the happiness of one class by asserting its supremacy and the inferiority of another class. Justice is pictured blind and her daughter, the Law, ought at least to be color-blind.

XII—The purpose and intent of the legislator as a rule of constitutional interpretation.

It is a remarkable fact connected with this decision, (the Slaughter House Cases,) and those which have followed it, that the rule that the purpose and intent of the lawmaker may be considered to explain doubt or ambiguity, seems in this case to have been used to *create* ambiguity and place upon this section a construction absolutely at variance with the plain and unquestioned purport of its words. No man can deny that the language employed is of the broadest and most universal character. "Every person," "no State," "any law," "any person" are the terms employed. The language has no more comprehensive or unmistakeable words. Yet in the face of these, the Court arrives at the conclusion that this section was intended *only to protect the rights of the colored citizen from infringment by State enactment*! This conclusion makes the "purpose and intent" inferred from external sources dominate and control the plain significance of the terms employed. Granting the assumption of the Court—which with deference, is only half-true—that the purpose of the section was to secure to the new-made colored citizen the same rights as white citizens had theretofore enjoyed, it does not follow that the language used should be wrested from its plain meaning to exclude all other force and consequence. One of the most common things in all corrective legislation is the use of terms including other acts than those it is sought specifically to restrain. A wrong done to specific individuals or classes, is prohibited, not as to those classes alone, but as to *all*; or a specific offence calls attention to possible kindred offences, and the whole class is prohibited instead of the particular evil. Whatever may have been the special controlling motive of the people of the United States in enacting this section, or of the Congress which proposed it, one thing is certain, the language used is not particular but universal. If it protects the colored citizen from discriminating legislation, it protects also, in an equal degree, the rights of the white citizen. "All" can never be made to mean "some," nor "every person" be properly construed to be only one class or race, until the laws of English speech are overthrown.

This decision wholly neglects the fact that an amendment giving colored persons *exclusively* the protection it is admitted that this was intended to give them, would have been obnoxious to the severest opprobrium as *class-legislation of the rankest sort*. It would have been giving to the colored citizen a security, a "privilege and immunity," not conferred on white citizens. It would have left the national citizenship of the whites *dependent on ancestry* while that of the blacks was *determined by the place of birth*. It would have protected the one from State aggression and oppression and left the other unprotected. Suppose the colored people to secure control of certain states as they ultimately will, for ten cannot always chase a thousand no matter how white the ten or how black the thousand may be, such a provision as has been supposed or such as the Court conceives this to have been intended to be, would leave the personal rights of a white minority wholly at the mercy of a colored majority, without possibility of national protection or redress. Indeed, if the construction which the Court puts upon it be the correct one, if only the rights of *colored* citizens are protected by this section from impairment by statal action or neglect, it is little wonder that the white people of the south declare themselves ready to resist even to the death, the domination of a colored majority in any state. If such is the law and *only colored* citizens are secured in their rights by this amendment, I do not hesitate to say that they are fully justified in anything they may have done or may hereafter do, to prevent control of the machinery of the state governments by colored citizens.

It was said above, that the assumption that this section was adopted for the protection of the colored citizen, was at best only half-true. The history of the times shows that exclusive state control over the persons and rights of the citizens of the state was not only the Gibraltar of slavery, but was the chief ingredient of that "paramount allegiance to the State," which was the twin of the doctrine of secession. Both rested on the same theory of the State's exclusive sovereignty over the inhabitance of the State. If slavery was one of the foundation stones of the Confederacy, as Mr. Stephens declared, the doctrine of "paramount allegiance" based on exclusive state-sovereignty over the personal rights of all inhabitants of the State, was certainly another. This exclusive sovereignty over the individual was well-founded, too, in the constitution. It came to be so fully accepted that Mr. Chief Justice Waite in Cruikshank's Case hereafter to be considered, even declares that it still exists. It was the nurse and secure defence of slavery and the excuse and justification of rebellion. A long and bloody war had just been concluded in which those in arms against the Union based the defence of their course wholly upon this theory. That the people of the United States should desire to eradicate this doctrine, is just as natural as that they should desire to secure the rights of the colored people they had freed. It was reasonable that they should seek to protect the nation against the recurrence of such peril. If they had such purpose, could they have effected it more fully than by the language of this section, creating a new and universal citizenship and making state-citizenship an incident of it? Thereby they would effect both ends with the same weapon. This they *meant* to do—and this they did, if the words of the constitution are to prevail, over a hypothetical limitation, based on a partial definition of the controlling purpose of the framers. It was the *real purpose* to destroy both "paramount allegiance" and discrimination based on race, at one blow; and this the section under consideration does, if the terms employed are given their usual and universal significance. The people of the United States were not building for to-day and its prejudices alone, but for justice, liberty and a nationality secure for all time.

XIII—The case of the United States *vs.* Cruikshank, 92 U. S., 542, proceeds upon the same, as we conceive, mistaken view, both of the character and effect of the XIVth amendment. It wholly neglects the apparent effect of the affirmative clauses and dwells entirely upon the restrictive provisions. While admitting that all rights *granted or secured* by the Constitution of the United States, are within the protection of the general government, it entirely ignores the evident facts that the citizenship granted by this amendment differs *both in character and extent* from the citizenship of the United States, existing theretofore, and that *State* citizenship with all its incidents, is directly *granted and secured* to classes never before entitled thereto, but expressly excluded therefrom. The opinion states, page 553, that it is the "duty of the States to protect all persons within their boundaries in the enjoyment of those inalienable rights with which they were endowed by their creator." And then, apparently oblivious of the fact that the States had failed to give such protection to the rights of their inhabitants and that their failure to do so in the past was *the sole reason* for the adoption of the XIIIth Amendment, and the apprehension that they might not do so in the future the sole reason for the adoption of the XIVth Amendment, the court proceeds to affirm that "sovereignty" for this purpose, (that is for the protection of the natural rights of the individual) "rests alone with the State." Truly, if this construction be the correct one, this section of the amendment is the absurdest piece of legislation ever written in a statute book. The States had many of them expressly denied a large portion of their population, not only liberty but *all natural rights.* The very definition of a slave was "a person without rights." (Code of Louisiana.) The nation conferred on more than half the population of this State liberty, national and state citizenship, embracing the inalienable rights of which they had been deprived and which were still denied by the State. Then, according to this construction, it said to the State: "The protection and security of these rights rests alone with you. I have made these people citizens and clothed them with the rights of citizens in the State and in the nation. You must not deny or impair these rights; *but if you do, it is your own affair.* I cannot prevent, restrain or hinder. Your sovereignty over them is paramount, exclusive and final. I cannot interfere to protect their rights or save their lives."

Does any man imagine—can any man believe when he recalls the heated war of words, the quarter-century of angry denunciation of this very theory, of the State's sole sovereignty over the lives and rights of its inhabitants, the years of bloody strife then just ended which resulted from this very theory, that the people of the United States meant to perpetuate this condition of affairs when they wrote these words in the Constitution which clothed these Ishmaels of our republic with the purple robe of citizenship? Does any one believe that they meant to restore *that very sovereignty* which was the excuse for resistance to national authority and which the bloody tide of war had only just overthrown? If that was their purpose, then Carlyle's grim designation of the people of Great Britain as "thirty millions of people—chiefly fools," should, when applied to the American people, be amended by leaving out the "chiefly" and saying "every last one a fool."

But the political aspect of these amendments was then to the fore and colored every man's thoughts. The old fetich of State-sovereignty which was essential to the stability of "a nation half-free and half-slave," still blinded the eyes which could not see that the system which was the Gibraltar of Slavery must, *ex necessitate*, be perilous to equal rights and liberty—that the Moloch of Slavery would never be the true God of Liberty. What was good for slavery must be bad for freedom.

This court, indeed, in Strauder *vs.* West Virginia, 100 U. S. 303, distinctly recognize the inconsistency of the ruling in Cruikshank's Case and admit that the effect of the amendment is to prohibit legislation prejudicial to *any* class of citizens whether colored or not.

"If in those states where the colored people constitute a majority of the entire population a law should be enacted excluding all white men from jury service, thus denying to them the privilege of participating equally with the blacks in the administration of justice, we apprehend no one would be heard to claim that it would not be a denial to white men of the equal protection of the laws. Nor, if a law should be passed excluding all naturalized Celtic Irishmen, would there be any doubt of its inconsistency with the spirit of the amendment."

It is but a step farther to what the Plaintiff in Error insists is the true construction, to wit, that "equal protection of the laws," is not a *comparative* equality—not merely equal as between one race and another, but a just and universal equality whereby the rights of life, liberty, and property are secured to all—the rights which belong to a citizen in every free country and every republican government.

In our case, the presentment does not allege the color or race of the Plaintiff in Error, but merely that he refused to abide by the assignment of the conductor to a compartment set aside for *his race* and *persisted* in sitting in one set apart for another race. He was by this presentment either a white man in a colored compartment or a colored man in a white compartment. In either case, assuming that he had paid his fare which is not in question, he had a right to ride where he chose, any law of the State to the contrary notwithstanding; for such a law discriminates in the enjoyment of a public right *solely* on the ground of race. The court will take notice of the fact that in all ages and all lands, it is the weak who suffer from all class discriminations and all caste legislation, and that, in this country, it is the colored race which must always be the victim of such legislation. In this case, if we take the evidence of the State's witnesses on which the presentment was evidently based, and the self-description of the plaintiff in error who swears that he is seven-eighths white and that the colored intermixture is not visible, we have the case of a man who believed he had a right to the privilege and advantage of being esteemed a white man, asserting that right against the action of the conductor who for some reason, we know not what, was intent on putting upon him the indignity of belonging to the colored race. The mere statement of the fact shows, in the strongest possible light, the discrimination based on race which is the sole object of the statute.

XIV—The Civil Rights Cases, 109 U. S. R. 3, while discussing at considerable length the provisions of this section of the XIVth Amendment is not applicable here, as it turns on the distinction between State acts and individual acts and considers only the effect of the prohibitive clauses of the section. It is to be noted, however, that although the learned Justice who delivered the opinion of the Court, mindful no doubt of his own dissenting opinion in the "Slaughter House Cases," declares that "positive rights and privileges are undoubtedly secured by the XIVth Amendment," yet shows that he has not considered its affirmative clauses as *grants of right*, since he adds: "But they are secured by way of prohibition against State laws and State proceedings affecting those rights and privileges."

Taken in its real significance, therefore, the opinion in the Civil Rights Cases, so far as it touches the questions at issue in this case, is strongly and expressly in favor of the Plaintiff in Error. The act of which he makes complaint is a "State act" and a "State proceeding" in regard to the rights granted by the XIVth Amendment.

The dissenting opinion of Mr. Justice Harlan in these cases is especially notable from the fact that we here first find formally and distinctly set forth the view that the national jurisdiction to protect the rights of the citizen is based on the affirmative as well as the prohibitive clauses of this amendment. He says:

"The first clause of this act is of a distinctly affirmative character. In its application to the colored race, *it created and granted*, as well citizenship of the United States as citizenship of the State in which they reside. It introduced all that race any of whose ancestors were imported and sold as slaves, into the political community, known as "The people of the United States." They became instantly citizens of the United States and of their respective States."

Not only were five millions of freedmen transformed into *national* and *state* citizens by this amendment, but every citizen of the United States was endowed with a national citizenship determinable in a new manner and a state citizenship made an incident thereof and based wholly upon the national grant.

XV—The relation of the leading cases in which this section is construed, to the construction contended for by the Plaintiff in Error.

The decisions mentioned are really the only ones necessary to be considered in connection with the construction of this section. The others neither materially add to nor detract from what is there determined. In all these cases there is dissent which wisely leaves the door open for farther consideration. While the opinions in all of them enter into a general discussion of the legal effect of the section, it may be said that the Slaughter House Cases determine merely that the State has exclusive jurisdiction of such police regulations as are therein defined; that the Civil Rights Cases decide that Congress has no right to legislate in regard to the rights of citizens in places of amusement, &c., *until* the states have by legislation improperly restricted them; while the opinion in the case of the United States *vs.* Cruikshank, decides that the State has the same sole and exclusive jurisdiction over the lives, liberties and rights of all citizens residing in its borders that it had before the enactment of this amendment when slavery and its interests, not the liberties of the individual, were the objects the constitution was intended to secure.

Only by the most strained construction can this wholesale and compulsory racial assortment of passengers upon a railroad train, where all as citizens have an equal right as on a public highway, and where all pay an equal price for the accommodations received, be termed a police regulation. In the history of English jurisprudence only slavery has demanded that distinctions in civil rights or the enjoyment of public privilege be marked by race distinctions. To introduce them again into our jurisprudence is to reanimate in effect the institution which is denounced in form by the XIIIth Amendment, and the destruction of which threatened the nation's life. It is not a sort of legislation that ought to be helped by strained construction of the fundamental law. Even under the decision in the Slaughter House Cases, this is not to be classed among those "police regulations" which are beyond the jurisdiction of the court.

It also comes squarely within the exception made in the Civil Rights Cases; it is a statute expressly ordained by State legislation and carried into effect by State agencies and tribunals.

The act in question is exactly such an one as these two cases assert to be within the purview of this court's jurisdiction to review. It is an act of race discrimination pure and simple. The experience of the civilized world proves that it is not a matter of public health or morals, but simply a matter intended to re-introduce the caste-ideal on which slavery rested. The court will take notice of a fact inseparable from human nature, that, when the law distinguishes between the civil rights or privileges of two classes, it always is and always must be, to the detriment of the weaker class or race. A dominant race or class does not demand or enact class-distinctions for the sake of the weaker but for their own pleasure or enjoyment. This is not an act to secure *equal* privileges; these were already enjoyed under the law as it previously existed. The object of such a law is simply to debase and distinguish against the inferior race. Its purpose has been properly interpreted by the general designation of "Jim Crow Car" law. Its object is to separate the Negroes from the whites in public conveyances for the gratification and recognition of the sentiment of white superiority and white supremacy of right and power.

It is freely admitted that Cruikshank's case is squarely against us. If the opinion in this case is to be held as law, the relation of the State to the personal rights of the citizens of the United States residing therein, is precisely what it was before the adoption of this section of the constitution, and there is nothing to prevent a State from re-enacting nearly all the caste-distinctions, which slavery created. If that is the law, what is there to prevent a State from enacting the old rule of slavery jurisprudence, that insulting words from a colored man justify an assault by a white man or negative the presumption of malice in homicide. See the State *vs.* Jowers, 11 Iredell, N. C., 555: State *vs.* Davis, 7 Jones, N. C., 52, and State *vs.* Caesar, 9 Iredell, for a full discussion of this legal presumption of inequality. What is there, if the State's jurisdiction over personal rights is to remain as it was before this section was adopted, to prevent the State from adopting as "police regulations," laws requiring a colored man to remove his hat on meeting or addressing a white man? Compelling him to give way to his white superior on the highway and other acts of enforced inferiority?

Our contention is that the opinion in Cruikshank's Case cannot stand, because it is based on the false hypothesis that this section does not create or secure *new rights* to the individual but merely defines pre-existent rights and prohibits the States from impairing or denying them. We contend that it creates a *new citizenship*—new in character, new in extent; new in method of determination, new in essential incident. That it endowed five millions of people with all the rights of national and state citizenship, both of which they were before forbidden by law to enjoy; that for these hitherto excluded classes, it created, granted and proclaimed a citizenship which embraced the old citizenship and added to it the privileges and immunities of the new one. That it enlarged the privileges and immunities of preexisting citizenship, by changing the method of determination and adding to it the right of State-citizenship to attach immediately upon residence obtained in the State, without regard to State legislation. We insist that the inference of right, obligation and power of the general government to enforce, maintain and secure the lives, liberties and personal rights of the citizenship created, granted and declared by this Amendment, is infinitely clearer, stronger and more imperative than the inference drawn from the assertion of the owner's right to regain control of his fugitive slave, set forth in Section 3 of article IV. Upon the effect of such inference of right and power we adopt the whole of the argument of Judge Story in Prigg *vs.* Pennsylvania. The only difference in the cases is that in our case the inference is much stronger than in that and that the result to be attained, in that case, was in derogation of liberty, while in this, its maintenance and security is sought. In that case, the result was to deprive the slave even of the hope of escape: in this case, it would be to give the colored man a hope that some time in the future the promise of liberty and equality of civil right in the United States may be peacefully fulfilled. The one is a presumption in favor of justice and liberty as the other was a presumption in favor of inconceivable wrong. Shall this court which was so ready to commit the government to the perpetuation of wrong, hesitate to apply the same rule to secure the rights of its citizens?

XVI—The construction insisted on by the Plaintiff in Error does not impair the "exclusive jurisdiction" of the State, except as to the *personal rights* of citizens. In other respects it still remains. Neither is it open to the common objection that it would require national legislation in regard to all the rights, privileges and immunities of citizens. It merely asserts the right of the Federal Courts to pass upon legislative acts of the States touching such rights and the power of

Congress to legislate in regard thereto, whenever it becomes necessary.

There are other parts of the Constitution which illustrate this relation. The power to provide uniform laws on the subject of bankruptcy and the inhibition of the States to pass laws impairing the obligation of contracts, are instances. In the absence of such national legislation, the States may pass insolvent laws and even exempt within certain limits, the property of the debtor from execution; but the Federal Courts will inquire in regard to all such laws when presented to them, and determine how far they are consistent with the constitutional requirement. The enactment of a bankrupt law wipes them all away unless affirmed by it. So, too, in the absence of national regulation of inter-state commerce, statutes affecting it were passed by the State; the Federal Courts merely considering whether they were in obstruction of it or not. While laws taxing traders from other states more heavily than dealers resident within the state, no one questions the right of the state to tax them equally with its own citizens. The federal courts only inquire into the *equality* of such laws. So in the case of the rights of the citizen as provided in this Amendment; as long as the State protects and secures the rights of all citizens without injustice or discrimination, there is no need for legislative assertion of the national prerogative: the supervisory control of the Federal Courts over State legislation is sufficient. But suppose a State, say the State of Louisiana where the common law never prevailed, should repeal all statutes in regard to murder—all laws defining the crime, giving jurisdiction of its trial and prescribing its punishment—is there any doubt that the government of the United States would be able to provide for the security of its citizens resident in the State? The XIVth Amendment did not destroy the jurisdiction of the State over the rights of its citizens, nor even its exclusive jurisdiction in regard to other matters, but simply made its legislation in regard to the rights of citizens and its judicial action in relation thereto, reviewable by the courts of the United States and subject to restraint when found to be in derogation of the rights, privileges and immunities of the citizens to whom the nation has guaranteed the rights of equal citizenship in the State.

XVII—It has been decided in the case of the Louisville Railway Co. *vs.* Mississippi 133 U. S. R., 589, that the State may compel a railroad operated under its charter, to provide separate cars or compartments equal in character and accommodation, to be used by individuals of different races, if it sees fit to do so. But in this case the exception is expressly made that the right to compel individuals of different races to use these separate coaches is not thereby decided.

The act in question in our case, proceeds upon the hypothesis that the State has the right to authorize and require the officers of a railway to assort the citizens who engage passage on its lines, according to race, *and to punish the citizen if he refuses to submit to such assortment.*

The gist of our case is the unconstitutionality of the assortment; *not* the question of equal accommodation; that much, the decisions of the court give without a doubt. We insist that the State has no right to compel us to ride in a car "set apart" for a particular race, whether it is as good as another or not. Suppose the provisions were that one of these cars should be painted white and the other black; the invidiousness of the distinction would not be any greater than that provided by the act.

But if the State has a right to distinguish between citizens according to race in the enjoyment of public privilege, by compelling them to ride in separate coaches, what is to prevent the application of the same principle to other relations? Why may it not require all red-headed people to ride in a separate car? Why not require all colored people to walk on one side of the street and the whites on the other? Why may it not require every white man's house to be painted white and every colored man's black? Why may it not require every white man's vehicle to be of one color and compel the colored citizen to use one of different color on the highway? Why not require every white business man to use a white sign and every colored man who solicits custom a black one? One side of the street may be just as good as the other and the dark horses, coaches, clothes and signs may be as good or better than the white ones. The question is not as to the *equality* of the privileges enjoyed, but *the right of the State to label one citizen as white and another as colored* in the common enjoyment of a public highway as this court has often decided a railway to be.

Neither is it a question as to the right of the common-carrier to distinguish his patrons into first, second and third classes, according to the accommodation paid for. This statute is really a restriction on that right, since the carrier is thereby compelled to provide two cars for each class, and so prevented from making different rates of fares by the expense which would be incurred by a multiplicity of coaches. In fact, its plain purpose and effect is to provide the white passenger with an exclusive first class coach *without requiring him to pay an extra fare for it.*

XVIII—Has a state power to punish as a crime, an act done by a person of one race on a public highway, which if done by an individual of another race on the same highway is no offense?

This is exactly what the act in question does, what it was intended to do and *all* it does. A man of one race taking his seat in a car and refusing to surrender it, is guilty of a crime, while another person belonging to another race may occupy the same without fault. The crime assigned depends not on the quality of the act, but on *the color of the skin.*

XIX—The criminal liability of the individual is not affected by inequality of accommodations.

While the act requires the accommodations for the white and black races to be "equal but separate," it by no means follows as a fact that they always are so. But the man who should refuse to go out of a clean and comfortable car into one reeking with filth at the behest of the conductor, would under this act be equally guilty of misdemeanor as if both were of equal desirability. The question of equality of accommodation cannot arise on the trial of a presentment under this statute. Equal or not equal, the refusal to obey the conductor's behest constitutes a crime. There is no averment in this case of equality of accommodation, but merely that the Plaintiff in Error was assigned "to the coach reserved for the race to which he the said Homer A. Plessy belonged" and that he "did then and there, unlawfully insist on going into a coach to which by race he did not belong." (See copy of information, printed Record, page 14.)

It does not appear to what race he belonged or what coach he entered, but, in the questionable language of the information, it is asserted that he did not belong to the *same race as the coach*. It is not asserted that the coach to which he was assigned was equal in accommodation to the one which it is alleged he committed a crime in entering. In his petition for certiorari (Printed Record, page one) the Plaintiff in Error avers himself to be "of mixed Caucasian and African descent, in the proportion of seven-eighths Caucasian and one-eighth African blood. That the mixture of colored blood is not discernable in him, that he is entitled to every right, privilege and immunity secured to citizens of the United States of the white race by the constitution of the United States, and that such right, privilege, recognition and immunity are worth to him the sum of Ten Thousand Dollars if the same be at all susceptible of being estimated by the standard value of money."

The affidavits of the state's witnesses, before the Recorder who bound over the Plaintiff in Error to the criminal court, where the same was filed before the information was entered therein, one of whom was the conductor of the train, (See printed Record, pages 4–5,) declare him to be "a person of the colored race" and that the car he entered and refused to leave was "assigned to passengers of the white race."

The crime, then, for which he became liable to imprisonment so far as the court can ascertain, was that a person of seven-eighths Caucasian blood insisted in sitting peacefully and quietly in a car the state of Louisiana had commanded the company to set aside exclusively for the white race. Where on earth should he have gone? Will the court hold that a single drop of African blood is sufficient to color a whole ocean of Caucasian whiteness?

XX—The exception which is made in section four of the Act in question should not be passed over without consideration: "Nothing in this act shall be construed as applying to nurses attending children of the other race."

The court will take notice of the fact that if there are any cases in the state of Louisiana in which nurses of the white race are employed to take charge of children of the colored race, they are so few that it is not necessary to consider them as a class actually intended to be favored by this exception. Probably there is not a single instance of such relation in the state. What then is the force and effect of this provision? It simply secures to the white parent travelling on the railroads of the state, the right to take a colored person into the coach set apart for whites in a menial relation, in order to relieve the passenger of the care of the children making the journey with the parents. In other words, the act is simply intended to promote the comfort and sense of exclusiveness and superiority of the white race. They do not object to the colored person in an inferior or menial capacity—as a servant or dependent, ministering to the comfort of the white race —but only when as a man and a citizen he seeks to claim equal right and privilege on a public highway with the white citizens of the state. The act is not only class-legislation but class-legislation which is self-condemned by this provision, as intended for the comfort and advantage of one race and the discomfort and disadvantage of the other, thereby tending directly to constitute a "step toward reducing them to the condition of a subject race"—the tendency especially condemned in Strauder *vs.* West Virginia, supra.

XXI—There is another point to be considered. The plaintiff insists that Act III of the Legislature of 1890, of the State of Louisiana is null and void because in tendency and purport it is in conflict with the Thirteenth Amendment of the Constitution of the United States; "Neither Slavery nor involuntary servitude—shall exist, &c."

What is meant by the word "Slavery" in this Amendment. It is evidently intended to embrace something more than a state of mere "involuntary servitude," since it is used in contradistinction to that term. It is the estate or condition of *being a slave.* What was the estate or condition of a slave? We have a right to suppose that this term is used in the Amendment with relation to the estate or condition of those who had up to that moment been slaves in the United States. What was that legal condition? The slave as defined by the Code of Louisiana, by the courts of the various states, and by this court in Scott *vs.* Sandford, was legally distinguished both from citizens and from "free persons of color," by one thing, he was a "person without rights." The fact that he was the property of another; that he was held in a state of involuntary servitude; that he might be bought and sold, —these were indeed incidents of his condition, striking and notable incidents, but they were all the results of one striking and distinctive feature of his legal relation to the body politic, which is expressed by the all-comprehensive statement that *he had no rights.* The master might grant him privilege, the State might restrain the master's brutality, but no right of person, of family, of marriage, of property, could attach to the slave. He was a person without rights before the law, and all the other distinctive facts of his status, flowed from this condition. He could not inherit, sue or be sued, marry, contract, or be seized of any estate, *because* he was "a person without rights."

The real distinction between the citizen and the slave was that the one was entitled to life, liberty, the pursuit of happiness and the protection of the law, while the other was beyond the domain of the law except when it took cognizance of his existence as the incident of another's right or as the violator of its behests. The law knew him only as a chattel or a malefactor.

This condition of utter helplessness and dependence came to be expressed in the public and private relations of the two classes. The slave was not only the property of his master, but he was also the defenceless and despised victim of the civil and political society to which he was subject as well as to his master. He could not resent words or blows from any citizen. Only in the last extremity was he permitted to defend his life. Impudent language from him was held the equivalent of a blow from one of the dominant class. He was in bondage to the whole white race as well as to his owner. This bondage was a more important feature of American slavery than chattelism—indeed it was the one feature which distinguished it from "involuntary servitude" which is the chief element of chattelism. Slavery was a caste, a legal condition of subjection to the dominant class, a bondage quite separable from the incident of ownership. The bondage of the Israelites in Egypt is a familiar instance, of this. It was unquestionably "Slavery;" but it was not chattelism. No single Egyptian owned any single Israelite. The political community of Egypt simply denied them the common rights of men. It did not go as far as American

Slavery in this respect since it did not by law deprive them of all natural and personal rights. It left the family and unlike our Christian slavery did not condemn a whole race to illegitimacy and adultery. It was this subjection to the control of the dominant race individually and collectively, which was the especially distinctive feature of slavery as contradistinguished from involuntary servitude. The slave was one who had no rights—one who differed from the citizen in that he had no *civil or political* rights and from the "free person of color" in that he had no *personal* rights.

The object of the XIIIth Amendment was to abolish this discrepancy of right, not only so far as the legal form of chattelism was concerned, but so far as civil rights and all that regulation of relation between individuals of specific race and descent which marked the slave's attitude to the dominant race both individually and collectively was concerned.

There were in all the slave states specific codes of law intended for the regulation and control of the slave-class. They marked and defined not only his relation to his master but to the white race. He was required to conduct himself, not only "respectfully," which term had a very different signification when applied to the slave than when applied to the white man, but was expected and required to demean himself "submissively" to them. His position was that of legal subjection and statutory inferiority to the dominant race.

It was this condition and all its incidents which the Amendment was intended to eradicate. It meant to restore to him the rights of person and property—the natural rights of man—of which he had been deprived by slavery. It meant to undo all that slavery had done in establishing race discrimination and collective as well as personal control of the enslaved race.

It is quite possible that the term "involuntary servitude" may have been employed to prevent that very form of personal subjection which, soon after the emancipation of the slave, manifested itself in the enactment of the "Black Codes" which assumed control on the part of the State of all colored laborers who did not contract within a certain time to labor for the coming year and hired them out by public outcry. At least, it is evident that the purpose of this Amendment was not merely to destroy chattelism and involuntary servitude but the estate and condition of subjection and inferiority of personal right and privilege, which was the result and essential concomitant of slavery.

XXII—"Privileges and Immunities of citizens of the United States."

It has been suggested that the omission of the term "rights" from the category of things exempted from impairment by State authority, was an intended reservation of state control. We beg to suggest that exactly the contrary is true.

"Right" as defined by Chancellor Kent, "is that which any one is entitled to have or do, or to require another to do, within the limits prescribed by law." Rights may be natural or conferred. The exercise of any right is a "privilege" in the legal sense. The distinction has been sought to be made between the exercise of natural and conferred rights, that the latter alone is the basis of privilege: but it does not rest on any solid ground. Privilege is the exercise of a legal right, however the same may attach.

"Immunity" is the legal guaranty of non-interference,—either with "right"—that is the abstract title on which the claim that one may "have or do or require another to do," any specific thing rests—or with the "privilege," which is based upon or constitutes the exercise or enjoyment of such right.

"Right," which is the basis both of "privilege" and "immunity" is, therefore, expressly included by the use of these terms. No "right," of any citizen of the United States, can be denied or contravened by the law of any State, without impairing the "privileges" and "immunities" of the citizen which correlatively depend thereon.

XXIII—The construction of the First Section of the Fourteenth Amendment contended for by the Plaintiff in Error, is in strict accord with the Declaration of Independence, which is not a fable as some of our modern theorists would have us believe, but the all-embracing formula of personal rights on which our government is based and toward which it is tending with a power that neither legislation nor judicial construction can prevent. Every obstacle which Congress or the Courts have put in its way has been brushed aside. Under its impulse, the Fugitive Slave law, and the Dred Scott decision, both specially designed to secure the perpetuation of slavery under the constitution, became active forces in the eradication of that institution. It has become the controlling genius of the American people and as such must always be taken into account in construing any expression of the sovereign will, more especially a constitutional provision which more closely reflects the popular mind. This instrument not only asserts that "All men are created equal and endowed with certain inalienable rights, among which are life, liberty and the pursuit of happiness," but it also declares that the one great purpose for which governments are instituted among men is to "secure these rights."

Applying this guiding principle to the case under consideration, what is it natural and reasonable to conclude was the purpose of the people of the United States, when in the most solemn manner, they ordered this broad, unmodified and supremely emphatic declaration to be enrolled among the mandates of our fundamental law? Were they thinking how to enlarge the power of the general government over individual rights so as to include all, or how to restrict it so as to include as few as possible? Were they thinking of State rights or human rights? Did they mean to perpetuate the caste-distinctions which had been injected into our law under a constitution expressly and avowedly intended to perpetuate slavery and prevent the spirit of liberty from growing so strong as to work its legal annihilation—were they seeking to maintain and preserve these discriminations, or to overthrow and destroy them?

The Declaration of Independence, with a far-reaching wisdom found in no other political utterance up to that time, makes the security of the individual's right to "the pursuit of happiness," a prime object of all government. This is the controlling idea of our institutions. It dominates the national as well as the state governments. In asserting national control over both state and national citizenship, in appointing the boundaries and distinctive qualities of each, in conferring on millions a status they had never before known and giving to every inhabitant of the country rights never before enjoyed and in restricting the rights of the states in regard thereto,—in doing this were the people consciously and actually intending to protect this right of the individual to the pursuit of happiness or not? If they were, was it the pursuit of happiness by all or by a part of the people which they sought to secure?

If the purpose was to secure the unrestricted pursuit of happiness by the four millions then just made free, now grown to nine millions, did they contemplate that they were leaving to the states the power to herd them away from her white citizens in the enjoyment of chartered privilege? Suppose a member of this court, nay, suppose every member of it, by some mysterious dispensation of providence should wake to-morrow with a black skin and curly hair—the two obvious and controlling indications of race—and in traveling through that portion of the country where the "Jim Crow Car" abounds, should be ordered into it by the conductor. It is easy to imagine what would be the result, the indignation, the protests, the assertion of pure Caucasian ancestry. But the conductor, the autocrat of Caste, armed with the power of the State conferred by this statute, will listen neither to denial or protest. "In you go or out you go," is his ultimatum.

What humiliation, what rage would then fill the judicial mind! How would the resources of language not be taxed in objurgation! Why would this sentiment prevail in your minds? Simply because you would then feel and know that such assortment of the citizens on the line of race was a discrimination intended to humiliate and degrade the former subject and dependent class—an attempt to perpetuate the caste distinctions on which slavery rested—a statute in the words of the Court "tending to reduce the colored people of the country to the condition of a subject race."

Because it does this the statute is a violation of the fundamental principles of all free government and the Fourteenth Amendment should be given that construction which will remedy such tendency and which is in plain accord with its words. Legal refinement is out of place when it seeks to find a way both to avoid the plain purport of the terms employed, the fundamental principle of our government and the controlling impulse and tendency of the American people.

ALBION W. TOURGÉE,
of Counsel for Plaintiff in Error.

UPHOLDING "EQUAL BUT SEPARATE"
ACCOMMODATIONS

HENRY B. BROWN
Opinion in Plessy v. Ferguson
May 18, 1896

MR. JUSTICE BROWN, after stating the case, delivered the opinion of the court.

This case turns upon the constitutionality of an act of the General Assembly of the State of Louisiana, passed in 1890, providing for separate railway carriages for the white and colored races. Acts 1890, No. 111, p. 152.

The first section of the statute enacts "that all railway companies carrying passengers in their coaches in this State, shall provide equal but separate accommodations for the white, and colored races, by providing two or more passenger coaches for each passenger train, or by dividing the passenger coaches by a partition so as to secure separate accommodations: *Provided*, That this section shall not be construed to apply to street railroads. No person or persons, shall be admitted to occupy seats in coaches, other than, the ones, assigned, to them on account of the race they belong to."

By the second section it was enacted "that the officers of such passenger trains shall have power and are hereby required to assign each passenger to the coach or compartment used for the race to which such passenger belongs; any passenger insisting on going into a coach or compartment to which by race he does not belong, shall be liable to a fine of twenty-five dollars, or in lieu thereof to imprisonment for a period of not more than twenty days in the parish prison, and any officer of any railroad insisting on assigning a passenger to a coach or compartment other than the one set aside for the race to which said passenger belongs, shall be liable to a fine of twenty-five dollars, or in lieu thereof to imprisonment for a period of not more than twenty days in the parish prison; and should any passenger refuse to occupy the coach or compartment to which he or she is assigned by the officer of such railway, said officer shall have power to refuse to carry such passenger on his train, and for such refusal neither he nor the railway company which he represents shall be liable for damages in any of the courts of this State."

The third section provides penalties for the refusal or neglect of the officers, directors, conductors and employés of railway companies to comply with the act, with a proviso that "nothing in this act shall be construed as applying to nurses attending children of the other race." The fourth section is immaterial.

The information filed in the criminal District Court charged in substance that Plessy, being a passenger between two stations within the State of Louisiana, was assigned by officers of the company to the coach used for the race to which he belonged, but he insisted upon going into a coach used by the race to which he did not belong. Neither in the information nor plea was his particular race or color averred.

The petition for the writ of prohibition averred that petitioner was seven eighths Caucasian and one eighth African blood; that the mixture of colored blood was not discernible in him, and that he was entitled to every right, privilege and immunity secured to citizens of the United States of the white race; and that, upon such theory, he took possession of a vacant seat in a coach where passengers of the white race were accommodated, and was ordered by the conductor to vacate said coach and take a seat in another assigned to persons of the colored race, and having refused to comply with such demand he was forcibly ejected with the aid of a police officer, and imprisoned in the parish jail to answer a charge of having violated the above act.

The constitutionality of this act is attacked upon the ground that it conflicts both with the Thirteenth Amendment of the Constitution, abolishing slavery, and the Fourteenth Amendment, which prohibits certain restrictive legislation on the part of the States.

1. That it does not conflict with the Thirteenth Amendment, which abolished slavery and involuntary servitude, except as a punishment for crime, is too clear for argument. Slavery implies involuntary servitude—a state of bondage; the ownership of mankind as a chattel, or at least the control of the labor and services of one man for the benefit of another, and the absence

of a legal right to the disposal of his own person, property and services. This amendment was said in the *Slaughter-house cases*, 16 Wall. 36, to have been intended primarily to abolish slavery, as it had been previously known in this country, and that it equally forbade Mexican peonage or the Chinese coolie trade, when they amounted to slavery or involuntary servitude, and that the use of the word "servitude" was intended to prohibit the use of all forms of involuntary slavery, of whatever class or name. It was intimated, however, in that case that this amendment was regarded by the statesmen of that day as insufficient to protect the colored race from certain laws which had been enacted in the Southern States, imposing upon the colored race onerous disabilities and burdens, and curtailing their rights in the pursuit of life, liberty and property to such an extent that their freedom was of little value; and that the Fourteenth Amendment was devised to meet this exigency.

So, too, in the *Civil Rights cases*, 109 U. S. 3, 24, it was said that the act of a mere individual, the owner of an inn, a public conveyance or place of amusement, refusing accommodations to colored people, cannot be justly regarded as imposing any badge of slavery or servitude upon the applicant, but only as involving an ordinary civil injury, properly cognizable by the laws of the State, and presumably subject to redress by those laws until the contrary appears. "It would be running the slavery argument into the ground," said Mr. Justice Bradley, "to make it apply to every act of discrimination which a person may see fit to make as to the guests he will entertain, or as to the people he will take into his coach or cab or car, or admit to his concert or theatre, or deal with in other matters of intercourse or business."

A statute which implies merely a legal distinction between the white and colored races—a distinction which is founded in the color of the two races, and which must always exist so long as white men are distinguished from the other race by color—has no tendency to destroy the legal equality of the two races, or reëstablish a state of involuntary servitude. Indeed, we do not understand that the Thirteenth Amendment is strenuously relied upon by the plaintiff in error in this connection.

2. By the Fourteenth Amendment, all persons born or naturalized in the United States, and subject to the jurisdiction

thereof, are made citizens of the United States and of the State wherein they reside; and the States are forbidden from making or enforcing any law which shall abridge the privileges or immunities of citizens of the United States, or shall deprive any person of life, liberty or property without due process of law, or deny to any person within their jurisdiction the equal protection of the laws.

The proper construction of this amendment was first called to the attention of this court in the *Slaughter-house cases,* 16 Wall. 36, which involved, however, not a question of race, but one of exclusive privileges. The case did not call for any expression of opinion as to the exact rights it was intended to secure to the colored race, but it was said generally that its main purpose was to establish the citizenship of the negro; to give definitions of citizenship of the United States and of the States, and to protect from the hostile legislation of the States the privileges and immunities of citizens of the United States, as distinguished from those of citizens of the States.

The object of the amendment was undoubtedly to enforce the absolute equality of the two races before the law, but in the nature of things it could not have been intended to abolish distinctions based upon color, or to enforce social, as distinguished from political equality, or a commingling of the two races upon terms unsatisfactory to either. Laws permitting, and even requiring, their separation in places where they are liable to be brought into contact do not necessarily imply the inferiority of either race to the other, and have been generally, if not universally, recognized as within the competency of the state legislatures in the exercise of their police power. The most common instance of this is connected with the establishment of separate schools for white and colored children, which has been held to be a valid exercise of the legislative power even by courts of States where the political rights of the colored race have been longest and most earnestly enforced.

One of the earliest of these cases is that of *Roberts* v. *City of Boston,* 5 Cush. 198, in which the Supreme Judicial Court of Massachusetts held that the general school committee of Boston had power to make provision for the instruction of colored children in separate schools established exclusively for them, and to prohibit their attendance upon the other schools. "The great principle," said Chief Justice Shaw, p. 206, "advanced by the learned and eloquent advocate for the plaintiff," (Mr. Charles Sumner,) "is, that by the constitution and laws of Massachusetts, all persons without distinction of age or sex, birth or color, origin or condition, are equal before the law. . . . But, when this great principle comes to be applied to the actual and various conditions of persons in society, it will not warrant the assertion, that men and women are legally clothed with the same civil and political powers, and that children and adults are legally to have the same functions and be subject to the same treatment; but only that the rights of all, as they are settled and regulated by law, are equally entitled to the paternal consideration and protection of the law for their maintenance and security." It was held that the powers of the committee extended to the establishment of separate schools for children of different ages, sexes and colors, and that they might also establish special schools for poor and neglected children, who have become too old to attend the primary school, and yet have not acquired the rudiments of learning, to enable them to enter the ordinary schools. Similar laws have been enacted by Congress under its general power of legislation over the District of Columbia, Rev. Stat. D. C. §§ 281, 282, 283, 310, 319, as well as by the legislatures of many of the States, and have been generally, if not uniformly, sustained by the courts. *State* v. *McCann*, 21 Ohio St. 198; *Lehew* v. *Brummell*, 15 S. W. Rep. 765; *Ward* v. *Flood*, 48 California, 36; *Bertonneau* v. *School Directors*, 3 Woods, 177; *People* v. *Gallagher*, 93 N. Y. 438; *Cory* v. *Carter*, 48 Indiana, 327; *Dawson* v. *Lee*, 83 Kentucky, 49.

Laws forbidding the intermarriage of the two races may be said in a technical sense to interfere with the freedom of contract, and yet have been universally recognized as within the police power of the State. *State* v. *Gibson*, 36 Indiana, 389.

The distinction between laws interfering with the political equality of the negro and those requiring the separation of the two races in schools, theatres and railway carriages has been frequently drawn by this court. Thus in *Strauder* v. *West Virginia*, 100 U. S. 303, it was held that a law of West Virginia limiting to white male persons, 21 years of age and citizens of the State, the right to sit upon juries, was a discrimination which implied a legal inferiority in civil society, which lessened the security of the right of the colored race, and was a step toward reducing them to a condition of servility. Indeed, the right of a colored man that, in the selection of jurors to pass upon his life, liberty and property, there shall be no exclusion of his race, and no discrimination against them because of color, has been asserted in a number of cases. *Virginia* v. *Rives*, 100 U. S. 313; *Neal* v. *Delaware*, 103 U. S. 370; *Bush* v. *Kentucky*, 107 U. S. 110; *Gibson* v. *Mississippi*, 162 U. S. 565. So, where the laws of a particular locality or the charter of a particular railway corporation has provided that no person shall be excluded from the cars on account of color, we have held that this meant that persons of color should travel in the same car as white ones, and that the enactment was not satisfied by the company's providing cars assigned exclusively to people of color, though they were as good as those which they assigned exclusively to white persons. *Railroad Company* v. *Brown*, 17 Wall. 445.

Upon the other hand, where a statute of Louisiana required those engaged in the transportation of passengers among the States to give to all persons travelling within that State, upon vessels employed in that business, equal rights and privileges in all parts of the vessel, without distinction on account of race or color, and subjected to an action for damages the owner of such a vessel, who excluded colored passengers on account of their color from the cabin set aside by him for the use of whites, it was held to be so far as it applied to interstate commerce, unconstitutional and void. *Hall* v. *De Cuir*, 95 U. S. 485. The court in this case, however, expressly disclaimed that it had anything whatever to do with the statute as a regulation of internal commerce, or affecting anything else than commerce among the States.

In the *Civil Rights case*, 109 U. S. 3, it was held that an act of Congress, entitling all persons within the jurisdiction of the United States to the full and equal enjoyment of the accommodations, advantages, facilities and privileges of inns, public conveyances, on land or water, theatres and other places of public amusement, and made applicable to citizens of every race and color, regardless of any previous condition of servitude, was unconstitutional and void, upon the ground that the Fourteenth Amendment was prohibitory upon the States only, and the legislation authorized to be adopted by Congress for enforcing it was not direct legislation on matters respecting which the States were prohibited from making or enforcing certain laws, or doing certain acts, but was corrective legislation, such as might be necessary or proper for counteracting and redressing the effect of such laws or acts. In delivering the opinion of the court Mr. Justice Bradley observed that the Fourteenth Amendment "does not invest Congress with power to legislate upon subjects that are within the domain of state legislation; but to provide modes of relief against state legislation, or state action, of the kind referred to. It does not authorize Congress to create a code of municipal law for the regulation of private rights; but to provide modes of redress against the operation of state laws, and the action of state officers, executive or judicial, when these are subversive of the fundamental rights specified in the amendment. Positive rights and privileges are undoubtedly secured by the Fourteenth Amendment; but they are secured by way of prohibition against state laws and state proceedings affecting those rights and privileges, and by power given to Congress to legislate for the purpose of carrying such prohibition into effect; and such legislation must necessarily be predicated upon such supposed state laws or state proceedings, and be directed to the correction of their operation and effect."

Much nearer, and, indeed, almost directly in point, is the case of the *Louisville, New Orleans &c. Railway* v. *Mississippi*, 133 U. S. 587, wherein the railway company was indicted for a violation of a statute of Mississippi, enacting that all railroads carrying passengers should provide equal, but separate, accommodations for the white and colored races, by providing two or more passenger cars for each passenger train, or by dividing the passenger cars by a partition, so as to secure separate accommodations. The case was presented in a different aspect from the one under consideration, inasmuch as it was an indictment against the railway company for failing to provide the separate accommodations, but the question considered was the constitutionality of the law. In that case, the Supreme Court of Mississippi, 66 Mississippi, 662, had held that the statute applied solely to commerce within the State, and, that being the construction of the state statute by its highest court, was accepted as conclusive. "If it be a matter," said the court, p. 591, "respecting commerce wholly within a

State, and not interfering with commerce between the States, then, obviously, there is no violation of the commerce clause of the Federal Constitution. . . . No question arises under this section, as to the power of the State to separate in different compartments interstate passengers, or affect, in any manner, the privileges and rights of such passengers. All that we can consider is, whether the State has the power to require that railroad trains within her limits shall have separate accommodations for the two races; that affecting only commerce within the State is no invasion of the power given to Congress by the commerce clause."

A like course of reasoning applies to the case under consideration, since the Supreme Court of Louisiana in the case of the *State ex rel. Abbott* v. *Hicks, Judge, et al.*, 44 La. Ann. 770, held that the statute in question did not apply to interstate passengers, but was confined in its application to passengers travelling exclusively within the borders of the State. The case was decided largely upon the authority of *Railway Co.* v. *State*, 66 Mississippi, 662, and affirmed by this court in 133 U. S. 587. In the present case no question of interference with interstate commerce can possibly arise, since the East Louisiana Railway appears to have been purely a local line, with both its termini within the State of Louisiana. Similar statutes for the separation of the two races upon public conveyances were held to be constitutional in *West Chester &c. Railroad* v. *Miles*, 55 Penn. St. 209; *Day* v. *Owen*, 5 Michigan, 520; *Chicago &c. Railway* v. *Williams*, 55 Illinois, 185; *Chesapeake &c. Railroad* v. *Wells*, 85 Tennessee, 613; *Memphis &c. Railroad* v. *Benson*, 85 Tennessee, 627; *The Sue*, 22 Fed. Rep. 843; *Logwood* v. *Memphis &c. Railroad*, 23 Fed. Rep. 318; *McGuinn* v. *Forbes*, 37 Fed. Rep. 639; *People* v. *King*, 18 N. E. Rep. 245; *Houck* v. *South Pac. Railway*, 38 Fed. Rep. 226; *Heard* v. *Georgia Railroad Co.*, 3 Int. Com. Com'n, 111; *S. C.*, 1 Ibid. 428.

While we think the enforced separation of the races, as applied to the internal commerce of the State, neither abridges the privileges or immunities of the colored man, deprives him of his property without due process of law, nor denies him the equal protection of the laws, within the meaning of the Fourteenth Amendment, we are not prepared to say that the conductor, in assigning passengers to the coaches according to their race, does not act at his peril, or that the provision of the second section of the act, that denies to the passenger compensation in damages for a refusal to receive him into the coach in which he properly belongs, is a valid exercise of the legislative power. Indeed, we understand it to be conceded by the State's attorney, that such part of the act as exempts from liability the railway company and its officers is unconstitutional. The power to assign to a particular coach obviously implies the power to determine to which race the passenger belongs, as well as the power to determine who, under the laws of the particular State, is to be deemed a white, and who a colored person. This question, though indicated in the brief of the plaintiff in error, does not properly arise upon the record in this case, since the only issue made is as to the unconstitutionality of the act, so far as it requires the railway to provide separate accommodations, and the conductor to assign passengers according to their race.

It is claimed by the plaintiff in error that, in any mixed community, the reputation of belonging to the dominant race, in this instance the white race, is *property*, in the same sense that a right of action, or of inheritance, is property. Conceding this to be so, for the purposes of this case, we are unable to see how this statute deprives him of, or in any way affects his right to, such property. If he be a white man and assigned to a colored coach, he may have his action for damages against the company for being deprived of his so called property. Upon the other hand, if he be a colored man and be so assigned, he has been deprived of no property, since he is not lawfully entitled to the reputation of being a white man.

In this connection, it is also suggested by the learned counsel for the plaintiff in error that the same argument that will justify the state legislature in requiring railways to provide separate accommodations for the two races will also authorize them to require separate cars to be provided for people whose hair is of a certain color, or who are aliens, or who belong to certain nationalities, or to enact laws requiring colored people to walk upon one side of the street, and white people upon the other, or requiring white men's houses to be painted white, and colored men's black, or their vehicles or business signs to be of different colors, upon the theory that one side of the street is as good as the other, or that a house or vehicle of one color is as good as one of another color. The reply to all this is that every exercise of the police power must be reasonable, and extend only to such laws as are enacted in good faith for the promotion for the public good, and not for the annoyance or oppression of a particular class. Thus in *Yick Wo* v. *Hopkins*, 118 U. S. 356, it was held by this court that a municipal ordinance of the city of San Francisco, to regulate the carrying on of public laundries within the limits of the municipality, violated the provisions of the Constitution of the United States, if it conferred upon the municipal authorities arbitrary power, at their own will, and without regard to discretion, in the legal sense of the term, to give or withhold consent as to persons or places, without regard to the competency of the persons applying, or the propriety of the places selected for the carrying on of the business. It was held to be a covert attempt on the part of the municipality to make an arbitrary and unjust discrimination against the Chinese race. While this was the case of a municipal ordinance, a like principle has been held to apply to acts of a state legislature passed in the exercise of the police power. *Railroad Company* v. *Husen*, 95 U. S. 465; *Louisville & Nashville Railroad* v. *Kentucky*, 161 U. S. 677, and cases cited on p. 700; *Daggett* v. *Hudson*, 43 Ohio St. 548; *Capen* v. *Foster*, 12 Pick. 485; *State ex rel. Wood* v. *Baker*, 38 Wisconsin, 71; *Monroe* v. *Collins*, 17 Ohio St. 665; *Hulseman* v. *Rems*, 41 Penn. St. 396; *Orman* v. *Riley*, 15 California, 48.

So far, then, as a conflict with the Fourteenth Amendment is concerned, the case reduces itself to the question whether the statute of Louisiana is a reasonable regulation, and with respect to this there must necessarily be a large discretion on the part of the legislature. In determining the question of reasonableness it is at liberty to act with reference to the established usages, customs and traditions of the people, and with a view to the promotion of their comfort, and the preservation of the public peace and good order. Gauged by this standard, we cannot say that a law which authorizes or even requires the separation of the two races in public conveyances is unreasonable, or more obnoxious to the Fourteenth Amendment than the acts of Congress requiring separate schools for colored children in the District of Columbia, the constitutionality of which does not seem to have been questioned, or the corresponding acts of state legislatures.

We consider the underlying fallacy of the plaintiff's argument to consist in the assumption that the enforced separation of the two races stamps the colored race with a badge of inferiority. If this be so, it is not by reason of anything found in the act, but solely because the colored race chooses to put that construction upon it. The argument necessarily assumes that if, as has been more than once the case, and is not unlikely to be so again, the colored race should become the dominant power in the state legislature, and should enact a law in precisely similar terms, it would thereby relegate the white race to an inferior position. We imagine that the white race, at least, would not acquiesce in this assumption. The argument also assumes that social prejudices may be overcome by legislation, and that equal rights cannot be secured to the negro except by an enforced commingling of the two races. We cannot accept this proposition. If the two races are to meet upon terms of social equality, it must be the result of natural affinities, a mutual appreciation of each other's merits and a voluntary consent of individuals. As was said by the Court of Appeals of New York in *People* v. *Gallagher*, 93 N. Y. 438, 448, "this end can neither be accomplished nor promoted by laws which conflict with the general sentiment of the community upon whom they are designed to operate. When the government, therefore, has secured to each of its citizens equal rights before the law and equal opportunities for improvement and progress, it has accomplished the end for which it was organized and performed all of the functions respecting social advantages with which it is endowed." Legislation is powerless to eradicate racial instincts or to abolish distinctions based upon physical differences, and the attempt to do so can only result in accentuating the difficulties of the present situation. If the civil and political rights of both races be equal one cannot be inferior to the other civilly or politically. If one race be inferior to the other socially, the Constitution of the United States cannot put them upon the same plane.

It is true that the question of the proportion of colored blood necessary to constitute a colored person, as distinguished from a white person, is one upon which there is a difference of opinion in the different States, some holding that any visible admixture of black blood stamps the person as belonging to the colored race, (*State* v. *Chavers*, 5 Jones, [N. C.] 1, p. 11); others that it depends upon the preponderance of blood, (*Gray* v. *State*, 4 Ohio, 354; *Monroe* v. *Collins*, 17 Ohio St. 665); and still others that the predominance of white blood must only be in the proportion of three fourths. (*People* v. *Dean*, 14 Michigan, 406; *Jones* v. *Commonwealth*, 80 Virginia, 538.) But these are questions to be determined under the laws of each State and are not properly put in issue in this case. Under the allegations of his petition it may undoubtedly become a question of importance whether, under the laws of Louisiana, the petitioner belongs to the white or colored race.

The judgment of the court below is, therefore,

Affirmed.

"THE WRONG THIS DAY DONE"
JOHN MARSHALL HARLAN
Dissenting Opinion in Plessy v. Ferguson
May 18, 1896

Mr. Justice Harlan dissenting.

By the Louisiana statute, the validity of which is here involved, all railway companies (other than street railroad companies) carrying passengers in that State are required to have separate but equal accommodations for white and colored persons, "by providing two or more passenger coaches for each passenger train, *or* by dividing the passenger coaches by a *partition* so as to secure separate accommodations." Under this statute, no colored person is permitted to occupy a seat in a coach assigned to white persons; nor any white person, to occupy a seat in a coach assigned to colored persons. The managers of the railroad are not allowed to exercise any discretion in the premises, but are required to assign each passenger to some coach or compartment set apart for the exclusive use of his race. If a passenger insists upon going into a coach or compartment not set apart for persons of his race, he is subject to be fined, or to be imprisoned in the parish jail. Penalties are prescribed for the refusal or neglect of the officers, directors, conductors and employés of railroad companies to comply with the provisions of the act.

Only "nurses attending children of the other race" are excepted from the operation of the statute. No exception is made of colored attendants travelling with adults. A white man is not permitted to have his colored servant with him in the same coach, even if his condition of health requires the constant, personal assistance of such servant. If a colored maid insists upon riding in the same coach with a white woman whom she has been employed to serve, and who may need her personal attention while travelling, she is subject to be fined or imprisoned for such an exhibition of zeal in the discharge of duty.

While there may be in Louisiana persons of different races who are not citizens of the United States, the words in the act, "white and colored races," necessarily include all citizens of the United States of both races residing in that State. So that we have before us a state enactment that compels, under penalties, the separation of the two races in railroad passenger coaches, and makes it a crime for a citizen of either race to enter a coach that has been assigned to citizens of the other race.

Thus the State regulates the use of a public highway by citizens of the United States solely upon the basis of race.

However apparent the injustice of such legislation may be, we have only to consider whether it is consistent with the Constitution of the United States.

That a railroad is a public highway, and that the corporation which owns or operates it is in the exercise of public functions, is not, at this day, to be disputed. Mr. Justice Nelson, speaking for this court in *New Jersey Steam Navigation Co.* v. *Merchants' Bank*, 6 How. 344, 382, said that a common carrier was in the exercise "of a sort of public office, and has public duties to perform, from which he should not be permitted to exonerate himself without the assent of the parties concerned." Mr. Justice Strong, delivering the judgment of this court in *Olcott* v. *The Supervisors*, 16 Wall. 678, 694, said: "That railroads, though constructed by private corporations and owned by them, are public highways, has been the doctrine of nearly all the courts ever since such conveniences for passage and transportation have had any existence. Very early the question arose whether a State's right of eminent domain could be exercised by a private corporation created for the purpose of constructing a railroad. Clearly it could not, unless taking land for such a purpose by such an agency is taking land for public use. The right of eminent domain nowhere justifies taking property for a private use. Yet it is a doctrine universally accepted that a state legislature may authorize a private corporation to take land for the construction of such a road, making compensation to the owner. What else does this doctrine mean if not that building a railroad, though it be built by a private corporation, is an act done for a public use?" So, in *Township of Pine Grove* v. *Talcott*, 19 Wall. 666, 676: "Though the corporation [a railroad company] was private, its work was public, as much so as if it were to be constructed by the State." So, in *Inhabitants of Worcester* v. *Western Railroad Corporation*, 4 Met. 564: "The establishment of that great thoroughfare is regarded as a public work, established by public authority, intended for the public use and benefit, the use of which is secured to the whole community, and constitutes, therefore, like a canal, turnpike or highway, a public easement." It is true that the real and personal property, necessary to the establishment and management of the railroad, is vested in the corporation; but it is in trust for the public."

In respect of civil rights, common to all citizens, the Constitution of the United States does not, I think, permit any public authority to know the race of those entitled to be protected in the enjoyment of such rights. Every true man has pride of race, and under appropriate circumstances when the rights of others, his equals before the law, are not to be affected, it is his privilege to express such pride and to take such action based upon it as to him seems proper. But I deny that any legislative body or judicial tribunal may have regard to the race of citizens when the civil rights of those citizens are involved. Indeed, such legislation, as that here in question, is inconsistent not only with that equality of rights which pertains to citizenship, National and State, but with the personal liberty enjoyed by every one within the United States.

The Thirteenth Amendment does not permit the withholding or the deprivation of any right necessarily inhering in freedom. It not only struck down the institution of slavery as previously existing in the United States, but it prevents the imposition of any burdens or disabilities that constitute badges of slavery or servitude. It decreed universal civil freedom in this country. This court has so adjudged. But that amendment having been found inadequate to the protection of the rights of those who had been in slavery, it was followed by the Fourteenth Amendment, which added greatly to the dignity and glory of American citizenship, and to the security of personal liberty, by declaring that "all persons born or naturalized in the United States, and subject to the jurisdiction thereof, are citizens of the United States and of the State wherein they reside," and that "no State shall make or enforce any law which shall abridge the privileges or immunities of citizens of the United States; nor shall any State deprive any person of life, liberty or property without due process of law, nor deny to any person within its jurisdiction the equal protection of the laws." These two amendments, if enforced according to their true intent and meaning, will protect all the civil rights that pertain to freedom and citizenship. Finally, and to the end that no citizen should be denied, on account of his race, the privilege of participating in the political control of his country, it was declared by the Fifteenth Amendment that "the right of citizens of the United States to vote shall not be denied or abridged by the United States or by any State on account of race, color or previous condition of servitude."

These notable additions to the fundamental law were welcomed by the friends of liberty throughout the world. They removed the race line from our governmental systems. They had, as this court has said, a common purpose, namely, to secure "to a race recently emancipated, a race that through many generations have been held in slavery, all the civil rights that the superior race enjoy." They declared, in legal effect, this court has further said, "that the law in the States shall be the same for the black as for the white; that all persons, whether colored or white, shall stand equal before the laws of the States, and, in regard to the colored race, for whose protection the amendment was primarily designed, that no discrimination shall be made against them by law because of their color." We also said: "The words of the amendment, it is true, are prohibitory, but they contain a necessary implication of a positive immunity, or right, most valuable to the colored race—the right to exemption from unfriendly legislation against them distinctively as colored—exemption from legal discriminations, implying inferiority in civil society, lessening the security of their enjoyment of the rights which others enjoy, and discriminations which are steps towards reducing them to the condition of a subject race." It was, consequently, adjudged that a state law that excluded citizens of the colored race from juries, because of their race and however well qualified in other respects to discharge the duties of jurymen, was repugnant to the Fourteenth Amendment. *Strauder* v. *West Virginia*, 100 U. S. 303, 306, 307; *Virginia* v. *Rives*, 100 U. S. 313; *Ex parte Virginia*, 100

U. S. 339; *Neal* v. *Delaware*, 103 U. S. 370, 386; *Bush* v. *Kentucky*, 107 U. S. 110, 116. At the present term, referring to the previous adjudications, this court declared that "underlying all of those decisions is the principle that the Constitution of the United States, in its present form, forbids, so far as civil and political rights are concerned, discrimination by the General Government or the States against any citizen because of his race. All citizens are equal before the law." *Gibson* v. *Mississippi*, 162 U. S. 565.

The decisions referred to show the scope of the recent amendments of the Constitution. They also show that it is not within the power of a State to prohibit colored citizens, because of their race, from participating as jurors in the administration of justice.

It was said in argument that the statute of Louisiana does not discriminate against either race, but prescribes a rule applicable alike to white and colored citizens. But this argument does not meet the difficulty. Every one knows that the statute in question had its origin in the purpose, not so much to exclude white persons from railroad cars occupied by blacks, as to exclude colored people from coaches occupied by or assigned to white persons. Railroad corporations of Louisiana did not make discrimination among whites in the matter of accommodation for travellers. The thing to accomplish was, under the guise of giving equal accommodation for whites and blacks, to compel the latter to keep to themselves while travelling in railroad passenger coaches. No one would be so wanting in candor as to assert the contrary. The fundamental objection, therefore, to the statute is that it interferes with the personal freedom of citizens. "Personal liberty," it has been well said, "consists in the power of locomotion, of changing situation, or removing one's person to whatsoever places one's own inclination may direct, without imprisonment or restraint, unless by due course of law." 1 Bl. Com. *134. If a white man and a black man choose to occupy the same public conveyance on a public highway, it is their right to do so, and no government, proceeding alone on grounds of race, can prevent it without infringing the personal liberty of each.

It is one thing for railroad carriers to furnish, or to be required by law to furnish, equal accommodations for all whom they are under a legal duty to carry. It is quite another thing for government to forbid citizens of the white and black races from travelling in the same public conveyance, and to punish officers of railroad companies for permitting persons of the two races to occupy the same passenger coach. If a State can prescribe, as a rule of civil conduct, that whites and blacks shall not travel as passengers in the same railroad coach, why may it not so regulate the use of the streets of its cities and towns as to compel white citizens to keep on one side of a street and black citizens to keep on the other? Why may it not, upon like grounds, punish whites and blacks who ride together in street cars or in open vehicles on a public road or street? Why may it not require sheriffs to assign whites to one side of a court-room and blacks to the other? And why may it not also prohibit the commingling of the two races in the galleries of legislative halls or in public assemblages convened for the consideration of the political questions of the day? Further, if this statute of Louisiana is consistent with the personal liberty of citizens, why may not the State require the separation in railroad coaches of native and naturalized citizens of the United States, or of Protestants and Roman Catholics?

The answer given at the argument to these questions was that regulations of the kind they suggest would be unreasonable, and could not, therefore, stand before the law. Is it meant that the determination of questions of legislative power depends upon the inquiry whether the statute whose validity is questioned is, in the judgment of the courts, a reasonable one, taking all the circumstances into consideration? A statute may be unreasonable merely because a sound public policy forbade its enactment. But I do not understand that the courts have anything to do with the policy or expediency of legislation. A statute may be valid, and yet, upon grounds of public policy, may well be characterized as unreasonable. Mr. Sedgwick correctly states the rule when he says that the legislative intention being clearly ascertained, "the courts have no other duty to perform than to execute the legislative will, without any regard to their views as to the wisdom or justice of the particular enactment." Stat. & Const. Constr. 324. There is a dangerous tendency in these latter days to enlarge the functions of the courts, by means of judicial interference with the will of the people as expressed by the legislature. Our institutions have the distinguishing characteristic that the three departments of government are coördinate and separate. Each must keep within the limits defined by the Constitution. And the courts best discharge their duty by executing the will of the law-making power, constitutionally expressed, leaving the results of legislation to be dealt with by the people through their representatives. Statutes must always have a reasonable construction. Sometimes they are to be construed strictly; sometimes, liberally, in order to carry out the legislative will. But however construed, the intent of the legislature is to be respected, if the particular statute in question is valid, although the courts, looking at the public interests, may conceive the statute to be both unreasonable and impolitic. If the power exists to enact a statute, that ends the matter so far as the courts are concerned. The adjudged cases in which statutes have been held to be void, because unreasonable, are those in which the means employed by the legislature were not at all germane to the end to which the legislature was competent.

The white race deems itself to be the dominant race in this country. And so it is, in prestige, in achievements, in education, in wealth and in power. So, I doubt not, it will continue to be for all time, if it remains true to its great heritage and holds fast to the principles of constitutional liberty. But in view of the Constitution, in the eye of the law, there is in this country no superior, dominant, ruling class of citizens. There is no caste here. Our Constitution is color-blind, and neither knows nor tolerates classes among citizens. In respect of civil rights, all citizens are equal before the law. The humblest is the peer of the most powerful. The law regards man as man, and takes no account of his surroundings or of his color when his civil rights as guaranteed by the supreme law of the land are involved. It is, therefore, to be regretted that this high tribunal, the final expositor of the fundamental law of the land, has reached the conclusion that it is competent for a State to regulate the enjoyment by citizens of their civil rights solely upon the basis of race.

In my opinion, the judgment this day rendered will, in time, prove to be quite as pernicious as the decision made by this tribunal in the *Dred Scott case*. It was adjudged in that case that the descendants of Africans who were imported into this country and sold as slaves were not included nor intended to be included under the word "citizens" in the Constitution, and could not claim any of the rights and privileges which that instrument provided for and secured to citizens of the United States; that at the time of the adoption of the Constitution they were "considered as a subordinate and inferior class of beings, who had been subjugated by the dominant race, and, whether emancipated or not, yet remained subject to their authority, and had no rights or privileges but such as those who held the power and the government might choose to grant them." 19 How. 393, 404. The recent amendments of the Constitution, it was supposed, had eradicated these principles from our institutions. But it seems that we have yet, in some of the States, a dominant race—a superior class of citizens, which assumes to regulate the enjoyment of civil rights, common to all citizens, upon the basis of race. The present decision, it may well be apprehended, will not only stimulate aggressions, more or less brutal and irritating, upon the admitted rights of colored citizens, but will encourage the belief that it is possible, by means of state enactments, to defeat the beneficent purposes which the people of the United States had in view when they adopted the recent amendments of the Constitution, by one of which the blacks of this country were made citizens of the United States and of the States in which they respectively reside, and whose privileges and immunities, as citizens, the States are forbidden to abridge. Sixty millions of whites are in no danger from the presence here of eight millions of blacks. The destinies of the two races, in this country, are indissolubly linked together, and the interests of both require that the common government of all shall not permit the seeds of race hate to be planted under the sanction of law. What can more certainly arouse race hate, what more certainly create and perpetuate a feeling of distrust between these races, than state enactments, which, in fact, proceed on the ground that colored citizens are so inferior and degraded that they cannot be allowed to sit in public coaches occupied by white citizens? That, as all will admit, is the real meaning of such legislation as was enacted in Louisiana.

The sure guarantee of the peace and security of each race is the clear, distinct, unconditional recognition by our governments, National and State, of every right that inheres in civil freedom, and of the equality before the law of all citizens of the United States without regard to race. State enactments, regulating the enjoyment of civil rights, upon the basis of race, and cunningly devised to defeat legitimate results of the war, under the pretence of recognizing equality of rights, can have no other result than to render permanent peace impossible, and to keep alive a conflict of races, the continuance of which must do harm to all concerned. This question is not met by the suggestion that social equality cannot exist between the white and black races in this country. That argument, if it can be properly regarded as one, is scarcely worthy of consideration; for social equality no more exists between two races when travelling in a passenger coach or a public highway than when members of the same races sit by each other in a street car or in the jury box, or stand or sit with each other in a political assembly, or when they use in common the streets of a city or town, or when they are in the same room for the purpose of having their names placed on the registry of voters, or when they approach the ballot-box in order to exercise the high privilege of voting.

There is a race so different from our own that we do not permit those belonging to it to become citizens of the United States. Persons belonging to it are, with few exceptions, absolutely excluded from our country. I allude to the Chinese race. But by the statute in question, a Chinaman can ride in the same passenger coach with white citizens of the United States, while citizens of the black race in Louisiana, many of whom, perhaps, risked their lives for the preservation of the Union, who are entitled, by law, to participate in the political control of the State and nation, who are not excluded, by law or by reason of their race, from public stations of any kind, and who have all the legal rights that belong to white citizens, are yet declared to be criminals, liable to imprisonment, if they ride in a public coach occupied by citizens of the white race. It is scarcely just to say that a colored citizen should not object to occupying a public coach assigned to his own race. He does not object, nor, perhaps, would he object to separate coaches for his race, if his rights under the law were recognized. But he objects, and ought never to cease objecting to the proposition, that citizens of the white and black races can be adjudged criminals because they sit, or claim the right to sit, in the same public coach on a public highway.

The arbitrary separation of citizens, on the basis of race, while they are on a public highway, is a badge of servitude wholly inconsistent with the civil freedom and the equality before the law established by the Constitution. It cannot be justified upon any legal grounds.

If evils will result from the commingling of the two races upon public highways established for the benefit of all, they will be infinitely less than those that will surely come from state legislation regulating the enjoyment of civil rights upon the basis of race. We boast of the freedom enjoyed by our people above all other peoples. But it is difficult to reconcile that boast with a state of the law which, practically, puts the brand of servitude and degradation upon a large class of our fellow-citizens, our equals before the law. The thin disguise of "equal" accommodations for passengers in railroad coaches will not mislead any one, nor atone for the wrong this day done.

The result of the whole matter is, that while this court has frequently adjudged, and at the present term has recognized the doctrine, that a State cannot, consistently with the Constitution of the United States, prevent white and black citizens, having the required qualifications for jury service, from sitting in the same jury box, it is now solemnly held that a State may prohibit white and black citizens from sitting in the same passenger coach on a public highway, or may require that they be separated by a "partition," when in the same passenger coach. May it not now be reasonably expected that astute men of the dominant race, who affect to be disturbed at the possibility that the integrity of the white race may be corrupted, or that its supremacy will be imperilled, by contact on public highways with black people, will endeavor to procure statutes requiring white and black jurors to be separated in the jury box by a "partition," and that, upon retiring from the court room to consult as to their verdict, such partition, if it be a moveable one, shall be taken to their consultation room, and set up in such way as to prevent black jurors from coming too close to their brother jurors of the white race. If the "partition" used in the court room happens to be stationary, provision could be made for screens with openings through which jurors of the two races could confer as to their verdict without coming into personal contact with each other. I cannot see but that, according to the principles this day announced, such state legislation, although conceived in hostility to, and enacted for the purpose of humiliating citizens of the United States of a particular race, would be held to be consistent with the Constitution.

I do not deem it necessary to review the decisions of state courts to which reference was made in argument. Some, and the most important, of them are wholly inapplicable, because rendered prior to the adoption of the last amendments of the Constitution, when colored people had very few rights which the dominant race felt obliged to respect. Others were made at a time when public opinion, in many localities, was dominated by the institution of slavery; when it would not have been safe to do justice to the black man; and when, so far as the rights of blacks were concerned, race prejudice was, practically, the supreme law of the land. Those decisions cannot be guides in the era introduced by the recent amendments of the supreme law, which established universal civil freedom, gave citizenship to all born or naturalized in the United States and residing here, obliterated the race line from our systems of governments, National and State, and placed our free institutions upon the broad and sure foundation of the equality of all men before the law.

I am of opinion that the statute of Louisiana is inconsistent with the personal liberty of citizens, white and black, in that State, and hostile to both the spirit and letter of the Constitution of the United States. If laws of like character should be enacted in the several States of the Union, the effect would be in the highest degree mischievous. Slavery, as an institution tolerated by law would, it is true, have disappeared from our country, but there would remain a power in the States, by sinister legislation, to interfere with the full enjoyment of the blessings of freedom; to regulate civil rights, common to all citizens, upon the basis of race; and to place in a condition of legal inferiority a large body of American citizens, now constituting a part of the political community called the People of the United States, for whom, and by whom through representatives, our government is administered. Such a system is inconsistent with the guarantee given by the Constitution to each State of a republican form of government, and may be stricken down by Congressional action, or by the courts in the discharge of their solemn duty to maintain the supreme law of the land, anything in the constitution or laws of any State to the contrary notwithstanding.

For the reasons stated, I am constrained to withhold my assent from the opinion and judgment of the majority.

MR. JUSTICE BREWER did not hear the argument or participate in the decision of this case.

1897–1909

AN INTERVIEW WITH BISHOP HENRY MCNEAL TURNER

THE WASHINGTON EVENING STAR
Negro Emigration
October 21, 1897

NEGRO EMIGRATION

Views of Bishop Turner, an Enthusiast on Subject.

AFRICA THE NATURAL HOME OF RACE

Perpetual Enslavement of Those Who Remain Here.

WHITES REIGN SUPREME

BISHOP HENRY M. TURNER of Georgia, who is one of the best-known and most highly educated negro ministers in the United States, was in Washington a few days this week, and gave The Evening Star the following interview touching the emigration of negroes to Africa, in which movement the bishop is the recognized head, and with which he has been identified for a number of years. Bishop Turner is an enthusiast on the emigration question, and does not hesitate to say that it is only a question of extermination or emigration for the negro. He has given the question years of study, and has been censured and abused by both the white and colored races, but this has not caused him to depart one iota from his beliefs and purposes regarding African emigration.

Replying to a question, Bishop Turner said

"Some of you gentlemen of the press have seen fit to give me an occasional roasting, but I am pleased to say that in most instances the press has been ready to give my followers and myself justice. We have done nothing in this matter except in an open and straightforward manner, and we have kept no one in the dark about anything connected with the movement. It has been our aim to give it the widest publicity possible, and I am even willing that I should be caricatured and lambasted by the press, if by so doing it will aid in any way in spreading the truths of our mission and our work.

THE NEGRO'S NATURAL HOME.

"I think the future of the negro race lies in Africa, his natural home, and the richest country on earth. Africa is the negro's fatherland, and the sooner he goes there the better for him. This movement is far-reaching and will change the entire history of our race. It has simply come down to extermination or emigration for the negro. Any intelligent man who has given the matter consideration realizes that. Why is it so? Simply from the fact that statistics show that the negro race is dying out. It is not growing healthier, wealthier, happier, wiser, or anything else which goes to make life worth living.

"God Almighty, in His infinite goodness and wisdom, made Africa for the negro and the negro for Africa. I believe this just as much as I do that the sun shines. If I had $5,000,000, I would invest every cent in ships, and would see that every negro who wished to go to Africa got there.

"Now, some of my people want to know why I do not go to Africa and stay there. I believe I am needed here, but the very moment I can get fifty thousand or one hundred thousand negroes to go with me, I am off like a quarter-horse, and I will think it the best day's work I ever accomplished."

"Do you not think that white and colored people get along very easily in this country?" he was asked.

WHITES WILL ALWAYS REIGN.

"Yes, but the negro race can never be more than hewers of wood and drawers of water here. The giant race—the white race—will always reign supreme in America. John Temple Graves, a gentleman for whom I have the highest regard, said in one of his speeches that the negro would never be allowed to control in this country, even where he has a majority. Mr. Graves also said that the price of the negro's peace was his subordination.

"This being true, how can the negro ever hope to attain here the full stature of a citizen or a man? Intelligent negroes well know that Mr. Graves has not uttered these truths from personal prejudice, for he has plead the negro's cause as but few men in the south have.

"And what does the great statesman, Senator Morgan of Alabama, say? He says the negro will never receive social recognition here, and that the negro had better be a slave than a free man without social recognition, if he expects to remain in this country."

"Has the African emigration movement met with the approval of a majority of the negro race?"

"No, indeed; but, on the contrary, a lot of ignorant negroes have opposed it from its very inception. They prate about the sickness of Africa and many other things of which they are in dense ignorance. The thoughtful and intelligent of the white race indorse the emigration policy, and it will yet prove a success and of untold blessings to the negro race.

MAY BE RE-ENSLAVED.

"There is some chance, too, of the negro being re-enslaved if he prefers to stay here. Some people are unkind enough to say that this kind of talk comes from a disordered brain, but that kind of stuff does not annoy me in the least.

"Africa is one of the very richest countries on earth, and with a line of steamers, owned and controlled by negroes, plying between that great country and the United States, the negro would soon grow rich and prosperous by selling to the whites of this country minerals, precious ores, gems, ivory and a thousand things which are found in abundance in that rich land and which would fetch good prices here. I believe that the press of this country would be doing incalculable benefit to humanity by giving this African emigration policy careful study and then giving the facts as wide publicity as possible."

"Is the movement growing satisfactorily?"

"Of course, with others, I am naturally somewhat impatient, but I can say that everything presents an encouraging look. The movement is one of vast magnitude and cannot be carried through in a hurry. It will be a glorious day when the first steamers sail for that land, which will be one of peace and plenty, and which was intended as the home for the negro race."

A WHITE SOUTHERN WOMAN DEFENDS LYNCHING

THE WILMINGTON MORNING STAR
Mrs. Felton Speaks

August 18, 1898

MRS. FELTON SPEAKS

She Makes a Sensational Speech
Before Agricultural Society.

Believes Lynching Should Prevail as Long
as Defenceless Woman Is Not
Better Protected.

[J. A. Holman, Special to Atlanta Journal.]

SOUTH BEND HOTEL, TYBEE, GA., August 12.—The feature of the session yesterday afternoon was the address by Mrs. W. H. Felton, of Bartow county, in which she discussed at length the public questions of interest in Georgia at this time, and dwelt with particular emphasis on the lynching problem. She reiterated her plea for co-education at the State University.

Mrs. Felton spoke of the necessity for the better education of farmers' daughters as a protection from the assaulter, and declared that instead of so much money being expended for foreign missions it might be used to even better advantage in educating the heathen at home, even in Georgia.

"I hear much of the millions sent abroad to Japan, China, India, Brazil and Mexico, but I feel that the heathen at home are so close at hand and need so much that I must make a strong effort to stop lynching, by keeping closer watch over the poor white girls on the secluded farms; and if these poor maidens are destroyed in a land that their fathers died to save from the invader's foot, I say the shame lies with the survivors who fail to be protectors for the children of their dead comrades.

"I do not discount foreign missions. I simply say the heathens are at your door, when our young maidens are destroyed in sight of your opulence and magnificence, and when your temples of justice are put to shame by the lynchers' rope. If your court houses are shams and frauds and the law's delay is the villain's bulwark, then I say let judgment begin at the house of God and redeem this country from the cloud of shame that rests upon it!

"When there is not enough religion in the pulpit to organize a crusade against sin; nor justice in the court house to promptly punish crime; nor manhood enough in the nation to put a sheltering arm about innocence and virtue—if it needs lynching to protect woman's dearest possession from the ravening human beasts—then I say lynch; a thousand times a week if necessary.

"The poor girl would choose any death in preference to such ignominy and outrage, and a quick death is mercy to the rapist compared to the suffering of innocence and modesty in a land of bibles and churches, where violence is becoming omnipotent except with the rich and powerful before the law.

"The crying need of women on the farms is security in their lives and in their homes. Strong, able-bodied men have told me they stopped farming and moved to town because their women folks were scared to death if left alone.

"I say it is a disgrace in a free country when such things are a public reproach and the best part of God's creation are trembling and crying for protection in their own homes. And I say, with due respect to all who listen to me, that so long as your politics takes the colored man into your embraces on election day to control the vote; and so long as the politicians use liquor to befuddle his understanding and make him think he is a man and a brother when they propose to defeat the opposition by honey-snuggling him at the polls, and so long as he is made familiar with their dirty tricks in politics so long will lynchings prevail, because the causes of it grow and increase."

[Mrs. Felton is one of the most distinguished women of Georgia, intellectually and socially. She is the wife of Dr. W. H. Felton, a former Representative in Congress, and takes a prominent part in everything pertaining to the advancement and protection of her sex.—EDITOR STAR.]

A BLACK EDITOR RESPONDS TO REBECCA FELTON

THE WILMINGTON MORNING STAR
A Horrid Slander
August 30, 1898

A HORRID SLANDER.

The Most Infamous That Ever
Appeared in Print in
This State.

The Alarmed Politicians are Trying to
Break the Force of it by Resorting
to Various Dodges,
But They are Too Thin.

THE INFAMOUS assault on the white women of this State which appeared on the 18th of August in the *Daily Record*, the negro paper published in this city, has aroused a storm of indignation from one end of the State to the other. We have received so many requests for copies of the STAR containing this article that we herewith reproduce it in full, the accuracy of which is certified to by Col. John D. Taylor, Clerk of the Superior Court of New Hanover county, and by a number of our well-known business men. The article is headed:

MRS. FELTON'S SPEECH.

"A Mrs. Felton, from Georgia, makes a speech before the Agricultural Society at Tybee, Ga., in which she advocates lynching as an extreme measure. This woman makes a strong plea for womanhood, and if the alleged crimes of rape were half so frequent as is ofttimes reported, her plea would be worthy of consideration.

"Mrs. Felton, like many other so-called Christians, loses sight of the basic principle of the religion of Christ in her plea for one class of people as against another. If a missionary spirit is essential for the uplifting of the poor white girls, why is it? The morals of the poor white people are on a par with their colored neighbors of like conditions, and if any one doubts the statement let him visit among them. The whole lump needs to be leavened by those who profess so much religion and showing them that the preservation of virtue is an essential for the life of any people.

"Mrs. Felton begins well for she admits that education will better protect the girls on the farm from the assaulter. This we admit and it should not be confined to the white any more than to the colored girls. The papers are filled often with reports of rapes of white women, and the subsequent lynching of the alleged rapists. The editors pour forth volleys of aspersions against all negroes because of the few who may be guilty. If the papers and speakers of the other race would condemn the commission of crime because it is crime and not try to make it appear that the negroes were the only criminals, they would find their strongest allies in the intelligent negroes themselves, and together the whites and blacks would root the evil out of both races.

"We suggest that the whites guard their women more closely, as Mrs. Felton says, thus giving no opportunity for the human fiend, be he white or black. You leave your goods out of doors and then complain because they are taken away. Poor white men are careless in the matter of protecting their women, especially on farms. They are careless of their conduct toward them and our experience among poor white people in the country teaches us that the women of that race are not any more particular in the matter of clandestine meetings with colored men, than are the white men with colored women. Meetings of this kind go on for some time until the woman's infatuation or the man's boldness, bring attention to them and the man is lynched for rape. Every negro lynched is called a 'big, burly, black brute,' when in fact many of those who have thus been dealt with had white men for their fathers, and were not only not 'black' and 'burly' but were sufficiently attractive for white girls of culture and refinement to fall in love with them as is well known to all.

"Mrs. Felton must begin at the fountain head if she wishes to purify the stream.

"Teach your men purity. Let virtue be something more than an excuse for them to intimidate and torture a helpless people. Tell your men that it is no worse for a black man to be intimate with a white woman, than for a white man to be intimate with a colored woman.

"You set yourselves down as a lot of carping hypocrites; in fact you cry aloud for the virtue of your women while you seek to destroy the morality of ours. Don't think ever that your women will remain pure while you are debauching ours. You sow the seed—the harvest will come in due time."

THE AFFIDAVIT OF THE CLERK.

An effort has been made by some of the politicians to fool the people by representing that this slander was a Democratic trick or was garbled, but the following affidavit from the Clerk of the Superior Court settles the question as to its accuracy:

NORTH CAROLINA,
NEW HANOVER COUNTY.

I, John D. Taylor, Clerk of the Superior Court of New Hanover county, do hereby certify that the foregoing is an accurate and true copy of an editorial in the *Daily Record*, a paper published in the city of Wilmington, of date Aug. 18, 1898.

I further certify that said paper has been published in said city at least eight months prior to this date; that Alex. L. Manly, the editor, is a negro, is well known as a Republican and has before this held the office of Deputy Register of Deeds of New Hanover county, by appointment from Charles W. Norwood, Republican Register of Deeds, of New Hanover county.

I further certify that John N. Goins, business manager; L. D. Manly, foreman; Jno. T. Howe, general traveling agent; and F. G. Manly, general manager, are all negroes, and are known as Republicans and the said Jno. T. Howe was a Republican Representative from New Hanover county in the Legislature of 1897. Witness my hand and seal this August 24th, 1898.

JOHN D. TAYLOR,
Clerk Superior Court of New Hanover Co.

WHO MANLY IS.

As the Republican politicians in this county could not call this assault a Democratic trick, or say it was garbled, they tried to break the force of it by repudiating the paper as a party organ and characterizing the editor as a "simpleton" who represents no one but himself. The following affidavit from a number of business men of Wilmington testifies to the accuracy of the published slander, tells who Manly and his associates on the *Record* are and shows that Manly was not regarded as a simpleton, or a nobody before he startled the bosses by the publication of that awful article:

CITIZENS TESTIFY.

B. G. Worth, of the Worth Co.; R. W. Hicks, wholesale grocer; C. E. Borden, president of Navassa Guano Co.; W. L. DeRosset, commander of N. C. Division Confederate Veterans, and John C. Springer, of the firm of W. E. Springer & Co., each being duly sworn says that he has read the foregoing paper, and that the said is an accurate and true copy of an editorial in the *Daily Record* of the date August 18th, 1898; that said paper, the *Daily Record*, has been published in the city of Wilmington at least eight months prior to this date, and Alex. L. Manly, the editor thereof, is a negro, is well known as a Republican and has held the position of Deputy Register of Deeds in New Hanover county under the Republicans.

Affiants further say that John N. Goins, business manager, L. D. Manly, foreman, John T. Howe, general travelling agent, and F. G. Manly, general manager, are all negroes, and Republicans, and the said John T. Howe was a Republican Representative from New Hanover county in the Legislature of 1897.

W. L. DeRosset,
John C. Springer,
B. G. Worth,
R. W. Hicks,
Chas. E. Borden.

State of North Carolina,
County of New Hanover.

Personally appeared before me, Wm. L. DeRossett, B. G. Worth, John C. Springer, R. W. Hicks and Charles E. Borden, shown to me to be the persons they represent themselves to be, and made oaths that the above statement is correct to the best of their knowledge and belief.

John Turrentine,
Notary Public.

INCITING THE WILMINGTON INSURRECTION

THE RALEIGH NEWS AND OBSERVER
Defamer Must Go
November 10, 1898

DEFAMER MUST GO

Mass Meeting of White Citizens
of Wilmington Pass Resolutions.

EXPULSION OF MANLY

AND RESIGNATIONS OF MAYOR
AND CHIEF OF POLICE DEMANDED.

MANLY GIVEN TWENTY-FOUR HOURS

Time for Negro Domination Forever Past,
Though they are to be Treated With
Justice and Consideration.
White Labor Favored.

Wilmington, N. C., Nov. 9.—There was a mass meeting of the business men of Wilmington today, attended by fully 800 of the best white citizens, at which the following resolutions were adopted:

"Believing that the constitution of the United States contemplated a Government to be carried on by an enlightened people; believing that its framers did not anticipate the enfranchisement of an ignorant population of African origin, and believing that the men of the State of North Carolina who joined in forming the Union did not contemplate for their descendants a subjection to an inferior race.

"We, the undersigned citizens of the city of Wilmington and county of New Hanover, do hereby declare that we will no longer be ruled, and will never again be ruled by men of African origin. This condition we have in part endured because we felt that the consequences of the war of secession were such as to deprive us of the fair consideration of many of our countrymen.

"We believe that, after more than thirty years, that this is no longer the case.

TIME FOR NEGRO RULE PAST.

"The stand we now pledge ourselves to is forced upon us suddenly by a crisis and our eyes are open to the fact that we must act now or leave our descendants to a fate too gloomy to be borne.

"While we recognize the authority of the United States, and will yield to it if exerted, we would not for a moment believe that it is the purpose of more than sixty millions of our own race to subject us permanently to a fate to which no Anglo-Saxon has ever been forced to submit.

"We therefore, believing that we represent unequivocally the sentiment of the white people of this county and city, hereby for ourselves, and representing them, proclaim:

"First—That the time has passed for the intelligent citizens of this community, owning 95 per cent of the property and paying taxes in like proportion, to be ruled by negroes.

"Second—That we will not tolerate the action of unscrupulous white men in affiliating with the negroes so that by means of their votes they can dominate the intelligent and thrifty element in the community, thus causing business to stagnate and progress to be out of the question.

"Third—That the negro has demonstrated by antagonizing our interest in every way and especially by his ballot, that he is incapable of realizing that his interests are and should be identical with those of the community.

THEY FAVOR WHITE LABOR.

"Fourth—That the progressive element in any community is the white population and that the giving of nearly all of the employment to negro laborers has been against the best interests of this county and city and is a sufficient reason why the city of Wilmington, with its natural advantages has not become a city of at least 50,000 inhabitants.

"Fifth—That we propose in future to give to white men a large part of the employment heretofore given to negroes, because we realize that white families cannot thrive here unless there are more opportunities for employment for the different members of said families.

"Sixth—That the white men expect to live in this community peaceably, to have and provide absolute protection for their families, who shall be safe from insult from all persons, whomsoever. We are prepared to treat the negroes with justice and consideration in all matters which do not involve sacrifices of the interest of the intelligent and progressive portion of the community. But we are equally prepared now and immediately to enforce what we know to be our rights.

MANLY TO BE EXPELLED.

"Seventh—That we have been, in our desire for harmony and peace, blinded both to our best interests and our rights. A climax was reached when the negro paper of this city published an article so vile and slanderous that it would in most communities have resulted in the lynching of the editor. We deprecate lynching and yet there is no punishment, provided by the laws adequate for this offense. We, therefore, owe it to the people of this community and of this city, as a protection against such license in future, that the paper known as the Record cease to be published and that its editor be banished from this community.

"We demand that he leave this city within twenty-four hours after the issuance of this proclamation. Second, that the printing press from which the Record has been issued be packed and shipped from the city without delay, that we be notified within twelve hours of the acceptance or rejection of this demand.

"If the demand is agreed to, within twelve hours we counsel forbearance on the part of all white men. If the demand is refused or if no answer is given within the time mentioned then the editor, Manly, will be expelled by force.

INTENSE EXCITEMENT.

"It is the sense of this meeting that Mayor S. P. Wright and Chief of Police J. R. Mullen, having demonstrated their utter incapacity to give the city a decent government and keep order therein, their continuance in office being a constant menace to the peace of this community ought forthwith to resign."

A committee of twenty-five citizens was appointed to direct the execution of the provisions of the resolutions.

This afternoon there was a conference between the committee and a number of the most influential negroes of the city at which it was agreed that the negroes report to the committee at 7 A.M. tomorrow as to whether or not Editor Manly would comply with the requirements of the resolutions. If he does not white men propose to go in full force at 8 A.M. and destroy the newspaper plant and forcibly expell the editor. There is intense excitement and many fear that the negroes will attempt to protect Manly. If they do the worst can be expected.

"THE TERRIBLE, STERN REALITY OF THE SITUATION"
W. H. COUNCILL
The Future of the Negro
The Forum, July 1899

THE FUTURE OF THE NEGRO.

THE recent political disturbances in the Carolinas have provoked much discussion of what is commonly called the Negro problem. The Negro has been brought into court, his case made out, and his plea entered by the "other side." The hearing has been entirely *ex parte*. But give the Negro himself a chance to present his own case freely, plainly, fairly, without being subjected to unfair criticism and misrepresentation,—seemingly intentionally prejudicial to him,—and other and more satisfactory conclusions will be reached. All discussions of the subject, so far, hold the Negro responsible for the solution of some problem which has never yet been stated.

Fairly stated, as I understand it, the problem is this: "Will the white man permit the Negro to have an equal part in the industrial, political, and civil advantages of the United States of America?" From this statement of the problem, it is clear that the Negro has no part in its solution. He is here by sufferance, and can remain only by grace. To talk of "rights" means but little. Rights, in the human vocabulary, are just what man gains by contention and struggle, or what the strong concede to the weak. Contention and struggle, in the Negro's case in this country, mean aggravation and death. Whatever comes must be concession. There has always been a race problem, and, I suppose, there always will be, until human nature shall have changed. Egypt, we are told, solved her race problem by divine intervention; ancient Asiatic empires, Greece, and Rome, by the sword: the early Briton was exterminated. The British Empire has its race problem to-day; and 150,000 white-skinned Anglo-Saxons control, soul and body, 250,000,000 dark-skinned Aryans, and exercise toward them a spirit of caste, bitter, blistering, and blighting. There will never be a time without a race problem, wherever two peoples with any points of difference live together. Race problems are in each case simply race prejudice. Race prejudice is unreasonable. It is as deep and abiding as it is unreasonable; and it is excusable because it is unreasonable.

There is a kind of indescribable dislike, founded on the differences in racial characteristics, which is manifested in antagonism at every opportunity. We hear of a high plane whereon all races "live, move, and have their being," devoid of race prejudice; but, so far, the world has seen it only in theory. Greek mind, standing tip-toe on the shoulders of the highest Oriental intellect and virtue, never so much as got a glimpse of this "universal racial equalization." Take one thousand white men and one thousand black men, representing the highest intellect, virtue, and industrial skill, trained in all the principles of the Gospel of Jesus of Nazareth, and place them, above want, remote from the contaminating influence of race-hating men, and before the end of the third generation the Race question would be raised and racial lines would be drawn. The black men would rally round their flag; the white men, round theirs. One flag would gain the ascendancy, or both would disappear in amalgamation. Racial identity on racial equality could not obtain. Races and peoples draw lines on the slightest differences regardless of merit. It is as difficult to equalize races as it is to equalize wealth.

Our Race problem is not a Southern problem, but a problem for the Anglo-Saxon people—in India, in Africa, in America.

Education, it is said, will solve the problem. Just how this will come about, we are not informed, and I cannot see. Without some kind of schooling different from that which mankind has had up to date, education will only aggravate the question. The educated Negro will feel that there is no disgrace attached to physical features or to his previous condition; hence, he will more and more love and honor his race, and grow into a kind of pardonable clannishness, or racial pride, which is the mainspring of racial achievement. A blind man can foresee the result.

I may be excused for saying here that the conclusion reached a few months ago by Georgia's distinguished Governor, that Negroes should not be educated because, by reason of education, they grow more criminal and clamor more for association with white people, is not justified by the facts. I do not hesitate to affirm that nine-tenths of the Negro criminals are uneducated. The distinguished Governor will also find, upon investigation, that the more education the Negro gets, the farther he is removed from the desire for social intermixture with the white race. He will find also that marriages of whites with blacks, in States where there is no statutory provision against such marriages, are too few to prove anything but palpable exceptions to the general rule.

The educated Negro, as a rule, does not desire and does not seek any social admixture with the white race. And, strange as it may appear, this very fact will ultimately vex the problem. Social equality has no place in discussions of race problems. Social equality is a matter of individual preference. No race with pride wishes annihilation, whether by absorption or amalgamation. The body of the Negro race in this country desires continuation of racial identity. It resists intermixture. I grant, however, that there are some Negroes —a part of the Hon. Robert H. Porter's 1,132,000 "colored people"—who are trying to get away from the Negro race.

We are told that if the Negro will get property, the problem will be solved. One orator declares that when a Negro gets what the white man wants—when a Negro gets a mortgage on a white man's farm—no one will bother him about voting. Now all this is just what I fear—this *battle over the loaf*. A casual retrospect of history tells me that the hard point in Negro life in America will not be reached until the Negro has to struggle with his white brother over the loaf. So far, we have had only a few skirmishes; and our losses in former bread-earning positions are not yet fully compensated by the new positions demanded by our new conditions as free men. What will be the result with increasing population and competition and with fiercer conflict? Will the conflict come? "I do not believe it will," says one. "I have faith in the upward tendency of the spirit of universal brotherhood," says another. There were those who expressed similar sentiments thousands of years ago; and still the world has gone on in the same old, hard, cruel way in solving its race problems. It has never changed at a single period in its history. Dollars never solve problems. They are as powerless in this as armies and navies. Problems are born in the souls of men, and, if solved at all, must be solved there.

Religion, it is claimed, will settle all these vexing matters. What is the record of religion on this question? Has it ever settled them? Christianity, as interpreted by races struggling for ascendancy, has been on trial for nearly two thousand years. What is the record? Do not men accommodate their religion to their prejudices? I admit that Jesus Christ is the perfect moral idea. Russia proclaims His peace principles, while in practice she strengthens her army and prepares for war. The world has never invented, nor has it had revealed to it, a religion which, as interpreted by ambitious men, has ever settled any phase of a race problem.

It is urged that if the Negro will stay out of politics, the Race problem will be solved! Whether he stays out or not has no bearing upon its ultimate solution. Whether he affiliates with Republicans or Democrats or any other political party, will not solve it. Political silence may remove the question a little *in time*. Meanwhile the gentle zephyrs will change to tornadoes, and, aggravated by the schoolroom and the struggle for wealth, will return with more deadly results. I have voted with the Democracy of the South for twenty-two years; and if every other Negro in the country had done the same, we should still have the same Race problem. I have advised, and now practise, political silence; but I know that such a course will not settle the question. The Negro will not go out of politics as long as he has the privilege to vote. If he desired to do so, white men, for personal gain, would drag him in. The genius and spirit of our government, as well as the ambition of the Negro, give him zest for politics. The Negro has political ambition, and ought to have it. It is a credit to him. If he had no such ambition, I should have no faith in his capacity to grow and take on civilization. He must vote and take part in government, or become a worthless, dangerous incubus on society. The Negro, trained and educated by the white man, has the same ambition and aspirations as the white man; and nothing but the white man's overshadowing competition and power can prevent the Negro from attaining his highest ideals. Having this capacity and ambition, these high aspirations, and feeling proud of his race, he enters into competition. These noble characteristics, these manly virtues, themselves will hasten and intensify conflict and, as I see it, the Negro's destruction.

I have said that the solution of the problem does not rest with the Negro. He has fulfilled every condition of civilization. He is a fervent, long-suffering, forgiving Christian. He is every man's friend. Every man is welcome to his humble cabin and to the best he has in it. He is a non-striker, a jolly, docile laborer, a loyal, sober, industrious citizen,—and a brave soldier. He has added much to the material, moral, and intellectual South since the War, as the following epitome of facts shows:

He has reduced his illiteracy 45 per cent in thirty-five years. Negro children in the common schools number 1,500,000; Negro students in higher institutions, 40,000; Negro teachers, 30,000; Negro students learning trades, 20,000; Negro students pursuing classical courses, 1,200; Negro students pursuing scientific courses, 1,200; Negro students pursuing business courses, 1,000; Negro graduates, 17,000. There are 250,000 volumes in Negro libraries; 156 Negro higher institutions; 500 Negro doctors; 300 books written by Negroes; 250 Negro lawyers; 3 Negro banks; 3 Negro magazines; and 400 Negro newspapers. The value of Negro libraries is $500,000; of Negro school property, $12,000,000; of Negro church property, $37,000,000; of 130,000 Negro farms, $400,000,000; of 150,000 Negro homes, besides farms, $325,000,000; and of Negro personal property, $165,000,000. Since the War the Negro has raised for his own education $10,000,000.

The friends of the Negro should not be ashamed of this record; and if he has any enemies, they surely must admire the battle which he has fought and won for himself and for the South. If we turn on the light of the Eleventh Census we find that:

1. Negroes are more eager for education than whites. The whites enrolled 14 per cent of their population in 1870, and only 22 per cent in 1890; the Negroes, 3 per cent in 1870, and 19 per cent in 1890.

2. The whites have 9 criminals to every 10,000 of their population; the Negroes, 33 to every 10,000. But the whites have 100 to 1 in educational advantages, have the entire machinery of the courts in their hands, and 100 chances to 1 to evade the law and to escape punishment.

3. Whites and Negroes each have 8 paupers to 1,000 population; while the whites are 64 to 1 in wealth, and 100 to 1 in good paying positions.

4. The Negroes die twice as fast as the whites; but the whites have greater comforts, and many advantages as regards skilled medical attention.

5. The whites have .61 of 1 per cent divorces; Negroes, .67 of 1 per cent. The whites have 2,000 years' advantage in civilization.

6. In the whole country there are 25 Negroes to 75 whites who own their homes: the proportion should be 1 Negro to 6 whites.

7. Of the Negro homes, 87 per cent are freeholds; of the white homes, but 71 per cent.

8. Of farms owned by Negroes 89 per cent are unencumbered; of those owned by whites, but 71 per cent.

9. Forty-one per cent of Negroes are engaged in gainful pursuits; while only 36 per cent of whites are thus engaged.

10. Government reports show that the Negro is the best soldier in the regular army.

But why present this evidence of Negro fitness for civilization? Why dig up the Census comparisons, to the disparagement of the white man? These things have no salutary influence upon the Race problem. They rather irritate the matter. They mean competition and combat, into which every differentiation of racial characteristics will be made to play a hurtful part.

The Negro should no longer deceive himself, nor suffer himself to be deceived, about Northern sympathy. Judge Tourgée, a few years ago, declared that the white men in this country who favor absolute justice, complete civil rights, and fairness in all things for the Negro, would not reach ten thousand. The average Northern politician of to-day is no more like Sumner or Lincoln or Phillips or Garrison than the mummy of Rameses II is like the real old king himself. The whites prate about constitutional liberty and civil rights while they shut out the Negro from the best means of gaining a livelihood, even mob him, and the President himself says that he cannot prevent white men from whipping Negroes from offices, destroying their property, and driving them from communities. Why continue this hypocritical farce of Dr. Jekyll and Mr. Hyde?

The Negro must just take his chances. That is all. When the old, gray-haired veterans who followed Gen. Lee's tattered banners to Appomattox shall have passed away, the Negro's best friends will have gone; for the Negro got more out of slavery than they did. "Now there arose up a new king over Egypt, which knew not Joseph."

Let the Negro lay aside his delusions and dreams, and recognize the terrible, stern reality of the situation. Whether North, South, East, or West be his ambition, his aspirations are chained to a stake, are circumscribed by Anglo-Saxon prejudice and might: his movements are circular. If he leap upward, it is only as the tide in its frantic and futile endeavor to reach the moon. If education, wealth, religion, cannot solve the question, then what can? There is no solution except (1) in complete surrender of racial pride and ambition; (2) in absorption by the very worst element of whites; or (3) in voluntary or involuntary deportation. I do not deny that there are and will be individual exceptions; but I am speaking of races, not individuals.

We have the rise and decay of nations pointed out; and we are told to stand still and wait upon the salvation of the Lord. Yesterday I heard the sound of martial strains. I looked, and saw the proud "Mistress of the world" in holiday attire celebrating the triumphant return of a Cæsar, leading three hundred kings among his captives. This morning I heard a requiem. I looked. The conquering Cæsar had turned to clay, the once invincible legions were rotting and their bones bleaching upon a thousand battle-fields. Rome had her toes turned toward the blue skies; and the barbarian was beating his tom-tom and dancing upon her lifeless bosom. Still race problems remain. The facts in our case to-day are steadfast.

This is a hard view. I know that there are thousands of kind souls—good-feeling, God-fearing white men and women in the North—who will throw up their hands in horror at these statements. But the facts remain the same. I know that there are thousands of noble and generous white men and women in the South who will be thrown into hysterical recitations of the virtues of countless "black mammas" and "Uncle Jims." But the facts are still stubborn. I know that fifty thousand Negro professors and ministers are on their feet at this minute, hurling anathemas of excommunication from the race,—aye, condemning to eternal exile "any person who has so little faith in the ultimate triumph of Christian tendencies toward the unification of all races on the American continent designed by God for the purpose." But, like *Banquo's* ghost, the facts will not down.

The Negro, I say again, may just as well understand, as President McKinley has said, that he is "not to attempt the unattainable," or he will be broken, shattered, destroyed, in proportion to the intensity of his attempt at President McKinley's "unattainable." Let him, without thought of solving this problem, go right on, educating himself in all the essential principles of the highest Christian civilization that he can get hold of, making of himself a polite, law-abiding, peaceful, industrious, dignified man, full of honor and integrity, *in his own sphere*, and he will have fulfilled what seems to be the highest law of being; and in God's eyes no race can climb higher. That people who have thrown into the world the best thoughts of divine truth,—the Jews,—have had their problem for forty or more centuries. They have suffered most, but have helped the world most. As freemen, they taught spiritual truth and right-doing as no other people have done. As slaves, they built the enigmatical pyramids and weird sphynx, constructed the wonderful walls and hanging gardens, and the gigantic coliseum. While they are not supreme in any nation, they are a power in all, and maintain their identity, personality, and integrity everywhere.

So far as the solution of the Race problem on American soil is concerned, I have presented, above, a very pessimistic view —as some people count pessimism. Yet to me, it is an iridescent picture. No sick man is likely to call in a physician until he feels the need of such assistance. Until he feels such need, he is in real danger; but the moment he recognizes his true condition, his danger is lessened.

Senator Morgan's ideas about repatriation, cruel and hard as they appear, seem to me to point to a glorious destiny for the Negro. Anglo-Saxon prejudice is but the voice of God calling to the Negro to arise, and go and make himself a people. Bishop Turner is looking through the telescope of prophecy, a hundred years ahead of us all, when he declares that he does not see any future for the Negro in America. I do not think, however, that there will be any wholesale emigration; for the present Negro is doubtless here to stay,—and it may be providential that he is. It requires a somewhat different Negro to settle and graft a new civilization in a foreign land. But the next few generations will see a Negro with views as far different from the views of the Negro leaders of to-day as day is different from night. There will be no statutory laws oppressing the Negro, no disposition by legal sanction to drive him from the country; *and yet he will go*. His own pride, the desire to redeem Africa from its darkness, and, last, the allurements of a thousand superior advantages for mental and material gain, to be attained through hardship and adversity, will be irresistible. He will no longer, as now, look for easy highways to success. This will check increase and, in a bloodless, natural way, solve the problem, which the pride and greed of the Anglo-Saxon race can never do.

The cultivation of the strongest, most manly traits of character by the present Negro will put into those future generations that which alone can make the desert blossom and the waste places rejoice, just as Luther, Zwingli, Melanchthon, and Calvin, one or two centuries in advance, moulded the manhood which conquered savage man and beast, and blessed the bleak shores of New England with a grand civilization.

THE DEADLY MANHUNT FOR ROBERT CHARLES

THE NEW ORLEANS DAILY PICAYUNE
To Protect the City;
End of a Desperado
July 28, 1900

TO PROTECT THE CITY.

THE cowardly mob, which had made itself infamous on Wednesday morning by attacking harmless negroes, women and old men, did not show its ugly head yesterday; but last night it appeared in the outlying district containing the Thomy Lafon Colored School, which was burned to the ground. This school was built by a wealthy colored man, who, at his death, left money for benefactions for both whites and negroes, and there was no sort of excuse for so wanton an outrage.

This evidence that the mob spirit is still alive will require that the Mayor shall continue to maintain at hand all the forces necessary for the preservation of the public peace. His admirable dispositions of the resources at command; his courage, promptness, firmness and decision under most trying circumstances, have proved to the people of this city that they have for their Chief Magistrate an able and distinguished man. The dangerous conditions could not have been better managed when it is considered that all preparations to meet the emergency had to be made after the emergency occurred.

Some short-sighted people hold to the notion that all the preparation that has been made was to protect the negroes. This is all wrong. It was to protect all the people and to maintain the safety of the city. A mob that will murder innocent negroes will murder whites. A mob that will plunder and destroy property under the pretense of hunting for negroes will rob and plunder for their own use whenever an opportunity occurs. A mob that will violate all the laws upon one pretense will violate them upon any other, and such a mob and the men who compose it are criminals, and need, for the public good, to be put down by the strong arm of the law.

END OF A DESPERADO.

YESTERDAY, until late in the afternoon, perfect order reigned in the city, when the quiet neighborhood of Clio and Saratoga streets was converted into a scene of the utmost excitement. It was caused by the discovery of Robert Charles, the negro murderer, in a house in that locality.

Many people supposed, after his escape from the house on Fourth street where he had slain Police Captain Day and Officer Lamb, on Wednesday morning, that the desperado had left the city. Those, however, who know that the best possible place to hide is in a great city, where sympathy and assistance could be secured, were confident that he was still secreted among the large negro population.

New Orleans has the largest negro population of any city in the world, or at least outside of Africa. Not less than 80,000 of people of that race are domiciled here, and they live, for the most part, in those quarters of the city where rents are lowest. The houses which they inhabit make up tangles and labyrinths of buildings jammed one against the others and reached by narrow alleys which usually have only one outlet. Into these places negro families and their lodgers are crowded, the settlement reminding one of an ant hill filled with dusky tenants when they are not absent on their own affairs. Once inside these peculiar precincts, a fugitive might lie long concealed, unless information of his whereabouts were secured.

It appears that such information of Charles' presence at Clio and Saratoga streets had come to the police, and yesterday afternoon Sergeant Porteous, with a squad, repaired to the place. They boldly entered the house, but before they even got a sight of the object of their search he opened on them, from a room upstairs, with his deadly fire, killing Sergeant Porteous and mortally wounding Corporal Lally, of the police force.

A crowd of people of both races and colors assembled, but there was no conflict between the races in the assemblage. All interest was centered on the desperate negro, who, from his fortress, which was approached only through devious passageways, delivered a terrible fusillade from his Winchester rifle and revolver. The scenes attending the exciting episode are fully described elsewhere, and it is only necessary here to remark that his stronghold was stormed and he was shot to death, but not until the negro had killed three men and wounded several others.

Robert Charles was the boldest, most desperate and dangerous negro ever known in Louisiana. He could read and write; but, so far from being possessed of any unusual intelligence, was only endowed with the qualities that go to make up a brutally, lustful and ferocious creature, desperate when brought to bay and fighting fiercely for his life. One of the most distinguishing features about him was his deadly shooting.

Charles was a fugitive from justice in Mississippi. He was morose, silent and savage in his manners, and appears to have had no friends. The people with whom he associated feared him, and they served him through fear only. It is a mistaken idea to suppose he was the victim of a mob in the sense that characterized the mob proceedings of Wednesday morning. His death was the central point in a tragedy that had brought together a great crowd of people to assist the police in the capture of the most noted criminal known in this city for a long time, and he was killed while he was resisting the laws which he had violated in every possible way and through a long course of crime and depravity.

The death of so ferocious and desperate a criminal is most beneficial and fortunate for the people of this city. No one man has ever before so profoundly aroused the rage and indignation of its citizens. He had forfeited his life by his numerous bloody crimes, and justice cried aloud for his life. It has been taken, and that fact will do more than all else to satisfy the people and quiet the popular indignation.

There is no doubt that Charles is the man who was slain in the Clio street building. His personal identity has been fully established, and corroboration is found in his terrible marksmanship. There is not another negro in the State who can perform such acts under like circumstances.

PRAISING ROBERT CHARLES:
"BOLD AND DEFIANT TO THE LAST"

THE RICHMOND PLANET
The Butchery at New Orleans;
With a Rifle in His Hand

August 4, 1900

THE BUTCHERY AT NEW ORLEANS.

THE action of the mob at New Orleans last week may well cause apprehension throughout the entire country, showing as it does the evident disposition of the people to disregard the law upon the slightest pretext.

Because ROBERT CHARLES, who is alleged to be a desperate character saw fit to shoot an officer, who attempted to arrest him without a warrant, and when he had committed no crime, the entire populace seems to have been aroused.

A mob was formed and indiscriminate shooting commenced. Colored people, who were peaceable and law-abiding were hunted and shot down in cold blood. It was a dark day in New Orleans.

To make a bad matter worse, the police authorities encouraged the murderous elements and afforded no protection to the innocent, but hunted blacks.

Two colored men were killed and four more beaten nearly to death. Throughout the day, Thursday, July 26th, the mob roamed at will and colored men and women were shot down. Business was practically suspended. In one night, one colored man was beaten to death and six so badly injured that they are not expected to live.

Scores of other persons were wounded. Only when the business interests found that it was paralyzing trade was the militia ordered out. Then the violence was deplored and the Mayor made efforts to check the outlawry.

Children were not even spared and in this great populous southern city hundreds of colored people are suffering as a result of these terrible conditions. Our situation in the

South-land is peculiar. In the midst of the white men, who are friendly toward us, we find thousands of others who are as ferocious as wild beasts.

It is unfortunate indeed that we must submit, and accept our surroundings, but we can do it if we try. Our progress has been phenomenal and it has only tended to increase the hatred of the lower elements against us.

They dislike to see colored families in good circumstances, and every species of misrepresentation are resorted to. Our plan is to accumulate money, if only a penny at a time, buy property, educate our children, improve our condition by being tidy and clean in appearance.

These critical conditions cannot last forever. They must give away in the face of progressive action. The lower strata of white men who oppose us will be forced to the wall, and our recognition by the better class of white men will surely follow.

Despite all of these outrages and butcheries, we are not as bad off as we were thirty years ago. The man who cannot see progress at the expense of blood is blind indeed.

It seems that the shedding of blood has preceded all great reformations and it may be that these sporadic outbreaks are indicators upon the dial plate of time of the final emancipation of the citizen of color.

When our people become financially independent and personally brave in defense of home, leaving it not to the lawless classes of our people to set the example as was done in the case of ROBERT CHARLES, then we may be content to announce the arrival of the race's millennium and the complete success of our people in all this land.

WITH A RIFLE IN HIS HAND.

ROBERT CHARLES, colored, charged with killing Captain DAY and Patrolman LAMB and badly wounding Officer MORA died game Friday, July 27th, in the city of New Orleans, La.

The city had been virtually turned over to an irresponsible mob and CHARLES knew what to expect if he was taken alive.

Single-handed and alone, but armed with a Winchester rifle, which he fired with deadly accuracy, he defied the entire police-force of the city, backed as it was by twenty thousand infuriated citizens.

It seems that upon learning that CHARLES was in a house on Clio Street, near Saratoga Street, the officers entered the side alley of the house. LALLY was shot in the abdomen and PORTEUS in the head. The other officers and the colored man, who betrayed CHARLES, ran as fast as their legs could carry them. ALFRED J. BLOOMFIELD, said to be a young boy was shot dead.

It was decided to smoke CHARLES out and the building was soon in flames. LECLERE, one of the leading confectioners of the city was fatally shot also ex-Policeman EVANS, JOHN BANVILLE, GEORGE H. LIONS, ANDY VAN KUREM, H. H. BALL and FRANK BERTURRE and J. W. BOFIL wounded.

With smoke and fire on every side yet grasping his trusty rifle he left the building, receiving as he did so a bullet in his breast. A moment later, he knew no more, dying in the midst of his enemies.

Soon thereafter, the mob exhibited its rage by firing into his body and certain fiendish members of it stamped his face into an unrecognizable mass of bleeding flesh.

Others wanted to burn the body. But ROBERT CHARLES had passed beyond the portals of human injury. His soul had returned to the God who gave it. His enemies could not do otherwise than admire his intrepid bravery. He lived like a colored man and died like a white one.

We do not know as to the merits or demerits of the charges against him. It is said that the officers, whom he is charged with killing attempted to arrest him when he had committed no crime.

Suffice it to say that he set an example which every colored man in the Southland should imitate. When we are assailed by lawless mobs, backed up by the officials, who are in league with them; we should imitate the white man to the extent of selling our lives as dearly as possible.

Death had no terrors for ROBERT CHARLES. Bold and defiant to the last he fought all comers, and only yielded up his life when his finger could no longer pull the trigger.

To have surrendered to the officers of the law would have been to place himself in the hands of a howling mob, who would no doubt have mutilated and burned him.

Colored men, we should be respectful to white people, observant of the law and industrious in our daily life; but greater than this, we should be manly and courageous. The world hates a coward and admires a champion.

Will the colored men of the United States understand this? Will they meet death fearlessly as they have done on the battlefields? If they will, respect will come to them in civil life, even as it has shone upon their banners during the days of war.

Live uprightly and die game. Oh, for a thousand ROBERT CHARLES throughout the Southland!

THE WHITE MAN'S UNION HOLDS A RALLY

THE NAVASOTA DAILY EXAMINER
Campaign Oratory
September 29, 1900

CAMPAIGN ORATORY.

A LARGE CROWD GREETS UNION CANDIDATES.

Appear a Bunch of Substantial,
Trustworthy and Even
Handsome Men.

A VERY LARGE CROWD of enthusiastic citizens assembled at the Columbia opera house last night mainly for the purpose of hearing some speeches announced to be delivered by citizens chosen by the White Man's Union association to stand for election to various offices of Grimes county. The gentlemen have now visited, or tried to visit, all parts of the county; and every place they have gone they have been received with marked attention and courtesy, both from political and personal stand points, and are greatly encouraged over prospects of success in November.

All candidates on the county ticket were present last night with the exception of Mr. Cross Baker, nominee for Sheriff. Capt. W. E. Barry was made master of ceremonies and first introduced Judge J. G. McDonald, candidate for county judge; he gave a plain, earnest and apparently convincing exposition of the county's business affairs during the present and other administrations; why some things were wrong and how they might be remedied.

Judge McDonald was followed by Henry Wilcox, Haynes Shannon, J. T. Presswood, Robert Oliphant, L. M. Bragg and W. S. Stampley. Each candidate in turn arose and disavowed claims to being possessor of oratorical powers; but each nevertheless acquitted themselves gracefully with words of thanks, timely, witty, and common sense remarks and observations —happily free from rash promises and no mixture of party politics. "Representer" J. M. Ackerman closed for the candidates and evened up with his preceding colleagues for their flings at him as the "big gun," "main guy," "band wagon," "orator," "figurer," etc. He kept the crowd under full head of enthusiasm generated by speeches of the evening, and added to it some. Among measures he favors going through the legislature are the Grubbs bill for establishment of Industrial school for girls, and a state reformatory for bad boys to be sent up by justices of the peace and in nowise treated as felons or convicts, to educate them rather than make life long criminals of them.

A. F. Brigance was then called upon, and came to taw with a red hot number; during the delivery of which he was continuously applauded—showing that he undoubtedly voiced the sentiments of his audience.

Next, the throng called for John M. King. He said he wasn't expecting to speak; but, just the same he kept the ball rolling, and rolling fast with brilliant flashes of his eloquence in presenting and eulogizing the Union, its principles, aims and purposes. He rounded off the evening's oratory in a fitting manner, indeed.

After the speaking several new members were added to the roll.

In concluding his remarks Mr. Bragg recited the following lines of his own original poetry.

> In all the annuals of legend and history,
>   Throughout continents, oceans and isles,
> There has never been a puzzling mystery,
>   Pervading the minds of the incredulous and wise,
>
> That the aggressive spirit of the Anglo-Saxon nation
>   Should meet with no power to thwart and correct,
> For history tells us that in all creation
>   There has never been a force sufficient to check.

That dominating spirit—that spirit of aggression,
    For wherever tested, in all known climes;
Was never found lacking, save in oppression,
    Nor do we expect it to weaken in Old Grimes!

From snow capped mountains of the far northern zone
    To the most southern tropical climes,
By power supreme the Anglo-Saxon is known—
    So shall this union be in grand Old Grimes.

That spirit of power implanted in the heart
    Dominates and rules the Anglo-Saxon race,
And we as integrate and recognized part,
    Must rule and dominate or give up our place.

Give up our place to an inferior race!
    It was never known thus in other climes,
Nor do we believe, from our present pace,
    Will it ever be done in grand Old Grimes.

Shall we rule our glorious commonwealth,
    Bequeathed to us by the fathers of old,
Or shall we turn it over to a party of pelf,
    And every mother's son of us hunt for his hole?

No! No! By the powers that be
    Will every one of us stand to his place,
And proclaim our heritage, forever free,
    From this notorious, vagabond race.

'Twas nature's laws that drew the lines
    Between the Anglo-Saxon and African races,
And we, the Anglo-Saxons of grand Old Grimes,
    Must force the African to keep his place.

A BLACK CONGRESSMAN'S VALEDICTORY ADDRESS

GEORGE H. WHITE
Speech in Congress in Defense of the Negro Race

January 29, 1901

SPEECH OF HON. GEORGE H. WHITE.

Mr. WHITE said:

Mr. CHAIRMAN: In the consideration of the bill now under debate the Committee on Agriculture has had a wide and very varied experience. We have had the farmers and their interests fully represented, and demand that the present seed list, giving to each Member and Delegate 9,000 packages, shall not be diminished, but rather increased. The beauties of their avocation have been elaborately portrayed. The increase of the agricultural industry has been shown beyond any possible doubt, and a little Department, but a few years ago controlled by a commissioner of agriculture, has now grown to wonderful proportion, and is now presided over by a Cabinet officer, Secretary of Agriculture, if you please, and a very good one he is. And with the present ratio of increase this Department is destined in a few years to be one of the largest, if not surpassing all other departments in the President's Cabinet. But this side of the question, with its heterogeneous interests and growth, is not without opposition.

We have been besought by the seed men from all parts of the country demanding that the appropriation for the free distribution of seed be once and forever hereafter dispensed with; that there can be no good reason assigned why the Government should continue to make appropriations for the free distribution of agricultural seeds, which are purchased, not from the first-class seed growers and sellers, but rather from a kind of junk or second or third rate establishments, whose headquarters can hardly be found by a search warrant, and stored away in some little 2 by 4 room up in the garret in our large cities—East, West, North, and South. This Government has no more right, so they say, to furnish these seeds for free distribution throughout the country, which purchasers could obtain at every crossroads store in each State, than it has the right to supply all persons desiring them ham and eggs, beefsteak and onions, hot rolls with biscuit and coffee, or any of the other necessities of life, either as food consumption or matters of home ornament or wearing apparel. But here we are, a custom once established soon becomes by common use a law, and it is exceedingly difficult to break away therefrom; hence the usual appropriation for the free distribution of seed will be found in this bill.

But the committee has been enlightened and greatly edified along other lines than that of distributing free agricultural seed. We have had scientists from every bureau and subordinate division in the Agricultural Department before us, each portraying the indispensability of his work and the absolute necessity for his department to be extended and the salaries of the heads of these bureaus and divisions respectively increased; that each in his peculiar sphere has spent a lifetime in becoming a specialist, and that he could get far more for his indispensable knowledge in the great colleges and universities of the land than "Uncle Sam" is paying him; but out of sheer charity for this Government and the fullness of patriotic hearts they continue to serve us, and beg that their salaries will be increased commensurate with their wisdom. There is no end to the demands for an increase in the laboring force, so far as numbers go, but not a word have we heard about the increase of the salary of men and women whose pay ranges between $25 and $75 per month, who, of necessity, must live upon the cheapest things of life, with the most humble surroundings, and doubtless after dinner each day the good wife and children of these humble homes must suck their thumbs as a kind of supplement to the poor meal their scanty earnings will afford.

But, Mr. Chairman, there are others on this committee and in this House who are far better prepared to enlighten the world with their eloquence as to what the agriculturists of this country need than your humble servant. I therefore resign to more competent minds the discussion of this bill. I shall consume the remainder of my time in reverting to measures and facts that have in them more weighty interests to me and mine than that of agriculture—matters of life and existence.

I want to enter a plea for the colored man, the colored woman, the colored boy, and the colored girl of this country. I would not thus digress from the question at issue and detain the House in a discussion of the interests of this particular people at this time but for the constant and the persistent efforts of certain gentlemen upon this floor to mold and rivet public sentiment against us as a people and to lose no opportunity to hold up the unfortunate few who commit crimes and depredations and lead lives of infamy and shame, as other races do, as fair specimens of representatives of the entire colored race. And at no time, perhaps, during the Fifty-sixth Congress were these charges and countercharges, containing, as they do, slanderous statements, more persistently magnified and pressed upon the attention of the nation than during the consideration of the recent reapportionment bill, which is now a law. As stated some days ago on this floor by me, I then sought diligently to obtain an opportunity to answer some of the statements made by gentlemen from different States, but the privilege was denied me; and I therefore must embrace this opportunity to say, out of season, perhaps, that which I was not permitted to say in season.

In the catalogue of members of Congress in this House perhaps none have been more persistent in their determination to bring the black man into disrepute and, with a labored effort, to show that he was unworthy of the right of citizenship than my colleague from North Carolina, Mr. KITCHIN. During the first session of this Congress, while the Constitutional amendment was pending in North Carolina, he labored long and hard to show that the white race was at all times and under all circumstances superior to the negro by inheritance if not otherwise, and the excuse for his party supporting that amendment, which has since been adopted, was that an illiterate negro was unfit to participate in making the laws of a sovereign State and the administration and execution of them; but an illiterate white man living by his side, with no more or perhaps not as much property, with no more exalted character, no higher thoughts of civilization, no more knowledge of the handicraft of government, had by birth, because he was white, inherited some peculiar qualification, clear, I presume, only in the mind of the gentleman who endeavored to impress it upon others, that entitled him to vote, though he knew nothing whatever of letters. It is true, in my opinion, that men brood over things at times which they would have exist until they fool themselves and actually, sometimes honestly, believe that such things do exist.

I would like to call the gentleman's attention to the fact that the Constitution of the United States forbids the granting of any title of nobility to any citizen thereof, and while it does not in letters forbid the inheritance of this superior caste, I believe in the fertile imagination of the gentleman promulgating it, his position is at least in conflict with the spirit of that organic law of the land. He insists and, I believe, has introduced a resolution in this House for the repeal of the fifteenth amendment to the Constitution. As an excuse for his peculiar notions about the exercise of the right of franchise by citizens of the United States of different nationality, perhaps it would not be amiss to call the attention of this House to a few facts and figures surrounding his birth and rearing. To begin with, he was born in one of the counties in my district, Halifax, a rather significant name.

I might state as a further general fact that the Democrats of North Carolina got possession of the State and local government since my last election in 1898, and that I bid adieu to these historic walls on the 4th day of next March, and that the brother of Mr. KITCHIN will succeed me. Comment is unnecessary. In the town where this young gentleman was born, at the general election last August for the adoption of the constitutional amendment, and the general election for State and county officers, Scotland Neck had a registered white vote of 395, most of whom of course were Democrats, and a registered colored vote of 534, virtually if not all of whom were Republicans, and so voted. When the count was announced, however, there were 831 Democrats to 75 Republicans; but in the town of Halifax, same county, the result was much more pronounced.

In that town the registered Republican vote was 345, and the total registered vote of the township was 539, but when the count was announced it stood 990 Democrats to 41

Republicans, or 492 more Democratic votes counted than were registered votes in the township. Comment here is unnecessary, nor do I think it necessary for anyone to wonder at the peculiar notion my colleague has with reference to the manner of voting and the method of counting those votes, nor is it to be a wonder that he is a member of this Congress, having been brought up and educated in such wonderful notions of dealing out fair-handed justice to his fellow-man.

It would be unfair, however, for me to leave the inference upon the minds of those who hear me that all of the white people of the State of North Carolina hold views with Mr. KITCHIN and think as he does. Thank God there are many noble exceptions to the example he sets, that, too, in the Democratic party; men who have never been afraid that one uneducated, poor, depressed negro could put to flight and chase into degradation two educated, wealthy, thrifty white men. There never has been, nor ever will be, any negro domination in that State, and no one knows it any better than the Democratic party. It is a convenient howl, however, often resorted to in order to consummate a diabolical purpose by scaring the weak and gullible whites into support of measures and men suitable to the demagogue and the ambitious office seeker, whose crave for office overshadows and puts to flight all other considerations, fair or unfair.

As I stated on a former occasion, this young statesman has ample time to learn better and more useful knowledge than he has exhibited in many of his speeches upon this floor, and I again plead for him the statute of youth for the wild and spasmodic notions which he has endeavored to rivet upon his colleagues and this country. But I regret that Mr. KITCHIN is not alone upon this floor in these peculiar notions advanced. I quote from another young member of Congress, hailing from the State of Alabama [Mr. UNDERWOOD]:

> Mr. Speaker, in five minutes the issues involved in this case can not be discussed. I was in hopes that this question would not come up at this session of Congress. When the fourteenth amendment was originally adopted it was the intention of the legislative body that enacted it and of the people who ratified it to force the Southern people to give the elective franchise to the negro. That was the real purpose of the fourteenth

amendment. It failed in that purpose. The fifteenth amendment was adopted for the same purpose. That was successful for the time being. It has proved a lamentable mistake, not only to the people of the South, but to the people of the North; not only to the Democratic party, but to the Republican party.

The time has now come when the bitterness of civil strife has passed. The people of the South, with fairness and justice to themselves and fairness to that race that has been forced among them—the negro race—are attempting to work away from those conditions; not to oppress or to put their foot on the neck of the negro race, but to protect their homes and their property against misgovernment and at the same time give this inferior race a chance to grow up and acquire their civilization. When you bring this resolution before this House and thrust it as a firebrand into the legislation here, you do more injury to the negro race of the South than any man has done since the fifteenth amendment was originally enacted. I tell you, sirs, there is but one way to solve this problem. You gentlemen of the North, who do not live among them and do not know the conditions, can not solve it.

We of the South are trying, as God is our judge, to solve it fairly to both races. It can not be done in a day or a week; and I appeal to you, if you are in favor of the upbuilding of the negro race, if you are in favor of honest governments in the Southern States, if you are willing to let us protect our homes and our property—yes, and the investments that you have brought there among us—then I say to you, let us send this resolution to a committee where it may die and never be heard of again. When we have done that, when we have worked out the problem and put it upon a fair basis, then if we are getting more representation than we are entitled to, five or six or ten years from now come to us with the proposition fairly to repeal both the fourteenth and fifteenth amendments and substitute in their place a constitutional amendment that will put representation on a basis that we can all agree is fair and equitable. Do not let us drive it along party lines.

It is an undisputed fact that the negro vote in the State of Alabama, as well as most of the other Southern States, have been effectively suppressed, either one way or the other—in some instances by constitutional amendment and State legislation, in others by cold-blooded fraud and intimidation, but whatever the method pursued, it is not denied, but frankly admitted in the speeches in this House, that the black vote has been eliminated to a large extent. Then, when some of us insist that the plain letter of the Constitution of the United States, which all of us have sworn to support, should be carried out, as expressed in the second section of the fourteenth amendment thereof, to wit:

> Representatives shall be apportioned among the several States according to their respective numbers, counting the whole number of persons in each State, excluding Indians not taxed. But when the right to vote at any election for the choice of electors for President and Vice-President of the United States, Representatives in Congress, the executive and judicial officers of a State, or the members of a legislature thereof, is denied to any of the male inhabitants of such State, being twenty-one years of age, and citizens of the United States, or in any way abridged, except for participation in rebellion, or other crime, the basis of representation therein shall be reduced in proportion which the number of such male citizens shall bear to the whole number of male citizens twenty-one years of age in such State.

That section makes the duty of every member of Congress plain, and yet the gentleman from Alabama Mr. UNDERWOOD says that the attempt to enforce this section of the organic law is the throwing down of firebrands, and notifies the world that this attempt to execute the highest law of the land will be retaliated by the South, and the inference is that the negro will be even more severely punished than the horrors through which he has already come.

Let me make it plain: The divine law, as well as most of the State laws, says, in substance: "He that sheddeth man's blood, by man shall his blood be shed." A highwayman commits murder, and when the officers of the law undertake to arrest, try, and punish him commensurate with the enormity of his crime, he straightens himself up to his full height and defiantly says to them: "Let me alone; I will not be arrested, I will not be tried, I'll have none of the execution of your laws, and in the event you attempt to execute your laws upon me, I will see to it that many more men, women, or children are murdered."

Here's the plain letter of the Constitution, the plain, simple, sworn duty of every member of Congress; yet these gentlemen from the South say "Yes, we have violated your Constitution of the nation; we regarded it as a local necessity; and now, if you undertake to punish us as the Constitution prescribes, we will see to it that our former deeds of disloyalty to that instrument, our former acts of disfranchisement and opposition to the highest law of the land will be repeated many fold."

Not content with all that has been done to the black man, not because of any deeds that he has done, Mr. UNDERWOOD advances the startling information that these people have been thrust upon the whites of the South, forgetting, perhaps, the horrors of the slave trade, the unspeakable horrors of the transit from the shores of Africa by means of the middle passage to the American clime; the enforced bondage of the blacks and their descendants for two and a half centuries in the United States, now, for the first time perhaps in the history of our lives, the information comes that these poor, helpless, and in the main inoffensive people were thrust upon our Southern brethren.

Individually, and so far as my race is concerned, I care but little about the reduction of Southern representation, except in so far as it becomes my duty to aid in the proper execution of all the laws of the land in whatever sphere in which I may be placed. Such reduction in representation, it is true, would make more secure the installment of the great Republican party in power for many years to come in all of its branches, and at the same time enable that great party to be able to dispense with the further support of the loyal negro vote; and I might here parenthetically state that there are some members of the Republican party to-day—"lily whites," if you please—who, after receiving the unalloyed support of the negro vote for over thirty years, now feel that they have grown a little too good for association with him politically, and are disposed to dump him overboard. I am glad to observe, however, that this class constitutes a very small percentage of those to whom we have always looked for friendship and protection.

I wish to quote from another Southern gentleman, not so young as my other friends, and who always commands attention in this House by his wit and humor, even though his speeches may not be edifying and instructive. I refer to Mr.

OTEY, of Virginia, and quote from him in a recent speech on this floor, as follows:

> Justice is merely relative. It can exist between equals. It can exist among homogeneous people. Among equals—among heterogeneous people—it never has and, in the very nature of things, it never will obtain. It can exist among lions, but between lions and lambs, never. If justice were absolute, lions must of necessity perish. Open his ponderous jaws and find the strong teeth which God has made expressly to chew lamb's flesh! When the Society for the Prevention of Cruelty to Animals shall overcome this difficulty, men may hope to settle the race question along sentimental lines, not sooner.
>
> These thoughts on the negro are from the pen, in the main, of one who has studied the negro question, and it was after I heard the gentleman from North Carolina, and after the introduction of the Crumpacker bill, that they occurred to me peculiarly appropriate.

I am wholly at sea as to just what Mr. OTEY had in view in advancing the thoughts contained in the above quotation, unless he wishes to extend the simile and apply the lion as a white man and the negro as a lamb. In that case we will gladly accept the comparison, for of all animals known in God's creation the lamb is the most inoffensive, and has been in all ages held up as a badge of innocence. But what will my good friend of Virginia do with the Bible, for God says that He created all men of one flesh and blood? Again, we insist on having one race—the lion clothed with great strength, vicious, and with destructive propensities, while the other is weak, good natured, inoffensive, and useful—what will he do with all the heterogeneous intermediate animals, ranging all the way from the pure lion to the pure lamb, found on the plantations of every Southern State in the Union?

I regard his borrowed thoughts, as he admits they are, as very inaptly applied. However, it has perhaps served the purpose for which he intended it—the attempt to show the inferiority of the one and the superiority of the other. I fear I am giving too much time in the consideration of these personal comments of members of Congress, but I trust I will be pardoned for making a passing reference to one more gentleman—Mr. WILSON of South Carolina—who, in the early part of this month, made a speech some parts of which did great credit to him, showing, as it did, capacity for collating, arranging, and advancing thoughts of others and of making a pretty strong argument out of a very poor case.

If he had stopped there, while not agreeing with him, many of us would have been forced to admit that he had done well. But his purpose was incomplete until he dragged in the reconstruction days and held up to scorn and ridicule the few ignorant, gullible, and perhaps purchasable negroes who served in the State legislature of South Carolina over thirty years ago. Not a word did he say about the unscrupulous white men, in the main bummers who followed in the wake of the Federal Army and settled themselves in the Southern States, and preyed upon the ignorant and unskilled minds of the colored people, looted the States of their wealth, brought into lowest disrepute the ignorant colored people, then hied away to their Northern homes for ease and comfort the balance of their lives, or joined the Democratic party to obtain social recognition, and have greatly aided in depressing and further degrading those whom they had used as easy tools to accomplish a diabolical purpose.

These few ignorant men who chanced at that time to hold office are given as a reason why the black man should not be permitted to participate in the affairs of the Government which he is forced to pay taxes to support. He insists that they, the Southern whites, are the black man's best friend, and that they are taking him by the hand and trying to lift him up; that they are educating him. For all that he and all Southern people have done in this regard, I wish in behalf of the colored people of the South to extend our thanks. We are not ungrateful to friends, but feel that our toil has made our friends able to contribute the stinty pittance which we have received at their hands.

I read in a Democratic paper a few days ago, the Washington Times, an extract taken from a South Carolina paper, which was intended to exhibit the eagerness with which the negro is grasping every opportunity for educating himself. The clipping showed that the money for each white child in the State ranged from three to five times as much per capita as was given to each colored child. This is helping us some, but not to the extent that one would infer from the gentleman's speech.

If the gentleman to whom I have referred will pardon me, I would like to advance the statement that the musty records of 1868, filed away in the archives of Southern capitols, as to what the negro was thirty-two years ago, is not a proper standard by which the negro living on the threshold of the twentieth century should be measured. Since that time we have reduced the illiteracy of the race at least 45 per cent. We have written and published near 500 books. We have nearly 300 newspapers, 3 of which are dailies. We have now in practice over 2,000 lawyers and a corresponding number of doctors. We have accumulated over $12,000,000 worth of school property and about $40,000,000 worth of church property. We have about 140,000 farms and homes, valued at in the neighborhood of $750,000,000, and personal property valued at about $170,000,000. We have raised about $11,000,000 for educational purposes, and the property per capita for every colored man, woman, and child in the United States is estimated at $75.

We are operating successfully several banks, commercial enterprises among our people in the Southland, including 1 silk mill and 1 cotton factory. We have 32,000 teachers in the schools of the country; we have built, with the aid of our friends, about 20,000 churches, and support 7 colleges, 17 academies, 50 high schools, 5 law schools, 5 medical schools, and 25 theological seminaries. We have over 600,000 acres of land in the South alone. The cotton produced, mainly by black labor, has increased from 4,669,770 bales in 1860 to 11,235,000 in 1899. All this we have done under the most adverse circumstances. We have done it in the face of lynching, burning at the stake, with the humiliation of "Jim Crow" cars, the disfranchisement of our male citizens, slander and degradation of our women, with the factories closed against us, no negro permitted to be conductor on the railway cars, whether run through the streets of our cities or across the prairies of our great country, no negro permitted to run as engineer on a locomotive, most of the mines closed against us. Labor unions—carpenters, painters, brick masons, machinists, hackmen, and those supplying nearly every conceivable avocation for livelihood have banded themselves together to better their condition, but, with few exceptions, the black face has been left out. The negroes are seldom employed in our mercantile stores. At this we do not wonder. Some day we hope to have them employed in our own stores. With all these odds against us, we are forging our way ahead, slowly, perhaps, but surely. You may tie us and then taunt us for a lack of bravery, but one day we will break the bonds. You may use our labor for two and a half centuries and then taunt us for our poverty, but let me remind you we will not always remain poor. You may withhold even the knowledge of how to read God's word and learn the way from earth to glory and then taunt us for our ignorance, but we would remind you that there is plenty of room at the top, and we are climbing.

After enforced debauchery, with the many kindred horrors incident to slavery, it comes with ill grace from the perpetrators of these deeds to hold up the shortcomings of some of our race to ridicule and scorn.

The new man, the slave who has grown out of the ashes of thirty-five years ago, is inducted into the political and social system, cast into the arena of manhood, where he constitutes a new element and becomes a competitor for all its emoluments. He is put upon trial to test his ability to be counted worthy of freedom, worthy of the elective franchise; and after thirty-five years of struggling against almost insurmountable odds, under conditions but little removed from slavery itself, he asks a fair and just judgment, not of those whose prejudice has endeavored to forestall, to frustrate his every forward movement, rather those who have lent a helping hand, that he might demonstrate the truth of 'the fatherhood of God and the brotherhood of man.'

Mr. Chairman, permit me to digress for a few moments for the purpose of calling the attention of the House to two bills which I regard as important, introduced by me in the early part of the first session of this Congress. The first was to give the United States control and entire jurisdiction over all cases of lynching and death by mob violence. During the last session of this Congress I took occasion to address myself in detail to this particular measure, but with all my efforts the bill still sweetly sleeps in the room of the committee to which it was referred. The necessity of legislation along this line is daily being demonstrated. The arena of the lyncher no longer is confined to Southern climes, but is stretching its hydra head over all parts of the Union.

> Sow the seed of a tarnished name—
> You sow the seed of eternal shame.

It is needless to ask what the harvest will be. You may dodge this question now; you may defer it to a more seasonable day; you may, as the gentleman from Maine, Mr. LITTLEFIELD, puts it—

> Waddle in and waddle out,
> Until the mind was left in doubt,
> Whether the snake that made the track
> Was going south or coming back.

This evil peculiar to America, yes, to the United States, must be met somehow, some day.

The other bill to which I wish to call attention is one introduced by me to appropriate $1,000,000 to reimburse depositors of the late Freedman's Savings and Trust Company.

A bill making appropriation for a similar purpose passed the Senate in the first session of the Fiftieth Congress. It was recommended by President Cleveland, and was urged by the Comptroller of the Currency, Mr. Trenholm, in 1886. I can not press home to your minds this matter more strongly than by reproducing the report of the Committee on Banking and Currency, made by Mr. Wilkins on the Senate bill above referred to, as follows:

> In March, 1865, the Freedman's Savings and Trust Company was incorporated by the Congress of the United States to meet the economic and commercial necessities of 7,000,000 of colored people recently emancipated.
>
> Its incorporators, 50 in number, were named in the act authorizing its erection, and embraced the names of leading philanthropic citizens of the United States, whose names, as was intended, commended the institution to those inexperienced, simple-minded people, who are to-day its principal creditors.
>
> The Freedman's Bank, as it is popularly called, was designed originally to perform for this trustful people the functions, as its name implies, of a savings bank, and none other than those hithertofore held in slavery or their descendants were to become its depositors.

Its purpose was (to quote the paragraph in the original law)—

> To receive on deposit such sums of money as may from time to time be offered therefor, by or in behalf of persons hitherto-fore held in slavery in the United States, or their descendants, and investing the same in the stocks, bonds, and Treasury notes, or other securities of the United States.

The distinction provided in the bill in favor of the payment of "such persons in whole or in part of African descent" rests upon the foregoing paragraph of the original law, and no persons other than those named have the right to make use of this institution in any manner; neither have they the right to acquire by any means any interest in its assets.

For four years after the organization of the Freedman's Savings and Trust Company the laws seemed to have been honestly observed by its officers and the provisions in its charter faithfully recognized. Congress itself, however, seems to have been derelict in its duty. One section of the original grant provided that the books of the institution were to be open at all times to inspection and examination of officers appointed by Congress to conduct the same, yet it does not appear that Congress ever appointed an officer for this purpose, nor has an examination of the character contemplated by Congress ever been made. The officers of the bank were to give bonds. There is nothing in the records to show that any bond was ever executed. Any proper examination would have developed this fact, and probably great loss would have been prevented thereby. In 1870 Congress changed or amended the charter without the knowledge or consent of those who had intrusted their savings to its custody.

This amendment embodied a radical change in the investment of these deposits by providing that instead of the safe, conservative, and prudent provision in the original charter "that two-thirds of all the deposits should be invested exclusively in Government securities," the dangerous privilege of allowing the irresponsible officers to loan one-half of its assets in bonds and mortgages and other securities, invest in and improve real estate without inspection, without examination, or responsibility on the part of its officers. The institution could only go on to a certain bankruptcy. In May, 1870, Congress amended the charter, and from that date began the speculative, dishonest transactions upon the part of those controlling the institution until resulting in ultimate suspension and failure, with consequent disastrous loss to this innocent and trustful people.

It is contended by your committee that there was a moral responsibility, at least, if not an equitable responsibility, assumed by the Government when Congress changed the original charter of the company as to the nature of its loans and investments, when it failed to have the consent of the depositors, because of which change most of its losses were incurred. This ought to be regarded a very strong argument in favor of this bill.

Then, again, Congress undertook the supervision of the trust and failed, so far as your committee can ascertain, to carry out their undertaking.

The attention of the House is directed to the following extract from the President's message to Congress in December, 1886:

> I desire to call the attention of the Congress to a plain duty which the Government owes to the depositors in the Freedman's Savings and Trust Company.
>
> This company was chartered by the Congress for the benefit of the most illiterate and humble of our people, and with the intention of encouraging in them industry and thrift. Most of its branches were presided over by officers holding the commissions and clothed in the uniform of the United States. These and other circumstances reasonably, I think, led these simple people to suppose that the invitation to deposit their hard-earned savings in this institution implied an undertaking on the part of their Government that their money should be safely kept for them.
>
> When this company failed it was liable in the sum of $2,939,925.22 to 61,131 depositors. Dividends amounting in the aggregate to 62 per cent have been declared, and the sum called for and paid of such dividends seems to be $1,648,181.72. This sum deducted from the entire amount of deposits leaves $1,291,744.50 still unpaid. Past experience has shown that quite a large part of this sum will not be called for. There are assets still on hand amounting to the estimated sum of $16,000.

I think the remaining 38 per cent of such of these deposits as have claimants should be paid by the Government, upon principles of equity and fairness.

The report of the commissioner, soon to be laid before Congress, will give more satisfactory details on the subject.

And also to extracts from the report to Congress of the commissioner having charge of the assets of the institution at the present time (the Comptroller of the Currency, Mr. Trenholm). See report for 1886 and emphasized in 1887:

> My predecessors have at various times urged upon Congress the justice of providing for the extinguishment of all outstanding claims of depositors, and, having had the opportunity to look into the matter, I most earnestly add my voice in invoking the attention of Congress to the importance of sustaining the honor of the Government by an immediate settlement of the claims of all depositors who can be identified.
>
> It seems plain that the honor of the Government became engaged in this undertaking when, in 1865, Congress, in the act of incorporation, held out to the lately emancipated slaves inducements to intrust their earnings to this institution by selecting as trustees the distinguished gentlemen whose names were incorporated in the charter, by requiring the deposits to be invested in securities of the United States, and by subjecting the books to Congressional examination.
>
> This last provision was especially significant, and bound Congress to provide for adequate examinations from time to time, since none of the 50 trustees lived in Washington and only 9 constituted a quorum.
>
> Under the sanction of the Government and in the name of the philanthropists, statesmen, and financiers thus united in a laudable purpose to secure the safe and profitable investment of the pay and bounty money of the colored troops, and of the savings of other classes among the newly emancipated negroes, Army officers on duty in the South and the officials and agents of the Freedman's Bureau were induced to urge the freedmen to bring their savings to be taken care of by their friends and protectors.
>
> Anson M. Sperry, in his examination before the Senate investigating committee, testified that he was employed in September, 1865, as general field agent to operate in the Twenty-fifth Army Corps; that he was commended by the Secretary of War

to the commanders of the colored troops, and received from General Brice authority to be present at the pay tables in order there to persuade the men as they were paid off to confide their money to the safe-keeping of this institution. Similar efforts were no doubt made everywhere.

The company had previously been promised the deposits already accumulated in the savings banks established at Norfolk by General Butler, and at Beaufort, S. C. by General Saxton, so that these officers must be presumed to have accepted it as a safe depositary.

The pass books issued to depositors in the Freedman's Savings and Trust Company bore on the covers likenesses of President Lincoln and of Generals Grant and Howard, and others whom the freedmen had learned to reverence as special benefactors of their race; the flag of the Union was depicted as sheltering and binding together the persons thus portrayed, while the remaining space was occupied with other pictorial devices adapted to the comprehension of those whose savings were sought after, and manifestly designed to assure them that the Government sanctioned the enterprise and would protect their interests.

The following citations are taken from a little pamphlet which appears to have been given to depositors and otherwise widely circulated at the South:

"I consider the Freedman's Savings and Trust Company to be greatly needed by the colored people, and have welcomed it as an auxiliary to the Freedman's Bureau." (Maj. Gen. O. O. Howard.)

"The whole institution is under the charter of Congress, and received the commendation and countenance of the President, Abraham Lincoln. One of the last official acts of his valued life was the signing of the bill which gave legal existence of this bank."

"Principal office, Washington, D. C., opposite the Treasury of the United States."

"This savings bank is established by act of Congress, approved March 3, 1865, by Abraham Lincoln.

"It is under the direction of a board of 50 trustees, who serve without pay. The branch offices are also under the supervision of local committees, chosen from the best men in the vicinity of each branch.

"The bank can not loan its deposits nor use them in any way, except to invest them, according to the act of Congress, in the bonds of the United States and in real-estate securities worth double the amount so invested.

"The profits of the bank are all returned to the depositors as interest, necessary expenses alone excepted. The income from deposits not called for goes to the 'educational fund' for the sole use of the freedmen and their descendants.

"The bank is obliged to keep its books open at all times to the inspection of such committees as Congress may from time to time appoint."

Everything done had the inevitable effect of impressing upon those whose savings were solicited the assurance that the Government of the United States had undertaken to secure their safe-keeping, and unless the good faith of the original promoters of the bank is doubted this was probably distinctly stated over and over again.

While there may have been some unprincipled persons engaged in the enterprise, it would be unjust to question the good faith of the many disinterested benefactors of the freedmen, such, for example, as Frederick Douglass, Charles Sumner, and others who were among its promoters, and therefore they must be presumed to have depended upon the terms of the charter and the character of the trustees to justify the earnestness and the energy which they threw into their efforts to gather in deposits.

Your committee report the bill back to the House with an amendment, and recommend the passage of the same.

May I hope that the Committee on Banking and Currency who has charge of this measure will yet see its way clear to do tardy justice, long deferred, to this much wronged and unsuspecting people. If individual sections of the country, individual political parties can afford to commit deeds of wrong against us, certainly a great nation like ours will see to it that a people so loyal to its flag as the black man has shown himself in every war from the birth of the Union to this day, will not permit this obligation to go longer uncanceled.

Now, Mr. Chairman, before concluding my remarks I want to submit a brief recipe for the solution of the so-called American negro problem. He asks no special favors, but simply demands that he be given the same chance for existence, for earning a livelihood, for raising himself in the scales of manhood and womanhood that are accorded to kindred nationalities. Treat him as a man; go into his home and learn of his social conditions; learn of his cares, his troubles, and his hopes for the future; gain his confidence; open the doors of industry to him; let the word "negro," "colored," and "black" be stricken from all the organizations enumerated in the federation of labor.

Help him to overcome his weaknesses, punish the crime-committing class by the courts of the land, measure the standard of the race by its best material, cease to mold prejudicial and unjust public sentiment against him, and my word for it, he will learn to support, hold up the hands of, and join in with that political party, that institution, whether secular or religious, in every community where he lives, which is destined to do the greatest good for the greatest number. Obliterate race hatred, party prejudice, and help us to achieve nobler ends, greater results, and become more satisfactory citizens to our brother in white.

This, Mr. Chairman, is perhaps the negroes' temporary farewell to the American Congress; but let me say, Phœnix-like he will rise up some day and come again. These parting words are in behalf of an outraged, heart-broken, bruised, and bleeding, but God-fearing people, faithful, industrious, loyal people—rising people, full of potential force.

Mr. Chairman, in the trial of Lord Bacon, when the court disturbed the counsel for the defendant, Sir Walter Raleigh raised himself up to his full height and, addressing the court, said:

> Sir, I am pleading for the life of a human being.

The only apology that I have to make for the earnestness with which I have spoken is that I am pleading for the life, the liberty, the future happiness, and manhood suffrage for one-eighth of the entire population of the United States. [Loud applause.]

"WHY ARE WE FORGOTTEN?"

THE INDEPENDENT
The Negro Problem: How It Appeals to a Southern Colored Woman
September 18, 1902

THE NEGRO PROBLEM

HOW IT APPEALS TO A SOUTHERN COLORED WOMAN

[This article and the one that follows are remarkable as being extraordinarily frank expressions of the views held on this painful question by the women of both races in the South. We print them anonymously, because both writers feel that it might actually imperil their lives if their names were known.—EDITOR.]

I AM a colored woman, wife and mother. I have lived all my life in the South, and have often thought what a peculiar fact it is that the more ignorant the Southern whites are of us the more vehement they are in their denunciation of us. They boast that they have little intercourse with us, never see us in our homes, churches or places of amusement, but still they know us thoroughly.

They also admit that they know us in no capacity except as servants, yet they say we are at our best in that single capacity. What philosophers they are! The Southerners say we negroes are a happy, laughing set of people, with no thought of to-morrow. How mistaken they are! The educated, thinking negro is just the opposite. There is a feeling of unrest, insecurity, almost panic among the best class of negroes in the South. In our homes, in our churches, wherever two or three are gathered together, there is a discussion of what is best to do. Must we remain in the South or go elsewhere? Where can we go to feel that security which other people feel? Is it best to go in great numbers or only in several families? These and many other things are discussed over and over.

People who have security in their homes, whose children can go on the street unmolested, whose wives and daughters are treated as women, cannot, perhaps, sympathize with the Southern negro's anxieties and complaints. I ask forbearance of such people.

It is asserted that we are dying more rapidly than other people in the South. It is not remarkable when the houses built for sale or rent to colored people are usually placed in the lowest and most unhealthy spots. I know of houses occupied by poor negroes in which a respectable farmer would not keep his cattle. It is impossible for them to rent elsewhere. All Southern real estate agents have "white property" and "colored property." In one of the largest Southern cities there is a colored minister, a graduate of Harvard, whose wife is an educated, Christian woman, who lived for weeks in a tumble down rookery because he could neither rent nor buy a house in a respectable locality.

Many colored women who wash, iron, scrub, cook or sew all the week to help pay the rent for these miserable hovels and help fill the many small mouths, would deny themselves some of the necessaries of life if they could take their little children and teething babies on the cars to the parks of a Sunday afternoon and sit under the trees, enjoy the cool breezes and breathe God's pure air for only two or three hours; but this is denied them. Some of the parks have signs, "No negroes allowed on these grounds except as servants." Pitiful, pitiful customs and laws that make war on women and babes! There is no wonder that we die; the wonder is that we persist in living.

Fourteen years ago I had just married. My husband had saved sufficient money to buy a small home. On account of our limited means we went to the suburbs, on unpaved streets, to look for a home, only asking for a high, healthy locality. Some real estate agents were "sorry, but had nothing to suit," some had "just the thing," but we discovered on investigation that they had "just the thing" for an unhealthy pigsty; others had no "colored property." One agent said that he had what we wanted, but we should have to go to see the lot after dark, or walk by and give the place a casual look; for, he said, "all the white people in the neighborhood would be down on me." Finally we bought this lot. When the house was being built we went to see it. Consternation reigned. We had ruined this neighborhood of poor people; poor as we, poorer in manners at least. The people who lived next door received the sympathy of their friends. When we walked on the street (there were no sidewalks) we were embarrassed by the stare of many unfriendly eyes.

Two years passed before a single woman spoke to me, and only then because I helped one of them when a little sudden trouble came to her. Such was the reception I, a happy young woman, just married, received from people among whom I wanted to make a home. Fourteen years have now passed, four children have been born to us, and one has died in this same home, among these same neighbors. Altho the neighbors speak to us, and occasionally one will send a child to borrow the morning's paper or ask the loan of a pattern, not one woman has ever been inside of my house, not even at the times when a woman would doubly appreciate the slightest attention of a neighbor.

The next door neighbor expressed sorrow about two years ago because she heard we were going to sell our home; for, said she, "I know we shan't have another such quiet family of folks as you for neighbors."

Now these people are not mean people; they have many good traits. The man who lives in the second house from us is a deacon in one of the poorer churches of the city; they are all respectable working people, and altho the women go in the houses of negro women who wash or scrub for them, and laugh and talk, somehow my home is different. My experience is only unusual in that it is better than most of my friends.

I have had friends tell me they would like to exchange neighbors with me, for their children could then go to the gate without being called "nigger" by the boy or girl next door to them.

The Southerner boasts that he is our friend; he educates our children, he pays us for our work and is most noble and generous to us. Did not the negro by his labor for over three hundred years help to educate the white man's children? Is thirty equal to three hundred? Does a white man deserve praise for paying a black man for his work?

The Southerner also claims that the negro gets justice. Not long ago a negro man was cursed and struck in the face by an electric car conductor. The negro knocked the conductor down and altho it was clearly proven in a court of "justice" that the conductor was in the wrong the negro had to pay a fine of $10. The judge told him: "I fine you that much to teach you that you must respect white folks." The conductor was acquitted. "Most noble judge! A second Daniel!" This is the South's idea of justice.

A noble man, who has established rescue homes for fallen women all over the country, visited a Southern city. The women of the city were invited to meet him in one of the churches. The fallen women were especially invited and both good and bad went. They sat wherever they could find a seat, so long as their faces were white; but I, a respectable married woman, was asked to sit apart. A colored woman, however respectable, is lower than the white prostitute. The Southern white woman will declare that no negro women are virtuous, yet she places her innocent children in their care. Many times she goes on long visits of days and weeks and leaves her children with these women. No amount of discussion will alter a fact, and it is a fact that a very great number of negro women are depraved. It is also a fact that those who now condemn the negro's depravity most, helped (they or their parents) to bring about this same depravity. Christian men and women of the South sold wives away from their husbands and then compelled them to live with other men. Fathers sold their own children. Beautiful girls brought large sums to their owners when sold, especially for mistresses to the fathers and brothers of these same women who now marvel that the negro is not chaste. The negro woman's immorality shows more plainly than her white sister's because she is poor and ignorant.

A few years ago, within the memory of us all, a prominent white Senator was being tried for seducing a young white girl, and it was brought out at the trial that five hundred illegitimate white children were born in a particular infirmary in one city in one year. This would never have been known but for the accident of this trial. The negro girl is too poor to hide her shame. Since God created men and women there has been sin and it is confined to no particular race.

A colored minister visited one of the white "temples of God." He was told that he must sit in a chair back by the door. He appealed to the pastor of this "holy place," a man with whom he was personally acquainted, and was told by this brave pastor, "You know it is the custom for colored people to sit apart in our churches." The colored minister walked out. God gave him the power to walk "as well as pray." Bob Ingersoll could raise his voice in condemnation of our frequent horrors, but the Christian ministers of the South are dumb. They have many crimes to account for—these crimes of omission. They preach against the dance, the theaters and the social card party, but not one word do they utter when a poor black woman is butchered, a father shot down and his children and wife left destitute, for no other reason than that he was appointed postmaster. Ministers of God, Christian Endeavor Societies, Epworth Leagues, Young Men's Christian Associations, are all deaf and dumb, while every week a new horror is added to the already long list.

The Southerner says the negro must "keep in his place." That means the particular place the white man says is his. The Southern white man is an enigma; he is full of contradictions. Social equality is riding on railroad trains with us, sitting in a church with us, going to school in the same building with us. On the other hand there is no class of people who draw the line of social demarcation among people of his own color so sharply as the Southerner. He by no means considers all white men his social equals because he rides, sits or studies with them. One of the aristocratic mothers of the South would throw up her hands in horror if she should see her daughter walking arm in arm with a poor white carpenter's daughter. Another contradiction is: A self respecting colored man who does not cringe, but walks erect, supports his family, educates his children, and by example and precept teaches them that God made all men equal, is called a "dangerous nigger;" "he is too smart;" "he wants to be white and act like white people." Now, we are told that the negro has the worst traits of the whole human family and the Southern white man the best; but we must not profit by his example or we are regarded as "dangerous niggers."

White agents and other chance visitors who come into our homes ask questions that we must not dare ask their wives. They express surprise that our children have clean faces and that their hair is combed. You cannot insult a colored woman, you know.

Southern railway stations have three waiting rooms, and the very conspicuous signs tell the ignorant that this room is for "ladies," and this is for "gents" and that for the "colored" people. We are neither "ladies" nor "gents," but "colored."

There are aristocrats in crime, in poverty, and in misfortune in the South. The white criminal cannot think of eating or sleeping in the same part of the penitentiary with the negro criminal. The white pauper is just as exclusive; and altho the blind cannot see color, nor the insane care about it, they must be kept separate, at great extra expense. Lastly, the dead white man's bones must not be contaminated with the dead black man's. I know one of the "black mammies" that the Southerner speaks of, in tones low and soft, who is compelled to go to the authorities of a certain Southern city for a "pass" to visit the grave of a man she nursed at her breast and whose children she afterward reared. It does not matter that this old woman gave herself in slavery and out of slavery for this man and his children, she must have a "pass" to visit his grave.

Whenever a crime is committed in the South the policemen look for the negro in the case. A white man with face and hands blackened can commit any crime in the calendar. The first friendly stream soon washes away his guilt and he is ready to join in the hunt to lynch the "big, black burly brute." When a white man in the South does commit a crime, that is simply one white man gone wrong. If his crime is especially brutal he is a freak or temporarily insane. If one low, ignorant black wretch commits a crime, that is different. All of us must bear his guilt. A young white boy's badness is simply the overflowing of young animal spirits; the black boy's badness is badness, pure and simple.

Young colored boys, too small for other work, who need the work more than the white boys, are not allowed to sell newspapers on the streets in most of our Southern cities.

When we were shouting for Dewey, Sampson, Schley and Hobson, and were on tiptoe to touch the hem of their garments, we were delighted to know that some of our Spanish-American heroes were coming where we could get a glimpse of them. Had not black men helped in a small way to give them their honors? In the cities of the South, where these heroes went, the white school children were assembled, flags were waved, flowers strewn, speeches made, and "My Country, 'Tis of Thee, Sweet Land of Liberty," was sung. Our children, who need to be taught so much, were not assembled, their hands waved no flags, they threw no flowers, heard no thrilling speech, sang no song of their country. And this is the South's idea of justice. Is it surprising that feeling grows more bitter, when the white mother teaches her boy to hate my boy, not because he is mean, but because his skin is dark? I have seen very small white children hang their black dolls. It is not the child's fault, he is simply an apt pupil. No self-respecting negro fails to condemn the rapist; but all just men condemn a mob, and especially for killing a suspected thief or barn burner. A negro woman is killed because she had used "abusive language." Her provocation was great. Her brother had been almost killed by a mob because he had been suspected of taking a pocketbook that had been dropped in the public road. If one of New York's "Four Hundred" gives an especially unique ball in his palatial stable, it is telegraphed and cabled around the globe. Things past, present and future stir the people of the United States; but its own citizens are butchered and burned alive and only a very mild wave of ever-lessening indignation sweeps by. Governors are vehement and determined (for a day) to discover the identity of the mobs of unmasked "best citizens."

When I think of these things, I exclaim, Why are we forgotten? Why does not the mistreatment of thousands of the citizens of our country call forth a strong, influential champion? It seems to me that the very weakness of the negro should cause at least a few of our great men to come to the rescue. Is it because an espousal of our cause would make any white man unpopular, or do most of our great men think that we are all worthless? Are there greater things to do than to "champion the rights of human beings and to mitigate human suffering?"

The way seems dark, and the future almost hopeless, but let us not despair,

> "For right is right, since God is God,
> And right the day must win."

Some one will at last arise who will champion our cause and compel the world to see that we deserve justice, as other heroes compelled it to see that we deserved freedom.

ALABAMA.

ADVOCATING WHITE SUPREMACY

BENJAMIN R. TILLMAN
from *Speech in the Senate on the Race Problem*

February 24, 1903

We have had three race problems in the nation's history. By common consent, North and South, we have acted upon the policy that there were no good Indians except dead ones. We have pushed the red man backward, westward, ever, ever westward, until by the overpowering, thronging white population the red men have been practically destroyed and the small remnant of those great tribes which once owned this continent are now corralled upon their reservations, without hope and without liberty or "equality." A few thousand, mainly mixed blood, are being given in the Indian Territory some little recognition of the obligations of this Government in parceling among them in severalty the lands set apart for those who had been transported across the Mississippi. In a few years those lands will also be owned by the palefaces.

Next we had the Chinese coming in from the Pacific, swarming over to develop our mines and build our railroads. But as soon as the competition between the Celestials and the Americans became sharp a universal demand arose that the Chinese should be excluded, and notwithstanding the fact that they are superior in every respect to the negroes, they have been kept out.

The negro alone of the three races other than the white with which we have had to deal as a people has excited a sympathy born of sentiment and his condition of slavery and has produced a conflagration the recollection and the magnitude of which will be a memory to be regretted by this people during the balance of their history, and history has no record of so grand and great a struggle in all its annals.

What has this race question, this negro question, cost us as a people? Speaking in general language, I want to remind you that from the very best sources of information I can get the cost in men—brave, gallant, heroic, patriotic men, the very flower of our country on both sides—was a half million or more. In money and property the least estimate is five billion dollars. Of the blood and the tears and the misery, the horrors of civil strife, I shall make no mention. But when we recall the facts which I have just repeated to you as to what this race problem has already cost us, and shall dwell as I shall do later on upon the conditions now confronting us, I ask you to meet me upon the same plane of patriotism, of race pride, and of civilization, and not to fall into the dirty cesspool of partisan politics. Ignorance and fanaticism were responsible for the Civil War. Have we not statesmanship to avoid the more direful struggle which threatens?

Returning to the thread of my story, because I want to get all the evidence in, for I am going to try this case just as impartially as if I myself was before the bar of God, I want to read you an extract from a letter published by the President of the United States on the 27th of last November. It was written in answer to two letters which he had received from some gentlemen in Charleston discussing a Federal appointment. Mr. Roosevelt in this communication uses the following language:

> The great majority of my appointments in every State have been of white men. North and South alike it has been my sedulous endeavor to appoint only men of high character and good capacity, whether white or black. But it is and should be my consistent policy in every State, where their numbers warranted it, to recognize colored men of good repute and standing in making appointments to office. These appointments of colored men have in no State made more than a small proportion of the total number of appointments. I am unable to see how I can legitimately be asked to make an exception for South Carolina. In South Carolina, to the four most important positions in the State, I have appointed three men and continued in office a fourth, all of them white men—three of them originally Gold Democrats—two of them, as I am informed, the sons of Confederate soldiers. I have been informed by the citizens of Charleston whom I have met that those four men represent a high grade of public service.

I do not intend to appoint any unfit man to office. So far as I legitimately can I shall always endeavor to pay regard to the wishes and feelings of the people of each locality; but I can not consent to take the position that the door of hope—the door of opportunity—is to be shut upon any man, no matter how worthy, purely upon the grounds of race or color. Such an attitude would, according to my convictions, be fundamentally wrong. If, as you hold, the great bulk of the colored people are not yet fit in point of character and influence to hold such positions, it seems to me that it is worth while putting a premium upon the effort among them to achieve the character and standing which will fit them.

The question of "negro domination" does not enter into the matter at all. It might as well be asserted that when I was governor of New York I sought to bring about negro domination in that State because I appointed two colored men of good character and standing to responsible positions—one of them to a position paying a salary twice as large as that paid in the office now under consideration; one of them as a director of the Buffalo exposition. The question raised by you and Mr. —— in the statements to which I refer is simply whether it is to be declared that under no circumstances shall any man of color, no matter how upright and honest, no matter how good a citizen, no matter how fair in his dealings with all his fellows, be permitted to hold any office under our Government. I certainly can not assume such an attitude, and you must permit me to say that in my view it is an attitude no man should assume, whether he looks at it from the standpoint of the true interest of the white man of the South or of the colored man of the South—not to speak of any other section of the Union. It seems to me that it is a good thing from every standpoint to let the colored man know that if he shows in a marked degree the qualities of good citizenship—the qualities which in a white man we feel are entitled to reward—then he will not be cut off from all hope of similar reward.

Without any regard as to what my decision may be on the merits of this particular applicant for this particular place, I feel that I ought to let you know clearly my attitude on the far broader question raised by you and Mr. ——, an attitude from which I have not varied during my term of office.

I have read this letter, Mr. President, for the purpose of giving to you that broad and high view which the President maintains. I want to be entirely just and fair to him. I have no purpose by implication or indirection to attack his motives, but I want to show how superficial is the view, how little and small and infinitesimal is the knowledge behind such a view.

First opening up the evidence, I want to say here and now that the facts I can bring to bear are overwhelming which go to prove that the masses of the Northern people have no more use for the colored man at close quarters than we have. If you occupy this attitude by reason of caste, the fact that you have not been brought in contact with negroes and you know nothing about them, still, let that number be ever so small, wherever there are any of them this race prejudice or caste feeling exists.

I have here a letter which appeared in the Washington Post a few days ago from a South Carolinian, a colored man by the name of Samuel H. Blythewood, describing his treatment and the environment to which he is subjected in the city of Philadelphia.

> SIR: I am a colored man, a mechanic by trade. There is nothing in the line of a house in wood that I can not make. I can build all the stairs, windows, make the sashes, blinds, and doors. I can build a house from the ground up and turn the keys over to the owner completed. I can draw the plans, make the blue prints, make the specifications, and give estimates. Yet I am debarred from employment on account of my color. The prejudice in this city is strong against me, much stronger than in the place I came from. No one wants me because I am a colored man. Why is this? I am 37 years old. I drew the plans of the colored church on Tasker street, above Twentieth. My name is on the corner-stone. I built the State Colored College of Orangeburg, S. C., and I have built cottages in Orangeburg and for the mayor of Beaufort, S. C., but still I am debarred from employment in Philadelphia.
>
> SAMUEL H. BLYTHEWOOD.

I have here a copy of the Hartford Daily Courant of March 28, 1902. It relates the pitiful condition of a well-to-do colored man by the name of Edwards, who owned a home immediately adjoining a school. The school board wanted his land to enlarge the playground or something. They bought it, and then he tried to go somewhere and buy another home. Here, in brief, is his experience:

> MR. EDWARDS'S HOME—HAVING SOLD IT, HE HAS TROUBLE GETTING ANOTHER—HARD LUCK OF A RESPECTABLE COLORED MAN IN TRYING TO BUY OR RENT A HOME FOR HIS FAMILY.
>
> William B. Edwards is one of the best known colored men in Hartford, a modest, retiring man, intelligent and self-respecting. He is employed by the Hartford Fire Insurance Company as messenger and janitor, and is well known to nearly everyone in the city as the janitor of the Center Church. Just now he is looking for a home for himself and family, and has hard luck in buying or renting.
>
> Mr. Edwards is at present living at No. 44 Wadsworth street, where he has made his home for the past twenty years, but having sold the house to the South School district, whose property it adjoins, he has been asked by the district committee to vacate as soon as possible; and this he is trying to do, but without signal success. To begin with, Mr. Edwards does not think he has been used quite fairly by the district in the purchase of the house. It seems that some years ago Mr. Baker, then chairman of the district committee, approached him with the statement that the district would probably want his house some time. Nothing happened under Mr. Baker's administration in the way of getting the property, however, and not until Gen. H. C. Dwight was chairman did negotiations for the house begin. Mr. Edwards was asked what he considered his property worth, and after consultation with Gen. William H. Bulkeley as to the probability of the district's ever buying it, he fixed the figure at $6,500.
>
> Another property directly in the rear of Mr. Edwards's lot is owned by Alonzo Edwards, who is a white man. This lot faces on Hudson street, and adjoins the school property very much as Mr. Edwards's property does. Mr. Edwards says he considered that his property was worth more than the Alonzo Edwards property, as it has a frontage of 90 feet and a depth of 153 feet, while the Hudson street property has a frontage of only 60 feet. At a meeting of the district held two years ago General Dwight reported that the Edwardses, both the colored and the white Edwards, wanted exorbitant prices for their property, and that the district ought not to buy at the figures. The proposed purchase was dropped, and just before the June meeting of the district in 1901 Mr. Edwards was again approached, this time by

Mr. Hansling, of the committee, as to what he would sell his property for. This time Mr. Edwards referred the matter to ex-Governor Bulkeley, but there was no satisfactory action taken by the meeting.

Mr. Edwards says that late in the fall of 1901 a real estate agent approached him on the matter and worried him a great deal about it. Finally he went to General Dwight and said that he wished to sell directly to the district and not through an agent. He was asked his lowest figure and said it was $5,500. The reason the figure was placed so low was that he was nervous and worried and had family afflictions and he agreed to let it go. At the same time he expected that he would be used as well as his white namesake. A meeting of the district was called and it was voted to buy both lots. No papers had been passed before he ascertained, as he says, that the district was going to pay Alonzo Edwards $7,000 for the Hudson street lot. He was worked up over this and consulted friends, saying that he did not think the district was using him right, and suggesting that he withdraw from the bargain. His friends advised him to stick to it and the house was sold to the district at the figure named. The house, which Mr. Edwards had bought of the Connecticut Mutual Life Insurance Company twenty years ago, had passed from his hands. To his surprise he read in a few days that the Alonzo Edwards property had been bought by the district for $8,000. "Then I kicked," he says. But it was too late.

But this is but the beginning of the story. Mr. Edwards immediately set himself about getting another home. Consulting Fred M. Lincoln, real estate agent, he got track of a new house down on Adelaide street and made a bargain to buy it for $3,250, the trading being done by the agent. The sum of $250 was paid to bind the bargain, and when the deed was prepared Mr. Edwards inspected it, and the owner of the property, a Mr. Kerns, came into the office of Francis Chambers to sign the document. Mr. Edwards was not in evidence, and left the office, supposing that the matter was adjusted. In the evening of last Thursday, however, some one met him on the street and told him that Kerns would not sign because the proposed purchasers were colored. He went to Mr. Chambers's office at once and Mr. Kerns was there, and the conversation between Mr. Chambers and Mr. Kerns was something like this:

"Did you not agree to sell this property through Mr. Lincoln to any respectable person?"

"Yes."

"You did not tell the agent not to sell to a Chinaman?"

"No."

"Nor to a Japanese?"

"No."

"You didn't tell Mr. Lincoln to sell to a Yankee and to no one else?"

"No."

"You didn't tell him not to sell to a negro?"

"No; I told him to sell to a respectable person; that's all."

"Well," said Mr. Chambers, "I have known Mr. Edwards many years and he is as respectable as any man of my acquaintance."

Just then Mr. Edwards stepped inside the office and Mr. Kerns "scooted out," to use Mr. Edwards's language, and Edwards has not seen him since. Mr. Lincoln returned the bargain money of $250 to Mr. Edwards and that transaction was closed, unfortunately for Mr. Edwards.

Another phase of the story was yet to develop. Mr. Edwards saw an advertisement in one of the evening papers to the effect that three tenements were to rent at No. 35 Sumner street, with the further information "to colored people only. Large families no objection." He thought the name of the street sounded rather large, but he investigated and found it to be the house of A. Goodman. He said to Mr. Goodman that if he really meant to have colored people live in his house he would like to rent it, but cautioned him that it would be to the disadvantage of the property for him to do so, owing to the prejudice against color. Mr. Goodman replied that the neighbors had found fault with his children and insulted them, and that he was going to let them live beside colored people and see how they would like that. Mr. Edwards assured him that his family was respectable, and that the only difficulty was that their skin was black.

He thought the rent was secured, and was congratulating himself on getting it, when on Monday Mr. Goodman appeared in distress, saying that the bank was going to call in its loan on the property. Mr. Edwards said that under those conditions he would not take the rent. Mr. Goodman assured him that if he could arrange the matter the rent was still his. Mr. Edwards told him the mistake he made was in putting such an advertisement in the papers. It had set the neighbors wild, and they had made a move against him. He did not suppose there would have been any objection to his living there, but "colored families only with large families" was something the people would resent. There the matter rests, and Mr. Edwards is still hunting for a comfortable rent for a respectable family of color.

Next I have a copy of the Boston Globe of June 2, 1902. I will read the headlines and merely print and insert, with the permission of the Senate, two articles. The first is as follows:

FEELING IS VERY BITTER—HOWARD AND MARSHALL GET SCANT COURTESY—COLORED BOYS AT EXETER ARE TREATED BY STUDENTS WITH CONTUMELY—RESENTMENT SHOWN OVER THEIR WITHDRAWAL FROM THE ATHLETIC TEAM.
EXETER, N. H., *June 1, 1902.*

It is the general belief in town that if Howard and Marshall, the colored boys until recently in the squad, were good enough to represent the school at the meet they were good enough to eat at the training table, and their resentment of insults by leaving the team is generally commended.

In student circles, however, feeling against them is very bitter, and in the march of the school from the campus after the meet they were treated with contumely.

This was in direct variance with the Exeter spirit. Twice has a colored man been elected class-day orator, and colored men, notably Jones, the star tackle, Lawton, Syphax, and Marshall, now a Boston lawyer, have repeatedly represented Exeter on elevens, nines, and track teams, eating at training tables.

It is almost a certainty that Howard would have won the mile in yesterday's meet, and that Marshall would have taken third place in the shot put. He was a substitute on last fall's eleven and was given an "E," being the single man who did not play in the Andover game to gain the distinction.

An unintentional omission was made in yesterday's report of the meet. McGovern and Marshall, of Andover, who tied for second place in the high jump at 5 feet 7½ inches, should have been credited with breaking a dual meet record, 5 feet 6 inches, established in the 1900 meet by Connor, of Exeter, and Botchford, of Andover.

The same Boston paper contains the following:

WOMAN ATTACKED—PLUCKY GIRL ESCAPED FROM NEGRO—MISS MARY R. GREEN DEFENDED HERSELF BRAVELY—WAS IN HER UNCLE'S GROUNDS AT WORCESTER—BURLY RUFFIAN TRIED TO DO HER VIOLENCE—FLED, BUT WAS CAPTURED A FEW HOURS AFTERWARDS. WORCESTER, *June 1, 1902.*

Mary R. Green, 28 years old, a niece of Andrew H. Green, of New York, was attacked by a burly negro on the grounds of her uncle, Martin Green, of Green Hill farm, this afternoon, and escaped from his clutches only after a most terrible struggle.

The man was drunk at the time, and to his condition as well as to the plucky fight put up in defense is due the escape of the young woman. She fought her assailant for five minutes, and then, frightened by her calls for help, the negro fled to the woods. He was captured three hours later.

The news of the assault did not spread, and few knew of it outside of the police, to whom it was reported at once, but this evening, when the news was circulated, there was great excitement.

Miss Green is a daughter of the late Dr. Samuel F. Green, for many years a missionary to India. She lived with her uncle, Martin Green, on his summer estate. She went to the Sabbath school of the Central church and was returning soon after 1 o'clock when she was attacked.

Green Hill is situated on the east side of Lincoln street, in the north part of the city, and the Green estate embraces many acres. The entrance gate is at the end of Green lane, which extends from Lincoln street, and Miss Green had entered the grounds to walk up to the house.

She had not gone far when she saw the man walking down the avenue from the house, but she paid no attention to him, as it is not uncommon for strangers to stroll through the grounds.

She was about to pass him when he rushed upon her and violently threw her to the ground. The young woman struggled and called for help, but this seemed only to exasperate the miscreant, who tore her clothing and held her to the ground.

When he became alarmed he started to run and was soon lost in the woods, but it was known that he had gone toward Lake Quinsigamond, and in that direction pursuit was taken. The bicycle squad and all the day force of the police department were ordered to search for the negro.

Sergeant Hill and Patrolmen Power, Thayer, Jackson, Knight, and Streeter were sent through the woods in the vicinity. Power and Thayer got a clew which led them in the direction of Bloomingdale, and there, near the engine house, they came upon him. He submitted quietly to arrest.

He had the appearance of just getting over a spree. One of the officers says he denied having committed any assault, but admitted having met a woman somewhere and taking hold of her. Even this much he would not admit later, but maintained that he had not committed any assault.

Miss Green and her uncle called at the police station, and the young woman positively identified her assailant.

The prisoner gave his name as William Johnson, and said he was 40 years old. He said he was born in Maryland and later moved to Harrisburg, and from there came to this city last fall. He was a laborer, and said he worked for a contractor named Barnard, whose other name he could not give.

Johnson is known to a few people in that vicinity of Hanover street. He roomed in a house on that street, near Arch street, and his quarters were frequently the scene of carousals, so his neighbors say.

The condition of Miss Green is not alarming. It was feared at first that she would suffer from the shock, but her uncle thinks she will be able to appear against her assailant in court to-morrow morning.

These may be isolated cases; they may not reflect the general feeling and sentiment of the Northern people or conditions there; but there are every day facts coming out going to show my contention to be true that the more the Northern people find out about the negro the less use they have for him. To use the expression which I have used once before, they love him according to the square of the distance. He is, they think, an admirable voter in the South and in the border States, where his vote counts for so much. Under the Constitution he is entitled to all the rights and privileges of other citizens, and many millions of unthinking Americans are drifting along that road absolutely ignorant and oblivious of where it is going to lead.

I will not spend more time to prove that there is prejudice and caste feeling among the Northern people in regard to the negro. If anyone wants to dispute it, let him produce his evidence and then I will be ready with some more facts to back up my position.

Right here, I think it very well to remind Senators that in this District we have the most striking example of the calm, considerate judgment of the leaders of the Republican party that the negro's ballot is a menace to good government. We had in this District in 1867 an enactment which gave the citizens, white and black, some control over local affairs and the levying of taxes and their expenditure. After five years the experiment had proven so absolute a failure that Congress, to save itself or save the city of Washington, felt constrained to repeal the act, and to institute the form of government we now have, which is as autocratic as that of Russia or China, or any other absolute government.

Why was it right or necessary to take the ballot from the negro here, and to take along with it the ballot of the white man, and yet it is right and proper to continue the partisan cry that there must be a free vote and a fair count in the South, and that every negro man should cast his ballot and have it counted, without regard to intelligence, or character, or anything else?

I leave those who are ready to defend this policy now, if there be any left, to specify. We have reached a period in the evolution of this question in which Northern sentiment has come to concede and to acknowledge that there was a blunder and a crime, or a mistake bordering on crime, when the negroes were enfranchised in the manner they were.

We have seen Southern State after Southern State exercise every possible ingenuity under the fourteenth and fifteenth amendments to reduce the number of negro voters and to minimize the danger from that source, and without protest almost from the North. Therefore I feel that we are approaching a period when this sane and patriotic view will obtain throughout the country, when the best thought North and South will come together and consider what can be possibly done for this colored brother, this man in black, and at the same time not jeopardize and destroy the white people who live where the negroes are thickest.

I shall approach that subject from the view point of a man living in a State where there are 235,000 more negroes than there are white people, and some 40,000 more negroes of voting age than there are white people. There is one other State similarly situated—Mississippi, while throughout the South the proportion of negroes to whites varies. There are over a million negroes in Georgia, and a majority of white voters of 30,000 or 40,000, and so on throughout the long catalogue. The table which I have prepared and which I have inserted will facilitate the examination by any person interested in it.

Now, the most striking phrase in the President's letter, the one which appeals strongest to the sentiment of everybody North and South, is that he is unwilling to "shut the door of hope and of opportunity in the face of a worthy and competent colored man." On first blush there is not a man alive who is a man, who has any of the elements of breadth and depth and liberality and Christianity and humanity, who would not agree with that sentiment.

Did it ever occur to those of you whose feelings are enlisted in that contention that in opening the door of hope and opportunity to this colored man you might be shutting it in the face of his white brother? We in my State for eight long years lived with the door of hope closed on us and the lock fastened by bayonets, keyed together by a bayonet, while rapine and murder and misgovernment and anarchy and every other thing which ought not to have been ran riot, with a travesty on government, an abomination in the sight of God and man presiding over the destinies of the Palmetto State.

We had the door shut, and it seemed to have closed for all time. We pried it open by force because we had to pry it open or suffocate. Even now the sunshine which comes to us from God's blue sky has up there the shadow of a negro with a ballot in his hand. We have exercised, as I said, our ingenuity and all the ability as lawyers and statesmen which we could under the fourteenth and fifteenth amendments to minimize and reduce the evil and to push it away from us. But it remains.

As chairman of the committee on suffrage in the constitutional convention, which I had struggled for four years as governor to have called for the express purpose of dealing with this question; as a man born on a slave plantation where there were one hundred of them belonging to my family; with experience, some little insight into the horrors of the war, and with a full knowledge of what happened during the reconstruction era when the carpetbag vampires and their negro dupes were running riot in South Carolina, I approached it with all the solemnity of a man resolved by every possible scheme that we could devise to take the ballot from every negro alive, if that had been allowed. But we could not do it, because the fifteenth amendment barred the way.

The fifteenth amendment prohibits any discrimination on

account of race, color, or previous condition. Therefore we had the simple and only alternative to provide for an educational qualification, with an elastic provision which enabled the illiterate whites to be registered, because we were unwilling to take the ballot from those of our own blood, some of them the best men we have, who had lost the opportunity to get an education in their youth because they were fighting.

We found after we had completed our work that there were some 15,000 negroes who were then ready to register. I suppose that the number has increased since by education to 25,000, while the number of whites who were able to register is something like a hundred thousand. So that for the time we have a breathing spell. We are at ease for the moment. But the relief is only temporary.

Along with the instrument which deprived the negroes of the right to vote because they could not read and write we placed in the constitution a provision which levied a 3-mill tax for public schools, and so again there was no discrimination on account of race, color, or previous condition. Therefore, the history of education in South Carolina for the last twenty-five years before the new constitution and since has been that there are more negro children in our public schools than there are white.

While we have opened the door of hope for a while to the whites, and shallow thinkers are ready to suppose that a solution of the race problem in the South has been reached, every man who can look beyond his nose can see that with the negroes constantly going to school, the increasing number of people who can read and write among the colored race, with such preponderance of numbers as they have, will in time encroach upon and reach and overbalance our white men. And then what will happen? Will the door of hope be closed again on us by submitting to negro domination? Take it home and sleep on it, and then give me your answer.

Why can we not afford it? This brings a long train of witnesses to show the difference between the Caucasian and the colored race, and to demonstrate to the satisfaction of every student of ethnology and history that the Southern white men can not, without absolute destruction to their civilization, submit to it.

I will begin in Washington. This city has been the very hotbed, the hothouse, where the effort to elevate the African and educate him and humanize him and civilize him and Christianize him has had its best development, or, rather, the effort has had unlimited money and encouragement. It has been right here under the ægis of the American eagle, in sight of the Dome of the Capitol, and what are the results?

I have here one of the most interesting, instructive and valuable compilations that I suppose has ever been written by anyone. I did not know it was in existence until I began the investigation of this subject. I should like for Congress to have it printed as a document if the consent of the owner of the copyright could be obtained, and let every student of our political and sociological and ethnological conditions get hold of it. It is termed "The Race Traits and Tendencies of the American Negro," a publication by the American Economic Association, volume 11, printed in 1896 by Macmillan & Co., New York. It is written by Frederick L. Hoffman, statistician to the Prudential Insurance Company of America; and in order that the astounding facts which this gentleman marshaled, purely as a scientific investigator, may receive such due credence as they appear to me to be entitled to, I will read briefly an extract from his preface. I want to introduce Mr. Hoffman to the Senate. I never knew of him until a few days ago myself.

> At the commencement of my investigation, especially in regard to longevity and physiological peculiarities among the colored population, I was confronted with the absence of any extensive collection of data free from the taint of prejudice or sentimentality. Being of foreign birth, a German, I was fortunately free from a personal bias which might have made an impartial treatment of the subject difficult. By making exclusive use of the statistical method and giving in every instance a concise tabular statement of the facts, I believe that I have made it entirely possible for my readers to arrive at their own conclusions, irrespective of the deductions that I have made.
>
> During the course of my inquiry it became more and more apparent that there lie at the root of all social difficulties or problems racial traits and tendencies which make for good or ill in the fate of nations as well as of individuals. It became more apparent as the work progressed that, in the great attempts at

world bettering, at the amelioration of the condition of the lower races by those of a higher degree of culture and economic well-being, racial traits and tendencies have been almost entirely ignored. Hence a vast sum of evil consequences is met as the natural result of misapplied energy and misdirected human effort.

He speaks here in regard to the city of Washington as follows:

> In Washington the colored race has had exceptional educational, religious, and social opportunities. Even in an economic sense the race is probably better off there than anywhere else. According to the census there were in Washington, in 1890, 77 churches for colored people, valued at $1,182,650, with 22,965 communicants. There were 250 colored teachers in charge of 13,332 colored pupils; but there were also during the year 483 young mothers whom neither education nor religion had restrained from open violation of the moral law.

I shall quote further presently, but before I give statistics I wish to bring as a witness the voluntary statement of one of our ex-District Commissioners. I have here a hearing before a subcommittee of the House Committee on Appropriations, consisting of Messrs. Grout, Bingham, McCleary, Allen, and Benton, in charge of the District of Columbia appropriation bill for 1901. Major Sylvester and Mr. Wight, the then Commissioner, having charge of the police department of the city government, were asking for more policemen. Here is what took place:

> Mr. BENTON. I would like to ask you if it is not a fact that there is not another city in this country of equal population to this as well patrolled as this. Is there another one?
>
> Major SYLVESTER. Yes; there are better patrolled cities.
>
> Mr. BENTON. There may be a good many more policemen; but is not the criminal class as successfully taken care of in Washington as in any other city of its size in the country?
>
> Major SYLVESTER. I believe so; but when I answer that statement I want to invite your attention to what I stated to you as to the hours of labor these men have.
>
> Mr. BENTON. I recollect what you said on that subject. You effect it, but you have to work your men more than you ought to.

Here is the Commissioner's statement:

> Mr. WIGHT. Perhaps I had better answer that, because it might be a little embarrassing to Major Sylvester. I think it is remarkably to the credit of the police department, with the small amount of men and the large amount of criminal classes——
> Mr. BENTON. I did not know that there was a very great amount. I know there is not a great deal of crime here, comparatively.
> The CHAIRMAN. They are not the worst criminals.
> Mr. WIGHT. I say it with all kindness, but I state it as a fact, that the 90,000 colored people here are equal to the criminal conditions in any city. They regard life as of no value whatever.

Here is a lifelong Republican, charged with the solemn duty of governing this city, and that is what he said. What corroborative evidence have I in regard to the conditions in Washington to sustain this terrible revelation, as it was to me? I will read first from Mr. Hoffman, because I can not be too long about this, and I am only citing gentlemen who wish to investigate, to this book which affords a fund of information about the colored race throughout the country, North and South, East and West. He gives here a table furnished from the report of the health officer of the District of Columbia for 1894, in which we have the illegitimacy in Washington for the years from 1879 to 1894. I wish to print it in my remarks, but I shall simply call attention to the facts that the average for the white race in 1894 was 2.92 per cent, while the average for the colored race was 22.49 per cent. That was the total of illegitimate births; and the saddest part of all of this is that in 1879 there were only 17.60 per cent of colored, while in 1898 there were 27 per cent and in 1894 26.46 per cent, and for the four preceding years there had been more than 25 per cent of births of illegitimate colored children in the city of Washington.

The explanation is made, or, rather, the bald fact is stated, that immorality of that kind, which lies at the very root of civilization and civilizing influences, is abroad; that it goes on in spite of religious teachings and educational opportunities. That is the appalling thing for us to consider.

The table referred to is as follows:

Illegitimacy in Washington, D. C., 1879–1894.
(Percentage of illegitimate in total number of births.)

	White.	Colored.
1879	2.32	17.60
1880	2.43	19.02
1881	2.33	19.42
1882	2.09	19.73
1883	3.14	20.95
1884	3.60	19.02
1885	3	22.88
1886	3.28	21.86
1887	3.34	21.27
1888	3.49	22.18
1889	3.59	23.45
1890	3.34	26.50
1891	2.90	25.12
1892	2.53	26.40
1893	2.82	27
1894	2.56	26.46
Average 1879–1894	2.92	22.49
SUMMARY 1879–1894.		
Total births, 1879–1894	34,803	27,211
Illegitimate births, 1879–1894	1,032	6,186
Percentage illegitimate births	2.92	22.49

Mr. TILLMAN. Now I will quote something from Mr. Hoffman. He says:

> I have given the statistics of the general progress of the race in religion and education for the country at large, and have shown that in church and school the number of attending members or pupils is constantly increasing; but in the statistics of crime and the data of illegitimacy the proof is furnished that neither religion nor education has influenced to an appreciable degree the moral progress of the race. Whatever benefit the individual

colored man may have gained from the extension of religious worship and educational processes, the race as a whole has gone backward rather than forward.

Next he says:

> It was a favorite argument of the opponents of slavery that freedom, education, and citizenship would elevate the negro to the level of the white in a generation or two. One writer, in a report to the Anti-Slavery Society, which was widely circulated, made use of the following language in regard to the effects of the emancipation of the slaves in the West Indies: "The abolition of slavery gave the death blow to open vice. Immediate emancipation, instead of opening the flood gates, was the only power strong enough to shut them down. Those great controllers of moral action, self-respect, attachment to law, and veneration of God, which slavery destroyed, freedom has resuscitated."

That is a quotation. Mr. Hoffman goes on and marshals some facts which utterly annihilate that contention. He says:

> The West India slaves were completely emancipated in 1838. About thirty years later the American Missionary, in commenting upon the people of Jamaica, used the following language: "A man may be a drunkard, a liar, a Sabbath breaker, a profane man, a fornicator, an adulterer, and such like, and be known to be such, and go to chapel and hold up his head there, and feel no disgrace from those things, because they are so common as to create a public sentiment in his favor."

About twenty-five years later James Anthony Froude, the great English historian, wrote of the negro in the West Indies in the following severe terms:

> Morals in the technical sense they have none, but they can not be said to sin, because they have no knowledge of the law and therefore can not commit a breach of the law. They are naked and not ashamed. They are married, as they call it, but not parsoned. The woman prefers a looser tie that she may be able to leave the man if he treat her unkindly. A missionary told me that a marriage connection rarely turned out well which begins

with legal marriage. The system is strange, but it answers. There is evil, but there is not the demoralizing effect of evil. They sin, but they sin only as animals sin, without shame, because there is no sense of wrongdoing; they eat the forbidden fruit, but it brings with it no knowledge of the difference between good and evil—in fact, these poor children of darkness have escaped the consequences of the fall, *and must come of another stock, after all.*

Mr. Hoffman resumes:

> The statements of the various writers on the social condition of the West India negro are supported by reliable statistical evidence. The table below, compiled from the annual reports of the registrar-general of Jamaica, bears mute testimony on this point:

Illegitimacy and illiteracy in Jamaica.

	Percentage of illegitimate births.	Percentage of females signing marriage register with mark.
1880–81	57.7	66.8
1881–82	58.2	67.7
1882–83	58.09	68.6
1883–84	58.9	68.8
1884–85	59.9	67.7
1885–86	59.6	64
1886–87	59.8	64.8
1887–88	60.6	64.8
1888–89	60.5	65.5
1889–90	61.7	64.9
1890–91	60.7	63.7
1891–92	60.6	61.6
1892–93	60.1	60
1893–94	60.6	59.4
1894–95	60.8	57.1

Indicating the increase in education. Mr. Hoffman sadly comments there. He says:

> After fifty years of educational and religious influence under conditions of freedom, sixty out of every hundred births are acknowledged to be illegitimate.

Further on Mr. Hoffman says:

> After nearly sixty years of freedom in the West Indies and after thirty years of freedom in this country, during which the most elaborate efforts have been made to improve the moral and social condition of the race, we find that its physical and moral tendency is downward.

One other quotation and I have done with this book for the present. Giving the percentage of criminals, he quotes from the official record of convicts in the Pennsylvania penitentiaries:

Convicts in the Pennsylvania penitentiaries, 1886 and 1894.

	Males.			Females.		
	Total.	Col-ored.	Percent-age of colored.	Total.	Col-ored.	Percent-age of colored.
1886.....	1,730	244	14.10	41	14	34.15
1894.....	2,312	384	16.61	52	18	34.61

	Males.	Females.
Percentage of colored in total population over 15 years of age in 1890............	2.23	2.09

This table shows that in Pennsylvania, in 1894, 16.61 per cent of the male inmates and 34.61 per cent of the females were colored; yet in the whole population of the State over 15 years of age only 2.23 per cent of the males and 2.09 per cent of the females were persons of African descent, showing an excessively high proportion of colored convicts.

It is rather strange that nearly all, or a large number, of the colored people who have gravitated North from our part of the world must be the bad negroes; and yet, coming in contact with this constantly increasing class of criminals, we find people up there who say that the stock from which they sprang is good enough to govern South Carolina. I will remark in passing that the conditions in our State are even worse. That is the astounding and the inexplicable situation to me. I have here a witness who speaks about Illinois. Benjamin G. Whitehead, of the New Orleans Times-Democrat, writing from Chicago, says:

A THREATENING CLOUD.

The more serious condition growing out of the negro problem is yet to come, criminologists and officers fear. The negro youth is the threatening cloud obscuring all hope of something better. As the first generation after slavery deteriorated in character and moral worth, the negro children of to-day tend toward vice and crime. In the John Worthy School at Chicago, an institution founded upon benevolent ideas and calculated to teach the mistaught boys the true path to upright citizenship, a most sickening scandal was brought to light from inquiry into the habits and practices of negro boys, and the investigation afforded a very good index to the inclination of even the very young negro children. The details of the scandal are too vile for publication, but the reader who is familiar with negro conduct may have some idea of the character of the testimony if not of the extent of the offenders' misconduct.

The negroes form 2 per cent of the population of Illinois.

Very nearly the same proportion that exists in Pennsylvania.

At the Illinois Home for Female Juvenile Offenders at Geneva 13 per cent of the inmates are negroes. At the boys' prison at Pontiac 18 per cent of those incarcerated are negroes. The negro lists in the juvenile prisons are constantly increasing. In the Chester penitentiary no statistics are furnished regarding the relative number of negroes and whites, but in the Joliet prison Warden Murphy affords the information that more than 16 per cent of the prisoners are negroes. In connection with this it may be stated that of the female prisoners there 27 are white and 38 are negroes.

It may appear in the eyes of some that I am bringing out all this for the sinister purpose of belittling the negro race—of dooming them to obloquy and mistreatment. I want to say to you—and I say it with all the sincerity of my nature—that I do not hate the negro. I was nursed by a black mammy. I have on my farm in South Carolina to-day a negro man of about my own age, Joe Gibson, who has been with me thirty years. He has charge of my keys and of everything I possess there in the way of a house, furniture, horses and carriages, and everything for a farm of 200 acres, worth some twelve or fifteen thousand dollars. I trust him implicitly. He can not read or write. He has got a wife who is as trustworthy as he is.

All negroes are not bad; a very small percentage of them are bad; but the bad ones are leading all the rest, and they are patted on the back by the politicians at the North. Every farmer throughout the South who is familiar with the locality in which he lives knows that there are on many of those plantations—in fact, on nearly all of them where any considerable number of negroes live—a large number of good, quiet, peaceable, orderly, and more or less industrious colored people, who are endeavoring to make a living with the least labor possible, and getting along pleasantly and peacefully with their white friends. But the younger generation is worthless—wholly unreliable—and in every community there are young vagabonds most of whom have a smattering of education who are doing all the devilment of which we read every day.

The condition which the President has precipitated by his revival of a worn-out policy, the discussion of the status of this man throughout the country and of his future, will not down. It is like Banquo's ghost, and the sooner we take hold of the question in a calm, statesmanlike way and endeavor to set in motion instrumentalities which will do something to stop the agitation and to help these people, if they can be helped, the better it will be for all concerned.

I am ready to lend any information I possess and to give the best thought I have, because I have given thought to this subject for the last thirty years, mainly from the point of view I have occupied up to now, that it was my duty to my own people and to my own State to stand forever opposed to any idea of political or social equality on the part of the negro with the whites of South Carolina. You have just had facts collected by a man whose statements with regard to himself would gain credit anywhere as to being an impartial observer and student of this great question. Opposed to that we have a vast amount of nebulous contention and assertion of claims; and I want to read here the latest that I have come across from the very highest negro authority, a man who stands highest in the estimation of white men North and South of any man of his race —Booker T. Washington.

In an address in New York on Washington's Birthday, Booker T. Washington, at a memorial meeting held in the Academy of Arts and Sciences, devoted his remarks to the consideration of the race problem. He said in part:

> Unlike the Indian, the original Mexican, or the Hawaiian, the negro, so far from dying out when in contact with a stronger and different race, has continued to increase in numbers to such an extent that whereas the race entered bondage 20 in number, there are now more than 9,000,000. So I want to emphasize the truth that whether we are of Northern or of Southern birth, whether we are black or white, we must face frankly the hard, stubborn fact that in bondage and in freedom the negro, in spite of all predictions to the contrary, has continued year by year to increase in numbers until he now forms about one-seventh of the entire population, and that there are no signs that the same ratio of increase will not hold good in the future. Further than this, despite of all the changing, uncertain conditions through which the race has passed and is passing in this country, whether in bondage or in freedom, he has made a steady gain in acquiring property, skill, habits of industry, education, and Christian character.
>
> To deal directly with the affairs of my own race, I believe that both the teachings of history, as well as the results of everyday observation, should convince us that we shall make our most enduring progress by laying the foundations carefully, patiently, in the ownership of the soil, the exercise of habits of economy, the saving of money, the securing of the most complete education of hand and head, and the cultivation of Christian virtues.
>
> I can not believe, I will not believe, that the country which invites into its midst every type of European, from the highest

to the very dregs of the earth, and gives these comers shelter, protection, and the highest encouragement, will refuse to accord the same protection and encouragement to her black citizens. The negro seeks no special privileges. All that he asks is opportunity—that the same law which is made by the white man and applied to the one race be applied with equal certainty and exactness to the other.

Here we have the apostle of technical and industrial education, a man who has warned his people against the folly of political office, showing in spite of his wisdom that he has the same dream.

I quote again:

> All that he asks is opportunity—that the same law which is made by the white man and applied to the one race be applied with equal certainty and exactness to the other.

I do not wish to comment on his utterances except to show that his hopes and aspirations are natural and even pathetic. But while he gives advice to his people that is wise, afar off he sees a vision of equality, and I say that his dream can never come to pass. His claims about the negro race are largely guesswork and can not stand against the facts as set out by Hoffman.

Mr. President, I do not want to tire the Senate, but I have here the work of a student of ethnology, of sociology, and of philosophy, one of the greatest minds of the last century, Max Muller, the famous Sanskrit scholar, who has delved deeper into the mine of Indian lore and East Indian traditions and religion than any other man, living or dead. In his Essay on Caste, he deals directly with the question which confronts us, and it is my desire, if you will be patient with me, to give you some quotations from this scholar, this man whose sole purpose and desire was to give to his countrymen the truth and the facts as his long years of laborious research had enabled him to arrive at them. And it is in regard to the question of caste—that inherent, irrepressible, indelible feeling which exists in the mind of every human being under certain conditions and circumstances, for which we are not responsible because it grows with our growth in childhood and becomes part and parcel of every fiber of flesh and bone of which our bodies are composed. In explanation of the conditions which he found in India, Muller says:

> As soon as we trace the complicated system of caste, such as we find it in India at the present day, back to its first beginnings, we find that it flows from at least three different sources, and that accordingly we must distinguish between ethnological, political, and professional caste.
>
> *Ethnological caste arises wherever different races are brought in contact. There is and always has been a mutual antipathy between the white and the black man, and when the two are brought together, either by conquest or migration, the white man has invariably asserted his superiority, and established certain social barriers between himself and his dark-skinned brother.* The Aryas and the Sudras seem to have felt this mutual antipathy. The difference of blood and color was heightened in ancient times by difference of religion and language; but in modern times also, and in countries where the negro has learned to speak the same language and to worship the same God as his master, the white man can never completely overcome the old feeling that seems to lurk in his very blood and makes him recoil from the embrace of his darker neighbor. And even where there is no distinction of color, an analogous feeling, the feeling of race, asserts its influence, as if inherent in human nature. Between the Jew and the Gentile, the Greek and the barbarian, the Saxon and the Celt, the Englishman and the foreigner, there is something—whether we call it hatred, or antipathy, or mistrust, or mere coldness—which in a primitive state of society would necessarily lead to a system of castes, and which, even in more civilized countries, will never be completely eradicated.

In tracing the condition in India as far back as he could get any authentic information, Muller tells us that caste existed there from the first settlement of that peninsula, and he goes on to describe the various strata of society and of population in the two hundred and odd millions of the inhabitants of Hindostan, and he winds up by saying that the word "caste" itself, in its primary significance, simply means color. He gives some very funny and ridiculous descriptions as to what the law of caste has forced those people to do and to believe and to feel. Here, for instance, is one:

> Low as the Sudra stood in the system of Manu, he stood higher than most of the mixed castes, the Varnasankaras. The son of a Sudra by a Sudra woman is purer than the son of a Sudra by a woman of the highest caste (Manu X, 30). Manu calls the Kandala one of the lowest outcasts, because he is the son of a Sudra father and a Brahmanic mother. He evidently considered the mésalliance of a woman more degrading than that of a man.

Just as we do.

> For the son of a Brahman father and a Sudra mother may in the seventh generation raise his family to the highest caste (Manu X, 64)—

In South Carolina we recognize octoroons as white people—

> while the son of a Sudra father and a Brahman mother belongs forever to the Kandalas. The abode of the Kandalas must be out of the town, and no respectable man is to hold intercourse with them. By day they must walk about distinguished by badges; by night they are driven out of the city.

He goes on to philosophize on this subject of race antagonism and association and contact, and of the laws of society even in England, and I will give a quotation without reading it all. He gives a remarkable illustration of the sense of indignation of one of the old-time English aristocracy, saying:

> Even in England the public service has but very lately been thrown open to all classes, and we heard it stated by one of the most eminent men that the Indian civil service would no longer be fit for the sons of gentlemen. Why? Because one of the elected candidates was the son of a missionary.

As illustrative of the intense cruelty, I may say, which this law in India has brought about, you all recollect the immolation of the child widows who had been married in their infancy, and if the husband to whom they had been married died, they were forbidden to marry anyone else. You all recall the Juggernaut car, with the idolators, so to speak, rushing in front and throwing themselves down to be crushed. You all remember the ceremony of burning, after maturity, a woman whose husband had died after marriage, and all that kind of thing. Muller states here:

> In former times a Pariah was obliged to carry a bell—the very name of Pariah is derived from that bell—in order to give warning to the Brahmans, who might be polluted by the shadow of an outcast. In Malabar a Nayadi defiles a Brahman at a distance of 74 paces—

If he gets within 74 paces the Brahman is polluted.

> and a Nayer, though himself a Sudra, would shoot one of these degraded races if he approached too near.

Here is what I want you gentlemen to consider:

> Those who know the Hindus best are the least anxious to see them without caste. Colonel Sleeman remarks:
> "What chiefly prevents the spread of Christianity is the dread of exclusion from caste and all its privileges, and the utter hopelessness of their ever finding any respectable circle of society of the adopted religion, which converts, or would-be converts, to Christianity now everywhere feel."

He says further:

> Caste can not be abolished in India, and to attempt it would be one of the most hazardous operations that was ever performed on a living political body. As a religious institution, caste will die; as a social institution, it will live and improve. Let the Sudras, or, as they are called in Tamil, the Petta Pittei, the children of the house, grow into free laborers, the Vaisyas into wealthy merchants, the Kahatriyas into powerful barons, and let the Brahmans aspire to the position of that intellectual aristocracy which is the only true aristocracy in truly civilized countries, and the four castes of the Veda will not be out of

date in the nineteenth century, nor out of place in a Christian country. But all this must be the work of time. "The teeth," as a native writer says, "fall off themselves in old age, but it is painful to extract them in youth."

Is this the genesis of the Booker Washington idea?

Muller, after devoting a lifetime to the study of the language, literature, and conditions in India, sums up with this declaration. It is worth all the schools and colleges, sermons and preachments, religious or political, that have ever been uttered on the subject of African regeneration. The mothers must lift the race or its doom is sealed.

> AS SOON AS THE FEMALE POPULATION OF INDIA CAN BE RAISED FROM THEIR PRESENT DEGRADATION; AS SOON AS A BETTER EDUCATION AND A PURER RELIGION WILL HAVE INSPIRED THE WOMEN OF INDIA WITH FEELINGS OF MORAL RESPONSIBILITY AND SELF-RESPECT; AS SOON AS THEY HAVE LEARNED—WHAT CHRISTIANITY ALONE CAN TEACH—THAT IN THE TRUE LOVE OF A WOMAN THERE IS SOMETHING FAR ABOVE THE LAW OF CASTE OR THE CURSES OF PRIESTS, THEIR INFLUENCE WILL BE THE MOST POWERFUL, ON THE ONE SIDE, TO BREAK THROUGH THE ARTIFICIAL FORMS OF CASTE, AND, ON THE OTHER, TO MAINTAIN IN INDIA, AS ELSEWHERE, THE TRUE CASTE OF RANK, MANNERS, INTELLECT, AND CHARACTER.

Senators will recollect that the Sepoy rebellion of 1857, with all its horrors, was produced by reason of the fact that the English officers forced the Sepoys simply to bite cartridges with hog grease on them. You will say, "That is all no good here; we are civilized Americans; we are the highest type of men." Bonaparte said, "If you scratch a Russian, you will find a Tartar." If you scratch the white man too deep, you will find the same savage whose ancestry used to roam wild in Britain when the Danes and Saxons first crossed over. I have seen doctors of divinity, I have seen the very highest and best men we have, lose all semblance of Christian human beings in their anger and frenzy when some female of their acquaintance or one of their daughters had been ravished, and they were as wild and cruel as any tiger of the jungle. You can not make us over by law. Constitutions do not change human nature.

I come now, after this imperfect portrayal, to another feature. There is much material here, and it covers much ground, in reference to racial antagonism. Look at the history of the Danube Valley, with its teeming millions of Slavs and Magyars and Bosnians and Servians and Dalmatians, and the Turks and the Macedonians, who have been cutting each other's throats for six centuries, all white people at that, but simply with a racial antagonism.

Look at India, with its two hundred and odd millions, nobody knows how many, governed by 400,000 Englishmen. Where in history can you point to an instance in which white men proper, the best type of white men, or even the lowest type, have been dominated very long by any colored people? It is not in our blood. When you force conditions, when you gentlemen relentlessly and remorselessly stand by your mistakes of the period from 1868 to 1872, when the fifteenth amendment was placed on our backs, and say, "It stands there sacred, and it must stay," you force us to face an alternative which in the future is bound to produce a conflict of races. That dire condition is ahead of us, and, like the sword of Damocles, it hangs by a very slender thread.

We ask you to pause and think. We beg you not to drive us to desperation. You say we must keep the door of hope open to the negro. Please consider the shutting of that door to the white man. If you could force that policy upon my State and we submitted to it quietly and peaceably, in the next fifty years at the outside we would have a majority of negroes in South Carolina who could outvote the whites. Give them a peaceful election, no resistance, absolute equality before the law, and what happens? The negroes capture the government. They do not own any of the property, or only a very small percentage. They have none of the intelligence, or so little that it does not count. They have none of the character, or so little that it does not count. They have none of the knowledge of government which is bred in our bones. But let us submit; let the negroes take possession; let them have a negro government; let them control taxation; and if we have sunk so low by that time as to forget all traditions of Anglo-Saxons, of Caucasians, then what follows?

The governing race in any community, where there is absolute equality before the law, and equality for which the

President contends before the law, and equality of opportunity, will in time come to amalgamation with any different race that may be there. The reason why we have not had any amalgamation in any of the racial antagonisms of which I have spoken, except in a limited degree, the reason why the Slavs and the Magyars in Hungary have never intermarried to any considerable degree, is because they hate each other, and whichever one crosses the line loses caste with his fellows and is absorbed into the other race.

What is the fundamental hope, what is the dream of the negro agitators, these men who are importuning the President now and are making his life a burden to him in regard to appointments to office of men of their race? I will produce a witness. He may not be a good one, but that is not my fault. In the Washington Post of January 27 I find this statement:

> HAYES STIRS HIS RACE—VIRGINIA NEGRO LEADER TALKS OF SWORD AND TORCH—WASHINGTON CROWD APPLAUD—JAMES H. HAYES PREDICTS FORCIBLE RESISTANCE TO THE VIRGINIA CONSTITUTION AND OTHER ACTS OF DISFRANCHISEMENT PASSED BY SOUTHERN LEGISLATURES—TEMPER OF A MASS MEETING AT LINCOLN CHURCH.

You all read it, at least most of you did. I will incorporate it in my speech, with the consent of the Senate.

> At a mass meeting of colored people at Lincoln Memorial Church, at 8 o'clock last night, under the auspices of the Afro-American Council, prominent speakers of the negro race made addresses upon the question of disfranchisement in the Southern States, and considerable feeling was manifested.
>
> James H. Hayes, of Richmond, the attorney who has been retained by the colored people of Virginia to test the disfranchisement laws of that State, delivered a speech in which he declared that the negro has now reached the limit of his endurance, and advocated the sword and torch as a means for the negro to maintain his manhood. His remarks were received with great enthusiasm.
>
> He referred to the fact that during the years which have elapsed since the war sectional feeling between the North and South has died out to such an extent that Virginia now proposes to place a monument of Lee in Statuary Hall in the National Capitol, but said that all this period has not been sufficient for

the negro to advance one inch beyond the place he held when liberated from slavery.

"There is nothing in Virginia for the negro," he said, "but degradation, unless the negroes make a firm stand, contend for their rights, and, if necessary, die for them. I am not an anarchist," he added, "and I don't mean to go out and kill anybody, but to let somebody else kill you." This veiled sally provoked loud applause and laughter. "In Virginia," added the speaker, "you are 'Jim Crows.' You opened the meeting to-night by singing 'My country, 'tis of thee,' but I wonder how negroes can sing that song. For myself, I am a man without a country.

"The time has come when the negro must fight, not theoretically, not intellectually; but fight with his hands. The disfranchisement of the children of Israel in Egypt has been followed letter for letter by the disfranchisement in the South."

He then spoke about Moses being called to lead the Israelites from their bondage and drew attention to the fact that slavery for four hundred years had made them cowards, so that they were obliged to turn back, drawing a parallel to the case of the negro in America.

"A second time," he continued, "the children of God arose. This time they had the leadership of Joshua, and when they went forth from the land of their bondage they did not go meekly, but carried the sword in one hand and the torch in the other. In this country," also he added, "a second generation has grown up in the forty years since the war. The Atlanta Constitution has threatened us with the Kuklux if the growth of Federal appointments in the South continues. I make the prediction that when the Southern people start to Kukluxing this time they will not have as the objects of their oppression the same timid people they Kukluxed in the sixties.

"Negroes are leaving the State of Virginia because of the treatment they are receiving. What we want to do is to start something, and keep it up until the white people stop something. We don't intend to be oppressed any longer. We don't intend to be crushed. I am afraid we are anarchistic, that we are anarchists, and I give the warning that if this oppression in the South continues the negro must resort to the sword and torch, and that the Southland will become a land of blood and desolation.

"I want to make the assertion right here that we are not going to be disfranchised in Virginia. It is written in the heavens and engraved upon the stars that the Virginia negro does not intend to submit to disfranchisement. We are told, 'Let the negro obtain education and wealth if he would gain the political equality which he desires.' I say that never was a bigger lie uttered. The more the negro advances the more will political rights be denied him. It is not the common negro in the South who is cut off the registration lists. It is not the ditch digger. It is the educated negro, the doctor and lawyer and preacher, who are deprived unlawfully of political rights and manhood by the iniquitous constitution of Virginia, which cost half a million dollars to frame. And I want to say that by the time we get through punching holes in the constitution it will cost the State of Virginia half a million more."

The sting of that speech is in the tail, and I want to read you what this colored orator, who made the members of his race in that tabernacle or church go wild with enthusiasm, as the report states, said:

"It is claimed that the negro industrial schools are the proper lines of effort for the race. Talk about education and wealth, and say that they make votes for the negro. It's a lie. No, they are destroying votes. Every negro who puts on a clean collar and tries to be a man is destroying a vote. I believe God will take care of us. And just one word about the question of the absorption of the races."

The speaker added significantly:

"No two people having the same religion and speaking the same tongue, living together, have ever been kept apart. This is well known, and it is one of the reasons why the dominant race is crushing out the strength of the negro in the South."

There is your open door and it is easy to see to what doom it leads. The purpose and hope of those who indorse this policy and are madly pressing it on us in the South is that we in time shall become a country or State of mulattoes. Wendell Phillips in his Fourth of July speech in 1863 openly advocated amalgamation. Theodore Tilton also advocated it. Thad. Stevens practiced it. It was not surprising. It was not to be wondered at that those men who had devoted their lives to the propaganda of abolition should have allowed their sentimentality to get the better of all judgment and race pride. Hayes is of a type of negroes who are growing in number daily. He is only more bold and less cunning and cautious than the rest. He repudiates Booker Washington and his teachings, but his race in Washington "go wild" over his ravings.

Look southward, if you please, over the Rio Grande, and tell me what you see from there to Cape Horn. You see no society that is pure blooded; you see no commonwealth that is self-governing. You see a mongrelized aggregation of Indians and Spaniards and negroes inhabiting that land who make orderly government a byword and a hissing. No such doom as that is possible to the Southern States. No such scheme will ever receive the indorsement of the American people, and if it does then God have mercy on this country, for there will be a hundred times more blood shed than ever was shed before "the stars in their courses fought against Sisera." I do not threaten you. I prayerfully warn you. I know those people. I know your stock as well as mine. You would not submit to it. We can not. We dare not. We will not!

I want to touch a moment on the effect of education on men. Under existing conditions we are left absolutely without any barrier in dealing with suffrage other than the ability to read and write. In my State we have enlarged that by permitting those who pay taxes on $300 worth of property, whether or not they read or write, to use the ballot. But who here is prepared to say that the mere acquirement of enough education to read and write makes a good citizen—that it fits a man for the complicated duties of self-government and participation in self-government? Pope declared that—

"A LITTLE LEARNING IS A DANGEROUS THING."

And it is the quintessence of folly to suppose that the African can emulate, or successfully imitate even, the Anglo Saxon in matters of government. The history of the race in the continent where it originated and still exists by the hundreds of millions is that of barbarism, savagery, cannibalism, and everything which is low and degrading.

This has been the story of all the centuries. It is idle to expect such beings to be transformed in a generation or two into good citizens capable of governing themselves.

My observation teaches me that where there is no moral training there is no character. If along with the training of the head—the mere ability to translate letters into words—there be not a training of the moral faculties, the realization of the difference between right and wrong, the instinct to tell the truth, to be virtuous and honest, what good do your three little r's do?

I did not want to say anything about what are the conditions in the South as I know them to be by personal contact and observation all my life. I have preferred to marshal the evidence of an unbiased witness, who has taken the official reports and the scientific data, and to tell you what he has to say about this race. But I am willing to say that the little smattering of education which negroes are receiving now has absolutely no influence upon their upbuilding as a people. It does not increase by one-quarter of an inch their stature in manhood. It is not elevating, but enervating and destructive of the original virtues of the negro race, and they have their virtues as well as we have.

I want to direct your attention to a remarkable fact in the history of this country, which can not be too much dwelt upon. When the Southern white men, from 16 to 60 years of age, all of them living in the cotton States, except a few in the mountains, had left their homes during the civil war to follow the standards of Lee and Jackson, of Johnston and Forrest, and when there were absolutely no men there except the old men above 60 and 65 and the little schoolboys—and the country then was much less thickly populated than it is now and altogether more agricultural—with over 4,000,000 negroes there were at least 1,000,000 males of adult age, slaves scattered throughout the breadth of the land, from the Potomac to the Rio Grande, and the wives and daughters of their masters were left to their care and protection.

The negroes knew the war was to settle the question of their future liberty or continued slavery. If there existed in their hearts any cause for hatred and resentment and a desire for revenge, such as you gentlemen in your youth were led to believe existed from reading Harriet Beecher Stowe's novel, and other sources of information and when oratory poured out its plea for the poor, downtrodden African—if these people had then been imbued with one-tenth of the hatred of the whites which exists to-day, if they had cause for hate, what would have been the consequences upon the helpless white women and children then living among them? The very imagination sickens at the picture of rapine and murder and of the cruelties and horrors of which we have read in Hayti and San Domingo, and which would have been repeated in the South. Yet they were slaves and had, as you believe, ample cause for revenge and hate.

But what are the facts, Senators? During those four dark years there is not of record a solitary case where a negro man wronged a white woman. What is the situation now? Take your morning paper and read it any day in the year, and there is hardly a day in which our sensibilities are not wrought up and our passions aroused or our pity aroused by some tale of horror and of woe.

I tell you from my own experience and observation that the old sense of security and of love and friendship on the part of the negro for his white master and his mistress and the children, which I myself experienced in my boyhood, has gone. With the remnant of the old negroes who were born in slavery and had some of that training (all of whom are now necessarily above 40) gone, the last restraining and conservative element among them will have disappeared. They have been taught that they are the equals of the whites. During the reconstruction period, when they had the ballot and professed to govern, and levied taxes and marched themselves in the statehouses, constantly squandering and stealing of our substances, they learned their lesson well. They tasted blood. They were inoculated with the virus of equality. A great poet tells us that those who love liberty must first deserve it.

Among the dusky millions who were held in bondage there were, of course, many who had been cruelly wronged and suffered injustice, but the overwhelming majority of them had no feeling for their masters and their families except love and veneration. They looked up to them as superior beings. They felt the obligations of the trusts which had been reposed in them, and many of them were true unto death. The fact which can not be disputed is one to give us pause when we undertake to analyze the present conditions.

So the poor African has become a fiend, a wild beast, seeking whom he may devour, filling our penitentiaries and our jails, lurking around to see if some helpless white woman can be murdered or brutalized. Yet he can read and write. He has a little of the veneer of education and civilization, according to New England ideas.

I do not blame the New England people. They have none, or few, of the negroes. The whole number beyond New York would not equal the negroes in my county. The people up there can afford to theorize and to determine upon the life and death of the civilization of the South from their standpoint of sentimentality, if they are willing, but I do not believe they are now willing. I do not believe they want to. I give them credit for more love of humanity and of their kind than to bring on a conflict of that sort. If there were no higher motives, I give them credit for more statesmanship. But, with the constantly increasing hatred between the races, with the older white men, acquainted with the better negroes, dying off, as they are doing rapidly; with the old negroes, the grandfathers of the race, dying off rapidly, as they are doing, in a very short while those who know anything of the relation of the slave and the master in the old days will have disappeared and gone.

And then the younger generation of white men, who are hating these negroes in return, whose animosity and antagonism grow apace with these acute situations and conditions, have got to face this problem. I thank God sometimes that I will not live to see the thing brought to a focus. I am endeavoring in my feeble way to beg you, for God's sake, not to help produce that acute stage of fever and race hatred and carry it through until you bring into people those angry passions which will put the races at each other's throats with the resolve on the part of the whites to die or maintain their supremacy. Everyone knows what will be the result.

What effect does it have to appoint a negro to office in a community, many of which I could mention in my State, where there are three or five negroes to one white, just as there are in Indianola three negroes to a white person in that entire community, and in the adjoining county of Washington there are absolutely ten to one, just as in Beaufort, S. C., there are ten to one? What effect does it have for the knowledge to go out all over and among them, at their churches and everywhere else, that the great President of the United States is still their friend; that he does not intend to allow the "door of hope to be shut upon them;" that he wants to offer them an opportunity in life; that he is going to recognize them and give them offices to represent the United States Government? Does that tend to peace, tend to good order, tend to produce that feeling of subordination which is their only salvation?

Some people have been ready to believe and to contend that the negro is a white man with a black skin. All history disproves that. Go to Africa. What do you find there? From one hundred and fifty million to two hundred million savages.

I happened in my boyhood, when I was about 12 years old, to see some real Africans fresh from their native jungles. The last cargo of slaves imported into this country were brought here in 1858 on the yacht *Wanderer*, landed on an island below Savannah, and sneaked by the United States marshal up the Savannah River and landed a little distance below Augusta, and my family bought some thirty of them.

Therefore I had a chance to see just what kind of people these were, and to compare the African as he is to-day in Africa with the African who, after two centuries of slavery, was brought side by side to be judged. The difference was as "Hyperion to a satyr." Those poor wretches, half starved as they had been on their voyage across the Atlantic, shut down and battened under the hatches and fed a little rice, several hundred of them, were the most miserable lot of human beings —the nearest to the missing link with the monkey—I have ever put my eyes on.

Now, I do not go into the philosophy of it, or undertake to act as God's interpreter, because I have no ambition of that sort and I would not presume to even suggest a thing more than to say that if we consider the destinies of this race from a broad standpoint, and compare the condition of the African in Africa to-day, the highest and best of them, with the condition of the American negroes, such as we now have them, or such as we had them in 1865, I do not hesitate to say that among the four million and odd slaves who were in the South in 1865 there were more good, Christian men and women and gentlemen and ladies than all Africa could show then or can show now.

Then if God in His providence ordained slavery and had these people transported over here for the purpose of civilizing enough of them to form a nucleus and to become missionaries back to their native heath, that is a question. I have a letter here from a distinguished African bishop who believes it, and I want to read it. But the thing I want to call your attention to is that slavery was not an unmitigated evil for the negro, because whatever of progress the colored race has shown itself capable of achieving has come from slavery; and whether among those four million there were not more good men and women than could be found among the nine million now is to my mind a question. I would not like to assert it; but I am strongly of that belief from the facts I know in regard to the demoralization that has come to those people down there by having liberty thrust upon them in the way it was, and then having the ballot and the burdens of government, and being subjected to the strain of being tempted and misled and duped and used as tools by designing white men who went there among them.

A little while back I received a letter from this man—I never met him—making some comment on something he had seen about my utterances in regard to the negro in some speech or lecture. My newspaper friends have always taken it upon themselves to quote everything that is lurid and hot and vitriolic that I say, and then to finish by saying, "The Senator from South Carolina made a characteristic speech," leaving anything that was sane and rational and decent and eloquent, if I ever rise to eloquence, out of the whole account. That is unintentional, doubtless. In their pursuit for sensation they have done me the great wrong to misrepresent me throughout this country. I do not fret over it. I know that the truth never has overtaken a lie, and I do not intend to undertake it; and I never will even make a start to run down the thousand and one lies that have been told on me.

But this man, this bishop, wrote me a letter and called my attention to a dream of his, an aspiration and a hope, and to suggest that I should submit his proposition to the Senate of the United States and lend it support. I wrote back to him the difficulty that lay in the way, the obstruction, the well-nigh impossibility of anything being done along that line to the extent he had dreamed of, and I went on to say something about my idea in regard to the negro, giving a little advice, as we are all so prone and ready to do. Advice is one of those commodities that nobody ever charges anything for except a lawyer. I got this letter in return:

> ATLANTA, GA., *January 24, 1903.*
>
> Hon. B. R. TILLMAN,
> *United States Senator.*
>
> SIR: Yours of the 19th instant was upon my table when I reached home from Memphis, Tenn.
>
> You say, if I know anything, I ought to know that the negro in the South must ever and forever remain subordinate or be destroyed and annihilated. I know that as well as you do, and even better, for a white man can not see the virus of this entire nation, from the Supreme Court of the United States down to the ward politician, as the colored man can see it and feel it. But this determination to degrade the negro and prevent his recognition as a man that God made is not only confined to the ruling masses of the South, but to the North as well. Color prejudice—

He seemed to agree with me in the idea I expressed in the beginning of my speech, that caste feeling, prejudice, whatever you call it, is just as strong in the North as it is with us, except that the provocation to exhibit it does not exist there. But let me go on with him—

> but to the North as well. Color prejudice is not a Southern institution alone, but of the United States. Hence my desire for my race to leave the nation and return to Africa. When I was a boy, 60 years ago, I thought then as I do now, that God allowed the negro to be brought to this country and civilized to redeem his kindred in Africa. And since I have traveled from one end of Africa to the other, I am stronger in my conviction than ever. And I did hope that, as Jefferson Davis was the negative force in the freedom of the negro, God had raised you up to be the negative force that should establish through governmental aid a highway for millions of our race to return to the land of our ancestors. I have been looking upon you as a creature of Providence—

Now, is not that a high compliment? [Laughter.] As you know—

> God moves in a mysterious way
> His wonders to perform—

and still think that your utterances in many instances will serve a purpose not even contemplated by yourself. Others of my race may denounce you, as they do in mass meetings and on the lecture platforms of this country, but I shall praise you and wish you godspeed; for I believe that you are serving a purpose of Providence that but few are aware of, and even yourself do not realize.

I judge you think, from the tone of your letter, that I am a politician—

I told him that if we could get the politicians to emigrate, God knows I would subsidize all the vessels Uncle Sam has and ship them to Africa or to heaven. He says:

I judge you think, from the tone of your letter, that I am a politician. But be politics far from me. I am no politician. Nor am I any office seeker for my race. I do not care if a negro never gets office in this country while the world stands. A little insignificant office in the face of all the laws that are enacted to prevent our rising to manhood is too small to merit my attention. The negro is a fool for wanting office. He is a fool for enlisting in the Army or Navy or in doing anything to protect a flag that gives white men all the stars and leaves nothing but the stripes for the negro. Please do not class me among the politicians.

You see this man has got some gray matter in his kinky head.

You say the natural increase of the negro by birth would be a bar to emigration solving the race problem. If I could talk with you I would make you see otherwise. For I know all about it— am acquainted with the statistics of immigration to this country. But I shall not intrude upon your time and patience. No reply to this letter will be expected.
    Truly,   H. M. TURNER.

H. M. Turner is a bishop of the African Methodist Episcopal Church. His scheme is before you to consider.

Now, Mr. President, a little brief summary, and I am done.

I have endeavored in my feeble and humble way to give you such historical light, such ethnological light, on this subject as I could come across in the brief time I have had, along with my other duties, to collect. I have relied mainly on the inner light of my own observations and my own feeling and knowledge of conditions.

I do not want to see the African driven to the wall. I do not want to shut the door of hope in his face. I am willing to give him every opportunity in life, all that the Declaration of Independence guarantees—life, liberty, and the pursuit of happiness. But that does not involve, and so help me God I can not consent to have it involve, the dominance of that people over my people.

Then what are we to do? We have, as I have told you, a large negro majority in South Carolina. Negroes constituted the wealth of that State before the war when these slaves were chattels. They are there, and they do not want to leave, and we do not want them to leave. What I mean by that is that to-day the superficial thought is that if they left our fields would go untilled, our lands would become worthless, there would be a vacuum in the productions of that State, and if you took them out of the South you would create a cataclysm in finance, and would knock down and destroy not only the financial prosperity of this nation, but of all Europe.

So you can not approach this problem at a double-quick. It has been coming on us for two centuries or more. We will have to take the time to study out the best way to go about settling it, and then begin. We had better never begin than to begin wrong. We have already begun wrong. The blunders which have been made since 1865 have produced the present unfortunate and, I might say, dangerous situation.

Consider for a moment what it means to undertake to deport these people, to encourage them to emigrate. You are face to face with a problem which in its magnitude in expense will approximate the national debt at the close of the war. The getting together even in small quantity of 200,000 a year, or whatever number might equal the birth rate, and giving them the aid and the assistance to go across the ocean, or to go to South America, or to Mexico, or to the Philippines, or to Cuba, or to Africa, or anywhere else, involves transportation by sea, the food necessary to sustain them while they are on the way and in the time they are on shipboard the food to support life; and then when you land them on the other shore you are compelled by humanity to furnish them with the means of support until they can make a start in the world, until they can plant a crop and gather it.

So I think upon a rough estimate you can not possibly hope or expect to accomplish it under $300 per capita at a very low estimate.

How many of them want to go? I do not know, and certainly there is no law to make them go and Congress can not pass one. Joe does not want to go—my Joe. I do not know whether I belong to Joe or Joe belongs to me. Anyhow, we have been together for thirty years, and we have agreed to live together until one or both of us die, and when I go away, if I go first, I know he will shed as sincere tears as anybody. I would die to protect him from injustice or wrong.

Now, what are you going to do about it? Throughout that broad land there are hundreds and thousands of Joes. They do not care anything about voting. They do not know anything about it. Left alone and in peace as they are now, they do not know anything about the elections. They have forgotten all they did know about them. They have not voted in South Carolina since 1881, long before they were disfranchised according to the constitution and the law of the State. When we took the government away from them in 1876 we made it so clear that we intended to keep it that, after one or two spasmodic efforts, they surrendered all desire or contention, and virtually were satisfied to go and pick cotton on the 6th or 7th of November, when the first Tuesday came.

It is only these pestiferous creatures who are organized, as I said, into little Republican machines to furnish delegates to nominate a Republican President who are bothering about it; and it is those fellows who are in these offices who stir up bad blood and create race antagonism and create a feeling of opposition in the minds of all those who are willing to be misled.

Then comes this other idea—I had forgotten it. I wish the Senator from Ohio [Mr. HANNA] was in his seat. I have here a bill which I should like to have him explain. I had almost let it slip my mind. It is Senate bill 7254, introduced by Mr. HANNA, "to provide pensions for freedmen," and so forth. "Be it enacted," and so on. The bill carries with it—how much I do not know—forty, or fifty, or sixty million dollars. Oh, Mr. President, did Mr. HANNA mean that, or is it a political dodge?

He can not answer, for he is not here. If he chooses to answer to-morrow, I shall be glad to hear him.

What has been the effect of this? There are passing up and down the South, from one end of it to the other, agents, shrewd, sharp fellows, mostly mulattoes, who have all the meanness of the white man, along with some intellectual superiority—many of them; some of them are good people. But these scoundrels are collecting at the negro churches and schools 10 cents, 20 cents, 30 cents, in accordance with the ability of the poor dupes to contribute to this fund, to hire lawyers to press this bill through Congress.

My God, was there ever a more infamous scheme to bamboozle and deceive since the Freedman's Bureau had those people contribute of their substance fifty-odd million dollars and then you allowed a lot of fellows to steal the best part of it?

Is there anybody on the other side willing to help me put this pension bill in one of the appropriation bills as a rider? I intend to move it—God knows I will—and let you vote on it, if I can get a chance. I want you to put yourselves on record whether you love these old negroes as well as I do. I am perfectly willing to give Joe and Kitty, both of whom were old slaves and who are ex-slaves, an appropriation of three or four hundred dollars or $10 a month apiece, and I will give them each a piece of land and let them stay on it, and when I want my shoes blacked and my carriage horses hitched up, or anything done for which I pay Joe, I will get it just the same without regard to the pension that Mr. HANNA is proposing to give.

Well, Mr. President, I am done. I have treated this subject but imperfectly, but I have spoken from the soul, from my very heart, to tell you the truth, so help me God. I warn you that in proportion as you arouse false hopes in these people's minds as to their future, keeping the door of hope open by giving them offices, you are only sowing the wind which will flame up into a whirlwind later on. You can not keep that door open without shutting it on the whites. The Northern millions which have gone down there have gone into negro colleges and schools to equip these people to compete with their white neighbors.

All of the millions that are being sent there by Northern philanthropy has been but to create an antagonism between the poorer classes of our citizens and these people upon whose level they are in the labor market. There has been no contribution to elevate the white people of the South, to aid and assist the Anglo-Saxon Americans, the men who are descended from the people who fought with Marion and Sumter. They are allowed to struggle in poverty and in ignorance, and to do everything they can to get along, and they see Northern people pouring in thousands and thousands to help build up an African domination.

Senators I leave the subject with you. May God give you wisdom and light to "do as you would have others do unto you."

THE LYNCHING OF THOMAS GILYARD

THE JOPLIN DAILY GLOBE
Murderer of Leslie Lynched by Angry Mob
April 16, 1903

MURDERER OF LESLIE
LYNCHED BY ANGRY MOB

City Officials Pleaded With the Mob to Let the Law Take Its Course, But Frenzied Citizens Demanded a Life for a Life and Appeals in Behalf of Law and Constitutional Justice Were Made in Vain.

A Sea of Enraged Humanity Surged Around the Jail—Occasionally the Tempest of Wrath Was Settled, Only to Break Forth Afresh With Renewed Fury—Finally the Battering Ram Was Applied, Entrance Effected, the Prisoner Taken From His Cell—And Then the End.

Mob Violence Was Rampant Last Night—A Number of Negro Hovels Were Burned in the North End and in the Negro Settlement on East Seventh Street—Frightened Negroes Flee to Neighboring Cities.

THE COWARDLY and unprovoked murder of Policeman Theodore Leslie has been avenged. The strange negro tramp who shot down the brave officer in the Kansas City Southern freight yards just north of Broadway at 7 o'clock Tuesday night was hanged to a telephone pole at the corner of Second and Wall streets yesterday afternoon and five thousand people witnessed the execution.

Never before in the history of Joplin has the passions of the people come to the surface with such force. Determination was depicted on every man's face when the unknown negro was brought face to face with his awful crime. It is doubtful if a mob ever lingered quite so long in an effort to establish the identity of the victim. For half an hour the big crowd jostled and listened to appeals from prominent officials and citizens, who begged that the law be allowed to take its course. But the reasons presented were not sufficiently convincing and suddenly, almost before the movements of the leaders could be followed, the wretch was dangling in mid-air.

There was a stifling stillness just after the gruesome task was done. People almost spoke in undertones. An hour or two after when the saloons, which had been ordered closed by Sheriff Owen, were opened and the crowds began to realize the enormity of the situation and the deed, excitement ran high. The small knots of men who first conversed on the street corners got together and shortly before 8 o'clock a band of two or three dozen, most of them from outlying mining camps, filed down Main street, yelling "Down with the negroes." "Hang the coons." Loud threats were made against the colored population.

At the corner of Fifth and Main streets the mob, now grown larger and more frenzical, declared that every negro must leave the city by tomorrow morning.

As they swarmed down Main street over a hundred boys, ranging in age from seven and eight years upward, followed in their wake and yelled like young demons. Within an hour the streets were alive with an animated and highly inflamed horde. They pushed and jostled one another and ran pell mell over everything in their path. Street cars were blockaded and vehicles of all sorts had to go over to Joplin street.

Every means was exhausted by the police and other officers to stay the carnage which seemed imminent. There was a thirst for blood in that motley crowd which nothing else but rapine could slake, and every appeal was in vain. Prominent business men were asked by the officers to address the seething mass and Mayor-elect Cunningham was brought unceremoniously from the session of the Joplin club, but the effort was for naught.

The mob swooped down on the negro settlement on the extreme northern end of Main street, with torches already prepared, and without a note of warning, except the one continuous cry for revenge, a half dozen negro shanties were set on fire.

The fire department rendered such assistance as it could to quench the flames, and regardless of the taunts and jeers of the mob, they did their duty well.

Then with a din that could be heard all over the down town districts the excited throng, numbering over a thousand, marched exultantly to another negro neighborhood in the eastern part of the city. Several negro cabins on East Seventh street were fired.

And through it all the name of Lee Fullerton was heard on every hand, the plucky young butcher apprentice who forced the desperate negro murderer in a slaughter house and with no other weapon than a carving knife effected his capture.

The name which would have been cursed and jeered, that of the victim of the first mob, was never learned. When he was taken to the police station shortly after 4 o'clock yesterday afternoon, Officer Frank Belford got a partial statement from him and he gave his name. He said that he came to Joplin Monday night direct from his home in Mississippi. He also declared that there were three other men with him in the box car where Officer Leslie was killed, none of whom he knew by name. He denied positively, however, that he had fired a shot.

Before he had talked more than a very few minutes an angry mob attacked the weather beaten, old jail and the conversation was cut short. Officer Belford was unable to remember the name which he had given.

NEGRO TAKEN FROM JAIL AND HANGED.

Soon after the negro suspect was locked in the city jail, the news had spread over the entire city, and within a quarter of an hour the streets about the jail were thronged with thousands of people. The crowd was composed of men, women and children, and shouts of

"Get a rope!"

"Hang the negro!"

"Hang the murderer!"

The larger the crowd grew the higher the excitement ran and it was only a short time before the officers realized that there was something desperate brewing. The negro was locked in a separate cell and all the other prisoners were locked in cells. The officers were determined that the negro should not be taken from the jail, but in case of their ability to prevent the mob from having its way they did not want the wrong prisoner taken.

While the excitement was at its highest City Attorney P. D. Decker came to the front door of the jail and made quite a lengthy speech. He advised the men that it would be best to allow the law to take its course, and that it was not certain that the negro suspect was the right man, and that they should wait and see. He talked at some length and had great influence over the crowd. The leaders seemed willing to give up the job and fully 200 people turned and left the streets about the jail, feeling the excitement was all over.

But shortly after that another set of leaders appeared upon the scene and they were equally as determined as the leaders who preceded them. Mayor Trigg and Mayor-elect Cunningham admonished the crowd to disperse, but they were heeded for only a few minutes.

The next sound that met the expectant ears of the vast crowd was the dull thuds of the butting ram which was in the hands of half a dozen strong and determined men.

They were battering in the wall of the jail.

This action began at five minutes of 5 o'clock and it was not more than ten minutes until the negro was in the hands of the angry mob, being carried to the scene of his death.

The first attempt to break into the jail was started from the police court room, but the iron door at that place was unrelenting, and in a short time a dozen men were at work in the alley east of the jail. At that place there was an iron door, in the lining of the jail, and a portion of this was exposed by a window in the wall. The mob began work on the bricks before this window and it was only a short time until a hole had been made and the iron door battered down. The men were working with a battering-ram fully ten feet long, and in spite of the efforts of the officers to prevent it, the entrance was effected.

As soon as the ram was taken from one mob by the officers another mob made its appearance and began work.

When the wall of the jail had been battered down a number of men went inside and began work on the lock of the cell in which the negro was confined. The breaking of this lock was but the work of a minute and then a rush was made for the victim.

During the time the crowd was at work on the wall of the jail and the lock of his cell the negro lay as if asleep in his cell.

But the instant the lock was broken on the cell door and the big iron grate swung open the black fellow jumped to his feet and fought like a demon. His blows were of little consequence, however, and in less time than it takes to tell it he was hustled into the alley east of the jail and into Second street at the north of the jail.

The people crowded in on all sides of him, and as soon as Second street was reached the mob with the negro turned west. There were as many people in front of them as on the sides or in the rear, and the negro was making desperate attempts to free his hands in order to deal out a blow to anybody who happened to be near him.

Down the street surged the mob of no less than 3,000 people. Excitement ran high. Men shouted and women and children screamed. The mob went on a run and the street was filled from curb to curb for a distance of more than a block.

When the corner of Second and Wall streets was reached a halt was made. Men and boys climbed trees, mounted the roofs of houses and sheds, in an effort to command a view of the lynching. The man who carried the rope was left behind and before he could get to the men with the negro, Attorney Decker rode into the mob on a horse and appealed to them to allow the negro to be taken back to the jail. He urged that he was not the right man and in support of his assertion placed Ike Clark, the seventeen year old lad on the horse to tell the people that the negro in their possession was not the one who had shot and killed Officer Leslie. Clark is the lad who followed the negro and fired at him immediately after the officer was killed.

Soon after this, Mayor-elect Cunningham mounted a wagon and requested that the negro be taken back to jail, and that the mob wait until it was certain that the negro in their possession was the man who killed the officer.

The mob hesitated and for a time it looked as though the members of the mob would relent, but suddenly there was another outburst of shouts and shrieks and the mob surged from the southeast corner of the streets to the southwest corner.

Here the rope was placed about the negro's neck and a big fellow climbed the pole with the rope in his hand. The rope was quickly placed over the arm of the pole, but as soon as the mob began pulling on the end of the rope in an effort to hoist the negro, equally as many took hold on the end to which the negro was tied in an effort to prevent the lynching.

It was like a tug of war for a time, but finally the men who were determined to hang the negro were successful and his body, almost naked, was hoisted high into the air, and one lone shot was fired at his dangling body.

It was then just 5:50 o'clock.

The arms and feet of the negro were not tied, but from the time his feet left the ground he scarcely moved a muscle. As he was being pulled from the ground some man grabbed the hand of the helpless negro and swung his whole weight on it in an effort to break his neck and put an end to his sufferings.

From the time the mob left the jail with the negro until he was strung to the telephone pole he was beat and cuffed and trampled and choked, until it is believed that before he was hung he was almost dead. Those who were in a position to see him, state that he was not able to stand. He made a plea of innocence soon after the mob arrived at the corner of Second and Wall streets, but before he was hung he became sullen and refused to talk. As he was being pulled into the air his hand grasped the rope as it tightened about his neck, but it was pulled away and all was over.

CAPTURE EFFECTED BY NERVE AND TACT.

The capture of the negro was effected at about 3 o'clock yesterday afternoon in the slaughter house of Bauer Bros., near Midway park, between the electric line and the Frisco tracks. The capture was made by Lee Fullerton and M. R. Bullock. Fullerton lives at 311 North Wall street and Bullock lives at Midway park. Fullerton related the story of the capture to the Globe soon after the negro was hanged last evening.

"I am in the employ of Bauer Bros.," said Fullerton, "and yesterday afternoon I was sent to the slaughter house to feed the stock and cut some tallow. I rode out in the wagon and walked through the slaughter house into the yard, and just as I did so I noticed a negro walking off up the hill. It is an unusual occurrence for anybody to be around the house as it is in such an out-of-the-way place. I was just the least frightened at first for the fellow was one of the meanest looking men I ever saw. He stopped and looked back and I spoke to him. Then he walked back to where I was and told me he had been in a shooting scrape the night before, and asked me if he could not hide in the slaughter house until he got well.

"He made all sorts of promises, saying he would befriend me some day, and said he would not disturb anything. I was alone and unarmed, and of course could not refuse him, as he was armed with a big gun.

"We walked into the house and the negro sat down on a bale of hay. Soon after this M. R. Bullock, who lives near by, came to the slaughter house, and we decided we would make an attempt to capture the fellow. I had read of the killing of Officer Leslie in the Globe and was satisfied in my own mind that the negro in the slaughter house was the man who had done the work. Bullock and I got outside and talked the matter over and decided upon a plan of action.

"We then returned and I busied myself in cutting some tallow within a couple of feet of the negro. Suddenly I made a lunge at him and before he knew it I had a big "skinning" knife within half an inch of his neck, and told him if he made a move I would cut his head off. He attempted to draw his gun and as he did so Bullock knocked his hand away and took the gun from his pocket.

"After we had the negro's gun we had no trouble with him, and after forcing him to get into the wagon we brought him to Joplin and he was placed in jail."

The negro admitted to Fullerton and to a number of the officials that he was in the car with him, two negroes and a white man but denied that he did the shooting. He claimed there were three other men in the car with him, two negroes and a white man. When he was placed under control at the slaughter house as many as 100 cartridges were taken from him. The gun taken from him was a Colts 38 calibre. When the men passed the scene of the murder of Officer Leslie as they were bringing the negro to Joplin, Fullerton pointed to the spot and asked the negro if he recognized the place. This seemed to confuse the fellow and he replied that he had not murdered anybody.

BODY OF THE VICTIM TAKEN DOWN FROM POLE.

At 6:20 last evening the body of the victim was cut down, after having been suspended in the air for half an hour. The body was taken charge of by Justice Potter, who instructed the Joplin Undertaking company to remove it to its rooms and prepare it for burial.

The body was taken there, but soon after the mob began to form last night it was deemed best to have the body removed to some other place, and it was secretly taken away. This was done for fear the mob might decide to get possession of the body and burn it. No examination of the body was made last night. The bullet wound in his leg will be examined today, but this does not promise to throw much light on the identity of the negro. He admitted that he was in the box car at the time of the shooting and that he was wounded there by a bullet from Leslie's gun. This is all that could be hoped to establish by an examination of the wound.

An examination of the box car in which the negro was located while the battle between him and Leslie was in progress shows that there are four bullet holes in it and were undoubtedly put there by bullets from Leslie's gun. The chambers of his gun were empty when examined soon after the shooting, and it is believed beyond a doubt that the bullet in the negro's leg was fired from Leslie's gun.

AFTER-SUPPER MOB FIRES NEGRO CABINS.

After the supper hour—after the lifeless body of the negro had been removed to the morgue—the mob which had dispersed again began to form and before 8 o'clock a surging, seething, infuriated mass of humanity was parading the streets, shouting at the top of their voices and shooting fire arms.

The mob was looking for negroes. It seemed that a preconcerted agreement had been reached that every negro in the city should be driven out.

The Imperial barbershop, where only negro barbers are employed, was the first place stormed, and as the mob entered the front door the barbers made their exit at the rear and escaped. Officer Ben May, who was standing on the opposite side of the street, rushed to the scene and ordered the mob out of the place. As there were no more negroes there the mob left and headed for the north end. Since the lewd women were driven from that section of the city a few months ago it has been inhabited by negroes, and as the mob reached the place the negroes fled in all directions.

The mob began at Broadway and from there to A street rocks and missiles of all descriptions were hurled at the houses, through windows and at fleeing negroes. One house was overturned and fire was set to two more, and they burned to the ground. There is scarcely a whole window pane in a window between Broadway and A street. Thousands of people from all sections of the city crowded the streets in the vicinity of the fires. The fire lads from both departments responded to an alarm, but they were unable to do much good. As fast as a line of hose was strung the mob stuck knives into it.

The negroes of the North End were expecting just what happened. Many of them were victims of the Peirce City mob, and the action of last night's mob was nothing new to them. Telephone messages from Webb City and Galena last night stated that those towns were black with Joplin negroes, who left the city as soon as possible after the mob began to form to hang the murderer of Theodore Leslie.

From the North End the mob marched South on Main street to Seventh street and turned east to another section of the city which is inhabited by negroes. Here the mob set fire to three buildings which were inhabited by negroes, and two of them were burned to the ground.

The negroes who inhabited that section of the city between Seventh street and Tenth street and west of the Kansas City Southern tracks, felt perfectly safe, as it was not expected that the mob would molest them, and they were taken quite by surprise. When they heard the mob approaching they deserted their homes only to see them burning from the distance a few minutes afterward.

"HICKORY BILL" WAS RELEASED ON DEMAND.

Soon after the mob began to reassemble after supper, "Hickory Bill," a Joplin character, was arrested for discharging a gun and creating a general disturbance. He was hustled off to the police station and placed in jail almost before the other members of the mob realized just what was happening.

In a few minutes a crowd of not less than 2000 people assembled in front of the jail and demanded that "Hickory Bill" be released from custody. They were in earnest in their demands and threatened to blow up the jail with dynamite if he was not released.

Many citizens with cooler heads addressed the mob, but they replied that talk didn't go—nothing but "Hickory Bill" would appease them. At first the officers were inclined to treat the matter as a jest, but after fully a half hour had passed, and the mob was more strenuous in its demands, "Hickory Bill" was released after the leaders of the mob had promised to see that he went straight home.

TWO SUSPECTS CAUGHT AT CARL JUNCTION.

Walter Scott, who was a member of a posse of men who went north yesterday morning, reported last night that they had arrested two negro suspects near Asbury.

The negroes claimed they had just been released from the Carthage jail and that they knew nothing of the murder. They were taken to Carl Junction and would have been brought to Joplin last night had it not been for the organization of the mob.

The negroes arrested were not armed, and there is no importance attached to the arrest.

MOB DISPERSED AND STREETS WERE CLEARED.

Before midnight the mob dispersed and all was serene. There were a number of people on the streets talking of the actions of the mob, but everything was quiet.

From 8 o'clock until early this morning there was not a negro to be seen on any of the streets in the down town section of the city.

NAME IS GILYARD.

Carthage, Mo., April 15.—The negro lynched in Joplin tonight was Thomas Gilyard, aged 20, a tramp. He had confessed he murdered Leslie, and he was crippled by a bullet fired by Leslie in last night's fight. Early today Sheriff Owen hurried off to the county jail at Carthage Dan Bullard, a negro, who was with Gilyard just before the policeman was killed. Tonight

Bullard was spirited away from Carthage for fear of attack on the county jail.

The above dispatch was received early this morning too late to be verified. Officer Belford, as stated elsewhere, could not remember the negro's name, but felt sure it began with B. It is possible the correspondent got the names confused and that the victim of yesterday's lynching was named Bullard.

RELIEF FUND FOR LESLIE FAMILY

Mr. Burt W. Lyon telephoned The Globe last night to put him down for a $25 subscription to a relief fund for the family of Officer Leslie. It is not known in what circumstances Mr. Leslie's family is left.

CRITICIZING WASHINGTON'S LEADERSHIP
W.E.B. DU BOIS
Of Mr. Booker T. Washington and Others
1903

OF MR. BOOKER T. WASHINGTON AND OTHERS

From birth till death enslaved; in word, in deed, unmanned!
. . . .
Hereditary bondsmen! Know ye not
Who would be free themselves must strike the blow?

BYRON.

EASILY the most striking thing in the history of the American Negro since 1876 is the ascendancy of Mr. Booker T. Washington. It began at the time when war memories and ideals were rapidly passing; a day of astonishing commercial development was dawning; a sense of doubt and hesitation overtook the freedmen's sons,—then it was that his leading began. Mr. Washington came, with a simple definite programme, at the psychological moment when the nation was a little ashamed of having bestowed so much sentiment on Negroes, and was concentrating its energies on Dollars. His programme of industrial education, conciliation of the South, and submission and silence as to civil and political rights, was not wholly original; the Free Negroes from 1830 up to wartime had striven to build industrial schools, and the American Missionary Association had from the first taught various trades; and Price and others had sought a way of honorable alliance with the best of the Southerners. But Mr. Washington first indissolubly linked these things; he put enthusiasm, unlimited energy, and perfect faith into this programme, and changed it from a by-path into a veritable Way of Life. And the tale of the methods by which he did this is a fascinating study of human life.

It startled the nation to hear a Negro advocating such a programme after many decades of bitter complaint; it startled and won the applause of the South, it interested and won the admiration of the North; and after a confused murmur of protest, it silenced if it did not convert the Negroes themselves.

To gain the sympathy and coöperation of the various elements comprising the white South was Mr. Washington's first task; and this, at the time Tuskegee was founded, seemed, for a black man, well-nigh impossible. And yet ten years later it was done in the word spoken at Atlanta: "In all things purely social we can be as separate as the five fingers, and yet one as the hand in all things essential to mutual progress." This "Atlanta Compromise" is by all odds the most notable thing in Mr. Washington's career. The South interpreted it in different ways: the radicals received it as a complete surrender of the demand for civil and political equality; the conservatives, as a generously conceived working basis for mutual understanding. So both approved it, and to-day its author is certainly the most distinguished Southerner since Jefferson Davis, and the one with the largest personal following.

Next to this achievement comes Mr. Washington's work in gaining place and consideration in the North. Others less shrewd and tactful had formerly essayed to sit on these two stools and had fallen between them; but as Mr. Washington knew the heart of the South from birth and training, so by singular insight he intuitively grasped the spirit of the age which was dominating the North. And so thoroughly did he learn the speech and thought of triumphant commercialism, and the ideals of material prosperity, that the picture of a lone black boy poring over a French grammar amid the weeds and dirt of a neglected home soon seemed to him the acme of absurdities. One wonders what Socrates and St. Francis of Assisi would say to this.

And yet this very singleness of vision and thorough oneness with his age is a mark of the successful man. It is as though

Nature must needs make men narrow in order to give them force. So Mr. Washington's cult has gained unquestioning followers, his work has wonderfully prospered, his friends are legion, and his enemies are confounded. To-day he stands as the one recognized spokesman of his ten million fellows, and one of the most notable figures in a nation of seventy millions. One hesitates, therefore, to criticise a life which, beginning with so little, has done so much. And yet the time is come when one may speak in all sincerity and utter courtesy of the mistakes and shortcomings of Mr. Washington's career, as well as of his triumphs, without being thought captious or envious, and without forgetting that it is easier to do ill than well in the world.

The criticism that has hitherto met Mr. Washington has not always been of this broad character. In the South especially has he had to walk warily to avoid the harshest judgments,—and naturally so, for he is dealing with the one subject of deepest sensitiveness to that section. Twice—once when at the Chicago celebration of the Spanish-American War he alluded to the color-prejudice that is "eating away the vitals of the South," and once when he dined with President Roosevelt—has the resulting Southern criticism been violent enough to threaten seriously his popularity. In the North the feeling has several times forced itself into words, that Mr. Washington's counsels of submission overlooked certain elements of true manhood, and that his educational programme was unnecessarily narrow. Usually, however, such criticism has not found open expression, although, too, the spiritual sons of the Abolitionists have not been prepared to acknowledge that the schools founded before Tuskegee, by men of broad ideals and self-sacrificing spirit, were wholly failures or worthy of ridicule. While, then, criticism has not failed to follow Mr. Washington, yet the prevailing public opinion of the land has been but too willing to deliver the solution of a wearisome problem into his hands, and say, "If that is all you and your race ask, take it."

Among his own people, however, Mr. Washington has encountered the strongest and most lasting opposition, amounting at times to bitterness, and even to-day continuing strong and insistent even though largely silenced in outward expression by the public opinion of the nation. Some of this opposition is, of course, mere envy; the disappointment of displaced demagogues and the spite of narrow minds. But aside from this, there is among educated and thoughtful colored men in all parts of the land a feeling of deep regret, sorrow, and apprehension at the wide currency and ascendancy which some of Mr. Washington's theories have gained. These same men admire his sincerity of purpose, and are willing to forgive much to honest endeavor which is doing something worth the doing. They coöperate with Mr. Washington as far as they conscientiously can; and, indeed, it is no ordinary tribute to this man's tact and power that, steering as he must between so many diverse interests and opinions, he so largely retains the respect of all.

But the hushing of the criticism of honest opponents is a dangerous thing. It leads some of the best of the critics to unfortunate silence and paralysis of effort, and others to burst into speech so passionately and intemperately as to lose listeners. Honest and earnest criticism from those whose interests are most nearly touched,—criticism of writers by readers, of government by those governed, of leaders by those led,—this is the soul of democracy and the safeguard of modern society. If the best of the American Negroes receive by outer pressure a leader whom they had not recognized before, manifestly there is here a certain palpable gain. Yet there is also irreparable loss, —a loss of that peculiarly valuable education which a group receives when by search and criticism it finds and commissions its own leaders. The way in which this is done is at once the most elementary and the nicest problem of social growth. History is but the record of such group-leadership; and yet how infinitely changeful is its type and character! And of all types and kinds, what can be more instructive than the leadership of a group within a group?—that curious double movement where real progress may be negative and actual advance be relative retrogression. All this is the social student's inspiration and despair.

Now in the past the American Negro has had instructive experience in the choosing of group leaders, founding thus a peculiar dynasty which in the light of present conditions is worth while studying. When sticks and stones and beasts form the sole environment of a people, their attitude is largely one of determined opposition to and conquest of natural forces. But when to earth and brute is added an environment of men and ideas, then the attitude of the imprisoned group may take three main forms,—a feeling of revolt and revenge; an attempt to adjust all thought and action to the will of the greater group; or, finally, a determined effort at self-realization and self-development despite environing opinion. The influence of all of these attitudes at various times can be traced in the history of the American Negro, and in the evolution of his successive leaders.

Before 1750, while the fire of African freedom still burned in the veins of the slaves, there was in all leadership or attempted leadership but the one motive of revolt and revenge,—typified in the terrible Maroons, the Danish blacks, and Cato of Stono, and veiling all the Americas in fear of insurrection. The liberalizing tendencies of the latter half of the eighteenth century brought, along with kindlier relations between black and white, thoughts of ultimate adjustment and assimilation. Such aspiration was especially voiced in the earnest songs of Phyllis, in the martyrdom of Attucks, the fighting of Salem and Poor, the intellectual accomplishments of Banneker and Derham, and the political demands of the Cuffes.

Stern financial and social stress after the war cooled much of the previous humanitarian ardor. The disappointment and impatience of the Negroes at the persistence of slavery and serfdom voiced itself in two movements. The slaves in the South, aroused undoubtedly by vague rumors of the Haytian revolt, made three fierce attempts at insurrection,—in 1800 under Gabriel in Virginia, in 1822 under Vesey in Carolina, and in 1831 again in Virginia under the terrible Nat Turner. In the Free States, on the other hand, a new and curious attempt at self-development was made. In Philadelphia and New York color-prescription led to a withdrawal of Negro communicants from white churches and the formation of a peculiar socio-religious institution among the Negroes known as the African Church,—an organization still living and controlling in its various branches over a million of men.

Walker's wild appeal against the trend of the times showed how the world was changing after the coming of the cotton-gin. By 1830 slavery seemed hopelessly fastened on the South, and the slaves thoroughly cowed into submission. The free Negroes of the North, inspired by the mulatto immigrants from the West

Indies, began to change the basis of their demands; they recognized the slavery of slaves, but insisted that they themselves were freemen, and sought assimilation and amalgamation with the nation on the same terms with other men. Thus, Forten and Purvis of Philadelphia, Shadd of Wilmington, Du Bois of New Haven, Barbadoes of Boston, and others, strove singly and together as men, they said, not as slaves; as "people of color," not as "Negroes." The trend of the times, however, refused them recognition save in individual and exceptional cases, considered them as one with all the despised blacks, and they soon found themselves striving to keep even the rights they formerly had of voting and working and moving as freemen. Schemes of migration and colonization arose among them; but these they refused to entertain, and they eventually turned to the Abolition movement as a final refuge.

Here, led by Remond, Nell, Wells-Brown, and Douglass, a new period of self-assertion and self-development dawned. To be sure, ultimate freedom and assimilation was the ideal before the leaders, but the assertion of the manhood rights of the Negro by himself was the main reliance, and John Brown's raid was the extreme of its logic. After the war and emancipation, the great form of Frederick Douglass, the greatest of American Negro leaders, still led the host. Self-assertion, especially in political lines, was the main programme, and behind Douglass came Elliot, Bruce, and Langston, and the Reconstruction politicians, and, less conspicuous but of greater social significance Alexander Crummell and Bishop Daniel Payne.

Then came the Revolution of 1876, the suppression of the Negro votes, the changing and shifting of ideals, and the seeking of new lights in the great night. Douglass, in his old age, still bravely stood for the ideals of his early manhood,—ultimate assimilation *through* self-assertion, and on no other terms. For a time Price arose as a new leader, destined, it seemed, not to give up, but to re-state the old ideals in a form less repugnant to the white South. But he passed away in his prime. Then came the new leader. Nearly all the former ones had become leaders by the silent suffrage of their fellows, had sought to lead their own people alone, and were usually, save Douglass, little known outside their race. But Booker T. Washington arose as essentially the leader not of one race but of two,—

a compromiser between the South, the North, and the Negro. Naturally the Negroes resented, at first bitterly, signs of compromise which surrendered their civil and political rights, even though this was to be exchanged for larger chances of economic development. The rich and dominating North, however, was not only weary of the race problem, but was investing largely in Southern enterprises, and welcomed any method of peaceful coöperation. Thus, by national opinion, the Negroes began to recognize Mr. Washington's leadership; and the voice of criticism was hushed.

Mr. Washington represents in Negro thought the old attitude of adjustment and submission; but adjustment at such a peculiar time as to make his programme unique. This is an age of unusual economic development, and Mr. Washington's programme naturally takes an economic cast, becoming a gospel of Work and Money to such an extent as apparently almost completely to overshadow the higher aims of life. Moreover, this is an age when the more advanced races are coming in closer contact with the less developed races, and the race-feeling is therefore intensified; and Mr. Washington's programme practically accepts the alleged inferiority of the Negro races. Again, in our own land, the reaction from the sentiment of war time has given impetus to race-prejudice against Negroes, and Mr. Washington withdraws many of the high demands of Negroes as men and American citizens. In other periods of intensified prejudice all the Negro's tendency to self-assertion has been called forth; at this period a policy of submission is advocated. In the history of nearly all other races and peoples the doctrine preached at such crises has been that manly self-respect is worth more than lands and houses, and that a people who voluntarily surrender such respect, or cease striving for it, are not worth civilizing.

In answer to this, it has been claimed that the Negro can survive only through submission. Mr. Washington distinctly asks that black people give up, at least for the present, three things,—

First, political power,

Second, insistence on civil rights,

Third, higher education of Negro youth,—

and concentrate all their energies on industrial education, the accumulation of wealth, and the conciliation of the South. This policy has been courageously and insistently advocated for over fifteen years, and has been triumphant for perhaps ten years. As a result of this tender of the palm-branch, what has been the return? In these years there have occurred:

1. The disfranchisement of the Negro.

2. The legal creation of a distinct status of civil inferiority for the Negro.

3. The steady withdrawal of aid from institutions for the higher training of the Negro.

These movements are not, to be sure, direct results of Mr. Washington's teachings; but his propaganda has, without a shadow of doubt, helped their speedier accomplishment. The question then comes: Is it possible, and probable, that nine millions of men can make effective progress in economic lines if they are deprived of political rights, made a servile caste, and allowed only the most meagre chance for developing their exceptional men? If history and reason give any distinct answer to these questions, it is an emphatic *No*. And Mr. Washington thus faces the triple paradox of his career:

1. He is striving nobly to make Negro artisans business men and property-owners; but it is utterly impossible, under modern competitive methods, for workingmen and property-owners to defend their rights and exist without the right of suffrage.

2. He insists on thrift and self-respect, but at the same time counsels a silent submission to civic inferiority such as is bound to sap the manhood of any race in the long run.

3. He advocates common-school and industrial training, and depreciates institutions of higher learning; but neither the Negro common-schools, nor Tuskegee itself, could remain open a day were it not for teachers trained in Negro colleges, or trained by their graduates.

This triple paradox in Mr. Washington's position is the object of criticism by two classes of colored Americans. One class is spiritually descended from Toussaint the Savior, through Gabriel, Vesey, and Turner, and they represent the attitude of revolt and revenge; they hate the white South blindly and distrust the white race generally, and so far as they agree on definite action, think that the Negro's only hope lies in emigration beyond the borders of the United States. And yet, by the irony of fate, nothing has more effectually made this programme seem hopeless than the recent course of the United States toward weaker and darker peoples in the West Indies, Hawaii, and the Philippines,—for where in the world may we go and be safe from lying and brute force?

The other class of Negroes who cannot agree with Mr. Washington has hitherto said little aloud. They deprecate the sight of scattered counsels, of internal disagreement; and especially they dislike making their just criticism of a useful and earnest man an excuse for a general discharge of venom from small-minded opponents. Nevertheless, the questions involved are so fundamental and serious that it is difficult to see how men like the Grimkes, Kelly Miller, J. W. E. Bowen, and other representatives of this group, can much longer be silent. Such men feel in conscience bound to ask of this nation three things:

1. The right to vote.
2. Civic equality.
3. The education of youth according to ability.

They acknowledge Mr. Washington's invaluable service in counselling patience and courtesy in such demands; they do not ask that ignorant black men vote when ignorant whites are debarred, or that any reasonable restrictions in the suffrage should not be applied; they know that the low social level of the mass of the race is responsible for much discrimination against it, but they also know, and the nation knows, that relentless color-prejudice is more often a cause than a result of the Negro's degradation; they seek the abatement of this relic of barbarism, and not its systematic encouragement and pampering by all agencies of social power from the Associated Press to the Church of Christ. They advocate, with Mr. Washington, a broad system of Negro common schools supplemented by thorough industrial training; but they are surprised that a man of Mr. Washington's insight cannot see that no such educational system ever has rested or can rest on any other basis than that of the well-equipped college and university, and they insist that there is a demand for a few such institutions throughout the South to train the best of the Negro youth as teachers, professional men, and leaders.

This group of men honor Mr. Washington for his attitude of conciliation toward the white South; they accept the "Atlanta Compromise" in its broadest interpretation; they recognize, with him, many signs of promise, many men of high purpose and fair judgment, in this section; they know that no easy task has been laid upon a region already tottering under heavy burdens. But, nevertheless, they insist that the way to truth and right lies in straightforward honesty, not in indiscriminate flattery; in praising those of the South who do well and criticising uncompromisingly those who do ill; in taking advantage of the opportunities at hand and urging their fellows to do the same, but at the same time in remembering that only a firm adherence to their higher ideals and aspirations will ever keep those ideals within the realm of possibility. They do not expect that the free right to vote, to enjoy civic rights, and to be educated, will come in a moment; they do not expect to see the bias and prejudices of years disappear at the blast of a trumpet; but they are absolutely certain that the way for a people to gain their reasonable rights is not by voluntarily throwing them away and insisting that they do not want them; that the way for a people to gain respect is not by continually belittling and ridiculing themselves; that, on the contrary, Negroes must insist continually, in season and out of season, that voting is necessary to modern manhood, that color discrimination is barbarism, and that black boys need education as well as white boys.

In failing thus to state plainly and unequivocally the legitimate demands of their people, even at the cost of opposing an honored leader, the thinking classes of American Negroes would shirk a heavy responsibility,—a responsibility to themselves, a responsibility to the struggling masses, a responsibility to the darker races of men whose future depends so largely on this American experiment, but especially a responsibility to this nation,—this common Fatherland. It is wrong to encourage a man or a people in evil-doing; it is wrong to aid and abet a national crime simply because it is unpopular not to do so. The growing spirit of kindliness and reconciliation between the North and South after the frightful differences of a generation ago ought to be a source of deep congratulation to all, and especially to those whose mistreatment caused the war; but if that reconciliation is to be marked by the industrial slavery and civic death of those same black men, with permanent legislation into a position of inferiority, then those black men, if they are really men, are called upon by every consideration of patriotism and loyalty to oppose such a course by all civilized methods, even though such opposition involves disagreement with Mr. Booker T. Washington. We have no right to sit silently by while the inevitable seeds are sown for a harvest of disaster to our children, black and white.

First, it is the duty of black men to judge the South discriminatingly. The present generation of Southerners are not responsible for the past, and they should not be blindly hated or blamed for it. Furthermore, to no class is the indiscriminate endorsement of the recent course of the South toward Negroes more nauseating than to the best thought of the South. The South is not "solid"; it is a land in the ferment of social change, wherein forces of all kinds are fighting for supremacy; and to praise the ill the South is to-day perpetrating is just as wrong as to condemn the good. Discriminating and broad-minded criticism is what the South needs,—needs it for the sake of her own white sons and daughters, and for the insurance of robust, healthy mental and moral development.

To-day even the attitude of the Southern whites toward the blacks is not, as so many assume, in all cases the same; the ignorant Southerner hates the Negro, the workingmen fear his competition, the money-makers wish to use him as a laborer, some of the educated see a menace in his upward development, while others—usually the sons of the masters—wish to help him to rise. National opinion has enabled this last class to maintain the Negro common schools, and to protect the Negro partially in property, life, and limb. Through the pressure of the money-makers, the Negro is in danger of being reduced to semi-slavery, especially in the country districts; the workingmen, and those of the educated who fear the Negro, have united to disfranchise him, and some have urged his deportation; while the passions of the ignorant are easily aroused to lynch and abuse any black man. To praise this intricate whirl of thought and prejudice is nonsense; to inveigh indiscriminately against "the South" is unjust; but to use the same breath in praising Governor Aycock, exposing Senator Morgan, arguing with Mr. Thomas Nelson Page, and denouncing Senator

Ben Tillman, is not only sane, but the imperative duty of thinking black men.

It would be unjust to Mr. Washington not to acknowledge that in several instances he has opposed movements in the South which were unjust to the Negro; he sent memorials to the Louisiana and Alabama constitutional conventions, he has spoken against lynching, and in other ways has openly or silently set his influence against sinister schemes and unfortunate happenings. Notwithstanding this, it is equally true to assert that on the whole the distinct impression left by Mr. Washington's propaganda is, first, that the South is justified in its present attitude toward the Negro because of the Negro's degradation; secondly, that the prime cause of the Negro's failure to rise more quickly is his wrong education in the past; and, thirdly, that his future rise depends primarily on his own efforts. Each of these propositions is a dangerous half-truth. The supplementary truths must never be lost sight of: first, slavery and race-prejudice are potent if not sufficient causes of the Negro's position; second, industrial and common-school training were necessarily slow in planting because they had to await the black teachers trained by higher institutions,—it being extremely doubtful if any essentially different development was possible, and certainly a Tuskegee was unthinkable before 1880; and, third, while it is a great truth to say that the Negro must strive and strive mightily to help himself, it is equally true that unless his striving be not simply seconded, but rather aroused and encouraged, by the initiative of the richer and wiser environing group, he cannot hope for great success.

In his failure to realize and impress this last point, Mr. Washington is especially to be criticised. His doctrine has tended to make the whites, North and South, shift the burden of the Negro problem to the Negro's shoulders and stand aside as critical and rather pessimistic spectators; when in fact the burden belongs to the nation, and the hands of none of us are clean if we bend not our energies to righting these great wrongs.

The South ought to be led, by candid and honest criticism, to assert her better self and do her full duty to the race she has cruelly wronged and is still wronging. The North—her copartner in guilt—cannot salve her conscience by plastering it with gold. We cannot settle this problem by diplomacy and suaveness, by "policy" alone. If worse come to worst, can the moral fibre of this country survive the slow throttling and murder of nine millions of men?

The black men of America have a duty to perform, a duty stern and delicate,—a forward movement to oppose a part of the work of their greatest leader. So far as Mr. Washington preaches Thrift, Patience, and Industrial Training for the masses, we must hold up his hands and strive with him, rejoicing in his honors and glorying in the strength of this Joshua called of God and of man to lead the headless host. But so far as Mr. Washington apologizes for injustice, North or South, does not rightly value the privilege and duty of voting, belittles the emasculating effects of caste distinctions, and opposes the higher training and ambition of our brighter minds,—so far as he, the South, or the Nation, does this,—we must unceasingly and firmly oppose them. By every civilized and peaceful method we must strive for the rights which the world accords to men, clinging unwaveringly to those great words which the sons of the Fathers would fain forget: "We hold these truths to be self-evident: That all men are created equal; that they are endowed by their Creator with certain unalienable rights; that among these are life, liberty, and the pursuit of happiness."

THE NULLIFICATION OF THE FIFTEENTH AMENDMENT
CHARLES W. CHESNUTT
The Disfranchisement of the Negro
1903

THE RIGHT of American citizens of African descent, commonly called Negroes, to vote upon the same terms as other citizens of the United States, is plainly declared and firmly fixed by the Constitution. No such person is called upon to present reasons why he should possess this right: that question is foreclosed by the Constitution. The object of the elective franchise is to give representation. So long as the Constitution retains its present form, any State Constitution, or statute, which seeks, by juggling the ballot, to deny the colored race fair representation, is a clear violation of the fundamental law of the land, and a corresponding injustice to those thus deprived of this right.

For thirty-five years this has been the law. As long as it was measurably respected, the colored people made rapid strides in education, wealth, character and self-respect. This the census proves, all statements to the contrary notwithstanding. A generation has grown to manhood and womanhood under the great, inspiring freedom conferred by the Constitution and protected by the right of suffrage—protected in large degree by the mere naked right, even when its exercise was hindered or denied by unlawful means. They have developed, in every Southern community, good citizens, who, if sustained and encouraged by just laws and liberal institutions, would greatly augment their number with the passing years, and soon wipe out the reproach of ignorance, unthrift, low morals and social inefficiency, thrown at them indiscriminately and therefore unjustly, and made the excuse for the equally undiscriminating contempt of their persons and their rights. They have reduced their illiteracy nearly 50 per cent. Excluded from the institutions of higher learning in their own States, their young men hold their own, and occasionally carry away honors, in the universities of the North. They have accumulated three hundred million dollars worth of real and personal property. Individuals among them have acquired substantial wealth, and several have attained to something like national distinction in art, letters and educational leadership. They are numerously represented in the learned professions. Heavily handicapped, they have made such rapid progress that the suspicion is justified that their advancement, rather than any stagnation or retrogression, is the true secret of the virulent Southern hostility to their rights, which has so influenced Northern opinion that it stands mute, and leaves the colored people, upon whom the North conferred liberty, to the tender mercies of those who have always denied their fitness for it.

It may be said, in passing, that the word "Negro," where used in this paper, is used solely for convenience. By the census of 1890 there were 1,000,000 colored people in the country who were half, or more than half, white, and logically there must be, as in fact there are, so many who share the white blood in some degree, as to justify the assertion that the race problem in the United States concerns the welfare and the status of a mixed race. Their rights are not one whit the more sacred because of this fact; but in an argument where injustice is sought to be excused because of fundamental differences of race, it is well enough to bear in mind that the race whose rights and liberties are endangered all over this country by disfranchisement at the South, are the colored people who live in the United States to-day, and not the low-browed, man-eating savage whom the Southern white likes to set upon a block and contrast with Shakespeare and Newton and Washington and Lincoln.

Despite and in defiance of the Federal Constitution, to-day in the six Southern States of Mississippi, Louisiana, Alabama, North Carolina, South Carolina and Virginia, containing an aggregate colored population of about 6,000,000, these have been, to all intents and purposes, denied, so far as the States can effect it, the right to vote. This disfranchisement is accomplished by various methods, devised with much transparent ingenuity, the effort being in each instance to violate the spirit of the Federal Constitution by disfranchising the Negro, while seeming to respect its letter by avoiding the mention of race or color.

These restrictions fall into three groups. The first comprises a property qualification—the ownership of $300 worth or more of real or personal property (Alabama, Louisiana, Virginia and South Carolina); the payment of a poll tax (Mississippi, North Carolina, Virginia); an educational qualification—the ability to read and write (Alabama, Louisiana, North Carolina). Thus far, those who believe in a restricted suffrage everywhere, could perhaps find no reasonable fault with any one of these qualifications, applied either separately or together.

But the Negro has made such progress that these restrictions alone would perhaps not deprive him of effective representation. Hence the second group. This comprises an "understanding" clause—the applicant must be able "to read, or understand when read to him, any clause in the Constitution" (Mississippi), or to read and explain, or to understand and explain when read to him, any section of the Constitution (Virginia); an employment qualification—the voter must be regularly employed in some lawful occupation (Alabama); a character qualification—the voter must be a person of good character and who "understands the duties and obligations of citizens under a republican (!) form of government" (Alabama). The qualifications under the first group it will be seen, are capable of exact demonstration; those under the second group are left to the discretion and judgment of the registering officer—for in most instances these are all requirements for registration, which must precede voting.

But the first group, by its own force, and the second group, under imaginable conditions, might exclude not only the Negro vote, but a large part of the white vote. Hence, the third group, which comprises: a military service qualification —any man who went to war, willingly or unwillingly, in a good cause or a bad, is entitled to register (Ala., Va.); a prescriptive qualification, under which are included all male persons who were entitled to vote on January 1, 1867, at which date the Negro had not yet been given the right to vote; a hereditary qualification, (the so-called "grandfather" clause), whereby any son (Va.), or descendant (Ala.), of a soldier, and (N. C.) the descendant of any person who had the right to vote on January 1, 1867, inherits that right. If the voter wish to take advantage of these last provisions, which are in the nature of exceptions to a general rule, he must register within a stated time, whereupon he becomes a member of a privileged class of permanently enrolled voters not subject to any of the other restrictions.

It will be seen that these restrictions are variously combined in the different States, and it is apparent that if combined to their declared end, practically every Negro may, under color of law, be denied the right to vote, and practically every white man accorded that right. The effectiveness of these provisions to exclude the Negro vote is proved by the Alabama registration under the new State Constitution. Out of a total, by the census of 1900, of 181,471 Negro "males of voting age," less than 3,000 are registered; in Montgomery county alone, the seat of the State capital, where there are 7,000 Negro males of voting age, only 47 have been allowed to register, while in several counties not one single Negro is permitted to exercise the franchise.

These methods of disfranchisement have stood such tests as the United States Courts, including the Supreme Court, have thus far seen fit to apply, in such cases as have been before them for adjudication. These include a case based upon the "understanding" clause of the Mississippi Constitution, in which the Supreme Court held, in effect, that since there was no ambiguity in the language employed and the Negro was not directly named, the Court would not go behind the wording of the Constitution to find a meaning which discriminated against the colored voter; and the recent case of Jackson vs. Giles, brought by a colored citizen of Montgomery, Alabama, in which the Supreme Court confesses itself impotent to provide a remedy for what, by inference, it acknowledges *may* be a "great political wrong," carefully avoiding, however, to state that it is a wrong, although the vital prayer of the petition was for a decision upon this very point.

Now, what is the effect of this wholesale disfranchisement of colored men, upon their citizenship. The value of food to the human organism is not measured by the pains of an occasional surfeit, but by the effect of its entire deprivation. Whether a class of citizens should vote, even if not always wisely—what class does?—may best be determined by considering their condition when they are without the right to vote.

The colored people are left, in the States where they have been disfranchised, absolutely without representation, direct or indirect, in any law-making body, in any court of justice, in any branch of government—for the feeble remnant of voters left by law is so inconsiderable as to be without a shadow of power. Constituting one-eighth of the population of the whole country, two-fifths of the whole Southern people, and a majority in several States, they are not able, because disfranchised where most numerous, to send one representative to the Congress, which, by the decision in the Alabama case, is held by the Supreme Court to be the only body, outside of the State itself, competent to give relief from a great political wrong. By former decisions of the same tribunal, even Congress is impotent to protect their civil rights, the Fourteenth Amendment having long since, by the consent of the same Court, been in many respects as completely nullified as the Fifteenth Amendment is now sought to be. They have no direct representation in any Southern legislature, and no voice in determining the choice of white men who might be friendly to their rights. Nor are they able to influence the election of judges or other public officials, to whom are entrusted the protection of their lives, their liberties and their property. No judge is rendered careful, no sheriff diligent, for fear that he may offend a black constituency; the contrary is most lamentably true; day after day the catalogue of lynchings and anti-Negro riots upon every imaginable pretext, grows longer and more appalling. The country stands face to face with the revival of slavery; at the moment of this writing a federal grand jury in Alabama is uncovering a system of peonage established under cover of law.

Under the Southern program it is sought to exclude colored men from every grade of the public service; not only from the higher administrative functions, to which few of them would in any event, for a long time aspire, but from the lowest as well. A Negro may not be a constable or a policeman. He is subjected by law to many degrading discriminations. He is required to be separated from white people on railroads and street cars, and, by custom, debarred from inns and places of public entertainment. His equal right to a free public education is constantly threatened and is nowhere equitably recognized. In Georgia, as has been shown by Dr. Du Bois, where the law provides for a pro rata distribution of the public school fund between the races, and where the colored school population is 48 per cent. of the total, the amount of the fund devoted to their schools is only 20 per cent. In New Orleans, with an immense colored population, many of whom are persons of means and culture, all colored public schools above the fifth grade have been abolished.

The Negro is subjected to taxation without representation, which the forefathers of this Republic made the basis of a bloody revolution.

Flushed with their local success, and encouraged by the timidity of the Courts and the indifference of public opinion, the Southern whites have carried their campaign into the national government, with an ominous degree of success. If they shall have their way, no Negro can fill any federal office, or occupy, in the public service, any position that is not menial. This is not an inference, but the openly, passionately avowed sentiment of the white South. The right to employment in the public service is an exceedingly valuable one, for which white men have struggled and fought. A vast army of men are employed in the administration of public affairs. Many avenues of employment are closed to colored men by popular prejudice. If their right to public employment is recognized, and the way to it open through the civil service, or the appointing power, or the suffrages of the people, it will prove, as it has already, a strong incentive to effort and a powerful lever for advancement. Its value to the Negro, like that of the right to vote, may be judged by the eagerness of the whites to deprive him of it.

Not only is the Negro taxed without representation in the States referred to, but he pays, through the tariff and internal revenue, a tax to a National government whose supreme judicial tribunal declares that it cannot, through the executive arm, enforce its own decrees, and, therefore, refuses to pass upon a question, squarely before it, involving a basic right of citizenship. For the decision of the Supreme Court in the Giles case, if it foreshadows the attitude which the Court will take upon other cases to the same general end which will soon come before it, is scarcely less than a reaffirmation of the Dred Scott decision; it certainly amounts to this—that in spite of the Fifteenth Amendment, colored men in the United States have no political rights which the States are bound to respect. To say this much is to say that all privileges and immunities which Negroes henceforth enjoy, must be by favor of the whites; they are not *rights*. The whites have so declared; they proclaim that the country is theirs, that the Negro should be thankful that he has so much, when so much more might be withheld from him. He stands upon a lower footing than any alien; he has no government to which he may look for protection.

Moreover, the white South sends to Congress, on a basis including the Negro population, a delegation nearly twice as large as it is justly entitled to, and one which may always safely be relied upon to oppose in Congress every measure which seeks to protect the equality, or to enlarge the rights of colored citizens. The grossness of this injustice is all the more apparent since the Supreme Court, in the Alabama case referred to, has declared the legislative and political department of the government to be the only power which can right a political wrong. Under this decision still further attacks upon the liberties of the citizen may be confidently expected. Armed with the Negro's sole weapon of defense, the white South stands ready to smite down his rights. The ballot was first given to the Negro to defend him against this very thing. He needs it now far more than then, and for even stronger reasons. The 9,000,000 free colored people of to-day have vastly more to defend than the 3,000,000 hapless blacks who had just emerged from slavery. If there be those who maintain that it was a mistake to give the Negro the ballot at the time and in the manner in which it was given, let them take to heart this reflection: that to deprive him of it to-day, or to so restrict it as to leave him utterly defenseless against the present relentless attitude of the South toward his rights, will prove to be a mistake so much greater than the first, as to be no less than a crime, from which not alone the Southern Negro must suffer, but for which the nation will as surely pay the penalty as it paid for the crime of slavery. Contempt for law is death to a republic, and this one has developed alarming symptoms of the disease.

And now, having thus robbed the Negro of every political and civil *right*, the white South, in palliation of its course, makes a great show of magnanimity in leaving him, as the sole remnant of what he acquired through the Civil War, a very inadequate public school education, which, by the present program, is to be directed mainly towards making him a better agricultural laborer. Even this is put forward as a favor, although the Negro's property is taxed to pay for it, and his labor as well. For it is a well settled principle of political economy, that land and machinery of themselves produce nothing, and that labor indirectly pays its fair proportion of the tax upon the public's wealth. The white South seems to stand to the Negro at present as one, who, having been reluctantly compelled to release another from bondage, sees him stumbling forward and upward, neglected by his friends and scarcely yet conscious of his own strength; seizes him, binds him, and having bereft him of speech, of sight and of manhood, "yokes him with the mule" and exclaims, with a show of virtue which ought to deceive no one: "Behold how good a friend I am of yours! Have I not left you a stomach and a pair of arms, and will I not generously permit you to work for me with the one, that you may thereby gain enough to fill the other? A brain you do not need. We will relieve you of any responsibility that might seem to demand such an organ."

The argument of peace-loving Northern white men and Negro opportunists that the political power of the Negro having long ago been suppressed by unlawful means, his right to vote is a mere paper right, of no real value, and therefore to be lightly yielded for the sake of a hypothetical harmony, is fatally short-sighted. It is precisely the attitude and essentially the argument which would have surrendered to the South in the sixties, and would have left this country to rot in slavery for another generation. White men do not thus argue concerning their own rights. They know too well the value of ideals. Southern white men see too clearly the latent power of these unexercised rights. If the political power of the Negro was a nullity because of his ignorance and lack of leadership, why were they not content to leave it so, with the pleasing assurance that if it ever became effective, it would be because the Negroes had grown fit for its exercise? On the contrary, they have not rested until the possibility of its revival was apparently headed off by new State Constitutions. Nor are they satisfied with this. There is no doubt that an effort will be made to secure the repeal of the Fifteenth Amendment, and thus forestall the development of the wealthy and educated Negro, whom the South seems to anticipate as a greater menace than the ignorant ex-slave. However improbable this repeal may seem, it is not a subject to be lightly dismissed; for it is within the power of the white people of the nation to do whatever they wish in the premises—they did it once; they can do it again. The Negro and his friends should see to it that the white majority shall never wish to do anything to his hurt. There still stands, before the Negro-hating whites of the South, the specter of a Supreme Court which will interpret the Constitution to mean what it says, and what those who enacted it meant, and what the nation, which ratified it, understood, and which will find power, in a nation which goes beyond seas to administer the affairs of distant peoples, to enforce its own fundamental laws; the specter, too, of an aroused public opinion which will compel Congress and the Courts to preserve the liberties of the Republic, which are the liberties of the people. To wilfully neglect the suffrage, to hold it lightly, is to tamper with a sacred right; to yield it for anything else whatever is simply suicidal. Dropping the element of race, disfranchisement is no more than to say to the poor and poorly taught, that they must relinquish the right to defend themselves against oppression until they shall have become rich and learned, in competition with those already thus favored and possessing the ballot in addition. This is not the philosophy of history. The growth of liberty has been the constant struggle of the poor against the privileged classes; and the goal of that struggle has ever been the equality of all men before the law. The Negro who would yield this right, deserves to be a slave; he has the servile spirit. The rich and the educated can, by virtue of their influence, command many votes; can find other means of protection; the poor man has but one, he should guard it as a sacred treasure. Long ago, by fair treatment, the white leaders of the South might have bound the Negro to themselves with hoops of steel. They have not chosen to take this course, but by assuming from the beginning an attitude hostile to his rights, have never gained his confidence, and now seek by foul means to destroy where they have never sought by fair means to control.

I have spoken of the effect of disfranchisement upon the colored race; it is to the race as a whole, that the argument of the problem is generally directed. But the unit of society in a republic is the individual, and not the race, the failure to recognize this fact being the fundamental error which has beclouded the whole discussion. The effect of disfranchisement upon the individual is scarcely less disastrous. I do not speak of the moral effect of injustice upon those who suffer from it; I refer rather to the practical consequences which may be appreciated by any mind. No country is free in which the way upward is not open for every man to try, and for every properly qualified man to attain whatever of good the community life may offer. Such a condition does not exist, at the South, even in theory, for any man of color. In no career can such a man compete with white men upon equal terms. He must not only meet the prejudice of the individual, not only the united prejudice of the white community; but lest some one should wish to treat him fairly, he is met at every turn with some legal prohibition which says, "Thou shalt not," or "Thus far shalt thou go and no farther." But the Negro race is viable; it adapts itself readily to circumstances; and being thus adaptable, there is always the temptation to

> "Crook the pregnant hinges of the knee,
> Where thrift may follow fawning."

He who can most skilfully balance himself upon the advancing or receding wave of white opinion concerning his race, is surest of such measure of prosperity as is permitted to men of dark skins. There are Negro teachers in the South—the privilege of teaching in their own schools is the one respectable branch of the public service still left open to them—who, for a grudging appropriation from a Southern legislature, will decry their own race, approve their own degradation, and laud their oppressors. Deprived of the right to vote, and, therefore, of any power to demand what is their due, they feel impelled to buy the tolerance of the whites at any sacrifice. If to live is the first duty of man, as perhaps it is the first instinct, then those who thus stoop to conquer may be right. But is it needful to stoop so low, and if so, where lies the ultimate responsibility for this abasement?

I shall say nothing about the moral effect of disfranchisement upon the white people, or upon the State itself. What slavery made of the Southern whites is a matter of history. The abolition of slavery gave the South an opportunity to emerge from barbarism. Present conditions indicate that the spirit which dominated slavery still curses the fair section over which that institution spread its blight.

And now, is the situation remediless? If not so, where lies the remedy? First let us take up those remedies suggested by the men who approve of disfranchisement, though they may sometimes deplore the method, or regret the necessity.

Time, we are told, heals all diseases, rights all wrongs, and is the only cure for this one. It is a cowardly argument. These people are entitled to their rights to-day, while they are yet alive to enjoy them; and it is poor statesmanship and worse morals to nurse a present evil and thrust it forward upon a future generation for correction. The nation can no more honestly do this than it could thrust back upon a past generation the responsibility for slavery. It had to meet that responsibility; it ought to meet this one.

Education has been put forward as the great corrective—preferably industrial education. The intellect of the whites is to be educated to the point where they will so appreciate the blessings of liberty and equality, as of their own motion to enlarge and defend the Negro's rights. The Negroes, on the other hand, are to be so trained as to make them, not equal with the whites in any way—God save the mark! this would be unthinkable!—but so useful to the community that the whites will protect them rather than to lose their valuable services. Some few enthusiasts go so far as to maintain that by virtue of education the Negro will, in time, become strong enough to protect himself against any aggression of the whites; this, it may be said, is a strictly Northern view.

It is not quite clearly apparent how education alone, in the ordinary meaning of the word, is to solve, in any appreciable time, the problem of the relations of Southern white and black people. The need of education of all kinds for both races is wofully apparent. But men and nations have been free without being learned, and there have been educated slaves. Liberty has been known to languish where culture had reached a very high development. Nations do not first become rich and learned and then free, but the lesson of history has been that they first become free and then rich and learned, and oftentimes fall back into slavery again because of too great wealth, and the resulting luxury and carelessness of civic virtues. The process of education has been going on rapidly in the Southern States since the Civil War, and yet, if we take superficial indications, the rights of the Negroes are at a lower ebb than at any time during the thirty-five years of their freedom, and the race prejudice more intense and uncompromising. It is not apparent that educated Southerners are less rancorous than others in their speech concerning the Negro, or less hostile in their attitude toward his rights. It is their voice alone that we have heard in this discussion; and if, as they state, they are liberal in their views as compared with the more ignorant whites, then God save the Negro!

I was told, in so many words, two years ago, by the Superintendent of Public Schools of a Southern city that "there was no place in the modern world for the Negro, except under the ground." If gentlemen holding such opinions are to instruct the white youth of the South, would it be at all surprising if these, later on, should devote a portion of their leisure to the improvement of civilization by putting under the ground as many of this superfluous race as possible?

The sole excuse made in the South for the prevalent injustice to the Negro is the difference in race, and the inequalities and antipathies resulting therefrom. It has nowhere been declared as a part of the Southern program that the Negro, when educated, is to be given a fair representation in government or an equal opportunity in life; the contrary has been strenuously asserted; education can never make of him anything but a Negro, and, therefore, essentially inferior, and not to be safely trusted with any degree of power. A system of education which would tend to soften the asperities and lessen the inequalities between the races would be of inestimable value. An education which by a rigid separation of the races from the kindergarten to the university, fosters this racial antipathy, and is directed toward emphasizing the superiority of one class and the inferiority of another, might easily have disastrous, rather than beneficial results. It would render the oppressing class more powerful to injure, the oppressed quicker to perceive and keener to resent the injury, without proportionate power of defense. The same assimilative education which is given at the North to all children alike, whereby native and foreign, black and white, are taught side by side in every grade of instruction, and are compelled by the exigencies of discipline to keep their prejudices in abeyance, and are given the opportunity to learn and appreciate one another's good qualities, and to establish friendly relations which may exist throughout life, is absent from the Southern system of education, both of the past and as proposed for the future. Education is in a broad sense a remedy for all social ills; but the disease we have to deal with now is not only constitutional but acute. A wise physician does not simply give a tonic for a diseased limb, or a high fever; the patient might be dead before the constitutional remedy could become effective. The evils of slavery, its injury to whites and blacks, and to the body politic, was clearly perceived and acknowledged by the educated leaders of the South as far back as the Revolutionary War and the Constitutional Convention, and yet they made no effort to abolish it. Their remedy was the same—time, education, social and economic development;—and yet a bloody war was necessary to destroy slavery and put its spirit temporarily to sleep. When the South and its friends are ready to propose a system of education which will recognize and teach the equality of all men before the law, the potency of education alone to settle the race problem will be more clearly apparent.

At present even good Northern men, who wish to educate the Negroes, feel impelled to buy this privilege from the none too eager white South, by conceding away the civil and political rights of those whom they would benefit. They have, indeed, gone farther than the Southerners themselves in approving the disfranchisement of the colored race. Most Southern men, now that they have carried their point and disfranchised the Negro, are willing to admit, in the language of a recent number of the *Charleston Evening Post*, that "the attitude of the Southern white man toward the Negro is incompatible with the fundamental ideas of the republic." It remained for our Clevelands and Abbotts and Parkhursts to assure them that their unlawful course was right and justifiable, and for the most distinguished Negro leader to declare that "every revised Constitution throughout the Southern States has put a premium upon intelligence, ownership of property, thrift and character."

So does every penitentiary sentence put a premium upon good conduct; but it is poor consolation to the one unjustly condemned, to be told that he may shorten his sentence somewhat by good behavior. Dr. Booker T. Washington, whose language is quoted above, has, by his eminent services in the cause of education, won deserved renown. If he has seemed, at times, to those jealous of the best things for their race, to decry the higher education, it can easily be borne in mind that his career is bound up in the success of an industrial school; hence any undue stress which he may put upon that branch of education may safely be ascribed to the natural zeal of the promoter, without detracting in any degree from the essential value of his teachings in favor of manual training, thrift and character-building. But Mr. Washington's prominence as an educational leader, among a race whose prominent leaders are so few, has at times forced him, perhaps reluctantly, to express himself in regard to the political condition of his people, and here his utterances have not always been so wise nor so happy. He has declared himself in favor of a restricted suffrage, which at present means, for his own people, nothing less than complete loss of representation—indeed it is only in that connection that the question has been seriously mooted; and he has advised them to go slow in seeking to enforce their civil and political rights, which, in effect, means silent submission to injustice. Southern white men may applaud this advice as wise, because it fits in with their purposes; but Senator McEnery of Louisiana, in a recent article in the *Independent*, voices the Southern white opinion of such acquiescence when he says: "What other race would have submitted so many years to slavery without complaint? *What other race would have submitted so quietly to disfranchisement?* These facts stamp his (the Negro's) inferiority to the white race." The time to philosophize about the good there is in evil, is not while its correction is still possible, but, if at all, after all hope of correction is past. Until then it calls for nothing but rigorous condemnation. To try to read any good thing into these fraudulent Southern constitutions, or to accept them as an accomplished fact, is to condone a crime against one's race. Those who commit crime should bear the odium. It is not a pleasing spectacle to see the robbed applaud the robber. Silence were better.

It has become fashionable to question the wisdom of the Fifteenth Amendment. I believe it to have been an act of the highest statesmanship, based upon the fundamental idea of this Republic, entirely justified by conditions; experimental in its nature, perhaps, as every new thing must be, but just in principle; a choice between methods, of which it seemed to the great statesmen of that epoch the wisest and the best, and essentially the most just, bearing in mind the interests of the freedmen and the Nation, as well as the feelings of the Southern whites; never fairly tried, and therefore, not yet to be justly condemned. Not one of those who condemn it, has been able, even in the light of subsequent events, to suggest a better method by which the liberty and civil rights of the freedmen and their descendants could have been protected. Its abandonment, as I have shown, leaves this liberty and these rights frankly without any guaranteed protection. All the education which philanthropy or the State could offer as a *substitute* for equality of rights, would be a poor exchange; there is no defensible reason why they should not go hand in hand, each encouraging and strengthening the other. The education which one can demand as a right is likely to do more good than the education for which one must sue as a favor.

The chief argument against Negro suffrage, the insistently proclaimed argument, worn threadbare in Congress, on the platform, in the pulpit, in the press, in poetry, in fiction, in impassioned rhetoric, is the reconstruction period. And yet the evils of that period were due far more to the venality and indifference of white men than to the incapacity of black voters. The revised Southern Constitutions adopted under reconstruction reveal a higher statesmanship than any which preceded or have followed them, and prove that the freed voters could as easily have been led into the paths of civic righteousness as into those of misgovernment. Certain it is that under reconstruction the civil and political rights of all men were more secure in those States than they have ever been since. We will hear less of the evils of reconstruction, now that the bugaboo has served its purpose by disfranchising the Negro, it will be laid aside for a time while the nation discusses the political corruption of great cities; the scandalous conditions in Rhode Island; the evils attending reconstruction in the Philippines, and the scandals in the postoffice department—for none of which, by the way, is the Negro charged with any responsibility, and for none of which is the restriction of the suffrage a remedy seriously proposed. Rhode Island is indeed the only Northern State which has a property qualification for the franchise!

There are three tribunals to which the colored people may justly appeal for the protection of their rights: the United States Courts, Congress and public opinion. At present all three seem mainly indifferent to any question of human rights under the Constitution. Indeed, Congress and the Courts merely follow public opinion, seldom lead it. Congress never enacts a measure which is believed to oppose public opinion; —your Congressman keeps his ear to the ground. The high, serene atmosphere of the Courts is not impervious to its voice; they rarely enforce a law contrary to public opinion, even the Supreme Court being able, as Charles Sumner once put it, to find a reason for every decision it may wish to render; or, as experience has shown, a method to evade any question which it cannot decently decide in accordance with public opinion. The art of straddling is not confined to the political arena. The Southern situation has been well described by a colored editor in Richmond: "When we seek relief at the hands of Congress, we are informed that our plea involves a legal question, and we are referred to the Courts. When we appeal to the Courts, we are gravely told that the question is a political one, and that we must go to Congress. When Congress enacts remedial legislation, our enemies take it to the Supreme Court, which promptly declares it unconstitutional." The Negro might chase his rights round and round this circle until the end of time, without finding any relief.

Yet the Constitution is clear and unequivocal in its terms, and no Supreme Court can indefinitely continue to construe it as meaning anything but what it says. This Court should be bombarded with suits until it makes some definite pronouncement, one way or the other, on the broad question of the constitutionality of the disfranchising Constitutions of the Southern States. The Negro and his friends will then have a clean-cut issue to take to the forum of public opinion, and a distinct ground upon which to demand legislation for the enforcement of the Federal Constitution. The case from Alabama was carried to the Supreme Court expressly to determine the constitutionality of the Alabama Constitution. The Court declared itself without jurisdiction, and in the same breath went into the merits of the case far enough to deny relief, without passing upon the real issue. Had it said, as it might with absolute justice and perfect propriety, that the Alabama Constitution is a bold and impudent violation of the Fifteenth Amendment, the purpose of the lawsuit would have been accomplished and a righteous cause vastly strengthened.

But public opinion cannot remain permanently indifferent to so vital a question. The agitation is already on. It is at present largely academic, but is slowly and resistlessly, forcing itself into politics, which is the medium through which republics settle such questions. It cannot much longer be contemptuously or indifferently elbowed aside. The South itself seems bent upon forcing the question to an issue, as, by its arrogant assumptions, it brought on the Civil War. From that section, too, there come now and then, side by side with tales of Southern outrage, excusing voices, which at the same time are accusing voices; which admit that the white South is dealing with the Negro unjustly and unwisely; that the Golden Rule has been forgotten; that the interests of white men alone have been taken into account, and that their true interests as well are being sacrificed. There is a silent white South, uneasy in conscience, darkened in counsel, groping for the light, and willing to do the right. They are as yet a feeble folk, their voices scarcely audible above the clamor of the mob. May their convictions ripen into wisdom, and may their numbers and their courage increase! If the class of Southern white men of whom Judge Jones of Alabama, is so noble a representative, are supported and encouraged by a righteous public opinion at the North, they may, in time, become the dominant white South, and we may then look for wisdom and justice in the place where, so far as the Negro is concerned, they now seem well-nigh strangers. But even these gentlemen will do well to bear in mind that so long as they discriminate in any way against the Negro's equality of right, so long do they set class against class and open the door to every sort of discrimination. There can be no middle ground between justice and injustice, between the citizen and the serf.

It is not likely that the North, upon the sober second thought, will permit the dearly-bought results of the Civil War to be nullified by any change in the Constitution. As long as the Fifteenth Amendment stands, the *rights* of colored citizens are ultimately secure. There were would-be despots in England after the granting of Magna Charta; but it outlived them all, and the liberties of the English people are secure. There was slavery in this land after the Declaration of Independence, yet the faces of those who love liberty have ever turned to that immortal document. So will the Constitution and its principles outlive the prejudices which would seek to overthrow it.

What colored men of the South can do to secure their citizenship to-day, or in the immediate future, is not very clear. Their utterances on political questions, unless they be to concede away the political rights of their race, or to soothe the consciences of white men by suggesting that the problem is insoluble except by some slow remedial process which will become effectual only in the distant future, are received with scant respect—could scarcely, indeed, be otherwise received, without a voting constituency to back them up,—and must be cautiously made, lest they meet an actively hostile reception. But there are many colored men at the North, where their civil and political rights in the main are respected. There every honest man has a vote, which he may freely cast, and which is reasonably sure to be fairly counted. When this race develops a sufficient power of combination, under adequate leadership,—and there are signs already that this time is near at hand,—the Northern vote can be wielded irresistibly for the defense of the rights of their Southern brethren.

In the meantime the Northern colored men have the right of free speech, and they should never cease to demand their rights, to clamor for them, to guard them jealously, and insistently to invoke law and public sentiment to maintain them. He who would be free must learn to protect his freedom. Eternal vigilance is the price of liberty. He who would be respected must respect himself. The best friend of the Negro is he who would rather see, within the borders of this republic one million free citizens of that race, equal before the law, than ten million cringing serfs existing by a contemptuous sufferance. A race that is willing to survive upon any other terms is scarcely worthy of consideration.

The direct remedy for the disfranchisement of the Negro lies through political action. One scarcely sees the philosophy of distinguishing between a civil and a political right. But the Supreme Court has recognized this distinction and has designated Congress as the power to right a political wrong. The Fifteenth Amendment gives Congress power to enforce its provisions. The power would seem to be inherent in government itself; but anticipating that the enforcement of the Amendment might involve difficulty, they made the superorogatory declaration. Moreover, they went further, and passed laws by which they provided for such enforcement. These the Supreme Court has so far declared insufficient. It is for Congress to make more laws. It is for colored men and for white men who are not content to see the blood-bought results of the Civil War nullified, to urge and direct public opinion to the point where it will demand stringent legislation to enforce the Fourteenth and Fifteenth Amendments. This demand will rest in law, in morals and in true statesmanship; no difficulties attending it could be worse than the present ignoble attitude of the Nation toward its own laws and its own ideals—without courage to enforce them, without conscience to change them, the United States presents the spectacle of a Nation drifting aimlessly, so far as this vital, National problem is concerned, upon the sea of irresolution, toward the maelstrom of anarchy.

The right of Congress, under the Fourteenth Amendment, to reduce Southern representation can hardly be disputed. But Congress has a simpler and more direct method to accomplish the same end. It is the sole judge of the qualifications of its own members, and the sole judge of whether any member presenting his credentials has met those qualifications. It can refuse to seat any member who comes from a district where voters have been disfranchised; it can judge for itself whether this has been done, and there is no appeal from its decision.

If, when it has passed a law, any Court shall refuse to obey its behests, it can impeach the judges. If any president refuse to lend the executive arm of the government to the enforcement of the law, it can impeach the president. No such extreme measures are likely to be necessary for the enforcement of the

Fourteenth and Fifteenth Amendments—and the Thirteenth, which is also threatened—but they are mentioned as showing that Congress is supreme; and Congress proceeds, the House directly, the Senate indirectly, from the people and is governed by public opinion. If the reduction of Southern representation were to be regarded in the light of a bargain by which the Fifteenth Amendment was surrendered, then it might prove fatal to liberty. If it be inflicted as a punishment and a warning, to be followed by more drastic measures if not sufficient, it would serve a useful purpose. The Fifteenth Amendment declares that the right to vote *shall not* be denied or abridged on account of color; and any measure adopted by Congress should look to that end. Only as the power to injure the Negro in Congress is reduced thereby, would a reduction of representation protect the Negro; without other measures it would still leave him in the hands of the Southern whites, who could safely be trusted to make him pay for their humiliation.

Finally, there is, somewhere in the Universe a "Power that works for righteousness," and that leads men to do justice to one another. To this power, working upon the hearts and consciences of men, the Negro can always appeal. He has the right upon his side, and in the end the right will prevail. The Negro will, in time, attain to full manhood and citizenship throughout the United States. No better guaranty of this is needed than a comparison of his present with his past. Toward this he must do his part, as lies within his power and his opportunity. But it will be, after all, largely a white man's conflict, fought out in the forum of the public conscience. The Negro, though eager enough when opportunity offered, had comparatively little to do with the abolition of slavery, which was a vastly more formidable task than will be the enforcement of the Fifteenth Amendment.

A SOUTHERN GOVERNOR
CELEBRATES DISFRANCHISEMENT

CHARLES BRANTLEY AYCOCK
from *Speech to the North Carolina Society*
December 18, 1903

These are some of the reasons for my being proud of North Carolina. I am proud of my State, moreover, because there we have solved the negro problem which recently seems to have given you some trouble. We have taken him out of politics and have thereby secured good government under any party and laid foundations for the future development of both races. We have secured peace, and rendered prosperity a certainty.

I am inclined to give to you our solution of this problem. It is, first, as far as possible under the Fifteenth Amendment to disfranchise him; after that let him alone, quit writing about him; quit talking about him, quit making him "the white man's burden," let him "tote his own skillet"; quit coddling him, let him learn that no man, no race, ever got anything worth the having that he did not himself earn; that character is the outcome of sacrifice and worth is the result of toil; that whatever his future may be, the present has in it for him nothing that is not the product of industry, thrift, obedience to law, and uprightness; that he cannot, by resolution of council or league, accomplish anything; that he can do much by work; that violence may gratify his passions but it cannot accomplish his ambitions; that he may eat rarely of the cooking of equality, but he will always find when he does that "there is death in the pot." Let the negro learn once for all that there is unending separation of the races, that the two peoples may develop side by side to the fullest but that they cannot intermingle; let the white man determine that no man shall by act or thought or speech cross this line, and the race problem will be at an end.

These things are not said in enmity to the negro but in regard for him. He constitutes one third of the population of my State: he has always been my personal friend; as a lawyer I have often defended him, and as Governor I have frequently protected him. But there flows in my veins the blood of the dominant race; that race that has conquered the earth and seeks out the mysteries of the heights and depths. If manifest destiny leads to the seizure of Panama, it is certain that it likewise leads to the dominance of the Caucasian. When the negro recognizes this fact we shall have peace and good will between the races.

But I would not have the white people forget their duty to the negro. We must seek the truth and pursue it. We owe an obligation to "the man in black"; we brought him here; he served us well; he is patient and teachable. We owe him gratitude; above all we owe him justice. We cannot forget his fidelity and we ought not to magnify his faults; we cannot change his color, neither can we ignore his service. No individual ever "rose on stepping stones of dead" others "to higher things," and no people can. We must rise by ourselves, we must execute judgment in righteousness; we must educate not only ourselves but see to it that the negro has an opportunity for education.

As a white man I am afraid of but one thing for my race and that is that we shall become afraid to give the negro a fair chance. The first duty of every man is to develop himself to the uttermost and the only limitation upon his duty is that he shall take pains to see that in his own development he does no injustice to those beneath him. This is true of races as well as of individuals. Considered properly it is not a limitation but a condition of development. The white man in the South can never attain to his fullest growth until he does absolute justice to the negro race. If he is doing that now, it is well for him. If he is not doing it, he must seek to know the ways of truth and pursue them. My own opinion is, that so far we have done well, and that the future holds no menace for us if we do the duty which lies next to us, training, developing the coming generation, so that the problems which seem difficult to us shall be easy to them.

CHALLENGING WASHINGTON'S LEADERSHIP

WILLIAM MONROE TROTTER
To W.E.B. Du Bois
March 26, 1905

Boston, March 26, 1905.

Dear Du Bois,

Your letter with enclosures received. Your answer was as encouraging as was Miller's and especially Grimké's letter disgusting. I showed all to Morgan and to my wife. My wife says you are a brick, all you need is a red head. Morgan said your letter was just what those two fellows needed. Myself and wife had lost faith in Grimké, but Morgan hung on. He is now disgusted with him. Grimké has been "throwing me down" for some time. He told me to my face he was "afraid of" me. I suppose you know he became a "staff correspondent" of the New York Age two weeks ago. That "upset" Morgan and myself completely. His course is especially helpful to Booker and especially embarrassing to me. Fortune had been treating you so nastily and had shown himself such a mean tool of Booker's in his treatment of Rev. Morris & James H. Hayes! Hershaw, of Washington, thinks Grimké has embarrassed himself. Fortune is paying him a salary. I had boomed Grimké so and he is president of the Boston Suffrage League, and now an employee of Tim Fortune! It certainly is hard.

Your course in coming out of that Secret Conference business is the only right course. No upright man ought to "come under" a man like Washington. Your letter was prime. You took care finely of all that flam-doodle of "bad faith." Kelly Miller made me sore when he was here along those lines and about item 5. Call on me at any and all times and I shall do anything I can to assist you. Any suggestions you have to make will always be carefully considered. A national "strategy board" for defensive and offensive and constructive action might be advisable. But no white man, especially like Ogden, can pay "expenses." That "expenses paid" is fatal to the "Committee of 12."

Wilkins will probably soon have the Conservator again. The "Voice of the Negro" seems to be your friend. Harry Smith at Cleveland seems to be O.K. Prof. L. M. Hershaw at Washington is true blue, a very valuable man, my Washington correspondent. He refused Tim's money. Hershaw has much influence with Chase of The Bee. The Pioneer Press at Martinsburg, W. Va. is reliable. I have great faith in Rev. O. M. Waller, now in Brooklyn, N.Y. and in Rev. Geo. Frazier Miller. John E. Bruce and Rev. Chas. S. Morris begin this week to start the Guardian in New York. What do you think of it?

What do you think of the revelation on Emmett Scott given by Alexander in my libel case? Is it not of value to you? Our trump card on Booker is his corrupt methods.

I have written Miss Pauline Hopkins for inside facts as to Booker and the Col. American Magazine. Hershaw is working on Cooper. Let me know whether what I have sent was of any service and what further I can do.

Am I at liberty to show your last correspondence, or copies of it to Hershaw and to Mrs Ida D. Bailey in confidence. They can be trusted and it would do them so *much* good, as well as John F. Cook. Grimké's connection with the Age, (how times have changed since he was helping me in The Guardian) has caused no end of talk at Washington. I believe he has hurt himself and hope he will return to us, a broken and empty vessel etc.

Booker must be checkmated and we must study to do it.

Shall I make any editorial comment about this Ogden business, of a general character?

Yours sincerely,
Wm. Monroe Trotter

A BLACK VAUDEVILLE STAR SPEAKS

AIDA OVERTON WALKER
Colored Men and Women on the Stage
The Colored American Magazine, October 1905

COLORED people on the stage have been given very little consideration by our colored writers and critics; perhaps they have considered them unworthy of their attention, or perhaps it has just been a matter of oversight; be that as it may, I beg leave to write briefly on the past, present, and if possible, future of colored men and women on the Stage.

In the past the profession which I am now following may have merited severe criticism, but like every other calling or profession, the Stage has improved with time, and I am proud to say that there are many clever, honest and well deserving men and women of color in professional life who will compare favorably with men and women of other races in the profession or in other professions. There are good and bad in all vocations, and it does seem rather strange that many outsiders should judge us all alike—bad! When white people refuse to classify, in dealing with us, we get highly indignant and say we should not all be judged alike, and yet we often fail to classify and make distinctions when judging ourselves. Consistency is still a jewel!

Some of our so-called society people regard the Stage as a place to be ashamed of. Whenever it is my good fortune to meet such persons, I sympathize with them for I know they are ignorant as to what is really being done in their own behalf by members of their race on the Stage.

In this age we are all fighting the one problem—that is the color problem! I venture to think and dare to state that our profession does more toward the alleviation of color prejudice than any other profession among colored people. The fact of the matter is this, that we come in contact with more white people in a week than other professional colored people meet in a year and more than some meet in a whole decade.

We entertain thousands of people in the course of a Season. We do a great deal of private entertaining in connection with our public performances and to do it all successfully requires much hard study. It is quite true that God has blessed us with much ability along musical lines, but even genius requires nursing to be used to good advantage. When a large audience leaves a theatre after a creditable two hours and a half performance by Negroes, I am sure the Negro race is raised in the estimation of the people.

It has been my good fortune to entertain and instruct, privately, many members of the most select circles—both in this country and abroad—and I can truthfully state that my profession has given me entree to residences which members of my race in other professions would have a hard task in gaining if ever they did. What I have done, other members of the Williams and Walker Company have also accomplished.

For example: When the Williams and Walker Company played in London, during the Season of 1903-4, Messrs Williams and Walker were invited to the renowned City of Oxford by students of the famous Oxford University, to attend a "stag-party" given in honor of Williams and Walker. Every attention possible was shown to the distinguished colored actors. Students of Oxford entertained the visitors by giving performances from plays written by Oxford men.

I am sure Williams and Walker's visit to Oxford reflected credit on the race and left a lasting impression in the minds of proud and highly cultured Englishmen.

Following are some of the distinguished people whom both Mr. Williams and Mr. Walker and their wives have had the honor to entertain privately. At these entertainments the entertainers were not screened off, nor were we slighted in any way. We have performed in the drawing rooms of Mrs. Arthur Paget, Miss Muriel Wilson, Mrs. Frank Avery, Lady Constance Mackenzie, and many others. At the entertainments given in London, English Nobility were present and expressed pleasure and delight at being entertained as we entertained them.

When Sir Thomas Lipton was presented with the silver service from the American Yacht Club, Williams and Walker entertained Sir Thomas and his party at the Hyde Park Hotel in

London. Much has been said about the occasion on which the Williams and Walker Company appeared at Buckingham Palace by special command from His Most Gracious Majesty King Edward VII., and therefore I need not make further mention of that. I might call attention to many other events in which we have figured, but those mentioned are sufficient to call attention to the work professional colored people have done, and which I am sure has reflected credit on them personally and indirectly on their race.

I do not mention the work of the Williams and Walker Company from an egotistic standpoint, but merely because with them I am better acquainted and know that they have appeared privately as well as publicly before and been appreciated by members of the better classes of white people on both sides of the ocean.

As individuals we must strive all we can to show that we are as capable as white people. In all other walks of life when colored people have had fair play, they have proved their ability, those before the lights must do their part for the cause. We must produce good and great actors and actresses to demonstrate that our people move along with the progress of the times and improve as they move. Our people are capable and with advantages they will succeed.

As yet our profession is young and as yet we have been permitted to do but little. We are often compelled by sheer force of circumstance, to work at a disadvantage, but I think the time is fast approaching when talent will speak for itself and be accepted for its real worth. White people used to allow for us and say "that is good for a colored person," but to-day we are criticized as severely as white actors and actresses, who have every advantage. This is a rather strange fact: the only time white newspaper men speak of us as the equal of white people, is when they are severely criticizing us and our ability to act well; when we fall short they cry out and think it strange that our acting is inferior; of course there is a method in all this we know. But at best, when it comes to singing and dancing, our critics find much difficulty in showing us up to disadvantage; they often acknowledge that it is wonderful that we have done so well and accomplished so much in spite of overwhelming difficulties that do not overwhelm.

I have stated that we ought to strive to produce great actors and actresses; in this I do not mean that all our men and women who possess talent for the Stage, should commence the study of Shakespeare. Already too many of our people wish to master Shakespeare. This is really a ridiculous notion. There are characteristics and natural tendencies in our people which make just as beautiful studies for the Stage as any to be found in the make up of any other race, and perhaps far better. By carefully studying our own graces we learn to appreciate the noble and the beautiful within us, just as other peoples have discovered the graces and beauty in themselves from studying and by acting that which is noble in them. Unless we learn the lesson of self appreciation and practice it, we shall spend our lives imitating other people and depreciating ourselves.

There is nothing so strong as originality, and I think much time is lost in trying to do something that has been done—and "over-done"—much better than you will ever be able to do it.

MORALITY ON THE STAGE.

I do not wish to moralize. I only wish to say a few common sense words in closing this article. I am aware of the fact that many well-meaning people dislike stage life, especially our women. On this point I would say, a woman does not lose her dignity to-day—as used to be the case—when she enters upon Stage life. In claiming Stage life as a profession, the emphasis should not be put upon the avocation, but rather upon the purpose for which you make the choice. If a girl is gay and easily dazzled by the brilliant side of life on the Stage or off, then I should say to that girl: "Choose some other line of work; look to some other profession, for the Stage is certainly no place for you." But if she be a girl of good thoughts and habits, and she chooses the Stage for the love of the profession and professional work, then I should say to her, "Come, for we need so many earnest workers in this field; and by hard work, I am sure the future will repay you and all of us."

One of the greatest needs of the times is a good school in which colored actors and actresses may be properly trained for good acting. With such an institution we could make a great record in the Artistic World. Of course, it takes time to do anything worth while, and especially to carry out great aims and accomplish good work, but when something has been accomplished we consider the time well spent, and so we must go on working in our profession, with the hope that the future will bring us more encouragement and better success and less criticism; not that we cannot stand criticism, for we can; but for the reason that our work is a great work and ought to be encouraged in these days when it needs help and encouragement.

Our Stage work is grand and our lives can be made beautiful. Just think; night after night we entertain people and make them laugh and be happy and forget all the troubles and sorrows with which they are burdened throughout the day. I am sure it is a pleasure to live and work and give pleasure to others as well as to receive pleasure ourselves.

When we look at the Stage from this standpoint, we can appreciate how much it means to ourselves and others. It is rather easy to stand the harsh things some people may say about us when we can feel that besides doing good for ourselves and our race, we are using the gifts that God has given us to a good purpose. With this view before us, we are bound to succeed.

My final word is to the men. You have your duties to perform on and off the stage, to women as well as to yourselves. Remember this fact: good men help women to be good; and remember also, that in helping women you are really helping yourselves. We must work together for the uplift of all and for the progress of all that is good and noble in life.

SEGREGATION IN WASHINGTON, D.C.

MARY CHURCH TERRELL
What It Means to Be Colored in the Capital of the United States
October 10, 1906

[The special interest in the present article rests in the fact that it describes conditions in Washington, a city governed solely by the United States Congress. It is our only city which represents the whole country. It lies between the two sections, North and South, and it has a very large negro population. The article is timely now that Senator Foraker has brought before the Senate the dismissal without honor of the negro battalion. The writer is a colored woman of much culture and recognized standing.—EDITOR.]

WASHINGTON, D. C., has been called "The Colored Man's Paradise." Whether this sobriquet was given to the national capital in bitter irony by a member of the handicapped race, as he reviewed some of his own persecutions and rebuffs, or whether it was given immediately after the war by an ex-slave-holder who for the first time in his life saw colored people walking about like freemen, minus the overseer and his whip, history saith not. It is certain that it would be difficult to find a worse misnomer for Washington than "The Colored Man's Paradise" if so prosaic a consideration as veracity is to determine the appropriateness of a name.

For fifteen years I have resided in Washington, and while it was far from being a paradise for colored people, when I first touched these shores it has been doing its level best ever since to make conditions for us intolerable. As a colored woman I might enter Washington any night, a stranger in a strange land, and walk miles without finding a place to lay my head. Unless I happened to know colored people who live here or ran across a chance acquaintance who could recommend a colored boarding-house to me, I should be obliged to spend the entire night wandering about. Indians, Chinamen, Filipinos, Japanese and representatives of any other dark race can find hotel accommodations, if they can pay for them. The colored man alone is thrust out of the hotels of the national capital like a leper.

As a colored woman I may walk from the Capitol to the White House, ravenously hungry and abundantly supplied with money with which to purchase a meal, without finding a single restaurant in which I would be permitted to take a morsel of food, if it was patronized by white people, unless I were willing to sit behind a screen. As a colored woman I cannot visit the tomb of the Father of this country, which owes its very existence to the love of freedom in the human heart and which stands for equal opportunity to all, without being forced to sit in the Jim Crow section of an electric car which starts from the very heart of the city—midway between the Capitol and the White House. If I refuse thus to be humiliated, I am cast into jail and forced to pay a fine for violating the Virginia laws. Every hour in the day Jim Crow cars filled with colored people, many of whom are intelligent and well to do, enter and leave the national capital.

As a colored woman I may enter more than one white church in Washington without receiving that welcome which as a human being I have a right to expect in the sanctuary of God. Sometimes the color blindness of the usher takes on that peculiar form which prevents a dark face from making any impression whatsoever upon his retina, so that it is impossible for him to see colored people at all. If he is not so afflicted, after keeping a colored man or woman waiting a long time, he will ungraciously show these dusky Christians who have had the temerity to thrust themselves into a temple where only the fair of face are expected to worship God to a seat in the rear, which is named in honor of a certain personage, well known in this country, and commonly called Jim Crow.

Unless I am willing to engage in a few menial occupations, in which the pay for my services would be very poor, there is no way for me to earn an honest living, if I am not a trained nurse or a dressmaker or can secure a position as teacher in the public schools, which is exceedingly difficult to do. It matters not what my intellectual attainments may be or how great is the need of the services of a competent person, if I try to enter many of the numerous vocations in which my white sisters are allowed to engage, the door is shut in my face.

From one Washington theater I am excluded altogether. In the remainder certain seats are set aside for colored people, and it is almost impossible to secure others. I once telephoned to the ticket seller just before a matinee and asked if a neat-appearing colored nurse would be allowed to sit in the parquet with her little white charge, and the answer rushed quickly and positively thru the receiver—NO. When I remonstrated a bit and told him that in some of the theaters colored nurses were allowed to sit with the white children for whom they cared, the ticket seller told me that in Washington it was very poor policy to employ colored nurses, for they were excluded from many places where white girls would be allowed to take children for pleasure.

If I possess artistic talent, there is not a single art school of repute which will admit me. A few years ago a colored woman who possessed great talent submitted some drawings to the Corcoran Art School, of Washington, which were accepted by the committee of awards, who sent her a ticket entitling her to a course in this school. But when the committee discovered that the young woman was colored they declined to admit her, and told her that if they had suspected that her drawings had been made by a colored woman they would not have examined them at all. The efforts of Frederick Douglass and a lawyer of great repute who took a keen interest in the affair were unavailing. In order to cultivate her talent this young woman was forced to leave her comfortable home in Washington and incur the expense of going to New York. Having entered the Woman's Art School of Cooper Union, she graduated with honor, and then went to Paris to continue her studies, where she achieved signal success and was complimented by some of the greatest living artists in France.

With the exception of the Catholic University, there is not a single white college in the national capital to which colored people are admitted, no matter how great their ability, how lofty their ambition, how unexceptionable their character or how great their thirst for knowledge may be.

A few years ago the Columbian Law School admitted colored students, but in deference to the Southern white students the authorities have decided to exclude them altogether.

Some time ago a young woman who had already attracted some attention in the literary world by her volume of short stories answered an advertisement which appeared in a Washington newspaper, which called for the services of a skilled stenographer and expert typewriter. It is unnecessary to state the reasons why a young woman whose literary ability was so great as that possessed by the one referred to should decide to earn money in this way. The applicants were requested to send specimens of their work and answer certain questions concerning their experience and their speed before they called in person. In reply to her application the young colored woman, who, by the way, is very fair and attractive indeed, received a letter from the firm stating that her references and experience were the most satisfactory that had been sent and requesting her to call. When she presented herself there was some doubt in the mind of the man to whom she was directed concerning her racial pedigree, so he asked her point-blank whether she was colored or white. When she confessed the truth the merchant expressed great sorrow and deep regret that he could not avail himself of the services of so competent a person, but frankly admitted that employing a colored woman in his establishment in any except a menial position was simply out of the question.

Another young friend had an experience which, for some reasons, was still more disheartening and bitter than the one just mentioned. In order to secure lucrative employment she left Washington and went to New York. There she worked her way up in one of the largest dry goods stores till she was placed as saleswoman in the cloak department. Tired of being separated from her family she decided to return to Washington, feeling sure that, with her experience and her fine recommendation from the New York firm, she could easily secure employment. Nor was she overconfident, for the proprietor of one of the largest dry goods stores in her native city was glad to secure the services of a young woman who brought such hearty credentials from New York. She had not been in this store very long, however, before she called upon me one day and asked me to intercede with the proprietor in her behalf, saying that she had been discharged that afternoon because it had been discovered that she was colored. When I called upon my young friend's employer he made no effort to avoid the issue, as I feared he would. He did not say he had discharged the young saleswoman because she had not given satisfaction, as he might easily have done. On the contrary, he admitted without the slightest hesitation that the young woman he had just discharged was one of the best clerks he had ever had. In the cloak department, where she had been assigned, she had been a brilliant success, he said. "But I cannot keep Miss Smith in my employ," he concluded. "Are you not master of your own store?" I ventured to inquire. The proprietor of this store was a Jew, and I felt that it was particularly cruel, unnatural and cold-blooded for the representative of one oppressed and persecuted race to deal so harshly and unjustly with a member of another. I had intended to make this point when I decided to intercede for my young friend, but when I thought how a reference to the persecution of his own race would wound his feelings, the words froze on my lips. "When I first heard your friend was colored," he explained, "I did not believe it and said so to the clerks who made the statement. Finally, the girls who had been most pronounced in their opposition to working in a store with a colored girl came to me in a body and threatened to strike. 'Strike away,' said I, 'your places will be easily filled.' Then they started on another tack. Delegation after delegation began to file down to my office, some of the women my very best customers, to protest against my employing a colored girl. Moreover, they threatened to boycott my store if I did not discharge her at once. Then it became a question of bread and butter and I yielded to the inevitable—that's all. Now," said he, concluding, "if I lived in a great, cosmopolitan city like New York, I should do as I pleased, and refuse to discharge a girl simply because she was colored." But I thought of a similar incident that happened in New York. I remembered that a colored woman, as fair as a lily and as beautiful as a Madonna, who was the head saleswoman in a large department store in New York, had been discharged, after she had held this position for years, when the proprietor accidentally discovered that a fatal drop of African blood was percolating somewhere thru her veins.

Not only can colored women secure no employment in the Washington stores, department and otherwise, except as menials, and such positions, of course, are few, but even as customers they are not infrequently treated with discourtesy both by the clerks and the proprietor himself. Following the trend of the times, the senior partner of the largest and best department store in Washington, who originally hailed from Boston, once the home of Wm. Lloyd Garrison, Wendell Phillips and Charles Sumner, if my memory serves me right, decided to open a restaurant in his store. Tired and hungry after her morning's shopping a colored school teacher, whose relation to her African progenitors is so remote as scarcely to be discernible to the naked eye, took a seat at one of the tables in the restaurant of this Boston store. After sitting unnoticed a long time the colored teacher asked a waiter who passed her by if she would not take her order. She was quickly informed that colored people could not be served in that restaurant and was obliged to leave in confusion and shame, much to the amusement of the waiters and the guests who had noticed the incident. Shortly after that a teacher in Howard University, one of the best schools for colored youth in the country, was similarly insulted in the restaurant of the same store.

In one of the Washington theaters from which colored people are excluded altogether, members of the race have been viciously assaulted several times, for the proprietor well knows that colored people have no redress for such discriminations against them in the District courts. Not long ago a colored clerk in one of the departments who looks more like his paternal ancestors who fought for the lost cause than his grandmothers who were victims of the peculiar institution, bought a ticket for the parquet of this theater in which colored people are nowhere welcome, for himself and mother, whose complexion is a bit swarthy. The usher refused to allow the young man to take the seats for which his tickets called and tried to snatch from him the coupons. A scuffle ensued and both mother and son were ejected by force. A suit was brought against the proprietor and the damages awarded the injured man and his mother amounted to the munificent sum of one cent. One of the teachers in the Colored High School received similar treatment in the same theater.

Not long ago one of my little daughter's bosom friends figured in one of the most pathetic instances of which I have ever heard. A gentleman who is very fond of children promised to take six little girls in his neighborhood to a matinee. It happened that he himself and five of his little friends were so fair that they easily passed muster, as they stood in judgment before the ticket-seller and the ticket taker. Three of the little girls were sisters, two of whom were very fair and the other a bit brown. Just as this little girl, who happened to be last in the procession, went by the ticket taker, that argus-eyed sophisticated gentleman detected something which caused a deep, dark frown to mantle his brow and he did not allow her to pass. "I guess you have made a mistake," he called to the host of this theater party. "Those little girls," pointing to the fair ones, "may be admitted, but this one," designating the brown one, "can't." But the colored man was quite equal to the emergency. Fairly frothing at the mouth with anger he asked the ticket taker what he meant, what he was trying to insinuate about that particular little girl. "Do you mean to tell me," he shouted in rage, "that I must go clear to the Philippine Islands to bring this child to the United States and then I can't take her to the theater in the National Capital?" The little ruse succeeded brilliantly, as he knew it would. "Beg your pardon," said the ticket taker, "don't know what I was thinking about. Of course she can go in."

"What was the matter with me this afternoon, mother?" asked the little brown girl innocently, when she mentioned the affair at home. "Why did the man at the theater let my two sisters and the other girls in and try to keep me out?" In relating this incident, the child's mother told me her little girl's question, which showed such blissful ignorance of the depressing, cruel conditions which confronted her, completely unnerved her for a time.

Altho white and colored teachers are under the same Board of Education and the system for the children of both races is said to be uniform, prejudice against the colored teachers in the public schools is manifested in a variety of ways. From 1870 to 1900 there was a colored superintendent at the head of the colored schools. During all that time the directors of the cooking, sewing, physical culture, manual training, music and art departments were colored people. Six years ago a change was inaugurated. The colored superintendent was legislated out of office and the directorships, without a single exception, were taken from colored teachers and given to the whites. There was no complaint about the work done by the colored directors no more than is heard about every officer in every school. The directors of the art and physical culture departments were particularly fine. Now, no matter how competent or superior the colored teachers in our public schools may be, they know that they can never rise to the height of a directorship, can never hope to be more than an assistant and receive the meager salary therefor, unless the present regime is radically changed.

Not long ago one of the most distinguished kindergartners in the country came to deliver a course of lectures in Washington. The colored teachers were eager to attend, but they could not buy the coveted privilege for love or money. When they appealed to the director of kindergartens, they were told that the expert kindergartner had come to Washington under the auspices of private individuals, so that she could not possibly have them admitted. Realizing what a loss colored teachers had sustained in being deprived of the information and inspiration which these lectures afforded, one of the white teachers volunteered to repeat them as best she could for the benefit of her colored co-laborers for half the price she herself had paid, and the proposition was eagerly accepted by some.

Strenuous efforts are being made to run Jim Crow street cars in the national capital. "Resolved, that a Jim Crow law should be adopted and enforced in the District of Columbia," was the subject of a discussion engaged in last January by the Columbian Debating Society of the George Washington University in our national capital, and the decision was rendered in favor of the affirmative. Representative Heflin, of Alabama, who introduced a bill providing for Jim Crow street cars in the District of Columbia last winter, has just received a letter from the president of the East Brookland Citizens' Association "indorsing the movement for separate street cars and sincerely hoping that you will be successful in getting this enacted into a law as soon as possible." Brookland is a suburb of Washington.

The colored laborer's path to a decent livelihood is by no means smooth. Into some of the trades unions here he is admitted, while from others he is excluded altogether. By the union men this is denied, altho I am personally acquainted with skilled workmen who tell me they are not admitted into the unions because they are colored. But even when they are allowed to join the unions they frequently derive little benefit, owing to certain tricks of the trade. When the word passes round that help is needed and colored laborers apply, they are often told by the union officials that they have secured all the men they needed, because the places are reserved for white men, until they have been provided with jobs, and colored men must remain idle, unless the supply of white men is too small.

I am personally acquainted with one of the most skilful laborers in the hardware business in Washington. For thirty years he has been working for the same firm. He told me he could not join the union, and that his employer had been almost forced to discharge him, because the union men threatened to boycott his store if he did not. If another man could have been found at the time to take his place he would have lost his job, he said. When no other human being can bring a refractory chimney or stove to its senses, this colored man is called upon as the court of last appeal. If he fails to subdue it, it is pronounced a hopeless case at once. And yet this expert workman receives much less for his services than do white men who cannot compare with him in skill.

And so I might go on citing instance after instance to show the variety of ways in which our people are sacrificed on the altar of prejudice in the Capital of the United States and how almost insurmountable are the obstacles which block his path to success. Early in life many a colored youth is so appalled by the helplessness and the hopelessness of his situation in this country that in a sort of stoical despair he resigns himself to his fate. "What is the good of our trying to acquire an education? We can't all be preachers, teachers, doctors and lawyers. Besides those professions there is almost nothing for colored people to do but engage in the most menial occupations, and we do not need an education for that." More than once such remarks, uttered by young men and women in our public schools who possess brilliant intellects, have wrung my heart.

It is impossible for any white person in the United States, no matter how sympathetic and broad, to realize what life would mean to him if his incentive to effort were suddenly snatched away. To the lack of incentive to effort, which is the awful shadow under which we live, may be traced the wreck and ruin of scores of colored youth. And surely nowhere in the world do oppression and persecution based solely on the color of the skin appear more hateful and hideous than in the capital of the United States, because the chasm between the principles upon which this Government was founded, in which it still professes to believe, and those which are daily practiced under the protection of the flag, yawns so wide and deep.

PROTESTING THE BROWNSVILLE DISMISSALS

THE NEW YORK TIMES
Negro Pastors Assail Roosevelt's Army Order
November 19, 1906

NEGRO PASTORS ASSAIL ROOSEVELT'S ARMY ORDER

One Calls Him a Judas for
Dismissing Colored Troops.

THREATEN A CHANGE IN VOTES

Mount Olivet Congregation Rises In a
Body to Condemn the President
—Much Feeling Shown.

DEEP RESENTMENT over the action of President Roosevelt in discharging without honor three companies of the colored Twenty-fifth United States Infantry was expressed yesterday by the preachers in the negro churches of the city. They protested against the arbitrary nature of the order and declared that the President never would have dared to give like treatment to white soldiers.

They saw in the selection of a Southerner to make the official investigation into the troubles at Brownsville a truckling to sectional prejudice, and they declared in so many words that the negroes of New York would seek revenge at the ballot box.

As the preachers expressed their feelings it was evident that the feelings of their congregations had been deeply touched also. They punctuated the telling points of the sermons with exclamations of approval. At Mount Olivet Baptist Church, Fifty-third Street and Seventh Avenue, the Rev. Dr. Gilbert presented resolutions condemning the President, and they were carried by the congregation rising in a body. In introducing the subject he said:

"You have often heard me speak in admiration of the President, but now we have lost confidence in him. He has yielded to the ungodly prejudice of the South and has acted as he never would have done with white people. You know colored people, and you know that those who committed the crime, which we as much as any condemn, would never have told their comrades. Yet he punishes all alike. His own son a few weeks ago refused to accuse his comrades, and no one approved more heartily than the President."

The resolutions offered recited the history of the Brownsville trouble and went on:

> As a church we object to the singling out of negro soldiers for a course of treatment that is unprecedented in the history of the country. We are unalterably opposed to the un-American idea of making the innocent suffer vicariously for the wrongdoing of a few guilty men, and we believe that the dismissal of all of the men of the three companies referred to is too great a concession to prejudice against our people. In view of the above-expressed sentiments be it
>
> Resolved, That the action of the President of the United States is most heartily disapproved by us, and is so much the more disapproved by us because of the high regard we have hitherto cherished for him.
>
> Resolved, further, That it is our conviction that the order of the President should be forthwith rescinded.
>
> Resolved, further, That a copy of these resolutions be given to the press for publication, and that a copy be sent to the President and also one to the War Department.

In the Memorial A. M. E. Zion Church of Brooklyn the Rev. Dr. F. M. Jacobs said:

> "The President might eat with a thousand Booker T. Washingtons and it would not hurt us as much as this action. The black man and woman do not want social equality; they do want justice and equity. In his ambition he has forgotten all the bravery and self-sacrifice of the negro troops, through which alone he is alive to-day."

Further references to the rescue of the Rough Riders at San Juan Hill by the negro troops were made at the Abyssinian Baptist Church, West Fortieth Street, by the Rev. Dr. Charles S. Morris. He said:

"When the President, whose life our soldiers saved on the red slopes of San Juan Hill, whose nomination to the Governorship of New York our votes ratified at the ballot box, sends a Southerner full of the prejudice of that section to investigate a case of lawless disorder, and brands with an ineffable stain 150 men for the crime of ten or twelve, a people with a million votes, which can be cast and counted, will smite with unforgiving condemnation the next Presidential candidate of the Republican Party.

"The President's decree was signed the day after the election. He shot us when our gun was empty. But we have two years to work, and our slogan shall be a Republican Congress to protect our people in the South, a Democratic President to resent the insult heaped upon us. Thus shall we answer Theodore Roosevelt, once enshrined in our love as our Moses, now enshrouded in our scorn as our Judas."

"VIOLATION OF THE THIRTEENTH AMENDMENT"

MARY CHURCH TERRELL
Peonage in the United States: The Convict Lease System and the Chain Gangs

The Nineteenth Century and After, August 1907

THE CONVICT LEASE SYSTEM AND THE CHAIN GANGS

IN the chain gangs and convict lease camps of the South to-day are thousands of coloured people, men, women, and children, who are enduring a bondage, in some respects more cruel and more crushing than that from which their parents were emancipated forty years ago. Under this modern *régime* of slavery thousands of coloured people, frequently upon trumped-up charges or for offences which in a civilised community would hardly land them in gaol, are thrown into dark, damp, disease-breeding cells, whose cubic contents are less than those of a good-sized grave, are overworked, underfed, and only partially covered with vermin-infested rags. As the chain gangs and the convict lease system are operated in the South to-day they violate the law against peonage, the constitutionality of which was affirmed by the Supreme Court two years ago. In the famous case of Clyatt *versus* the United States, Attorney-General Moody, recently placed upon the bench of the Supreme Court, represented the Government, while Senator Bacon and others appeared for Clyatt, a resident of Georgia, who had been convicted in the Federal Courts of that State and sentenced to four years' hard labour on the charge of having held two coloured men in peonage on account of debt, in violation of the law. In his brief, Attorney Moody declared that the executive arm of the law, so far as the enforcement of the statute against peonage was concerned, has been practically paralysed.

'Notwithstanding the fact that several United States Courts have held this law to be constitutional' [said Judge Moody], 'the Government is powerless to compel its enforcement or observance, even in the most typical and flagrant cases. We think we may truthfully say' [continues Judge Moody], 'that upon the decision of this case (Clyatt *v.* the United States) hangs the liberty of thousands of persons, mostly coloured, it is true, who are now being held in a condition of involuntary servitude, in many cases worse than slavery itself, by the unlawful acts of individuals, not only in violation of the thirteenth amendment to the constitution, but in violation of the law which we have under consideration.'

With one or two exceptions, perhaps, no case decided by the Supreme Court within recent years involved graver considerations than were presented by the questions raised in the Clyatt case, for the constitutionality of the law against peonage was thereby affirmed.

If anybody is inclined to attach little importance to Judge Moody's description of the conditions under which thousands of peons are living in the South to-day, on the ground that they may be simply the exaggerated statement of a Northerner who, at best, has received his information second hand, let him listen to the words of a man, born and reared in the South, who was commissioned a few years ago to investigate the convict camps of his own State. After Colonel Byrd, of Rome, Ga., had inspected every county camp in the State which it was possible for him to discover, he addressed himself to Governor Atkinson, who for years had been trying to improve existing conditions, as follows:

'Your Excellency never did a more noble deed nor one that has been more far reaching in good or beneficent results to a helpless and friendless class of unfortunates than when you sent Special Inspector Wright into the misdemeanour camps of Georgia two years ago. His one visit did valiant service for human beings that were serving a bondage worse than slavery. True they were law-breakers and deserved punishment at the hands of the State, but surely the State has no right to make helpless by law and then to forsake the helpless to the mercies of men who have no mercy. Surely there can be no genuine civilisation when man's inhumanity to man is so possible, so plainly in evidence.'

Immediately after the constitutionality of the law against peonage was affirmed by the Supreme Court in March 1904, Judge Emory Speer, of Savannah, Georgia, one of the most eminent jurists in the country, began to attack the chain gangs of the South on the ground that they violate both the thirteenth amendment and the law against peonage. Since the thirteenth amendment declares that 'involuntary servitude except as punishment for crime, whereof the party shall have been duly convicted, shall not exist in the United States,' Judge Speer attacked the chain gangs, because men, women, and children by the hundreds are forced into involuntary servitude by being sentenced to work upon them, who are not even charged with crime, but are accused of some petty offence, such as walking on the grass, expectorating upon the side walk, going to sleep in a depot, loitering on the streets, or other similar misdemeanours which could not by any stretch of the imagination be called a crime. Judge Speer also declared it to be his opinion that even those who sentence these helpless and friendless people to the chain gangs, and thus force them into involuntary servitude, are guilty of violating the law and are liable to punishment therefore; since it was explicitly stated in the decision rendered by the Supreme Court that even though 'there might be in the language of the court either a municipal ordinance or State law sanctioning the holding of persons in involuntary servitude, Congress has power to punish those who thus violate the thirteenth amendment' and the law against peonage at one and the same time.

In spite, however, of the overwhelming weight of evidence showing that atrocities are daily being perpetrated upon American citizens in almost every State of the South, with the connivance of those who administer the law, which are as shocking and unprintable as those endured by the Russian Jew, in spite of the power which the Supreme Court asserts is possessed by Congress, but feeble efforts are being put forth to suppress the chain gangs and the convict lease camps of the South. It is surprising how few there are among even intelligent people in this country who seem to have anything but a hazy idea of what the convict lease system means.

The plan of hiring out short term convicts to an individual or a company of individuals who needed labourers was adopted by the southern States shortly after the war, not from choice, it is claimed, but because there was neither a sufficient number of gaols nor money enough to build them. Those who need labourers for their farms, saw mills, brick yards, turpentine distilleries, coal or phosphate mines, or who have large contracts of various kinds, lease the misdemeanants from the county or State, which sells them to the highest bidder with merciless disregard of the fact that they are human beings, and practically gives the lessee the power of life and death over the unfortunate man or woman thus raffled off. The more work the lessee gets out of the convict, the more money goes into his gaping purse. Doctors cannot be employed without the expenditure of money, while fresh victims may be secured by the outlay of little cash when convicts succumb to disease and neglect. From a purely business standpoint, therefore, it is much more profitable to get as much work out of a convict as can be wrung from him at the smallest possible expense, and then lay in a fresh supply, when necessary, than it is to clothe, and shelter, and feed him properly, and spend money trying to preserve his health. It is perfectly clear, therefore, that it is no exaggeration to say that in some respects the convict lease system, as it is operated in certain southern States, is less humane than was the bondage endured by slaves fifty years ago. For, under the old *régime*, it was to the master's interest to clothe and shelter and feed his slaves properly, even if he were not moved to do so by considerations of mercy and humanity, because the death of a slave meant an actual loss in dollars and cents, whereas the death of a convict to-day involves no loss whatsoever either to the lessee or to the State.

Speaking of this system a few years ago, a governor of Kentucky said:

> 'I cannot but regard the present system under which the State penitentiary is leased and managed as a reproach to the commonwealth. It is the *system* itself and not the officer acting under it with which I find fault. Possession of the convict's person is an opportunity for the State to make money—the amount to be made is whatever can be wrung from him without regard to moral or mortal consequences. The penitentiary which shows the largest cash balance paid into the State treasury is

the best penitentiary. In the main the notion is clearly set forth and followed that a convict, whether pilferer or murderer, man, woman, or child, has almost no human right that the State is bound to be at any expense to protect.'

Again, at a meeting of the National Prison Association which was held in New Orleans a few years ago, a speaker who had carefully studied the convict lease system declared that the convicts in the South, most of whom are negroes, are in many cases worse off than they were in the days of slavery. 'They are bought as truly,' said he, 'are more completely separated from their families, are irretrievably demoralised by constant evil association and are invariably worse off when they leave the camps than when they entered.' 'Over certain places where the convicts of Alabama are employed,' said an authority on penology, 'should be written the words "All hope abandon, ye who enter here," so utterly demoralising is the entire management.' And so it would be possible to quote indefinitely from men all over the country in every station of life, from judges, governors of States, prison experts, and private citizens, whose testimony without a single exception proves conclusively that the convict lease system in particular, and the chain gang on general principles, are an insult to the intelligence and humanity of an enlightened community.

It is frequently asserted that the convict lease camps and other forms of peonage are dying out in the south. First one State and then another passes laws against leasing convicts to private individuals or attempts to pass such a law, or, if it still adheres to the convict lease system, it tries to provide for the inspection of the camps by men appointed to do this work by the State. But facts which have been brought to light during the last year or two show that those who extract comfort from the reports which announce the disappearance of the convict camps and the chain gangs build their hope upon a foundation of sand. During the year 1906 allegations of the existence of slavery in Florida were made to the department of justice, and evidence was produced to show that hundreds of men, the majority of whom were coloured, but a few among the number white, were virtually reduced to the condition of slaves.

Facts were produced which showed that the officers of the law, the sheriffs themselves, were parties to reducing to a condition of slavery the coloured people who work in the phosphate and coal mines, in the lumber mills or on the turpentine farms of Florida, for instance. These camps were inspected by a woman who was commissioned, it is said, by those high in authority to secure the facts. Only last September a government detective disguised as a man anxious to purchase timber lands, visited the railroad camps of Blount Co., Tenn., and secured evidence against some of the most prominent contractors in that section, which showed that hundreds of coloured men have systematically been deprived of their liberty, while it is impossible to state how many of them lost their lives.

Before the grand jury the victims of this barbarous system of peonage, many of whom had been brought to Tennessee from North and South Carolina, told pitiable tales of their suffering and maltreatment and related stories of seeing men killed, dragged to the river in blankets, weighted, and then sunk into the water, which are too horrible to believe. As a result of this trial one of the largest railroad contractors of Knoxville, Tenn., was indicted by the grand jury on the charge of peonage, the indictment containing twenty-five counts.

Upon the evidence of a coloured soldier who was with President Roosevelt in Cuba, and who sawed his way to freedom through the floor of the shack in which he was confined at night, together with a large number of peons, the man who thus held him in bondage in Missouri was sentenced to three and a half years in the penitentiary of Fort Leavenworth, Kansas, in addition to paying a fine of five thousand dollars and costs. Several others who were engaged in conducting this particular camp, among them the son of the chief offender, were also sentenced to the penitentiary, fined, and obliged to pay the costs. Last spring six coloured people filed suits against a family by whom they had been held in a state of peonage in Ashley Co., Ark. Their complaint set forth inhuman treatment, imprisonment in gaols in various places, that they were bound like beasts, paraded through public streets, and then imprisoned on plantations, where they were compelled to do the hardest kind of labour without receiving a single cent.

While coloured people were originally the only ones affected to any great extent by the practice of peonage in the southern States, in recent years white people in increasingly large numbers have been doomed to the same fate. For instance, only last July the chairman of the Board of Commissioners of Bradford Co., Florida, was arrested for holding in a state of peonage an orphan white girl sixteen years old. The girl declares that she was so brutally treated, she started to walk to Jacksonville, Fla. When she had gone six miles, she was overtaken, she says, by her hard task-master and forced to walk back by a road covered with water in places, so that she was obliged to wade knee deep. When she returned, she declared her master beat her with a hickory stick and showed bruises to substantiate the charge. Last October a wealthy family, living in Arkansaw, was convicted of holding two white girls from St. Louis, Mo., in peonage, and was forced to pay one of the white slaves one thousand dollars damages, and the other 625 dollars. The farmer had induced the girls to come from Missouri to Arkansaw, and then promptly reduced them to the condition of slaves. In the same month of October came the startling announcement that one thousand white girls, who are rightful heiresses to valuable timber lands in the wilds of the Florida pine woods, wear men's clothing and work side by side with coloured men who are held in slavery as well as the girls. Stories of the treatment accorded these white slave girls of Florida, which reached the ears of the Washington officials, equal in cruelty some of the tales related in *Uncle Tom's Cabin* by Harriet Beecher Stowe. In the black depths of pine woods, living in huts never seen by civilised white men other than the bosses of the turpentine camps, girls are said to have grown old in servitude. These girls are said to be the daughters of crackers who, like fathers in pre-historic times, little value the birth of a girl, and sell the best years of their daughters' lives to the turpentine or sulphur miners and to the lumber men for a mere song. To be discharged from one of these camps means death to an *employé*. Since they receive nothing for their services, their dismissal is no revenge for an angered foreman or boss. The slaves are too numerous to be beaten, and it is said to be a part of the system never to whip an *employé*, but invariably to shoot the doomed man or woman upon the slightest provocation, so that the others might be kept in constant subjection.

Two white men of Seymour, Indiana, went to Vance, Mississippi, not very long ago, to work for a large stave company, as they supposed; but when they reached Vance, they were told they must go to the swamp and cut timber. When they demurred, the foreman had them arrested for securing their transportation money 'on false pretences.' The squire before whom they were taken fined each of them 45 dollars and costs. They were then obliged to ride twenty-three miles on horseback to Belen, the county seat, where they were kept three days and given one meal. Then they were taken to Essex, Mississippi, turned over to the owner of a plantation, placed in a stockade at night and forced to work under an armed guard. They were ordered to work out their fine at *fifteen cents a day*, such a contract being made by the *court officers themselves*. These Indiana men learned during the nine days they were in this Mississippi stockade that there were men on the plantation who had been there for ten years trying to work out their fines. Before one fine could be worked out a new charge would be trumped up to hold them. Only last August a young white man who had lived in New York returned to his home, half starved, his body covered with bruises, resulting from unmerciful beatings he had received in a State camp in North Carolina, and related a story which was horrifying in its revelations of the atrocities perpetrated upon the men confined in it. This young white man claimed that at the time he escaped there were no less than twenty other youths from New York unable to return to their homes, and enduring the torture to which he was subjected by inhuman bosses every day. According to this young New Yorker's story, there were about one thousand men at work in this camp, each of whom was obliged to contribute 50 cents a week toward the support of a physician.

> 'On one occasion' [said he] 'the foreman threw heavy stones at me, one of which struck me on the head, knocking me senseless, because I sat down to rest. For hours I lay on the cot in my shack without medical aid, and I bear the mark of that stone to-day. For refusing to work because of lack of nourishment, for our meals consisted only of a slice of bread and a glass of water, I saw the foreman take a revolver, shoot a young negro through

the leg and walk away, leaving him for dead. This fellow lay for days without medical aid and was finally taken away, nobody knows where. Three Italians were killed and two others were severely injured in a fight between the foreman and labourers, and yet not one of these men was arrested. Since the post office was under the control of the men running the camp, the letters written by the New York boys to their friends and relatives never reached their destination.'

The cases just cited prove conclusively that not only does peonage still rage violently in the southern States and in a variety of forms, but that while it formerly affected only coloured people, it now attacks white men and women as well.

From renting or buying coloured men, women, and children, who had really fallen under the ban of the law, to actually trapping and stealing them was a very short step indeed, when labour was scarce and the need of additional hands pressed sore. Very recently, incredible as it may appear to many, coloured men have been captured by white men, torn from their homes and forced to work on plantations or in camps of various kinds, just as truly as their fathers before them were snatched violently by slave catchers from their native African shores. Only last February (1906) two cotton planters of Houston Co., Texas, were arrested for a kind of peonage which is by no means uncommon in the South to-day. The planters needed extra help, so they captured two strong, able-bodied negroes, whom they charged with being indebted to them, and with having violated their contracts. Without resort to law they manacled the negroes and removed them to their plantations, where they forced them to work from twelve to sixteen hours a day without paying them a cent. The sheriff who arrested the planters admitted that this practice of capturing negroes when labour is needed on the plantations has prevailed for a long time in Madison Co., Texas, where the population is mainly negro. The captured men are worked during the cotton-planting season, are then released with empty pockets and allowed to return to their homes as best they can, where they remain until they are needed again, when they are recaptured.

But the methods generally used by the men who run the convict camps of the South or who own large plantations, when they need coloured labourers, are much more skilful and less likely to involve them in trouble than those which the Texans just mentioned employ. Coloured men are convicted in magistrates' courts of trivial offences, such as alleged violation of contract or something of the kind, and are given purposely heavy sentences with alternate fines. Plantation owners and others in search of labour, who have already given their orders to the officers of the law, are promptly notified that some available labourers are theirs to command and immediately appear to pay the fine and release the convict from gaol only to make him a slave. If the negro dares to leave the premises of his employer, the same magistrate who convicted him originally is ready to pounce down upon him and send him back to gaol. Invariably poor and ignorant, he is unable to employ counsel or to assert his rights (it is treason to presume he has any) and he finds all the machinery of the law, so far as he can understand, against him. There is no doubt whatever that there are scores, hundreds perhaps, of coloured men in the South to-day who are vainly trying to repay fines and sentences imposed upon them five, six, or even ten years ago. The horror of ball and chain is ever before them, and their future is bright with no hope.

In the annual report of the 'Georgia State Prison Commission,' which appeared only last June, the secretary shows that during the year 1905–06, there was a decrease of fully 10 per cent. in the number of misdemeanour convicts on the county chain gangs in Georgia, notwithstanding the fact that there has been an increase among the felony convicts. This decrease in the number of misdemeanants is explained as follows: 'Owing to the scarcity of labour, farmers who are able to do so pay the fines of able-bodied prisoners and put them on their plantations to work them out.' 'Had it not been for the fact that many farmers have paid the fines of the men convicted,' explains the prison commission, 'in order to get their labour, there is no doubt that there would be an increase instead of a decrease in the number on the misdemeanour gangs.' This very frank admission of the open manner in which the law against peonage is deliberately broken by the farmers of Georgia is refreshing, to say the least. Surely they cannot be accused by prudish and unreasonable persons of violating the thirteenth amendment by mysterious methods hard to detect and transgressing the peonage law in secret, when the decrease in the number of misdemeanants of a sovereign State is attributed in a printed report to the fact that the farmers are buying up able-bodied negroes a bit more briskly than usual.

While the convict lease camps of no State in the South have presented conditions more shocking and cruel than have those in Georgia, it is also true that in no State have more determined and conscientious efforts to improve conditions been put forth by a portion of its citizens than in that State. In spite of this fact it is well known that some of the wealthiest men in the State have accumulated their fortunes by literally buying coloured men, women, and children, and working them nearly, if not quite, to death. Reference has already been made to the report submitted to the Georgia legislature a few years ago by Colonel Byrd, who was appointed special commissioner to investigate the convict lease camps of his State. In reviewing this report the *Atlanta Constitution* summed up the charges against the convict lease system as follows: 'Colonel Byrd's report was not written by a Northerner, who does not understand conditions in the South, or the people living in that section' (as is so frequently asserted, when one who does not live in the sunny south dares to comment on anything which takes place below Mason's and Dixon's line); 'but it is written by one of the South's most distinguished citizens who did not deal in glittering generalities, but in facts.' Colonel Byrd gave a truthful account of his trips to the camps, of his visits in the day time and at night, when none knew of his coming. He made it a rule, he said, to arrive at each camp unannounced, and he has told us exactly what he saw with his eyes and heard with his ears. Of the fifty-one chain gangs visited, Colonel Byrd discovered that at least half were operated exclusively by private individuals who had practically the power of life and death over the convicts. Seldom was provision made for the separation of the sexes, either during work by day or sleep by night. Little or no attention was given to the comfort or sanitary condition of the sleeping quarters, and women were forced to do men's work in men's attire. The murder of the men and the outrage of the women in these camps, the political pulls by which men occupying lofty positions in the State were shielded and saved from indictment by grand juries, formed the subjects of many indignant editorials in the *Atlanta Constitution*.

Briefly summed up, the specific charges preferred by one of the South's most distinguished sons who had made a most painstaking and exhaustive investigation of the convict lease camps of Georgia are as follow:

(1) Robbing convicts of their time allowances for good behaviour. According to Colonel Byrd, there were not five camps in the State that had complied with the law requiring them to keep a book in which the good or bad conduct of each convict shall be entered daily. In the event of good conduct the law provides that a prisoner's term of confinement shall be shortened four days during each month of service. In fifteen out of twenty-four private camps the contractors did not give the convicts a single day off for good service, nor did they even make pretence of doing so.

(2) Forcing convicts to work from fourteen to twenty hours a day.

(3) Providing them no clothes, no shoes, no beds, no heat in winter, and no ventilation whatever in single rooms in summer in which sixty convicts slept in chains.

(4) Giving them rotten food.

(5) Allowing them to die, when sick, for lack of medical attention.

(6) Outraging the women.

(7) Beating to death old men too feeble to work.

(8) Killing young men for the mere sake of killing.

(9) Suborning jurors and county officers, whose sworn duty it is to avenge the wrongdoing of guards.

It is when he struck the convicts leased to private individuals that Colonel Byrd took off his gloves, as the *Atlanta Constitution* well said, and dipped his pen in red ink. In these private camps Colonel Byrd found the convicts, men committed at the most for some trivial offence or perhaps none at all, had no clothes except greasy, grimy garments, which in many cases were worn to threads and were worthless as protection. These men, women, and children, for there were children only eight years old in the camps inspected by Colonel Byrd a few years ago, were badly shod and in the majority of cases went barefoot the year round. In many of the pine belt gangs, where the convicts were buried in the fastness of mighty pine forests, they went from year's end to year's end without a taste of vegetables. Usually after the convicts returned from their fourteen hours' work they were given raw chunks of meat to prepare for their own dinner. In the matter of buildings the report was no less severe. In a camp owned by a well-known Georgian, Colonel Byrd found eleven men sleeping in a room ten feet square and but seven feet from floor to ceiling, with no window at all, but one door which opened into another room. In another camp the convicts slept in tents which had no bunks, no mattresses, and not even a floor. Fully thirteen of the camps out of twenty-four contained neither bunks nor mattresses, and the convicts were compelled to sleep in filthy, vermin-ridden blankets on the ground. And the men were obliged to sleep chained together.

Many of the camps had no arrangements and scarcely miserable excuses for means of warming the barn-like buildings in which the convicts were confined during stormy days and wintry nights. The suffering the helpless inmates were forced to endure in winter, according to Colonel Byrd's description, must have been terrible, while in the summer they were locked into the sweat boxes without ventilation, in order that the lessee might save the expense of employing night guards.

'In two instances,' said Colonel Byrd, 'I found by the bedside of sick convicts tubs that had been used for days without having been emptied and in a condition that would kill anything but a misdemeanour convict.' But Colonel Byrd's description of the insanitary condition of some of the camps and the horrors of convict life are unprintable. He calls attention to the fact that the death rate in the private camps is double that of the county camps. In one of the camps one out of every four convicts died during their incarceration. In another camp one out of every six unfortunates who had committed some slight infraction of the law, if he were guilty at all, was thrust into a camp which he never left alive. In twenty-one out of twenty-four private camps there were neither hospital buildings nor arrangements of any kind for the sick. After describing the lack of bathing facilities, which Colonel Byrd says gave the convicts a mangy appearance, he refers to the inhuman beatings inflicted upon the convicts. A leather strop was the instrument of punishment found by the commissioner in all the camps, 'and my observation has been,' said he, 'that where the strap has been used the least the best camps exist and the best work is turned out by the convicts.'

In the camp in which the negroes looked worst the commissioner found very few reported dead. On the very date of inspection, however, there were three men, all new arrivals, locked in the filthy building, sick. They said they had been there a week, and two of them looked as though they could not recover. In another camp there was not even a stove, and the negroes had to cook on skillets over log fires in the open air. There were no beds at all and the few blankets were reeking with filth, as they were scattered about over a dirty floor.

In his report Colonel Byrd called particular attention to a few of the many cases of brutality, inhumanity, and even murder which came under his own personal observation. In the banner camp for heavy mortality the commissioner found two men with broken legs, so terribly surrounded as practically to make it impossible for them to recover. Both in this camp and in others there were numerous instances of sudden deaths among convicts, which were attributed to brain trouble and other diseases. On reliable authority Colonel Byrd learned that the guards in one of the camps visited had just a short while before his arrival literally beaten one of the convicts to death and then burned his remains in his convict suit with his shackles on. 'A reputable citizen,' said Colonel Byrd, 'told me that he had seen the guards beating this convict, and that in their anger they had caught him by the shackles and run through the woods, dragging him along feet foremost.' He stated he had gone before the grand jury of Pulaski Co., where the camp was situated, and had sworn to these facts, but that Mr. Allison, who ran this camp, had friends on the jury and that other citizens had thought it would be best to hush the whole deplorable affair up, so as to keep it out of the newspapers and courts. The superintendent of the camp simply claimed that the murdered negro had died of dropsy and was buried in his stripes and shackles to save time.

The camp of W. H. and J. H. Griffin in Wilkes Co. was described as being 'very tough.' It was in that camp that Bob

Cannon, a camp guard, beat to death an aged negro named Frank McRay. The condition in this camp was too horrible to describe. The prison was an abandoned kitchen or outhouse in the yard of a large *ante bellum* residence. Every window in it had been removed and the openings closely boarded up and sealed. It was a small square box with not even an augur hole for air or light.

> 'When the door was opened' [said Colonel Byrd], 'and I had recovered from the shock caused by the rush of foul air, I noticed a sick negro sitting in the room. How human beings could consign a fellow being to such an existence I cannot understand any more than I can understand how a human being could survive a night of confinement in such a den. There was an open can in the centre of the room and it looked as if it had not been emptied in a fortnight. A small bit of cornbread lay on a blanket near the negro, and that poor victim, guilty of a misdemeanour only, while sick, confined in this sweat-box dungeon, humbly asked to be furnished with a drink of water.
>
> 'It was in this gang that I found Lizzie Boatwright, a nineteen-year-old negress sent up from Thomas, Ga., for larceny. She was clad in men's clothing, was working side by side with male convicts under a guard, cutting a ditch through a meadow. The girl was small of stature and pleasant of address, and her life in this camp must have been one of long drawn out agony, horror, and suffering. She told me she had been whipped twice, each time by the brutal white guard who had beaten McRay to death, and who prostituted his legal right to whip into a most revolting and disgusting outrage. This girl and another woman were stripped and beaten unmercifully in plain view of the men convicts, because they stopped on the side of the road to bind a rag about their sore feet.'

Be as sanguine as one may, he cannot extract much comfort from the hope that conditions at present are much better, if any, than they were when Col. Byrd made this startling, shocking revelation, as the result of a careful investigation of these camps several years ago, since camps for misdemeanour convicts are being conducted by private individuals to-day just as they were then. The eighth annual report of the Prison Commission, issued May 1905, shows that thirteen of the misdemeanour convict camps in the State of Georgia are worked for and in some cases by private individuals, contrary to law, who hire them directly from the authorities having them in charge after conviction with no legal warrant from the county authorities in those counties where they are worked. These convicts, according to the last year's report from Georgia, are entirely in the custody and control of private individuals. The officials hire them in remote counties, never seeing them after delivery, and the county authorities where they are worked never exercise supervision over or control of them.

The law explicitly states that the Prison Commission of Georgia shall have general supervision of the misdemeanour convicts of the State.

> 'It shall be the duty of one of the Commissioners, or, in case of emergency, an officer designated by them, to visit from time to time, at least quarterly, the various camps where misdemeanour convicts are at work, and shall advise with the county or municipal authorities working them, in making and altering the rules for the government control and management of said convicts. . . . And if the county or municipal authorities fail to comply with such rules, or the law governing misdemeanour chain gangs [reads the statute], then the Governor with the Commission shall take such convicts from said county or municipal authorities. Or the Governor and Commission in their discretion may impose a fine upon each of the said county or municipal authorities failing to comply with such rules or the law.'

But this law is easily evaded, because the county authorities where the convict is sentenced have established no chain gang, and the county authorities where the convict is worked none, so that neither can be proceeded against by the Commission. 'The Prison Commission of Georgia has repeatedly called the attention of the General Assembly to this condition,' says the report, and cannot refrain from again doing so, hoping that some means may be devised by which this violation of the law may be prevented.

Again and again efforts put forth by humane people, both in Georgia and in other southern States, to correct abuses in the camps have been frustrated by men high in authority, who belong to the State legislatures and who make large fortunes out of the wretches they abuse. Colonel Byrd called attention to the fact that the whole political machinery of the State and county stood in with the lessees, because the first money earned by the poor victims paid the cost of trial and conviction. Not a dollar of the rental for the convicts reached the county treasury, he declared, till sheriff, deputy sheriff, county solicitor, bailiffs, court clerks, justice of the peace, constables and other officials who aided to put the convict in the chain gang were paid their fees in full. 'It is not to be supposed,' said Colonel Byrd, 'that these people would be in favour of destroying a system profitable to themselves.' The following incident throws some light on this point. A coloured man was convicted of larceny and sentenced to twelve months on the chain gang. The county solicitor personally took charge of him, carried him to a private camp, where the contractor gave him 100 dollars in cash for this prisoner. A few months later it was discovered that the man was innocent of the crime. Both the judge and the jury before whom he was convicted signed a petition to the Governor praying for the prisoner's release. The county solicitor refused to sign it, however, because he had received his 100 dollars in advance and distributed it among the other court officials and did not want to pay it back.

There are in Georgia at the present time 1,500 men who were sold to the highest bidder the 1st of April, 1904, for a period of five years. The Durham Coal and Coke Co. leased 150 convicts, paying for them from 228 dollars to 252 dollars apiece per annum. The Flower Brothers Lumber Co. leased one hundred and paid 240 dollars a piece for them for a year. Hamby and Toomer leased five hundred, paying 221 dollars a head. The Lookout Mountain Coal and Coke Co. took 100 at 223.75 dollars a head.

The Chattahoochee Brick Co. secured 175 men at 223.75 dollars apiece per annum. E. J. McRee took one hundred men and paid 220.75 dollars for each. In its report the Prison Commission points with great pride to the fact that for five years, from the 1st of April, 1904, to the 1st of April, 1909, this batch of prisoners alone will pour annually into the State coffers the gross sum of 340,000 dollars with a net of 225,000 dollars, which will be distributed proportionately among the various counties for school purposes.

In 1903 a man whose barbarous treatment of convicts leased to him by Tallapoosa and Coosa Counties, Alabama, had been thoroughly exposed, and who had been indicted a number of times in the State courts, succeeded in leasing more convicts for a term of three years without the slightest difficulty, in spite of his record. The grand jury for the May term, 1903, of the District Court of the middle of Alabama returned ninety-nine indictments for peonage and conspiring to hold parties in a condition of peonage. In these ninety-nine true bills only eighteen persons were involved. Under the convict lease system of Alabama the State Board of Convicts then had no control whatever over the County convicts, and if they were leased to an inhuman man there was absolutely nothing to prevent him from doing with them what he wished. During the trial of the cases in Alabama to which reference has been made, a well-known journalist declared over his signature that when the chief of the State Convict Inspecting Bureau, who had been sent to Tallapoosa Co. to investigate conditions obtaining in the penal camps there, reported that some of the largest landowners and planters in the State were engaged in the traffic of selling negroes into involuntary servitude, the Governor took no further steps to bring about the conviction of the guilty parties.

In Alabama a justice of the peace in criminal cases has power to sentence a convicted prisoner to hard labour for a term not exceeding twelve months. He is required under law to make a report of such cases to the Judge of Probate of his respective county, and to file a mittimus with the gaoler of each man who is tried before him who has been convicted and fails to give bond. As soon as a man was convicted in Tallapoosa and Coosa counties by a Justice of the Peace, who was in collusion with the party or parties who had a contract with the county for leasing the county convicts, he would turn each of them over to the lessee without committing them to the county gaol, and without filing a certificate of these convictions with the Judge of Probate. Since there was no public examiner to go over the books of the Justice of the Peace, it was easy, when they were examined by order of the grand jury, to explain away as a mistake any discrepancies upon the docket. Since there was nothing on the docket of the Justice of the Peace to show the length of time the man was to serve, he was held by the lessee, until he broke down or managed to escape. Moreover, the prosecution of the cases mentioned showed that trumped-up charges would be frequently made against negroes in the two counties mentioned for the most trivial offences, such as happened in the case of one convict who was arrested for letting one man's mule bite another man's corn. It also came out in the trial that when the sentence of two convicts expired at the same time they were often provoked into a difficulty with each other and then each man would be taken down before a Justice of the Peace without the knowledge of the other, and persuaded to make an affidavit against the other man for an affray. Both would then be tried before a Justice, convicted and sentenced to imprisonment at hard labour for six months, and this would go on indefinitely. It was also developed at this Alabama trial that there was often no trial at all. An affidavit would be sworn out, but never entered upon the docket, and after a mock trial the man would be sentenced for three months or six and the judgment never entered up.

If there was an examination by the grand jury of the county, there would be no way for it to secure the facts, and no one in the community seemed to think it was his duty to make any charges. Between A and B, both of whom were convicted of peonage in Alabama in 1903, it is said that there was an understanding that the men arrested in A's neighbourhood were to be tried before C, one of B's brothers-in-law, while those whom B wanted would be tried before one of the A's, who was Justice of the Peace. If material ran short, the men held by the A's were taken down and tried before B's brother-in-law and turned over to B and *vice versa*. It can easily be seen that negroes—friendless, illiterate, and penniless—had no salvation at all except when the strong arm of the United States Government took them under its protection. Although the grand jury at the May term in 1903 declared that Tallapoosa and Coosa counties were the only localities in the State where peonage existed, subsequent arrests of persons who were bound over by a United States Commissioner to await the action of the United States grand jury at the December term of 1903 proved conclusively that there were many cases of peonage in Covington,

Crenshaw, Pike, Coffee, Houston, and other counties in the State of Alabama.

Describing the convict lease system, as it is operated in Mississippi, one of the best attorneys in that State said:

> 'This institution is operated for no other purpose than to make money, and I can compare it with nothing but Dante's Inferno. Hades is a paradise compared with the convict camps of Mississippi. If an able-bodied young man sent to one of these camps for sixty or ninety days lives to return home, he is fit for nothing the rest of his natural life, for he is a physical wreck at the expiration of his term.'

As in other States, the convict camps of Mississippi are operated by planters or others who have secured a contract from the County Board to work all prisoners sent up by the magistrates or other courts. A stipulated sum per capita is paid for the prisoners, who have to work out their fines, costs, and living expenses, receiving practically nothing for their labour. As spring comes on, officers of the law become exceedingly busy looking up cases of vagrancy or misdemeanour, so as to supply their regular patrons.

It is interesting and illuminating to see what class of men have been indicted for holding their fellows in bondage in the stockades of the South. A few years ago a leading member of the Georgia legislature, together with his brothers, operated an extensive camp in Lowndes Co. Witnesses testified before the grand jury that in this camp, owned by a member of the legislature, the brutalities practised were too revolting to describe. It is also interesting to know that a member of that same family was awarded 100 convicts on the 1st of April 1904, and this lease is good for five years. Witnesses testified that this member of the Georgia legislature operated a camp in which prisoners were stripped and unmercifully lashed by the whipping bosses for the slightest offence. It was also alleged that this lawmaker for a sovereign State and his brothers were accustomed to go into counties adjoining Lowndes, pay the fines of the misdemeanour convicts, carry them into their Ware county camp and there keep them indefinitely.

The grand jury claimed that at least twenty citizens of Ware Co. were held as slaves in the camp owned by the brothers to whom reference has been made, long after their terms had expired. An ex-sheriff of Ware Co. and a well-known attorney of Georgia pleaded guilty not very long ago to the charge of holding citizens in a condition of peonage, and were each fined 1,000 dollars (500 dollars of which was remitted) by Judge Emory Speer. A sheriff in Alabama was recently indicted for peonage. Manufacturers of Georgia and railroad contractors in Tennessee have recently been indicted for holding men and women in involuntary servitude. The chairman of the Board of Commissioners of Bradford Co., Fla., was indicted not long ago for the same offence. In March 1905 the Federal Grand Jury indicted the city of Louisville and the superintendent of the workhouse for violating the federal statute against peonage.

There is no doubt whatever that every misdemeanour convict in the chain gangs and convict lease camps in the South operated by private individuals could appeal to the courts and secure release. Incarceration of misdemeanour convicts in these camps is as much disobedience of the laws as the original offence which led to conviction. There is no doubt that every misdemeanour camp in the southern States which is controlled by private individuals is a nest of illegality. Every man employing misdemeanour convicts for private gain is a law-breaker. Every county official who leases or permits to be leased a misdemeanour convict for other than public work transgresses one of the plainest statutes on the law books of some of the States in which the offence is committed, and violates an amendment to the constitution of the United States besides. There is no lack of law by which to punish the guilty, but they are permitted to perpetrate fearful atrocities upon the unfortunate and helpless, because there are thousands of just and humane people in this country who know little or nothing about the methods pursued in the chain gangs, the convict lease system and the contract labour system, which are all children of one wicked and hideous mother, peonage.

The negro was armed with the suffrage by just and humane men, because soon after the War of the Rebellion the legislatures of the southern States began to enact vagrant or peonage laws, the intent of which was to reduce the newly emancipated slaves to a bondage almost as cruel, if not quite as cruel, as that from which they had just been delivered. After the vote had been given the negro, so that he might use it in self-defence, the peonage laws became a dead letter for a time and lay dormant, so to speak, until disfranchisement laws were enacted in nearly every State of the South. The connection between disfranchisement and peonage is intimate and close. The planter sees the negro robbed of his suffrage with impunity, with the silent consent of the whole country, and he knows that political preferment and great power are the fruits of this outrage upon a handicapped and persecuted race. He is encouraged, therefore, to apply the same principle for profit's sake to his business affairs. The politician declares that the negro is unfit for citizenship and violently snatches from him his rights. The planter declares the negro is lazy and forces him into involuntary servitude contrary to the law. Each tyrant employs the same process of reasoning to justify his course.

REMEMBERING A BLACK TOWN IN THE SOUTHWEST

SALLY NASH
Interview about Life in Rentiesville, Oklahoma, 1903–1908

June 22, 1937

SALLY (LOVE) NASH—Creek Freedman
Rentieville, Oklahoma
Interview—June 22, 1937.
Jas. S. Buchanan, Field Worker
Indian-Pioneer History

I (Sally Nash) was born February 19, 1871 near where the town of Rentieville now stands.

My father was June Love, Chickasaw freedman.

My mother was Dorcas (Robertson) Love, Creek freedman.

The Creek Nation had no public schools in this district during my school age, therefore the only schooling I received was in a subscription school established by William F. McIntosh with a tuition fee of $1.00 per month. Many months my parents didn't have the dollar, consequently, those months I missed school.

When allotments were made to the Indians and freedmen, I drew my allotment near Council Hill. Through misfortune, I lost my allotment several years ago.

In 1904 I was married to Joe Nash, colored, of Texas. No children were born to us.

For several years William McIntosh and his brother, John McIntosh were the only preachers in this part of the Creek Nation. They both preached at the old Honey Springs church which was a log structure that stood near the Honey Springs burial ground. The little log church rotted down and passed out of existence many years ago.

In the early days when the old Texas trail was the only north and south trail through the Indian Territory, Honey Springs was a noted camping ground and watering place for the travelers passing over the old trail. The trail crossed Spring Creek at the spring.

I saw the little town of Rentieville come into existence and grow into a thriving little town. It was established by William Rentie, a Creek freedman, who, at that time was quite wealthy, a good citizen and was always ready to help anyone that was in need and worthy of assistance.

In the beginning there were several good families that settled and built homes in the little town of Rentieville, people who were a credit to the community, but the tough element that congregated in the place made life so unpleasant that the better class soon moved away.

In 1908 William Rentie, being a county officer and the only officer of the law in the town, was compelled to arrest a man by the name of Garfield Walker, a negro, for drunkenness and disorderly conduct. Later, for revenge, an uncle of Garfield Walker called William Rentie from his home one evening after dark, and Garfield Walker, hiding in the darkness, shot and killed William Rentie. Walker was arrested and placed in jail at Eufaula where he was later stabbed and killed by another prisoner while in jail.

William Rentie was a good man and his death was mourned by all good people. His death was the result of lust for revenge by a ruthless killer, like many other similar crimes that were committed in the Indian Territory in the early days.

It seemed as though his death spelled the doom of Rentieville, for since he was killed Rentieville has been going down, and today is nothing more than a ghost town.

SAN PEDRO DAILY NEWS
The Candidates and the Negro
October 14, 1908

THE CANDIDATES AND THE NEGRO

THE most remarkable fact in connection with the American negro is that in the former slave states he is worse off politically and no better off socially than he was forty years ago. By devices which are a matter of current history and which have been so adroitly framed as to evade reversal by the supreme court he has been deprived of the ballot conferred on him by the Republican party, compelled to ride in cars separate from the whites and in every way made to feel that the change from legal bondage to freedom has made no difference in the attitude of the white race toward him.

These are the conditions brought about by Democrats in states where Democrats rule. The Democratic party has spared no effort to degrade the negro to nearly as possible the level of slavery times and has made wider than ever the dividing line which separates the two races. In taking this position the Democrats of the former slave states have the express approval of the Democratic candidate for the presidency, William J. Bryan, who, when questioned on the subject immediately after an address which he had delivered in New York city on "Universal Brotherhood," took ground firmly in favor of negro disfranchisement.

In states controlled by Republicans the negro has the right to vote and votes on an equality with the white citizens. The rights of white and black are identical not only in law, but in practice. The condition of the negro in Republican states has improved instead of retrograding. He is an American citizen in all that the title implies.

The Republican platform adopted at Chicago explicitly demands justice for all men without regard to race or color and just as explicitly declares for the enforcement without reservation in letter and spirit of the thirteenth, fourteenth and fifteenth amendments to the constitution of the United States. "It is needless to state," says Mr. Taft in his speech accepting the Republican nomination for president, "that I stand with my party squarely on that plank in the platform and believe that equal justice to all men and the fair and impartial enforcement of these amendments are in keeping with the real American spirit of fair play."

Here we have Bryan, the candidate of the Democracy, approving the policy of disfranchising the negro and keeping him under, and here, again, we have William H. Taft, the Republican candidate, declaring in the clearest language possible for the enforcement of the amendments which made the negro a freeman, a citizen and a voter.

A vote for Bryan would be a vote approving the policy of negro disfranchisement which he approves; a vote for Taft is a vote to elect president one who has solemnly proclaimed his purpose to see that the amendments which gave to the negro citizenship and the ballot shall not be nullified.

How any negro loyal to his race and not sunk in self abasement, any negro who is unwilling to grovel in the dust at the feet of southern lynchers and ballot robbers, can vote for Bryan and against Taft is beyond the grasp of reason.

A vote for Bryan would be a vote to indorse his views in favor of negro disfranchisement and might be construed as a vote to bring about general disfranchisement of the colored race. A vote for Taft would be a vote to intrust the great powers of the president to one who has the will, the courage and the ability to enforce the negro's rights so far as the federal law will permit.

No intelligent negro will waver as to his duty. No negro who has any practical knowledge of the situation of his race in the former slave states will hesitate to do what he can to bring about the emancipation of his brethren by helping to elect Taft and Sherman president and vice president of the United States.

To think any considerable number of negros capable of opposing the Republican ticket would be to doubt the capacity of the negro for his duties as an American citizen.

"THE RENEWAL OF THE STRUGGLE FOR CIVIL AND
POLITICAL LIBERTY"

THE NEW YORK EVENING POST
Conference on Negroes
February 13, 1909

CONFERENCE ON NEGROES

A CALL IS ISSUED BY MEN AND WOMEN OF PROMINENCE.

Signers Represent Various Sections of the Country—Present Conditions that Would Astonish Abraham Lincoln and the Others Who Died After Striving for Race Freedom.

A CALL FOR a national conference, to discuss the present state of the negro, has been issued, signed by men and women representing nearly every section of the country. The call reads as follows:

"The celebration of the centennial of the birth of Abraham Lincoln, widespread and grateful as it may be, will fail to justify itself if it takes no note of and makes no recognition of the colored men and women to whom the great emancipator labored to assure freedom. Besides a day of rejoicing, Lincoln's birthday in 1909 should be one of taking stock of the nation's progress since 1865.

"How far has it lived up to the obligations imposed upon it by the Emancipation Proclamation? How far has it gone in assuring to each and every citizen, irrespective of color, the equality of opportunity and equality before the law, which underlie our American institutions and are guaranteed by the Constitution?

"If Mr. Lincoln could revisit this country in the flesh, he would be disheartened and discouraged. He would learn that on January 1, 1909, Georgia had rounded out a new confederacy by disfranchising the negro, after the manner of all the other Southern States. He would learn that the Supreme Court of the United States, supposedly a bulwark of American liberties, had refused every opportunity to pass squarely upon this disfranchisement of millions, by laws avowedly discriminatory and openly enforced in such manner that the white men may vote and black men be without a vote in their government; he would discover, therefore, that taxation without representation is the lot of millions of wealth-producing American citizens, in whose hands rests the economic progress and welfare of an entire section of the country.

BEREA COLLEGE CASE.

"He would learn that the Supreme Court, according to the official statement of one of its own judges in the Berea College case, has laid down the principle that if an individual State chooses, it may 'make it a crime for white and colored persons to frequent the same market place at the same time, or appear in an assemblage of citizens convened to consider questions of a public or political nature in which all citizens, without regard to race, are equally interested.'

"In many States Lincoln would find justice enforced, if at all, by judges elected by one element in a community to pass upon the liberties and lives of another. He would see the black men and women, for whose freedom a hundred thousand of soldiers gave their lives, set apart in trains, in which they pay first-class fares for third-class service, and segregated in railway stations and in places of entertainment; he would observe that State after State declines to do its elementary duty in preparing the negro through education for the best exercise of citizenship.

"Added to this, the spread of lawless attacks upon the negro, North, South, and West—even in the Springfield made famous by Lincoln—often accompanied by revolting brutalities, sparing neither sex nor age nor youth, could but shock the author of the sentiment that 'government of the people, by the people, for the people, shall not perish from the earth.'

"Silence under these conditions means tacit approval. The indifference of the North is already responsible for more than one assault upon democracy, and every such attack reacts as unfavorably upon whites as upon blacks. Discrimination once permitted cannot be bridled; recent history in the South shows that in forging chains for the negroes the white voters are forging chains for themselves. 'A house divided against itself cannot stand'; this government cannot exist half-slave and half-free any better to-day than it could in 1861.

"Hence we call upon all the believers in democracy to join in a national conference for the discussion of present evils, the voicing of protests, and the renewal of the struggle for civil and political liberty."

>Jane Addams, Chicago.
>Samuel Bowles (Springfield "Republican.")
>Prof. W. L. Bulkley, New York.
>Harriet Stanton Blatch, New York.
>Ida Wells Barnett, Chicago.
>E. H. Clement, Boston.
>Kate Claghorn, New York.
>Prof. John Dewey, New York.
>Prof. W. E. B. Du Bois, Atlanta.
>Mary E. Dreier, Brooklyn.
>Dr. John L. Elliott, New York.
>William Lloyd Garrison, Boston.
>The Rev. Francis J. Grimke, Washington, D. C.
>William Dean Howells, New York.
>Rabbi Emil G. Hirsch, Chicago.
>The Rev. John Haynes Holmes, New York.
>Prof. Thomas C. Hall, New York.
>Hamilton Holt, New York.
>Florence Kelley, New York.
>The Rev. Frederick Lynch, New York.
>Helen Marot, New York.
>John E. Milholland, New York.
>Mary E. McDowell, Chicago.
>Prof. J. G. Merrill, Connecticut.
>Dr. Henry Moskowitz, New York.
>Leonora O'Reilly, New York.
>Mary W. Ovington, New York.
>The Rev. Dr. Charles H. Parkhurst, New York.
>Louis F. Post, Chicago.
>The Rev. Dr. John P. Peters, New York.
>Dr. Jane Robbins, New York.
>Charles Edward Russell, New York.

Joseph Smith, Boston.
Anna Garlin Spencer, New York.
William M. Salter, Chicago.
J. G. Phelps Stokes, New York.
Judge Wendell Stafford, Washington.
Helen Stokes, New York.
Lincoln Steffens, Boston.
President Thwing, Western Reserve University.
W. I. Thomas, Chicago.
Mrs. Mary Church Terrell, Washington, D. C.
Rabbi Stephen S. Wise, New York.
Bishop Alexander Walters, New York.
Dr. William H. Ward, New York.
Horace White, New York.
William English Walling, New York.
Dr. J. Milton Waldron, Washington, D. C.
Mrs. Rodman Wharton, Philadelphia.
Susan P. Wharton, Philadelphia.
Prof. Charles Zneblin, Boston.
President Mary E. Woolley, Mt. Holyoke College.
Lillian D. Wald, New York.

FOUNDING THE NAACP

Platform Adopted by the National Negro Committee
June 1, 1909

NATIONAL NEGRO COMMITTEE
500 FIFTH AVENUE
NEW YORK

Rev. W. H. BROOKS, New York.
Prof. JOHN DEWEY, New York.
PAUL KENNADAY, New York.
JACOB W. MACK, New York.
Mrs. M. D. MACLEAN, New York.
Dr. HENRY MOSKOWITZ, New York.
JOHN E. MILHOLLAND, New York.
Miss LEONORA O'REILLY, New York.
CHARLES EDWARD RUSSELL, New York.
Prof. EDWIN R. A. SELIGMAN, New York.
Rev. JOSEPH SILVERMAN, New York.
OSWALD G. VILLARD, New York.
Miss LILLIAN D. WALD, New York.
WM. ENGLISH WALLING, New York.
Bishop ALEXANDER WALTERS, New York.
Dr. STEPHEN S. WISE, New York.
Miss MARY W. OVINGTON, Brooklyn.
Dr. O. M. WALLER, Brooklyn.
Rev. J. H. HOLMES, Yonkers, N. Y.
Prof. W. L. BULKLEY, Ridgefield Park, N. J.
Miss MARIA BALDWIN, Boston.
ARCHIBALD H. GRIMKE, Boston.
ALBERT E. PILLSBURY, Boston.
MOORFIELD STOREY, Boston.
Pres. CHAS. P. THWING, Cleveland, O.
Pres. W. S. SCARBOROUGH, Wilberforce, O.
Miss JANE ADDAMS, Chicago.
Mrs. IDA WELLS BARNETT, Chicago.
Dr. C. E. BENTLEY, Chicago.
Mrs. CELIA PARKER WOOLLEY, Chicago.
Dr. WILLIAM SINCLAIR, Philadelphia.
Miss SUSAN WHARTON, Philadelphia.
R. R. WRIGHT, Jr., Philadelphia.
L. M. HERSHAW, Washington.
Judge WENDELL P. STAFFORD, Washington.
Mrs. MARY CHURCH TERRELL, Washington.
Rev. J. MILTON WALDRON, Washington.
Prof. W. E. B. DU BOIS, Atlanta, Ga.
LESLIE PINCKNEY HILL, Manassas, Va.

Platform Adopted by the National Negro Committee, 1909

We denounce the ever-growing oppression of our 10,000,000 colored fellow citizens as the greatest menace that threatens the country. Often plundered of their just share of the public funds, robbed of nearly all part in the government, segregated by common carriers, some murdered with impunity, and all treated with open contempt by officials, they are held in some States in practical slavery to the white community. The systematic persecution of law-abiding citizens and their disfranchisement on account of their race alone is a crime that will ultimately drag down to an infamous end any nation that allows it to be practiced, and it bears most heavily on those poor white farmers and laborers whose economic position is most similar to that of the persecuted race.

The nearest hope lies in the immediate and patiently continued enlightenment of the people who have been inveigled into a campaign of oppression. The spoils of persecution should not go to enrich any class or classes of the population. Indeed persecution of organized workers, peonage, enslavement of prisoners, and even disfranchisement already threaten large bodies of whites in many Southern States.

We agree fully with the prevailing opinion that the transformation of the unskilled colored laborers in industry and agriculture into skilled workers is of vital importance to that race and to the nation, but we demand for the Negroes, as for all others, a free and complete education, whether by city, State or nation, a grammar school and industrial training for all and technical, professional, and academic education for the most gifted.

But the public schools assigned to the Negro of whatever kind or grade will never receive a fair and equal treatment until he is given equal treatment in the Legislature and before the law. Nor will the practically educated Negro, no matter how valuable to the community he may prove, be given a fair return for his labor or encouraged to put forth his best efforts or given the chance to develop that efficiency that comes only outside the school until he is respected in his legal rights as a man and a citizen.

We regard with grave concern the attempt manifest South and North to deny black men the right to work and to enforce this demand by violence and bloodshed. Such a question is too fundamental and clear even to be submitted to arbitration. The late strike in Georgia is not simply a demand that Negroes be displaced, but that proven and efficient men be made to surrender their long-followed means of livelihood to white competitors.

As first and immediate steps toward remedying these national wrongs, so full of peril for the whites as well as the blacks of all sections, we demand of Congress and the Executive:

(1). That the Constitution be strictly enforced and the civil rights guaranteed under the Fourteenth Amendment be secured impartially to all.

(2). That there be equal educational opportunities for all and in all the States, and that public school expenditure be the same for the Negro and white child.

(3). That in accordance with the Fifteenth Amendment the right of the Negro to the ballot on the same terms as other citizens be recognized in every part of the country.

I herewith subscribe $_____ to the National Negro Committee, and desire to become a member of the permanent organization growing out of the present Conference.

_____

(Make checks payable to Oswald G. Villard, Treasurer).

1909–1919

SEVENTY VICTIMS OF MOB VIOLENCE

HANFORD DAILY JOURNAL
Lynching Bees in Present Year Numerous

December 17, 1909

LYNCHING BEES IN PRESENT YEAR NUMEROUS

SEVENTY VICTIMS OF "NECKTIE PARTIES" IN 1909, ACCORDING TO STATISTICS.

11 WHITES AND 59 NEGROES HUNG BY MOBS: ALL SAVE TWO IN THE SOUTH.

WASHINGTON, D. C., Dec. 17.—Lynchings in 1909 have numbered 70, the highest number recorded since 1904. The victims numbered 11 whites and 59 negroes. The lynchings occurred in 12 states and one territory—New Mexico. As in previous years, crimes or alleged crimes against white women and murders caused most of these summary executions. One case, occurring in Cairo, Ill., combined both causes and resulted in the placing of the city under military control for several days. The Cairo lynchings were the only cases of the kind that occurred north of the Ohio river during the year. Several double lynchings occurred at various points in the south, and Oklahoma furnished a quadruple lynching, with four cattlemen as the victims.

In the following record the word "lynching" has been held to apply only to the summary punishment inflicted by a mob or by any number of citizens on a person alleged to have committed a crime. By states the 70 lynching cases here recorded are classified as follows:

Georgia	11
Texas	10
Florida	8
Louisiana	7

Mississippi 7
Alabama. 6
Oklahoma 5
Kentucky 4
South Carolina. 3
Arkansas 3
Illinois 2
New Mexico 2
Missouri. 1
West Virginia 1

The detailed record for 1909 is as follows:

Jan. 6—Lexington, S. C.; Unidentified negro; attempted criminal assault.

Jan. 8—Marthaville, La.; Jim Gilbert, negro; accused of counterfeiting.

Jan. 10—Poplarville, Miss.; Pink Willis, negro; attempted criminal assault.

Jan. 18—Hope, Ark.; Hilliard, negro; insulting white woman.

Jan. 23—Mobile, Ala.; Douglas Roberson, negro; murder of deputy sheriff.

Jan. 24—Leighton, Ala.; Sam Davenport, negro; incendiarism.

Feb. 7—Mexia, Ala.; Will Parker, negro; criminal assault.

Feb. 9—Houston, Miss.; Roby Daskin, negro; murder of Rev. W. T. Hudson.

Feb. 13—Gainesville, Fla.; Jake Wads, negro; criminal assault.

Feb. 11—Hearn, Texas; Rolly Wyatt, negro; shooting a white man.

Mch. 4—Blakely, Ga.; John Fowler, negro; murder of deputy sheriff.

Mch. 7—Rockwall, Texas; Anderson Ellis, negro; attempted criminal assault.

Mch. 12—Eden, Miss.; Joe Gordon, negro; shooting and blinding a white man.

Mch. 19—Elkins, W. Va.; Joseph Brown, white; shooting chief of police.

Mch. 25—Cuervo, N. M.; Daniel Johnson, negro, and Manuel Sandoval, a Mexican, kidnapping young girl.

Mch. 29—Dawson, Texas; Joe Redden, negro; insulting white woman.

Apr. 6—Pensacola, Fla.; Dave Alexander, negro; murder of policeman.

Apr. 9—Lafayette, Ky.; Ben Brame, negro; attempted criminal assault.

Apr. 11—Yazoo City, Miss.; Howard Montgomery, negro; assaulting an officer.

Apr. 11—Arcadia, Fla.; John Smith, negro; attempted criminal assault.

Apr. 19—Ada, Okla.; J. B. Miller, B. B. Burrell, Jesse West and Joe Allen, all white; charged with murder.

Apr. 25—Bessemer, Ala.; John Thomas, negro; criminal assault.

Apr. 26—Bartow, Fla.; Charles Scarborough; attempted criminal assault.

Apr. 30—Marshall, Texas; Creole Mose, Pie Hill and Mat Chase, negroes; murder.

May 1—Tyler, Texas; Jim Hodges, negro; criminal assault.

May 8—Camden, Fla.; Unidentified negro; criminal assault.

May 24—Lincolnton, Ga.; Albert Aiken, negro; shooting white man.

May 24—Pine Bluff, Ark.; Livett Davis, negro; attempted criminal assault.

May 28—Abilene, Texas; Tom Barnett, white; shot to death in his cell; convicted of murder.

May 30—Portland, Ark.; Joseph Blakeley, negro; threatening murder.

June 3—Frankfort, Ky.; John Maxey, negro; shooting a white man.

June 6—Tallahassee, Fla.; Maik Morris, negro; convicted of murder.

June 11—Smoaks, S. C.; Quillie Simmons and Frank Samuels, white; charged with murder.

June 15—Arcadia, Fla.; Unidentified negro; attempted criminal assault.

June 22—Talbotton, Ga.; William Caneker, negro; murder.

June 24—Cuthbert, Ga.; Albert Reese, negro; assaulting white woman.

June 26—Wilburton, Okla.; Sylvester Stennien, negro; murder of deputy constable.

July 1—Barwick, Ga.; Unidentified negro, found hiding under a bed in the home of a white family.

July 20—Paris, Ky.; Albert Lawson, negro; shooting a sheriff.

July 20—Gum Branch, Ga.; Unidentified negro; attempted theft of horse and buggy.

July 29—Opelousas, La.; Onesime Thomas and Emile Antoine, negroes; assault.

July 31—Wellston, Ga.; Sim Anderson, negro; peeping into a white woman's bedroom.

Aug. 2—Platte City, Mo.; George Johnson, white; murder.

Aug. 9—Cadiz, Ky.; Joe Miller, negro; criminal assault.

Aug. 12—Greenville, Miss.; Will Robinson, negro; insulting white girl.

Aug. 27—Tarrytown, Ga.; John Sweeney, negro; aiding a negro murderer to escape.

Sept. 4—Jackson, Ala.; Josh and Lewis Balaam, negroes; murder of deputy sheriff.

Sept. 5—Clarksdale, Miss.; Herman McDaniels, negro; accused of being concerned in a murder committed by his brother.

Sept. 7—Mangham, La.; Henry Hill, negro; drowned by mob; attempted criminal assault.

Sept. 25—Perry, Fla.; Charley Anderson, negro; murder.

Oct. 5—Greensburg, La.; Aps Ard, negro; murder.

Oct. 21—Greenville, Texas; Frank Williams and "Louis," negroes; criminal assault.

Nov. 12—Cairo, Ill.; Henry Salzner, white, charged with wife murder, and Will James, negro, confessed assailant and murderer of young white woman.

Nov. 20—Delhi, La.; James Estes, negro; shooting city marshal.

Nov. 25—Meehan, Miss.; Morgan Chambers, negro; criminal assault.

Nov. 26—West Shreveport, La.; Henry Rachel, negro; attempted criminal assault.

Dec. 1—Cochran, Ga.; John Harvard, negro; burned at stake; shooting white man.

THE JOHNSON-JEFFRIES FIGHT

LOS ANGELES TIMES
The Fight and Its Consequences
July 6, 1910

THE FIGHT AND ITS CONSEQUENCES.

IT was a fight between a white man and a black man, but it is well at the outset not to pin too much racial importance on the fact. The conflict was a personal one, not race with race. There are other black men who can whip other white ones, and a greater number of whites who can whip blacks. Even if it were a matter of great racial import, the whites can afford the reflection that it is at best only a triumph of brawn over brain, not of brain over brawn. The black pugilist may be able to deliver stunning blows, but the stupidest mule in Missouri can hit harder. Johnson may spar cleverly, but a kitten can feint and ward better than any man. If the white race has no greater claim to superiority than that of pugilistic fitness, the sooner it abdicates in favor of its betters the happier it will be.

Pugilism and civilization bear no direct connection, but are in inverse ratio. The Roman boxers may have been less clever than the winner of the fight at Reno; but as to taking punishment, the man who stood up against the sole-leather cestus shod with brass nails could claim superiority over any modern fighter who has yet stood in the ring. In war (a vastly higher type of conflict) there are those who consider the African fresh from the jungle the making of the best soldier in the world. But the question is, how would they fare in battle commanded by one of their own race with an army of Europeans under the leadership of Napoleon, Gen. Grant or Von Moltke.

The white man's mental supremacy is fully established, and for the present cannot be taken from him. He has arithmetic and algebra, chemistry and electricity; he has Moses, David, Homer, Shakespeare, Milton, Byron and Burns; he has Herschel, Tyndall, Darwin and Edison, to fall back upon. His superiority does not rest on any huge bulk of muscle, but on brain development that has weighed worlds and charmed the most subtle secrets from the heart of nature.

The members of the white race who are not a disgrace to it will bear no resentment toward the black race because of this single victory in the prize ring. That would be to manifest lamentable weakness, not strength; stupid foolishness, not wisdom; a cowardly disposition, not manliness.

Let the white man who is worthy of the great inheritance won for him by his race and handed down to him by his ancestors "take his medicine" like a man. If he put his hope and the hope of his race in the white man who went into the ring, let him recognize his foolishness, and in his disappointed hope let him take up this new "white man's burden" and bear it like a man, not collapse under it like a weakling.

And now

A WORD TO THE BLACK MAN.

Do not point your nose too high. Do not swell your chest too much. Do not boast too loudly. Do not be puffed up. Let not your ambitions be inordinate or take a wrong direction. Let no treasured resentments rise up and spill over. Remember you have done nothing at all. You are just the same member of society today you were last week. Your place in the world is just what it was. You are on no higher plane, deserve no new consideration, and will get none. You will be treated on your personal merits in the future as in the past. No man will think a bit higher of you because your complexion is the same as that of the victor at Reno. That triumph is the personal asset of Arthur Johnson, a negro to be sure, but not the particular person who stands in your own shoes.

Remember that if it did establish the fact that, man for man all through the two races, yours was capable of being wrought into the best pugilists (which is not the case,) even then there would be no room for becoming swollen with pride. That would not justify your jumping at the very illogical conclusion that you are "on top." You are no nearer that mark than you were before the fight took place. You must depend on other influences to put your race on higher ground, and you must depend on personal achievement to put yourself on higher ground.

Never forget that in human affairs brains count for more than muscle. If you have ambition for yourself or your race, you must try for something better in development than that of the mule.

As to the white man who attempts to insult you because of the fair victory won by one of your race from one of the white race, you can well afford to ignore him and respect yourself. The fact that the man's skin is white does not make him more or less brutal or cowardly. He is no credit to the white race and would be none to any race. Such conduct is more than foolish. It is asinine. No savage fresh from the jungle could manifest more brutish traits of character than this. White men who are men worthy of the name will not join in any fresh crusade against your race, already too long and too cruelly persecuted.

Do not dwell too much on matters of race, particularly when it relates to the characteristics in which the dullest of the brute creation is superior to men of all races and colors. Think rather of your own individuality, of your personal achievements. Be ambitious for something better than the prize ring. Cultivate patience, grow in reasonableness, increase your stock of useful knowledge, try for new things which distinguish man from the beasts that perish and leave no results of their life behind them. Endurance is part of Johnson's qualities which stood him in good stead; hopefulness and good nature are others. Try to emulate this member of your race in these qualities. Their possession will do you more good and count for more in behalf of your race than it would if a black man were to "knock out" a white man every day for the next ten years.

CELEBRATING JACK JOHNSON'S VICTORY

WILLIAM PICKENS
Talladega College Professor Speaks on Reno Fight
The Chicago Defender, July 30, 1910

TALLADEGA COLLEGE PROFESSOR SPEAKS ON RENO FIGHT

The Fight Looked Upon as Pugilistic Contest. Northern & Southern Newspapers (White) Insisted That it Was Race Issue—Negro Not Inferior Race Only in Money.

JACK JOHNSON THE UNAFRAID.

White Editors Have Dumped 585 Tons of Editorials in Triumph in Waste Basket—687,000,000 Pounds of Metal Already Set up Remelted and Put to Better Use.

Special to the Chicago Defender.

TALLADEGA, Ala., July 29.—"If I whip that white man, he never will forget it; if that white man whips me, I'll forget it in about fifteen minutes." These are the reported words of Jack Arthur Johnson, heavy-weight pugilistic champion of the world, a day or so before the fight at Reno, Nev. These words pretty accurately express the difference in the feelings of the two races. The average Negro wished to look at the fight as only a pugilistic contest between individuals, while certain clamorous newspapers of the white race, north and south, insisted and kept insisting that it was to be "a great race battle." This was indeed a very untactful insistence, since no earthly power could foresee the result. For although Johnson was known to be the better man the better man does not always win in a contest of any kind.

HAD JEFFRIES WON FIGHT.

If Jeffries had won the fight, it would have aroused no resentment in the Negro race against the white race. The

Negroes would have forgotten it "in about fifteen minutes." They would have taken it as a matter of fact and a matter of history. And this does not mean that they were not both proud and hopeful of their champion. But hard common-sense says that in the natural course of events in such a contest ONE MUST WIN and one must lose. We knew that many of these clamorous newspapers were ready to preach insulting homilies to us about our inferiority; we knew that many of the editors had already composed and pigeon-holed their editorials of mockery and spite—and we shall not conceal the fact of our satisfaction at having these homilies and editorials all knocked into the waste basket by the big fist of Jack Johnson. In this he did missionary work,—although pugilism is that end of civilization that is adjacent to barbarism.

We are not sorry that Johnson showed other points of superiority besides more physical superiority. Most of us had already conceded the latter. But during all the months of preparation and clear through the battle he has carried the sunshine and good-nature of his race. His good-nature was impregnable against insult and unshaken by the battle itself. Right in the midst of the fight, when Jeffries jabbed him on the head by one clever hook which Johnson had not intended to receive, the Negro champion laughed out loud. Think of it! Imagine Jeffries tickled by a clever blow from Johnson! Neither Jeffries nor any other white man I have ever met could have been capable of that. When the fight waxed hot the only unexcited man in all the fifteen thousand or more, was Jack Johnson.

DOUGLASS LIKEN THEM TO ASSES.

Even the insulting words of Corbett, the "bully," could not shake him. The jeers of the audience fell on him like rain upon the testudinate back of a turtle. Fred Douglass once said, when asked how he felt when people jeered at him on the streets on account of his color: "I feel as if an ass had kicked, but had hit nobody." Such a feeling is not devoid of its humor. Under it one's humor is likely to get the better of his contempt.

JOHNSON HUGS JEFF AND JOKES.

The black man was merry all through the game. Corbett had trained Jeffries, and had ridiculed Johnson,—and when Jeffries made one great swing at Johnson's body, his fist passed harmlessly under the black man's arm, and thus coming to a close hug, Johnson hung his head over the white man's shoulder and said with an arch smile to Corbett: "Hello Jimmy!"

GIVE JEFF PLEASANT CORNER.

And not only in physical and temperamental qualities, but in magnanimity the black man was superior. His race has noted with pride that he has never tried to bully his enemies or to detract from the worth of his opponent. When on the platform of battle he was asked by the other side to "toss" for choice of "corners," he gave them choice of corners without "tossing" —and they deliberately chose the best corner, leaving him with the sun in his eyes.

NO HARM DONE IF FEW BLACKS ARE KILLED.

White editors who so nobly fought Jeffries' battles before the fight, have found one consoling reflection since the fight, viz: that the victory of the black man "will do the Negro race harm." How, I ask, in the name of heaven can it harm a race to show itself excellent? Does it harm the Negro race to kill a score of Negroes as a result of the fight? The Persian King could as easily harm the sea by whipping it. These results have simply impressed the Negro with an undue sense of its importance. It was poor tact again on the part of white people.

But, sincerely now, it was a good deal better for Johnson to win and a few Negroes be killed in body for it, than for Johnson to have lost and all Negroes to have been killed in spirit by the preachments of inferiority from the combined white press. It is better for us to succeed, though some die, than for us to fail, though all live. The fact of this fight will outdo a mountain peak of theory about the Negro as a physical man,—and as a man of self-control and courage.

BRUTE FORCE, OR SKILL, WHICH?

It is by no means "bad for his race." It was an action at the rag-tag end of civilization, but it was a point at which the Negro's advance was disputed and his equality denied. It is just as important as is the carrying of the "outer-works" of an enemy. It makes the "inner-works" the next point of defense and attack. It will awaken a good deal of sober reflection about the soundness of the grounds of charging the Negro with inferiority in any other lines. It will do Johnson's race good and no one knows this better than the white men who are responsible for the over-estimation of the event—before the event. After the event, however, it is called a pure contest of brutality, and Johnson is represented as simply the "best brute." It is not necessary to say to intelligence that the mightiest brute in the world could have been no match for the skill of Jeffries. And if it were a mere trial of the animal, is it not well for the Negro to show that the animal in him is equal in power and skill to the animal in the white man? The first condition of good manhood is sound animalhood.—Alabamian.

LESTER A. WALTON
Concert at Carnegie Hall
The New York Age, May 9, 1912

IT HAS LONG been my wish that the local colored musicians appear in a concert at one of the leading music halls of the city and give the white citizens an opportunity to hear music written and played by colored people. My aspirations in that direction increased after hearing the first concert given by the Clef Club at the Manhattan Casino, and it was not until Thursday evening at Carnegie Hall was my wish gratified. The colored musicians made an excellent showing, and many of their admirers would have been sadly disappointed had the affair been labeled other than a success.

At some time or another I have spoken in complimentary terms of the work of all the colored artists appearing on Thursday evening's program, the Clef Club in particular. Were I to comment on each number in detail I fear I would be charged with repetition and lacking in originality. For instance, I have been profuse in my praise of the enjoyable and artistic manner in which the Clef Club previously rendered the majority of selections used Thursday evening. However, it behooves me before going further to confess that I spent most of my time watching the white auditors, as I was particularly anxious to know just what they thought of the concert.

It is extremely unfortunate, as well as ofttimes inconvenient, that color prejudice, with its inconsistencies and un-American spirit (due in the main to a state of ignorance relative to conditions), is running riotously rampant in this country. It is unfortunate for those who are compelled to battle daily against such unnecessary odds as well as for those who know about as much concerning the home life and qualifications of our colored citizens as a whole as they do of the Hottentot, despite the fact that both races live side by side in this country.

So when a golden opportunity is afforded us to show that we are no different from other human beings and that although we possess strong racial characteristics the same as other races still we are making great strides in this great era of civilization and advancement, it is a source of great pleasure to take advantage of such a chance as given Thursday evening at Carnegie Hall.

The concert was unique in many respects. Some of the leading white citizens sat in evening dress in seats next to some of our highly respectable colored citizens, who were also in evening clothes. No color line was drawn in any part of the house, both white and colored occupying boxes. Carnegie Hall was packed to the doors with members of both races and hundreds were turned away. Yet no calamity occurred because the colored citizens were not segregated in certain parts of the house as some of our theatre managers think it necessary to do, despite laws forbidding discrimination. And it should not be overlooked that the whites present represented the best element of their race; so did the colored people in attendance.

Many white composers and writers do their best to disparage syncopated music, commonly known as ragtime, and do their utmost to show wherein this brand of music does not even merit passing consideration. Yet I noticed that not until the Clef Club had played "Panama" did the audience evince more than ordinary interest. White men and women then looked at each other and smiled, while one lady seated in a prominent box began to beat time industriously with her right hand, which was covered with many costly gems. It was then that after a brief mental soliloquy I was forced to conclude that despite the adverse criticism of many who are unable to play it that syncopation is truly a native product—a style of music of which the Negro is originator, but which is generally popular with all Americans.

Although the Clef Club Orchestra of 125 musicians, under the direction of James Reese Europe, assisted by William H. Tyers, was the feature of the program, there were other meritorious attractions. J. Rosamond Johnson so pleased in his singing of "Li'l Gal" that he was compelled to respond to an encore. Then there was the Poinciana Quintet, consisting of Messrs. Hilliard, Hawkes, Sutton, Jones and Foster, which scored a hit despite the fact that the singers were first handicapped by opening with a number more suitable for a rathskeller. "Dearest Memories" and "The Belle of the Lighthouse" evoked hearty applause.

A fine appearance was presented by the choir of St. Philip's Church, under Paul C. Bohlen. The choristers won favor in the singing of Coleridge-Taylor's "By the Waters of Babylon" and "Benedictus," from an original mass composed by Prof. Bohlen.

Mrs. Elizabeth Payne was down on the program for two numbers—"Jean," by Harry Burleigh, and "Suwanee River." She was pleasing in "Jean," but instead of singing "Suwanee River" as billed, gave as an encore "Mon Coeur s'Ouvre ta Voix," which did not show her at her best.

There was one number on the program well worth the price of admission—the rendition of Will Marion Cook's "Swing Along," by the Clef Club chorus, the members singing and playing this delightful Negro melody. There was something invigorating and inspiring in the manner in which "Swing Along" was put on which provoked applause. Three times did the Clef Club musicians sing and play the number before the enthusiastic audience was satisfied. Will Marion Cook rehearsed the men in the song, and it was the hit of the program. The artistic way in which it was rendered bore out the statement often made that classical music is not the only kind that requires preparation and intelligent interpretation.

Another number that struck the fancy of the audience was "The Rain Song," by Cook and Rogers, which was one of the hits of "Bandanna Land." The Cleftites sang and played this number in lively fashion, with "Deacon" Johnson's Martinique Quartet leading the song.

The concert was given in the interest of the Music School Settlement for Colored People, of which David Mannes is the moving spirit. Mr. Mannes is a sincere friend of the Negro and believes that the race is going to make an enviable reputation in the musical world. He is devoting time and money to further the project, and it was mainly through his efforts that Carnegie Hall was secured for Thursday evening's entertainment as well as the deep interest manifested by the white citizens.

In looking over the list of directors of the settlement school I note that more than three-fourths of the members are white. To my mind it would be a capital idea if the board were composed of half white and half colored at least, taking into consideration that the institution is conducted for colored people.

Those who took part in the concert gave their services free, and the members of the Clef Club put in many hours in preparation for an event which should always occasion memories fond and pleasant to those present.

CELEBRATING JUNETEENTH

THE AUSTIN DAILY STATESMAN
Negroes to Gather Here by Thousands

May 20, 1912

NEGROES TO GATHER HERE BY THOUSANDS

BIG PLANS FOR THE MAKING
FOR JUNETEENTH CELEBRATION.

IT'S TO BE AT EAST END PARK

Baseball Game Between Austin and
Beaumont Nines to Be Feature
of the Affair.

EMANCIPATION DAY this year is to be celebrated by an ingathering of the Afro-American clans from all points of the compass, and the black battalions, several thousand strong, will converge here in the State Capital. To mix in the throng that will overflow East End (or Idle Hour) Park that day will be like an excursion into plantation-land in the days "befo' de wah." Or rather it will be like this—and then some. For there will be all sorts of amusements, both ancient and modern, and all sorts of negroes, both ancient and young.

Old uncles and aunties who have scarce wandered out of sight of the old cabin door for years will be drawn along with the crowds, in the wagon or on board train, and there'll be many a quaint old story told, and many an old half-forgotten superstition revived when those old slave time darkies get together on this occasion of jubilation.

And there'll be singing and dancing till you can't rest, for where is the real negro who isn't a natural musician or who wouldn't rather cut the pigeon's wing or trip the light fantastic than—well, anything, except eat watermelon. In this connection, it can be said with confidence that the supply of this juicy fruit of the Texan fields will be measured only by the carloads.

Among the many surrounding cities and towns which will send large delegations to participate in this almost Statewide rally of the race is Beaumont. Wilson Carroll, one of the leaders in arranging the celebration, is in receipt of a letter from that city saying that it will send a thousand on a special train, among them a trained quartet, dancers and a baseball team. The baseball aggregation has challenged a local negro nine, and a picturesque performance may be counted on.

Special rates have been obtained over the railroads and the negroes say they are going to pull off the biggest thing ever done by them in Central Texas. They count on at least 10,000 comers. They say that the race in this city is united now, whereas for the past several years each party or faction has had its own "Juneteenth" celebration. There were four or five last year. Now all will pull together and by their united efforts stage something really big, something that will be a credit to them and a benefit to the city.

Some of the prominent men of the race will be on hand to extol "Marse Abe Linkum's" historic act and to urge on the rising generation the virtues of industry and sobriety.

Everybody will be fed. Beeves and porkers by the half-dozen will be slain and then barbecued over fires that will burn all through the previous night in long trenches. Bread by the ton, pickles by the barrel and coffee by the tankful will supply sustenance to the hungry multitude.

PROTESTING THE SEGREGATION OF FEDERAL WORKERS

MOORFIELD STOREY, W.E.B. DU BOIS, OSWALD GARRISON VILLARD
To Woodrow Wilson
The New York Evening Post, August 15, 1913

PLEA FOR NEGRO WORKERS

COLORED PEOPLE'S ASSOCIATION
APPEALS TO PRESIDENT.

Charge that Members of Race in Federal Employ Are Being Made Objects of Discrimination—Set Apart As If Contact with Them Were Contamination—No Promotion.

An appeal, in which it charged that the Government is discriminating against the negroes among its civilian employees, has been sent to President Wilson for the National Association for the Advancement of Colored People. The letter bears the signatures of Moorfield Storey, president of the Association; Oswald Garrison Villard, chairman of the board of directors, and W. E. B. Du Bois, director of publicity. The letter follows:

New York, August 15 1913.
To Woodrow Wilson, President of the United States.
Dear Mr. President: The National Association for the Advancement of Colored People, through its Board of Directors, respectfully protests against the policy of your Administration in segregating the colored employees in the departments at Washington. It realizes that this new and radical departure has been recommended, and is now being defended, on the ground that, by giving certain bureaus or sections wholly to colored employees they are thereby rendered safer in possession of their offices and are less likely to be ousted or discriminated against. We believe this reasoning to be fallacious. It is based on a failure

to appreciate the deeper significance of the new policy; to understand how far reaching the effects of such a drawing of caste lines by the Federal Government may be, and how humiliating it is to the men thus stigmatized.

Never before has the Federal Government discriminated against its civilian employees on the ground of color. Every such act heretofore has been that of an individual State. The very presence of the Capitol and of the Federal flag has drawn colored people to the District of Columbia in the belief that, living there under the shadow of the National Government itself, they were safe from the persecution and discrimination which follow them elsewhere because of their dark skins. To-day they learn that, though their ancestors have fought in every war in behalf of the United States, in the fiftieth year after Gettysburg and Emancipation, this Government, founded on the theory of complete equality and freedom for all citizens, has established two classes among its civilian employees. It has set the colored apart as if mere contact with them were contamination. The efficiency of their labor, the principles of scientific management are disregarded, the possibilities of promotion, if not now, will soon be severely limited. To them is held out only the prospect of mere subordinate routine service, without the stimulus of advancement to high office by merit, a right deemed inviolable for all white natives, as for the children of the foreign born, of Italians, French and Russians, Jews and Christians, who are now entering the Government service. For to such limitation this segregation will inevitably lead. Who took the trouble to ascertain what our colored clerks thought about this order, to which their consent was never asked? Behind screens and closed doors they now sit apart as though leprous. Men and women alike have the badge of inferiority pressed upon them by Government decree. How long will it be before the hateful epithets of "nigger" and "Jim Crow" are openly applied to these sections? Let any one experienced in Washington affairs, or any trained newspaper correspondent, answer. The colored people themselves will tell you how soon sensitive and high-minded members of their race will refuse to enter the Government service which thus decrees what is to them the most hateful kind of discrimination. Indeed, there is a widespread belief among them that this is the very purpose of these unwarrantable orders. And wherever there are men who rob the negroes of their votes, who exploit and degrade and insult and lynch those whom they call their inferiors, there this mistaken action of the Federal Government will be cited as the warrant for new racial outrages that cry out to high Heaven for redress. Who shall say where discrimination once begun shall cease? Who can deny that every act of discrimination the world over breeds fresh injustice?

For the lowly of all classes you have lifted up your voice and not in vain. Shall ten millions of our citizens say that their civic liberties and rights are not safe in your hands? To ask the question is to answer it. They desire a "New Freedom," too, Mr. President, yet they include in that term nothing else than the rights guaranteed them by the Constitution under which they believe they should be protected from persecution based upon a physical quality with which Divine Providence has endowed them.

They ask, therefore, that you, born of a great section which prides itself upon its chivalry towards the humble and the weak, prevent a gross injustice which is an injustice none the less because it was actuated in some quarters by a genuine desire to aid those now discriminated against.

Yours, for justice,

The National Association for the Advancement of Colored People.

By Moorfield Storey, President.
W. E. Burghardt Du Bois,
Director of Publicity.
Oswald Garrison Villard,
Chairman of the Board.

"A GRATUITOUS BLOW AGAINST
EVER-LOYAL CITIZENS"

WILLIAM MONROE TROTTER
Address to Woodrow Wilson
November 12, 1914

Full Text of the Protest Against Segregation—The Speech That Upset the Equilibrium of the Nation's Chief Executive.

(Special to the Chicago Defender.)

WASHINGTON, D. C., Nov. 20.—William Monroe Trotter's address to President Woodrow Wilson Thursday, November 12, is as follows:

One year ago we presented a national petition, signed by Afro-Americans in thirty-eight states, protesting against the segregation of employes of the national government whose ancestry could be traced in whole or in part to Africa, as instituted under your administration in the treasury and postoffice departments. We then appealed to you to undo this race segregation in accord with your duty as president and with your pre-election pledges. We stated that there could be no freedom, no respect from others, and no equality of citizenship under segregation for races, especially when applied to but one of the many racial elements in the government employ. For such placement of employes means a charge by the government of physical indecency or infection, or of being a lower order of beings, or a subjection to the prejudices of other citizens, which constitutes inferiority of status. We protested such segregation as to working positions, eating tables, dressing rooms, rest rooms, lockers and especially public toilets in government buildings. We stated that such segregation was a public humiliation and degradation, entirely unmerited and far-reaching in its injurious effects, a gratuitous blow against ever-loyal citizens and against those many of whom aided and supported your elevation to the presidency of our common country.

INSTANCES CITED.

At that time you stated you would investigate conditions for yourself. Now, after the lapse of a year, we have come back, having found that all the forms of segregation of government employes of African extraction are still practiced in the treasury and postoffice department buildings, and to a certain extent have spread into other government buildings.

Under the treasury department, in the bureau of engraving and printing, there is segregation not only in dressing rooms, but in working positions, Afro-American employes being herded at separate tables, in eating, and in toilets. In the navy department there is herding at desks and separation in lavatories; in the postoffice department there is separation in work for Afro-American women in the alcove on the eighth floor, of Afro-American men in rooms on the seventh floor, with forbidding even of entrance into an adjoining room occupied by white clerks on the seventh floor, and of Afro-American men in separate rooms just instituted on the sixth floor, with separate lavatories for Afro-American men on the eighth floor; in the main treasury building in separate lavatories in the basement; in the interior department separate lavatories, which were specifically pointed out to you at our first hearing; in the state and other departments in separate lavatories; in marine hospital service building in separate lavatories, though there is but one Afro-American clerk to use it; in the war department in separate lavatories; in the postoffice department building separate lavatories; in the sewing and bindery divisions of the government printing office on the fifth floor there is herding at working positions of Afro-American women and separation in lavatories, and now segregation instituted by the division chief since our first audience with you. This lavatory segregation is the most degrading, most insulting of all. Afro-American employes who use the regular public lavatories on the floors where they work are cautioned and are then warned by superior officers against insubordination.

We have come by vote of this league to set before you this definite continuance of race segregation and to renew the protest and to ask you to abolish segregation of Afro-American employes in the executive department.

HUMILIATION ALLEGED.

Because we cannot believe you capable of any disregard of your pledges we have been sent by the alarmed American citizens of color. They realize that if they can be segregated and thus humiliated by the national government at the national capital the beginning is made for the spread of that persecution and prosecution which makes property and life itself insecure in the South, the foundation of the whole fabric of their citizenship is unsettled.

They have made plain enough to you their opposition to segregation last year by a national anti-segregation petition, this year by a protest registered at the polls, voting against every Democratic candidate save those outspoken against segregation. The only Democrat elected governor in the eastern states was Governor Walsh of Massachusetts, who appealed to you by letter to stop segregation. Thus have the Afro-Americans shown how they detest segregation.

In fact, so intense is their resentment that the movement to divide this solid race vote and make peace with the national Democracy, so suspiciously revived when you ran for the presidency, and which some of our families for two generations have been risking all to promote, bids fair to be undone.

Only two years ago you were heralded as perhaps the second Lincoln, and now the Afro-American leaders who supported you are hounded as false leaders and traitors to their race. What a change segregation has wrought!

ASK EXECUTIVE ORDER.

You said that your "Colored fellow citizens could depend upon you for everything which would assist in advancing the interests of their race in the United States." Consider that pledge in the face of the continued color segregation! Fellow citizenship means congregation. Segregation destroys fellowship and citizenship. Consider that any passerby on the streets of the national capital, whether he be black or white, can enter and use the public lavatories in government buildings, while citizens of color who do the work of the government are excluded.

As equal citizens and by virtue of your public promises we are entitled at your hands to freedom from discrimination, restriction, imputation and insult in government employ. Have you a "new freedom" for white Americans and a new slavery for your "Afro-American fellow citizens"? God forbid!

We have been delegated to ask you to issue an executive order against any and all segregation of government employes because of race and color, and to ask whether you will do so. We await your reply, that we may give it to the waiting citizens of the United States of African extraction.

A WHITE HOUSE CONFRONTATION
WOODROW WILSON AND WILLIAM MONROE TROTTER
An Exchange
November 12, 1914

[Wilson] Now let me see—because, in the first place, let us leave politics out of it. If the colored people made a mistake in voting for me, they ought to correct it and vote against me if they think so. I don't want politics brought into it at all, because I think that lowers the whole level of the thing. I am not seeking office. God knows that any man that would seek the presidency of the United States is a fool for his pains. The burden is all but intolerable, and the things that I have to do are just as much as a human spirit can carry. So that I don't care the least in the world for the political considerations involved. I want you to understand that. But we are dealing with a human problem, not a political problem. It's a human problem.

Now, I think that I am perfectly safe in stating that the American people, as a whole, sincerely desire and wish to support, in every way they can, the advancement of the Negro race in America. They rejoice in the evidences of the really extraordinary advances that the race has made—in its self-support, in its capacity for independent endeavor, in its adaptation for organization, and everything of that sort. All of that is admirable and has the sympathy of the whole country.

But we are all practical men. We know that there is a point at which there is apt to be friction, and that is in the intercourse between the two races. Because, gentlemen, we must strip this thing of sentiment and look at the facts, because the facts will get the better of us whether we wish them to or not.

Now, in my view the best way to help the Negro in America is to help him with his independence—to relieve him of his dependence upon the white element of our population, as he is relieving himself in splendid fashion. And the problem, as I have discussed it with my colleagues in the departments, is this, for I had taken it very seriously after my last interview with a committee of this organization. If you will leave with me all the instances you have just cited, I will look into them again. But the point that was put to me, in essence, was that they were seeking, not to put the Negro employees at a disadvantage, but they were seeking to make arrangements which would prevent any kind of friction between the white employees and the Negro employees.

Now, they may have been mistaken in judgment. But their objective was not to do what you gentlemen seem to assume— to put the Negro employees at an uncomfortable disadvantage —but to relieve the situation that does arise. We can't blink the fact, gentlemen, that it does arise when the two races are mixed.

Now, of course color outside is a perfectly artificial test. It is a race question. And color, so far as the proposition itself, is merely an evidence of the development from a particular continent; that is to say, from the African continent.

Now, it takes the world generations to outlive all its prejudices. Of course they are prejudices. They are prejudices which are embarrassing the Government of the United States just as much with other races, that is, some other races, as they are embarrassing us about the race that is derived from African descent. And so we must treat this thing with a recognition of its difficulties.

Now, I am perfectly willing to do anything that is just. I am not willing to do what may turn out to be unwise. Now, it is the unwise part that is debatable—whether we have acted in a wise way or not. If my colleagues have dealt with me candidly —and I think they have—they have not intended to do an injustice. They have intended to remedy what they regarded as creating the possibility of friction, which they did not want ever to exist. They did not want any white man made uncomfortable by anything that any colored man did, or a colored man made uncomfortable by anything that a white man did in the offices of the government. That, in itself, is essentially how they feel—that a man of either race should not make the other uncomfortable. It works both ways. A white man can make a colored man uncomfortable, as a colored man can make a white man uncomfortable if there is a prejudice existing between them. And it shouldn't be allowed on either end.

Now, what makes it look like discrimination is that the colored people are in a minority as compared with the white employees. Any minority looks as if it were discriminated against. But suppose that the Negroes were in the majority in the departments in the clerkships and this segregation occurred? Then it would look like discrimination against the whites, because it is always the minority that looks discriminated against, whereas the discrimination may not be intended against anybody, but for the benefit of both.

I am not deciding this question, you understand. I am only saying that everything that has been done is just. I have not inquired into it recently enough to be sure of that. But I want to get you gentlemen to understand this thing from the point of view of those who are trying to handle it. It is a very difficult question. Nobody can be cocksure about what should be done. I am not cocksure about what should be done. I am certain that I have been dependent upon the advice of the men who were in immediate contact with the problem in the several departments. They have assured me that they have not put Negro employees at a disadvantage in regard to rooms and lighting that was inconvenient. I have put that up to them again. I haven't had time to look at the conditions myself, but I have again and again said that the thing that would distress me most would be that they should select the colored people of the departments to be given bad light or bad ventilation yet worse than the others, and inferior positions, physically considered.

Now, they have not intended to do that, I am quite sure, from the assurances of many of the cabinet. It may be that some have been taking information from their subordinates without going to look at what was actually done. But, at any rate, that is the spirit of the heads of the departments, for I consulted with them very gravely about this, and I think their spirit is mine in the matter.

I want to help the colored people in every way I can, but there are some ways, some things that I could do myself that would hurt them more than it would help them.

Now, you may differ with me in judgment. It is going to take generations to work this thing out. And mark these pages, it will come quickest if these questions aren't raised. It will come quickest if you men go about the work of your race, if you will go about it and see that the race makes good and nobody can say that there is any kind of work that they can't do as well as anybody else.

That is the way to solve this thing. It is not a question of intrinsic equality, because we all have human souls. We are absolutely equal in that respect. It is just at the present a question of economic equality—whether the Negro can do the same things with equal efficiency. Now, I think they are proving that they can. After they have proved it, a lot of things are going to solve themselves.

Now, that is the whole thing. We must not misunderstand one another in these things. We must not allow feelings to get the upper hands of our judgments. We must try to do what judgment demands now, as has been said to Mr. Trotter. I think you have the memoranda, and I will look into it again. I will look into it, and I accept the assurances that were given me, and I have repeated them to you. That is all I can do.

[Trotter] May I ask one question, Mr. President? What do you think about the result of this present condition in the departments, where it has already operated to the detriment of so many of the employees, where some of them have been placed in a position where they are now humiliated and indisposed as a result of this humiliating condition: having to go so far from their work to the toilet rooms, and then the condition also where employees in the government have not only been reduced from clerkships to laborers, but have next been forced right out of the departments entirely.

[Wilson] I haven't known of such incidents. My question would be this: If you think that you gentlemen, as an organization, and all other Negro citizens of the country, that you are being humiliated, you will believe it. If you take it as a humiliation, which it is not intended as, and sow the seed of that impression all over the country, why the consequences will be very serious. But if you should take it in the spirit in which I have presented it to you, it wouldn't have serious consequences. Now, that is what I think about it. It is the misunderstanding, as I honestly believe it to be, that is going to be serious, much more serious than the facts justify.

Now, as for demotions and things of that sort, I haven't taken them up. I didn't know about that.

[An unknown person] Mr. President, these colored clerks, and clerks of other nationalities, have been working together, side by side, in peace and harmony and friendship for fifty years without distinction and separation based upon their race. Mr. President, it is entirely untenable to say that race feeling or race friction necessitates any of this separation of Afro-American clerks. It is absolutely contrary to the facts of the case. Mr. Trotter has told you that, even under a Democratic administration, it was not found to be necessary to separate clerks.

[Trotter] We are not here as wards. We are not here as dependents. We are not here looking for charity or help. We are here as full-fledged American citizens, vouchsafed equality of citizenship by the federal Constitution. Separation and distinction marking, because of a certain kind of blood in our veins, when it is not made against other different races, is something that must be a humiliation. It creates in the minds of others that there is something the matter with us—that we are not their equals, that we are not their brothers, that we are so different that we cannot work at a desk beside them, that we cannot eat at a table beside them, that we cannot go into the dressing room where they go, that we cannot use a locker beside them, that we cannot even go into a public toilet with them.

Think of it, Mr. President, that any pedestrian walking the streets of the national capital, whether he be white or black, can enter and use any of these public toilets in the government buildings, and that Americans of color who are doing the work of the government cannot do so.

Now, Mr. President, there cannot be any friction with regard to going into a public toilet. They have been going into the public toilets for fifty years. They were going into the public toilets when your administration came in. When your administration came in, under Mr. John Skelton Williams, a drastic segregation was put into effect almost at once.

Mr. President, we insist that the facts in the case bear us out in truth—that this segregation is not due to any friction between the races, but is due to race prejudice on the part of the official who puts it into operation.

Mr. President, citizens, as they are picked out, especially in a country where there are many races and many nationalities—and everyone is picked out to be subjected to a prejudice of theirs—they are going to be subjected to all kinds of mistreatment and persecution everywhere throughout the country. They are necessarily objects of contempt and scorn, because segregation is not only a natural order of things, but it is the way of progression and more segregation. The very fact of any racial element of government employees being by themselves is an invitation in the public mind. That fact cannot be denied nor disputed.

Now, Mr. President, this is a very serious thing with us. We are sorely disappointed that you take the position that the separation itself is not wrong, is not injurious, is not rightly offensive to you. You hold us responsible for the feeling that the colored people of the country have—that it is an insult and an injustice; but that is not in accord with the facts, Mr. President. We, if anything, lag behind. Why, Mr. President, two years ago among our people, and last year, you were thought to be perhaps the second Abraham Lincoln.

[Wilson] Please leave me out. Let me say this, if you will, that if this organization wishes to approach me again, it must choose another spokesman. I have enjoyed listening to these other gentlemen. They have shown a spirit in the matter that I have appreciated, but your tone, sir, offends me. You are an American citizen, as fully an American citizen as I am, but you are the only American citizen that has ever come into this office who has talked to me with a tone with a background of passion that was evident. Now, I want to say that if this association comes again, it must have another spokesman. You wouldn't do me, then, a possible injustice.

[Trotter] I am from a part of the people, Mr. President.

[Wilson] You have spoiled the whole cause for which you came.

[Trotter] Mr. President, I am sorry for that. Mr. President, America that professes to be Christian cannot condemn that which [ ]

[Wilson] I expect those who profess to be Christians to come to me in a Christian spirit.

[Trotter] Mr. President, I have—now, don't misunderstand me, I have not condemned the Christian spirit. I am pleading for simple justice. Mr. President, I am from a part of the people who will take me at my word. I am from a part of the people. If my tone has seemed so contentious, why my tone has been misunderstood. I am from a part of the people, and I would like to be able to say, and do so, without prejudice.

[Wilson] Please leave me out and argue the case.

[Trotter] I was simply trying to show how my people feel, Mr. President, because it is the truth that we who led in this movement are today, among our people, branded as traitors to our race on segregation.

[Wilson] As traitors to your race?

[Trotter] As traitors to our race, because we advised the colored people to support the ticket. That is the reason we do it. I am sincere in this feeling. I want to show, Mr. President, their feeling in the matter, not my feeling. I am telling you the truth. We ought to be truthful, Mr. President. We ought to be frank and truthful. I hope you want to be frank and true and not be false to your faith. Now, Mr. President, you know it would be an unmanly thing to appear to be false.

[Wilson] These other gentlemen are not—

[Trotter] Believe me because I have been in the midst, and I work in this cause. And we have tried to get the colored people to reason in this matter. Their feeling is more [   ] than on others. Any portrayal, we found, led them to resent this thing. No, Mr. President, that is God's earnest truth, that we are as we seem to be, Mr. President—that we cannot be respected by our fellow citizens if we are to be segregated by the federal government. Our plea to you, Mr. President, from the bottom of my heart, is not to have the federal government make concessions to the prejudices of anybody.

We grew up in this country, and we know these various racial elements—the Latin, the Slavic, the Oriental, the differences, the conglomeration of races. And when they look around, they find we are treated differently from the way they are treated. I have given my life to this work of trying to relieve our people. God knows I want to relieve it, but I am trying to find the right way.

Mr. President, my whole desire is to let you know the truth we know. We see how it is impossible to make you feel what this thing is like, which injures. And they feel alienated by bringing any kind of separation in the public service. Because, Mr. President, it has been taken as an example in our every turn of our daily lives, in every turn of it. The government employees, if it were possible to have a separation without humiliation—if that position is adopted outside these limits—then for us, you know, this, if that is the position that is adopted, it is going to be inconceivable for colored clerks to concur with that separation.

There are great dangers, Mr. President, far more than there are advantages. We of course—of course, we do feel that there is a political aspect of the case, because, you know, we felt that there might be a question about this thing, and you know that we went on your declaration and things that you said. And, as I say, we are simply asking that conditions obtain that have obtained before. We would be false, Mr. President, false to ourselves and false to you, if we went out and led you to believe that we could convince the colored people that there was anything but degradation.

[Wilson] I don't think it's degradation. That is your interpretation of it.

[Trotter] Mr. President, as for your expression about having the two races work together without the dissatisfaction of either party, I want just to ask this question: If I am appointed to a government position, and a white man is in the same office, and either one becomes dissatisfied with the other, without any reason for it, should either be considered? Should it not be ignored simply as a dispute? Unless all those things occur in the abstract.

[Wilson] That is, if you do the work being done. If you harm the one, you are doing an injury to the other. It seems to me that is the situation.

Well, I am very much obliged to you. I will look into it again.

[Trotter] Mr. President, I hope that you don't feel toward me as you did a little while ago. I think you made a mistake. I assume great responsibility in the whole matter.

[Wilson] But that part we must leave out. Politics must be

left out, because, don't you see, to put it plainly, that is a form of blackmail. I am only saying that you are conscious of that, or that you would tell me contrary to that. But you must reflect that, when you call upon an officer and say you can't get certain votes if you don't do certain things, that is the kind of course which ought never to be attempted. I would resent it from one set of men as from another. You can vote as you please, provided I am perfectly sure that I am doing the right thing at the right time.

[Trotter] Just one word, Mr. President. We were trying to bring about racial harmony throughout the country.

PLOTTING THE OVERTHROW OF "YANKEE TYRANNY"
PROVISIONAL DIRECTORATE OF THE REVOLUTIONARY PLAN
The Plan of San Diego
January 6, 1915

WE, who in turn sign our names, assembled in the revolutionary plot of San Diego, Tex., solemnly promise each other, on our word of honor, that we will fulfill, and cause to be fulfilled and complied with, all the clauses and provisions stipulated in this document, and execute the orders and the wishes emanating from the provisional directorate of this movement and recognize as military chief of the same Mr. Agustin S. Garza, guaranteeing with our lives the faithful accomplishment of what is here agreed upon.

1. On the 20th day of February, 1915, at 2 o'clock in the morning, we will rise in arms against the Government and the country of the United States of North America, one as all and all as one, proclaiming the liberty of the individuals of the black race and its independence of Yankee tyranny which has held us in iniquitous slavery since the remote times; and at the same time and in the same manner we will proclaim the independence and segregation of the States bordering on the Mexican Nation, which are: Texas, New Mexico, Arizona, Colorado, and Upper California, of which States the Republic of Mexico was robbed in a most perfidious manner by North American Imperialism.

2. In order to render the foregoing clause effective, the necessary army corps will be formed under the immediate command of military leaders named by the Supreme Revolutionary Congress of San Diego, Tex., which shall have full power to designate a supreme chief, who shall be at the head of said army. The banner which shall guide us in this enterprise shall be red, with a white diagonal fringe, and bearing the following inscription: "Equality and independence," and none of the subordinate leaders or subalterns shall use any other flag

(except only the white flag for signals). The aforesaid army shall be known by the name of "liberating army for races and peoples."

3. Each one of the chiefs will do his utmost, by whatever means possible, to get possession of the arms and funds of the cities which he has beforehand been designated to capture, in order that our cause may be provided with resources to continue the fight with better success, the said leaders each being required to render an account of everything to his superiors, in order that the latter may dispose of it in the proper manner.

4. The leader who may take a city must immediately name and appoint municipal authorities, in order that they may preserve order and assist in every way possible the revolutionary movement. In case the capital of any State we are endeavoring to liberate be captured, there will be named in the same manner superior municipal authorities for the same purpose.

5. It is strictly forbidden to hold prisoners, either special prisoners (civilians) or soldiers; and the only time that should be spent in dealing with them is that which is absolutely necessary to demand funds (loans) of them; and whether these demands are successful or not, they shall be shot immediately without any pretext.

6. Every stranger who shall be found armed and who can not prove his right to carry arms shall be summarily executed, regardless of his race or nationality.

7. Every North American over 16 years of age shall be put to death, and only the aged men, the women, and children shall be respected; and on no account shall the traitors to our race be spared or respected.

8. The Apaches of Arizona, as well as the Indians (redskins) of the Territory shall be given every guaranty; and their lands which have been taken from them shall be returned to them, to the end that they may assist us in the cause which we defend.

9. All appointments and grades in our army which are exercised by subordinate officers (subalterns) shall be examined (recognized) by the superior officers. There shall likewise be

recognized the grades of leaders of other complots which may be connected with this, and who may wish to cooperate with us; also those who may affiliate with us later.

10. The movement having gathered force, and once having possessed ourselves of the States above alluded to, we shall proclaim them an independent republic, later requesting (if it be thought expedient) annexation to Mexico, without concerning ourselves at the time about the form of government which may control the destinies of the common mother country.

11. When we shall have obtained independence for the Negroes, we shall grant them a banner, which they themselves shall be permitted to select, and we shall aid them in obtaining six States of the American Union, which States border upon those already mentioned, and they may form from these six States a republic, and they may therefore be independent.

12. None of the leaders shall have power to make terms with the enemy, without first communicating with the superior officers of the army, bearing in mind that this is a war without quarter; nor shall any leader enroll in his ranks any stranger, unless said stranger belong to the Latin, the Negro, or the Japanese race.

13. It is understood that none of the members of this complot (or any one who may come in later) shall, upon the definite triumph of the cause which we defend, fail to recognize their superiors, nor shall they aid others who, with bastard designs, may endeavor to destroy what has been accomplished by such great work.

14. As soon as possible each local society (junta) shall nominate delegates who shall meet at a time and place beforehand designated, for the purpose of nominating a permanent directorate of the revolutionary movement. At this meeting shall be determined and worked out in detail the power and duties of the permanent directorate and this revolutionary plan may be revised or amended.

15. It is understood among those who may follow this movement that we shall carry in a singing voice the independence of the negroes, placing obligations upon both races and that on no account will we accept aid, either moral or pecuniary, from

the Government of Mexico; and it need not consider itself under any obligation in this, our movement.

Equality and independence.

SAN DIEGO, TEX., *January 6, 1915.*

    (Signed)   L. PERRIGO, *President.*
            A. GONZALES, *Secretary.*
            A. A. SAENZ.
            E. CISNEROS.
            PORFIRIO SANTOS.
            A. S. GARZA.
            MANUEL FLORES.
            B. RAMOS, JR.
            A. G. ALMARAZ.

REVIEWING THE BIRTH OF A NATION:
"VICIOUS AND DEFAMATORY"

FRANCIS HACKETT
Brotherly Love
The New Republic, March 20, 1915

BROTHERLY LOVE

The Birth of a Nation, a motion picture drama in two acts, founded on Thomas Dixon's story, The Clansman. Presented at the Liberty Theatre, New York.

IF history bore no relation to life, this motion picture drama could well be reviewed and applauded as a spectacle. As a spectacle it is stupendous. It lasts three hours, represents a staggering investment of time and money, reproduces entire battle scenes and complex historic events, amazes even when it wearies by its attempt to encompass the Civil War. But since history does bear on social behavior, "The Birth of a Nation" cannot be reviewed simply as a spectacle. It is more than a spectacle. It is an interpretation, the Rev. Thomas Dixon's interpretation, of the relations of the North and South and their bearing on the negro.

Were the Rev. Thomas Dixon a representative white Southerner, no one could criticize him for giving his own version of the Civil War and the Reconstruction period that followed. If he possessed the typical Southern attitude, the paternalistic, it would be futile to read a lecture on it. Seen from afar, such an attitude might be deemed reactionary, but at any rate it is usually genial and humane and protective, and because it has experience back of it, it has to be met with some respect. But the attitude which Mr. Dixon possesses and the one for which he forges corroboration in history is a perversion due largely to his personal temperament. So far as I can judge from this film, as well as from my recollection of Mr. Dixon's books, his is the sort of disposition that foments a great deal of the trouble in civilization. Sometimes in the clinical laboratory the doctors are reputed to perform an operation on a dog so that he loses the power to restrain certain motor activities. If he is started running in a cage, the legend goes, he keeps on running incessantly, and nothing can stop him but to hit him on the head with a club. There is a quality about everything Mr. Dixon has done that reminds me of this abnormal dog. At a remote period of his existence it is possible that he possessed a rudimentary faculty of self-analysis. But before that faculty developed he crystallized in his prejudices, and forever it was stunted. Since that time, whenever he has been stimulated by any of the ordinary emotions, by religion or by patriotism or by sex, he has responded with a frantic intensity. Energetic by nature, the forces that impel him are doubly violent because of this lack of inhibition. Aware as a clergyman that such violence is excessive, he has learned in all his melodramas to give them a highly moral twang. If one of his heroes is about to do something peculiarly loathsome, Mr. Dixon thrusts a crucifix in his hand and has him roll his eyes to heaven. In this way the very basest impulses are given the sanction of godliness, and Mr. Dixon preserves his own respect and the respect of such people as go by the label and not by the rot-gut they consume.

In "The Birth of a Nation" Mr. Dixon protests sanctimoniously that his drama "is not meant to reflect in any way on any race or people of to-day." And then he proceeds to give to the negro a kind of malignity that is really a revelation of his own malignity.

Passing over the initial gibe at the negro's smell, we early come to a negrophile senator whose mistress is a mulatto. As conceived by Mr. Dixon and as acted in the film, this mulatto is not only a minister to the senator's lust but a woman of inordinate passion, pride and savagery. Gloating as she does over the promise of "negro equality," she is soon partnered by a male mulatto of similar brute characteristics. Having established this triple alliance between the "uncrowned king," his diabolic colored mistress and his diabolic colored ally, Mr. Dixon shows the revolting processes by which the white South is crushed "under the heel of the black South." "Sowing the wind," he calls it. On the one hand we have "the poor bruised heart" of the white South, on the other "the new citizens inflamed by the growing sense of power." We see negroes shoving white men off the sidewalk, negroes quitting work to dance, negroes beating a crippled old white patriarch, negroes slinging up "faithful colored servants" and flogging them till they drop, negro courtesans guzzling champagne with the would-be head of the Black Empire, negroes "drunk with wine and power," negroes mocking their white master in chains, negroes "crazy with joy" and terrorizing all the whites in South Carolina. We see the blacks flaunting placards demanding "equal marriage." We see the black leader demanding a "forced marriage" with an imprisoned and gagged white girl. And we see continually in the background the white Southerner in "agony of soul over the degradation and ruin of his people."

Encouraged by the black leader, we see Gus the renegade hover about another young white girl's home. To hoochy-coochy music we see the long pursuit of the innocent white girl by this lust-maddened negro, and we see her fling herself to death from a precipice, carrying her honor through "the opal gates of death."

Having painted this insanely apprehensive picture of an unbridled, bestial, horrible race, relieved only by a few touches of low comedy, "the grim reaping begins." We see the operations of the Ku Klux Klan, "the organization that saved the South from the anarchy of black rule." We see Federals and Confederates uniting in a Holy War "in defence of their Aryan birthright," whatever that is. We see the negroes driven back, beaten, killed. The drama winds up with a suggestion of "Lincoln's solution"—back to Liberia—and then, if you please, with a film representing Jesus Christ in "the halls of brotherly love."

My objection to this drama is based partly on the tendency of the pictures but mainly on the animus of the printed lines I have quoted. The effect of these lines, reinforced by adroit quotations from Woodrow Wilson and repeated assurances of impartiality and goodwill, is to arouse in the audience a strong sense of the evil possibilities of the negro and the extreme propriety and godliness of the Ku Klux Klan. So strong is this impression that the audience invariably applauds the refusal of the white hero to shake hands with a negro, and under the circumstances it cannot be blamed. Mr. Dixon has identified the negro with cruelty, superstition, insolence and lust.

We know what a yellow journalist is. He is not yellow because he reports crimes of violence. He is yellow because he distorts them. In the region of history the Rev. Thomas Dixon corresponds to the yellow journalist. He is a clergyman, but he is a yellow clergyman. He is yellow because he recklessly distorts negro crimes, gives them a disproportionate place in life, and colors them dishonestly to inflame the ignorant and the credulous. And he is especially yellow, and quite disgustingly and contemptibly yellow, because his perversions are cunningly calculated to flatter the white man and provoke hatred and contempt for the negro.

Whatever happened during Reconstruction, this film is aggressively vicious and defamatory. It is spiritual assassination. It degrades the censors that passed it and the white race that endures it.

"AN EXALTATION OF RACE WAR"

OUTLOOK
The Birth of a Nation
April 14, 1915

"THE BIRTH OF A NATION"

CRITICISM OF moving pictures comes perhaps more properly within the field of a weekly journal than criticism of the "legitimate stage." The acted play, whatever its literary merits, may not live to pass beyond the dramatic confines of the metropolis. The "movie" drama, whatever its defects, will not improbably reach every city, if not every town, in the country. Of the great feature films costing thousands of dollars, advertised more extensively than any all-star play of the past, this is particularly true.

Such a film is "The Birth of a Nation," a drama of the Reconstruction period based upon the writings of the Rev. Thomas Dixon. In interest and technical mastery of the moving-picture art this film is one of the best yet produced by a modern director. Apparently neither expense nor time has been spared in preparing for the screen the story of the Civil War and the unhappy period which followed. The opportunity, indeed, was one that would have been the delight of any great and careful novelist, and one which would have taxed the knowledge of a great historian. Unhappily for the value of "The Birth of a Nation," Mr. Dixon is neither.

The story of "The Birth of a Nation," as Mr. Dixon sees it, is briefly this: Slavery is brought to the South by the traders of New England. Under slavery the Negroes are happy, working, as we are told in large letters, only from six in the morning to six at night, with two hours off in the middle of the day. The spirit of abolition grows in the North and the spirit of secession in the South. The war comes. Lincoln, Grant, Lee, the burning of Atlanta, Gettysburg and Appomattox, are passed in august review upon the screen. The North triumphs. Lincoln is killed, and the radical element in his party, led by a Congressman with a Negro mistress, adopts a policy of reconstruction involving social as well as political intercourse between the black and white races. Reconstruction means Negro domination of the white civilization of the South. Confronting this menace the Kuklux Klan springs into being, marshaled in legions that never were, and redeems the South from destruction.

The difficulty with Mr. Dixon as a purveyor of history is that he is not a historian. A historian not only presents true incidents from the past, but, if he is fair-minded and impartial, takes care that the incidents are representative and typical. Many of the most effective and most misleading scenes in "The Birth of a Nation" doubtless occurred some time, somewhere, in the South. Chosen as the whole picture of the Reconstruction period, however, they are unfair and vicious. Mr. Dixon has "a single-track mind," and the track leads only through a very unpleasant country. He is a partisan, and a dangerous one. He can see questions only in broad splotches of black and white. He knows but one side of Southern life, the sex problem of "Aryan and African."

As Mr. Dixon rightly believes and dramatically shows, the American Nation was born from the travail of civil war and the injustice of the Reconstruction period, and therefore his photo drama threatens no reopening of the wounds of the white North and the white South. The evil in "The Birth of a Nation" lies in the fact that the play is both a denial of the power of development within the free Negro and an exaltation of race war.

It would be difficult, indeed, to paint in colors dark enough the shame of the Reconstruction period. To say this is not to excuse the offense of a writer who distorts this shame and labels the blurred picture—"history."

WARTIME OPPORTUNITIES

W.E.B. DU BOIS
"We Should Worry"
The Crisis, June 1917

"WE SHOULD WORRY."

THE American Negro more unanimously than any other American group has offered his services in this war as officer and soldier. He has done this earnestly and unselfishly, overlooking his just resentment and grievous wrongs.

Up to the present his offer has been received with sullen and ungracious silence, or at best in awkward complaisance.

Nevertheless, the offer stands as it stood in 1776, 1812, 1861, and 1898.

But——

Certain Americans,—Southern Bourbons, and Northern Copperheads—fear Negro soldiers. They do not fear that they will not fight—they fear that they WILL fight and fight bravely and well. Just as in Reconstruction days, it was not bad Negro voters they feared but good, intelligent ones.

Selah!

These Bourbons and Copperheads know that if Negroes fight well in this war they will get credit for it. They cannot "Carrizal" the news and boost the white putty-head who blundered, forgetting the very name of the brave black subalterns. No! those fool French will tell the truth and the Associated Press will not be able to edit "Niggers"; so the Copperheads and Bourbons do not want Negro soldiers. They think they can trust Southern state officers to juggle that little "agricultural laborer joker" and keep us out of the ranks.

Very good.

"We should worry."

If they do not want us to fight, we will work. We will walk into the industrial shoes of a few million whites who go to the front. We will get higher wages and we cannot be stopped from migrating by all the deviltry of the slave South; particularly with the white lynchers and mob leaders away at war.

Will we be ousted when the white soldiers come back?

THEY WON'T COME BACK!

So there you are, gentlemen, and take your choice,——

We'll fight or work.

We'll fight and work.

If we fight we'll learn the fighting game and cease to be so "aisily lynched."

If we don't fight we'll learn the more lucrative trades and cease to be so easily robbed and exploited.

Take your choice, gentlemen.

"We should worry."

MOB ATTACKS ON BLACK WORKERS

THE NEW YORK TIMES
Mob of 3,000 Rules in East St. Louis
May 29, 1917

MOB OF 3,000 RULES IN EAST ST. LOUIS

*Attack and Beat Imported Negro
Workers—Police and Militia
Unable to Control Rioters.*

EAST ST. LOUIS, Ill., Tuesday, May 29.—A mob, estimated at 3,000 persons, determined, as they said, to rid the city of negroes imported to work in factories and munition plants, swept through the streets last night and early this morning, attacking and beating negroes wherever found. Several negroes have been injured so severely that they will probably die.

The mob stopped street cars and interurban cars in its search, and at 1 o'clock was threatening to storm the jail, where a score of negroes had been taken for safekeeping. Ambulances made the rounds of streets where the mob had traveled to pick up injured negroes and take them to hospitals.

The police were helpless against the mob, and Mayor Fred Mollman appealed for aid to Major R. W. Cavanaugh, commanding two companies of the Sixth Illinois Infantry, quartered here. Major Cavanaugh sent 125 men, who helped to fight back the mob, while several negroes were rescued, but this small force of soldiers proved inadequate. Thereupon Mayor Mollman telegraphed Governor Lowden to send additional troops for duty.

The riot started after a delegation of sixty members of the trades and labor union visited the City Council to protest against the importation of negroes from Mississippi to fill positions in the factories of the city. It is estimated that 8,000 negroes had been brought into the city since Jan. 1.

A DEADLY RIOT IN EAST ST. LOUIS

CARLOS F. HURD
Post-Dispatch Man, An Eye-Witness, Describes Massacre of Negroes

St. Louis Post-Dispatch, July 3, 1917

POST-DISPATCH MAN, AN EYE-WITNESS, DESCRIBES MASSACRE OF NEGROES

Victims Driven From Home by Fire, Stoned, Beaten and Hanged When Dying—Women Fight Militiamen and Assist in Work.

A Staff Reporter of the Post-Dispatch.

FOR an hour and a half last evening I saw the massacre of helpless negroes at Broadway and Fourth street, in downtown East St. Louis, where a black skin was a death warrant.

I have read of St. Bartholomew's night. I have heard stories of the latter-day crimes of the Turks in Armenia, and I have learned to loathe the German army for its barbarity in Belgium. But I do not believe that Moslem fanaticism or Prussian frightfulness could perpetrate murders of more deliberate brutality than those which I saw committed, in daylight by citizens of the State of Abraham Lincoln.

I saw man after man, with hands raised, pleading for his life, surrounded by groups of men—men who had never seen him before and knew nothing about him except that he was black—and saw them administer the historic sentence of intolerance, death by stoning. I saw one of these men, almost dead from a savage shower of stones, hanged with a clothesline, and when it broke, hanged with a rope which held. Within a few paces of the pole from which he was suspended, four other negroes lay dead or dying, another having been removed, dead, a short time before. I saw the pockets of two of these negroes searched, without the finding of any weapon.

ROCK DROPPED ON NEGROES NECK.

I saw one of these men, covered with blood and half conscious, raise himself on his elbow, and look feebly about, when a young man, standing directly behind him, lifted a flat stone in both hands and hurled it upon his neck. This young man was much better dressed than most of the others. He walked away unmolested.

I saw negro women begging for mercy and pleading that they had harmed no one, set upon by white women of the baser sort, who laughed and answered the coarse sallies of men as they beat the negresses' faces and breasts with fists, stones and sticks. I saw one of these furies fling herself at a militiaman who was trying to protect a negress, and wrestle with him for his bayonetted gun, while other women attacked the refugee.

What I saw, in the 90 minutes between 6:30 P.M. and the lurid coming of darkness, was but one local scene of the drama of death. I am satisfied that, in spirit and method, it typified the whole. And I cannot somehow speak of what I saw as mob violence. It was not my idea of a mob.

CROWD MOSTLY WORKINGMEN.

A mob is passionate, a mob follows one man or a few men blindly; a mob sometimes takes chances. The East St. Louis affair, as I saw it, was a man hunt, conducted on a sporting basis, though with anything but the fair play which is the principle of sport. The East St. Louis men took no chances, except the chance from stray shots, which every spectator of their acts took. They went in small groups, there was little leadership, and there was a horribly cool deliberateness and a spirit of fun about it. I cannot allow even the doubtful excuse of drink. No man whom I saw showed the effect of liquor.

It was no crowd of hot-headed youths. Young men were in the greater number, but there were the middle-aged, no less active in the task of destroying the life of every discoverable black man. It was a shirt-sleeve gathering, and the men were mostly workingmen, except for some who had the aspect of mere loafers. I have mentioned the peculiarly brutal crime committed by the only man there who had the appearance of being a business or professional man of any standing.

I would be more pessimistic about my fellow-Americans than I am today, if I could not say that there were other workingmen who protested against the senseless slaughter. I would be ashamed of myself if I could not say that I forgot my place as a professional observer and joined in such protests. But I do not think any verbal objection had the slightest effect. Only a volley of lead would have stopped those murderers.

"Get a nigger," was the slogan, and it was varied by the recurrent cry, "Get another!" It was like nothing so much as the holiday crowd, with thumbs turned down, in the Roman Coliseum, except that here the shouters were their own gladiators, and their own wild beasts.

When I got off a State street car on Broadway at 6:30, a fire apparatus was on its way to the blaze in the rear of Fourth street, south from Broadway. A moment's survey showed why this fire had been set, and what it was meant to accomplish.

FIRE DRIVES OUT NEGROES.

The sheds in the rear of negroes' houses, which were themselves in the rear of the main buildings on Fourth street, had been ignited to drive out the negro occupants of the houses. And the slayers were waiting for them to come out.

It was stay in and be roasted, or come out and be slaughtered. A moment before I arrived, one negro had taken the desperate chance of coming out, and the rattle of revolver shots, which I heard as I approached the corner, was followed by the cry, "They've got him!"

And they had. He lay on the pavement, a bullet wound in his head and his skull bare in two places. At every movement of pain which showed that life remained, there came a terrific kick in the jaw or the nose, or a crashing stone, from some of the men who stood over him.

At the corner, a few steps away, were a Sergeant and several guardsmen. The Sergeant approached the ring of men around the prostrate negro.

"This man is done for," he said. "You'd better get him away from here." No one made a move to lift the blood-covered form, and the Sergeant walked away, remarking, when I questioned him about an ambulance, that the ambulances had quit coming. However, an undertaker's ambulance did come 15 minutes later, and took away the lifeless negro, who had in the meantime been further kicked and stoned.

By that time, the fire in the rear of the negro houses had grown hotter, and men were standing in all the narrow spaces through which the negroes might come to the street. There was talk of a negro in one of the houses, who had a Winchester, and the opinion was expressed that he had no ammunition left but no one went too near, and the fire was depended on to drive him out. The firemen were at work on Broadway, some distance east, but the flames immediately in the rear of the negro houses burned without hindrance.

MILITIAMEN TRY TO CURB MOB.

A half-block to the south, there was a hue and cry at a railroad crossing, and a fusillade of shots was heard. More militiamen than I had seen elsewhere, up to that time, were standing on a platform and near a string of freight cars, and trying to keep back men who had started to pursue negroes along the track.

As I turned back toward Broadway, there was a shout at the alley, and a negro ran out, apparently hoping to find protection. He paid no attention to missiles thrown from behind, none of which had hurt him much, but he was stopped, in the middle of the street by a smashing blow in the jaw, struck by a man he had not seen.

"Don't do that," he appealed. "I haven't hurt nobody." The answer was a blow from one side, a piece of curbstone from the other side, and a push which sent him on the brick pavement. He did not rise again, and the battering and kicking of his skull continued until he lay still, his blood flowing half way across the street. Before he had been booted to the opposite curb, another negro appeared, and the same deeds were repeated. I did not see any revolver shots fired at these men. Bullets and ammunition were saved for use at longer range. It was the last negro I have mentioned who was apparently finished by the stone hurled upon his neck by the noticeably well-dressed young man.

The butchering of the fire-trapped negroes went on so rapidly that, when I walked back to the alley a few minutes later, one was lying dead in the alley on the west side of Fourth street and another on the east side.

And now women began to appear. One frightened black girl, probably 20 years old, got as far as Broadway with no worse treatment than jeers and thrusts. At Broadway, in view of militiamen, the white women, several of whom had been watching the massacre of the negro men, pounced on the negress. I do not wish to be understood as saying that these women were representative of the womanhood of East St. Louis. Their faces showed, all too plainly, exactly who and what they were. But they were the heroines of the moment with that gathering of men, and when one man, sick of the brutality he had seen, seized one of the women by the arm to stop an impending blow, he was hustled away, with fists under his nose, and with more show of actual anger than had been bestowed on any of the negroes. He was a stocky, nervy chap, and he stood his ground until a diversion elsewhere drew the menacing ring of men away.

"Let the girls have her," was the shout as the women attacked the young negress. The victim's cry, "Please, please, I ain't done nothing," was stopped by a blow in the mouth with a broomstick, which one of the women swung like a baseball bat. Another woman seized the negress' hands, and the blow was repeated as she struggled helplessly. Finger nails clawed her hair, and the sleeves were torn from her waist, when some of the men called, "Now let her see how fast she can run." The women did not readily leave off beating her, but they stopped short of murder, and the crying, hysterical girl ran down the street.

An older negress, a few moments later, came along with two or three militiamen, and the same women made for her. When one of the soldiers held his gun as a barrier, the woman with the broomstick seized it with both hands, and struggled to wrest it from him, while the others, striking at the negress, in spite of the other militiamen, frightened her thoroughly and hurt her somewhat.

From negress baiting, the well-pleased procession turned to see a lynching. A negro, his head laid open by a great stonecut, had been dragged to the mouth of the alley on Fourth street and a small rope was being put about his neck. There was joking comment on the weakness of the rope, and everyone was prepared for what happened when it was pulled over a projecting cable box, a short distance up the pole. It broke, letting the negro tumble back to his knees, and causing one of the men who was pulling on it to sprawl on the pavement.

STOUTER ROPE OBTAINED.

An old man, with a cap like those worn by street car conductors, but showing no badge of car service, came out of his house to protest. "Don't you hang that man on this street," he shouted. "I dare you to." He was pushed angrily away, and a rope, obviously strong enough for its purpose, was brought.

Right here I saw the most sickening incident of the evening. To put the rope around the negro's neck, one of the lynchers stuck his fingers inside the gaping scalp and lifted the negro's head by it, literally bathing his hand in the man's blood.

"Get hold, and pull for East St. Louis!" called a man with a black coat and a new straw hat, as he seized the other end of the rope. The rope was long, but not too long for the number of hands that grasped it, and this time the negro was lifted to a height of about seven feet from the ground. The body was left hanging there.

While this lynching was in preparation I walked to Broadway, found a Corporal's guard of militiamen, who had just come from where the firemen were working, and called their attention to what was going on. I do not know that they could have done anything to stop it. I know that they did not try to.

In the first hour that I was there I saw no sufficient body of militiamen anywhere, and no serious effort, on the part of the few who were about to prevent bloodshed. Most of the men in uniform were frankly fraternizing with the men in the street. But beginning at 7:30, I did see instances of what national guardsmen, in reasonable numbers, and led by worthy officers, can do.

RESCUE SOME NEGROES.

First, there came a hollow square of soldiers from the fire zone along Broadway. In the front row of the frightened group within the square was a mulatto boy, not more than 6 years old. Further within the group were other children with their mothers. The negro men were marching with their hands raised, and some of the women were also holding up their hands.

The natural point of attack was in the rear, and the soldiers, under sharp commands from an officer, repeatedly turned about and made room with their bayonets. The pitiful procession got safely around the corner and to the police station.

Some smaller rescues of a similar kind were carried out in the next few minutes.

Following one of these rescue parties to the police station, I suddenly became aware that a new man, and a new spirit of soldiery, had entered into the situation. A man in a light suit and a straw hat, who had just come into town, was listening to a few details of what had happened in the neighborhood. He gave some quick commands, and in a moment, the first adequate body of guardsmen that I had seen was marching toward Broadway. The soldiers were from B company and other companies of the Fourth Illinois, and the apparent civilian in command was Col. Stephen O. Tripp of the Adjutant-General's office in Springfield.

As they turned into Broadway, double-quick was ordered, and it was none too quick, for another lynching was being prepared. This lynching was apparently to be on Broadway, and a negro, his head cut, but still conscious and struggling, was being dragged along the pavement with a rope around his neck.

"Get those men!" was the command, and a moment later several white men were in line on the south sidewalk, some of them with hands raised, while guardsmen faced them with bayonets. On the opposite sidewalk, the soldiers merely told the men to "move on," and this brought a sharp reprimand from Col. Tripp. "Don't let them get away," he ordered. "Make them prisoners." Most of these men were again lined up, and the two lines of prisoners, 25 or 30 men in all, were then marshaled in the car tracks, and the march to the station began, a guard being left behind to protect the negro, and to keep the street clear. I did not learn what became of this negro.

TEMPER OF CROWD CHANGES.

The temper of the men in the street showed a change after the first encounter with Tripp methods. It began to seem that the situation had found its master. But the most efficient Colonel cannot be everywhere at once, and while the uniformed line was busy keeping a crowd from forming about the police station, scattered shooting began in the neighborhood of the recent killings.

One negro ran the gauntlet on Broadway. Several shots were fired at him in a reckless fashion that explains the number injured by stray bullets earlier in the day. But it appeared that he got away.

It was nearly dark, and the fire on Broadway was becoming more threatening. A half-hour before, some lines of hose, though apparently in insufficient number, had been in use, but now the use of water had ceased, and it was said that the hose had been cut. The fire was nearing the Mollman harness establishment, in which the mayor of East St. Louis is interested, and the big wooden horse on top of the building was silhouetted in the twilight.

As I returned from a look at the fire, I saw an ambulance drive into Fourth street, to get the bodies which had been lying there for nearly an hour. I saw one body placed in the ambulance. I heard it said, as I was leaving town, that the men in the street had prevented the removal of one of the bodies, saying that the negro was not dead, and must lie there until he died. I did not verify this, and I do not state it as a fact. Everything which I have stated as a fact came under my own observation. And what I saw was, as I have said, but a small part of the whole.

I must add a word about the efficiency of the East St. Louis police. One of them kept me from going too near the fire. Absolutely the only thing that I saw policemen do was to keep that fire line. As the police detail marched to the fire, two of the men turned aside into Fourth street, apparently to see if two negroes, lying on the pavement within a few steps of Broadway, were dead. These policemen got a sharp call into line from their sergeant. They were not supposed to bother themselves about dead negroes.

In recording this, I do not forget that a policeman—by all accounts a fine and capable policeman—was killed by negroes the night before. I have not forgotten it in writing about the acts of the men in the street. Whether this crime excuses or palliates a massacre, which probably included none of the offenders, is something I will leave to apologists for last evening's occurrence, if there are any such, to explain.

RACIAL TENSIONS IN EAST ST. LOUIS

JOHN PERO
from *Testimony to the House Select Committee*

October 24, 1917

Mr. Raker: Where were you on the 28th and 29th of May, this year?

Mr. Pero: The 28th of May—was that the night of the first riot?

Mr. Raker: Yes.

Mr. Pero: I was in my room at the Hotel that night—the 28th of May. I remember that very well.

Mr. Raker: By what occurrence do you remember it?

Mr. Pero: Because I heard the crowd when I was ready for bed. I heard the noise of the crowd at the intersection of these four streets here.

Mr. Raker: And you didn't go out to see what was going on?

Mr. Pero: No.

Mr. Raker: Well, did you inquire the next day as to the conditions?

Mr. Pero: Yes, I heard the next day what it was.

Mr. Raker: What was it that you heard?

Mr. Pero: I heard the next day that there had been a meeting in the City Hall and that the crowd came out from the City Hall and assaulted or attacked some colored people.

Mr. Raker: Well, did you make any investigation as to the cause of this riot?

Mr. Pero: No.

Mr. Raker: Have you or your firm, or anyone interested, or did they at that time make any inquiry as to the cause of the riot?

Mr. Pero: No.

Mr. Raker: Do you know?

Mr. Pero: Not that I know of.

Mr. Raker: From your observation here what was the cause of the May 28 and 29 riot?

Mr. Pero: You must remember I am under oath to tell the truth.

Mr. Raker: That is what I am asking you.

Mr. Pero: In my opinion that riot was directly caused by the meeting in the City Hall that night. That is my opinion of it. The crowd came out, as the newspapers reported it, and I heard that the crowd came directly from the City Hall and began very shortly after that to make trouble.

Mr. Raker: What I am trying to get at is, what is the moving cause for a riot of that kind? What is back of it? You live here now, and stop at the Illmo Hotel right across from the center of the town and you hear a good many people talk as to what is going on in East St. Louis. What is the prime, moving cause, if you know?

Mr. Pero: Why, I should think, in my opinion—which may or may not be right—my opinion is it is the antagonism of the labor unions to colored people. That is my opinion of it. That may or may not be right.

Mr. Raker: What did you or your firm do now to alleviate the situation between the 28th of May this year and the 1st of July?

Mr. Pero: I don't know of anything we could do. We did nothing. We pursued the even tenor of our way. We assumed that that was a little spasm and that was all there was of it.

Mr. Raker: What?

Mr. Pero: We assumed that this thing had come up and was over. We did nothing. We knew of no condition that existed with us that we could in any way alleviate. We knew no condition existed with us that would cause anything of that kind. Our men were working for us; were satisfied and were working steadily.

Mr. Raker: And there was no complaint?

Mr. Pero: No complaint. We had no trouble of any kind. Everyone was satisfied with their work and wages, and we were getting along very happily. We had no trouble in our plant, and we knew of no trouble in our plant.

Mr. Raker: Well, I think that is all.

Mr. Foss: You were speaking about the cause of the riot, in your judgment. Have you ever given any study to the remedies for a situation such as existed in East St. Louis? What is the preventive of a recurrence of such a condition again, in your judgment?

Mr. Pero: That is a pretty broad question.

Mr. Foss: Yes, I want to ask you if you have ever given any study to the subject.

Mr. Pero: Yes, it is a matter that has come up in that time. It is a matter to which a great deal of thought has been given. I have believed in segregation, for one thing. I don't know that that would stop the trouble.

Mr. Foss: In segregation you say?

Mr. Pero: Yes.

Mr. Foss: What would be your idea on that point?

Mr. Pero: My idea would be to get the colored people in a certain portion of the city; give them every facility and every convenience that the white people have; be sure that they have comfortable homes; get the colony sufficiently large—if you want to call it a "colony." I have talked to some of the negroes along these lines, get a section of the city sufficiently large so that they might have their own little grocery stores, and instead of every other store building being used as a church, that they might have a church of each of the different denominations sufficiently large to secure an able man for pastor and support him, a man who could be not only their spiritual adviser but their temporal adviser as well. Now I believe that might remove some of the ill feeling that there is against the blacks in East St. Louis.

Mr. Raker: Did you say that they were opposed to segregation?

Mr. Pero: Well, they don't like it.

Mr. Raker: They don't?

Mr. Pero: No, but I told them not to consider it segregation. I told them in that case they would have a ward of their own; and undoubtedly if they were in the ward they would have representation in the city government, and I thought eventually all those things would work out for the best interests of the white and colored people in East St. Louis. Now if the commission form of govenment comes up, that will take away the possibility of their representation in the city council. I believe that is the solution of the question in East St. Louis. Give them decent living conditions in a section by themselves, where they can have good ministers, able ministers and men who will advise them not only in spiritual matters but in temporal matters.

Mr. Foster: What do you notice as to the attitude of colored people coming from the South into the North, to a place like East St. Louis?

Mr. Pero: I don't believe I grasp the question.

Mr. Foster: What is the attitude of a colored man coming from the South into the North, say to a place like East St. Louis? I mean does he put on an air of importance more than he had—would likely have where he came from?

Mr. Pero: Well, sir, I don't know from my own observation that he does or does not. But some of the colored people tell me that these fellows coming from the South are not like the colored men who have lived here. Now, some of the colored people tell me that, but from my own observation I don't know.

Mr. Foster: You don't know as to that?

Mr. Pero: No, I don't.

Mr. Johnson: What do they say is the difference between them?

Mr. Pero: Well, they seem to have a sense of freedom or wrong idea of the freedom that they have here.

Mr. Raker: They have a misconception?

Mr. Pero: A misconception of freedom, yes. A man told me the other day—one of the prominent colored men of the town—that in the South the whites had control of them and when they got up here they seemed to think that nobody had control of them.

Mr. Foster: They sort of turned loose, didn't they?

Mr. Pero: Yes. I don't know that that applies to all of them. I don't know that from my own observation.

Mr. Cooper: They acted sort of like the white peasantry of Russia just released from thraldom is said to be acting in Russia?

Mr. Pero: That may be the case.

Mr. Cooper: They act as any human being will who has been kept down for a century. Not knowing he had any rights, he misunderstands what his liberty is, white or black. Is that so?

Mr. Pero: I think likely, from what they think, that would be the explanation of it.

Mr. Foster: In your opinion, has that anything to do with the clashes that have occurred here in the last year?

Mr. Pero: No, I don't think that attained such an extent as to cause anything of that kind.

Mr. Foster: You think that had nothing to do with it?

Mr. Pero: I don't think so.

Mr. Foster: I believe that is all.

Mr. Johnson: You have made reference to the Southern negro having liberties and privileges here that he does not enjoy in the South. The Southern people came to the full realization of that enjoyment of liberty and freedom for the negro on the second day of July last, did they not?

Mr. Pero: I don't know I am sure.

Mr. Johnson: And in consequence of that there was a general exodus across the Mississippi River into another state to get away from that extreme liberty and enjoyment he was accorded here?

Mr. Pero: License, yes, sir.

Mr. Johnson: When you wanted the Southern negro to come here there was not such an exodus from the South to this land of liberty and freedom for the southern negro, that there was to get out of here, was there, on the 2nd of July?

Mr. Pero: I think the exodus across the bridge was any colored man who could get to the bridge whether he was a northern negro or a southern negro. I guess anybody who could get to the bridge made tracks for it.

Mr. Johnson: That is all.

Mr. Johnson: Again referring to the subject, do you know of anybody in Illinois who last July undertook to deprive the people of the right to be shot, beaten up and burned up here?

Mr. Pero: No, I don't: simply because, as I say, I was not in town and I have no knowledge of anything that took place.

Mr. Johnson: Haven't you understood that that right to be shot up and burned up and beat was fairly established by the State Militia indulging in it on the 2d day of July last?

Mr. Pero: I saw something of that in the papers, but I don't know that I have seen a single person who saw anything of that kind.

Mr. Johnson: I don't recall ever meeting anybody who said he saw it. The papers spoke of that to some extent. Do you know Mr. Rogers, the president of the chemical company here?

Mr. Pero: Yes, sir, I do.

Mr. Johnson: Have you ever talked to him relative to the July riots?

Mr. Pero: No, sir. I know him but I have never talked to him much.

Mr. Johnson: If you had, and he had told you what he testified to before this committee, he would have told you that he saw a member of the State troops here guaranteed the negro that right by shooting one of them himself (Laughter).

Mr. Pero: No; I have seen something of that in the different papers, but I have not seen anybody who saw it.

Mr. Johnson: And it has been testified to here by an eyewitness—and as the Committee believes by a reputable man —that four or five soldiers selected from among the citizens of the State of Illinois, guaranteed to two negroes who were running out of a house that was on fire the right to be shot, and left there to be burned. Have you heard of that?

Mr. Pero: I saw something of that in the papers, but I haven't heard of it otherwise. The only man that I have heard express himself on the riot matter was Rev. Allison, and I heard him tell of something he saw at the riot.

Mr. Johnson: But you don't know of anybody in Illinois, citizen or soldier, who has undertaken during your troubles to deprive the negro of his right in Illinois to be shot, beat up and burned up? (Laughter).

Mr. Pero: No, sir.

Mr. Johnson: Very well. That is all.

A SILENT MARCH IN NEW YORK CITY

JAMES WELDON JOHNSON
An Army with Banners
The New York Age, August 2, 1917

Last Saturday the silent protest parade came off, and it was a greater success than even the committee had dared to hope it would be. Some of the New York papers estimated the number of marchers in line as high as fifteen thousand. It was indeed a mighty host, an army with banners.

No written word can convey to those who did not see it the solemn impressiveness of the whole affair. The effect could be plainly seen on the faces of the thousands of spectators that crowded along the line of march. There were no jeers, no jests, not even were there indulgent smiles; the faces of the onlookers betrayed emotions from sympathetic interest to absolute pain. Many persons of the opposite race were seen to brush a tear from their eyes. It seemed that many of these people were having brought home to them for the first time the terrible truths about race prejudice and oppression.

The power of the parade consisted in its being not a mere argument in words, but a demonstration to the sight. Here were thousands of orderly, well-behaved, clean, sober, earnest people marching in a quiet, dignified manner, declaring to New York and to the country that their brothers and sisters, people just like them, had been massacred by scores in East St. Louis for no other offense than seeking to earn an honest living; that their brothers and sisters, people just like them, were "Jim Crowed" and segregated and disfranchised and oppressed and lynched and burned alive in this the greatest republic in the world, the great leader in the fight for democracy and humanity.

The impact of this demonstration upon New York city was tremendous. And it is not strange that it was so. More than twelve thousand of us marching along the greatest street in the world, marching solemnly to no other music than the beat of muffled drums, bearing aloft our banners on which were inscribed not only what we have suffered in this country, but what we have accomplished for this country, this was a sight as has never before been seen.

But, after all, the effect on the spectators was not wholly in what they saw, it was largely in the spirit that went out from the marchers and overpowered all who came within its radius. There was no holiday air about this parade. Every man, woman and child that took part seemed to feel what it meant to the race. Even the little six year old tots that led the line seemed to realize the full significance of what was being done. And so it was that these thousands and thousands moving quietly and steadily along created a feeling very close to religious awe.

When the head of the procession paused at 30th Street I looked back and saw the long line of women in white still mounting the crest of Murray Hill, the men's column not yet in sight; and a great sob came up in my throat and in my heart a great yearning for all these people, my people, from the helpless little children just at my hand back to the strong men bringing up the rear, whom I could not even see. I turned to Dr. Du Bois at my side and said, "Look!" He looked, and neither of us could tell the other what he felt.

It was a great day. An unforgettable day in the history of the race and in the history of New York City.

WATCHING A "RADICAL COLORED MAN"

RALPH VAN DEMAN
Army Intelligence Memorandum on William Monroe Trotter

October 2, 1917

October 2, 1917.
From: Chief, Military Intelligence Section.
To: Intelligence Officer, Northeastern Department.
Subject: Monroe Trotter (Radical colored man)

1. The attention of this office has been called to the possibility that a colored man named Monroe Trotter, who is editor of the "Boston Guardian" and is very radical in his views on the race question, might make some trouble.

2. I wish you would watch his publication and see if he is stirring up anything.

3. Major Parsons of this office says that in inquiring about him, you could undoubtedly get the cooperation of W. H. Lewis, a colored man who was formerly an Assistant Attorney General. He lives in Boston or Cambridge, and practices law thereabouts.

R H VAN DEMAN
Lt. Col., General Staff.

A REBELLION BY BLACK SOLDIERS

MARTHA GRUENING
Houston: An N.A.A.C.P. Investigation
The Crisis, November 1917

THE primary cause of the Houston riot was the habitual brutality of the white police officers of Houston in their treatment of colored people. Contributing causes were (1) the mistake made in not arming members of the colored provost guard or military police, (2) lax discipline at Camp Logan which permitted promiscuous visiting at the camp and made drinking and immorality possible among the soldiers.

Houston is a hustling and progressive southern city having the commission form of government and, as southern cities go, a fairly liberal one. Its population before the Negro exodus, which has doubtless decreased it by many thousands, was estimated at 150,000. Harris County, in which it is situated, has never had a lynching, and there are other indications, such as the comparative restraint and self-control of the white citizens after the riot, that the colored people perhaps enjoy a greater degree of freedom with less danger than in many parts of the South. It is, however, a southern city, and the presence of the Negro troops inevitably stirred its Negrophobe element to protest. There was some feeling against the troops being there at all, but I could not find that it was universal. Most of the white people seem to have wanted the financial advantages to be derived from having the camp in the neighborhood. The sentiment I heard expressed most frequently by them was that they were willing to endure the colored soldiers if they could be "controlled." I was frequently told that Negroes in uniform were inevitably "insolent" and that members of the military police in particular were frequently "insolent" to the white police of Houston. It was almost universally conceded, however, that the members of the white police force habitually cursed, struck, and otherwise maltreated colored prisoners. One of the important results of the riot has been an attempt on the part of the Mayor and the Chief of Police of Houston to put a stop to this custom.

In deference to the southern feeling against the arming of Negroes and because of the expected co-operation of the city Police Department, members of the provost guard were not armed, thus creating a situation without precedent in the history of this guard. A few carried clubs, but none of them had guns, and most of them were without weapons of any kind. They were supposed to call on white police officers to make arrests. The feeling is strong among the colored people of Houston that this was the real cause of the riot. "You may have observed," one of them said to me, "that Southerners do not like to fight Negroes on equal terms. This is at the back of all the southern feeling against Negro soldiers. If Corporal Baltimore had been armed, they would never have dared to set upon him and we should not have had a riot." This was the general feeling I found among the colored people of Houston.

Several minor encounters took place between the military and civil police shortly after the troops arrived. As a result, Chief of Police Brock issued an order calling on his men to co-operate with the military police, to give them full assistance, and to refer to them as "colored" and not as "nigger" officers. Chief Brock is a northern man and though apparently sincere and well-meaning, does not seem to have the full confidence of all his men for this and other reasons. The order was obeyed in a few instances and more often disregarded.

On the afternoon of August 23, two policemen, Lee Sparks and Rufe Daniels—the former known to the colored people as a brutal bully—entered the house of a respectable colored woman in an alleged search for a colored fugitive accused of crap-shooting. Failing to find him, they arrested the woman, striking and cursing her and forcing her out into the street only partly clad. While they were waiting for the patrol wagon a crowd gathered about the weeping woman who had become hysterical and was begging to know why she was being arrested. In this crowd was a colored soldier, Private Edwards. Edwards seems to have questioned the police officers or remonstrated with them. Accounts differ on this point, but they all agree that the officers immediately set upon him and beat him to the ground with the butts of their six-shooters, continuing to beat and kick him while he was on the ground, and arrested him. In the words of Sparks himself: "I beat that nigger until his heart got right. He was a good nigger when I got through with him." Later Corporal Baltimore, a member of the military police, approached the officers and inquired for Edwards, as it was his duty to do. Sparks immediately opened fire, and Baltimore, being unarmed, fled with the two policemen in pursuit shooting as they ran. Baltimore entered a house in the neighborhood and hid under a bed. They followed, dragged him out, beat him up and arrested him. It was this outrage which infuriated the men of the 24th Infantry to the point of revolt. Following is the story of the arrest as given by its victim, Mrs. Travers, and by eyewitnesses whose names are in the possession of the Association, but are withheld for their protection.

Mrs. Travers, an evidently respectable, hardworking colored woman, said:

"I was in my house ironing. I got five children. I heard shooting and I'd run out in my yard to see what was happening. Sparks he came into my house and said, 'Did you see a nigger jumping over that yard?' and I said, 'No, sir.' He came in the house and looked all around. Went in back. Then Daniels, the other policeman, he came around the corner on his horse. I called to Mrs. Williams, my friend that lives across the street, and asked her what was the matter. She said, 'I don't know; I think they were shooting at crap-shooters.'

"He (Sparks) came in again just then and said, 'You're a God damn liar; I shot down in the ground.' I looked at her and she looked at me and he said, 'You all God damn nigger bitches. Since these God damn sons of bitches of nigger soldiers come here you are trying to take the town.' He came into the bedroom then and into the kitchen and I ask him what he want. He replied to me, 'Don't you ask an officer what he want in your house.' He say, 'I'm from Fort Ben and we don't allow niggers to talk back to us. We generally whip them down there.' Then he hauled off and slapped me. I hollered and the big one—this Daniels—he ran in, and then Sparks said to him, 'I slapped her and what shall we do about it?' Daniels says, 'Take and give her ninety days on the Pea Farm 'cause she's one of these biggety nigger women.' Then they both took me by the arm and commenced dragging me out. I asked them to let me put some clothes on and Sparks says, 'No, we'll take you just as you are. If you was naked we'd take you.' Then I take the baby in my arms and asked him to let me take it. He took it out of my arms and threw it down on the sidewalk. Took me with my arms behind my back and Daniels, he says, if I didn't come he'd break them. They took me out on Tempson Street. He rung up the Police Department. Whilst I was standing crowd began a-coming (all I had on was this old dress-skirt and a pair panties and a ol' raggedy waist. No shoes or nothing) —crowd and a colored soldier man came. [Private Edwards.] Sparks, he says to me, 'YOU STAND HERE,' and I did and a lady friend brought me shoes and a bonnet and apron and he (Sparks) says, 'Stay here,' and went over, and before the soldier could say a word he said, 'What you got to do with this,' and he raised his six-shooter and he beat him—beat him *good*. He didn't do a thing but just raise his hand to ward them off. Didn't even tell them to quit, nor nothing. Then another soldier, this Sergeant Somebody, came, and the first one called to him and the policeman said to him, 'If you come here, we'll give you the same.' Edwards said, 'Must I go with them?' and the second one says, 'Yes, go with them and we'll come along after you.' I hear they shot that second soldier but I didn't see it, for they took me away. They take me to the Police Department and locked me up for using 'abusive language'—but they dismissed the case today.

"I ain't never been before no court of inquiry, no ma'am. Only just to the court when they dismissed the case against me, and there ain't no generals nor no one been out to see me or ask anything. I don't know why they don't come to me. They been to most everyone else around here, and I could tell them the truth. Seems like they might ask me, when I'm the one it happened to, and I'm not afraid to tell, even if Sparks do come back afterwards and do some more to me, but you're the only one yet that's come to ask me."

When interviewed a second time, Mrs. Travers added the following to her statement:

"I been down to the Prosecutor's office to-day. He asked me what did I know about the riot. I said, 'I don't know nothing about it. I was in bed with my children when it happened.

Where else would I be at that time of night?' He said to me didn't I know beforehand that the soldiers were coming; didn't none of them tell me beforehand. I told him no, but I could tell him what happened before the riot to make it happen, and I started to tell him that Sparks came into my house and hit me. He say he didn't want to hear anything more about that and he sent me home. That's what I had to spend my carfare for."

One eye-witness said:

"I didn't see them arrest Mrs. Travers. I don't know what happened in the house, but I saw her afterwards and I know she said they slapped her in the house and pinched her arms and threw her baby under the bed. They had her right outside here waiting for the patrol wagon. She hadn't on but two pieces of clothes—and she was hollering and asking what she'd done to be arrested. Then Private Edwards came up and asked if he could take her. I heard the policeman say, 'Stand back,' and landed him on the head with his six-shooter. Then Baltimore he came and asked him about the other soldier. They beat him, too, and he ran and they shot after him. I saw Sparks fire after him three times, myself. Daniels shot, too, but I don't know if it was more than once. Baltimore ran away around the corner, with them firing after him, and his head was bloody. I thought he'd drop any time, but he didn't get hit. They said afterward they fired at the ground—but they didn't. They shot right straight at him and (they fired) into a street full of women and children. They haven't found any bullet holes in the sidewalk either, and it wasn't there that they fired. It was at Baltimore, and no mistake."

A second eye-witness said:

"I drive a butcher wagon. I make deliveries all about here and I saw a lot of what happened about here before the riot. When Sparks and Daniels came along that day I was driving past where three boys were shooting craps at the corner of Felipe and Bailey Streets. They fired a shot to scare the boys and they ran. Then the officers couldn't locate them. When I rode by again they had this woman, whose arrest was the cause of the riot, by the patrol box. She was insufficiently dressed to be out on the street and barefoot. There was a young soldier there (Private Edwards) who came up and asked the officers to let her put on shoes and clothes. The officers struck at him with their six-shooters. He put up his hand and blocked the first blow. The second hit him on the head and made him bloody. They followed that up and beat him to the ground. When he was down, one of them took the muzzle of his gun and punched him in the side, and Sparks said, 'That's the way we do things in the South. We're running things not the d—— niggers.'

"It was later—at the same spot—the policemen were still there when the military officer (Baltimore) came. I didn't hear what he said, but whatever was said between him and the police officers made him stop about half a block away and fold his arms, and at that one of the officers took out his revolver and commenced firing at him—right at him. He ran away around the corner of Mr. May's place. That's all I saw then."

When word of the outrage reached camp, feeling ran high. It was by no means the first incident of the kind that had occurred. A few days before a Negro had been beaten on a car by city detective Ed Stoermer, who, according to his own testimony before the Citizens Investigating Committee, cleared the car of its white passengers, telling them that he "might have to kill the nigger." I was reliably informed that on another occasion two colored soldiers were brutally beaten up by city detectives who boarded the car in which they sat from a Ford machine; that this machine drew up alongside of the car which was halted by the conductor long enough for the beating to take place, after which the detectives again got into the car and drove off.

Baltimore was popular among the men of the 24th Infantry, and for some time the rumor persisted that he had been killed. To quell the excitement Major Snow telephoned in to Police Headquarters to ascertain the facts and asked that Baltimore be returned to the camp immediately. At roll call that evening Snow addressed the men, telling them what had happened and stating that Sparks was to blame and would be punished. The men, however, were by that time beyond his control. In this connection it has been pointed out several times that Sparks has been suspended and is under indictment for the assault on Baltimore and for murder for the shooting of another Negro. There is no reason to believe that this indictment is anything but a bluff, the purpose of which is to show that there was no excuse for the soldiers taking the law into their hands. Chief Brock, who throughout has given evidence of good faith, did his duty in suspending Sparks, but there is no reason to believe that Sparks will receive any punishment at the hands of a white jury, and if he is acquitted, he probably cannot be kept off the police force. "Of course, Sparks will be let off with a fine. Our policemen have to beat the niggers when they are insolent. You can't expect them to let a nigger curse them," one white man told me. The same man, in reply to my question whether Sparks did not have a reputation as a bully, replied, "Oh, no; at least only among the colored people." The feeling of the colored people in regard to Sparks and the police in general is best illustrated by the statement of another colored man whose name I was unable to learn:

"It's like this, lady—I could talk all right, but I'm afeard. I know a lot, but I live here, and my family lives here, and all I got—all my savings of a lifetime is here—and there's prejudice here—and you see how 'tis. I made up my mind—I took like an oath to myself I wouldn't say nothing. I just made up my mind that I didn't *know* nothing. Only that my friend here says you're all right, I wouldn't say this much—but I got confidence in him.

"There's been a lot of dirty work here. I'm not saying nothing, but you find out who it was killed that colored man who was drafted into the army on Washington Street, and who shot that colored man, Williams, in the back, they say was killed in a crap game on Dallas Avenue. They can't find out that no one did it—but we *know* Sparks was in the gang that did the shooting. And that soldier man—the police shot him running —I saw *him* and he was hit in the back of the neck. And, what's more, I've seen three more colored men beat up without any cause by the police since the riot. There's a lot more I *could* say, only I'm afeard."

It is the Negro mentioned in this statement, Williams, for whose murder Sparks has been indicted. While I was in Houston the other Negro fugitive mentioned, who turned out to be an enlisted man under the selective draft law, was shot by a city detective simply for refusing to halt. The detective was "amicably" arrested by the Chief of Detectives and almost immediately released on a five hundred dollar bond. Sparks is also at liberty and although without the prestige given him by his position on the police force, was, at last report, using that liberty to further molest the colored people. About a week after the riot he entered the house of a respectable colored physician on Robbin Avenue early in the morning while the latter was in his bath and his wife partly dressed, on the pretext of looking for a fugitive, insulted and bullied them both when they protested, and threatened them with a drawn gun. On the same day he threatened a colored woman that he would "blow her damned head off" because he thought she had laughed at him. It was in pursuit of this woman that he entered several colored houses in this block, threatening and cursing the colored people.

When investigation made it apparent that the police were to blame for the beginning of the riot, a systematic attempt was made to shift the blame for this also on to the colored people. Strange stories began to be circulated in the papers and by word of mouth as to the real cause of the friction between the soldiers and the police. It was again the insolence of the Negro soldiers which in this case took the form of ignoring the "Jim Crow" regulations of Houston, particularly on the Houston Street cars. Testimony to this effect, which was obviously absurd, was given and reported apparently in all seriousness before the Citizen's Board of Inquiry. Several motormen and conductors were subpoenaed to testify to this effect, and one of them told a pathetic story of one occasion on which his car was boarded by a number of Negro soldiers (unarmed) who threw the "Jim Crow" screen out of the car window, over ran the car, forcing white passengers to get up and give them their seats, and who escaped unscathed to tell the tale. He was unable to give the names of any witnesses to this occurrence, although he stated that many of the white passengers left the car in great anger threatening that he would be reported and lose his job. The legend continued to the effect that white police officers were finally called in to deal with the Negro soldiers who were terrorizing the peaceable white citizens and demoralizing colored civilians, and that the former by merely doing their duty won the undying enmity of the colored soldiers.

Another outrageously false impression which was deliberately given by the white press was that Mrs. Travers was a woman of the underworld and that her arrest was the result of drunken and disorderly conduct. Mrs. Travers is unmistakably a hardworking, respectable woman. She had no connection with either Edwards or Baltimore, whom she had never seen before the day of the riot. The story, however, was never denied, and was still being circulated while I was in Houston, although so many white people who had employed her testified to her good character that it was necessary to acquit her at her trial for "using abusive language." She was also never called before the Citizen's Board of Inquiry.

Police brutality and bad discipline among the soldiers led up to the riot, which cost the city of Houston eighteen lives. Among them was that of Daniels, the policeman who had taken part in the beating of Baltimore and Edwards. There is abundant testimony from both white and colored people that there was excessive drinking and immorality among the soldiers at the camp, and there is testimony by white people to the effect that Edwards was drunk when he was arrested. While this may have been the case, it does not seem to materially affect the situation, as Baltimore, who was sober, received even worse treatment at the hands of the police officers. It is also very probable that some of the leaders were inflamed with drink at the time of the outbreak. That outbreak, according to a statement made by Major Snow before he received orders not to talk, was not an out and out mutiny, although the men were undoubtedly guilty of repeated disobedience to orders before they left the camp. If they did, as is alleged, shoot at their officers, they did not kill or wound any of them, though they did wound a colored soldier who was guarding the ammunition supply and who later died of his wounds. When the soldiers left the camp their slogan was, "On to the Police Station," where their idea was to punish the police for their attack on Edwards and Baltimore. Even the white people of Houston do not believe that their original intention was to shoot up the town. When on the way to the police station they met with opposition, they gave battle with terrible results. As in every riot, innocent bystanders were killed, one very pathetic case being that of a little white girl who was killed by a stray bullet which penetrated the room where she slept. The bitterness of the white people over this and other casualties is understandable, but the worst features of the Houston riot do not for one moment make it comparable with the massacre of East St. Louis. It was not a cold-blooded slaughter of innocents but the work of angry men whose endurance of wrong and injustice had been strained to the breaking point, and who in their turn committed injustices. There was no burning of women and children, no hanging, no torturing of innocent victims. The only atrocity reported being the bayoneting of Captain Mattes of the Illinois National Guard, spoken of by the Houston papers as the work of "black fiends," although bayoneting is not a practice discouraged by the United States Army.

All the men who are alleged to have taken part in the outbreak have been captured and are facing a court martial at El Paso. The one fact which admits of no uncertainty is that if they are found guilty they will be fully and sufficiently punished.

After the riot the white citizens of Houston behaved with unusual coolness and restraint and they have taken unto themselves full credit for so doing. The presence of United States troops undoubtedly assisted materially in keeping order. A half hour after the riot started Governor Ferguson had declared martial law which lasted for several days and order was restored without any lynching or other form of reprisal on the part of the white people. It was not to be expected that martial law or any other kind of law could be enforced impartially under the circumstances, and it was not so enforced. White citizens were given arms "to protect their homes" and the homes of Negro civilians were visited and their arms taken away from them. Many Negroes were also unjustly arrested, locked up for several days, and then dismissed without any charge having been made against them. That further disorder did not occur under such circumstances is one of the most remarkable things about the situation, and credit for it should be given to both races. The Houston *Post* and the white people generally explained it as another illustration of the well-known fact that "the South is the Negro's best friend"; that race riot and bloodshed are really indigenous to northern soil; and that the relations between black and white in the South are highly cordial. The colored people of Houston, however, are migrating North, and to this more than to any element in the case I attribute the new restraint in the attitude of white Houstonians. While I was in Houston,

130 colored people left in one day. In June, one labor agent exported more than nine hundred Negroes to points along the Pennsylvania Railroad. The Houston Chamber of Commerce became so alarmed over the Negro exodus that it telegraphed to the head of the railroad asking that this exportation be discontinued. The railroad complied with this request, but the colored people continued to leave. Colored men and women in every walk of life are still selling their homes and household goods at a loss and leaving because, as one of them, a physician, put it to me, "Having a home is all right, but not when you never know when you leave it in the morning if you will really be able to get back to it that night." White Houston, especially its business men, are beginning to realize this. For the first time they are showing some slight signs of seeking to make the South safe for the Negro. While the northern exodus of the Negroes, which began with the war, is largely responsible for this, occurrences such as the Houston riot must be admitted to quicken the sense of justice which has so long lain dormant in the white southern breast. However much the riot is to be condemned from the standpoint of justice, humanity, and military discipline, however badly it may be held to have stained the long and honorable record of Negro soldiers, however necessary it may be that the soldiers should be severely punished, it seems to me an undeniable fact that one of its results will be a new respect and consideration for the Negro in the South.

THE GREAT MIGRATION NORTH

THE CHICAGO DEFENDER
Migration and Its Effect
April 20, 1918

VARIOUS estimates have been made of the number of people who have left the South for other parts of the country in the past eighteen months, the figures ranging from 500,000 to 2,000,000. Whatever the number, it was great enough to upset the labor field in this country and establish us as permanent factors in the economic world. Naturally, we say supply and demand regulate everything, and in a great measure, it is true, the war came and left a great gap in the industries of the North, East and West. When shops, mills and factories close for want of labor, the pocketbooks of the owners suffer, and when a man's pocketbook is touched everything else is forgotten in the mad rush to replenish it.

With foreign immigration cut off and no prospect of being able to draw on foreign countries for labor for some years to come, the captains of industry LOWERED THEIR GLASSES, AND INSTEAD OF LOOKING OVER OUR HEADS, AS THEY HAVE BEEN DOING FOR YEARS, GAZED DIRECTLY AT US AND, CATCHING OUR EYE, BECKONED TO US TO COME TO THEM, SHOWING A PICTURE THE WHILE THAT LURED US ON. THOUSANDS LEFT THEIR SUNNY SOUTHERN HOMES with bitter-sweet, mostly the bitter, memories. Anxiety was felt on all sides. The employers of the rest of the country were experimenting with what the South has pronounced a failure. They were experimenting, not because they wished to prove that the South was in error, but because it was either the black workmen or no workmen at all, and between the two evils they wisely chose to have workmen.

The black workmen left the South with trembling and fear. They were going—they didn't know where—among strange people, with strange customs. The people who claimed to know best how to treat them painted frightful pictures of what would befall the migrators if they left the land of cotton and sugar cane. But they left in droves, are still leaving, and only a few have returned. The effect has been to paralyze the industries of the South while the other sections of the country have prospered. The experiment proved a success. NECESSITY MADE THE WHITE AND THE BLACK WORK SIDE BY SIDE WITHOUT FRICTION, A FEAT THE SOUTH SAID COULD NOT BE PERFORMED.

There is no denying the fact that prejudice is rife everywhere; but we, like other animate persons and things, follow the line of least resistance. What has been established for several hundred years cannot be broken down in a day. There is a long fight still ahead of us—a fight with brains, not brawn. Our entrance into the economic world sounds the death knell of discrimination and oppression. We must hold fast every inch we have gained, remembering always the many are judged by the few in our case. There is such a thing as STAYING IN ONE PLACE TOO LONG, and while the rolling stone never gathers any moss, when it stops rolling IT IS MORE POLISHED THAN WHEN IT BEGAN. The scattering of the South's shaded population all over the country is a real blessing. Every day fresh evidence of this fact is apparent. THE WHITE MAN SEEKS THE FARTHEST CORNERS OF THE GLOBE IF HE THINKS HE CAN BETTER HIMSELF. WHY SHOULD WE NOT DO LIKEWISE?

THE CONSTITUTIONALITY
OF A FEDERAL LAW

LEONIDAS C. DYER
*Speech in Congress on
the Anti-Lynching Bill*

May 7, 1918

Mr. Speaker, I am in favor of this legislation and all necessary laws that are needed to produce law and order in the United States. The whole citizenship of America should aid in maintaining law and order and not permit mob violence in any place. We set a poor example for our soldiers and sailors that are sent to France to destroy tyranny and oppression there when we at home tolerate lynchings and attacks upon persons and property without regard to law. This country alone stands in shame and disgrace before the civilized bar of public opinion in that it has for years tolerated lynchings. The lynching and murder of hundreds of colored people at East St. Louis a short time ago and the lynching of Praeger last month at Collinsville, Ill., horrible and disgraceful as they were, are but instances of thousands of a similar nature just as bad that have taken place in this country annually in past years.

On April 8 I introduced a bill designed to protect citizens of the United States against lynching in default of protection by the States. When it is taken up by the Judiciary Committee of the House for consideration I shall offer some amendments to perfect it in details, and then I will ask to have it reported to the House and passed by the Congress, so that it may become a law at an early date. I believe its enactment into law and enforcement will result in wiping out for all time to come the most damnable crime known to civilized man. Since and before I introduced this bill I have received many strong indorsements of its provisions. I believe that the public conscience of America is now fully aroused to its necessity. The States can not be depended upon to do their duty in all instances. Gov. McCall, of Massachusetts, on April 10 last, in discussing lynchings, said:

> The brutality of lynching does not at all surpass its cowardice. Nothing more contemptibly cowardly can be imagined than for a crowd of armed men to seize a single, unarmed man and put him to death. If such cowardice could be regarded as distinctive of a nation, no amount of heroism on the part of its soldiers in the field could make atonement for it.
>
> There has been quite too much talk in our politics, even before the war, of hanging people to lamp-posts. The spirit of lawlessness has received an impulse from men who should be the leaders and teachers of the people. The first duty upon us, after supporting to the utmost our soldiers and our allies, is sternly to repress those barbarous exhibitions of lawlessness that have too often disgraced our country.

The Attorney General of the United States, on the 16th of April last, in an address to the executive committee of the American Bar Association at Richmond, Va., spoke in the same vein when he said:

> We must set our faces against lawlessness within our own borders. Whatever we may say about the causes for our entering this war, we know that one of the principal reasons was the lawlessness of the German nation—what they have done in Belgium and in northern France, and what we have reason to know they would do elsewhere. For us to tolerate lynching is to do the same thing that we are condemning in the Germans.
>
> Lynch law is the most cowardly of crimes. Invariably the victim is unarmed, while the men who lynch are armed and large in numbers. It is a deplorable thing under any circumstances, but at this time, above all others, it creates an extremely dangerous condition. I invite your help in meeting it.

I have recently made an investigation to get some idea of the number of people who have been lynched in the last three years, and I find a record in 1915 where there were 43 white and 49 colored lynched. Most of the white men lynched were Mexicans. In 1916 I find the number to be 8 white and 51 colored, and, in 1917, 2 white and 44 colored. Of the total number for these three years lynched, I find them charged with different crimes and offenses, but not in one-tenth of the cases was there a charge of that crime which some people consider lynching specially appropriate.

The horribleness of lynchings and mob violence is evident to all decent and civilized people. Congress should put an end to it, since the States in so many cases are unable to do so. The bill (H. R. 11279) which I have introduced on this subject is as follows:

> A bill (H. R. 11279) to protect citizens of the United States against lynching in default of protection by the States.
>
> *Be it enacted, etc.*, That the putting to death within any State of a citizen of the United States by a mob or riotous assemblage of three or more persons openly acting in concert, in violation of law and in default of protection of such citizen by such State or the officers thereof, shall be deemed a denial to such citizen by such State of the equal protection of the laws and a violation of the peace of the United States and an offense against the same.
>
> SEC. 2. That every person participating in such mob or riotous assemblage by which such citizen is put to death, as described in section 1 hereof, shall be deemed guilty of murder and shall be liable to prosecution and, upon conviction, to punishment therefor, according to law, in any court of the United States having jurisdiction in the place where such putting to death occurs.
>
> SEC. 3. That every county in which such putting to death as described in section 1 hereof occurs shall be subject to a forfeiture of not less than $5,000 nor more than $10,000, which may be recovered by action therefor in the name of the United States against such county for the use of the dependent family, if any, of the citizen so put to death; and if none, for the use of the United States, which action shall be brought and prosecuted by the attorney of the United States for the district in which such county is situated in any district court of the United States having jurisdiction therein. If such forfeiture is not paid upon recovery of judgment therefor, such court shall have jurisdiction to enforce payment thereof by extent or levy of execution upon any property of the county, or may compel the levy and collection of a tax therefor, or otherwise compel payment thereof by mandamus or other appropriate process; and every officer of such county and every other person who disobeys or fails to comply with any lawful order of the court in

the premises shall be liable to punishment according to law as for contempt and to any other penalty provided by law therefor.

SEC. 4. That every State or municipal officer having the duty or power of preservation or conservation of the peace at the time and place of any such putting to death as described in section 1 hereof, who, having reasonable cause to believe that the same is being or is to be attempted, neglects or omits to make all reasonable efforts to prevent the same, and every State or municipal officer having the duty or power of prosecuting criminal offenses at such time and place who neglects or omits to make all reasonable efforts to prosecute to judgment under the laws of such State all persons participating in such mob or assemblage as described in section 1 hereof, except such, if any, as have been or are held to answer therefor in a circuit court of the United States, as provided in section 2 hereof, shall be deemed guilty of an offense against the United States, and shall be liable to prosecution therefor in any district or circuit court of the United States having jurisdiction in such place, and upon conviction thereof shall be punished by imprisonment not exceeding five years or by fine not exceeding $5,000 or by both such fine and imprisonment.

SEC. 5. That every State or municipal officer having the custody within a State of a citizen of the United States charged with or held to answer for any crime or offense who suffers such citizen to be taken from his custody by a mob or riotous assemblage of three or more persons openly acting in concert in violation of law with the purpose of putting such citizen to death or inflicting bodily violence upon him in default of protection of such citizen by such State or officers thereof, shall be deemed guilty of an offense against the United States and shall be liable to prosecution therefor in any district court of the United States having jurisdiction in the place where the same occurs, and upon conviction thereof shall be punished by imprisonment not exceeding five years or by fine not exceeding $5,000, or by both such fine and imprisonment.

SEC. 6. That any prosecution for either of the offenses defined in sections 2, 4, or 5 hereof, and in any action for the forfeiture imposed by section 3 hereof, every person who has participated in lynching or in the putting to death of or of the infliction of great bodily violence upon any person without authority of law, and every person who entertains or has expressed any opinion in favor of lynching or in justification or excuse thereof, or whose character, conduct, or opinions have been or are such as, in the judgment of the court, may tend to disqualify him for the impartial and unprejudiced trial of the cause, shall be disqualified to serve as a juror; and the attorney for the United States in such action or prosecution shall be entitled to make full inquiry thereof and to produce evidence thereon; and every person who refuses to answer any inquiry touching his qualifications on the ground that he may thereby criminate himself shall be disqualified as aforesaid.

Some people and some writers seem to think that such a law would not be constitutional. I differ with them in regard to this. The fourteenth amendment of the Constitution says in part:

> Nor shall any State deprive any person of life, liberty, or property without due process of law, nor deny to any person within its jurisdiction the equal protection of the law. Congress has the power to enforce this provision of the fourteenth amendment.

The early theory that the United States has no police power, so called, or power to protect life or punish crimes of violence within the States, is already superseded by judicial decision. It is now determined by the highest authority that the United States has such power, when a Federal right or duty is invaded or involved. This principle is neither new nor startling, though modern applications of it have attracted attention. For example, it is now held that the United States, by the hand of its marshal, may lawfully kill one who assaults a Federal judge traveling through a State in the course of his duty, and that the State can not hold the marshal to account for such killing (In re Neagle, 135 U. S., 1); and that the United States may punish, as for murder, one who kills a prisoner in the custody of a Federal officer within a State (Logan *v.* United States, 144 U. S., 263). The principle is that the persons so assailed are within the peace of the United States; that the United States owes them the duty of protection; and that the power of protection follows upon the duty.

The equality clause of the fourteenth amendment forbids the States to deny to any person within their jurisdiction the equal protection of the laws. This clause is judicially held to confer immunity from any discrimination as a Federal right. The protection which the State extends to one person must be extended to all. It does not forbid discrimination merely in the making of laws, but in the equal protection which the laws are designed to afford. Forbidding the State to deny equal protection is equivalent to requiring the State to provide it. Equal protection is withheld if a State fails to provide it, and the guaranteed immunity is infringed. The constitutional requirement may be violated by acts of omission no less than by acts of commission. The omission of the proper officers of the State to furnish equal protection in any case is the omission of the State itself, since the State can act only by its officers. (Tenn. *v.* Davis, 100 U. S., 257, 266; Strauder *v.* W. Va., 100 U. S., 303, 306, 310; Va. *v.* Rives, 100 U. S., 313, 318; Ex parte Va., 100 U. S., 339, 345; U. S. *v.* Harris, 106 U. S., 629, 639; Civil Rights Cases, 100 U. S., 3, 13, 23; Ex parte Yarbrough, 110 U. S., 651, 660 et seq.; Yick Wo *v.* Hopkins, 118 U. S., 356, 373; Baldwin *v.* Franks, 120 U. S., 683 and (Harlan, J.) 700; In re Coy, 127 U. S., 731; Carter *v.* Texas, 177 U. S., 442, 447.) It would seem to follow that when a citizen or other person is put to death by a lawless mob, in default of the protection which the State is bound to provide for all alike, there is a denial of equal protection by the State, in the sense of the equality clause, which Congress may prevent or punish by legislation applying to any individuals who participate in or contribute to it, directly or indirectly.

The United States has, as all governments have, a political and legal interest in the lives of its citizens. If it had not full power to protect them in their lives within the States as it has elsewhere, it can be, as already observed, only because that duty rests solely upon the States. If so, it is a duty owed to the United States as well as to individual citizens. It would seem that open and notorious neglect or omission of this duty on the part of the State, by suffering lawless mobs to murder citizens for want of legal protection, may be declared an offense against the United States, and if so, that the United States may punish all persons who contribute to it.

Section 5508 of the Revised Statutes, which is taken from the act of May 31, 1870, is as follows:

> If two or more persons conspire to injure, oppress, threaten, or intimidate any citizen in the free exercise or enjoyment of any privilege secured to him by the Constitution or laws of the

United States, or because of his having so exercised the same, or if two or more persons go in disguise on the highway or on the premises of another, with intent to prevent or hinder his free exercise or enjoyment of any right or privilege so secured, they shall be fined not more than $5,000 and imprisoned not more than 10 years, and shall, moreover, be ineligible to any office or place of honor, profit, or trust created by the Constitution or laws of the United States.

A part of section 1980 of the Revised Statutes is as follows:

If two or more persons in any State or Territory conspire or go in disguise on the highway or on the premises of another for the purpose of depriving, either directly or indirectly, any person or class of persons of the equal protection of the law; or of equal privileges and immunities under the law; or for the purpose of preventing or hindering the constituted authorities of any State or Territory from giving or securing to all persons within such State or Territory the equal protection of the law; or if two or more persons conspire to prevent by force, intimidation, or threat any citizen who is lawfully entitled to vote, from giving his support or advocacy in a legal manner toward or in favor of the election of any lawfully qualified person as an elector for President or Vice President, or as a Member of Congress of the United States, or to injure any citizen in person or property on account of such support or advocacy in any case of conspiracy set forth in this section, if one or more persons engaged therein do, or cause to be done, any act in furtherance of the object of such conspiracy whereby another is injured in person or property, or deprived of having or exercising any right or privilege of a citizen of the United States, said person so injured or deprived may have an action for the recovery of damages occasioned by such injury or deprivation against any one or more of the conspirators.

This is taken from the acts of July 31, 1861.

These acts are construed to apply only to such rights as are granted by or dependent upon the Constitution, and valid and constitutional laws of the United States.

One of the matters which has been determined by the Supreme Court to be within the protection of these laws is the right of the Federal Government by penal laws to prevent discrimination against negroes serving on juries; and in ex parte Virginia (100 U. S., 339) the prosecution was maintained and conviction upheld, when the judge of a county court, whose duty it was to draw the juries for service, had discriminated against negroes in such jury service.

In Neal *v.* Delaware (103 U. S., 370) it was held that the exclusion because of their race and color of citizens of African descent from the grand jury that found and from the petit jury that was summoned to try the indictments, if made by the jury commissioners, without authority derived from the Constitution and laws of the State, was a violation of the prisoner's rights under the Constitution and laws of the United States, which the trial court was bound to redress, and the remedy for any failure in that respect is ultimately in this court upon writ of error. The court held that the exclusion of negroes from such grand and petit juries by officers charged with their selection, although such exclusion was no doubt by State constitution or laws, denies the equality of protection of law, denies the equality of protection secured by the Federal Constitution and law.

It has been more than once held that rights and immunities created by or dependent upon the Constitution of the United States can be protected by Congress. The form and manner of protection will be such as Congress, in the legitimate exercise of its legislative discretion, shall provide. These may be varied to meet the necessities of the particular rights to be protected.

In the case of Strauder *v.* West Virginia (100 U. S., 303) a law which denied colored persons the right to sit on juries was declared void. The court said:

> It (the fourteenth amendment) was designed to assure to the colored race the enjoyment of all the civil rights that under the law are enjoyed by white persons and to give to that race the protection of the General Government in that enjoyment whenever it should be denied by the States.

The court also said:

> It is not easy to comprehend how it can be said that while every white man is entitled to a trial by a jury selected from persons of his own race or color, or rather selected without discrimination against his color, and a negro is not, the latter is

equally protected by the law with the former. Is not protection of life and liberty against race or color prejudice a right, a legal right, under the constitutional amendment?

The act of Congress of March 1, 1875 (18 Stat., par. 3, p. 336), enacts that:

> No citizen, possessing all other qualifications which are or may be prescribed by law, shall be disqualified from service as grand or petit juror in any court of the United States, or of any State, on account of race, color, or previous condition of servitude; and any officer or other person charged with any duty in the selection or summoning of jurors, who shall exclude or fail to summon any citizen for the cause aforesaid, shall, on conviction thereof, be deemed guilty of a misdemeanor and be fined not more than $5,000.

This was held to be constitutional in the case of Ex Parte Virginia, supra. The court laid stress upon the provisions of the fourteenth amendment, especially:

> No state shall make or enforce a law which shall abridge the privileges or immunities of citizens of the United States. * * * Nor deny to any person within its jurisdiction the equal protection of the law.

And upon the last section, which gives Congress the power to enforce its provisions by appropriate legislation.

One of the privileges or rights granted the colored man by this amendment is citizenship; another is that no State shall make or enforce any law which shall abridge the privileges or immunities of citizens of the United States; another is, nor shall any State deprive any person of life, liberty, or property without due process of law; another is, nor deny to any person within its jurisdictions the equal protection of the laws.

If a county judge can be punished for refusing to draw his jury so as to include any of the negro race, and if exclusion of negroes from the jury list is sufficient to deny equal protection of the law to a defendant who is to be tried by a jury to be drawn therefrom, the question arises as to why may not the Federal authority protect one of its citizens while in confinement or custody awaiting trial by a jury with the composition of which it has exercised material power?

Why is not a refusal to put into operation the laws against lynching as much within the jurisdiction of Congress as is the refusal to obey a State law by a judge in drawing a jury?

If Congress can punish a judge for refusing to include any negroes in the jury list for the purpose of trying a negro, why can it not punish a sheriff for refusing to protect a negro while awaiting trial?

If Congress has the power to enforce, by appropriate legislation, the provisions which prevent a State from taking life and liberty or property of its citizens by due process of law, why may it not determine that in order to fulfill this guaranty it may make the sheriff directly amenable to its jurisdiction in such matters?

The Supreme Court has said:

> The equality of the rights of citizens is a principle of republicanism. Every republican government is in duty bound to protect all its citizens in the enjoyment of this principle if within its power. The duty was originally assumed by the States, and it still remains there. The only obligation resting upon the United States is to see that the States do not deny the right. This the amendment guarantees, but no more. (United States *v.* Cruikshank, 92 U. S., 542, 555.)

The power in the right of the Federal Government to see that the States do not deny any person the right to due process of law, and to see that they do not deny him the equal protection of the law will be construed to be equal to the task. No one of us dare say that the limit of this power has been reached. No person who genuinely believes in the necessity for the exercise of State rights in full vigor will desire to tempt the Federal Government to the full awakening of these latent powers. If the States fail to give adequate protection, how shall the Federal Government exercise its power to fulfill the guaranty of the fourteenth amendment?

The amendment itself says that this shall be done by appropriate legislation. Who shall determine what is appropriate legislation? Manifestly Congress in the first instance, finally the courts.

The States lagged in the making of adequate pure-food laws. The result is that this is now nearly entirely regulated by the Federal Government.

The States did not adequately meet the narcotic-drug nuisance; the result is that the Federal Government is now reaching down into the daily lives of the citizens in this respect to a degree which would have been thought impossible a few years ago.

Congress has exercised its rights in enacting legislation with reference to child labor in the various States. It has done likewise with reference to intoxicating liquors. If Congress has felt its duty to do these things, why should it not also assume jurisdiction and enact laws to protect the lives of citizens of the United States against lynch law and mob violence? Are the rights of property, or what a citizen shall drink, or the ages and conditions under which children shall work, any more important to the Nation than life itself? I believe that Congress has ample power to enact the legislation that I have recommended. I believe it would stand the test of the courts and be a great blessing, as well as aid in wiping out the greatest blot upon the honor of the American Nation.

"THE CRISIS OF THE WORLD"

W.E.B. DU BOIS
Close Ranks
The Crisis, July 1918

THIS is the crisis of the world. For all the long years to come men will point to the year 1918 as the great Day of Decision, the day when the world decided whether it would submit to military despotism and an endless armed peace—if peace it could be called—or whether they would put down the menace of German militarism and inaugurate the United States of the World.

We of the colored race have no ordinary interest in the outcome. That which the German power represents today spells death to the aspirations of Negroes and all darker races for equality, freedom and democracy. Let us not hesitate. Let us, while this war lasts, forget our special grievances and close our ranks shoulder to shoulder with our own white fellow citizens and the allied nations that are fighting for democracy. We make no ordinary sacrifice, but we make it gladly and willingly with our eyes lifted to the hills.

"HATRED OF THE UNLIKE"

CYRIL BRIGGS
The American Race Problem
The Crusader, September–December 1918

NO. I. WHAT IS IT.

THE American Race Problem is the problem of Black and White. Other race problems there are in this country, but before this problem of Black and white all others sink into pale insignificance. It is one of the most written of and talked about of American public questions and the one least understood.

It is based upon hatred of the unlike—the white man's hatred for his racial opposite and for other types that are in any way different from his selected standard. It derives most of its virulence from the firm conviction in the white man's mind of the inequality of races—the belief that there are superior and inferior races and that the former are marked with a white skin and the latter with dark skin and that only the former are capable and virtuous and therefore alone fit to vote, rule and inherit the earth. This belief finds strength and support in the partial decadence and almost complete submergence of Negro culture from the time Arabs over-ran North Africa and the Sudan offering, by virtue of SUPERIOR FORCE, the Sword or the Koran, and implanting the Mohammedan religion and Arab civilization where formerly had flourished Negro theology and culture of such a type as to excite the whole-hearted admiration and emulation of the ancient Hebrews and Greeks.

The American Race Problem is further accentuated by the history of the country and the fact that the Negro a little more than a half a century ago occupied here a most subservient and helpless position. He was a slave and unlike the Anglo-Saxon and other European races who made up the mass of the slaves of the Roman Empire, the freed Negro, on account of his color, was not able to merge with the rest of the free citizens. He remained, therefore, a thing apart. In the American body but not accepted of it. In many sections of the country he has not the status of an American citizen—since an American citizen VOTES; And in those sections he is not alone disfranchised but made to feel in many other ways the caucasion-proclaimed inferiority of his Race. So that he may know that he is inferior he is Jim-crowed on public conveyances, segregated into undesirable and unhealthy locations, and even in the public schools, theatres and moving picture houses the controlling white man assiduously toils to convince him of his inferiority. This caucasion propaganda aims to exalt the white races into the heaven of the little tin gods by the blatant declaration of the inferiority of the darker races and the more or less effective attempt to cover up their achievements in the past so that the white man may claim credit for all that has been done in the development of civilisation. And when all this fails, and the Negro still feels himself a Man, the "superior" caucasion descends to the savagery and terrorism of lynching!

Such are some of the most salient phases of the American Race Problem. To fully appreciate the difficulties of the problem, however, it is necessary to go afield a bit. In the first place we must remember that racial antipathy is not exclusively confined to the caucasion, that the Negro dislikes the white man almost as much as the latter dislikes the Negro. We must remember secondly, that this racial antipathy is not of modern origin, that it probably existed before the dawn of history, that it certainly has been a factor in all times and countries of which there are any records, that never before in history have the two races lived together on terms of peace, justice and equality. That to-day, only in Brazil and for the first time is this phenomena presented and that between the NEGRO, INDIAN AND LATIN RACES, but nowhere on earth in the present or in the past between the Negro and the Nordic—Anglo-Saxon, Teuton, Scandinavian. And that in Brazil the darker races enjoy equal opportunities and complete equality merely because they greatly outnumber the white races in that country. But that in ancient lands, as in most modern countries, the relations of the two races have always been on the basis of slave and master, inferior and superior. And so strong was this racial antipathy which the Negro in the past felt for his racial antipodes that history records that the Negro women of a Sudan town about to be captured by besieging white enemies committed suicide by flinging themselves from the walls rather than fall into the hands of the hated caucasian.

Is race prejudice then so light a thing, so shallow an emotion that we can airily prate of an ultimate solution while allowing matters to drift along their own way or rather, the way of the white man, and without taking some action to assure the future "security of life" and happiness of our Race? The solution this magazine has to offer is not easy. It calls for Sacrifice and Service! But at least it leads to Glory and Respect! The other way leads to degradation and hell upon earth.

NO. 2. THE WHITE MAN'S SOLUTION.

> Is it for this we all have felt the flame.
> This newer bondage and this deeper shame?
> —Dunbar.

While the Negro has been drifting and letting things take care of themselves, trusting in that great illusion, the Ultimate Equitable Peaceful Solution the white man in the South has been solving the Negro Problem in his own way. And in this he has had the acquiescence of the white man in the North.

Now, the white man's solution of the Negro Problem is great—for himself. For the Negro it is hell and worse! The white man's solution is simply that the Negro should behave himself and keep his place. To this end he has instituted jim-crowism, segregation, the terrorism of lynching, and peonage and convict-labor. If the Negro will stand for this, in the end he will be the dehumanized, servile, unambitious and abject creature that the white man evidently desires to see him. And lest we be accused of exaggeration we call the white man himself to the witness stand. Read what white men, naturally in half-sympathy with the South and only protesting when cracker cruelty went too far, have to say in the white man's solution then consider whether the Northern Negro can afford to stand by in smug complacency of mistaken geographical safety while his brother is being dehumanized in the South. The first we shall call to testify is William P. Pickett, a resident of Brooklyn and author of "The Negro Problem: Abraham Lincoln's

Solution", a book we have lately read with great interest. Says Mr. Pickett:

"One of the most alarming aspects of the Southern situation is the constantly increasing tendency towards reducing the Negro to a condition of peonage. A chapter might be profitably devoted to this view of the subject, did space permit.

"From Virginia to Texas various state laws are in force which virtually operate to restrain the Negro farm-hand from leaving the farm, or the common laborer under contract from leaving his employment, and enable the employer through a system of fines or imprisonment to control the personal liberty of his employee.

". . . . this amounts substantially to selling into enforced public service or the retaining in private involuntary servitude, persons who fail to pay alleged debts, frequently extortionate or fraudulent. The crime appears to be on the increase throughout the South, . . .

"No more may be said upon this point here than that this system, with the barbarous and inhuman convict-labor system of the extreme Southern States, has a general tendency compulsorily to retain the Negro upon his native soil, and *is leading towards a system of complete physical subjugation which promises to be fruitful of the greatest injury to the race.*

"The practice prevails throughout the range of states extending from Virginia to Texas, of leasing persons convicted of crime (the great majority being Negroes) to the highest bidder, who thus acquires the right to avail himself of their labor as a matter of speculation. Statistics relating to this barbarous practice are simply incredible. The usual custom is for the bidder, frequently some favored politician, to sublet the convicts by hundreds to contracts for road-making, lumbering, working in the turpentine industry, or other similar exhausting labor. The prices paid for the labor of these convicts by those employing their services appears almost beyond belief.

". . . . and when we take in consideration the ordinary wages paid to unskilled labor in that section, or even the highest compensation of the same class in the North, and reflect upon what must be exacted in the way of production from an ill-fated convict for whom a sub-contractor is paying $47.50 per month, with the expense of keeping, the horrors of the system must at once impress themselves on the mind of any person possessing the least spirit of humanity."

Mr. Pickett's testimony is substantiated by other whites who have written on the subject. Prof. Albert Bushnell Hart in "The Southern South" bears witness that

"Even without a contract a Negro may be legally obliged to labor for a white man under vagrancy laws, by which Negroes who are not visibly supporting themselves may be convicted for that crime, and then sent to the County Farm, or hired out to somebody who will pay their fine. Once in the hands of a master, they are helpless. For instance, one Glenny Helms, who was apparently guilty of no offense, was in 1907 arrested, fined and sold to one Turner, who in this case thought it prudent to plead guilty of peonage. The son of this Turner was the agent in the most frightful case of peonage as yet recorded. A woman was accused of a misdemeanor; it is doubtful whether she had committed any; but at any rate she was fined fifteen dollars; Turner paid the fine; she was assigned to him and he set her to the severe labor of clearing land. And then what happened? What was a hustling master to do with a woman who would not pile brush as fast as the men brought it, but to whip her, and if she still did not reform, to whip her again, and when she still would not do the work, to string her up by the wrists for two hours, and when she still 'shirked,' God Almighty at last came to the rescue; she was dead!"

This much testimony does space allow for peonage and convict-labor. Of the cruelty of the system there can be no doubt. Of the menace to the future of the Race let thinking Negro men and women judge for themselves. Of "Jimcrowism" William P. Pickett says:

"Of all devices employed for the purpose of marking the distinction between the white and Negro races in the South, probably the most offensive to the Negro is what are commonly known as the 'Jim Crow' laws.

"Nothing more destructive of the natural pride of an intelligent and self-respecting man or woman can be conceived than the treatment to which the better class of Negroes in the South are subjected in this ruthless enforcement of the mortifying regulations for the separation of the races. Yet all protest is unavailing. The laws which accomplish this degrading discrimination against the black man are denounced by the enlightened members of the race, but have been steadily upheld by the courts and sanctioned by the Interstate Commerce Commission as constituting proper and reasonable regulations of travel. The Negro asserts that these unjust laws result in the dwarfing of the manhood and womanhood of his people, and bitterly denounces the practice of exacting payment for first-class accomodations and then compelling the members of his race, theoretically equal before the law, to submit themselves to such obnoxious requirements."

Of lynching, the weapon of terrorism used by the Southern whites when all else have failed to break the spirit on lynching, let Walter F. White, assistant secretary of the N. A. A. C. P., and investigator of the recent lynchings in Brooks and Lowndes County, Ga., speak. We quote from his report in the September Crisis:

"The murder of the Negro men was deplorable enough in itself, but the method by which Mrs. Mary Turner was put to death was so revolting and the details are so horrible that it is with reluctance that the account is given. It might be mentioned that each detail given is not the statement of a single person but each phase is related only after careful investigation and corroboration. Mrs. Turner made the remark that the killing of her husband on Saturday was unjust and that if she knew the names of the persons who were in the mob that lynched her husband, she would have warrants sworn out against them and have them punished in the courts.

"This news determined the mob to 'teach her a lesson,' and although she attempted to flee when she heard that they were after her, she was captured at noon on Sunday. The grief-striken and terrified woman was taken to a lonely and secluded spot, down a narrow road over which the trees touch at their tops, which, with the thick undergrowth on either side of the road, made a gloomy and appropriate spot for the lynching. Near Folsom's Bridge over the Little River a tree was selected for her execution—a small oak tree extending over the road.

At the time she was lynched, Mary Turner was in her eight month of pregnancy. The delicate state of her health, one month less previous to delivery, may be imagined, but this had no effect on the tender feelings of the mob. Her ankles were tied together and she was hung to the tree, head downward. Gasoline and oil from the automobiles were thrown on her clothing and while she writhed in Agony and the mob howled in glee, a match was applied and her clothes burned from her person. When this had been done and while she was yet alive, a knife, evidently one such as is used in splitting hogs, was taken and *the woman's abdomen was cut open, the unborn babe falling from her womb to the ground. The infant, prematurely born, gave two feeble cries and then its head was crushed by a member of the mob with his heel. Hundreds of bullets were then fired into the body of the woman, now mercifully dead, and the work was over.*

Of the general attitude toward the Negro, Prof. Hart says:

"So far as can be judged, the average frame of mind in the South includes much injustice, and unwillingness to permit the Negro race to develop up to the measure of its limitations.

"Observe that this ferocity is not directed against the Negro simply because he does ill, *but equally if he does well.*"

And William Pickett admits that

"The conditions under which the great majority of the Negro race live, the handicap imposed upon them by their color, the implacable hostility which they encounter in their endeavors to compete industrially with the white man, their exclusion from the unions, all combine to constitute them a class apart in the realm of productive activity, and to compel them to accept the most meagre wages for their unskilled efforts, and in like manner to accomodate themselves to the lowest scale of living."

NO. 3   THE NEGRO'S SOLUTION.

While lynching, jim-crowism, peonage, convict slave labor, segregation and other forms of oppression leading to the ultimate dehumanization of the Negro constitute the white man's "Solution" to the American Race Problem, the Negro's Solution, until recently, has been more of a hope against hope, a dream in a realm of fact, than any definite attempt towards a solution that would be just and honorable to his race as well as acceptable to the white man.

Whether it was the advice to "buy pigs" or the declaration that white men would learn to respect and honor Negroes as soon as Negroes acquired sufficient property and education it was all diametrically opposed to human nature, the lessons of history and the facts in the case. The South has long since proved the fallacy of the theory that the ownership of pigs (and other property) will secure one in the rights of life and property. "Observe," says Prof. Hart, "that this ferocity is not directed against the Negro simply because he does ill, but equally if he does well." While William P. Picket, a keen observer of conditions in the South, says:

"Now the fallacy of this view (that education or wealth will solve) lies in the assumption that the higher the state of education and ability the Negro can attain, the more wealth he can accumulate and the greater his prosperity, the more he will be liked and appreciated by the white race in the South.

"The contrary is always the case. The Southern Negro who performs humble duties, who is content with menial occupation, who bears himself meekly, stands in the attitude of hat in hand, is not ordinarily the subject of aggressive racial animosity. It is the Negro who asserts himself to the level, social or political of the white man, who meets with the sternest opposition."

Another profered solution for the problem is "simple justice". A beautiful theory, indeed, but one that absolutely ignores the kind of human nature that made the poet exclaim that "man's inhumanity to man makes countless millions mourn". In the face of the fact that the white race (nor, in truth, any other race) has never been just in its dealings with unorganised and (therefore) weak peoples it would seem that Negro leaders who are expected to be versed in the human records (called history) would hesitate to offer seriously such a solution as "simple justice," yet a sea of talk has been sent out along this line and much good mental energy wasted.

Still yet another beautiful solution is "to leave it to God". This is the advice of those who would have us egoistically look for a special dispensation of Providence in our own particular case, forgetful of the fact that "God helps those who help themselves".

All these beautiful theories come together to form the "Ultimate Equitable Solution", the great illusion of the Negro in an alien civilization. But the fact is that beautiful theories and eloquent harangues upon justice, liberty and the guarantees of the Constitution little avails in the face of the many-sided race problem, imbedded as the latter is in the natural fortressess of human nature (caucasian nature in particular) and the cold reality of racial antipathy.

Latterly, however, a new solution has been offered as the Negro began to recognise that the salvation of his race and an honorable solution of the American Race Problem call for action and decision in preference to the twaddling, dreaming and indecision of 'leaders'.

This new solution is nothing more or less than independent, separate existence. "Government of the (Negro) people, for the (Negro) people and by the (Negro) people".

"When two ride a horse one must ride behind" is an old adage the truth of which has yet to be questioned. Then, too, Negroes have had the opportunity of observing how quickly the Japanese adaptation of their Government and philosophies to the caucasian gospel of force won for them the respect and consideration still denied the Jew after centuries of achievement and much accumulation of weath. Negroes are rapidly learning that superior force (not sentiment whether of justice or liberty) dominates the thoughts and actions of men.

THE MENACE OF THE FUTURE.

The end of the war is in sight. In the sharp industrial competition which will follow the war (and which was on the way war or no war) the Negro Race in America and in the sub-tropical sections of Africa will face annihilation and economic death unless protected economically—as other and wiser races have seen fit to protect themselves —by the ownership of territories large and rich enough in resources to supply present needs and guarantee future requirements. All the dead and dying races were not conquered by the sword; many were victims of economic warfare.

For years the white man has been assiduously fencing off the earth while the darker races slept. The vast Dominion of Canada, the illimitable expanse of Siberia, the entire continent of Australia have been fenced off to supply the future territorial needs of the white race while, at the present moment supporting puny white populations who, backed by mother nations in Europe, plainly tell the Colored races to keep out, that they will have none of them, that these vast territories, once the habitat of Colored races, and capable of supporting millions upon millions of human beings, are to be held by sparse white populations—backed by militant Europe—for white posterity.

Here we have an example of the white man looking hundreds of years into the future and taking steps now to safeguard the white men of a far distant future day.

His action is wise and deserves applause—*from white men*. To Negroes, however, his action is a menace and from them deserves the sharpest and swiftest opposition.

In the economic war that is to follow the war—that in fact, is already upon us—Negroes in countries dominated by a numerically superior white population will be at a deadly disadvantage.

Ownership and control of large and rich territories is necessary to safeguard the existence of the race and to guarantee it political equality and justice and the freest opportunity for development. Without control of resources we are lost. Only the race that is in possession and control of such resources can hope to survive the stern economic competition of the future.

A BLACK REGIMENT RETURNS FROM FRANCE

THE RIGHT-ABOUT
Hell-Fighters Cheered on Homecoming
February 19, 1919

HELL-FIGHTERS CHEERED ON HOMECOMING

Crowds Line Fifth Avenue As 369th Regiment Parades

FIRST REAL WELCOME

Col. "Bill" Hayward Marches at Head
of His Victorious Black Troops

BLACK men, yes, but with bravery of the whitest, cleanest sort, and with streams of red, valiant blood in their veins—this was the verdict of thousands of soldiers and civilians on the sidelines, as the men of the 369th Infantry, the old 15th New York National Guard Regiment, filed by in parade along Fifth Avenue on Monday.

It was New York's first view en masse of the men who had brought fear into the marrow of the bones of the Prussian Guard. The old town forgot color and creed. It simply let itself go. It was the same spirit of pure exuberance which must have been manifest when Rome welcomed under victory arches her legionnaires brimming over with conquest.

No finer tribute could have been accorded the dark skinned troopers than that given by fellow soldiers. Only those who fought beside them in France could fully appreciate their worth as warriors. They knew and were not lax in making this clear by their cheers and shouts.

The inevitable toll had been paid by the black soldiers. Not a few are buried in friendly soil overseas. Many more there are who still know the pain of open wounds. There was evidence of this in the rear-guard of the procession made up of hospital cases conveyed in motor cars and ambulances. But their hurts could have received no more balsam salve than that of the acclaimed welcome of the by-standers.

As the procession ended one in the crowd was overheard to say: "Bell-hops and waiters before the war heroes to-day; tomorrow what?"

ANSWER IN WELCOME

An answer to that was the welcome itself. If ever there was evidence of the fulfillment of Lincoln's promise that some day the sun would rise on an America united despite all bonds and barriers of creed and race, it was during the course of the parade of the old Fifteenth on Monday.

To those who have contributed so nobly in redeeming democracy, no avenue of democracy shall be denied. Education, opportunity, fair and equal judgment on merit to negro soldiers and their race, must result or else victory will be relieved of its full meaning. This seemed to be the subsurface conviction of the on-looking multitudes. It was not difficult to grasp it on mingling with the crowds.

Led by their beloved commander, Colonel William Hayward, 3,000 gallant colored men saw fifth avenue a blaze of flags and banners, and the sidewalks solidly packed with white and black folks alike who turned out to do them homage. A Croix de Guerre was emblazoned on their regimental colors and 171 of them were decorated for personal bravery.

The veterans were all togged out in fighting regalia, from big hopnailed trench shoes to the steel helmets. There was plenty of living rag-time music furnished by the police band and the 15th's own "jazz" band which has become internationally famous.

FLAGS FLUTTER GREETING

The soldiers were preceded up the Avenue by wave after wave of cheers and applause. Men, women and children shouted themselves fairly hoarse, and from the groups in the windows of the buildings on the avenue, fluttered clouds of paper clippings, and streamers of every hue. Automobiles parked in side streets shrieked a welcome with their horns. This was the scene from 23rd Street and Fifth Avenue to Lenox Avenue and 135th Street, where the procession broke up and the men gave themselves over to celebrating with their thousands of colored friends and relatives in Harlem.

At the 71st regiment armory, after the parade had disbanded, the soldiers were treated to a spread and entertainment. In the evening they returned to Camp Upton, where they will be mustered out of service.

The members of the old 15th returned to the United States on the Swedish-American line steamer *Stockholm*, and landed in New York on February 12th, the anniversary of the birth of their Emancipator.

As for Colonel Hayward, the gallant commander of the "Fighting 15th," he wears a wound chevron, and still limps slightly from a wound in the ankle received last June, at Belleau Ridge. Of his dusky heroes, Colonel Hayward says:

"I am proud of my men. There isn't a braver or cleaner lot of soldiers in the United States Army or any other army than the old 15th regiment of the New York National Guard."

During its services abroad, the 15th regiment passed through 191 days of fighting, with only one week's rest. This record is unique.

"THIS COUNTRY . . . IS YET A SHAMEFUL LAND"

W.E.B. DU BOIS
Returning Soldiers
The Crisis, May 1919

WE are returning from war! THE CRISIS and tens of thousands of black men were drafted into a great struggle. For bleeding France and what she means and has meant and will mean to us and humanity and against the threat of German race arrogance, we fought gladly and to the last drop of blood; for America and her highest ideals, we fought in far-off hope; for the dominant southern oligarchy entrenched in Washington, we fought in bitter resignation. For the America that represents and gloats in lynching, disfranchisement, caste, brutality and devilish insult—for this, in the hateful upturning and mixing of things, we were forced by vindictive fate to fight, also.

But today we return! We return from the slavery of uniform which the world's madness demanded us to don to the freedom of civil garb. We stand again to look America squarely in the face and call a spade a spade. We sing: This country of ours, despite all its better souls have done and dreamed, is yet a shameful land.

It *lynches*.

And lynching is barbarism of a degree of contemptible nastiness unparalleled in human history. Yet, for fifty years we have lynched two Negroes a week, and we have kept this up right through the war.

It *disfranchises* its own citizens.

Disfranchisement is the deliberate theft and robbery of the only protection of poor against rich and black against white. The land that disfranchises its citizens and calls itself a democracy lies and knows it lies.

It encourages *ignorance*.

It has never really tried to educate the Negro. A dominant minority does not want Negroes educated. It wants servants, dogs, whores and monkeys. And when this land allows a reactionary group by its stolen political power to force as many black folk into these categories as it possibly can, it cries in contemptible hypocrisy: "They threaten us with degeneracy; they cannot be educated."

It *steals* from us.

It organizes industry to cheat us. It cheats us out of our land; it cheats us out of our labor. It confiscates our savings. It reduces our wages. It raises our rent. It steals our profit. It taxes us without representation. It keeps us consistently and universally poor, and then feeds us on charity and derides our poverty.

It *insults* us.

It has organized a nation-wide and latterly a world-wide propaganda of deliberate and continuous insult and defamation of black blood wherever found. It decrees that it shall not be possible in travel nor residence, work nor play, education nor instruction for a black man to exist without tacit or open acknowledgment of his inferiority to the dirtiest white dog. And it looks upon any attempt to question or even discuss this dogma as arrogance, unwarranted assumption and treason.

This is the country to which we Soldiers of Democracy return. This is the fatherland for which we fought! But it is *our* fatherland. It was right for us to fight. The faults of *our* country are *our* faults. Under similar circumstances, we would fight again. But by the God of Heaven, we are cowards and jackasses if now that that war is over, we do not marshal every ounce of our brain and brawn to fight a sterner, longer, more unbending battle against the forces of hell in our own land.

> We *return*.
> We *return from fighting*.
> We *return fighting*.

Make way for Democracy! We saved it in France, and by the Great Jehovah, we will save it in the United States of America, or know the reason why.

"STRIKING TERROR INTO . . . THE WHITE MOB"
JEANNETTE CARTER
Negroes of Washington Were Forced to Protect Themselves
The New York Age, August 2, 1919

WASHINGTON, D. C.—The colored people of the District of Columbia have shown what a people can do when assailed on all hands by mob fury and deserted by the police power of the District and by the Federal Government, both of which to all intents and purposes threw their organized influence against the colored people, the victims of the fury of the mob.

Disorganized as they were, and without leadership, when the rioting was started Saturday night and continuing through Sunday and Sunday night, without any effective interference on the part of the police, colored people were prepared on Monday to defend themselves, after a fashion, and began to do so with a grim determination to exact a life for a life. They entered into the strife with more determination than the whites who started it, and they stuck to the job all the week like heroes of many battles.

On Monday the Negroes had three machine guns placed in high-powered automobiles, with hand grenades, and before the riot ended had begun to make bombs. They had plenty of ammunition and guns which were handed around to all colored people who were not able to buy them. The bootleggers who had been making plenty of money went to Baltimore and bought ammunition and guns amounting to more than fifteen thousand dollars worth and gave them out to Negroes.

Too much cannot be said in praise of the so-called common people who equipped themselves to meet the emergency. It was splendid. The poolroom hangers-on and men from the alleys and side streets, people from the most ordinary walks of life were the people who really saved the day by striking terror into the hearts of the white mob. They had a regular organization of their own, with a private code. They had a flying automobile squadron that took in every section of the city, including the school of Miss Nannie H. Burroughs, on Lincoln Heights, and places thereabouts, they made several trips to the school, after a report got into circulation that the white mob intended to attack the school.

They made their trip in their high-powered automobiles, every man in the trucks being armed, while the chauffeurs who ran the trucks, steered with one hand and held a gun with the other. They kept one truck with a plenty of ammunition, stationed in the neighborhood of Lincoln Heights. The daily newspapers did not report one-half the deaths or casualties.

The white newspapers, which did so much to stir up race strife in the District of Columbia, got very weak and tired of the dirty business just as soon as the colored mob got busy on the job with the white mob and began to put the white mob guessing. They were the first to start the rioting, and they were the first to sue for peace.

COLORED GIRL PROTECTS HERSELF.

The suggestion has been made that a Croix de Guerre, with palm, be given to the seventeen-year-old girl who is accused of picking off a detective when he went into her bedroom at night without a warrant and when no riot call had come from that house. But the colored girl may not have killed the detective, because Inspector Grant, in his excitement and fearing that the colored gang was behind him, ran across two street car platforms, on his way to the hospital, and ploughed through the door of the hospital on his way into it. He was sure some scared.

Your correspondent personally visited the scene of the rioting, realizing withal that I was in much danger of getting a stray bullet, but having no fear of being attacked, because I was surrounded by that splendid crowd of brave young men.

While these splendid men of ours were standing to the fight I noticed that Mrs. Mary Church Terrell, Mr. and Mrs. Henry E. Baker, Dr. A. M. Curtis, Prof. Neval Thomas, Prof. Carter G. Woodson, Dr. Henry F. Freeman, Attorney Charles S. Hill, Editor J. Finley Wilson, Prof. B. B. Church, and many others, mingled freely in the thick of the trouble, and showed no fear of danger.

COLORED MEMBERS NOT CALLED OUT.

The one colored man who shot the two Home Defense Guards was sufficient to disband that mighty organization of 2,000 members, the colored members of which were not called to duty, but were supposed to remain at home and do nothing, as were the colored policemen, who were detached from active service and to their homes during the life of the rioting.

Judge Robert H. Terrell played a splendid, I might say, a heroic part in the rioting. He was not afraid to go anywhere and was always at the point where he should be. Early in the rioting he and a committee of our lawyers visited Judge McMahon's court, where he was handing out sentences of two years to men for carrying concealed weapons. Judge Terrell told him that he represented those colored men who were being grossly discriminated against; that white men were allowed to go free while colored men were given two-year sentences. He told them plainly that he wanted what his people wanted, and that was justice before the law; that the colored men accused were within their rights in seeking to protect their lives. After that the same Judge reduced the sentences to sixty days and placed the alleged offenders on probation.

A committee of preachers also visited the Department of Justice to protest against the unjust sentences.

The next time that the crackers start a riot in this town, whether fomented by the white newspapers and a bunch of white soldiers and sailors or by themselves, they will think a long, deep think, as the colored men in Washington who do not belong to the criminal classes have resolved to front the white mob by the colored mob and exact life for life. If they can't have protection of the Federal Government, and it has been shown that they had not had it, they have determined to defend themselves. And that is as it should be.

"LYNCH HIM"

JAMES E. SCOTT
Statement on Attack by Rioters in Washington, D.C.
Recorded August 4, 1919

STATEMENT OF JAMES E. SCOTT, ATTACKED BY RIOTERS

Monday Night July 21, 1919.

I was returning to Washington after having been out of town since Friday July 18, 1919. I arrived at the Union Station at 12 P.M. Monday Night and on entering the station noticed nothing unusual. I boarded a street car which went to Rockcreek Bridge via. New Jersey Ave. and got a transfer to the Brightwood car line. When I reached 7th & Florida Ave. N. W. the place of transfer I noticed that things were as quiet as is usually the case at that hour of the night. I waited there about five minutes for the Brightwood car and when it came I and a Captain boarded it. I walked into the car and soon noticed that I was the only member of my race present except a lady whom I noticed later but not at this time. As I started to get a vacant seat a soldier put his arm across me and said "where are you going nigger?" I said to him that I was going to get a seat. As I was telling him that I heard some others in the car saying "Lynch him", "Kill him", "Throw him out of the car window" and at that time I was being grabbed from all sides. I forced my way to the rear door and was hit by something as I stepped off, which cut my ear and bruised my head. As the car moved away the conductor fired three shots at me. It was as I got off the car that I noticed the lady on the car, what became of her I do not know.

"THEY WILL FIGHT"
MARTINA SIMMS
Washington Riot

The Baltimore Afro-American, August 15, 1919

WASHINGTON RIOT

You have heard about the riot
   In Washington, D. C.
You can't come fooling around
   Aunt Dinah's boys you see.

They went to France and fought
   For Democracy
They might as well shed their blood
   For their rights in Washington D. C.

You read about Carrie Johnson
   Who was only seventeen
She killed a detective, wasn't she
   brave and keen.

They will fight,— of course they will
   fight
If the white folks don't give Aunt
   Dinah's boys their rights.

               By MARTINA SIMMS.
               1527 E. MADISON ST.
               BALTIMORE, MD.
                   Age eleven years.

A CITY ERUPTS

THE CHICAGO DAILY TRIBUNE
Report Two Killed, Fifty Hurt, in Race Riots
July 28, 1919

BATHING BEACH FIGHT
SPREADS TO BLACK BELT

All Police Reserves
Called to Guard
South Side.

TWO COLORED men are reported to have been killed and approximately fifty whites and negroes injured, a number probably fatally, in race riots that broke out at south side beaches yesterday. The rioting spread through the black belt and by midnight had thrown the entire south side into a state of turmoil.

Among the known wounded are four policemen of the Cottage Grove avenue station, two from west side stations, one fireman of engine company No. 9, and three women.

One Negro was knocked off a raft at the Twenty-ninth street beach after he had been stoned by whites. He drowned because whites are said to have frustrated attempts of colored bathers to rescue him. The body was recovered, but could not be identified.

A colored rioter is said to have died from wounds inflicted by Policeman John O'Brien, who fired into a mob at Twenty-ninth street and Cottage Grove avenue. The body, it is said, was spirited away by colored men.

DRAG NEGROES FROM CARS.

So serious was the trouble throughout the district that Acting Chief of Police Alcock was unable to place an estimate on the injured. Scores received cuts and bruises from flying stones and rocks, but went to their homes for medical attention.

Minor rioting continued through the night all over the south side. Negroes who were found in street cars were dragged to the street and beaten.

They were first ordered to the street by white men and if they refused the trolley was jerked off the wires.

Scores of conflicts between the whites and blacks were reported at south side stations and reserves were ordered to stand guard on all important street corners. Some of the fighting took place four miles from the scene of the afternoon riots.

When the Cottage Grove avenue station received a report that several had drowned in the lake during the beach outbreak, Capt. Joseph Mullen assigned policemen to drag the lake with grappling hooks. The body of a colored man was recovered, but was not identified.

BOATS SCOUR LAKE.

Rumors that a white boy was a lake victim could not be verified. The patrol boats scoured the lake in the vicinity of Twenty-ninth street for several hours in a vain search.

John O'Brien, a policeman attached to the Cottage Grove avenue station, was attacked by a mob at Twenty-ninth and State streets after he had tried to rescue a fellow cop from a crowd of howling Negroes. Several shots were fired in his direction and he was wounded in the left arm. He pulled his revolver and fired four times into the gathering. Three colored men dropped.

MAN COP SHOT DIES.

When the police attempted to haul the wounded into the wagon the Negroes made valiant attempts to prevent them. Two were taken to the Michael Reese hospital, but the third was spirited away by the mob. It was later learned that he died in a drug store a short distance from the shooting.

Fire apparatus from a south side house answered an alarm of fire which was turned in from a drug store at Thirty-fifth and State streets. It was said that more than fifty whites had sought refuge here and that a number of Negroes had attempted to "smoke them out." There was no semblance of a fire when the autos succeeded in brushing through the populated streets.

PARTIAL LIST OF WOUNDED.

An incomplete list of the wounded follows:

POLICEMAN JOHN F. O'BRIEN, Cottage Grove avenue station; white; shot in left arm; taken to his home at 7151 South Michigan avenue.

POLICEMAN JOHN O'CONNELL, same station; white; knocked down and beaten.

POLICEMAN JOHN CALLAHAN, same station; white; beaten and bruised by mob.

POLICEMAN THOMAS J. GALLAGHER, same station; white; scalp wounds.

EDWARD HAUSNER, white, 4347 S. State street, cut about legs and face.

ARTHUR CARROLL, white, 2979 Prairie avenue, head bruised by stone.

JAMES CRAWFORD, colored, 2959 Federal street, shot through abdomen; probably will die; taken to Michael Reese hospital.

CHARLES CORMIER, white, 2839 Cottage Grove avenue, shot in head by stray bullet.

WILLIAM LONG, white, 2215 S. State street; cut in head and back.

JOSEPH WIGGINS, colored, 2417 Wabash avenue, beaten about head.

PHIL GRIFFIN, colored, 912 East Thirty-third street, shot in both legs.

GEORGE STAUBER, white, 2904 Cottage Grove avenue, beaten and cut.

HERMAN RABISOHN, white, 1804 South State street, bruised by missiles.

JOHN O'NEIL, white, 1828 West Thirty-fifth street, struck on head by brick.

WALTER CARSON, white, same address, face cut by rock.

WILLIAM CHEESHIRE, white, 3529 South Hermitage avenue; stabbed in face; taken to Provident hospital.

ANTON DUGO, white, 627 East Twenty-fifth street; shot in leg; taken to St. Anthony's hospital.

WILLIAM SCOTT, colored, 3611 Vernon avenue; scalp wounds.

MISS MAMIE McDONALD, white, 2901 Emerald avenue; head cut by brick.

MISS FRANCES McDONALD, sister, same address; back injured by rock.

MRS. GLADYS WILLIAMS, white, 2818 Indiana avenue; face bruised by stone.

MELVIN DAVIS, colored, 2816 Cottage Grove avenue, beaten while waiting for Halsted street car.

HARRY SPEEZ, colored, 3142 West Fifteenth street, knocked unconscious by whites at Thirty-first and Halsted streets.

LEWIS PHILLIPS, colored, 452 East Thirty-ninth street, shot in groin while riding in Thirty-ninth street car; taken to Provident hospital.

FRANK WALLS, white, pipeman of Engine company 9, struck in neck by rock.

EVELYN BOYDE, white, 530 West Twenty-seventh street, hit on face and hip by stones.

FRANCES BOYDE, sister, same address, knocked down by rock.

LEWIS B. KNIGHT, white, 6400 Dorchester avenue; beaten about head with club.

SHOT AT HIS WINDOW.

Charles Cromier was sitting in his window at 2839 Cottage Grove avenue watching the clashing mobs. A stray bullet lodged in his head and he fell back into the room. Spectators saw him being helped to a chair by a woman.

Racial feeling, which had been on a par with the weather during the day took fire shortly after 5 o'clock when white bathers at the Twenty-ninth street improvised beach saw a colored boy on a raft paddling into what they termed "white" territory.

A snarl of protest went up from the whites and soon a volley of rocks and stones were sent in his direction. One rock, said to have been thrown by George Stauber of 2904 Cottage Grove avenue, struck the lad and he toppled into the water.

COP REFUSES TO INTERFERE.

Colored men who were present attempted to go to his rescue, but they were kept back by the whites, it is said. Colored men and women, it is alleged, asked Policeman Dan Callahan of the Cottage Grove station to arrest Stauber, but he is said to have refused.

Then, indignant at the conduct of the policeman, the Negroes set upon Stauber and commenced to pommel him. The whites came to his rescue and then the battle royal was on. Fists flew and rocks were hurled. Bathers from the colored Twenty-fifth street beach were attracted to the scene of the battling and aided their comrades in driving the whites into the water.

NEGROES CHASE POLICEMAN.

Then they turned on Policeman Callahan and drove him down Twenty-ninth street. He ran into a drug store at Twenty-ninth street and Cottage Grove avenue and phoned the Cottage Grove avenue police station.

Two wagon loads of cops rolled to the scene, and in a scuffle that ensued here Policeman John O'Brien and three blacks were shot.

Riot calls were sent to the Cottage Grove avenue station and more reserves were sent into the black belt. By this time the battling had spread along Cottage Grove avenue and outbreaks were conspicuous at nearly every corner.

Meanwhile the fighting continued along the lake. Miss Mamie McDonald and her sister, Frances, had been bathing with a friend, Lieut. Runkle, a convalescing soldier. A colored woman walked up to the trio and made insulting remarks, it is said.

Runkle attempted to interfere, but the colored woman voiced a series of oaths and promptly struck the soldier in the face. Negroes in the vicinity hurled stones and rocks at the women and both were slightly injured.

RESERVES CALLED OUT.

In less than a half hour after the beach outbreak, Cottage Grove avenue and State street from Twenty-ninth south to Thirty-fifth were bubbling caldrons of action.

When the situation had gotten beyond the control of the Cottage Grove police, Acting Chief of Police Alcock was notified. He immediately sent out a call to every station in the city to rush all available men to the black belt.

Before they arrived colored and white men were mobbed in turn. The blacks added to the racial feeling by carrying guns and brandishing knives. It was not until the reserves arrived that the rioting was quelled.

WHITES ARM SELVES.

News of the afternoon doings had spread through all parts of the south side by nightfall, and whites stood at all prominent corners ready to avenge the beatings their brethren had received. Along Halsted and State streets they were armed with clubs, and every Negro who appeared was pommeled.

Lewis Phillips, colored, was riding in a Thirty-ninth street car, when a white man took a pot shot from the corner as the car neared Halsted street. Phillips was wounded in the groin and was taken to the Provident hospital.

Melvin Davis, colored, of 2816 Cottage Grove avenue, was waiting for a Thirty-fifth street car at Parnell avenue when he was slugged from behind. His assailants disappeared.

"THE CAUSES AND CURE" FOR THE RIOT

THE CHICAGO DAILY TRIBUNE
Negroes Call on Mayor, Lowden, to Stop Riots
July 31, 1919

VISIT CITY HALL; BLAME THE POLICE IN PART FOR RACE CLASHES.

COLORED LEADERS of Chicago joined with others yesterday in bringing about Mayor Thompson's decision to call out the state troops as a means of quitting the race riots.

They called on him in the afternoon and made a formal request to this effect, declaring police protection was inadequate, calling certain of the police indifferent, and blaming the alleged refusal of the police to arrest white lawbreakers for "the condition of anarchy which reigns today."

The colored delegation consisted of Ald. R. R. Jackson, Dr. A. J. Carey, the Rev. L. H. Williams, Ferdinand L. Barnett and F. A. Denison. They presented the mayor with two documents, approved by a conference of colored ministers, social workers, professional and business men, after two days of discussion at the Olivet Baptist church, of which the Rev. Mr. Williams is pastor.

POLICE LAX, CHARGE.

One document was entitled "An Appeal to the Public by Negro Citizens." It declared that through "this carnival of murder and assault some members of the police department have been indifferent and inadequate in furnishing protection to our people."

This appeal called on the mayor and governor to "stop the wholesale murder of our defenseless race or be held responsible by the judgment of the world for their failure to do their plain duty," and requested the mayor to appoint a committee of fifty persons, half of its members white and half colored, to consider the causes of the riots and prevent their recurrence.

FORM RACE COUNCIL.

The mayor also was informed that at the two day conference a colored council was formed, composed of the heads of all Chicago colored organizations, which is to have for its specific work the safeguarding of the colored race.

The other document was headed "The Causes and Cure for the Present Riot and Unsettled Conditions in Chicago," and represented, the delegates said, two days of deliberation. This was left with the mayor for his consideration.

"The mayor told us in his opinion this is not the time to investigate the causes of the rioting, or to appoint a committee to consider the question of preventing its recurrence," said Ald. Jackson. "He indicated, however, that when times are normal again he will grant our request that a mixed committee be appointed.

BLAME RACE ANTIPATHY.

The statement setting forth the causes and cure for the riots which, Mr. Williams said, was drafted after many conferences and prolonged discussion, is as follows:

"It is believed by many who have had a fair chance to know that the following are some of the contributing causes for the present unrest in Chicago:

"1. That race antipathy is the primary and fundamental one.

"2. That this race prejudice has manifested itself recently in many instances in minor race clashes, assaults, bomb throwing, efforts against colored people moving into certain districts, and finally in an assault made upon a colored boy last Sunday that resulted in his death.

"3. That this assault and the murder of this young colored boy by white persons was committed because he passed over the imaginary line made on the Chicago beach by whites which marked the limits in which the colored people were supposed to bathe.

BLAME POLICE NEGLIGENCE.

"4. That had the police authorities present done their duty, or showed a disposition to do so, the riot would not have found in this unfortunate occurrence anything like a just provocation.

"5. That even now the police powers of the city are inadequate in efforts to cope with the present situation.

"6. That all idlers and lawless dens of vice are contributing causes to the growth of the riot, spirit, and work; that certain laborers or industrial workers, with grievances against colored people because they have become a keen competitor with them for certain jobs, and likewise contributing causes to the life and sweep of this mob.

"7. That inflammatory newspaper writeups and comments on the race situation everywhere are fanning the flames and keeping alive the spirit of anarchy that seems to have settled down upon us.

REFER TO WAR RECORD.

"8. That many of the white people do not realize they have in Chicago's colored population a new type to deal with, one that has a distinct race consciousness, that has helped to fight its country's every battle, and that will content itself with nothing less than the full enjoyment of the privileges and rights granted under the law, one that is not seeking social contact with any race or person that bases such contact upon color and not character, past history, and not the present worth of the individual.

IRRESPONSIBLES AT FAULT.

"9. That irresponsible members of both races, persons with no property, families, no education, and sometimes no employment or anything else that would check their passions or move them to moderation are the ones making up largely, if not wholly, this riot.

"10. That, as a result of this outbreak, many innocent persons, persons who are taking no part, have had their homes burned, been assaulted, injured, murdered.

"11. That thieves and thugs have in most subtle ways incited this riot in order that they might pillage, plunder and confiscate the property of others."

HOW TO STOP THE RIOTING.

On means of curbing the riots, the document says:

"1. There should be no needless appearances and assembling of persons on the streets.

"[a] Let this be done by speakers and recognized leaders making appeals to persons disposed to frequent or congregate needlessly on the street.

"[b] By increasing the number and efficiency of police power to the extent of calling out the state militia and sufficient troops.

"2. Restore and increase the confidence of parties participating in the riot in the competency and fairness of the public powers.

"3. Close up all vice hovels, which are the breeders of crime, the covert of the lawless and the retreat of an idle, irresponsible element which feed the reckless passions so essential to the growth and life of mobs.

"ASSURE WORKERS' SAFETY."

"4. See that every man goes to work, and guarantee, by adequate police protection, his safety going to and returning from his work.

"5. Stop all public street agitation, such as is now being made by a selfish, illiterate, designing, self appointed, would be leadership. These would take this serious situation to further some veiled ends or foster some cherished selfish ambition.

"6. Have at once a joint meeting of representatives or responsible persons from both the white and colored races and publish an address to cover this situation and help prevent the spread of the spirit of lawlessness.

"7. Stop all inflammatory newspaper writeups and comments on this and other events and race differences.

ASK INDUSTRIES' AID.

"8. Let industries employing laborers help guarantee their safety and protection in going to and returning from their work.

"9. Let colored men, wherever they can, join organized labor and obtain the protection and privileges growing therefrom.

"10. Let all be calm and possess their souls, and assist in maintaining law and order."

A PROGRAM FOR "NEGRO LABOR RADICALISM"

A. PHILIP RANDOLPH
Our Reason for Being
The Messenger, August 1919

FIRST, as workers, black and white, we all have one common interest, viz., the getting of more wages, shorter hours, and better working conditions.

Black and white workers should combine for no other reason than that for which individual workers should combine, viz., to increase their bargaining power, which will enable them to get their demands.

Second, the history of the labor movement in America proves that the employing class recognize no race lines. They will exploit a white man as readily as a black man. They will exploit women as readily as men. They will even go to the extent of coining the labor, blood and suffering of children into dollars. The introduction of women and children into the factories proves that capitalists are only concerned with profits and that they will exploit any race or class in order to make profits, whether they be black or white men, black or white women or black or white children.

Third, it is apparent that every Negro worker or non-union man is a potential scab upon white union men and black union men.

Fourth, self-interest is the only principle upon which individuals or groups will act if they are sane. Thus, it is idle and vain to hope or expect Negro workers, out of work and who receive less wages when at work than white workers, to refuse to scab upon white workers when an opportunity presents itself.

Men will always seek to improve their conditions. When colored workers, as scabs, accept the wages against which white workers strike, they (the Negro workers) have definitely improved their conditions.

That is the only reason why colored workers scab upon white workers or why non-union white men scab upon white union men.

Every member, which is a part of the industrial machinery, must be organized, if labor would win its demands. Organized labor cannot afford to ignore any labor factor of production which organized capital does not ignore.

Fifth, if the employers can keep the white and black dogs, on account of race prejudice, fighting over a bone; the yellow capitalist dog will get away with the bone—the bone of profits. No union man's standard of living is safe so long as there is a group of men or women who may be used as scabs and whose standard of living is lower.

The combination of black and white workers will be a powerful lesson to the capitalists of the solidarity of labor. It will show that labor, black and white, is conscious of its interests and power. This will prove that unions are not based upon race lines, but upon class lines. This will serve to convert a class of workers, which has been used by the capitalist class to defeat organized labor, into an ardent, class conscious, intelligent, militant group.

This statement of the Negro's labor problem, together with the presentation of the radical whites, who recognize no race or color line, brought to the attention of the Union League Club's billionaires, and the Washington Chamber of Commerce, what the new Negro is thinking and Mr. Samuel Gompers, who is a member of the Chamber of Commerce himself, was no doubt promptly informed that the Negroes were getting unruly and from under control of the reactionaries and that some sop would have to be handed out or else the more radical unions would get control of them.

Sixth: The Industrial Workers of the World commonly termed, the I. W. W., draw no race, creed, color or sex line in their organization. They are making a desperate effort to get the colored men into the One Big Union. The Negroes are at least giving them an ear, and the prospects point to their soon giving them a hand. With the Industrial Workers Organization already numbering 800,000, to augment it with a million and a half or two million Negroes, would make it fairly rival the American Federation of Labor. This may still be done anyhow and the reactionaries of this country, together with Samuel Gompers, the reactionary President of the American

Federation of Labor, desire to hold back this trend of Negro labor radicalism.

Seventh: The Providence Sunday Journal of June 1st, 1919, one of the chief plutocratic mouth pieces of the country, carries a whole half page on THE MESSENGER and its labor agitation, entitled "Enrolling American Negroes Under Banners of Bolshevism." In speaking of THE MESSENGER it says: "What is advocated by THE MESSENGER, is a policy of evolution—one that will bring the Negro workers of this country into closer relationship with the white unionists—one that will make a great combination of the white and black laboring vote of this country, and, therefore, one which if brought to a successful culmination would dominate the politics and policies of the entire country."

The Providence Journal continues, "The publication in the U. S., spreading this insidious propaganda among Negroes, is THE MESSENGER. It is published at 2305 Seventh Avenue, New York City, *by two as well read, well educated and competent Negroes as there are in the United States.* They are A. Philip Randolph and Chandler Owen, and as a contributing editor, they have Dr. George Frazier Miller, one of the best known Negro divines in New York City. The publication is well gotten up, well printed and in every way put together in a manner which would appeal to the people that it is intended to reach."

After writing a whole half page on the propaganda being carried on by THE MESSENGER magazine and the National Association for the Promotion of Labor Unionism Among Negroes the Providence Journal also quotes the preamble of the National Association for the Promotion of Labor Unionism Among Negroes.

Eighth: The New York World, the mouth piece of the present administration, and also a plutocratic mouth piece, says in its issue of June 4, 1919, "The radical forces in New York City have recently embarked on a great new field of revolutionary endeavor, the education through agitation of the southern Negro into the mysteries and desirability of revolutionary Bolshevism. There are several different powerful forces in N. Y. City behind this move. The chief established propaganda is being distributed through THE MESSENGER, which styles itself

—"The only magazine of scientific radicalism in the world, published by Negroes." Its editors are A. Philip Randolph and Chandler Owen, with George Frazier Miller, contributing editor. This radical journal is published at 2305 Seventh Ave., New York City. With the exception of The Liberator, it is the most radical journal printed in the U. S.

In the issue of the New York World, June 8th, Sunday edition, a special article, almost a page long on "Methods Used by Radicals to Destroy the Influence of The American Federation of Labor," the following quotation was taken from the MESSENGER: "The dissolution of the American Federation of Labor would inure to the benefit of the Labor Movement in this country in particular, and to the International Labor Movement in general. Why? In the first place it is organized upon unsound principles. It holds that there can be a partnership between capital and labor. Think of it! A partnership between the exploiter and the exploited! Between the spider and the fly! Between the lion and the lamb! Between the cat and the mouse!"

The foregoing comments from such powerful organs as The Providence Sunday Journal, The New York Sunday World, The National Civic Federation Review and the Union League Club of New York, followed by action of the Legislature of the State of New York—demonstrates how powerful is the influence of a well written, logical publication, fighting for the interests of twelve million Negroes in particular and the working masses in general. These are the real reasons why the American Federation of Labor decided to lay aside its infamous color line. There is no change of heart on the part of the Federation, but it is acting under the influence of fear. There is a new leadership for Negro workers. It is a leadership of uncompromising manhood. It is not asking for a half loaf but for the whole loaf. It is insistent upon the Negro workers exacting justice, both from the white labor unions and from the capitalists or employers.

The Negroes who will benefit from this decision are indebted first to themselves and their organized power, which made them dangerous. Second, to the radical agitation carried on by the MESSENGER; and third, to the fine spirit of welcome shown by the Industrial Workers of the World, whose rapid growth and increasing power the American Federation of

Labor fears. These old line Negro political fossils know nothing of the Labor Movement, do not believe in labor unions at all, and have never taken any active steps to encourage such organizations. We make this statement calmly, coolly and with a reasonable reserve. The very thing which they are fighting is one of the chief factors in securing for Negroes their rights. That is Bolshevism. The capitalists of this country are so afraid that Negroes will become Bolshevists that they are willing to offer them almost anything to hold them away from the radical movement. Nobody buys pebbles which may be picked up on the beach, but diamonds sell high. The old line Negro leaders have no power to bargain, because it is known that they are Republicans politically and job-hunting, me-too-boss-hat-in-hand-Negroes, industrially. Booker Washington and all of them have simply advocated that Negroes get more work. The editors of the MESSENGER are not interested in Negroes getting more work. Negroes have too much work already. What we want Negroes to get is less work and more wages, with more leisure for study and recreation.

Our type of agitation has really won for Negroes such concessions as were granted by the American Federation of Labor and we are by no means too sanguine over the possibilities of the sop which was granted. It may be like the Constitution of the United States—good in parts, but badly executed. We shall have to await the logic of events. In the meantime, we urge the Negro labor unions to increase their radicalism, to speed up their organization, to steer clear of the Negro leaders and to thank nobody but themselves for what they have gained. In organization there is strength, and whenever Negroes or anybody else make organized demands, their call will be heeded.

"FOR A FREE AND INDEPENDENT RACE"
MARCUS GARVEY
Speech in New York City
August 25, 1919

Lady Chairman, Ladies and Gentlemen: I am here tonight to represent the interests of the Universal Negro Improvement Association and African Communities League of the World.

I am here, not representing 100,000 people in New York of the race, but 15,000,000 negroes in the United States of America; 15,000,000 negroes in the West Indian Islands, and the negroes of South and Central America, and the 280,000,000 on the continent of Africa. (Applause).

We speak tonight from Carnegie Hall to the 400,000,000 of our people scattered all over the world.

We are here because the times demand that we be here. We are now living in a world that is reorganizing itself. It is reorganizing itself out of a bloody war as fought for four and one-half years, a war in which men were called out from all parts of the world, from the four corners of the world, to die for the sacred cause of democracy; to give liberty to all mankind; to make all men free; and in the war as fought for 4 1/2 years, they took out 2,000,000 black men from America, from the West Indies and Africa, to fight for this farcical democracy they told us about; and now we are, after winning the fight, winning the battle, we realize that we are without democracy; and we come before the world, therefore, as the Universal Improvement Association, to demand our portion of democracy (applause); and we say woe betide the man or the nation who stands in the way of the negro fighting for democracy!

We stand here tonight as the Universal Negro Improvement Association, on the same uncompromising platform as the Irish stand, as the Hindu stands, as the Egyptian stands, and we say "We shall not yield one inch of our rights until we get all belonging to us". (Applause). For three hundred years, the white tyrant of the world encompassed us as slaves and made us peons. Between 1914 and 1918, a new doctrine was taught to the world, the doctrine of right.

To maintain that doctrine, thousands of negroes out of 2,000,000 called, died on the battle-fields of France and Flanders. We died there gladly, thinking that we were shedding our blood for a real cause. After that blood is shed we now realize that it was a farcical cause; that we have found out our mistake before it is too late; we say we shall continue the war until we get democracy. (Applause).

We stand here determined and absolute in our rights. President Woodrow Wilson entered this war on the principle of democracy. He mobilized the strength of this country for that sacred cause. England, that great Anglo-Saxon Empire or Nation, heralded to the world that she was fighting the cause of humanity, and caused President Wilson to deliver to her the strength of the American Nation; and through the declaration of England, the negroes scattered in the West Indies, in Central America, and Africa, rallied to the colors of the Allied Nations.

We fought, and after the battle what was done to us? They mobbed us in Liverpool, in London and Manchester. The English in Wales stopped the funeral procession of the West Indian negro, smashed the coffin, cut off the head of the dead man and made a football of it (cries of "Shame"). The British did that in Great Britain.

In America, below the Mason and Dixon Line, what did they do to Mary Turner? Oh, I will not repeat because it is common knowledge to the world.

Now, in the face of the continuity of such outrages, how can the new negro of today, that same negro who fought in France and Flanders be satisfied with this farcical democracy in the world? (Applause and Cries of "No").

We shall not be satisfied. Therefore we declare this: We, who have survived the war, that the same blood our brothers gave in France and Flanders to free the whites, the Belgians and the Serbians, the same blood we are prepared at any time to shed in the emancipation of the negro race. (Great applause).

The white man of the world has been accustomed to deal with the Uncle Tom cringing negro. Up to 1918, he knew no other negro than the negro represented through Booker

Washington. Today he will find that a new negro is on the stage representing the spirit of the [   ].

We are fifteen millions in America; we are fifteen or twenty millions in the West Indies; and two hundred and eighty millions on the continent of Africa, and we have declared for a free and independent race.

In this re-construction period, when the Irishman is striking homewards towards Ireland to make Ireland a free and independent country, when the Hindu is striking homeward toward India to make India a free and independent nation and empire, the negro says—the negroes of the world say "We are striking homewards towards Africa to make her the big black republic" (applause), and in the making of Africa a big, black republic, what is the barrier? The barrier is the white man; and we say to the white man who now dominates Africa, that it is to his interests to clear out of Africa now (applause), because we are coming, not as in the time of Father Abraham, 200,000 strong, but we are coming 400,000,000 strong (applause); and we mean to re-take every square inch of the 12,000,000 square miles of African territory belonging to us by right divine. (Applause).

They say to us in East St. Louis, "We do not want you here". They say to us in Chicago, "We don't want you here". They say to us in Washington, "We don't want you here", in America— They say to us in Liverpool, "We don't want you here", and so in Manchester and Cardiff, and in other parts of Great Britain —the audacity of the white man after keeping the negro in America in slavery for 250 years! That negro, through his sacrifice, through his blood, has made America what it is today. (Great applause).

That same audacious white man kept the negro in the West Indies in slavery for 230 years, and through the blood and sacrifice of the West Indian negro, the British Empire became a possibility; and the Englishman says "We don't want you— I don't want you in Liverpool, in Manchester or in London —black man". Aint it time now for the black man to think of turning to the white man and saying "I don't want you here"? (Applause). And if we have come to that stage in America, where the white man is in America ninety million whilst we are only fifteen, and if he says it in England where he dominates the country, must we not say it therefore in the world where we dominate by numbers? That is the question; and as the Englishman asked the negro in Liverpool and Manchester what he is doing there, so the new negro means, within the next 20 years, to ask the white man in the continent of Africa, "What are you doing here?" (Applause).

This African question is one that every negro must understand now or never. Every American negro and every West Indian negro must understand now that there is but one fatherland for the negro, and that is Africa. (Applause). And as the Germans fought and struggled for the fatherland of Germany; as the Irishman is struggling and fighting for the fatherland of Ireland, so must the new negro of the world fight for the fatherland of Africa (applause), because if we allow the white man to continue in his old-time ways, it will mean that in the next fifty years there will be very few negroes left in the world. (Laughter.)

You remember what the white man did to the North American Indian. What he did—he exterminated him. When the white man wanted to find a place and the Indians stood in his path, he cleared the Indians from his path; and today the Indian is underground. When he did that, he was building up civilization for himself. He was building a new world for himself. He succeeded in building the new world, but what happened? Between 1914 and 1918, the white man of the world destroyed what it took him 2,000 years to build. (Applause). And today he is where he was two thousand years ago (applause).

Therefore, he is going to restart something. What is that something? He is going to restart that thing he started hundreds of years ago—exterminating and robbing all those who stand in his way; and not long ago you remember what he did to us. Three hundred years ago only, he made slaves of us; and at the time when he made slaves of us, he was better off than he is now (laughter), because he was not nearly bankrupt. Today he is a bankrupt (laughter). The Englishman is a bankrupt. The Frenchman is a bankrupt. The German, the Austrian, the Russian—all are bankrupts (laughter); AND YOU KNOW a hungry man makes no fuss. If a man is hungry and he sees bread in his way he is going to take it and grab it, caring not to whom it belongs. A bankrupt man is like a hungry man.

It means, therefore, that the one country in the world that has wealth, mineral, agricultural and otherwise, is the great continent of Africa, and this arch-lover of the world—his eyes are now centered on the Continent of Africa. The Englishman's eyes are centered on the Continent of Africa. The Frenchman's eyes are centered on Africa; so with the Italians and the Germans; but the poor Germans have not a look-in. (Laughter).

It is their fault, anyhow. The Kaiser had no right to start any war; but anyhow, the wars that the Kaiser started suited our purpose (great applause); and therefore we are not indebted to the Kaiser at all. We have no fault to find with this man at all because in four and a half years he had negroes in New York who, in 1913 used to work for $20 a week—he helped them to get $80 a week. (Laughter and Applause). And if he had kept up this thing a little longer, some of us would have been better off tonight. But anyhow, he was defeated, and who defeated him—the black man. (Applause). It took the black man to whip the Kaiser's soldiers, and up to now there is not a more glorious record in the history of the war than the record of those two boys from the New York 15th (applause)—Needham Roberts and Johnson have proved to the Kaiser that the negro is more than a match for the German soldier; but Needham Roberts and Johnson were fighting somebody else's battle, and even though they knew they were fighting for someone else, they did half of their best, now. (Applause).

Now, when those boys and the four hundred millions of us start to fight for ourselves, what will happen? (Great applause). That is the question—that is the question for the white man to solve; and if he takes my advice, he will solve it quick (applause), because the new negro means business.

If any Englishman, if any German, if any Frenchman, if any white American man thinks that the new negro is going down on his knees to beg anything to-day, he makes a big mistake (Applause).

We are out to get what has belonged to us, politically, socially, economically and in every way (applause); and what fifteen millions of us can not get, we will call in the four hundred millions to help us get. (Applause).

Hence the Universal Negro Improvement Association comes before you tonight, not representative of any one section of negroes in the world, but of all the sections.

We are as much American as we are British; we are as much British as we are French; we are as much French as we are German (laughter)—because there is a terrible mix-up (laughter). We did not mix ourselves up; they mixed us up (laughter).

In the fight of the Universal Negro Improvement Association, as the Chairlady said to you a while ago, this Association was first founded on the Island of Jamaica, and 21 months ago was founded in the United States of America. We started in New York with thirteen members, and in the space of 21 months, what has happened? We have made 5,500 members in the district of Harlem alone. We are scattered with twelve branches, and some of the branches out of New York are stronger than the New York branch.

We are at places like Virginia. In Newport News, Virginia, there are 5,000 members there (applause). We have branches of our Association in 25 States of the Union. We have branches of our Association in every West Indian Island (laughter) and Central America, and more than all men, we stand doubly strong on the West coast of Africa. (Applause).

All that we have to do in New York is to press the button, and later on—(great applause)—and later on we really mean to press the button.

Those crackers of the South who have been lynching our brothers and sisters, our mothers and our fathers and our children for over 15 years, they have been doing that thing, because they realize that in America there are ninety millions of white people, whilst there are only 15,000,000 of black. They realize by strength of numbers they will be able to take advantage of us; and they have been getting away with their cowardice, because we were not an organized people; but in the next few months we will be so organized so that when they lynch a negro below the Mason and Dixon Line, if we can not lynch a white man there, and since it is not safe to lynch a white man in any part of America, we shall press the button and lynch him in the great continent of Africa. (Great applause and much excitement).

From time immemorial, we have been told that the white man represents God (laughter); that the angels are white (laughter); that the very Heavens are draped in white; and all that is pure, all that is good and sublime, is white. They were able to tell us that for 300 years. Now, I wonder *if* they have the nerve to continue to think that they can tell us that now. (Laughter). We have caught the new doctrine. The white man says that everything that is pure is white. The yellow man of Asia is saying that everything that is pure is yellow. The black man is saying that everything that is pure is black (applause); and according to the white man's doctrine, if the Beings who preside over the two worlds other than this one, and I mean the eternal worlds, the one called God, and the one called the devil, if those two Beings have the semblance of mankind, then, as the white man has been saying all the time that the devil is black, and God is white, we are going to say that God is black and the devil is white (laughter), because if you are to compare men by their ways, if you are to compare the Deities therefore, that have connection with man both ways, we can easily see who is the devil today. Why? Tell me how many people the blacks have killed within recent years on their own initiative? I can not think of any. How many have the whites killed, of their own initiative—over ten millions, just a few days ago, and they were not satisfied in doing the killing themselves. They had to call out two million black men to help them kill (applause); and because we were unable to help ourselves, because we had no organization, we had to go out and kill, even though we had no cause against those who were killing. (Cries of "No" and applause). But why were we not organized—because we had negroes of America like Booker Washington, to be succeeded by Russey Moton. We had negroes in the West Indies like those frothy negroes there who have been always bowing down to white men, because we had not the right kind of negroes in Africa, and therefore, the white man found us napping in 1914, and he was able to say, "Come on here, negro of America, go fight and die"; "Come out here, West Indian negro, go fight and die"; "Come out here African negro and fight and die. You are fighting for democracy", and we had to go.

But there is one thing we are going to do now. We are going

to so organize ourselves all over the world that when the white men say—any white man wants a black man to die in the future, they have to tell us what we are going to die for. (Applause).

The first dying that is to be done by the black man in the future will be done to make himself free. (Applause). And then when we are finished, if we have any charity to bestow, we may die for the white man; but, as for me, I think I have stopped dying for him. I do not know what you have to say about that (uproar and cries of "Yes"). Thank you. Therefore, all of us who are here representing the spirit of the new negro (cries of "We do" and applause), and that therefore will give the lie to the New York Times of a few days ago, that published yesterday, that published some news from Washington wherein it said that in New York City there is a movement led by the Bolshevists and the I.W.W. and the movement is striking out to make the negro independent. I want to answer the Times from Carnegie Hall tonight. The Times seems to believe (applause) —the Times still seems to believe that they are dealing still with Booker Washington.

Now, I hope the Times will correct that wrong impression and go out tomorrow morning and tell the world as was told on Sunday, that the new negro need no other leadership but his own (applause). We are in this Universal movement that is encircling the world. We are neither Democrats nor Republicans nor Socialists nor Bolshevists nor I.W.W.'s (applause), because whether we are Democrats, Republicans, Socialists or I.W.W.'s, all of them are white men, and when they were robbing us from Africa, they robbed us with all parties—Republicans, Socialists, Democrats, I.W.W.'s, and everybody settled us and brought us here (laughter); therefore, we are not going to waste time over the white man's politics. All the time we have to waste is with pro-negro politics (applause).

We belong to a new party—the party that means we will never stop fighting constitutionally—in countries like America and Africa, where we respect no constitution we will continue to fight, and fight until we make ourselves a great people—the new race that is to be (applause).

My allegiance to America has been questioned. Now, let me answer that accusation from Carnegie Hall. If there is one country in the world I love, that country is America.

(Applause). Why do I love America? Because America was founded upon the principles of liberty, and America has always offered the opportunity and inducements to all peoples who were in search of liberty to come here and agitate the question of liberty. (Applause).

America helped the Irish. America helped the Jew. America helped the people of the Eastern states of Russia to air their grievance to the world, and for those principles I love America —and for those principles only. (Applause).

And, as the Irish came and spoke from this Carnegie Hall; as the Russians came and spoke from this Carnegie Hall; and some will get what they agitated for—and the Irish are going to get theirs—so do we come tonight to agitate so as to get ours.

The Irish have been fighting for over 700 years to free Ireland. From the time when Robert Emmett, when he lost his head, to the time of Roger Casement, Ireland has been fighting, agitating and offering up her sons as martyrs.

As Emmett bled and died for Ireland, so we who are leading the Universal Negro Improvement Association, are prepared at any time to free Africa and free the negroes of the world. (Applause).

So I trust that everybody understands the platform on which the Universal Negro Improvement Association stands. It is on a platform of manhood rights. We say if it is right for the white man to rule, to dominate, if it is right for the yellow man of Asia to rule and dominate, it is time for the negro to rule and to dominate (applause), because God created of one blood all nations of men to dwell upon the earth. He never said to the white man,—"You are to be the perpetual master and lord, and negroes must be your slaves". Although the white man had been so bad and wicked as to write a thing called the Bible and put in there and say that black men shall be "hewers of wood and drawers of water" (applause and laughter)—The white man put that there and expects that 20th Century negroes to believe that (laughter). Now, we believe in everything in the Bible except that. (Cries of "No").

Now, if there is any one man in the world, whether he is an American white man or an English white man, or a French white man who thinks he can get me to chop his wood, let him come—or draw his water—let him come.

So, I want you all to understand, therefore, that the Universal Negro Improvement Association stands on a platform of manly rights. We want to see our men occupying positions in the world as white men are occupying; (Applause); as Asiatic men are occupying. We want to see our women occupying positions and stations in life as white women and yellow women are occupying (applause).

We say that the time for the negro woman to leave the kitchen is now (applause); and we of the Universal Negro Improvement Association swear by everything that is in this creation, swear by the Almighty God, that we are going to make a new race out of this negro race (applause); and that brings me to our great proposition known as the Black Star Line. (Applause).

There is a corporation organized and chartered by the State of Delaware, known as the Black Star Line; and fortunately, or unfortunately, I am also President of that corporation, and also President of the Universal Negro Improvement Association. (Applause).

I am lending my influence, the influence I have in America, and the influence I have in the West Indies, Central America and South America, places where I have lived and travelled for years before I came to America—I am using my influence to make the Black Star Line a possibility on the 31st of October of this year. (Applause).

That corporation is capitalized at $500,000. Within a few months its capital will increase to $10,000,000 (applause); and we are now putting on the market the $500,000 of common stock of par value of $5.00 a share, and we are asking every negro in New York City to own as many shares as possible in the Black Star Line. If you cannot own 100 shares, own 50; if not 50, own 20, 10, 5 or one; but we want every negro in Carnegie Hall tonight to be a stockholder in the Black Star Line, so as to be one of its owners. (Applause).

The West Indian negroes in the West Indies, and the South American negroes and Central American negroes are doing their part. We are selling as many shares through our branches in the West Indies and in Central America, as we are selling in America; and tonight I am asking when the ushers present to you the application slips for stocks, to write your names down, and put down as many shares as you can afford to buy. Pin your money on to the application blank. The usher will give you a receipt for the money, and tonight or tomorrow or any day of this week you can get your stock certificates. Those of you who can remain behind long enough, you can get your certificates from the Treasurer here tonight. Those of you who can not wait to get your stock certificates, you can call at our office, 56 West 135th Street tomorrow, or any day next week, and get your stock certificate; but tonight we want every one of you to subscribe for shares in the Black Star Line, as the ushers hand you subscription blanks, and I want you to do it quietly while Dr. Shaw will speak.

I am called an orator, but Dr. Shaw is a greater orator, and you are going to hear him tonight. (Applause).

The things I can not touch on, the things I can not touch on because I am not an American citizen, Dr. Shaw will touch on because he is an American citizen. (Applause). I am not an American citizen not because I do not want to be an American citizen. I would have been too glad to become an American citizen tomorrow morning, but time will not permit me, because in the very near future I will have to travel into other parts of the world; and with the Universal Negro Improvement movement, the country that has the most negroes under her flag today is Great Britain, and I was born under the flag of Britain. (Applause). Britain kept me a slave for 230 years, and Britain will have to tell me the reason why; and when I go to Britain I do not want them to say to me "You are an American citizen", because those Britons are the greatest camoufleurs in the world. When they wanted the help of America, there is nobody as dear as the American. When the American wants justice, there is nobody so hideous as the American; but I say Britain will have to tell me why she kept me a slave for 230 years.

If David Lloyd George, if Herbert Asquith, if Bonar Law, and Arthur J. Balfour think that I, standing here tonight, am afraid of them, then wait until I get in London when I meet them in the Royal Albert Hall. (Applause). They might have succeeded in driving those Africans and West Indian negroes out of London, but they will have to do some driving to get me out (applause), because they say—"You are a British subject; you are a British citizen"; and I shall claim my right of citizenship, and I shall go to Trafalgar Square, as Mrs. Pankhurst went there; as Ramsay MacDonald went there; as all the other fighters for the cause of liberty went there. I shall go to Clapham Common, Hyde Park, Trafalgar Square, and I will go also to the Royal Albert Hall and tell the white man in England what I think of him; and I feel sure that the Bonar Law and A. J. Balfour class, when they are ready to fight the negroes of Africa, they will have to fight themselves, when I am through with the English workman.

My duty is to let the English workman know that his cause is the negro's cause; (applause); and that he has absolutely no right to fight the negro, to make Balfour, Bonar Law, and those idle bluffing class, continue to fool the world.

So I am going to take my seat now.

I want every one of you here to subscribe for as many shares in the Black Star Line as possible. Buy them up tonight, writing your names down, or addresses, and the number of stocks you want and pass the money and the application blanks to the ushers. I thank you. (Applause).

"THE NEW NEGRO HAS ARRIVED"

W. A. DOMINGO AND CLAUDE MCKAY
If We Must Die
The Messenger, September 1919

AMERICA won the war that was alleged to be fought for the purpose of making the world safe for democracy, but in the light of recent happenings in Washington, the Capital city, and Chicago, it would seem as though the United States is not a part of the world. In order to win the war President Wilson employed "force, unstinted force," and those who expect to bring any similar desirable termination to a just cause can do no less than follow the splendid example set them by the reputed spokesman of humanity. That the lesson did not take long to penetrate the minds of Negroes is demonstrated by the change that has taken place in their demeanor and tactics. No longer are Negroes willing to be shot down or hunted from place to place like wild beasts; no longer will they flee from their homes and leave their property to the tender mercies of the howling and cowardly mob. They have changed, and now they intend to give men's account of themselves. If death is to be their portion, New Negroes are determined to make their dying a costly investment for all concerned. If they must die they are determined that they shall not travel through the valley of the shadow of death alone, but that some of their oppressors shall be their companions.

This new spirit is but a reflex of the great war, and it is largely due to the insistent and vigorous agitation carried on by younger men of the race. The demand is uncompromisingly made for either liberty or death, and since death is likely to be a two-edged sword it will be to the advantage of those in a position to do so to give the race its long-denied liberty.

The new spirit animating Negroes is not confined to the United States, where it is most acutely manifested, but is simmering beneath the surface in every country where the race is oppressed. The Washington and Chicago outbreaks should be regarded as symptoms of a great pandemic, and the Negroes as courageous surgeons who performed the necessary though painful operation. That the remedy is efficacious is beyond question. It has brought results, for as a consequence the eyes of the entire world are focused upon the racial situation in the United States. The world knows now that the New Negroes are determined to observe the primal law of self-preservation whenever civil laws break down; to assist the authorities to preserve order and prevent themselves and families from being murdered in cold blood. Surely, no one can sincerely object to this new and laudable determination. Justification for this course is not lacking, for it is the white man's own Bible that says "Those who live by the sword shall perish by the sword," and since white men believe in force, Negroes who have mimicked them for nearly three centuries must copy them in that respect. Since fire must be fought with hell fire, and diamond alone can cut diamond, Negroes realize that force alone is an effective medium to counteract force. Counter irritants are useful in curing diseases, and Negroes are being driven by their white fellow citizens to investigate the curative values inherent in mass action, revolvers and other lethal devices when applied to social diseases.

The New Negro has arrived with stiffened back bone, dauntless manhood, defiant eye, steady hand and a will of iron. His creed is admirably summed up in the poem of Claude McKay, the black Jamaican poet, who is carving out for himself a niche in the Hall of Fame:

IF WE MUST DIE

If we must die, let it not be like hogs
    Hunted and penned in an inglorious spot,
While round us bark the mad and hungry dogs,
    Making their mock at our accursed lot.
If we must die, oh, let us nobly die,
    So that our precious blood may not be shed
In vain; then even the monsters we defy
    Shall be constrained to honor us, though dead!

Oh, kinsmen! We must meet the common foe;
    Though far outnumbered, let us still be brave,
And for their thousand blows deal one death-blow!
    What though before us lies the open grave?
Like men we'll face the murderous, cowardly pack,
    Pressed to the wall, dying, but—fighting back!

                                        W. A. D.

CHRONOLOGY

NOTE ON THE TEXTS

NOTES

INDEX

Chronology

1877   Congress creates fifteen-member commission to resolve disputed 1876 presidential election between Republican Rutherford B. Hayes and Democrat Samuel J. Tilden. The commission awards all of the contested electoral votes to Hayes in a series of 8–7 votes. Democrats drop plans to obstruct the final count in the House of Representatives with the understanding that Hayes will end military protection for the remaining Republican state governments in the South. In April President Hayes withdraws federal troops guarding the statehouses in Columbia and New Orleans, allowing Democrats to take over the governorships of South Carolina and Louisiana, completing the "redemption" of the South and signaling the end of Reconstruction. (The commission awarded Hayes the electoral votes of South Carolina, Florida, and Louisiana. Republican candidates will win six out of the ten presidential elections held from 1880 to 1916 without receiving any electoral votes from the former Confederate states.) The new Forty-fifth Congress meets in the fall with one black senator and three black representatives, compared with one senator and seven representatives in the preceding Forty-fourth Congress, all from southern states. (There will be no black representation in the Senate after 1881 until 1967, and the number of black representatives serving in the House will vary from three to none from 1879 to 1901.) Georgia adopts state constitution making the payment of poll tax a prerequisite for voting. Black settlers found the town of Nicodemus as part of ongoing black migration to Kansas from Kentucky, Tennessee, and Mississippi.

1878   In *Hall v. Decuir* the U.S. Supreme Court unanimously rules that an 1869 Louisiana law forbidding racial discrimination in transportation unconstitutionally infringes on the power of Congress to regulate interstate commerce. Congress passes Posse Comitatus Act severely restricting the use of the army in domestic law enforcement. In fall elections Democrats gain control of both houses of Congress for the first time since 1859. Republicans protest widespread violence, intimidation, and fraud used to suppress the black vote in Louisiana, South Carolina, and Mississippi. Soprano Marie Selika Williams, the "queen of staccato," performs for President Hayes and First Lady Lucy Webb Hayes, making her the first black artist to perform at the White House.

1879 About six thousand black "Exodusters" migrate to Kansas from Louisiana, Mississippi, and Texas. Biracial coalition of white and black voters gives control of the Virginia legislature to the Readjuster Party, which seeks to refinance the state debt to preserve funding for the segregated public school system established during Reconstruction.

1880 U.S. Senate select committee holds hearings to investigate the highly publicized "Negro Exodus" from the South. U.S. Supreme Court rules in *Strauder v. West Virginia* that laws excluding black men from jury service violate the Fourteenth Amendment while holding in *Virginia v. Rives* that black defendants are not constitutionally entitled to a racially mixed jury.

1881 Tennessee legislature enacts a law requiring railroads to provide separate accommodations for black travelers. Tuskegee Normal School for Colored Teachers (later known as the Tuskegee Normal and Industrial Institute, now Tuskegee University) is founded in Macon County, Alabama on July 4, with Booker T. Washington as its principal.

1882 South Carolina legislature passes "eight box law," a complex balloting procedure designed to disenfranchise black voters. Readjuster majority in the Virginia legislature eliminates poll tax as requirement for voting.

1883 In *Pace v. Alabama*, the U.S. Supreme Court unanimously upholds the convictions of Tony Pace and Mary J. Cox, who were indicted in 1881 for violating a section of Alabama Code making it illegal for black and white people to "intermarry or live in adultery or fornication." The *Pace* decision sets a precedent upholding the constitutionality of state laws prohibiting interracial marriage. A white conductor forcibly removes Ida B. Wells from a train on the Chesapeake, Ohio & Southwestern Railroad in Tennessee on September 15 after Wells refuses to give up her seat in the first-class ladies' car. In the *Civil Rights Cases* the U.S. Supreme Court overturns almost all the provisions of the

1875 Civil Rights Act, ruling 8–1 that the Thirteenth and Fourteenth Amendments do not forbid private businesses from engaging in racial discrimination. After a riot on November 3 in Danville, Virginia, white Democrats seize control of the local government. Democrats defeat Readjusters in Virginia elections and regain control of the legislature.

1884   Grover Cleveland becomes the first Democrat to win a presidential election since 1856. Wells wins lawsuit against Chesapeake, Ohio & Southwestern when circuit court judge awards her $500 in damages, ruling that the railroad had failed to provide her with the accommodations her first-class ticket entitled her to. (Her lawsuit is one of several brought by black plaintiffs in the 1880s challenging the segregation policies of railroad and steamship companies.)

1886   In Carroll County, Mississippi, Ed and Charley Brown, two brothers of black and Indigenous ancestry, press charges against James Liddell, a white attorney and newspaper editor, for attempted murder. About fifty armed white men attack the courthouse in Carrollton, Mississippi, on March 17 and open fire, killing the Brown brothers and eleven other black men.

1887   Tennessee Supreme Court reverses circuit court decision in Wells's lawsuit. Florida legislature passes law requiring railroads to segregate passengers by race.

1888   Mississippi passes railroad segregation law. Benjamin Harrison defeats Cleveland in the presidential election as Republicans win control of the House and retain their Senate majority, giving the party control of the White House and both chambers of Congress for the first time since 1875.

1889   Texas passes railroad segregation law. Florida legislature enacts "eight box law" and makes payment of poll tax requirement for voting. Reports later compiled by the Tuskegee Institute record the lynching of 534 black persons in the United States from 1882 to 1889.

1890   T. Thomas Fortune, editor of the *New York Age*, organizes the first meeting of the National Afro-American League (NAAL) in January. In *Louisville, New Orleans & Texas Railway Co. v. Mississippi*, the Supreme Court rules 7–2 that the 1888 Mississippi railroad segregation law requiring separate but equal accommodations for black and white passengers does not violate the interstate commerce clause of the Constitution. Black settlers begin founding autonomous towns in Oklahoma. In an attempt to protect black suffrage in the South, Republicans introduce bill authorizing federal officials to supervise voter registration, polling procedures, and ballot counting in congressional elections. The bill passes the House, 155–149, but is filibustered in the Senate. Louisiana legislature passes law requiring railway companies to provide "equal but separate accommodations" for white and black passengers. Mississippi convention controlled by white Democrats adopts a new state constitution that uses poll taxes and literacy tests to disenfranchise black and poor white voters. In the fall elections the Democrats regain control of the House of Representatives.

1891 Alabama, Arkansas, Georgia, and Tennessee enact laws mandating railroad segregation.

1892 A white mob lynches Thomas Moss, owner of the successful People's Grocery in Memphis, along with two store employees, Calvin McDowell and Will Stewart. The murders prompt their friend Ida B. Wells to publish her pamphlet *Southern Horrors: Lynch Law in All Its Phases* and begin public speaking tour against lynching. Arkansas makes payment of poll tax a requirement for voting. Kentucky passes railroad segregation law. Cleveland defeats Harrison in presidential election as Democrats gain control of both houses of Congress.

1893 Henry Smith is tortured and burned alive in Paris, Texas, before a crowd of ten thousand spectators. Lack of resources and political support causes National Afro-American League to disband. Ida B. Wells and Frederick Douglass collaborate on pamphlet *The Reason Why the Colored American is not in the World's Columbian Exposition*.

1894 Democrats in Congress repeal several acts passed during Reconstruction to enforce the Fifteenth Amendment. So-called Fusion alliance of black and white Republicans and white Populists wins control of the North Carolina legislature.

1895 Ida B. Wells publishes pamphlet *A Red Record*, which uses newspaper coverage to document the rise in lynching in the South. Booker T. Washington gives an address on race and southern society at the Cotton States and International Exposition in Atlanta that propels him into the national spotlight. The National Baptist Convention is formed from the merger of three earlier conventions and emerges as a denomination distinct from the white Northern Baptist and Southern Baptist conventions. Voyages organized by Bishop Henry McNeal Turner carry over five hundred emigrants to Liberia in West Africa (some of the migrants later return). South Carolina adopts new constitution that uses poll taxes and literacy tests to disenfranchise black voters. (South Carolina and Mississippi constitutions have "understanding" clauses that allow election officials to register illiterate white voters.)

1896 The U.S. Supreme Court rules 7–1 in *Plessy v. Ferguson* that the Louisiana railroad segregation law does not violate the Fourteenth Amendment. The National Association of Colored Women forms on July 21 and elects Mary Church Terrell as its president. Booker T. Washington appoints George Washington Carver as director of agricultural research at Tuskegee Institute. Fusion alliance elects governor in North Carolina.

1898 In *Williams v. Mississippi*, the U.S. Supreme Court unanimously rejects a challenge to the 1890 Mississippi constitution, ruling that its suffrage provisions do not violate the Fourteenth Amendment because they "do not on their face discriminate between the races, and it has not been shown that their actual administration was evil; only that evil was possible under them." Louisiana adopts new constitution that uses poll taxes and literacy tests to disenfranchise black voters and a grandfather clause that permits the registration for a limited time of white voters who fail to meet the literacy requirement. South Carolina passes railroad segregation law. T. Thomas Fortune and Bishop Alexander Walters form the Afro-American Council (AAC) in Rochester, New York, to combat segregation and discrimination. Democrats regain control of the North Carolina legislature in election marked by widespread intimidation and fraud. On November 10, two days after the election, a white supremacist militia stages a violent coup that overthrows the biracial Fusionist city government in Wilmington; at least fourteen and perhaps as many as sixty black men are murdered during the insurrection.

1899   A white mob lynches Sam Hose (Wilkes), a black farmworker, in Newnan, Georgia, on April 23. Later in the year Ida B. Wells-Barnett describes his torture and mutilation at the hands of the mob in her pamphlet *Lynch Law in Georgia*. Tuskegee Institute archives record the lynching of 1,111 black persons from 1890 to 1899. North Carolina enacts law segregating passengers on railroads and steamboats.

1900   George H. White of North Carolina, the only black representative in Congress, introduces a bill on January 20 to make lynching a federal crime and treat it as "treason against the Government of the United States." The bill is referred to the House Judiciary Committee and never acted upon. Virginia enacts law requiring segregation on railroads and steamboats. Robert Charles kills two white New Orleans police officers after an altercation on the night of July 23, triggering rioting in which white mobs kill five black persons. Violence continues until July 27, when Charles kills two more police officers and three white onlookers before being shot to death. North Carolina adopts constitutional amendment on suffrage imposing poll taxes and literacy requirement and containing grandfather clause.

1901   House of Representatives debates proposal to reduce the congressional representation of Louisiana, Mississippi, South Carolina, and North Carolina because of their disenfranchisement of black voters. The proposal is rejected, 136–94. George H. White gives valedictory address in the House of Representatives on January 29. (After White's term ends in March, no black representative will serve in Congress until 1929, when Oscar De Priest, a Republican from Chicago, takes his seat.) Alabama convention adopts new state constitution designed to disenfranchise black voters through literacy and property qualifications and poll taxes; the suffrage provisions include a grandfather clause. Booker T. Washington becomes the first black American to dine at the White House when he has dinner with President Theodore Roosevelt and his family on October 16. The dinner is widely condemned in the South as a move toward "social equality." (No other black American will be a social guest at the White House until 1929, when Jessie De Priest, the wife of Representative De Priest, has tea with First Lady Lou Hoover and several other congressional wives.)

1902	Virginia adopts new constitution intended to disenfranchise black voters, with suffrage provisions that include literacy and property qualifications, poll taxes, and a grandfather clause. Texas adopts constitutional amendment instituting a poll tax. Louisiana enacts law segregating streetcar passengers.
1903	*The Souls of Black Folk*, a collection of essays on race and black life in the United States by the sociologist W.E.B. Du Bois, is published. In *Giles v. Harris* the U.S. Supreme Court rejects, 7–2, a challenge brought under the Fourteenth and Fifteenth Amendments to the disenfranchisement provisions of the new Alabama constitution, ruling that the federal courts have no power to "enforce political rights" through equitable relief. Arkansas passes streetcar segregation law.
1904	Maryland enacts a railroad segregation law. Mississippi passes legislation segregating streetcars.
1905	Tennessee and Florida pass streetcar segregation laws. Responding to a call from Du Bois and William Monroe Trotter, editor of the *Boston Guardian*, twenty-nine black activists meet in Fort Erie, Ontario, on July 11–14 and form the Niagara Movement, a militant civil rights organization.
1906	Virginia and North Carolina pass streetcar segregation laws. White residents of Brownsville, Texas, accuse soldiers of the black 25th Infantry Regiment of committing shooting spree on August 13 that kills a white bartender and wounds a police lieutenant. After newspapers print sensational stories alleging a series of attacks by black men on white women, white mobs in Atlanta, Georgia, attack black neighborhoods, September 22–25; at least ten black and two white persons are killed in the rioting. In a decision criticized widely by black Americans, President Roosevelt orders the discharge without honor of 167 soldiers from the 25th Infantry for not identifying the alleged perpetrators of the Brownsville shooting. Seven undergraduate men at Cornell University in Ithaca, New York, found Alpha Phi Alpha Fraternity, Inc., the first black Greek-letter organization, on December 4.
1907	Oklahoma enacts legislation mandating segregation on railroads and streetcars.

1908	On January 15 twenty undergraduate women at Howard University in Washington, D.C., establish Alpha Kappa Alpha Sorority, Inc. (AKA), the oldest Greek-letter organization created by black women. After failing to lynch two black prisoners held in the county jail, a white mob in Springfield, Illinois, destroys the black business district, burns black homes, and lynches two black residents, August 14–16. The racial violence in the hometown of President Abraham Lincoln attracts national attention. Niagara Movement holds last annual meeting. Georgia adopts constitutional amendment that establishes a literacy test for suffrage and includes a grandfather clause. In *Berea College v. Kentucky*, the U.S. Supreme Court upholds 7–2 a Kentucky state law forbidding schools from teaching both white and black students.

1909	An interracial group of more than fifty activists issues a call on February 12, the centenary of Lincoln's birth, for a national conference on racial discrimination and democracy, resulting in meeting of National Negro Committee in New York City, May 31–June 1. On April 6 black explorer Matthew Henson is part of the first expedition credited with reaching the North Pole. Tuskegee Institute archives record the lynching of 791 black persons from 1900 to 1909.

1910	Second annual meeting of the National Negro Committee, May 12–14, results in the founding of a permanent organization, the National Association for the Advancement of Colored People. Black heavyweight boxing champion Jack Johnson defeats former champion James Jeffries, "the Great White Hope," in a fifteenth-round knockout in Reno, Nevada, July 4. Following the fight riots break out throughout the country in which at least eleven and as many as twenty-six persons, almost all of them black, are killed. Oklahoma adopts constitutional amendment on suffrage that includes a literacy requirement and a grandfather clause. The first issue of *The Crisis*, the official magazine of the NAACP, edited by W.E.B. Du Bois, is published in November.

1912	Led by James Reese Europe, the Clef Club Symphony Orchestra presents "An Evening of Negro Music," becoming the first black orchestra to play at Carnegie Hall in New York City.

	CHRONOLOGY	629

1913   With approval from President Woodrow Wilson, several federal departments in Washington, D.C., begin segregating black employees into separate offices, restrooms, and cafeterias.

1914   Marcus Mosiah Garvey establishes the Universal Negro Improvement Association (UNIA) in Kingston, Jamaica. World War I begins in Europe. The United States will supply Britain, France, and other Allied Powers with food, raw materials, and manufactured goods; the growing need for industrial labor will increase black migration from the rural South into cities in the South, Midwest, and Northeast.

1915   A small group of ethnic Mexicans in South Texas draft the Plan de San Diego, which calls for the execution of Anglo men, the return of southwestern lands to Mexico, the establishment of an independent black republic in North America, and the recruitment of a liberating army made up of members of "the Latin, the Negro, or the Japanese race." Director D. W. Griffith screens his film *The Birth of a Nation*, a celebration of the Reconstruction-era Ku Klux Klan, for President Wilson and his family at the White House on February 18. The film is shown the next day at the National Press Club for Chief Justice Edward Douglass White, thirty-three senators, and fifty congressmen. The NAACP mounts a campaign against the film but is unable to prevent its exhibition throughout the United States. In a case brought by the NAACP, the U.S. Supreme Court unanimously rules in *Guinn v. Oklahoma* that the state's grandfather clause violates the Fifteenth Amendment. (The ruling does not affect other states whose grandfather clauses were time-limited in their operation. Oklahoma passes a highly restrictive voter registration law in 1916 that the Supreme Court will overturn in 1939.) Inspired by *The Birth of a Nation*, a second version of the Ku Klux Klan is founded at Stone Mountain, Georgia, on Thanksgiving night. While still committed to antiblack racism, the new Klan is also vocally anti-Semitic and anti-Catholic. (Klan membership totals a few thousand men by 1920, but then expands rapidly as chapters form across the United States.)

1916   Marcus Garvey moves to Harlem in New York and begins speaking tour across the United States. Governor Charles Whitman establishes the 15th Infantry, the first black regiment of the New York National Guard. James Reese Europe serves as a lieutenant and leads the regiment's marching band. (The regiment will serve in World War I as the U.S. 369th Infantry and become popularly known as the "Harlem Hellfighters"; the 8th Illinois, a black National Guard regiment formed in 1898, will serve as the U.S. 370th Infantry.)

1917 President Wilson asks Congress for a declaration of war against Germany, April 2, declaring that the "world must be made safe for democracy." More than 380,000 black men will serve in the army during World War I, and about 200,000 will be sent to Europe, where approximately 40,000 of them will fight in combat units. White mobs attack black residents in East St. Louis, Illinois, July 2–3, during rioting in which at least thirty-nine black and nine white persons are killed. On July 28 approximately 10,000 black New Yorkers silently march down Fifth Avenue to protest lynching and mob violence. After two of their comrades are beaten by the police, black soldiers stationed at Camp Logan near Houston march on the city on August 23 and kill nine civilians, five police officers, and two soldiers; four black soldiers also die that night. (The military will hang nineteen black soldiers found guilty of participating in the rebellion.) In another case brought by the NAACP, the U.S. Supreme Court unanimously rules in *Buchanan v. Warley* that a Louisville, Kentucky, ordinance prohibiting black people from living in white majority neighborhoods violates the Fourteenth Amendment. Chandler Owen and A. Philip Randolph, two black members of the Socialist Party, begin publishing radical monthly magazine *The Messenger* in November.

1918 American Expeditionary Forces engage in widespread combat in France, with black American soldiers fighting under both American and French commanders. West India–born journalist Cyril Briggs begins publishing radical magazine *The Crusader* in September. Armistice signed on November 11 ends fighting in World War I.

1919 The 369th Infantry Regiment ("Harlem Hellfighters") marches in victory parade down Fifth Avenue in New York City on February 17. Racially motivated mob violence erupts in at least twenty-five U.S. cities and towns during the "Red Summer." At least four black and three white persons are killed in Washington, D.C., July 18–22, and twenty-three black and fifteen white persons are killed in Chicago, July 27–31. Tuskegee Institute archives record the lynching of 534 black persons from 1910 to 1919. Cyril Briggs founds the African Blood Brotherhood for African Liberation and Redemption (ABB), headquartered in Harlem. White mobs and U.S. troops kill more than 100 persons in Phillips County, Arkansas, September 30–October 4, in response to false reports of an uprising by black sharecroppers. Organized self-defense of black neighborhoods during Washington and Chicago riots leads to commentary in the black press about the emergence of the "New Negro."

Note on the Texts

This volume collects late nineteenth- and early twentieth-century American writing about the political, legal, social, economic, and cultural aspects of the system of racial discrimination, segregation, disenfranchisement, and violence known as "Jim Crow." It brings together speeches, pamphlets, manifestos, essays, newspaper and magazine articles, public and private letters, congressional testimony, judicial opinions and legal briefs, interviews, memoranda and affidavits, and poems and songs written by participants and observers and dealing with events in the period from 1876 to 1919. Some of these documents were not written for publication, and some of them existed only in manuscript or typescript during the lifetimes of their creators. With four exceptions, the texts presented in this volume are taken from printed sources. In cases where there is only one printed source for a document, the text offered here comes from that source. Where there is more than one printed source for a document, the text printed in this volume is taken from the source that appears to contain the fewest editorial alterations in the spelling, capitalization, paragraphing, and punctuation of the original. In four instances where no printed source was available, the text in this volume is printed from a manuscript or typescript.

This volume prints texts as they appear in the sources listed below, but with a few alterations in editorial procedure. In *The Papers of Woodrow Wilson* the text presented of the exchange between President Woodrow Wilson and William Monroe Trotter on November 12, 1914, is taken from a later typed transcription of the contemporaneous shorthand notes made by Wilson's stenographer Charles Lee Swem. In one instance the editors of *The Papers of Woodrow Wilson* indicated missing material in the shorthand record by printing "[blank]"; in this volume the missing material is indicated at page 510.37 by a bracketed two-em space, i.e., [   ]. In three other instances the editors of *The Papers of Woodrow Wilson* offered bracketed conjectural readings where they believed words had been omitted in the shorthand record. This volume rejects a conjectural reading in one instance where other readings are possible and instead prints a bracketed two-em space at page 511.25, and in two instances where it is possible that no words were omitted this volume deletes the bracketed conjectural reading and accepts the wording recorded in the shorthand notes, i.e., "and do so, without prejudice" at 511.7 and "relieve our people" at 511.37.

The text of the speech delivered by Marcus Garvey in New York City on August 25, 1919, presented in *The Marcus Garvey and Universal Negro Improvement Association Papers*, is taken from a typed transcription of shorthand notes made by William F. Smart, a stenographer hired by the special committee of the New York legislature charged with investigating "seditious activities" in the state. In one instance the editors of *The Marcus Garvey and Universal Negro Improvement Association Papers* indicated missing material in the shorthand record by printing "[*omission*]"; in this volume the missing material is indicated at page 606.2 by a bracketed two-em space, i.e., [   ]. The bracketed editorial insertion used by the editors to identify a person at page 610.31, i.e., "Russey [*Russa*] Moton," is omitted in this volume. In *The Marcus Garvey and Universal Negro Improvement Association Papers* two additions or corrections made above or below the line in the typescript are brought into the body of the text and printed within virgules; this volume omits the virgules and prints the incorporated material.

Four typesetting errors that appeared in the printed source texts are corrected in this volume: at 143.16, "but" becomes "but for"; at 368.13, "Diura" becomes "Sisera"; at 386.31–32, "and a but" becomes "and a white man but."; at 445.10, "after election" becomes "after the election." Two slips of the pen in the manuscript of the letter from William Monroe Trotter to W.E.B. Du Bois dated March 26, 1905, are also corrected: at 426.18, "especially embarassing to me" becomes "especially embarrassing to me," and at 427.24, "broken an empty" becomes "broken and empty."

The following is a list of the documents included in this volume, in the order of their appearance, giving the source of each text. Four sources are indicated by these abbreviations:

Address   *Address of Booker T. Washington, Principal of the Tuskegee Normal and Industrial Institute, Tuskegee, Alabama, delivered at the opening of the Cotton States and International Exposition, at Atlanta, Ga., September 18, 1895, with a letter of congratulation from the President of the United States* (Tuskegee, 1895).

Reason   Frederick Douglass, Ida B. Wells, Irvine Garland Penn, Ferdinand L. Barnett, *The Reason Why The Colored American is not in the World's Columbian Exposition: The Afro-American's Contribution to Columbian Literature* (Chicago, 1893).

Report   *Report and Testimony of the Select Committee of the United States Senate to Investigate the Causes of the Removal of*

	the Negroes from the Southern States to the Northern States (3 pts., Washington, D.C.: Government Printing Office, 1880).
Speeches	*Speeches at the Constitutional Convention, by Gen. Robt. Smalls: with the right of suffrage passed by the Constitutional Convention: compiled by Miss Sarah V. Smalls* (Charleston, SC: Enquirer Print, 1896).

1876–1896

Frederick Douglass: Speech to the Republican National Convention, June 14, 1876. *The Frederick Douglass Papers, Series One: Speeches, Debates, and Interviews*, vol. 4, ed. John W. Blassingame and John R. McKivigan (New Haven, CT: Yale University Press, 1991), 440–42. Copyright © 1991 by Yale University Press. Used by permission of the publisher.

Denver Daily Tribune: "A Threatening Power." *Denver Daily Tribune*, January 12, 1877.

St. Louis Globe Democrat: The Future of the Negro. *St. Louis Globe Democrat*, April 27, 1877.

National Colored Colonization Society to Rutherford B. Hayes, September 15, 1877. *Report*, pt. II, 156.

Hester Hickman: The Land That Gives Birth to Freedom; Extending Our Voices to Heaven. Lyric sheet, Nashville, Tennessee, 1877.

The New York Times: New Homes for Freedmen. *The New York Times*, January 23, 1879.

The Chicago Tribune: The Debtor South. *Chicago Tribune*, May 13, 1879.

Benjamin Singleton: from Testimony to the Senate Select Committee, April 17, 1880. *Report*, pt. III, 379–86.

Stephen Field: Opinion in *Pace v. Alabama*, January 29, 1883. U.S. Reports: 106 U.S. 583 (1883), 583–85.

John Marshall Harlan: Dissenting Opinion in *Civil Rights Cases*, October 15, 1883. U.S. Reports: 109 U.S. 3 (1883), 26–62.

New York Globe: The Civil Rights Decision. *New York Globe*, October 20, 1883.

Nathaniel S. Shaler: The Negro Problem. *The Atlantic Monthly*, November 1884.

George Washington Cable: The Freedman's Case in Equity. *The Century Magazine*, January 1885.

Thomas Miller: Speech in Congress on the Elections Bill, January 12, 1891. *Congressional Record*, 51st Congress, 2nd Session, 1216.

Ida B. Wells: *Southern Horrors: Lynch Law in All Its Phases*. Ida B. Wells, *Southern Horrors: Lynch Law in All Its Phases* (New York: The New York Age Print, 1892).

Frederick Douglass: from *The Reason Why the Colored American is not in the World's Columbian Exposition*. *Reason*, 2–12.

Ida B. Wells: from *The Reason Why The Colored American is not in the World's Columbian Exposition*. *Reason*, 13–24.

Richard T. Greener: The White Problem. *Lend a Hand: A Record of Progress*, May 1894.

Ida B. Wells: from *A Red Record*. Ida B. Wells, *A Red Record: Tabulated Statistics and Alleged Causes of Lynchings in the United States, 1892–1893–1894* (Chicago: Donohue & Henneberry, 1895), 7–15.

Booker T. Washington: Address at the Atlanta Exposition, September 18, 1895. *Address*, 6–11.

Clark Howell: To the Editor of *The World*, September 19, 1895. *Address*, 4–5.

Republican Members of the South Carolina Convention: To the Editor of *The World*, September 30, 1895. *Speeches*, 26–29.

Grover Cleveland: To Booker T. Washington, October 6, 1895. *Address*, 3.

Robert Smalls: from Speech in the South Carolina Convention, October 26, 1895. *Speeches*, 4–10.

Albion W. Tourgée: Brief for the Plantiff in *Plessy v. Ferguson*, c. 1895. *Landmark Briefs and Arguments of the Supreme Court of the United States: Constitutional Law*, vol. 13, ed. Philip B. Kurland and Gerhard Casper (Arlington, VA: University Publications of America, 1975), 32–63.

Henry B. Brown: Opinion in *Plessy v. Ferguson*, May 18, 1896. U.S. Reports: 163 U.S. 537 (1896), 540–52.

John Marshall Harlan: Dissenting Opinion in *Plessy v. Ferguson*, May 18, 1896. U.S. Reports: 163 U.S. 537 (1896), 552–64.

1897–1909

The Washington Evening Star: Negro Emigration. *The Washington Evening Star*, October 21, 1897.

The Wilmington Morning Star: Mrs. Felton Speaks. *The Wilmington Morning Star*, August 18, 1898.

The Wilmington Morning Star: A Horrid Slander. *The Wilmington Morning Star*, August 30, 1898.

The Raleigh News and Observer: Defamer Must Go. *The Raleigh News and Observer*, November 10, 1898.

W. H. Councill: The Future of the Negro. *The Forum*, July 1899.

The New Orleans Daily Picayune: To Protect the City; End of a Desperado. *The New Orleans Daily Picayune*, July 28, 1900.

The Richmond Planet: The Butchery at New Orleans; With a Rifle in His Hand. *The Richmond Planet*, August 4, 1900.

The Navasota Daily Examiner: Campaign Oratory. *The Navasota Daily Examiner*, September 29, 1900.

George H. White: Speech in Congress in Defense of the Negro Race, January 29, 1901. *Speech of the Hon. George H. White, of North Carolina, in the House of Representatives, January 29, 1901. Defense of the Negro Race—Charges Answered* (Washington, D.C.: 1901), 3–14.

The Independent: The Negro Problem: How It Appeals to a Southern Colored Woman. *The Independent*, September 18, 1902.

Benjamin R. Tillman: from Speech in the Senate on the Race Problem, February 24, 1903. *Congressional Record*, 57th Congress, 2nd Session, 2558–66.

The Joplin Daily Globe: Murderer of Leslie Lynched by Angry Mob. *The Joplin Daily Globe*, April 16, 1903.

W.E.B. Du Bois: Of Mr. Booker T. Washington and Others. W. E. Burghardt Du Bois: *The Souls of Black Folk: Essays and Sketches* (Chicago: A. C. McClurg & Co., 1903), 41–59.

Charles W. Chestnutt: The Disfranchisement of the Negro. *The Negro Problem: A Series of Articles by Representative Negroes of To-day* (New York: James Pott & Company, 1903), 79–124.

Charles Brantley Aycock: from Speech to the North Carolina Society, December 18, 1903. R.D.W. Connor and Clarence Poe, *The Life and Speeches of Charles Brantley Aycock* (Garden City, NY: Doubleday, Page & Company, 1912), 161–63.

William Monroe Trotter: To W.E.B. Du Bois, March 26, 1905. W.E.B. Du Bois Papers (MS 312), Robert S. Cox Special Collections and University Archives Research Center, University of Massachusetts Amherst Libraries. Used by permission.

Aida Overton Walker: Colored Men and Women on the Stage. *The Colored American Magazine*, October 1905.

Mary Church Terrell: What It Means to Be Colored in the Capital of the United States. *The Independent*, January 24, 1907.

The New York Times: Negro Pastors Assail Roosevelt's Army Order. *The New York Times*, November 19, 1906.

Mary Church Terrell: Peonage in the United States: The Convict Lease System and the Chain Gangs. *The Nineteenth Century and After*, August 1907.

Sally Nash: Interview about Life in Rentiesville, Oklahoma, 1903–08. Indian-Pioneer Papers, vol. 66, interview by Sally (Love) Nash, June 22, 1937, Western History Collections, University of Oklahoma Libraries, Norman, Oklahoma.

San Pedro Daily News: The Candidates and the Negro. *San Pedro Daily News*, October 14, 1908.

The New York Evening Post: Conference on Negroes. *The New York Evening Post*, February 13, 1909.

Platform Adopted by the National Negro Committee, June 1, 1909. NAACP Records, Manuscript Division (024.00.00), Library of Congress. The publishers wish to thank the National Association for the Advancement of Colored People for the use of this document.

1909–1919

Hanford Daily Journal: Lynching Bees in Present Year Numerous. *Hanford Daily Journal*, December 17, 1909.

Los Angeles Times: The Fight and its Consequences. *Los Angeles Times*, July 6, 1910.

William Pickens: Talladega College Professor Speaks on Reno Fight. *Chicago Defender*, July 30, 1910.

Lester A. Walton: Concert at Carnegie Hall. *The New York Age*, May 9, 1912.

The Austin Daily Statesman: Negroes to Gather Here by Thousands. *The Austin Daily Statesman*, May 20, 1912.

Moorfield Storey, W.E.B. Du Bois, Oswald Garrison Villard to Woodrow Wilson, August 15, 1913. *New York Evening Post*, August 18, 1913.

William Monroe Trotter: Address to President Woodrow Wilson, November 12, 1914. *The Chicago Defender*, November 21, 1914.

Woodrow Wilson and William Monroe Trotter: An Exchange, November 12, 1914. *The Papers of Woodrow Wilson*, vol. 31, ed. Arthur S. Link (Princeton NJ: Princeton University Press, 1979), 301–8.

Provisional Directorate of the Revolutionary Plan: The Plan of San Diego, January 6, 1915. *Investigation of Mexican Affairs, Report and Hearing before a Subcommittee on Foreign Relations*, Senate Document 285, 66th Congress, 2nd Session, vol. 1 (Washington, D.C.: Government Printing Office, 1920), 1205–7.

Francis Hackett: Brotherly Love. *The New Republic*, March 20, 1915.

Outlook: The Birth of a Nation. *Outlook*, April 14, 1915.

W.E.B. Du Bois: "We Should Worry." *The Crisis*, June 1917.

The New York Times: Mob of 3,000 Rules in East St. Louis. *The New York Times*, May 29, 1917.

Carlos F. Hurd: Post-Dispatch Man, An Eye-Witness, Describes Massacre of Negroes. *St. Louis Post-Dispatch*, July 3, 1917.

John Pero: from Testimony to the House Select Committee, October 24, 1917. *Transcripts of the Hearings of the House Select Committee that Investigated the Race Riots in East St. Louis, Illinois, 1917*

(Washington, D.C.: Government Printing Office, 1918), microfilm edition, vol. 4, 714–16, 722–23, 726–27, 734–35, 746–48.

James Weldon Johnson: An Army with Banners. *The New York Age*, August 2, 1917.

Ralph Van Deman: Army Intelligence Memorandum on William Monroe Trotter, October 2, 1917. National Archives and Records Administration, RG 165 War Department: General and Special Staffs, Military Intelligence Division, Series 10218, Case file 10218-26.

Martha Gruening: Houston: An N.A.A.C.P. Investigation. *The Crisis*, November 1917.

The Chicago Defender: Migration and Its Effect. *The Chicago Defender*, April 20, 1918.

Leonidas C. Dyer: Speech in Congress on the Anti-Lynching Bill, May 7, 1918. *Congressional Record*, 65th Congress, 2nd Session, 6176–79.

W.E.B. Du Bois: Close Ranks. *The Crisis*, July 1918.

Cyril Briggs: The American Race Problem. *The Crusader*, September–December 1918.

The Right-About: Hell-Fighters cheered on Homecoming. *The Right-About*, February 19, 1919.

W.E.B. Du Bois: Returning Soldiers. *The Crisis*, May 1919.

Jeannette Carter: Negroes of Washington Were Forced to Protect Themselves. *The New York Age*, August 2, 1919.

James E. Scott: Statement on Attack by Rioters in Washington, D.C., August 4, 1919. Typescript, NAACP Records, Manuscript Division (044.00.00), Library of Congress. The publishers wish to thank the National Association for the Advancement of Colored People for the use of this document.

Martina Simms: Washington Riot. *Baltimore Afro-American*, August 15, 1919.

The Chicago Daily Tribune: Report Two Killed, Fifty Hurt, in Race Riots. *The Chicago Daily Tribune*, July 28, 1919.

The Chicago Daily Tribune: Negroes Call on Mayor, Lowden, to Stop Riots. *The Chicago Daily Tribune*, July 31, 1919.

A. Philip Randolph: Our Reason for Being. *The Messenger*, August 1919.

Marcus Garvey: Speech in New York City, August 25, 1919. *The Marcus Garvey and Universal Negro Improvement Association Papers*, vol. I, *1826–August 1919*, ed. Robert A. Hill (Berkeley: University of California Press, 1983), 500–509. Copyright © 1983 by The Regents of the University of California. Reprinted by permission.

W. A. Domingo and Claude McKay: If We Must Die. *The Messenger*, September 1919.

This volume presents the texts of the printings, typescripts, and manuscript chosen as sources here but does not attempt to reproduce features of their typographic design or physical layout. The texts are printed without alteration except for the changes previously discussed and for the correction of typographical errors. Spelling, punctuation, and capitalization are often expressive features, and they are not altered, even when inconsistent or irregular. The text of "Peonage in the United States: The Convict Lease System and the Chain Gangs" by Mary Church Terrell is taken from the August 1907 number of *The Nineteenth Century and After*, an English publication, and retains the English spellings (e.g., "gaol" for "jail") and punctuation (e.g., the use of single quotation marks) in that printing. The following is a list of typographical errors corrected, cited by page and line number: 12.1, maintainance; 17.10, offices such; 20.21, planter, who; 20.32–33, extortinate; 21.7, neees; 23.15, agred; 29.12, it; 30.30, Tennesee; 32.3, you; 35.18, thot it; 41.30, enfore; 47.20, *Sanford*; 54.16, becaused; 91.15, as as; 130.22, thread bare; 132.25, miscegnation; 135.5, horified; 136.31, miscegnationists; 137.38, lynch a; 138.11, Hanifan; 138.39, suppported; 138.40, liasion; 139.18, insiduous; 139.29, Ellerton; 139.30, Layfayette; 140.15, Carrolton; 142.22, beastial; 143.16, but the; 143.28, the the state; 145.28, lesson? The; 147.2, insiduous; 148.33–34, him, The; 149.10–11, justice, No; 150.5, others; 150.6, every every; 150.6, pas; 150.11, effected; 151.15, Jarvis; 151.24, money and; 151.32, *liason*; 151.39, inconsistant; 156.19, villanies; 156.40, arrrive; 157.16, inperfections; 159.17, monster; 163.5, repentence; 165.27, regisration; 167.12, 1884; 167.14, state's rights'; 167.16–17, Alabama Georgia; 170.19–20, Parish; 170.20, Extein; 171.21, penetentiary; 175.21, Glidden; 180.35, 1828; 182.3, Saltoum,; 182.13, Nero; 182.33, Henning; 182.35–36, * * notwithstanding; 186.4, "What; 192.25, have have; 206.29, Sept., 30; 209.17, Pesidential; 211.39, it You; 212.27, interterest; 213.28, capitalist; 213.30, Representative; 219.2, compell; 219.5, spoilation; 222.40, Section 3; 223.11, migbt; 223.25, the the; 224.18, regulations.; 224.19–20, jurisdicdiction; 226.37, Case"; 227.11, discrimation; 228.5, limbs health; 228.39, opprobious; 232.29, controling; 235.33, Case,; 236.24, States.; 241.3, compell; 244.21, Slaudter; 244.38, vs Sanford,; 277.7, Enthsiast; 278.30, rawers; 281.29, the; 283.38, all."; 284.6, You; 304.40, mutillated; 307.6, preceeding; 308.1, of of; 308.14, know; 313.16, degredation; 320.18, "The; 320.30, man.'"; 326.28, individuals; 337.12, fanateceism; 340.28, Gen-; 340.34, does Mr.; 341.20, suprise; 356.9, Benjamin C.; 370.24, innoculated; 380.19, shop; 381.3, stiffling; 381.12, coons. Loud; 381.23, sorts and to; 386.4, stoppped; 388.mo bbegan; 396.5, Shad; 404.3, Disenfranchisement; 408.40, DuBois; 427.19, Ida L.; 429.23–24, performaces;

430.3, commad; 431.22, loose; 439.26, afternoon? mother; 440.10, hight; 461.11, misdemeanor; 469.15, drunkeness; 484.22, Ape; 489.18, caried; 490.10, has; 494.2, Bell; 500.21, Moorefield; 514.20, iniquituous; 516.22, Japenese; 517.4, *1919.*; 526.16, sorm; 537.36, undoubtly; 542.21, DuBois; 552.19, effect; 552.23, acccording; 552.27, alleged; 569.18, virtous; 570.39, Suden; 571.36, Picket; 574.36, executian; 575.7, abdoman; 575.8, prematuraly; 575.16, *well.*; 575.36, pigs'; 576.28, records called; 580.3, what?; 584.15, peolice; 586.26, formented; 588.13, C; 589.13, spred; 593.23–24, Mame; 594.15, Davies; 600.18, group.”; 601.14, country.; 607.35, Englishmen; 609.17, Virginia, In; 610.19, Dieties; 612.33, be hewers; 613.33, Line. if; 614.17, Applause); 614.35, Brittonain; 615.2, have do.

Notes

In the notes below, the reference numbers denote page and line of this volume (the line count includes headings, but not rule lines). No note is made for material included in the eleventh edition of *Merriam-Webster's Collegiate Dictionary*. Biblical references are keyed to the King James Version. Quotations from Shakespeare are keyed to *The Riverside Shakespeare*, ed. G. Blakemore Evans (Boston: Houghton Mifflin, 1974). Footnotes and bracketed editorial notes within the text were in the originals. For further historical background and references to other studies, see Leon Litwack, *Been in the Storm So Long: The Aftermath of Slavery* (New York: Alfred A. Knopf, 1979); Grace Elizabeth Hale, *Making Whiteness: The Culture of Segregation in the South, 1890–1940* (New York: Pantheon Books, 1998); Henry Louis Gates Jr., *Stony the Road: Reconstruction, White Supremacy, and the Rise of Jim Crow* (New York: Penguin Press, 2019); Nell Irvin Painter, *Standing at Armageddon: The United States, 1877–1919* (New York: W. W. Norton & Company, 1989); Jackson Lears, *Rebirth of a Nation: The Making of Modern America, 1877–1920* (New York: HarperCollins Publishers, 2009); Richard White, *The Republic for Which It Stands: The United States During Reconstruction and the Gilded Age, 1865–1896* (New York: Oxford University Press, 2017); and *Encyclopedia of African-American Civil Rights, From Emancipation to the Present*, ed. Charles D. Lowery and John F. Marszalek (Westport, CT: Greenwood Press, 1992).

1876–1896

3.3–4 *Speech . . . Republican National Convention*] The convention was held in Cincinnati, Ohio, June 14–16, 1876.

4.16–18 the Israelites . . . their jewels] See Exodus 12:35–36.

4.20–21 Russian serfs . . . their liberty] Russian serfs were emancipated in 1861 by an edict issued by Tsar Alexander II (1818–1881).

6.5 House Committee at New Orleans] The 1876 presidential election between Rutherford B. Hayes, the Republican governor of Ohio, and Samuel J. Tilden, the Democratic governor of New York, resulted in a disputed electoral count caused by conflicting returns in South Carolina, Florida, and Louisiana, and a disqualification controversy over an Oregon elector. On December 5, the Democratic-controlled House of Representatives appointed three select committees to investigate the elections held in the disputed southern states. The committee that traveled to Louisiana later in the month collected hundreds of pages of testimony, including allegations that black women had actively sought to keep black men from voting for the Democratic ticket. Witnesses from several different parishes variously testified that "every colored woman is a radical"; that black women belonged to secret "Councils of Freedom"; that they armed themselves with "cane-knives and forks" as well as clubs; that they snatched Democratic tickets away from voters at the polls and forced Republican tickets into their hands; that they illegally voted themselves; and that they would "blackguard and abuse" would-be Democratic voters with "all kinds of vile language," subjecting them to "insults and mockery," threatening them with ostracism, and accusing them of "selling themselves, their wives and their families" back into slavery. The *Denver Daily Tribune*, a Republican newspaper, commented on the hearings in the editorial printed here.

6.28 White Leaguers] A white supremacist militia formed in Louisiana in 1874 that used murder and intimidation in its efforts to overthrow the state's Republican government.

6.35–7.1 Sam. Randall . . . John Morrissey] Samuel Randall (1828–1890), Democratic congressman from Pennsylvania, 1863–90, and Speaker of the House of Representatives, 1875–81; Fernando Wood (1812–1881), Democratic congressman from New York, 1841–43, 1863–65, 1867–81, and mayor of New York City, 1855–57 and 1860–61; William Springer (1836–1903), Democratic congressman from Illinois, 1875–95; Henry Banning (1836–1881), a former Union Army officer and Democratic congressman from Ohio, 1875–79; Henry Watterson (1840–1921), Democratic congressman from Kentucky, 1876–77; Abram Hewitt (1822–1903), Democratic congressman from New York, 1875–79 and 1881–87, and mayor of New York City, 1887–88; John Morrissey (1831–1878), a former boxer, was a Democratic congressman from New York, 1867–71, and a Democratic state senator, 1876–78.

8.6 early acts . . . Florida Legislature] In 1876 the Democrats gained control of the Florida legislature for the first time since the adoption of the Reconstruction state constitution in 1868.

10.3 Council . . . Venice] The Council of Ten, a powerful ruling body in the Venetian republic, 1310–1797.

10.19–20 Hampton and Nicholls] The 1876 election resulted in the establishment of rival Republican and Democratic state governments in South Carolina and Louisiana. Wade Hampton (1818–1902), a former Confederate lieutenant general, became governor of South Carolina on April 11, 1877, after President Hayes ordered the federal troops guarding the statehouse in Columbia withdrawn and the Republican governor, Daniel H. Chamberlain, surrendered his office. Hampton served as governor until 1879 and then as a U.S. senator, 1879–91. Francis T. Nicholls (1834–1912), a former Confederate brigadier general, became governor of Louisiana on April 25, 1877, after federal troops were withdrawn from the statehouse in New Orleans and Republican governor Stephen Packard left office. Nicholls served until 1880 and was later elected to a second term as governor, 1888–92. He then served as chief justice of the Louisiana Supreme Court, 1892–1904, and as an associate justice of the court, 1904–11.

11.2–4 NATIONAL COLORED COLONIZATION . . . *Hayes*] This document was read into the record of a hearing held in March 1880 by the Senate select committee investigating the "exodus" of black people from the South. It was entered as part of the testimony of Henry Adams (1843–?), one of the leaders of the colonization society. Adams was a freedman who learned to read while serving in the army after the Civil War. He settled in northwestern Louisiana and in 1870 joined a group of former soldiers known as "the Council" or "the Committee" who helped tenant farmers with labor contracts and gathered information about racial violence and exploitation across the South. Adams told the senators that "the Council" became increasingly pessimistic about the future of black people in the South during the violent Louisiana state election in 1874, and soon saw their worst fears come to pass. "In 1877 we lost all hopes," Adams testified. "We said that the whole South—every State in the South—had got into the hands of the very men that held us slaves—from one thing to another—and we thought that the men that held us slaves was holding the reins of government over our heads in every respect almost, even the constable up to the governor. We felt we had almost as well be slaves under these men." In response "the Council" became increasingly committed to promoting black colonization outside the South. On July 9, 1877, it submitted a petition bearing 3,186 signatures to President Hayes calling for a "territory for our Selves." Adams told the Senate that five thousand people attended the mass meeting held in Shreveport on September 15, 1877, that adopted the address to Hayes printed here. There is no record that either petition ever received a reply from the president.

12.24 the Freedman's Bank] The Freedman's Savings and Trust Company was founded by a group of white philanthropists and chartered by Congress in 1865 as a mutual savings bank investing in federal securities. Although the bank was a private company, it often shared offices with the Freedman's Bureau, and many depositors believed it was a government institution. After the bank had its charter revised in 1870, it began making highly speculative investments in railroad securities and Washington real estate. The Freedman's Bank was among the financial institutions severely impacted by the Panic of 1873, and it collapsed on June 28, 1874. Only about half of the bank's sixty-one thousand depositors received any funds when the company was liquidated, and none of them received the full value of their deposits.

14.12 Mr. Singleton] Benjamin (Pap) Singleton (1809–1900); see pp. 28–39 and note 28.2 in this volume.

16.6 SENATOR WINDOM'S] William Windom (1827–1891), a Republican, was a congressman from Minnesota, 1859–69, and a senator, 1870–71, 1871–81, and 1881–83; he also served as secretary of the treasury, March–November 1881.

16.16 his resolution] Windom introduced a resolution on January 16, 1879, calling for the Senate to appoint a committee to inquire "as to the expediency and practicability of encouraging and promoting by all just and proper methods the partial migration of colored persons from those States and congressional districts where they are not allowed to freely and peacefully exercise and enjoy their constitutional rights as American citizens, into such States as may desire to receive them and will protect them in said rights, or into such Territory or Territories of the United States as may be provided for their use and occupation." The Senate rejected the resolution on February 24.

16.17 Prof. Greener] Richard T. Greener (1844–1922) was born in Philadelphia and in 1870 became the first black graduate from Harvard College. Greener taught Latin, Greek, and law at South Carolina College (later the University of South Carolina), 1873–76, and was the head of the law department at Howard University, 1877–80. He later practiced law in Washington, D.C., helped raise funds to build Grant's Tomb, and became the first black American to hold a diplomatic post in a white country, serving as U.S. consul at Vladivostok, Russia, 1898–1905.

18.4 Congressmen Rainey, Cain, and Smalls] Born into slavery in South Carolina, Joseph H. Rainey (1832–1887) was elected to Congress as a Republican in 1870, becoming the first black American in the House of Representatives, and served until March 1879. Richard Harvey Cain (1825–1887) was born to free parents in Virginia and became a minister in the African Methodist Episcopal Church. Cain served as a Republican congressman from South Carolina, 1873–75 and 1877–79. Robert Smalls (1839–1915) was born into slavery in South Carolina, where he learned to be a ship's pilot. In 1862 Smalls and several other enslaved crew members commandeered the Confederate transport steamer *Planter* and sailed it out of Charleston Harbor to join the Union blockade fleet, an exploit that freed sixteen black men, women, and children. Smalls later served as a Republican in the South Carolina house of representatives, 1868–70; in the state senate, 1870–74; in Congress, 1875–79, 1882–83, and 1884–87; and as a delegate to the South Carolina constitutional conventions of 1868 and 1895.

19.2–3 *THE CHICAGO TRIBUNE / The Debtor South*] This is the eighth in a series of eleven reports on "the Negro Exodus" from the South that appeared in the *Chicago Tribune* April 30–May 3, May 6–7, May 9, May 13–15, and May 17, 1879. The articles were sent from Mississippi and Louisiana by Robert Wilson Patterson (1850–1910), who later served as editor-in-chief of the *Chicago Tribune*, 1899–1910.

22.8 turn-rows] Strips of land at the end or side of a field where a plow can be turned around.

24.11–12 $6.84 . . . 8.09] These are the figures that appeared in the *Chicago Tribune*, although the sum of $6.84 and $1.24 is actually $8.08.

26.24–30 Constitutional Convention . . . poll-tax] The 1879 Louisiana constitutional convention did not adopt a poll tax or a literacy requirement for voting.

27.37 R. W. P.] See note 19.2–3.

28.2 BENJAMIN SINGLETON] Born into slavery in Tennessee, Benjamin Singleton (1809–1900) escaped to Canada in 1846 and settled in Detroit. After the Civil War Singleton returned to Tennessee, where he worked as a carpenter. He visited Kansas in 1873 and soon became a major promoter of black migration to that state. In the 1880s, after black settlement in the American West had slowed, Singleton advocated emigration to Cyprus (then under British administration) and West Africa.

28.4 *Senate Select Committee*] In 1879 thousands of black people left the South, including about six thousand who migrated from Louisiana, Mississippi, and Texas in the spring. The U.S. Senate appointed a select committee of three Democrats and two Republicans on December 18, 1879, to "investigate the causes which have led" to the migration. From January 16 to April 27, 1880, the committee heard from 153 witnesses from six southern and three northern states. The Democratic majority submitted a six-page report on June 1 concluding that the migration "was undoubtedly induced in a great degree by northern politicians, and by negro leaders in their employ, and in employ of the railroad lines" and "that the sooner" the black population of the South "are taught to depend upon themselves, the sooner they will learn to take care of themselves." In a seventeen-page minority report, the Republican senators quoted testimony detailing the violence and exploitation experienced by black people in the South and wrote that the migrants, "unable longer to endure the intolerable hardships, injustice, and suffering inflicted upon them by a class of Democrats in the South," had sought "passage to the land of freedom, where the rights of citizens are respected and honest toil rewarded by honest compensation."

28.9 Mr. Windom] See note 16.6.

30.23 Governor St. John] John Pierce St. John (1833–1916), a Republican, was governor of Kansas, 1879–83.

32.22–23 Mrs. Governor Brown . . . Mrs. Sanders] Cynthia Pillow Saunders Brown (1810–1892), the second wife of Aaron Venable Brown (1795–1859), Democratic governor of Tennessee, 1845–47.

32.25 Ex-Governor Brown] Probably John Calvin Brown (1827–1889), Democratic governor of Tennessee, 1871–75.

33.25 the outside box] A wooden grave liner.

36.21 The CHAIRMAN] Daniel W. Voorhees (1827–1897) was a Democratic congressman from Indiana, 1861–67 and 1869–73, and a senator, 1877–97.

39.3 governor's—Brownlow's?] William G. (Parson) Brownlow (1805–1877), a Methodist minister and newspaper editor, was a leading East Tennessee Unionist during the Civil War. Brownlow was elected governor in 1865 as a Unionist and reelected in 1867 as a Radical. He later served in the U.S. Senate as a Republican, 1869–75.

40.2 STEPHEN FIELD] A Democrat, Field (1816–1899) served on the California state supreme court, 1857–63. He was appointed to the U.S. Supreme Court by President Abraham Lincoln in 1863 and served until his retirement in 1897.

41.7 opinion of the court] The decision was unanimous.

43.2 JOHN MARSHALL HARLAN] Born in Danville, Kentucky, John Marshall Harlan (1833–1911) was an enslaver who opposed secession and served as an officer in the Union Army, 1861–63. Elected attorney general of Kentucky as a Unionist in 1863, Harlan opposed the ratification of the Thirteenth and Fourteenth Amendments. After being defeated for reelection in 1867 he became a Republican, endorsed the Reconstruction amendments, and ran unsuccessfully for governor twice. In 1877 Harlan was appointed to the Supreme Court by President Hayes and served until his death.

43.3 Civil Rights Cases] The *Civil Rights Cases* were a consolidation of five lawsuits brought under the 1875 Civil Rights Act, involving the denial of accommodation because of race by hotels in Hiawatha, Kansas, and Jefferson City, Missouri, theaters in San Francisco and New York City, and the refusal by a railroad conductor to seat a black woman in a whites-only "ladies' car" in Tennessee.

43.6 The opinion in these cases] The opinion of the court was written by Justice Joseph P. Bradley (1813–1892), who served as an associate justice, 1870–92. The other justices in the majority were Samuel F. Miller (1816–1890), associate justice, 1862–90; Stephen Field (1816–1899), associate justice, 1863–97; Morrison R. Waite (1816–1888), chief justice, 1874–88; William B. Woods (1824–1887), associate justice, 1881–87; Stanley Matthews (1824–1889), associate justice, 1881–89; Horace Gray (1828–1902), associate justice, 1882–1902; and Samuel Blatchford (1820–1893), associate justice, 1882–93. All eight justices had been appointed by Republican presidents: Miller and Field by Abraham Lincoln, Bradley and Waite by Ulysses S. Grant, Woods by Rutherford B. Hayes, Matthews by James A. Garfield, and Gray and Blatchford by Chester A. Arthur.

43.10–12 "It is not . . . law is the soul."] Harlan paraphrases comments made by Sir Edmund Plowden (1518–1585) on the case of *Eyston v. Studd* (1574) in *The Commentaries, or Reports of Edmund Plowden, of the Middle-Temple, Esq.* (London: 1761).

44.25 said this court in *Fletcher* v. *Peck*] Chief Justice John Marshall (1755–1835) ruled in *Fletcher v. Peck* (1810) that a Georgia state law rescinding the corrupt Yazoo land purchases violated the contracts clause of the Constitution.

44.30–31 in *Sinking Fund Cases* . . . we said] In the *Sinking Fund Cases* (1878) Chief Justice Waite upheld the power of Congress to amend corporate charters for legitimate public purposes.

45.22–25 *Prigg* v. *Commonwealth* . . . MR. JUSTICE STORY] Justice Joseph Story (1779–1845) wrote the opinion of the court in *Prigg v. Commonwealth of Pennsylvania* (1842).

47.15 *Ableman* v. *Booth*] Chief Justice Roger B. Taney (1777–1864) wrote the opinion of the court in *Ableman v. Booth* (1859).

47.19–20 *Dred Scott* v. *Sanford*] The case was decided on March 6, 1857.

47.38 speaking by Chief Justice Taney] In her posthumous memoir *Some Memories of a Long Life, 1854–1911* (2001), Malvina Shanklin Harlan (1838–1916) wrote that when her husband was having difficulty drafting his opinion in the *Civil Rights Cases*, she placed on his desk the inkwell Taney had used to write the *Dred Scott* opinion, which Justice Harlan then used to complete his dissent.

50.30 *ex industria*] Latin: by design, on purpose.

50.37–38 *United States* v. *Reese* . . . *Strauder* v. *West Virginia*] In *United States v. Reese* (1876) the court dismissed indictments brought under the Enforcement Act of 1870 against two Kentucky election inspectors for refusing to let a black man vote in a municipal election. Declaring that the Fifteenth Amendment "does not confer the right of suffrage upon any one," the court held, 8–1, that the relevant section of the Enforcement Act failed to explicitly mention the denial of suffrage on account of race, thereby exceeding the enforcement power granted to Congress under the Fifteenth Amendment. In *Strauder v. West Virginia* (1880) the court held, 6–2, that a West Virginia law excluding black men from jury service violated the equal protection clause of the Fourteenth Amendment.

52.30 *Slaughter-house Cases*] In the *Slaughterhouse Cases* (1873) the court ruled, 5–4, that a Louisiana law regulating slaughterhouses in New Orleans did not violate the privileges and immunities clause of the Fourteenth Amendment.

54.7–9 *New Jersey Steam* . . . Mr. Justice Nelson] The opinion in the case, decided in 1848, was written by Samuel Nelson (1792–1873), who served as an associate justice, 1845–72.

54.13–14 *Munn* v. *Illinois* . . . *Olcott* v. *Supervisors*] *Munn* was decided by the Supreme Court in 1877, *Olcott* in 1872.

54.28 *Township of Queensbury* v. *Culver*] The case was decided by the Supreme Court in 1873.

54.31–34 *Township of Pine Grove* . . . the State."] From the opinion of the court (1873) by Noah Swayne (1804–1884), who served as an associate justice, 1862–81.

54.36–55.6 Supreme Judicial Court . . . trust for the public."] From the opinion of the court (1842) by Lemuel Shaw (1781–1861), chief justice of the Massachusetts Supreme Judicial Court, 1830–60.

55.6–16 *Erie, Etc., R.R. Co.* . . . exercisable within them."] From the opinion of the Pennsylvania Supreme Court by Justice Jeremiah S. Black (1810–1883) in *Erie & North East Railroad v. Casey* (1856).

55.39–56.3 "Personal liberty consists . . . course of law."] Cf. William Blackstone (1723–1780), *Commentaries on the Laws of England*, Book One (1765), ch. I, 130.

56.27–28 Redfield on Carriers, etc.] Isaac F. Redfield (1804–1876), *The Law of Carriers of Goods and Passengers, Private and Public, Inland and Foreign, by Railway, Steamboat, and Other Modes of Transportation; also, the Construction, Responsibility, and Duty of Telegraph Companies, the Responsibility and Duty of Innkeepers, and the Law of Bailments of Every Class, Embracing Remedies* (1869).

56.39–40 Story on Bailments] Joseph Story, *Commentaries on the Law of Bailments, with illustrations from the Civil and Foreign Law* (1832).

57.1–2 *Rex* v. *Ivens* . . . Mr. Justice Coleridge] An English case decided in 1835 by John Taylor Coleridge (1790–1876), a justice of the King's Bench.

58.6–7 *Peik* v. *Chicago & N. W. Railway Co.*] The case was decided by the Supreme Court in 1877.

58.13 remark . . . Lord Chief Justice Hale] Matthew Hale (1609–1676) was chief justice of the King's Bench, 1671–75. The quotation is from his posthumous treatise on the law of seaports, *De Portibus Maris* (1787).

58.15 *juris privati*] Latin: of private right, private property.

58.16–24 "Property does become . . . to the control."] From the opinion of the court in *Munn v. Illinois* (1877) by Chief Justice Waite.

60.9–13 "the freedom of . . . dominion over him."] From the opinion of the court in the *Slaughterhouse Cases* by Justice Samuel F. Miller.

60.30 *Ex parte Virginia*] In *Ex parte Virginia* the court upheld 6–2 the clause in the 1875 Civil Rights Act prohibiting racial discrimination in jury service in a case involving a Virginia county judge who refused to qualify black men as potential jurors. *Ex parte Virginia* was decided on March 1, 1880, the same day as *Strauder v. West Virginia* and *Virginia v. Rives*, a third case involving race and jury service. In *Virginia v. Rives* two black defendants charged with murdering a white man sought to have their cases removed from state to federal court because they had been indicted and faced trial by all-white juries in a county that was one-third black. The court rejected their petition, ruling that black defendants were not constitutionally entitled to trial by a racially mixed jury.

63.20–21 *Ward* v. *Maryland . . . Paul* v. *Virginia*] *Ward v. Maryland* (1870), a Supreme Court case involving state taxes levied on nonresident traders; *Corfield v. Coryell* (1823), a circuit court case decided by Justice Bushrod Washington (1762–1829) regarding a state law forbidding nonresidents from harvesting oysters; *Paul v. Virginia* (1869), a Supreme Court case regarding state regulation of out-of-state insurance companies.

64.32 *United States* v. *Cruikshank*] A case that arose from the Colfax Massacre in Louisiana on April 13, 1873, in which a heavily armed white posse attacked an improvised militia of black residents guarding the Grant Parish courthouse in the aftermath of a disputed election. The white posse drove the poorly armed militiamen from their defensive positions, set fire to the courthouse, and began killing prisoners. At least sixty-two, and possibly as many as eighty-one, black men were killed in the fighting and subsequent massacre. In the spring of 1874 James R. Beckwith (1838–1912), the U.S. attorney for Louisiana, obtained convictions against three white defendants charged under the Enforcement Act of 1870 with conspiring to deprive the Colfax victims of their constitutional rights. The verdicts were overturned in 1876 by the Supreme Court in a unanimous decision in which Chief Justice Waite severely limited the reach of the Enforcement Act, ruling that the Fourteenth Amendment did not protect the right to assemble, to bear arms, or to vote, nor did it protect citizens against the criminal acts of private individuals.

65.7 *Neal* v. *Delaware*] In 1881 the Supreme Court overturned, 4–2, the conviction of William Neal, a black man who had been sentenced to death for the rape of a white woman after being indicted and tried by all-white juries. Justice Harlan wrote in his opinion for the court that the prosecution had conceded that no black citizen had ever served as a juror in Delaware, and quoted the assertion by the state's chief justice that "the great body of black men residing in this State are utterly unqualified by want of intelligence, experience, or moral integrity to sit on juries." Neal was retried and acquitted.

66.12–17 "right and immunities . . . to be protected."] From the opinion of the court in *United States v. Reese* (1876) by Chief Justice Waite.

66.19–21 "a right or immunity . . . protected by Congress."] From the opinion of the court in *Strauder v. West Virginia* (1880) by William Strong (1808–1895), who served as an associate justice, 1870–80.

67.6–10 *United States* v. *Fisher . . .* by the Constitution."] From the opinion of the court in *United States v. Fisher* (1805) by Chief Justice Marshall, holding that the United States was entitled to priority of payment from a bankrupt debtor.

67.19–20 *McCulloch* v. *Maryland*] The case, decided in 1819, in which the Marshall court upheld the constitutionality of the Second Bank of the United States.

67.38 I Story Const. § 422] Joseph Story, *Commentaries on the Constitution of the United States* (1833), vol. I, bk. III, ch. 5, para. 422.

73.28–74.6 "The constitutional provision . . . *Ex parte Virginia*] From the opinion of the court by Justice Strong.

75.31–32 *Robinson and Wife . . . Railroad Company*] See note 43.3.

76.11–15 *Hall* v. *De Cuir* . . . from the States."] From the opinion of the court (1878) by Chief Justice Waite. The decision was unanimous.

76.23–30 "when a man has . . . rights are protected."] Harlan quotes from the majority opinion by Justice Bradley. In an earlier paragraph Bradley had written that a refusal of accommodation at an inn, public conveyance, or place of amusement on account of race "has nothing to do with slavery or involuntary servitude," and continued: "It would be running the slavery argument into the ground to make it apply to every act of discrimination which a person may see fit to make as to the guests he will entertain, or as to the people he will take into his coach or cab or car, or admit to his concert or theatre, or deal with in other matters of intercourse or business."

76.38–39 "to help the feeble . . . support him after."] *Timon of Athens*, I.i.107–8.

77.7–11 contemporary English historian . . . a single despot."] William Edward Hartpole Lecky (1838–1903), *A History of England in the Eighteenth Century*, vol. I (1878), ch. II.

78.2–3 *NEW YORK GLOBE . . . Rights Decision*] This editorial was probably written by the managing editor of the *Globe*, T(imothy) Thomas Fortune (1856–1928). Born into slavery in Florida, Fortune attended Howard University and learned the printing trade before moving to New York City. Fortune was the managing editor of the *Globe* from 1881 to 1884, when the newspaper collapsed financially. He was later editor of the *New York Freeman*, 1884–87, and its successor the *New York Age*, 1889–1907, and of *The Negro World*, the official newspaper of the United Negro Improvement Association.

78.13 carried the war into Africa] A common phrase referring to the decision of the Roman general Scipio Africanus (236–183 BCE) to invade North Africa during the Second Punic War.

78.17–18 Supreme Court . . . Ku Klux law was unconstitutional] In *United States v. Harris*, decided on January 22, 1883, the Supreme Court dismissed federal indictments brought against twenty men for beating four prisoners, one fatally, in the custody of a Tennessee deputy sheriff. The defendants were prosecuted under a section of the 1871 Enforcement Act, also known as the Ku Klux Klan Act, which made it a crime to conspire to deprive any person of the equal protection of the laws. In his opinion for the court, Justice Woods held that the relevant section of the Klan Act was unconstitutional because the Fourteenth Amendment was directed at state action, not the acts of private individuals. Justice Harlan dissented from the decision on jurisdictional grounds but did not express an opinion on the merits of the case. (It is not clear if the court was aware that the mob had been led by the county sheriff.)

80.3 NATHANIEL S. SHALER] The son of a slaveholding Kentucky physician, Shaler (1848–1906) graduated from the Lawrence Scientific School at Harvard in 1862. After serving in the Union Army he returned to Lawrence School, where he was professor of paleontology, 1869–88, professor of geology, 1888–1906, and dean of the school, 1891–1906. Shaler published more than twenty books on geology, natural history, and other subjects.

80.29–31 General S. C. Armstrong . . . Hon. D. H. Chamberlain] Samuel C. Armstrong (1839–1893) commanded black troops during the Civil War before becoming the founding principal of Hampton Normal and Industrial School (now Hampton University), 1868–93. Thomas Wentworth Higginson (1823–1911) was a Unitarian minister and radical abolitionist who helped finance John Brown's raid on the federal arsenal at Harpers Ferry in 1859. Higginson served as colonel of the 1st South Carolina Volunteers, a regiment of freedmen raised in the Sea Islands, 1862–64, and later wrote *Army Life in a Black Regiment* (1870). A former Union Army officer from Massachusetts, Daniel H. Chamberlain (1835–1907) moved to South Carolina in 1866. He was a Republican delegate to the state constitutional convention in 1868, the state attorney general, 1868–72, and governor from 1874 to 1877, when he surrendered his office (see note 10.19–20).

85.19–21 increase in the number of blacks . . . of 1880] The 1870 census recorded the black population of the United States as 4.88 million, while the 1880 census reported a black population of 6.58 million, an increase of 35 percent. (During the same decade the total U.S. population grew from 38.55 million to 50.15 million, an increase of 30 percent.)

86.36 General Saxton's brief answer] Brigadier General Rufus Saxton (1824–1906) was the Union military governor of coastal South Carolina and Georgia, 1862–65. In his memoir *Army Life in a Black Regiment* (1870) Higginson wrote: "General Saxton, examining with some impatience a long list of questions from some philanthropic Commission at the North, respecting the traits and habits of the freedmen, bade some staff-officer answer them all in two words,—'Intensely human.' We all admitted that it was a striking and comprehensive description."

87.24 my late master, Louis Agassiz] The Swiss American zoologist, paleontologist, and geologist Louis Agassiz (1807–1873) was Shaler's teacher at the Lawrence Scientific School at Harvard.

87.25–26 his residence at Charleston] Agassiz taught at the Medical College of South Carolina in the winters of 1851–52 and 1852–53.

87.42 our Indians] Hampton Normal and Industrial School began admitting Indigenous men and women in 1878.

90.3 *exceptio probat*] Latin: *exceptio probat regulam*, the exception proves the rule.

100.23 Joseph Bannecker] Probably a reference to Benjamin Banneker (1731–1806). The son of a formerly enslaved man and a free woman, Banneker was born and lived in Maryland. A farmer, astronomer, surveyor, and almanac author, he helped plot the boundaries of the District of Columbia and publicly corresponded with Thomas Jefferson regarding slavery.

101.2 GEORGE WASHINGTON CABLE] Born into a slaveholding New Orleans family, Cable (1844–1925) served in the Confederate cavalry before becoming a journalist, essayist, and fiction writer. His early works included the story collection *Old Creole Days* (1879), the novels *The Grandissimes* (1880), *Madame Delphine* (1881), and *Dr. Sevier* (1884), and the exposé "The Convict Lease System in the Southern States" (1884). Cable responded to the controversy caused by the publication of "The Freedman's Case in Equity" in "The Silent South," an essay published in *The Century* in September 1885.

106.35 old Louisiana Black Code] The code was adopted in 1806 when Louisiana became an American territory.

107.12–23 I am a Southerner . . . behind the smoke!] From "To the South" by Maurice Thompson (1844–1901), published in *The Independent*, September 11, 1884.

113.16 "Whereas we were blind, now we see"] Cf. John 9:25.

114.33–34 following extract . . . not six months ago] The piece appeared in the *Selma Times* on July 22, 1884, under the heading "Too Much Civil Rights."

114.36 E.T., V & G.] East Tennessee, Virginia & Georgia.

117.24–40 when in June last] Cable delivered an early version of "The Freedman's Case in Equity" as an address to the Alabama Historical Society in Tuscaloosa on June 18, 1884, given as part of the University of Alabama commencement exercises.

117.39 'Is it nominated . . . in the bond.'"] *The Merchant of Venice*, IV.i.259, 262.

124.2 THOMAS MILLER] Born in South Carolina and raised by two freed people, Miller (1849–1938) graduated from Lincoln University in 1872 and was admitted to the South Carolina bar in 1875. He served as a Republican in the state house of representatives, 1874–80, 1886–87, and 1894–96, and in the state senate, 1880–82. In 1888 Miller ran for the U.S. House of Representatives against a Democratic incumbent, William Elliott, who claimed victory and was seated in the new Congress. He contested the election on the grounds that many black voters had been prevented from casting ballots, and on September 23, 1890, the Republican-controlled House voted to seat him in Elliott's place. Miller served for the remainder of the Fifty-first Congress and defeated Elliott in the November 1890 election but lost his seat when the canvassing board threw out most of his ballots for being improperly printed. He again contested the election results, but the Democratic-controlled Fifty-second Congress seated Elliott. Miller later served as a delegate to the 1895 state constitutional convention and became the first president of the Colored Normal, Industrial, Agricultural, and Mechanical College (now South Carolina State University), 1896–1911.

124.3 *Elections Bill*] The 1888 election gave the Republicans simultaneous control of the White House, the Senate, and the House of Representatives for the first time since 1875 and resulted in a renewed effort to protect black suffrage in the South from fraud and discrimination. On June 19, 1890, Henry Cabot Lodge of Massachusetts introduced a bill in the House authorizing federal officials to supervise voter registration, polling procedures, and ballot counting in congressional elections. The bill passed the House, 155–149, on July 2 with no Democrats voting in favor. In August the Senate Republican caucus voted to delay consideration of the elections bill until after the election in order to pass a protectionist tariff measure. When the Senate began its new session in December 1890 the elections bill was filibustered by the Democrats and lacked universal support from Republican senators. On January 22, 1891, the Senate voted, 35–34, to postpone further debate on the bill, and it was never again brought up for consideration.

124.5 Mr. Chairman] The House had resolved itself into a Committee of the Whole House on the State of the Union in order to debate an army appropriations bill, with Nelson Dingley (1832–1899) of Maine presiding. At the beginning of the debate William J. Stone (1848–1918), a Democrat from Missouri, had announced that he would propose an amendment to the bill prohibiting the use of federal troops at polling places. (Although the 1890 elections bill did not contain provisions for a military role in elections, its Democratic opponents sought to associate the bill with the use of federal troops to guard polling places during Reconstruction.)

124.25–26 the speech . . . Mr. HEMPHILL] John J. Hemphill (1849–1912) was a Democratic congressman from South Carolina, 1883–93, and the opposition floor leader during the House debate on the elections bill. In a speech delivered on June 26, 1890, Hemphill claimed that the bill was intended to put "the colored man" in "control of the government of the Southern States," but that "the honest and intelligent people" of South Carolina would refuse to let their "great and noble State" be "over-ridden and down-trodden by a race whom God never intended to rule over us."

125.15–16 the newly elected governor] Benjamin R. Tillman (1847–1918) was the Democratic governor of South Carolina, 1890–94, and a U.S. senator, 1895–1918.

125.17–18 Jefferson's principles . . . equal rights] In his inaugural address, delivered on December 4, 1890, Tillman said, "We deny, without regard to color, that 'all men are created equal;' it is not true now and was not true when Jefferson wrote it."

125.24 Mr. CUTCHEON] Byron M. Cutcheon (1836–1908) was a Republican congressman from Michigan, 1883–91.

125.30 constitutional guaranty of a 2-mill tax] An amendment to the South Carolina state constitution adopted in 1878 provided for the levying of a .2 percent state property tax in support of public education.

126.7–8 He recommends the abolishment of two colleges] In his inaugural address Tillman questioned the value of state aid to the Citadel and called for the University of South Carolina to be stripped of its agricultural and mechanical department and reorganized as a smaller liberal arts college.

127.10–11 South Carolina represented . . . seven Democrats] South Carolina had been represented in the Fifty-first Congress by seven Democrats until September 23, 1890, when the House voted to seat Miller (see note 124.2).

128.2 IDA B. WELLS] Born to enslaved parents in Holly Springs, Mississippi, Ida B. Wells (1862–1931) was educated at Shaw University (now Rust College), a school for freed people in Holly Springs. Wells taught in rural schools in Mississippi and Arkansas before moving to Memphis in 1881, where she taught in the nearby town of Woodstock, 1881–84, and in the Memphis schools, 1884–91. She began writing for *Living Way*, a Baptist weekly, and *Evening Star*, a lyceum publication, before becoming editor and part owner of the *Memphis Free Speech and Headlight* in 1889. A mob destroyed the offices of the *Free Speech* in 1892 after Wells wrote a series of articles denouncing lynching. She went into exile in the North and began a campaign against lynching, delivering public lectures and publishing pamphlets on racial violence, including *Southern Horrors* (1892), *A Red Record* (1895), *Lynch Law in Georgia* (1899), *Mob Rule in New Orleans* (1900), *The East St. Louis Massacre* (1917), and *The Arkansas Race Riot* (1920).

128.20–21 Sampsons . . . Deliahs] See Judges 16:4–31.

130.3 Wednesday evening May 24th, 1892] May 24, 1892, was a Tuesday.

132.7 J.C. Duke . . . "The Herald"] Jesse Chisholm Duke (1853–1916), a leader in the black Baptist Church in Alabama, founded the *Montgomery Herald* in May 1886. After his editorial on lynching appeared on August 13, 1887, Duke left Montgomery and settled in Pine Bluff, Arkansas, where he edited the *Weekly Echo* and the *Weekly Herald*.

132.34 "Cleveland Gazette"] A black weekly newspaper, founded in 1883 and edited by Harry Clay Smith (1863–1941).

136.9–10 Edward Coy . . . January 1, 1892] Coy was burned alive before a crowd of about one thousand people in Texarkana, Arkansas, on February 20, 1892.

136.11–12 Bystander . . . Chicago Inter-Ocean, October 1, 1892] The civil rights lawyer and novelist Albion W. Tourgée (see note 214.3) wrote a weekly column, "A Bystander's Notes," for the *Chicago Daily Inter Ocean*, 1888–98. Tourgée addressed the lynching of Coy in his column for September 24, 1892.

137.34 Bishop Fitzgerald] Oscar Penn Fitzgerald (1829–1911), editor of the *Nashville Christian Examiner*, 1878–90, and bishop of the Methodist Episcopal

Church, South, 1890–1911. In an interview printed in the *Atlanta Constitution* on May 23, 1892, Fitzgerald said that "the unspeakable crime" punished by lynch mobs "outlaws the perpetrator, whether black or white, in every part of the United States." He continued: "It is notable that in all the spasms of indignation against the Southern people because of these lynchings, no word of sympathy has been spoken for the white women who were their victims." Fitzgerald was responding to a resolution adopted by the General Conference of the Methodist Episcopal Church on May 17 calling on the federal and state governments to take action against the "outrages" and "cruelties" of lynching.

137.35–39 Governor Tillman . . . a *white* woman."] On December 28, 1889, a white mob removed eight black men from the jail in Barnwell, South Carolina, tied them to trees, and shot them to death. Two of the prisoners had been accused of murdering white men in separate cases, while the other six were being held as accessories or witnesses. An Associated Press article dated June 8, 1892, reported that Governor Benjamin Tillman (see note 125.15–16) had opened his reelection campaign under "the grove of trees" in Barnwell where the eight men had been lynched and declared: "There is only one crime that should bring lynching. I, as Governor, would head a party to lynch any negro that would criminally assault a white woman."

138.11–14 Pat Hanifin . . . a detective] Patrick J. Hanifin (1856–1899) was indicted in Nashville on January 22, 1884, for the rape of a ten-year-old black girl and held without bond. He was released after the jury in his trial divided 7–5 in favor of acquittal on March 14. His second trial ended in an acquittal on October 15, 1884, and Hanifin resumed his career as a detective. He was shot to death in 1899 in the offices of his loan collection agency by Thomas Johnson, a black employee who claimed self-defense. Johnson testified that Hanifin had fired first during a quarrel over money Johnson said was owed to him and was acquitted at trial.

138.15–16 a white man outraged an Afro-American girl] Lem Thompson Jr., a thirteen-year old white boy working as a drugstore clerk, was arrested in Nashville on May 23, 1892, for attempting to criminally assault Maggie Reese, an eight-year-old black girl. The case was presented to the grand jury, which apparently did not vote for an indictment.

138.23 Eph. Grizzard] Two white sisters who lived near Goodlettsville, Tennessee, reported on April 28, 1892, that they had been sexually assaulted by two black men who broke into their home. Henry Grizzard was seized by a white mob that morning and hanged, while his brother Ephraim was sent to the Nashville jail. In the early hours of April 30, a mob attempted to break into the jail. Governor John P. Buchanan urged the crowd to let the law take its course, but the mob did not disperse until two white men outside the jail were wounded, one fatally, in an exchange of gunfire. A second assault on the jail on the afternoon of April 30 met little resistance, and the mob took Ephraim Grizzard to the Woodland Street Bridge, where he was hanged and repeatedly shot.

138.24–25 Governor Buchanan] John P. Buchanan (1847–1930), Democratic governor of Tennessee, 1891–93.

139.8–9 Ellerton L. Dorr . . . Russell Hancock's widow] Elizabeth Gwynn Hancock (1853–1911) had married Ellerton Dorr (1863–1943), a cotton buyer, in 1891. She was the widow of Russell Hancock (1850–1884), the son of Major General Winfield Scott Hancock (1824–1886), the Democratic candidate for president in 1880 and a former corps commander in the Army of the Potomac.

139.28 White Liners] A white supremacist militia that used murder and intimidation to suppress the Republican vote in the 1875 Mississippi state election, resulting in the Democrats winning control of the state legislature and forcing the Republican governor to resign the following year.

139.29 Hamburg and Ellenton, S. C.] White supremacists killed six black men in Hamburg, July 18, 1876, and about thirty black people in and around Ellenton, September 16–19, 1876, during the 1876 election campaign.

139.30 Copiah County Miss., . . . Lafayette Parish, La.] Copiah County is in western Mississippi, south of Jackson. It is possible that Wells is referring to events in neighboring Hinds County during the Mississippi state elections in 1875, where a Democratic attempt to disrupt a Republican election rally in Clinton on September 4 led to an exchange of gunfire in which three white and at least five black persons were killed. Over the next two days several hundred members of the "White Line" militia moved through Hinds County and murdered between thirty and fifty black residents. White supremacist groups committed several massacres in Louisiana during Reconstruction, including at Opelousas in St. Landry Parish in 1868, at Colfax in Grant Parish in 1873, and at Coushatta in Red River Parish in 1874.

140.15–16 Barnwell, S. C. . . . Memphis, Tenn.] For the mass lynching in Barnwell, South Carolina, in 1889, see note 137.35–39. About fifty armed white men attacked the Carroll County Courthouse in Carrollton, Mississippi, on March 17, 1886, as the trial was about to begin of a white man charged with the attempted murder of Ed and Charley Brown, two brothers of black and Indigenous ancestry. The gunmen killed or fatally wounded at least thirteen black men, including the Brown brothers. There was no local, state, or federal investigation of the Carrollton murders. Wells's reference to Waycross, Georgia, may refer to the attack on the Waycross jail on December 13, 1891, in which a mob unsuccessfully tried to kill Welcome Golden and Robert Knight, two black men charged with murdering two white men during a land dispute. (The attackers fired repeatedly into their darkened cell but failed to hit the two prisoners, who hid along the walls.) Fearing that they would be lynched if they were acquitted, Golden and Knight pled guilty in February 1892 and received long prison sentences; they were released in 1908. For the lynching of three of Wells's friends in Memphis in March 1892, see pp. 144.30–146.21 in this volume.

144.5 bloody riot of 1866] A confrontation between white police officers and recently discharged black soldiers sparked three days of racial violence in Memphis, May 1–3, 1866, in which forty-six black and three white persons were killed. A three-member select committee of the House of Representatives investigated the riot and submitted two reports. The Republican majority report described the violence as "an organized and bloody massacre of the colored people" caused by racial prejudice and hostility toward the federal government, while the Democratic minority report concluded that future violence could best be avoided by restoring the political rights of former Confederates and abolishing the Freedmen's Bureau.

144.30–31 lynched . . . three of the best] The three men were Thomas Moss (1853–1892), the president of the People's Grocery and a close friend of Wells; Calvin McDowell, the twenty-one-year-old manager of the grocery; and Will Stewart, the store's clerk.

146.24–25 Henry W. Grady . . . New York] Henry W. Grady (1850–1889) was the managing editor of the *Atlanta Constitution*, 1879–89. In his widely reported speech "The New South," delivered in New York City on December 21, 1886, he characterized race relations in the South as "close and cordial" and declared that the future of "the negro" should "be left to those among whom his lot is cast, with whom he is indissolubly connected." In "The Race Problem in the South," delivered in Boston on December 12, 1889, Grady vowed that the South would never be "surrendered to the control of an ignorant and inferior race" and described "purchasable" black southern voters as "clannish, credulous, impulsive, and passionate—tempting every demagogue, but insensible to the appeal of the statesmen."

147.10–13 great M. E. Church . . . Omaha last May] See note 137.34.

147.16–17 Republican platform . . . June 7th] The Republican National Convention met in Minneapolis, June 7–10, 1892, and adopted a platform that denounced "the continued inhuman outrages perpetrated upon American citizens for political reasons in certain Southern States of the Union" and declared that the "free and honest popular ballot, the just and equal representation of all the people, as well as their just and equal protection under the laws, are the foundation of our Republican institutions."

147.18–20 The President . . . he has jurisdiction] In a public letter to the Virginia State Baptist Convention sent on May 21, 1892, President Benjamin Harrison wrote: "Lynchings are a reproach to any community; they impeach the adequacy of our institutions for the punishment of crime; they brutalize the participants and shame our Christian civilization. I have not time to explain to you the limitations of the Federal power further than to say that under the Constitution and laws I am, in a large measure, without the power to interfere for the prevention or punishment of these offenses. You will not need to be assured that the Department of Justice will let no case pass that is one of

Federal jurisdiction without the most strenuous endeavors to bring the guilty persons to punishment."

147.20–21 Governor Northern and Chief Justice Bleckley] William J. Northern (1835–1913), a Democrat, was governor of Georgia, 1890–94. Logan E. Bleckley (1827–1907) served as an associate justice of the Georgia Supreme Court, 1875–80, and as its chief justice, 1887–94.

147.30 A. S. Colyar] Arthur St. Clair Colyar (1818–1907), a Nashville attorney and businessman.

148.14 murder at Shelbyville] William Bates, a white farmer from Bedford County, Tennessee, was charged on June 25, 1892, with the murder of Ida Koonce Bates, his wife. A mob took Bates from the jail in Shelbyville on June 27 and hanged him.

150.29–30 proposed lynching . . . Paducah, Ky.] On the afternoon of July 4, 1892, Benjamin Reed, a black teamster, was arrested after he fatally injured Frank Burrows, a white shipping clerk, during a fight in a brewery in Jacksonville, Florida. Hundreds of armed black men guarded the jail until a strong force of state militia arrived in the city on July 7. Reed was convicted of murder in 1893 and sentenced to life at hard labor. Charles Hill, a black man, was lynched in Paducah, Kentucky, on June 10, 1892, after being accused of assaulting a white woman while robbing her home. When Thomas Burgess was arrested on July 11 and accused of being a "night prowler" in white neighborhoods, armed black men gathered around the jail, resulting in an exchange of gunfire with state militia in which a militiaman was fatally wounded.

151.15 lynching occurred at Port Jarvis, N. Y.] Lena McMahon, a young white woman, reported on June 2, 1892, that she had been assaulted by a black man along the banks of the Neversink River in Port Jervis, New York. Robert Lewis, a twenty-eight-year-old black man, was apprehended in a nearby village and brought back to town, where a mob seized him outside the jail and hanged him before as many as two thousand onlookers. It was reported that while in custody Lewis had implicated Philip Foley, McMahon's white suitor, in the assault. Foley was arrested and later charged with blackmailing McMahon but was released on bail in November 1892 and never tried. Although several men were named as participants in the lynching by witnesses at the coroner's inquest, no one was charged for taking part in Lewis's murder.

152.36–37 hung . . . thirteen year old Mildrey Brown] Mildrey (or Milbry) Brown, a domestic servant, was convicted of poisoning an eleven-month-old baby with carbolic acid after the child's mother scolded her for sweeping too slowly. Brown, who was variously reported to be thirteen, fourteen, or sixteen years old, was hanged in Spartanburg, South Carolina, on October 7, 1892.

154.3–4 *The Reason Why . . . Exposition*] The World's Columbian Exposition was held in Chicago from May 1 to 31, 1893. To protest the exclusion of black Americans from the boards that planned the exposition and the absence

NOTES

of exhibits devoted to black life in the United States, Frederick Douglass and Ida B. Wells decided to publish "a carefully prepared pamphlet, setting forth the past and present condition of our people and their relations to American civilization." *The Reason Why the Colored American is not in the World's Columbian Exposition: The Afro-American's Contribution to Columbian Literature* was printed in the late summer of 1893, with an afterword dated August 30. It featured an unsigned preface, an introductory chapter by Douglass, three chapters by Wells, a chapter titled "The Progress of the Afro-American since Emancipation" by the journalist and educator Irvine Garland Penn (1867–1930), and a chapter by the lawyer and newspaper publisher Ferdinand L. Barnett (1852–1936) on the attempts to have black Americans represented in the exposition. (Wells and Barnett would marry in 1895.)

156.9 whited sepulcher] See Matthew 23:27.

156.18–22 John Wesley . . . cannot sleep forever."] Wesley wrote in his journal on February 12, 1772, about "that execrable sum of all villainies, commonly called the Slave Trade." Douglass quotes from Jefferson's *Notes on the State of Virginia* (1785), query XVIII.

164.7 CLASS LEGISLATION] The second and third chapters in the pamphlet, "Class Legislation" and "The Convict Lease System," appeared without attribution, while the fourth chapter, "Lynch Law," was credited to Wells. It is likely that she wrote the second and third chapters, possibly using information supplied by the civil rights lawyer Albion Tourgée (see note 214.3).

165.25–28 Mississippi made . . . Mississippi Constitution] Mississippi adopted a new state constitution in 1890 that made payment of a poll tax a prerequisite for voting and also required that every voter "be able to read any section of the constitution of this State; or he shall be able to understand the same when read to him, or give a reasonable interpretation thereof." The new franchise qualifications went into effect on January 1, 1892.

166.12 M. & V.] Misdemeanors and Violations.

167.10 Johnson's History . . . America] Edward A. Johnson, *A School History of the Negro Race in America, from 1619 to 1890, with a short introduction as to the origin of the race; also a short sketch of Liberia* (1890). Johnson (1860–1944) was the principal of the Washington School in Raleigh, North Carolina, 1885–91. He later taught law at Shaw University, 1893–1907, before moving to New York City. In 1917 Johnson became the first black person elected to the New York legislature and served a single one-year term in the assembly.

168.2–12 colored young school teacher . . . damages.] Wells was forcibly removed from the ladies' coach while traveling on the Chesapeake, Ohio & Southwestern Railroad in September 1883 and in May 1884. She sued the railroad after both incidents and was awarded a total of $700 in damages by the circuit court, but the decisions were overturned by the Tennessee Supreme Court in April 1887.

170.18–20   Rev. John Frank . . . Rev. C. H. Parrish] John H. Frank (1859–1941) was the pastor of the Fifth Street Baptist Church in Louisville, 1887–1937; Charles Henry Parrish (1859–1931) became president of Eckstein Norton University shortly after its founding in 1890 and served until 1912, when the school merged with the Lincoln Institute.

171.12   George W. Cable] See note 101.2.

172.17   Chicago *Inter-Ocean* recently printed an interview] "On a Convict Farm," October 3, 1892.

173.36–40   Alabama a new warden . . . of the age.'] John H. Bankhead, "Warden's Report," *Biennial Report of the Inspectors of the Alabama Penitentiary, from September 30, 1880, to September 30, 1882* (1882). Bankhead (1842–1920) was warden of the Alabama state penitentiary, 1881–85. He later served as a Democratic congressman, 1887–1907, and senator, 1907–20.

174.9   Mildred Brown] See note 152.36–37.

174.14–15   second colored female hanged . . . one month] Anna Tribble was hanged in Newberry, South Carolina, on October 7, 1892, for killing her newborn child.

174.18   Alabama . . . ten year old Negro boy] This may be an inaccurate report. Sam Smith, described in newspaper accounts as being eighteen years old, was hanged in Birmingham, Alabama, on February 2, 1893, for the murder the previous year of Isaac Berger (or Burger), a peddler.

175.2   RICHARD T. GREENER] See note 16.17.

175.4   *Lend a Hand*] *Lend a Hand: A Record of Progress* was a magazine edited by the Unitarian minister, reformer, and writer Edward Everett Hale (1822–1909) from 1886 to 1897.

175.8–9   Thomas Jefferson's "Notes on Virginia"] *Notes on the State of Virginia* (1785), queries XIV and XVIII.

175.10   the *Forum*] *The Forum* was a magazine published monthly (quarterly, 1902–8) in New York City from 1886 to 1930, when it merged with *The Century*.

175.14   Imlay and Abbé Grégoire] The views on race and slavery expressed by Jefferson in *Notes on the State of Virginia* were criticized by the American writer and land speculator Gilbert Imlay (1754?–1828?) in *Topographical Description of the Western Territory of North America* (1792) and by the French bishop Henri Jean-Baptiste Grégoire (1750–1831) in *De la littérature des Nègres* (1808).

175.15–16   Benjamin Banneker] See note 100.23.

175.21   Nott & Gliddon, DeLeon, DeBow] The American physician John C. Nott (1804–1873) and the Anglo-American Egyptologist George R. Gliddon

(1809–1857) co-authored *Types of Mankind* (1854) and co-edited *Indigenous Races of the Earth* (1857). Edwin de Leon (1818–1891) was co-editor of *The Southern Press* (1850–52) and published the pamphlet *The Truth About the Confederate States of America* (1862) while serving as a Confederate envoy in Europe. James D. B. DeBow (1820–1867), an economist and statistician, defended slavery as the editor of the *Commercial Review of the South and West*, commonly known as *DeBow's Review*, 1846–62.

175.21 *alius, alii*] Latin: one to another.

176.7 sand-hiller] Term for a poor southern white person.

176.19 *novi homines*] Latin: new men.

176.24–30 Wut *is* there . . . an' they duller] From "Mr. Hosea Biglow's Speech in March Meeting" by James Russell Lowell (1819–1891), published in *The Atlantic Monthly*, May 1866, and collected in *The Biglow Papers, Second Series* (1867).

177.8–11 heights of Abraham . . . from Bunker Hill] British general James Wolfe (1727–1759) won a major victory on the Plains of Abraham outside Quebec City in 1759 during the French and Indian War. General Edward Braddock (1695–1755) led British and colonial forces to defeat in the Battle of Monongahela in 1755. Crispus Attucks (c. 1723–1770), a sailor of African and Indigenous ancestry, was one of five men killed by British soldiers in the Boston Massacre of 1770. John Trumbull (1756–1843) depicted the battle in his painting *The Death of General Warren at the Battle of Bunker's Hill, 17 June, 1775* (1786).

177.18–24 Andrew Jackson . . . entitle you to."] From "Address to the Free People of Color," issued on December 18, 1814, three weeks before the battle of New Orleans.

177.24–26 fought with Lawrence . . . Old Ironsides] James Lawrence (1781–1813) commanded the frigate USS *Chesapeake* in its battle with the frigate HMS *Shannon* off Boston in 1813 and was mortally wounded in the engagement, which ended with the capture of the *Chesapeake* by the British. "Old Ironsides" was the popular name for the frigate USS *Constitution*, which defeated five British warships during the War of 1812.

177.28–29 Port Hudson and Battery Wagner] Black troops took part in the Union assaults on Port Hudson, Louisiana, May 27, 1863, and Fort Wagner, South Carolina, July 18, 1863.

177.30 Negro historians . . . or Wilson] William Nell (1816–1874), author of *Services of Colored Americans in the Wars of 1776 and 1812* (1851) and *The Colored Patriots of the American Revolution* (1855); George Washington Williams (1849–1891), author of *History of the Negro Race in America* (1885) and *A History of the Negro Troops in the War of the Rebellion, 1861–1865* (1887); Joseph T. Wilson (1837–1890), author of *The Black Phalanx: A History of the Negro Soldiers of the United States in the Wars of 1775–1812, 1861–'65* (1887).

178.7   Palatines] Inhabitants of the German Palatinate.

178.31   from 1808] The year the congressional act prohibiting the importation of enslaved persons took effect.

178.37–38   Benezet . . . Rittenhouse] Anthony Benezet (1713–1784), French-born Pennsylvania Quaker antislavery writer and activist; Abbé Grégoire, see note 175.14; the Marquis de Condorcet (1713–1794), French philosopher who wrote *Reflections on Negro Slavery* (1781); Jacques Pierre Brissot de Warville (1754–1793), French journalist and revolutionary who cofounded the abolitionist Society of the Friends of the Blacks in 1788; Benjamin Franklin (1706–1790) and the physician Benjamin Rush (1746–1813) reorganized the Pennsylvania Abolition Society in 1787; the surveyor, astronomer, and inventor David Rittenhouse (1732–1796) denounced slavery in his 1775 oration to the American Philosophical Society and endorsed Benjamin Banneker's work as an almanac maker.

179.2–6   Abbé Raynal, 1779 . . . in particular."] Guillaume-Thomas Raynal, abbé de Raynal (1713–1796), *A Philosophical and Political History of the British Settlement and Trade in North America* (1779). Raynal first made the observation in *Histoire philosophique et politique, des établissements et du commerce des Européens dans les deux Indes* (1770).

179.7–12   Fisher Ames . . . considerable talents,"] Fisher Ames (1758–1808), Massachusetts lawyer and orator, "American Literature" (1807); Sydney Smith (1771–1845), English clergyman and essayist, in a letter to Lord Grey, November 30, 1818.

179.14   Ferguson's Astronomy] *Astronomy Explained on Sir Isaac Newton's Principles* (1756) by Scottish astronomer James Ferguson (1710–1776).

179.19   Lundy] Benjamin Lundy (1789–1839), a Quaker abolitionist, founded the antislavery newspaper *Genius of Universal Emancipation* in 1821 and published it intermittently for the rest of his life.

179.20   Mr. Howells . . . streets of "Nigger Hill"] Possibly a reference to the first chapter of the novel *An Imperative Duty* (1891) by William Dean Howells (1837–1920), in which the white protagonist walks from Boston Common to the black neighborhood along Cambridge Street. (The term "Nigger Hill" does not appear in Howells's text.)

179.25   Big Dick . . . Jackson] Richard Crafus (c. 1791?–1831), known as "Big Dick" and "King Dick," was a seaman who was captured by the British during the War of 1812 and imprisoned in Dartmoor prison in England. After his release he settled in Boston and became a well-known boxer. Born in St. Croix in the West Indies, Peter Jackson (1861–1901) became the Australian heavyweight champion and also fought in Britain, Ireland, and the United States during the bareknuckle era.

179.26–27   Prince Hall, and Easton, Master Paul] Prince Hall (c. 1735–1807) was a freedman who became a leader of the Boston black community, an

NOTES 663

abolitionist campaigner, and the founder of the first black Masonic lodge in North America. James Easton was a black ironworker who opened a trade school for black youth in Boston in 1816; his son, Hosea Easton (1798–1837), was an abolitionist minister in Boston and Hartford, Connecticut. Thomas Paul (1773–1831) became the founding pastor of the First African Baptist Church (also known as the African Meeting House) in Boston in 1805. The church building, opened in 1806, housed a school for black children.

179.29–33 "On that dismal . . . to be resisted."] Oliver Johnson (1809–1889), *William Lloyd Garrison and His Times* (1879).

179.37–38 Mr. Garrison, at Exeter Hall . . . sixty years ago] Garrison spoke at Exeter Hall on July 13, 1833.

180.16–17 Cary . . . Cook] Isaac Newton Cary (c. 1806–1884), a free black man, owned a successful barbershop in Washington, D.C., and distributed abolitionist newspapers. In 1836 he successfully challenged in court a recently adopted municipal law prohibiting black people from obtaining commercial licenses. John Fleet was a barber and friend of Cary. John Francis Cook (1810–1855), a freedman who worked as a shoemaker and as a messenger for the U.S. Land Office, founded a "Moral and Literary Society" for young black men in Washington. In 1834 he became the principal of Union Seminary, a school for free black children, and the following year he served as the secretary of the fifth Convention for the Improvement of Free People of Color.

180.17–18 Forten . . . Purvis] James Forten (1766–1842), born to free parents in Philadelphia, became a highly successful sailmaker. An opponent of the American Colonization Society and advocate for the rights of free black people in Pennsylvania, Forten became a financial supporter of William Lloyd Garrison and was elected vice president of the American Anti-Slavery Society in 1834. Richard Allen (1760–1831), a freedman, became a Methodist preacher and leader of the black community in Philadelphia. In 1816 he helped found the African Methodist Episcopal Church and was elected as its first bishop. John Pierre Burr (1792–1864), a barber who hid fugitives in his home, was an active member of the Pennsylvania Anti-Slavery Society and the American Moral Reform Society. (Burr was the son of Mary Emmons, a free woman of color born in Kolkata [Calcutta], India; it is likely that his father was the politician Aaron Burr.) Robert Purvis (1810–1898), the son of a white father and a freedwoman, helped found the American Anti-Slavery Society in 1833 and was active in other reform movements.

180.18 Grice . . . Watkins] Hezekiah Grice (c. 1801–1863), a free machinist and businessman living in Baltimore, helped organize the first Convention for the Improvement of Free People of Color in 1830 and cofounded the Legal Rights Association with William Watkins the following year. Grice immigrated to Haiti around 1834. Jacob Greener, Richard T. Greener's grandfather, was the principal of a school for indigent and orphaned children in Baltimore. William Watkins (c. 1801–1858) was a shoemaker, lay Methodist preacher, and contributor to *Genius of Universal Emancipation* and *The Liberator*. William

Lloyd Garrison later acknowledged that his conversations with Grice, Greener, and Watkins influenced him to reject colonization and embrace immediate emancipation as a goal for the antislavery movement.

180.19 Paul . . . Walker] For Thomas Paul and Hosea Easton, see note 179.26–27. James G. Barbadoes (1796–1841), a barber who operated a rooming house, was an active Freemason and a founding member of the American Anti-Slavery Society. Born free in North Carolina, David Walker (1796–1830) eventually settled in Boston, where he worked as a used clothing merchant and became an agent for *Freedom's Journal*, the country's first black-owned and black-operated newspaper. In 1829 Walker published *Walker's Appeal, in Four Articles, together with a Preamble, to the Colored Citizens of the World, but in particular and very expressly to those of the United States of America*, a pamphlet in which he called for the forcible overthrow of slavery and racial oppression.

180.26 abolitionists . . . in 1860] A mob violently disrupted an abolitionist meeting held at Tremont Temple on December 3, 1860, to commemorate the first anniversary of John Brown's execution. The meeting later reconvened at the First African Baptist Church and was addressed by Frederick Douglass and Wendell Phillips.

180.31–32 emancipation . . . Russwurm] Samuel E. Cornish (1795–1858), a Presbyterian minister, and John Brown Russwurm (1799–1851), the first black graduate of Bowdoin College, began publishing *Freedom's Journal* in New York City on March 16, 1827; the remaining enslaved people in New York State were legally emancipated on July 4, 1827. Cornish resigned from the newspaper in September 1827, and as sole editor Russwurm began to support colonization. Russwurm closed the newspaper in 1829 and emigrated to Liberia, where he served as governor of the Maryland Colony from 1836 until his death.

180.38 "old clo' merchants"] Used clothing merchants.

181.1 reward set for the author's head] After the publication of Walker's *Appeal* it was reported that a group of wealthy southern planters offered a $3,000 reward for his assassination and $10,000 if he was delivered alive to a southern state.

181.4–5 Butler, Walker's son . . . in Boston] Edward Garrison Walker (1830–1901) was admitted to the Massachusetts bar in 1861 and appointed to the municipal court in Charlestown in 1883 by Governor Benjamin F. Butler (1818–1893). Although Butler, a former Union general, had served in Congress after the Civil War as a Republican, he was elected governor on a Greenback-Democratic ticket, and the Republican-controlled executive council blocked Walker's judicial appointment.

181.21 *J'y suis reste*] French: Here I am; here I remain.

182.3–12 Fletcher of Saltoun . . . —*Dvorak.*] The Scottish political leader Andrew Fletcher of Saltoun (1655–1716) wrote in *An Account of a Conversation concerning a right Regulation of Governments for the Common Good of Mankind* (1704): "If a man were permitted to make all the Ballads, he need not care who should make the Laws of a Nation." The quotations from the Bohemian composer Antonín Dvořák (1841–1904) are from an interview that appeared in the *New York Herald* on May 21, 1893, under the headline "Real Value of Negro Melodies." (In the *Herald* the last quoted sentence reads, "There is nothing in the whole range of composition that cannot be supplied with themes from this source.")

182.26–28 Galton . . . brain of Athens!] The English statistician and eugenicist Francis Galton (1822–1911) wrote in *Hereditary Genius: An Inquiry into its Laws and Consequences* (1869) that the "average ability of the Athenian race" of 530–430 BCE was "very nearly two grades higher than our own—that is, about as much as our race is above that of the African negro."

182.33 *partus sequiter patiem*] Latin: the offspring follows the father, i.e., the legal status of the father determines the status of the child.

182.33–36 Hening . . . their importation."] "An act concerning Servants and Slaves," (1705), *The Statutes at large; being a collection of all the Laws of Virginia*, vol. III (1812), 447–48, edited by William Waller Hening (1768–1828).

183.7–33 "Consider him at . . . patience and tolerance."] From Walter H. Page, "The Last Hold of the Southern Folly," *The Forum*, November 1893. Page (1855–1918), a native of North Carolina, was the editor of the *Raleigh State Chronicle*, 1885–87, and of *The Forum*, 1891–95. He later served as U.S. ambassador to Great Britain, 1913–18.

184.10 Mr. Lowell] The poet, essayist, and editor James Russell Lowell (1819–1891).

184.21 Professor Price] Born free in North Carolina, Joseph Charles Price (1854–1893) graduated from Lincoln University in 1879 and was ordained in the African Methodist Episcopal Church. He served as president of Zion Wesley Institute (later Livingstone College) in Salisbury, North Carolina, from 1882 until his death.

184.23 Professor Scarborough] Born into slavery in Georgia, William Sanders Scarborough (1852–1926) graduated from Oberlin in 1875. He was professor of ancient languages at Wilberforce University, 1877–91 and 1897–1920, president of the university, 1908–20, and the author of *First Lessons in Greek* (1881) and *The Birds of Aristophanes: A Theory of Interpretation* (1886).

185.8 Bishop Potter] Henry C. Potter (1834–1908) was the Episcopal bishop of New York, 1883–1908.

185.10–15 Cable . . . and high-minded.] A garbled quotation from "The Freedman's Case in Equity" by George Washington Cable; see p. 118.19–23 in this volume.

185.15–18 We hear much . . . moral guide."] See p. 121.10–14 in this volume.

185.19–33 Bishop Dudley . . . the Creator's law."] Thomas Underwood Dudley, "How Shall We Help the Negro?," *The Century Magazine*, June 1885. Dudley (1837–1904) was the Episcopal bishop of Kentucky, 1884–1904.

185.35–186.15 Archbishop Ireland . . . with white citizens."] John Ireland, "No Barrier Against Color: Oration Delivered, January 1, 1891." Ireland (1838–1918), the Roman Catholic archbishop of St. Paul, 1888–1918, delivered his speech at a banquet held by the Afro-American League of St. Paul to commemorate the anniversary of the Emancipation Proclamation.

186.20–23 Edmund Burke's . . . *in the right.*"] Cf. Edmund Burke (1729–1797), *Speech at the Guildhall, in Bristol, Previous to the late Election in that City, upon Certain Points Relative to his Parliamentary Conduct* (1780).

186.26–29 Slaves of Gold . . . question ours.] The final stanza of "The Negro's Complaint" (1788) by the English poet William Cowper (1731–1800).

189.25–26 Frederick Douglass . . . recent date] "Lessons of the Hour," an address delivered in Washington, D.C., on January 9, 1894, that was printed as a pamphlet and in several newspapers and journals.

190.29–30 Yazoo, Hamburg, Edgefield, Copiah] White supremacists killed one white and several black Republicans in Yazoo City, Mississippi, September 1–2, 1875. For Hamburg, see note 139.29. Edgefield, South Carolina, was the home of Martin Gary (1831–1881), author of what became known as the "Edgefield Plan" for suppressing the black vote for Republican candidates in the 1876 election through fraud, bribery, intimidation, and violence. For Copiah, see note 139.30.

193.33–38 Bishop Haygood . . . and daughters."] Atticus G. Haygood, "The Black Shadow in the South," *The Forum*, October 1893. Haygood (1839–1896) was president of Emory College, 1875–84, and the Methodist Episcopal Church, South, bishop of California, 1890–93.

195.15–17 "great dark faced mobs . . . roof trees."] A suffragist and social reformer, Frances Willard (1839–1898) was president of the Woman's Christian Temperance Union, 1879–98. In an interview titled "The Race Problem: Miss Willard on the Political Puzzle of the South," *The New York Voice*, October 23, 1890, she said, "'Better whisky and more of it' has been the rallying cry of great dark-faced mobs" in the South. Willard continued: "The colored race multiplies like the locusts of Egypt. The grog shop is the centre of its power. The safety of women, of childhood, of the home is menaced in a thousand localities at the moment, so that men dare not go beyond the sight of their own roof-tree." Wells had criticized Willard during her anti-lynching speaking tours, resulting in a public controversy addressed in chapter VIII of *A Red Record*, "Miss Willard's Attitude."

196.29–30 the incidents hereinafter reported] That is, in the subsequent chapters of *A Red Record*.

NOTES   667

197.2 BOOKER T. WASHINGTON] Born into slavery in Virginia, Washington (1856–1915) graduated from Hampton Normal and Agricultural Institute in 1875 and taught at Hampton, 1879–81. Washington became the first principal of Tuskegee Normal and Industrial Institute in 1881 and served in that position until his death. His autobiography *Up from Slavery* was published in 1901.

197.3 *Address at the Atlanta Exposition*] Washington delivered this address, which became known as the "Atlanta Compromise Speech," to a segregated audience at the opening of the Cotton States and International Exposition.

199.23–24 "blessing him . . . that takes."] Cf. *The Merchant of Venice*, IV.i.187.

199.27–30 "The laws . . . fate abreast."] John Greenleaf Whittier (1807–1892), "Song of the Negro Boatmen" (1862).

202.3 CLARK HOWELL] A graduate of the University of Georgia, Howell (1863–1936) joined *The Atlanta Constitution* in 1884 and was its managing editor, 1889–97, editor-in-chief, 1897–1936, and principal owner, 1901–36. He served as a Democrat in the Georgia house of representatives, 1887–93, and the state senate, 1901–05.

204.3 SOUTH CAROLINA CONVENTION] In November 1894 voters in South Carolina approved, 31,402–29,523, calling a convention to replace the state constitution adopted in 1868 during Reconstruction. A series of county conventions chose 160 delegates, of whom 112 were supporters of the Reform faction of the state Democratic Party led by Benjamin Tillman, 42 were Conservative Democratic opponents of Tillman, and 6 (all black) were Republicans. The convention met on September 10 and adjourned on December 4 after adopting a new constitution that went into effect on December 31, 1895, without having been submitted to the voters for ratification.

204.26 Benjamin Ryan Tillman] See note 125.15–16.

205.1–4 58,086 Negroes . . . 74,851 votes] The sum of 58,086 and 74,851 is 132,937, not the figure of 132,949 reported in the 1890 census.

206.14 Mr. Creelman] James Creelman (1859–1915) was a correspondent for *The New York Herald*, 1878–92, *The New York Evening Telegram*, 1892–94, *The New York World*, 1894–96 and 1900–1906, and *The New York Journal*, 1896–1900.

206.23–27 ROBERT SMALLS . . . ISAIAH REED] Robert Smalls, see note 18.4; Thomas E. Miller, see note 124.2; James E. Wigg (born c. 1850), a freedman who became a landowning cotton farmer on Beaufort Island, served in the South Carolina house of representatives, 1890–91; Robert E. Anderson, a schoolteacher from Georgetown who served in the state house of representatives, 1890–98; Isaiah Reed, an attorney from Beaufort.

208.24 disqualified . . . the Constitution] That is, persons disqualified under section 3 of the Fourteenth Amendment from holding federal or state office.

209.22–23 In all elections . . . but one ballot box] In 1882 the South Carolina legislature passed the "eight box law," requiring separate ballot boxes for eight different categories of political office and making ballots cast in the wrong box invalid. Election officials were required to read the box labels to illiterate voters who asked for assistance, but there was no mechanism to ensure they did so fairly. The eight box law also introduced stricter registration procedures, with the result that the number of black voters in South Carolina declined from about fifty-eight thousand in 1880 to about fourteen thousand in 1888.

209.32 MR. PRESIDENT] John Gary Evans (1863–1942), the Democratic governor of South Carolina, 1894–97, served as president of the convention.

209.38–210.1 the speeches made . . . my county] Beaufort County delegates Thomas Miller (see note 124.2) James E. Wigg (see note 206.23–27), and William James Whipper spoke against the proposed disenfranchisement clauses on October 25–26, 1895. Whipper (1834–1907) had served as a delegate to the 1868 South Carolina constitutional convention and as a Republican in the state house of representatives, 1868–72 and 1875–76.

210.12–13 chairman . . . ex-governor No. 1] John Calhoun Sheppard (1823–1888) was lieutenant governor of South Carolina, 1882–86, and served as governor, July–November 1886, after his predecessor resigned. Benjamin Tillman, another former governor, was also a member of the Edgefield County delegation.

210.30–31 a history . . . written by Neil] Possibly a reference to the American historian Edward D. Neill, author of *History of the Virginia Company of London* (1869) and *Virginia Vetusta, during the reign of James the First* (1885).

211.12–15 a good leader . . . uses only one eye] Benjamin Tillman had his left eye removed in 1864 after it became seriously inflamed.

213.38 let us make a Constitution] The convention adopted suffrage provisions that required prospective voters to pay a poll tax and be able to read any section of the new state constitution presented to them by a registration officer. Up to January 1, 1898, prospective voters would be registered if they could "understand and explain" a section of the constitution read to them by the registration officer, but after that date, only men who owned $300 or more in taxable property would be exempt from the literacy requirement.

214.3 ALBION W. TOURGÉE] A native of Ohio, Albion Tourgée (1838–1905) fought in the Civil War as a Union officer. He opened a law practice in Greensboro, North Carolina, in 1865 and served as a state superior court judge, 1868–74, before leaving the state in 1879. Tourgée published the novels *A Fool's Errand* (1879) and *Bricks Without Straw* (1880), set in North Carolina during Reconstruction, and *The Invisible Empire* (1880), a documentary account of the Ku Klux Klan, and advocated racial equality, national support for public schools, and anti-lynching legislation in a weekly column for the *Chicago Daily Inter Ocean*, 1888–98. In 1891 he became the chief legal adviser to the Citizens' Committee that had been formed in New Orleans to test the constitutionality of the 1890 Louisiana Separate Car Act.

214.4 *Brief for . . . Plessy v. Ferguson*] Homer Plessy (c. 1862/63–1925), a racially ambiguous shoemaker, was arrested in New Orleans on June 7, 1892, as part of a legal challenge to Louisiana's railroad segregation law. Plessy appeared before Judge John H. Ferguson (1838–1915) in the city criminal court in October 1892, represented by James C. Walker (1837–1898), a local white attorney. When Ferguson rejected his argument that the railroad law violated the Fourteenth Amendment, Walker appealed the case to the Louisiana Supreme Court and submitted a brief cowritten by him and Tourgée. The court upheld the law, and Walker filed an appeal to the U.S. Supreme Court in January 1893. In addition to the brief by Tourgée printed in this volume, Walker and Tourgée submitted a joint brief to the Supreme Court, as well as a separate brief by Walker. Another brief for the plaintiff was submitted by two Washington attorneys, Samuel F. Phillips (1824–1903) and Frederick D. McKenney (1863–1949). Phillips had served as solicitor general of the United States, 1872–85, and helped argue the *Civil Rights Cases* in 1883. Tourgée and Phillips appeared together when *Plessy* came before the Supreme Court on April 13, 1896, but their oral argument was not recorded.

218.29–30 *anglice*] Latin: in English.

219.4 *pro tanto*] Latin: to that extent.

222.32 Section 3 Article II] Possibly an error for section 2, Article IV.

223.6 Prigg vs. Pennsylvania] See note 45.22–25.

225.18 "Slaughter House Cases"] See note 52.30.

225.31–32 Chief justice Chase . . . Bradley] Salmon P. Chase (1808–1873) served as a senator from Ohio, 1849–55 and 1860–61, governor of Ohio, 1855–59, secretary of the treasury, 1861–64, and chief justice of the Supreme Court, 1864–73. For Field, Swayne, and Bradley, see notes 43.6 and 54.31–34.

226.28 opinion of the Court] The majority opinion in the *Slaughterhouse Cases* was written by Justice Samuel F. Miller.

226.34 Strauder *vs.* West Virginia] See notes 50.37–38 and 66.19–21.

228.3 Thorpe *vs.* Rutland and Burlington Railroad] An 1854 decision by Chief Justice Isaac F. Redfield (1804–1876) of the Vermont Supreme Court upholding a state law imposing liability on railroads that failed to build fences and cattle guards along their lines.

229.35–37 Haman . . . Kings gate] See Esther 3:1–5.

230.9–10 Justice is . . . to be color-blind.] Cf. Justice Harlan's dissent in *Plessy v. Ferguson*, p. 268.28–29 in this volume: "Our Constitution is color-blind, and neither knows nor tolerates classes among citizens." It is possible that Tourgée was familiar with a published speech given by the Republican lawyer and orator Robert G. Ingersoll (1833–1899) at a mass meeting held in Washington, D.C., on October 22, 1883, to protest the Supreme Court's decision in the *Civil Rights Cases*. Ingersoll said that "the obvious purpose" of the Thirteenth Amendment was "to forbid all shades and conditions of slavery, no matter of what sort or kind—all marks of legal inferiority. Each citizen was to be absolutely free. All his rights complete, whole, unmaimed and unabridged. From the moment of the adoption of that amendment, the law became color-blind."

231.21–22 ten cannot . . . a thousand] Cf. Deuteronomy 32:30.

232.5–7 If slavery was . . . Mr. Stephens declared] In a speech delivered at Savannah, Georgia, on March 21, 1861, Alexander Stephens (1812–1883), the Confederate vice president, said that the "corner-stone" of the new Confederacy "rests upon the great truth, that the negro is not equal to the white man; that slavery—subordination to the superior race—is his natural and normal condition."

232.12 Cruikshank's Case] See note 64.32.

234.11–13 Carlyle's grim . . . chiefly fools,"] In *Latter-Day Pamphlets* (1850), "No. VI Parliaments," the British essayist Thomas Carlyle (1795–1881) repeatedly described the population of Great Britain and Ireland as "twenty-seven million, mostly fools."

235.38 the learned Justice] See note 43.6.

236.12 dissenting opinion of Mr. Justice Harlan] See pp. 43–77 in this volume.

238.23–25 State *vs.* Jowers . . . State *vs.* Caesar] Tourgée cites three antebellum decisions of the North Carolina Supreme Court. The court ruled in *State v. Jowers* (1850) that "insolence from a free person of color to a white man will excuse a battery in the same manner and to the same extent as in the case of a slave." In *State v. Davis* (1859) the court overturned the conviction of a free black man who had struck a town constable trying to arrest him, finding that the constable had exceeded his authority and ruling that "while the law will not allow a free negro to return blow for blow, and engage in a fight with a white man, under ordinary circumstances," a free black man could claim self-defense if he could "prove that it became necessary for him to strike in order to protect himself from great bodily harm or grievous oppression." In *State v. Caesar* the court reversed the murder conviction and death sentence of an enslaved man who killed a drunken white man who was beating his friend, ruling that if "a white man wantonly inflicts upon a slave, over whom he has no authority, a severe blow or repeated blows, under unusual circumstances" an enslaved person could kill him "*at the instant*" and be only guilty of manslaughter.

241.1–2 Louisville Railroad Co. *vs.* Mississippi] In *Louisville, New Orleans and Texas Railway Company v. Mississippi* (1890) the U.S. Supreme Court ruled, 7–2, with Justices Harlan and Bradley dissenting, that the 1888 Mississippi law segregating railroad passengers within the state was not an unconstitutional regulation of interstate commerce.

247.10–12 "Right," as defined by Chancellor Kent . . . by law."] James Kent (1763–1847), *Commentaries on American Law*, vol. II (4th ed., 1840), lecture XXIV, "Of the Absolute Rights of Persons." Kent served as an associate justice of the New York Supreme Court of Judicature, 1798–1804, as its chief justice, 1804–14, and as chancellor of New York, 1814–23.

250.3 HENRY B. BROWN] After serving as a federal district judge in Michigan, 1875–90, Brown (1836–1913) was appointed as an associate justice of the U.S. Supreme Court by President Benjamin Harrison in 1890 and served until his retirement in 1906. The other justices in the majority were Stephen Field and Horace Gray (see note 43.6); Melville W. Fuller (1833–1910), chief justice, 1888–1910; George Shiras Jr. (1832–1924), associate justice, 1892–1903; Edward Douglass White (1845–1921), associate justice, 1894–1910 and chief justice, 1910–21; and Rufus Peckham (1838–1909), associate justice, 1895–1909. Fuller, White, and Peckham were appointed by President Grover Cleveland, Siras by President Benjamin Harrison.

253.35–36 *Roberts* v. *City of Boston*] The case was decided in 1850.

254.1 Chief Justice Shaw] See note 54.36–55.6.

254.22–23 District of Columbia . . . 319] The cited laws were enacted by Congress in 1862, 1864, and 1866.

254.25–28 *State* v. *McCann* . . . *Dawson* v. *Lee*] The first six cases cited are cases in which courts ruled that various state laws establishing racial segregation in public schools did not violate the Fourteenth Amendment: *State v. McCann* (1871), decided by the Ohio Supreme Court; *Lehew v. Brummell* (1891), decided by the Missouri Supreme Court; *Ward v. Flood* (1874), decided by the California Supreme Court; *Bertonneau v. School Directors* (1878), decided by the U.S. Circuit Court for Louisiana; *People v. Gallagher* (1883), decided by the New York Court of Appeals; and *Cory v. Carter* (1874), decided by the Indiana Supreme Court. In *Dawson v. Lee* (1885), the Kentucky Court of Appeals held that a state law excluding schools for black children from a share of the state's common school fund violated the Fourteenth Amendment.

254.32 *State* v. *Gibson*] The Indiana Supreme Court ruled in 1871 that the state law prohibiting marriage between white and black people did not violate the Fourteenth Amendment or the 1866 Civil Rights Act.

255.6–8 *Virginia* v. *Rives* . . . *Gibson* v. *Mississippi*] *Virginia* v. *Rives*, see note 60.30; *Neal* v. *Delaware*, see note 65.7. In *Bush v. Kentucky* (1883) the Supreme Court set aside, 6–3, the indictment of John Bush, a black servant convicted of the fatal shooting of the adolescent daughter of his white employer. Justice Harlan wrote in his opinion for the court that the indictment violated the Fourteenth Amendment because it had been voted by a grand jury chosen under an 1873 Kentucky statute restricting jury duty to white men. Bush was reindicted, convicted, and hanged in 1884. In *Gibson v. Mississippi* (1896) the court unanimously affirmed the conviction of John Gibson, a black laborer sentenced to death for the murder of a white plantation manager. Gibson sought to have his case removed to federal court on the grounds that the exclusion of black people from the grand jury that indicted him violated the Fourteenth Amendment. In his opinion for the court Justice Harlan held that Gibson could not prove his indictment was "due to the prejudice of race" because there were no provisions in the "constitution and laws of the state" restricting jury service on racial grounds. Gibson was hanged in 1897.

255.16 *Railroad Company* v. *Brown*] Kate Brown, a black woman who attended to the "ladies' retiring room" of the U.S. Senate, was forcibly removed by a railroad policeman when she attempted to board the ladies' car in Alexandria, Virginia, in February 1868 while returning to Washington. Brown sued the Washington, Alexandria & Georgetown Railroad Company and was awarded $1,500 in damages by the Supreme Court of the District of Columbia. The U.S. Supreme Court unanimously affirmed the judgment in 1873, citing the clause in the charter granted by Congress to the railroad in 1863 providing that "no person shall be excluded from the cars on account of color." In his opinion for the court Justice David Davis (1815–1886) rejected the railroad's claim that it had complied with the charter by providing accommodations for black passengers in separate cars: "It was the discrimination in the use of the cars on account of color where slavery obtained which was the subject of discussion at the time, and not the fact that the colored race could not ride in the cars at all."

255.26 *Hall* v. *De Cuir*] See note 76.11–15.

256.39–257.11 "If it be . . . commerce clause."] The opinion of the court in *Louisville, New Orleans and Texas Railway Company v. Mississippi* (see note 241.1–2) was written by David Brewer (1837–1910), who served as an associate justice from 1890 until his death.

257.14 *State ex rel. Abbott* . . . *et al.*] The case was decided by the Louisiana Supreme Court in 1892.

257.25–33 *West Chester* . . . *Georgia Railroad Co.*] In four of the cases cited, courts ruled against black plaintiffs suing railroad or steamboat companies, holding that the common law required common carriers to serve all passengers but allowed them to assign accommodations on the basis of race: *West Chester & Philadelphia Railroad Company v. Miles* (1867), decided by the

Pennsylvania Supreme Court; *Day v. Owen* (1858), decided by the Michigan Supreme Court; *Logwood v. Memphis & Central Railroad* (1885), decided by the U.S. District Court for Western Tennessee; and *McGuinn v. Forbes* (1889), decided by the U.S. District Court for Maryland. In three of the cited cases, courts upheld damages awarded to black plaintiffs for their unequal treatment by railroad or steamboat companies while holding that providing separate but equal accommodations was permitted by the law of common carriers: *Chicago & Northwest Railway Company v. Williams* (1870), decided by the Illinois Supreme Court; *The Sue* (1885), decided by the U.S. District Court for Maryland; and *Houck v. Southern Pacific Railway* (1888), decided by the U.S. Circuit Court for the Western District of Texas. *Chesapeake, Ohio & Southwestern Railroad v. Wells* (1887) was the decision by the Tennessee Supreme Court overturning the damages awarded to Ida B. Wells (see note 168.2–12). In *Memphis & Charleston Railroad v. Benson* (1887), the Tennessee Supreme Court held that an unaccompanied man did not have the right to be seated in the ladies' car in order to avoid sitting with smokers. *People v. King* (1888) was a decision by the New York Court of Appeals upholding a state law prohibiting racial exclusion from a variety of public accommodations. *Heard v. Georgia Railroad Co.* (1888, 1889) were two complaints brought before the Interstate Commerce Commission by a black passenger forced to ride in a "Jim Crow" car while traveling between states. The commission ruled that the railroad had violated the Interstate Commerce Act of 1887, which made it unlawful for a common carrier "to subject any person . . . to any undue or unreasonable prejudice or disadvantage," but stated that separate but equal accommodations would not violate the law. None of the cases cited addressed whether a state law could require segregation or involved provisions of the Thirteenth or Fourteenth Amendment.

257.33 *S. C.*] Same case.

259.6 *Yick Wo v. Hopkins*] The Supreme Court ruled 9–0 in 1886 that the San Francisco ordinance violated the equal protection clause of the Fourteenth Amendment.

259.21–26 *Railroad Company . . . Orman v. Riley*] In *Railroad Company v. Husen* (1877) the U.S. Supreme Court ruled that a Missouri law prohibiting the driving of Texas, Mexican, or Indian cattle into the state violated the interstate commerce clause of the Constitution, while in *Louisville & Nashville Railroad v. Kentucky* (1896) the court upheld a provision of the Kentucky state constitution prohibiting the consolidation of competing railroad lines within the state, holding that the prohibition was a "legitimate exercise of the police power" that did not interfere with interstate commerce. (The "cases cited on p. 700" refers to page 700 of volume 161 in the *U. S. Reports* series of Supreme Court opinions.) In three of the cases cited by Justice Brown, courts ruled on the validity under their respective state constitutions of various voter registration statutes: in *Daggett v. Hudson* (1885), decided by the Ohio Supreme Court, the law was overturned, while in *Capen v. Foster* (1832), decided by the

Massachusetts Supreme Judicial Court, and *State ex rel. Wood v. Baker* (1875), decided by the Wisconsin Supreme Court, the laws were upheld. A law allowing election officials to challenge prospective voters with a "visible admixture of African blood" was ruled by the Ohio Supreme Court in *Monroe v. Collins* (1868) to violate the state constitution. (Under the 1851 Ohio constitution suffrage was limited to "white male citizens," but the state supreme court had previously ruled that an individual having "more white than black blood" was "a *white man* within the meaning of the constitution.") In *Hulseman v. Rems* (1861) the Pennsylvania Supreme Court ruled that even though a Philadelphia municipal election had been decided by fraudulent votes, it could not invalidate the certificates of election issued by officials unaware of the fraud, while in *Orman v. Riley* (1860) the California Supreme Court refused to overturn the results of an election for county sheriff because the evidence of fraud was deemed insufficient.

260.23–31 "this end can . . . it is endowed."] From the opinion in *People v. Gallagher* by William C. Ruger (1824–1892), chief justice of the New York State Court of Appeals, 1883–92.

261.4–9 *State* v. *Chavers . . . Jones* v. *Commonwealth*] In *State v. Chavers* (1858) the North Carolina Supreme Court ruled that "a person must have in his veins less than one-sixteenth part of negro blood" before they could be considered to be white under the law. The other cases cited are *Gray v. Ohio* (1831), decided by the Ohio Supreme Court; *Monroe v. Collins* (1868), see note 259.21–26; *People v. Dean* (1866), decided by the Michigan Supreme Court; and *Jones v. Commonwealth* (1885), decided by the Virginia Supreme Court.

263.16–18 Mr. Justice Nelson . . . *Merchants' Bank*] See note 54.7–9.

263.22 Mr. Justice Strong] See note 66.19–21.

263.23 *Olcott* v. *The Supervisors*] See note 54.13–14.

263.38–39 *Township of Pine Grove* v. *Talcott*] See note 54.31–34.

264.2–11 *Inhabitants of Worcester . . .* the public."] See note 54.36–55.6.

265.17–35 "to a race . . . a subject race"] From the opinion of the court in *Strauder v. West Virginia* (see notes 50.37–38 and 66.19–21).

265.40–266.2 *Virginia* v. *Rives . . . Bush* v. *Kentucky*] *Virginia v. Rives* and *Ex parte Virginia*, see note 60.30; *Neal v. Delaware*, see note 65.7; *Bush v. Kennedy*, see note 255.6–8.

266.3–8 "underlying all . . . *Gibson* v. *Mississippi*] From Justice Harlan's opinion for the court in *Gibson v. Mississippi* (see note 255.6–8).

266.30–34 "Personal liberty . . . course of law."] See note 55.39–56.3.

267.33–38 Mr. Sedgwick . . . particular enactment."] Theodore Sedgwick (1811–1859), *A Treatise on the Rules which Govern the Interpretation and Construction of Statutory and Constitutional Law* (2nd ed., 1874).

269.8–13 "considered as . . . to grant them."] From the opinion of the court by Chief Justice Taney.

270.24–28 a race so different . . . Chinese race] The Chinese Exclusion Act of 1882 prohibited the entry of "skilled and unskilled" Chinese laborers and miners into the United States for ten years and continued the existing ban on the naturalization of Chinese immigrants. Congress renewed the act for another ten years in 1892 and required Chinese laborers already in the country to obtain residency certificates or face deportation, a measure upheld by the Supreme Court the following year. In 1898 the court would rule 6–2 in *United States v. Wong Kim Ark* that children of Chinese immigrants born in the United States were American citizens under the terms of the Fourteenth Amendment.

273.12–13 MR. JUSTICE BREWER . . . this case.] Brewer missed the oral argument in *Plessy v. Ferguson* because of the fatal illness of his daughter Frances Adele Brewer (1870–1896).

1897–1909

277.1 BISHOP HENRY MCNEAL TURNER] Turner (1834–1915) was born into a free black family in Newberry Courthouse, South Carolina. He became a licensed minister in the African Methodist Episcopal (AME) Church in 1853 and traveled as an itinerant preacher. During the Civil War he helped organize the 1st U.S. Colored Infantry Regiment and served as its chaplain, becoming one of the first black chaplains in the history of the U.S. Army. After the war he became a Republican organizer in Georgia and served as a delegate to the state constitutional convention, 1867–1868. Turner was elected to the Georgia assembly in 1868 but was expelled along with the other black members by the white majority and was unable to take his seat until 1870. After being defeated for reelection in 1870 he left politics and focused on religion and education. Turner served as pastor of St. Phillips AME Church in Savannah, Georgia, and, beginning in 1876, as president of Morris Brown College in Atlanta. He was appointed a bishop in the AME Church in 1880. Convinced that black Americans could not attain political equality in the United States, Turner founded two newspapers, *The Voice of Missions* (1893–1900) and the *Voice of the People* (1901–4), that promoted emigration to West Africa, and in 1895–96 organized two voyages that carried over five hundred emigrants to Liberia.

278.31–34 John Temple Graves . . . a majority] Graves (1856–1925) was an Atlanta newspaper editor, writer, and orator.

279.4–5 Senator Morgan of Alabama] John Tyler Morgan (1824–1907) was a Democratic senator from Alabama, 1877–1907.

280.4 *Mrs. Felton Speaks*] The speech quoted in this article was originally delivered before the Georgia Agricultural Society on August 11, 1897, and published in *The Atlanta Journal* the following day. It was reprinted in the *Wilmington Morning Star* of August 18, 1898, during the Democratic campaign to regain control of the state government from the biracial Fusion alliance of Populists and Republicans. Rebecca Latimer Felton (1835–1930) was an advocate for public education, prohibition, and the abolition of convict lease labor, and in the early twentieth century became a prominent supporter of white women's suffrage.

280.12–13 *J.A. Holman . . . SOUTH BEND HOTEL*] In the original *Atlanta Journal* text of this article, *Holman* is spelled *Hollomon*, and "SOUTH BEND" appears as "SOUTH END."

282.4 *A Horrid Slander*] On August 18, 1898, the *Wilmington Daily Record*, a black newspaper edited by Alex L. Manly (1866–1944), published an editorial in response to Rebecca Felton's 1897 speech on lynching. Born in Raleigh, North Carolina, and educated at Hampton Institute in Virginia, Manly moved to Wilmington and began publishing the *Daily Record* in 1895. The *Wilmington Morning Star* reprinted the text of the *Daily Record* editorial on August 30 and continued to run it under the headline "A Horrid Slander" in the weeks leading up to the election on November 8. This volume prints the text that appeared in the *Wilmington Morning Star* because copies of the *Daily Record* for August 18, 1898, are not known to be extant.

286.4 *Defamer Must Go*] This article appeared in the *Raleigh News and Observer* two days after the election of November 8, 1898. Although Democrats won the majority of votes, Fusionist candidates, representing a biracial coalition of Republicans and Populists, still held some offices in Wilmington, including the position of mayor. The *News and Observer* had been edited since 1894 by Josephus Daniels (1862–1948), a leading advocate for white supremacy during the 1898 election. Daniels later served as secretary of the navy under Woodrow Wilson, 1913–21, and as U.S. ambassador to Mexico, 1933–41.

288.31 the editor, Manly] Alex Manly fled Wilmington sometime between November 7, the eve of the election, and November 10, the day of the white supremacist insurrection in the city (see Chronology). After taking refuge in Washington, D.C., he eventually settled in Philadelphia. The offices of the *Daily Record* were burned by a white mob on November 10, 1898.

288.33–34 Mayor S. P. Wright . . . Mullen] Dr. Silas P. Wright (1839–1922), a white Republican born in Massachusetts, was elected mayor of Wilmington by the board of aldermen in 1897. On November 10, 1898, armed insurrectionists led by Alfred Moore Waddell (1834–1912) forced Wright, the white chief of police, John R. Melton (misidentified as Mullen in the *News and Observer*), and the board of aldermen to resign. The insurrectionists then installed Waddell as the new city mayor, a position he held until 1906.

290.2 W.H. COUNCILL] Born enslaved in Fayetteville, North Carolina, William Hooper Councill (1848–1909) founded the State Colored Normal School in Huntsville, Alabama (now Alabama A&M University) in 1875 and served as its principal until his death. His publications included *The Negro*

Laborer: A Word to Him (1887) and *Lamp of Wisdom; or, Race History Illuminated* (1898).

291.9 "live, move, . . . being,"] Cf. Acts 17:28.

291.39 Georgia's distinguished Governor] Allen D. Candler (1834–1910), Democratic governor of Georgia from 1898 to 1902.

292.20–21 Hon. Robert H. Porter's . . . people"] Porter (1852–1917) was superintendent of the census from 1889 to 1893. The eleventh census, conducted in 1890, reported a total of 7,470,040 "Persons of Negro Descent," including a total of 1,132,060 persons recorded as either "Mulattoes," "Quadroons," or "Octoroons."

295.28 Judge Tourgée] See note 214.3.

296.5–6 "Now there arose . . . not Joseph."] Exodus 1:8.

297.4 *Banquo's* ghost] See *Macbeth*, III.iv.

297.7–8 President McKinley . . . the unattainable,"] President William McKinley visited the Tuskegee Institute in Alabama on December 16, 1898, as part of his tour of the South. McKinley praised Booker T. Washington and the institute for their efforts to "promote an amicable relationship between the races" and then said, "An evidence of the soundness of the purpose of this institution is that those in charge of its management evidently do not believe in attempting the unattainable, and their instruction in self-reliance and practical industry is most valuable."

297.34 Senator Morgan's ideas about repatriation] Beginning in 1884, Morgan (see note 279.4–5) had advocated the "repatriation" of black Americans to the Congo Free State.

297.38 Bishop Turner] See note 277.1.

299.1 ROBERT CHARLES] Born in Mississippi in 1865, Robert Charles moved sometime in the 1890s to New Orleans, where he worked as a laborer, distributed literature promoting emigration to Liberia, and sold copies of Bishop Henry McNeal Turner's newspaper *Voice of Missions*. On the night of July 23, 1900, he was sitting on a stoop with a friend when they were approached by three white policemen. One of the officers grabbed Charles and drew his billy club, but Charles managed to break free. Both men drew revolvers, exchanged shots, and were wounded. Charles managed to return to his boardinghouse, where he armed himself with a Winchester rifle. When the police came to arrest him, Charles killed two officers and escaped. As the police hunted him white mobs attacked black residents in the streets at random, murdering five men and one woman. A tip led the police on the afternoon of July 27 to the house where Charles was hiding. Using his rifle and homemade bullets, Charles killed two policemen and three white onlookers before being fatally shot by a member of the "citizen police" formed by the mayor to restore order during the riots.

299.9 Wednesday morning] The morning of July 25, 1900.

299.17 the Mayor] Paul Capdievielle (1842–1922) served as mayor of New Orleans from May 9, 1900, until December 5, 1904.

300.10–11 Police Captain Day . . . Wednesday morning] Charles killed Captain John T. Day and Patrolman Peter J. Lamb in the early hours of Tuesday, July 24, 1900.

302.4–5 *The Butchery . . . in His Hand*] It is likely that these editorials were written by John Mitchell (1863–1929), editor of the *Richmond Planet* from 1884 to 1929. Mitchell served as president of the Afro-American Press Association, 1890–94, and as a Republican on the Richmond board of aldermen, 1892–96.

304.6–7 colored man, who betrayed CHARLES] Charles was hiding in the home of Silas Jackson, who denied knowing of his whereabouts when questioned by Sergeant Gabriel Porteous and Corporal John Lally. Jackson was indicted in August 1900 for murder and harboring a fugitive, but the charges were eventually dropped.

304.8 ALFRED J. BLOOMFIELD . . . young boy] Albert J. Blumfield, who was nineteen years old.

304.10–13 LECLERE . . . BOFIL] Andrew Van Kuren and H. H. Batte were killed during the gun battle while A. V. Leclerc, Frank Evans, John Banville, George J. Lyons, Frank Bertucci, and J. W. Bofill were wounded.

306.1 THE WHITE MAN'S UNION] White Man's Union Associations were political organizations founded in Texas after Reconstruction to gain control of regions with large black or ethnic Mexican populations. The White Man's Union in Grimes County was organized in 1899. It used murder and intimidation during the 1900 election campaign to overthrow the alliance of white Populists and black Republicans that controlled the county government, prevailing in the 1900 election and retaining power in the county until the late 1950s.

307.16 came to taw] Stepped up to the mark. (A "taw" is the line from which players throw or shoot in a game of marbles.)

309.2 GEORGE H. WHITE] Born in Rosindale, North Carolina, White (1852–1918) studied at Howard University, worked as a school principal, became a lawyer, and then served as a Republican in the North Carolina house of representatives in 1881 and in the state senate in 1885. White won election to Congress as a Republican in 1896 and was reelected in 1898. He fought against efforts to disenfranchise black citizens and introduced the first federal anti-lynching legislation. White decided not to seek reelection in 1900 after an amendment to the North Carolina constitution was adopted that disenfranchised black voters. He moved to Washington, D.C., and then to Philadelphia, where he established a commercial bank.

309.8 Mr. CHAIRMAN] The House was sitting as a Committee of the Whole in order to debate the appropriations bill for the Department of Agriculture.

309.16–19 commissioner of agriculture . . . good one he is.] The Department of Agriculture, established in 1862, was headed by a commissioner until 1889, when the department was granted cabinet status by Congress. James Wilson (1835–1920) of Iowa served as secretary of agriculture from 1897 to 1913, in the administrations of William McKinley, Theodore Roosevelt, and William Howard Taft.

311.13–14 Fifty-sixth Congress] The Congress that met from 1899 to 1901.

311.17 consideration . . . recent reapportionment bill] On January 8, 1901, the House concluded its debate on a bill reapportioning representatives among the states based on the 1900 census. White spoke briefly in support of a proposal by Edgar D. Crumpacker (1851–1920), a Republican from Indiana, to reduce the representation of Louisiana, Mississippi, North Carolina, and South Carolina under section 2 of the Fourteenth Amendment because the four states had adopted constitutional measures disenfranchising black voters. The Crumpacker motion was rejected, 136–94.

311.28 Mr. KITCHIN] William Walton Kitchin (1866–1924), a North Carolina Democrat who served as a congressman from 1897 to 1909 and as governor from 1909 to 1913.

312.21–22 Halifax, a rather significant name] The town of Halifax in Halifax County, North Carolina, saw the adoption of the first official colonial resolution calling for independence from Great Britain on April 12, 1776, later known as the Halifax Resolves.

312.26–27 the brother . . . will succeed me] Claude Kitchin (1869–1923), a Democrat, served in the House of Representatives from 1901 until his death.

313.25 stated on a former occasion] In his remarks on January 8, 1901.

313.31–314.36 I quote . . . party lines.] From remarks regarding the reapportionment bill made in the House on January 4, 1901, by Oscar Underwood (1862–1929), a Democrat from Alabama who served as a congressman from 1897 to 1915 and as a U.S. senator from 1915 to 1927.

315.28–30 The divine law . . . be shed."] Genesis 9:6.

316.29 "lily whites,"] This epithet for Republicans who sought to exclude black people from the party has been attributed to Norris Wright Cuney (1846–1898), a black Texas Republican who first used it in 1888.

316.39–317.17 I refer to Mr. OTEY . . . peculiarly appropriate.] Peter J. Otey (1840–1902) was a Democratic congressman from Virginia, 1895–1902. Otey made the remarks quoted by White on January 8 during the debate on the reapportionment bill. The first paragraph of the extract is a quotation taken from *The Virginia Constitutional Convention and Its Possibilities* (1901), a pamphlet by Alsen Franklin Thomas (1862–1943).

318.1–3 Mr. WILSON . . . made a speech] Stanyarne Wilson (1860–1928), a Democratic congressman from South Carolina, 1895–1901, gave a lengthy speech in opposition to the Crumpacker proposal on January 7, 1901.

320.34–36 The first . . . cases of lynching] White introduced the bill on January 20, 1900, and gave a lengthy speech presenting his case for its passage on February 23. The bill was referred to the judiciary committee and never acted upon.

321.3–4 Sow the seed . . . eternal shame] From "What Shall the Harvest Be?" (1850), a hymn by Emily Sullivan Oakey (1829–1883).

321.7–12 Mr. LITTLEFIELD . . . coming back.] Charles E. Littlefield (1851–1915), a Republican congressman from Maine from 1899 to 1908, quoted this quatrain on the House floor on January 5, 1901, during the debate on the reapportionment bill.

321.19 first session of the Fiftieth Congress] The session met from December 1887 to October 1888.

321.21 Comptroller . . . Mr. Trenholm] William L. Trenholm (1836–1901) was comptroller of the currency from 1886 to 1889.

321.24 Mr. Wilkins] Beriah Wilkins (1846–1905), an Ohio Democrat who served in Congress, 1883–89, was chairman of the Committee on Banking and Currency from 1887 to 1889.

323.19 the President's] Grover Cleveland.

325.2 General Brice] Benjamin Brice (1809–1892) was paymaster general of the U.S. Army from 1864 to 1872.

325.24–25 Maj. Gen. O. O. Howard] Oliver Otis Howard (1830–1909) was commissioner of the Freedmen's Bureau, 1865–72, and president of Howard University, 1869–74.

327.21–25 Lord Bacon . . . a human being.] During his trial for treason on November 17, 1603, Sir Walter Raleigh (1552–1618) insisted on being confronted with the main witness against him, saying: "Were the case but for a small copyhold, you would have witnesses or good proof to lead the jury to the verdict. And I am here for my life." Francis Bacon (1561–1626) later published *A Declaration of the demeanor and cariage of Sir Walter Raleigh, Knight, as well in his voyage, as in, and sithence his Returne; And of the true motives and inducements which occasioned His Majestie to Proceed in doing justice upon him, as hath bene done* (1618), a pamphlet justifying the decision of King James I to order Raleigh's execution.

328.8 article . . . that follows] "The Negro: How It Appeals to a Southern White Woman." Its author, a thirty-five-year-old woman from Alabama, wrote about the "immorality" and "inferiority" of black people.

332.11 Bob Ingersoll] Ingersoll (1833–1899), a writer and orator most widely known for his agnosticism, also spoke out in favor of racial equality.

331.38 white Senator . . . young white girl] Probably a reference to the trial of William Breckinridge (1837–1904), a Democratic congressman from Kentucky, 1885–95, who was successfully sued for breach of promise in 1894 by Madeline Pollard (1863?–1945).

332.19–20 Epworth Leagues] Social clubs for young Methodist adults, named after Epworth, England, the birthplace of John Wesley (1703–1791) and Charles Wesley (1707–1788).

334.1–2 Dewey, Sampson, Schley and Hobson] George Dewey (1837–1917), William Thomas Samson (1840–1902), Winfield Scott Schley (1839–1911), and Richmond P. Hobson (1870–1937), naval officers celebrated for their roles in the Spanish-American War of 1898.

334.23–24 New York's "Four Hundred"] The principal members of New York society, as imagined (and, in 1892, listed in print) by Ward McAllister (1827–1895), author of *Society As I Have Found It* (1890).

335.3–4 "For right is right . . . day must win"] From "The Right Must Win" by Frederick William Faber (1814–1863), first collected in *Jesus and Mary; or, Catholic Hymns* (1849).

336.2 BENJAMIN R. TILLMAN] See note 125.15–16.

337.18–21 a letter published . . . a Federal appointment] President Roosevelt wrote to James A. Smyth (1837–1920), the Democratic mayor of Charleston, 1895–1903, about his appointment of William Crum (1859–1912), a black physician and businessman, as collector of customs at Charleston.

338.19 Mr. ——] James C. Calvin (1850–1927), editor of the *Charleston News and Courier*, 1888–1910.

337.36 Gold Democrats] Members of a faction of the Democratic Party who favored the gold standard over the looser "free silver" monetary policies of the party's 1896 and 1900 presidential candidate, William Jennings Bryan.

346.39 The table . . . inserted] The table gave figures for "Persons of negro descent, 1900" and "Negroes of voting age, 1900" for all the states and federal territories as well as the District of Columbia.

348.17 3-mill tax] A tax of $3 per $1,000 of assessed property.

353.11–16 "The abolition of slavery . . . resuscitated."] A quotation, condensed, from James A. Thome and J. Horace Kimball's *Emancipation in the West Indies: A Six Months' Tour in Antigua, Barbadoes, and Jamaica in the Year 1837*, published by the American Anti-Slavery Society in 1838.

353.20–26 About thirty years . . . his favor."] From a letter by the missionary Rev. H. B. Hall quoted in *The Ninth Annual Report of the American Missionary Association* (1855).

353.27–354.8 James Anthony Froude . . . *stock, after all*] See Froude's *The English in the West Indies; or, the Bow of Ulysses* (1888).

356.9–27 Benjamin C. Whitehead . . . population of Illinois] See Ben G. Whitehead, "Negroes in Illinois," *Times-Democrat* (New Orleans), February 8, 1903.

362.19–24 Colonel Sleeman . . . everywhere feel."] See *Rambles and Recollections of an Indian Official* (1844) by William Henry Sleeman (1788–1856).

363.2–4 "The teeth . . . in youth."] See *The Thoughts of a Native of Northern India on the Rebellion, Its Causes and Remedies*, published anonymously in London in 1858.

363.24 the Sepoy rebellion of 1857] An uprising against British rule in India in 1857–58, begun among the sepoys in a British East India Company garrison north of Delhi.

367.32 Theodore Tilton . . . Thad. Stevens] Tilton (1835–1907) was an abolitionist newspaper editor. Thaddeus Stevens (1792–1868), a radical Republican from Pennsylvania who served in the House from 1859 until his death, may have had a romantic relationship with Lydia Hamilton Smith (1813–1884), his widowed black housekeeper and business manager.

368.12–13 "the stars . . . against Sisera."] Judges 5:20.

368.26–27 Pope . . . DANGEROUS THING."] See Pope's *Essay on Criticism* (1711).

369.21 Lee and Jackson, of Johnston and Forrest] Confederate generals Robert E. Lee (1807–1870), Stonewall Jackson (1824–1863), Joseph E. Johnson (1807–1891), and Nathan Bedford Forrest (1821–1877).

369.34 Harriet Beecher Stowe's novel] *Uncle Tom's Cabin* (1852).

370.1–2 the cruelties . . . San Domingo] Also known as the Haitian Revolution, slave rebellions in the French colony of Saint-Domingue beginning in 1791 led to Haitian independence in 1804.

372.20–21 "Hyperion to a satyr."] *Hamlet*, I.ii.140. In Greek mythology, Hyperion was a sun god, one of the Titans.

374.38–39 God moves . . . to perform—] From the poem "Light Shining out of Darkness" by William Cowper (1731–1800), first published in 1774 and subsequently sung as a hymn.

379.4 Marion and Sumter] Francis Marion (c. 1732–1795) and Thomas Sumter (1734–1832), both South Carolinians who fought in the southern theater of the American Revolutionary War.

388.35–36 "Hickory Bill"] Ellsworth "Hickory Bill" Fields and two other white men, Bartimeus H. Barnes and Sam Mitchell, were tried for the lynching of Thomas Gilyard. Fields and Barnes were acquitted while Mitchell was convicted of second-degree murder. His conviction was overturned on a technicality, and he was acquitted on retrial.

391.2 W.E.B. DU BOIS] Born in Great Barrington, Massachusetts, Du Bois (1868–1963) enrolled at Fisk, a historically black college in Nashville, Tennessee, in September 1885. He later earned three degrees from Harvard, the last his 1895 Ph.D. In 1896 the University of Pennsylvania invited him to conduct a study of the Philadelphia's seventh ward; his research resulted in *The Philadelphia Negro* (1899). Du Bois then took a position at Atlanta University. Along with his books *The Souls of Black Folk* (1903) and *John Brown* (1909), he edited two magazines, *Moon* (1905–6) and *Horizon* (1907–10), and was a cofounder of both the Niagara Movement and, in 1909, the National Association for the Advancement of Colored People. He left Atlanta in 1910 to work as an officer in the NAACP and to edit its monthly magazine, *The Crisis*. Du Bois resigned in 1934 and accepted a position at Atlanta University as chair of the sociology department. He founded and edited a new journal, *Phylon*, from 1940 to 1944, and published *Black Reconstruction in America: An Essay toward a History of the Part Which Black Folk Played in the Attempt to Reconstruct Democracy in America, 1860–1880* (1935) and *Dusk of Dawn: An Essay toward an Autobiography of a Race Concept* (1940). Du Bois moved to Accra, the capital of Ghana in 1961, at the invitation of President Kwame Nkrumah, and died there in 1963.

391.3 *MR. BOOKER T. WASHINGTON*] See note 197.2.

391.7–10 From birth . . . BYRON] From *Childe Harold's Pilgrimage*, a narrative poem by George Gordon, Lord Byron (1788–1824), first published from 1812 to 1818.

391.25 Price] See note 184.21.

392.13 Tuskegee] See note 197.2.

392.15–17 the word spoken . . . mutual progress."] From Washington's September 18, 1895, address at the Atlanta Exposition, subsequently described as his "Atlanta Compromise" speech; see pp. 197–201 in this volume.

392.34–36 a lone black boy . . . absurdities.] See Washington's *Up from Slavery* (1901), ch. 6 ("Early Days at Tuskegee and Teaching School").

393.17–19 once when at the Chicago . . . the South,"] Addressing the National Peace Jubilee in Chicago on October 16, 1898, Washington said: "We have succeeded in every conflict, except the effort to conquer ourselves in the blotting out of racial prejudices . . . Until we thus conquer ourselves, I make no empty statement when I say that we shall have a cancer gnawing at the heart of the republic that shall one day prove as dangerous as an attack from an army without or within." On November 10, responding to criticism of the speech in the southern press, he wrote to the editor of *The Birmingham Age-Herald* to clarify that he did not intend to raise or agitate "questions of social equality."

395.12–13 the terrible Maroons . . . Stono] Historical incidents of violent resistance by enslaved black people. Groups of fugitive slaves called Maroons formed communities in the swamps and forests of the southern United States, occasionally raiding nearby settlements, but Du Bois may refer specifically to the Maroons of Jamaica and to the First Maroon War (c. 1728–40), in which the English were fought to a stalemate. In 1733, enslaved rebels gained control of St. John in the Danish West Indies (now the U.S. Virgin Islands) and held it for six months; an international force broke the insurrection and many of the enslaved rebels committed suicide rather than accept reenslavement. Cato of Stono, also known as Jemmy, led a force of over one hundred enslaved rebels in insurrection and flight from Stono, South Carolina, in 1739. They intended to flee to the Spanish colony of Florida. While many were captured and executed, it is believed that some escaped successfully. The Stono Rebellion is said to be the cause of the South Carolina colonial legislature's restriction, for the first time, of the importation of enslaved rebels from Africa, as black people had become a majority in that colony.

395.17–20 the earnest songs of Phyllis . . . the Cuffes] Phillis Wheatley (c. 1753–1784), author of *Poems on Various Subjects, Religious and Moral* (1733); Crispus Attucks (c. 1723–1770), traditionally described as the first American casualty of the American Revolution; Peter Salem (1750–1816) and Salem Poor (1747–1802), soldiers of the Revolutionary War, both of whom fought at Bunker Hill; Benjamin Banneker (1731–1806) and James Derham (1762–c. 1802), the former an author of astronomical almanacs and the latter a pioneering physician; and the Cuffe brothers Paul (1759–1817) and John (1752–1836), early advocates for the abolition of slavery.

395.27–28 Gabriel in Virginia . . . Nat Turner] Du Bois refers to people who plotted or led insurrections against southern slavery: Gabriel (c. 1775–1800), Denmark Vesey (c. 1767–1822), and Nat Turner (1800–1831).

395.36 Walker's wild appeal] See note 180.19.

396.4–6 Forten and Purvis . . . of Boston] Free black abolitionists of the urban North, all active around 1830: James Forten Sr. (1766–1842), with whose financial support *The Liberator* was established in 1831, and a frequent contributor to that paper; Robert Purvis (1810–1898), cofounder in 1833 of the American Anti-Slavery Society; Abraham Doras Shadd (1801–1882), who also helped to found the American Anti-Slavery Society, and an anticolonization activist; Alexander Du Bois (1803–1887), W.E.B. Du Bois's grandfather; and James George Barbadoes (c. 1796–1841), cofounder of the Massachusetts General Colored Association in 1826.

396.16 Remond, Nell, Wells-Brown] Charles Lenox Redmond (1810–1874), born in Salem, Massachusetts, was a journalist, lecturer, and an active member of the Massachusetts Anti-Slavery Society. William Cooper Nell (1816–1874), born in Boston, was a lecturer, journalist, and historian, and was active in the Underground Railroad. William Wells Brown (c. 1814–1884) wrote the famous *Narrative of William W. Brown, a Fugitive Slave* (1847), *Clotel, or The President's Daughter* (1853), and other works.

396.20 John Brown's raid] Brown (1800–1859) led a biracial group of men in a raid on the federal arsenal at Harpers Ferry, Virginia, on October 16, 1859. Brown was executed on December 2.

396.25–27 Elliot, Bruce . . . Payne] Robert Brown Elliot (1842–1884) was born and educated in Liverpool, England, where he learned the printing trade. He arrived in Boston in 1867 after service in the British navy and worked as a typesetter. After a few months he moved to South Carolina to become an editor of the *South Carolina Leader*. He was elected to the South Carolina house of representatives and then, from 1871 to 1874, served as a U.S. congressman from South Carolina's third district. His brief tenure as South Carolina's attorney general (1876–77) ended with the return of Democratic rule in that state. Blanche K. Bruce (1841–1898), fugitive from enslavement, teacher, and planter, served as a U.S. senator from Mississippi, from 1875 to 1881; he later held appointed offices in government under Republican administrations. John Mercer Langston (1829–1897), lawyer, founder and dean of the law department at Howard University (1868–73), Howard's acting president (1873–75), and president of Virginia Normal and Collegiate Institute in Petersburg, Virginia (1885–87). He served as chargé d'affaires to the Dominican Republic from 1877 to 1885 and became the first black congressman in 1890. Alexander Crummell (1819–1898), an Episcopal priest born in New York, spent twenty years in Liberia as an evangelist and advocate for black emigration. He returned to the United States in 1872 and moved to Washington, D.C., where he helped to establish St. Luke's Episcopal Church. Daniel A. Payne (1811–1893), educator, church historian, civic leader, and bishop of the African Methodist Episcopal Church, was instrumental in the founding of Wilberforce University and served as its president, 1863–76.

398.36 Toussaint the Savior] Toussaint Louverture (1743–1803), a leader of the Haitian Revolution sometimes described as the "Father of Haiti."

399.14 the Grimkes . . . Bowen] Archibald H. Grimké (1849–1930), lawyer, editor, and author, and his brother Francis J. Grimké (1850–1937), clergyman and author, were both active civil rights leaders. Kelly Miller (1863–1939) taught at Howard University from 1890 to 1934 and was dean of the College of Arts and Sciences from 1907 to 1919. A mathematician by training, he added sociology to the Howard curriculum; as a journalist and pamphleteer he attempted to resolve conflicts among black leaders. John Wesley Edward Bowen (1855–1933), a Methodist clergyman and noted lecturer, earned a Ph.D. in philosophy from Boston University and later taught at a number of institutions; he was an unsuccessful candidate for the office of bishop, and worked for the integration of black clergymen into the Methodist establishment.

401.39–402.1 Governor Aycock . . . Tillman] Charles Brantley Aycock (1859–1912), governor of North Carolina from 1901 to 1905, championed educational reform in his state, attempting to overcome the illiteracy of both blacks and whites by funding public education. John Tyler Morgan

(1824–1907), senator from Alabama from 1876 to 1907, was a strong advocate of white supremacy. Thomas Nelson Page (1853–1922) wrote novels that promoted a romantic view of the Old South and plantation life. Benjamin Ryan ("Pitchfork Ben") Tillman (1847–1918), a demagogue, orator, and advocate of "white democracy," was governor of South Carolina from 1890 to 1894 and senator from 1894 to 1918.

404.2 CHARLES W. CHESNUTT] Born in Cleveland, Ohio and raised in Fayetteville, North Carolina, Chesnutt (1858–1932) attended a Freedmen's Bureau school; he began a teaching career, and in 1880 became principal of the Fayetteville State Normal School for Negroes. Moving back to Cleveland in 1883, he passed the bar exam and started a legal stenography firm. He published his first short story, "The Goophered Grapevine," in *The Atlantic Monthly*, and followed this debut with story collections *The Conjure Woman* (1899), *The Wife of His Youth and Other Stories of the Color-Line* (1899), novels *The House Behind the Cedars* (1900), *The Marrow of Tradition* (1901), and *The Colonel's Dream* (1905), and a biography, *Frederick Douglass* (1899).

407.27–28 the recent case of Jackson vs. Giles] *Giles v. Harris*, decided on April 27, 1903.

413.21–22 "Crook the pregnant . . . follow fawning."] *Hamlet*, III.ii.61–62.

416.32–35 in the language . . . the republic."] See the editorial "First Principles," *The Evening Post* (Charleston), April 4, 1903.

416.35–36 our Clevelands and Abbotts and Parkhursts] Northern white apologists for disenfranchisement, including Grover Cleveland (1837–1908), the former president, who in a speech in support of the Tuskegee Institute on April 14, 1903, attributed the present "Negro problem" to "a perilous flood of indiscriminate, unintelligent and blighting negro suffrage" during Reconstruction; Lyman Abbott (1832–1927), an editor and reformer whose essay "The Race Problem" (*Outlook*, March 14, 1903) praised white southerners' solutions; and the Rev. Charles Parkhurst (1842–1933), who felt that black voting rights were "one of those blunders that it is not easy to escape from" ("Relations of North and South," *New York Times*, April 29, 1901).

416.37–40 the most distinguished Negro . . . character."] From a letter of Booker T. Washington to the editor of the Birmingham (Alabama) *Age-Herald* dated November 24, 1902, published in the *Age-Herald* on November 28 and widely reprinted thereafter.

417.26–32 Senator McEnery of . . . the white race."] See "The Race Problem in the South" (*Independent*, February 19, 1903) by Samuel Douglas McEnery (1837–1910), who served as a Louisiana senator from 1897 to 1910.

419.21–28 a colored editor in Richmond . . . unconstitutional."] See "Another Decision" (*Richmond Planet*, May 2, 1903) by John R. Mitchell (1863–1929).

420.30 Judge Jones of Alabama] Thomas G. Jones was a federal district judge in Alabama, 1901–14.

423.18–19 "Power that works for righteousness,"] In his 1875 sermon "Antidotes to Atheism," Octavius Brooks Frothingham (1822–1895) writes, "The abolitionist did not abolish human slavery, but there was behind him this power that works for righteousness, the accumulated conscience of generations of the past." Robert G. Ingersoll (1833–1899) subsequently used the phrase as the title of a lecture, first collected in *What Is Religion?* (1899).

424.3–4 CHARLES BRANTLEY . . . *Society*] Aycock (1859–1912), governor of North Carolina from 1901 to 1905, addressed the first annual dinner of the North Carolina Society of Baltimore, a social club.

424.27–28 "there is death in the pot."] 2 Kings 4:40.

425.4 the seizure of Panama] Panama declared its independence from Colombia on November 3, 1903, and was promptly recognized by the United States, which acquired the Panama Canal Zone by treaty on November 18.

425.15 "rose on stepping stones . . . higher things,"] See the first canto of Alfred, Lord Tennyson's elegy "In Memoriam A.H.H." (1850).

426.2 WILLIAM MONROE TROTTER] Born in Hyde Park, Massachusetts, Trotter (1872–1934) graduated from Harvard and in 1896 earned his master's degree there. In 1901 he cofounded *The Guardian*, a Boston weekly that often criticized the accommodationist positions of Booker T. Washington. Trotter was a principal organizer of the Niagara Movement of 1905 but split from the group, later joining the National Equal Rights League. He met with President Wilson in 1914, publicly criticizing Wilson's tolerance of resegregation within the federal bureaucracy.

426.8–9 Miller's . . . Morgan] George Frazier Miller (1864–1943), rector of St. Augustine's Episcopal Church in Brooklyn; Archibald Grimké (1849–1930), Boston lawyer and orator; Clement R. Morgan (1859–1929), one of Du Bois's Harvard classmates and a civil rights lawyer.

426.18 Fortune] Timothy Thomas Fortune (1856–1928), editor of *The New York Age* and advisor to Booker T. Washington.

426.20 Hershaw] Lafayette M. Hershaw (1863–1945), a longtime land examiner for the Department of the Interior beginning in 1890, was active in District of Columbia literary and intellectual circles and was one of the original organizers of the Niagara Movement.

426.28 Kelly Miller] See note 399.14.

426.34 Ogden] Robert Curtis Ogden (1836–1913), a Philadelphia businessman with a philanthropic interest in southern education; he was a trustee of the Hampton Institute in Hampton, Virginia, and a supporter of Booker T. Washington.

426.35 the "Committee of 12"] In July 1904, with support from philanthropist Andrew Carnegie, Booker T. Washington formed a "Committee of Twelve for the Advancement of the Interests of the Negro Race." Du Bois played a prominent role in the establishment of the committee but by March 1905 had resigned in frustration over Washington's leadership and influence.

427.1 Wilkins . . . the Conservator] Daniel Robert Wilkins (1852–1908), a former pastor, took over the management of *The Conservator*, Chicago's oldest black newspaper, in 1900, and later bought out its owners. The paper generally allied itself with Du Bois and the Niagara Movement; Booker T. Washington subsidized a rival Chicago paper, *The Leader*.

427.2 The "Voice of the Negro"] A monthly magazine published in Atlanta beginning in June 1904; after the Atlanta riot of September 1906, its operations were moved to Chicago.

427.2–3 Harry Smith at Cleveland] Harry Clay Smith (1863–1941) cofounded *The Cleveland Gazette*, a weekly, in 1883, and later became its sole proprietor, publishing continuously until his death. He was one of the Niagara Movement's original twenty-nine members.

427.6 Chase of The Bee] William Calvin Chase (1854–1921) edited *The Washington Bee*, a weekly paper, from 1882 until his death.

427.6–7 The Pioneer Press at Martinsburg] West Virginia's first black newspaper, founded by John Robert ("J. R.") Clifford (1848–1933) in 1882 and published weekly until 1917.

427.11–12 the revelation on Emmett Scott . . . libel case?] Trotter sued for libel after the Boston *Colored Citizen*, edited by Charles Alexander (1868–1923), published an article ("Doing the Circus Act," datelined New York, September 26, 1904) alleging, without naming him, that Trotter had set aside his principles to beg for "political cash" from the Roosevelt presidential campaign. In his testimony, Alexander admitted that Trotter was the subject of the article and that the article had been sent to him for publication by Emmett Jay Scott (1873–1957) of Tuskegee, advisor and secretary to Booker T. Washington.

427.14–15 Miss Pauline Hopkins . . . Col. American Magazine] Hopkins (1859–1930) was a major contributor to *The Colored American Magazine*, published from 1900 to 1909, and became its literary editor in 1903; in 1904 the magazine was purchased by Fred R. Moore (1857–1943), an ally of Booker T. Washington, who replaced her. Washington supported the magazine financially and had significant editorial control during Moore's tenure.

427.16 Cooper] Probably Edward E. Cooper (1859–1908), editor and publisher of *The Colored American*, a Washington, D.C., weekly, and an ally of Booker T. Washington.

427.19–21 Mrs Ida L. Bailey . . . John F. Cook] John F. Cook Jr. (1833–1910), an educator and investor, was reputed, around the turn of the century, to be the richest black man in Washington, D.C.; Bailey (1864–1908) worked with his wife Helen A. Cook (1837–1913) in the efforts of the Colored Women's League of the District of Columbia, later part of the National Association of Colored Women.

428.2 AIDA OVERTON WALKER] Sometimes described as the "Queen of the Cakewalk," Walker (1880–1914) was a vaudeville performer who acted, sang, danced, and choreographed. Marrying fellow vaudevillian George Walker (c. 1872–1911) in 1899, she appeared in the musical *Sons of Ham* (1900) and, with Walker and his partner Bert Williams (1874–1922), in *In Dahomey* (1903), *In Abyssinia* (1906), and *Bandanna Land* (1908).

429.15–16 the Williams and Walker Company] Vaudeville performers Bert Williams (1874–1922) and George Walker (c. 1872–1911) met in San Francisco in 1893 and began to tour as a duo. Their 1903 musical comedy *In Dahomey* —the first full-length black Broadway musical—ran for a total of four years and toured both the United States and the United Kingdom. They later appeared in *In Abyssinia* (1906) and *Bandanna Land* (1908).

429.32–34 Mrs. Arthur Paget . . . Constance Mackenzie] White Edwardian socialites Lady Mary Paget (1853–1919), Muriel Thetis Wilson (1875–1964), Mrs. Frank Avery (née May Clark, 1878–1952), and Lady Constance Mackenzie (1882–1932). Paget and Avery were American heiresses.

429.37 Sir Thomas Lipton] Lipton (1848–1931), owner of a British grocery store chain, founded the Lipton tea company in 1890.

433.2 MARY CHURCH TERRELL] Born in Memphis to formerly enslaved parents, Terrell (1863–1954) was an activist for racial equality and women's suffrage. Her father was one of the first black millionaires in the South, and her mother owned a hair salon. Terrell attended Antioch College and Oberlin College, earning a B.A. and an M.A. In 1887 she moved to Washington, D.C., to teach at the M Street Colored High School. She became more active in politics in 1892 when her friend, Thomas Moss, was lynched by whites in Memphis. Terrell served as the first president of the National Association of Colored Women from 1896 to 1901, and in 1909 helped to establish the National Association for the Advancement of Colored People. Her autobiography, *A Colored Woman in a White World*, was published in 1940.

433.3–5 *What It Means . . . 1906*] Originally presented as a speech to the United Women's Club in Washington, D.C., this piece was published anonymously in *The Independent* on January 24, 1907.

433.11–13 Senator Foraker . . . negro battalion] Joseph B. Foraker (1846–1917), an Ohio Republican who served in the U.S. Senate from 1897 to 1909, opposed President Roosevelt's decision to discharge without honor 167 soldiers of the black 25th Infantry Regiment (see Chronology, 1906).

433.14 EDITOR] William Hays Ward (1835–1916), editor of *The Independent* from 1896 to 1913.

433.30 a stranger in a strange land] Exodus 2:22.

435.19–35 A few years ago a colored woman . . . in France.] Terrell describes the career of the painter Annie E. Anderson Walker (1855–1929).

436.1 the Columbian Law School] Now the law school of George Washington University.

440.32 Representative Heflin] James T. Heflin (1869–1951) was a Democratic congressman from Alabama from 1904 to 1920, and a senator from 1920 to 1930.

443.1 THE BROWNSVILLE DISMISSALS] See Chronology, 1906.

443.20–21 Southerner . . . official investigation] Brigadier General Ernest A. Garlington (1853–1934), the army inspector general, was a native of South Carolina.

444.9–10 His own son . . . accuse his comrades.] Theodore Roosevelt Jr. (1887–1944) and three other Harvard students were apprehended on the night of September 27, 1906, after an altercation on Boston Common in which a policeman was injured. When questioned Roosevelt refused to name the student who had tripped the officer. (His roommate, Shaun Kelley, later came forward and was acquitted at trial.)

444.33–34 "The President . . . Booker T. Washingtons] See Chronology, 1901.

446.24 Senator Bacon] Augustus O. Bacon (1839–1914), a Democratic senator from Georgia from 1895 to 1914.

447.23–39 Colonel Byrd . . . plainly in evidence.'] From Phill G. Byrd (1861–1939), *Report of Special Inspector of Misdemeanor Convict Camps in Georgia* (1897). Byrd had been appointed by William Y. Atkinson (1854–1899), Democratic governor of Georgia, 1894–98.

448.3 Judge Emory Speer] Speer (1848–1918) was U.S. district judge for the southern district of Georgia, 1885–1918.

449.31–36 governor of Kentucky . . . I find fault.] Preston Leslie (1819–1907), Democratic governor of Kentucky, 1871–75, in his message to the Kentucky general assembly, December 1, 1873, as quoted by George Washington Cable (see note 101.2) in "The Convict Lease System in the Southern States," *The Century Magazine*, February 1884.

449.36–450.4 Possession of the . . . to protect.'] From "The Convict Lease System in the Southern States." Terrell conflated the quotation from Leslie's message with this passage in Cable's article.

450.6–13 a speaker . . . when they entered.'] See "Louisiana's Convicts," *The Independent*, February 2, 1899.

453.21–454.8 Only last August . . . their destination.'] As reported in a widely published Hearst wire story; see, for instance, "Barbarous Treatment of

NOTES 691

White Men, Slaves in North Carolina Camp," *The Washington Times*, August 6, 1906. The young New Yorker's name was Louis Gross.

460.8–31 'When the door . . . sore feet.'] See note 447.23–39.

468.21 When allotments were made . . . freedmen] Under the terms of the Dawes Act of 1887 and the Curtis Act of 1898, communally held Creek tribal lands in Indian Territory were subdivided for private ownership; some were sold to outsiders, and some were allotted to tribal members. Sallie Love (1871–fl. 1940) applied for a 159-acre allotment on April 8, 1899. Creeks of any degree of African descent, most of them formerly enslaved by tribal members or descended from those formerly enslaved, and many of them of mixed ancestry, became known as "Creek Freedmen." In subsequent decades the Muscogee (Creek) Nation excluded the Freedmen from tribal membership and benefits, a policy that continues to be subject to legal challenges.

470.22–26 William J. Bryan . . . negro disfranchisement] In response to a question from the audience after his speech at Cooper Union on April 21, 1908, Bryan said the "negro of the South may fit himself to claim his vote" by meeting the educational requirements for suffrage, adding: "The white man, as it is, gives the black man a better government than the black man would give the white."

471.9 the Democracy] The Democratic Party.

472.12–13 A CALL . . . has been issued] Authorship of the call has been attributed to Oswald Garrison Villard (1872–1949), president of *The New York Evening Post*.

473.10–18 BEREA COLLEGE CASE . . . equally interested,'] In *Berea College v. Kentucky*, decided on November 9, 1908, by a vote of 7 to 2, the Supreme Court upheld a Kentucky law that prohibited integrated schools. The quoted text is from the dissenting opinion of Associate Justice John Marshall Harlan (1833–1911).

473.32–33 'government of the people . . . the earth.'] The conclusion of Lincoln's Gettysburg Address of November 19, 1863.

474.1–2 'A house divided . . . cannot stand'] From Lincoln's "House Divided" speech of June 16, 1858.

477.39 late strike in Georgia] White locomotive firemen went on strike against the Georgia Railroad, May 17–29, 1909, to protest the company's hiring of black firemen. The strike ended when both sides agreed to federal arbitration.

1909–1919

481.2 *HANFORD DAILY JOURNAL*] A newspaper published in Hanford, California.

485.1 THE JOHNSON-JEFFRIES FIGHT] When Jack Johnson (1878–1946) became the first black heavyweight boxing champion of the world in 1908, white promoters began searching for a "great white hope" to challenge him. They convinced Jim Jeffries (1875–1953), the undefeated heavyweight champion from 1899 to 1905, to return to the ring and fight Johnson in an event billed as the "Battle of the Century." Johnson defeated Jeffries in a fifteenth-round technical knockout on July 4, 1910, in Reno, Nevada. After Johnson's victory, dozens of riots broke out across the nation in which at least eleven and as many as twenty-six persons, almost all of them black, were killed.

485.29 Von Moltke] Helmuth von Moltke (1800–1891), chief of the Prussian (later German) general staff, 1858–88, who led the Prussian army to victory in wars against Denmark (1864), Austria (1866), and France (1870–71). His nephew, Helmuth von Moltke (1848–1916), sometimes known as "Moltke the Younger," was chief of the German general staff, 1906–14.

486.27–28 Arthur Johnson] John Arthur Johnson, i.e., Jack Johnson.

488.2 *WILLIAM PICKENS*] A graduate of Talladega College and Yale, Pickens (1881–1954) was professor of foreign languages at Talladega, 1904–14, and later served as a field secretary for the NAACP, 1920–41. His autobiography *The Heir of Slaves* (1911) was later published in expanded form as *Bursting Bonds* (1923).

489.29 Corbett] Jim Corbett (1866–1933), the heavyweight champion, 1892–97, helped train Jeffries for his match with Johnson and shouted insults at Johnson from ringside during the fight.

489.31–34 Fred Douglass . . . hit nobody."] See *Life and Times of Frederick Douglass* (1893), ch. XVII.

490.20–21 The Persian King . . . whipping it.] According to the Greek historian Herodotus (c. 484–c. 425 BCE), Xerxes I (c. 518–465 BCE) ordered the Hellespont (Dardanelles) to be whipped after a bridge he was building to cross was destroyed in a storm.

491.13 Alabamian] Probably *The Colored Alabamian*, published in Montgomery from 1907 to 1916. Copies of the paper published in July 1910 are not known to be extant.

492.2 LESTER A. WALTON] Walton (1882–1965), born in St. Louis, was a songwriter and pioneering journalist who wrote on theater and film for the *New York Age*, 1906–14. He later wrote for the *New York World* and *New York Herald Tribune* while campaigning to have the word "Negro" capitalized in the press. Walton served as U.S. ambassador to Liberia, 1935–46.

492.10 the Manhattan Casino] A large dance hall located at Eighth Avenue and West 155th Street that was also used as a venue for basketball games and political meetings.

492.33 the Hottentot] An outdated term once used to refer to a group of Khoisan people indigenous to southern Africa.

493.22 "Panama"] Song (1911), originally published as "Panama: A Characteristic Novelty," by the black composer William H. Tyers (1870–1924).

493.33 James Reese Europe] Born in Mobile, Alabama, Europe (1880–1919) studied violin and piano in Washington, D.C., and joined the Memphis Students, a New York–based troupe of black musicians and dancers, in 1905. After serving as musical director for several theatrical productions he formed the Clef Club, a labor organization and booking agency for black musicians, and the Clef Club Orchestra. Europe would become the first black bandleader to record in the United States, cutting eight sides in 1913–14. He enlisted in the 15th New York, a black National Guard regiment later known as the 369th Infantry, in 1916 and saw combat in France in 1918. Europe led the regimental band when the 369th, now known as the "Harlem Hellfighters," marched down Fifth Avenue in February 1919. Later that year he was stabbed to death in Boston by one of the drummers in his band.

493.35 J. Rosamond Johnson] Composer and singer John Rosamond Johnson (1873–1954) was the younger brother of the writer, editor, and civil rights activist James Weldon Johnson (1871–1938). They collaborated as composer and lyricist on a number of songs, including "Lift Ev'ry Voice and Sing" (1900).

493.36 "Li'l Gal"] Song (1901) by J. Rosamond Johnson, set to a text by Paul Laurence Dunbar (1872–1906).

494.2 "Dearest Memories"] Song (1911) with music by black composer Will Vodery (1885–1951) and words by black lyricist Henry Creamer (1879–1930).

494.6 Coleridge-Taylor's . . . Waters of Babylon"] Musical setting (1899) of Psalm 137 by the Afro-British composer and conductor Samuel Coleridge-Taylor (1875–1912). Coleridge-Taylor attended the first Pan-African conference in London in 1900, and his music often reflected his interests in the African diaspora. During his first tour of the United States in 1904, President Theodore Roosevelt received him at the White House.

494.10 "Jean" . . . "Suwanee River"] "Jean" (1903), song by black composer Henry T. Burleigh (1866–1949), with words by the white journalist and lyricist Frank Lebby Stanton (1857–1927); "Suwanee River" (1851), also known as "Old Folks at Home," song by Stephen Foster (1826–1864).

494.12–13 "Mon Coeur s'Ouvre ta Voix,"] Aria from the opera *Samson et Delilah* (1877) by Camille Saint-Saëns (1835–1921), with a libretto by Ferdinand Lemaire (1832–1879), a Creole from Martinique.

494.15 Will Marion Cook] Cook (1869–1944) was a composer, conductor, performer, and teacher born in Washington, D.C. His 1898 musical, *Clorindy, or The Origin of the Cakewalk* (with lyrics by Paul Lawrence Dunbar), was the first Broadway musical to feature an all-black cast. "Swing Along" is the first song in his collection *3 Negro Songs* (1912).

494.27–28 "The Rain Song" . . . "Bandanna Land"] Song with music by Will Marion Cook and lyrics by black poet and songwriter Alex Rogers (1876–1930), from the musical *Bandanna Land* (1908).

494.29 "Deacon" Johnson's] Fred "Deacon" Johnson (1878–1944), a vaudeville performer and music contractor.

494.31–32 the Music School . . . David Mannes] The Music School Settlement for Colored People was founded in New York City in 1911 by violinist David Mannes (1866–1959) and others to provide training for black children who were excluded from other music schools, including the original Music School Settlement, founded on the Lower East Side in 1894.

497.19 "Marse Abe Linkum's" historic act] The Emancipation Proclamation, issued by Abraham Lincoln on January 1, 1863, was not enforced in Texas until June 19, 1865, the date commemorated in celebrations of Juneteenth.

498.2 MOORFIELD STOREY] Storey (1845–1929), a Boston attorney, was the founding president of the National Association for the Advancement of Colored People, serving from 1910 until his death.

498.4 OSWALD GARRISON VILLARD] Villard (1872–1949), the grandson of abolitionist William Lloyd Garrison, was the president of the *New York Evening Post*, 1897–1918, and chairman of the NAACP board of directors, 1910–14.

500.8 "New Freedom"] Name for the program of tariff reduction, banking regulation, and antitrust legislation outlined by Woodrow Wilson in his 1912 presidential campaign.

501.3–4 WILLIAM MONROE TROTTER . . . *Woodrow Wilson*] Trotter (1872–1934), a graduate of Harvard, famously opposed Booker T. Washington's "accommodationist" approach to racial progress. Disillusioned with Theodore Roosevelt and William Howard Taft, Trotter had supported Woodrow Wilson's 1912 bid for the presidency.

501.12 One year ago] Trotter and Wilson had met in the White House on November 6, 1913.

503.15 Governor Walsh] David Ignatius Walsh (1872–1947) was governor of Massachusetts from January 1914 to January 1916. He later served in the U.S. Senate, 1919–25 and 1926–47.

503.28–30 You said that . . . the United States."] On October 16, 1912, Wilson wrote to Alexander Walters (1858–1917), a bishop of the African Methodist Episcopal Zion Church and vice president of the NAACP, that his "sympathy" with the "colored people of the United States" was "of long standing." He continued: "I want to assure them through you that should I become President of the United States, they may count upon me for absolute fair dealing and for everything by which I could assist in advancing the interests of their race."

NOTES   695

509.14 *Plan of San Diego*] The Plan of San Diego came to the attention of U.S. authorities on January 23, 1915, when Basilo Ramos, one of its signers, was arrested in McAllen, Texas, carrying a copy of the document. When questioned, Ramos claimed it had actually been signed in a jail in the Mexican city of Monterrey. Charged with conspiring against the United States, Ramos was released on bail in May 1915 and fled to Mexico. While the general uprising called for in the manifesto never took place, a series of raids in the summer and fall of 1915 targeted ranches, farms, railroads, and rural settlements in the lower Rio Grande valley, resulting in the deaths of around twenty soldiers and civilians. Anglo vigilantes, local sheriffs, and the Texas Rangers lynched approximately three hundred Mexican citizens and Tejanos in retaliation.

509.34 John Skelton Williams] Williams (1865–1926) served as comptroller of the currency, 1914–21.

514.12 Agustin S. Garza] Agustín Solis de la Garza (1881–1970) was a clothing merchant with no military experience who had organized protests against the United States in Veracruz, Mexico, in 1913. Garza remained in northern Mexico during the violence in south Texas in 1915–16, and eventually settled in Mexico City.

518.1 THE BIRTH OF A NATION] A silent film directed by D. W. Griffith, the story depicts the South during and after the Civil War, portraying the Ku Klux Klan as heroic and free black men as sexual predators. The screenplay was adapted from *The Clansman: An Historical Romance of the Ku Klux Klan* (1905), a novel by Thomas Dixon (1864–1946) that had previously been adapted for the stage. William Monroe Trotter and activists in the NAACP protested the film but were unable to prevent its exhibition. The success of the film helped to inspire the rebirth of the Ku Klux Klan in November 1915.

518.3 FRANCIS HACKETT] Born in Ireland, Hackett (1886–1962) emigrated to the United States in 1901 and began writing for the *Chicago Evening News* in 1906. Hackett helped found *The New Republic* in 1914 and was an editor and critic for the magazine until 1922. He later published a number of works of fiction and nonfiction, including the novels *That Nice Young Couple* (1925) and *The Green Lion* (1936).

518.18 Rev. Thomas Dixon's] Dixon was a Baptist minister.

520.27 "Lincoln's solution"—back to Liberia] Abraham Lincoln joined the American Colonization Society in 1856, and as president encouraged various schemes for settling emancipated black Americans in Liberia, Central America, and the Caribbean.

520.33 quotations from Woodrow Wilson] *The Birth of a Nation* included three title cards quoting from the chapter on Reconstruction in Wilson's *A History of the American People* (1902).

524.23–24 "Carrizal" . . . blundered] On June 21, 1916, during the expedition into Mexico to capture revolutionary leader Francisco "Pancho" Villa

(1878–1923), a detachment from the black 10th Cavalry Regiment led by white officers attempted to pass through Carrizal, in Chihuahua, despite the presence of superior Mexican army forces. In the fighting two officers and seven troopers were killed and twenty-four troopers were captured (they were later released).

526.14 they will probably die] The mob violence on May 29, 1917, did not result in any fatalities.

526.20–21 Mayor Fred Mollman] A Democrat, Mollman (1869–1961) was the mayor of East St. Louis, 1915–19.

526.26 Governor Lowden] Frank Lowden (1861–1943) was the Republican governor of Illinois, 1917–21.

527.2 CARLOS F. HURD] Hurd (1876–1950) worked as a reporter for the *St. Louis Post-Dispatch* from 1900 until his final illness. In April 1912 he witnessed the rescue of the survivors from the *Titanic* while a passenger on board the *Carpathia*; Hurd wrote a five-thousand-word story on the sinking that he delivered to an editor on a tugboat in New York Harbor, scooping the competition.

527.15 St. Bartholomew's night] The St. Bartholomew's Day massacre of 1572 involved Catholic violence against Huguenots during the French Wars of Religion.

535.2–4 JOHN PERO . . . *House Select Committee*] The committee, which held hearings in an East St. Louis courtroom beginning on October 18, 1917, had five members: John E. Raker (1863–1926), Democrat of California, 1911–26; George E. Foss (1863–1936), Republican of Illinois, 1895–1919; Martin D. Foster (1861–1919), Democrat of Illinois, 1907–19; its chairman, Ben Johnson (1858–1950), Democrat of Kentucky, 1907–27; and Henry A. Cooper (1850–1931), Republican of Wisconsin, 1893–1919 and 1921–31. John P. Pero (1856–1922) was superintendent of the Missouri Malleable Iron Company.

540.31 Rev. Allison] Noted for his campaigns for social reform, George W. Allison (1882–1958) was minister at the First Baptist Church of East St. Louis.

541.1–2 A SILENT MARCH . . . JOHNSON] Organized by writer and civil rights activist James Weldon Johnson (1871–1938) and the NAACP in the aftermath of the East St. Louis massacre, the Silent Protest Parade was held on Fifth Avenue in New York City on July 28, 1917.

543.2–18 RALPH VAN DEMAN] Beginning in May 1917, Van Deman (1865–1952) headed the newly established Military Intelligence Section of the War Department.

543.17 W.H. Lewis] William Henry Lewis (1868–1949) was one of the first black attorneys admitted to the American Bar Association; in 1903 he became the first black man appointed as an assistant United States attorney. In 1910,

President Taft nominated him as assistant attorney general, a position in which he served until 1913.

544.2 MARTHA GRUENING] Gruening (1889–1937) graduated from Smith College in 1909 and received a law degree from New York University five years later. A suffragist and opponent of conscription, she wrote for *The Dawn*, a pacifist magazine, and became an assistant secretary to the National Board of the NAACP. In July 1917, she went to East St. Louis with Du Bois to investigate the city's recent race riot, and later that year, she went to Houston to report on the black soldiers' uprising in that city.

545.36 Private Edwards] Alonzo Edwards, of Company "L," 24th Infantry Regiment.

546.34–39 Fort Ben . . . the Pea Farm] Fort Bend County, southwest of Houston, was an agricultural area with an economy based on black plantation labor before the Civil War. In 1917, it was the site of Imperial Sugar Company and the Central State Prison Farm at Sugar Land.

549.30–32 Major Snow . . . Baltimore be returned] Major Kneeland S. Snow (1880–1941), the commander of the Third Battalion, 24th Infantry, succeeded in having Corporal Charles Baltimore (1893–1917) released. Baltimore left camp later that night and was charged with participating in the mutiny. He was found guilty and hanged on December 11, 1917.

550.35 Sparks has been indicted] Sparks was acquitted on October 15, 1917, the *Houston Post* reporting that jurors in his trial returned their verdict in "less than one minute."

553.8 the bayoneting of Captain Mattes] Oliver W. Mattes (1875–1917) of the 2nd Illinois Field Artillery was shot to death after mutineers mistook him for a police officer. The undertaker who prepared his body testified that he saw no evidence of bayonet wounds.

553.12–15 All the men   sufficiently punished] A total of 118 men were court-martialed in three separate trials, resulting in 110 convictions. Of those found guilty, twenty-nine were sentenced to death, fifty-three to life terms, and twenty-eight defendants received terms ranging from two to fifteen years. Thirteen of the condemned were hanged on December 11, 1917, and another six men were executed in the fall of 1918, while ten of the death sentences were commuted by President Wilson. All of the men sentenced to prison were released by 1938.

557.3–5 LEONIDAS C. DYER . . . *Anti-Lynching Bill*] Dyer (1871–1957), a white Republican congressman from Missouri, introduced an anti-lynching bill in 1918. The House of Representatives passed the Dyer Bill on January 26, 1922, but southern Democrats defeated it by filibuster. In 2022, President Joseph Biden signed the Emmett Till Anti-Lynching Act, making lynching a federal crime punishable by up to thirty years in prison.

557.18 the lynching of Praeger] Robert Paul Praeger (1888–1918), a German immigrant, was lynched by a mob on April 5, 1918, for ostensible disloyalty to the United States.

563.30 acts of July 31, 1861] Statutes originally enacted during the Civil War to punish insurrection, which were amended by the Third Enforcement (Ku Klux Klan) Act of April 20, 1871.

564.4–26 Neal *v.* Delaware . . . Strauder *v.* West Virginia] *Neal v. Delaware* and *Strauder v. West Virginia* were 1880 U.S. Supreme Court decisions.

569.2 CYRIL BRIGGS] Briggs (1888–1966), who immigrated to the United States from Nevis in 1905, founded *The Crusader* in 1918.

571.13–15 Is it for this . . . Dunbar] See Paul Laurence Dunbar's poem "To the South. On Its New Slavery," first collected in *Lyrics of Love and Laughter* in 1903.

571.35–572.1 William Pickett . . . Solution."] See *The Negro Problem: Abraham Lincoln's Solution* (1909), by William P. Pickett (1855–1936), a white lawyer.

574.18 Mrs. Mary Turner] A white mob in southern Georgia lynched Mary Turner, a black woman who was eight months pregnant, on May 19, 1918.

575.12–17 Prof. Hart says . . . *does well.*] See *The Southern South* (1910) by Harvard historian Albert Bushnell Hart (1854–1943).

576.23–24 "man's inhumanity . . . mourn"] See "Man Was Made to Mourn," by Robert Burns (1759–1796), first published in 1784.

579.9 Col. "Bill" Hayward] Born in Nebraska City, Nebraska, Hayward (1877–1944) served as a captain of the 2nd Nebraska Volunteer Infantry during the Spanish-American War. In 1910 he unsuccessfully ran for Congress as a Republican, then moved to New York City to practice law. During World War I he commanded the 369th Infantry Regiment, one of several black regiments that saw combat in France. He later served as U.S. attorney for the Southern District of New York, 1921–25.

580.19 the old Fifteenth] The 15th New York National Guard, organized in 1916, became known as the U.S. Army's 369th Regiment.

582.3 *Returning Soldiers*] Du Bois traveled to France in December 1918 to investigate the treatment of black soldiers for the NAACP. While in Paris he helped organize a Pan-African Congress, held in February 1919, which called on the peace conference to protect the rights of Africans living under colonial rule. He returned to the United States in April with material for "An Essay Toward a History of the Black Man in the Great War," published in *The Crisis* in June, and with documentation of attempts by the U.S. military to prevent black soldiers from fraternizing with French civilians. "Documents of the War" appeared in the May issue along with the editorial "Returning Soldiers."

Postmaster General Burleson considered withholding mailing privileges from the magazine, but he relented. The May 1919 *Crisis* sold 106,000 copies, its highest circulation ever.

584.2 JEANNETTE CARTER] Carter (1886–1964), a suffragist, attorney, and labor organizer, was appointed manager of the Washington bureau of the *New York Age* in 1917.

585.2 Miss Nannie H. Burroughs] Burroughs (1879–1961) founded the National Training School for Women and Girls in 1909. The school was renamed the Nannie Helen Burroughs School in 1964.

585.18 COLORED GIRL PROTECTS HERSELF] Detectives Pat Grant and Harry Wilson entered the front door of Ben Johnson's home with guns drawn on July 21, 1919. His seventeen-year-old daughter, Carrie Johnson, shot Wilson, who later died from the gunshot wound. Both Johnsons were charged with first-degree murder. The charges against her father were dropped, but Carrie Johnson stood trial in 1921. A jury of twelve white men convicted her of manslaughter, but a judge overturned the verdict. The U.S. attorney dropped the charges and Johnson was freed on June 21, 1921.

585.34–37 I noticed that Mrs. Mary Church Terrell . . . and many others] Carter names prominent activists, such as Terrell, an early president of the National Association for Colored Women. Neval Thomas (1874–1930) provided aid to black residents during and after the Washington, D.C., riots. He served as NAACP branch president from 1925 to 1930. Carter G. Woodson (1875–1950) founded the Association for the Study of Negro Life and History and the *Journal of Negro History*.

586.9 Judge Robert H. Terrell] Born in Charlottesville, Virginia, Terrell (1857–1925) married Mary Church in 1891; he graduated from Harvard in 1899 and then from Howard University Law School. He became the first black judge in Washington, D.C., in 1910, serving until his death.

588.9 Aunt Dinah's] Aunt Dinah is a cook and kitchen maid in Harriet Beecher Stowe's *Uncle Tom's Cabin* (1852), and a stereotypical "mammy" character, like Aunt Jemima, in other works.

595.3 *Lowden*] Frank Lowden (1861–1943) was governor of Illinois from 1917 to 1921.

595.15 R.R. Jackson] Robert R. Jackson (1870–1942), a veteran of the Spanish-American War, was elected to the Illinois house of representatives in 1912. He served as an alderman for two different wards in the Chicago City Council from 1918 to 1939. He also cofounded Chicago's first black baseball team and served as commissioner of the Negro American League.

595.15–16 Dr. A.J. Carey] Rev. Archibald Carey Sr. (1868–1931) was an activist, writer, and religious leader within the African Methodist Episcopal Church. He served as chaplain of the black 370th Infantry Regiment during World War I.

595.16 Ferdinand L. Barnett] Barnett (1858–1936) was an attorney, writer, and editor. He founded Chicago's first black newspaper, the *Chicago Conservator*, in 1878. He married Ida B. Wells in 1895. Barnett became the first black assistant state's attorney in 1896.

595.17 F.A. Denison] Franklin A. Denison (1862–1932), a lawyer, helped organize the black 8th Illinois National Guard regiment in 1898 and led it in Cuba in the Spanish-American War. He also commanded the regiment, now the 370th Infantry, while it trained in the U.S. during World War I but was replaced by a white officer when it was sent to France.

605.26 Mary Turner] See note 574.18.

608.21–22 Needham Roberts and Johnson] On May 15, 1918, Pvt. Needham Roberts (1901–1949) and Sgt. Henry Johnson (1892–1929) of the 369th Infantry Regiment held back a surprise attack by a German raiding party in the Argonne Forest, later receiving the Croix de Guerre for their heroism. Johnson was posthumously awarded the Medal of Honor in 2015.

610.31 Russey Moton] Robert Russa Moton (1867–1940) served as principal of the Tuskegee Institute from 1915 to 1935, succeeding Booker T. Washington.

614.15 Dr. Shaw] Rev. Dr. Matthew A. N. Shaw (1871–1923) was a Jamaica-born clergyman who led the Twelfth Baptist Church of Boston beginning in 1899.

614.37–38 If David Lloyd George . . . Arthur J. Balfour] David Lloyd George (1863–1945) served as prime minister of the United Kingdom from 1916 to 1922, Herbert Asquith (1852–1928) from 1908 to 1916, Andrew Bonar Law (1858–1923) from 1922 to 1923, and Arthur J. Balfour (1848–1930) from 1902 to 1905.

615.5–6 Trafalgar Square . . . Ramsay MacDonald] Emmeline Pankhurst (1858–1928) hosted a rally for women's suffrage in Trafalgar Square in October 1908, during which she urged her supporters to storm the Houses of Parliament. She was subsequently arrested and sent to Holloway Prison. Ramsay MacDonald (1866–1937) was present on "Bloody Sunday" in the square—November 13, 1887—when police clashed with protestors against the government's labor and Irish policies. He later wrote "Remember Trafalgar Square: Tory Terrorism in 1887," about the protests, during which hundreds were arrested and many injured.

Index

Abbott, Lyman, 416
Abilene, Texas, 483
Ableman v. Booth, 47
Abolitionism, xix, 179–80, 353, 367, 393, 396, 522
Abraham (biblical patriarch), 606
Abyssinian Baptist Church, 444–45
Accommodations, public, segregation in, 43–44, 54, 56–57, 59, 74, 78, 80, 112–13, 115, 167, 252, 255, 408, 434
Ackerman, J. M., 307
Acme Quartette, 615
Actors/actresses, 428–32
Ada, Okla., 483
Adams, John, 152
Addams, Jane, xxx, 474, 476
Africa, 47, 78, 89, 96, 98, 291, 300, 308, 492, 501, 506, 569, 605, 611–12, 615; Algeria, 160; alleged savagery in, 81, 84–88, 368, 372; Congo, 84; Dahomey, 160; Egypt, 160, 245, 290, 295–97, 366, 604; and European imperialism, 608, 610; Guinea coast, 84, 88; Liberia, xxix, 12–13, 180, 250; migration to (colonization), xxix, xxxiii–xxxiv, 11–13, 16, 81, 277–79, 297–98, 373–76, 396, 398–99, 520; missionaries in, 194; history of black race in, 368; population of, 604–5; potential of, 279, 298, 363, 374, 485, 577, 606–10; slave trade from, 97, 102, 104, 210–11, 269, 316, 372, 454, 522; Sudan, 160, 570–71; Tunisia, 160
African Blood Brotherhood, xxxiii–xxxiv
African Communities League, 604, 615
African Meeting House, 179–80
African Methodist Episcopal Church, xxix, 375, 395
Afro-American Council, 365
Agassiz, Louis, 87
Agricultural laborers, xxvi, 19–27, 93, 198–200, 411, 524, 536; peonage of, 449, 454–56, 472–73, 477

Agricultural slaves, 20, 81–82, 98–99, 176, 522
Agriculture, 82, 85, 212, 309–11; credit system for sharecroppers, 19–27
Agriculture Department, U.S., 309–10
Aiken, Albert, 483
Alabama, 32, 116, 135, 279, 313–15, 335, 440, 491; anti-miscegenation laws in, 40–42; constitution, 407, 420; constitutional convention, 402; convict lease system in, 169; disenfranchisement in, 405–8, 419–20; intermarriage prohibited in, 166; lynching in, 130, 143, 152, 192, 482–84; prisons in, 173–74, 450, 463–66; separate railroad cars in, 167; voting rights in, 405–10, 419–20
Alcock, John, 589, 593
Aldrich, Robert, 213
Alexander, Charles, 427
Alexander, Dave, 483
Algeria, 160
Alienism, 104, 109
Allen, Ethan, 177
Allen, Joe, 483
Allen, John Mills, 350
Allen, Richard, 180
Allison, George, 540
Almaraz, A. G., 517
Amazon River, 198
American Bar Association, 558
American Federation of Labor, 327, 600–603
American Historical Society, 184
Americanization, 91, 98
American Missionary Association, 353, 391
American Philological Society, 184
American Quarterly Review, 180
Ames, Fisher, 179
Amsterdam News, xxxiii
Amusement places, public, segregation in, 43–44, 54, 57–59, 74, 78, 112–13, 167, 252, 255, 408, 435, 438–39, 473, 493, 570
Anderson, Charley, 484

701

Anderson, R. B., 206
Anderson, Sim, 484
Anderson, Texas, xxv
Andover, Mass., 343
Anglo-Saxons, 169, 290–91, 296–98, 307–8, 364, 368, 379, 569–70, 605
Anniston, Ala., 130, 142, 192
Anti-Lynching Bill, 557–67
Anti-miscegenation laws, 40–42
Anti-Slavery Society, 353
Antoine, Emile, 484
Apache nation, 515
Appointments, federal, 337–38, 365–66, 371–72, 409
Appomattox, surrender at, 296, 522
Arabs, 569
Arcadia, Fla., 483
Ard, Aps, 484
Arizona, 514–15
Arkansas, 135; convict lease system in, 169; intermarriage prohibited in, 166; lynching in, 130, 140, 143, 192, 482–83; prisons in, 451; separate railroad cars in, 167
Armenia, 527
Armstrong, Samuel C., 80, 82–83, 87–89, 91–93, 96, 98–100
Army, Confederate, 82, 115, 143, 159, 193, 211, 285, 296, 337, 348, 406
Army, Union: black soldiers in, 3, 12, 79, 160–61, 177, 305, 324–25, 499, 524
Army, U.S.: black soldiers in, xxx–xxxii, 178, 295, 375, 433, 443–45, 524–25, 544–54, 579–83, 597, 604–5, 608; intelligence memorandum on William Monroe Trotter, 543; in World War I, 524–25, 557–58, 568, 579–83, 597, 604–5, 608
Articles of Confederation, 177
Ashley County, Ark., 451
Asia, 160, 290–91, 336, 511, 610, 612–13
Asquith, Herbert, 614
Assimilation, 395–96
Associated Press, 399, 524
Atkinson, William Y., 447, 462
Atlanta, Ga., xxviii, xxx, xxxiii, 171, 197–203, 207, 374, 392, 400, 474, 477, 522
Atlanta Constitution, 203, 366, 456–57
Atlanta Journal, 280
Atlantic Monthly, xx, 80

Attucks, Crispus, 395
Augusta, Ga., 372
Austin, Texas, xxx, 496–97
Austin Daily Statesman, 496–97
Austria, 607
Avery, Mrs. Frank, 429
Aycock, Charles B., 401; speech to North Carolina Society, 424–25

Bacon, Augustus O., 446
Bacon, Francis, 327
Bailey, Ida D., 427
Bailey, Lillie, 134–35
Baker, Cross, 306
Baker, Henry E., 585
Baker, Mr. (of Hartford school committee), 340
Balaam, Josh, 484
Balaam, Lewis, 484
Baldwin, Maria, 476
Baldwin v. Franks, 562
Balfour, Arthur J., 614–15
Ball, H. H., 304
Baltimore, Charles, 545–46, 548–49, 552
Baltimore, Md., 138, 178, 180, 588
Baltimore Afro-American, 588
Baltimore Sun, 140–41
Banneker, Benjamin, 100, 175, 179, 395
Banning, Henry B., 6
Banville, John, 304
Baptists, xxix, 170, 179–80
Barbadoes, James G., 180, 396
Barlow, Joel, 179
Barnett, Ferdinand L., 595
Barnett, Ida Wells. *See* Wells, Ida B.
Barnett, Tom, 483
Barnwell, S.C., 137–38, 140, 213
Barrett, Mr. (of Memphis), 144–45
Barry, W. E., 306
Barton, Fla., 483
Bartow County, Ga., 280
Barwick, Ga., 483
Baseball, 496–97
Beaufort County, S.C., 213, 325, 339, 371
Beaumont, Texas, 496–97
Belen, Miss., 453
Belford, Frank, 382, 390
Belgium, 527, 558, 605
Belleau Wood, battle of, 581
Benezet, Anthony, 178

Bentley, C. E., 476
Benton, Maecenas E., 350–51
Berea College v. Kentucky, 473
Bertonneau v. School Directors, 254
Berturre (Bertucci), Frank, 304
Bessemer, Ala., 483
Bible, 11–12, 99, 106, 229, 245, 281, 296, 298, 315, 317, 331, 366, 368, 403, 485, 612, 617
Bingham, Henry H., 350
Birth of a Nation, The, 518–23
Bisbee, Ariz., xxxiv
Black codes, 106, 213, 246
Blackface minstrelsy, xix–xx
Black Star Line, 613–15
Blackstone, William, 55–56
Blakeley, Joseph, 483
Blakely, Ga., 482
Blatch, Harriet Stanton, 474
Bleckley, Logan E., 147
Bloomfield (Blumfield), Alfred J., 304
Blount County, Tenn., 451
Blues, xxx
Bluffton, S.C., 213
Blythewood, Samuel H., 339
Boatwright, Lizzie, 460
Bofill, J. W., 304
Bohlen, Paul C., 494
Bolshevism, 601, 603, 611
Borden, Charles E., 285
Bosnians, 364
Boston, Mass., 177, 184, 343, 426, 543; black churches in, 179–80; and civil rights, 474–76; free persons of color in, 178–81, 396; public schools in, 253–54; segregation in, 438
Boston Globe, 343–45
Boston Guardian, xxx, 543
Boston Suffrage League, 426
Bowen, J.W.E., 399
Bowles, Samuel, 474
Boxing, 485–91
Boycotts, 149–50, 153
Boyde, Evelyn, 592
Boyde, Frances, 592
Braddock, Edward, 177
Bradford County, Fla., 452, 466
Bradley, Joseph P., 225, 252, 256
Bragg, L. M., 306–8
Brame, Ben, 483
Brazil, 280, 570
Brewer, David J., 273

Brice, Benjamin, 325
Brickyards, 449, 462
Brigance, A. F., 307
Briggs, Cyril, xxxiii–xxxiv; "The American Race Problem," 569–78
Brissot, Jacques-Pierre, 178
Britain, xxvii, 97, 105, 178, 180, 234, 360, 609; and Africa, 608; and American Revolution, 47, 177; black people in, 185, 429–30, 605, 614–15; capitalist investors from, 213; immigrants from, 181; and India, 361, 363–64; and Ireland, 612; and Jamaica, 83; Magna Charta, 421; race relations in, 290, 606–7, 614–15; and slavery, 237, 614; in World War I, xxxiii, 605
Britton & Koontz (bankers), 26–27
Brock, Clarence, 545, 550
Brooklyn, N.Y., 128–29, 427, 444, 474, 476, 571
Brooks, W. H., 476
Brooks County, Ga., 574
Brotherhood of Sleeping Car Porters, xxxiv
Brown, Aaron Venable, 32
Brown, Henry B.: Opinion in *Plessy v. Ferguson*, 250–61
Brown, John, 11, 178, 396
Brown, John C., 32
Brown, Joseph, 482
Brown, Mildred, 152, 174
Brown, William Wells, 396
Brownlow, William G., 39
Brownsville, Texas, 443–45
Bruce, Blanche K., 396
Bruce, John E., 427
Bryan, William Jennings, 470–71
Buchanan, James S., 468
Buchanan, John P., 138, 169
Buffalo, N.Y., 338
Buffalo Soldiers, xxxi
Bulkeley, William H., 340–41
Bulkley, William L., 474, 476
Bullard, Dan, 389–90
"Bulldozing," 25–27, 31, 33, 36–37
Bullock, M. R., 385–86
Bunker Hill, battle of, 177
Burke, Edmund, 186
Burleigh, Harry, 494
Burns, Robert, 485
Burr, John Pierre, 180

Burrell, B. B., 483
Burroughs, Nannie H., 585
Bush v. Kentucky, 255, 266
Butler, Benjamin, 177, 181, 325
Buzzards Bay, Mass., 207
Byrd, Phill G., 447, 456–60, 462
Byron, Lord (George Gordon), 485; *Childe Harold's Pilgrimage*, 391

Cable, George Washington, 185; "The Convict Lease System," 171–72; "The Freedman's Case in Equity," 101–23
Caddo Parish, La., 11
Cadiz, Ky., 484
Cahn, Samuel, 24
Cain, Richard H., 18
Cairo, Ill., 481, 484
Calhoun, John C., 178
California, 254, 259, 514, 516
Callahan, John (Dan), 591–92
Calvin, John, 298
Cambridge, Mass., 543
Camden, Fla., 483
Camphor, Miss (of Baltimore), 138
Camp Logan, xxxi, 544
Camp Upton, 581
Canada, xxx, 37, 577
Candler, Allen D., 291–92
Caneker, William, 483
Cane Spring, Ky., 170
Cannon, Bob, 459–60
Capdevielle, Paul, 299, 302
Capen v. Foster, 259
Capitalists, 149, 599–603
Cardiff, Wales, 606
Carey, A. J., 595
Carlyle, Thomas, 234
Carnegie Hall, 492–95, 604, 611–13
Carpetbaggers, 27, 176, 347
Carrizal, battle of, 524
Carroll, Arthur, 591
Carroll, William, 497
Carrolton, Miss., 140
Carson, Walter, 591
Carter, Jeannette: "Negroes of Washington Were Forced to Defend Themselves," 584–86
Carter v. Texas, 562
Carthage, Mo., 389–90
Cary, Isaac, 180

Casement, Roger, 612
Cash, Ellerbe Boggan, 210
Caste, 106, 182, 184–85, 220, 224, 238, 245, 248–49, 312, 339, 345, 359–63, 365, 374, 398, 403, 499, 582
Catholics, 178, 185
Catholic University, 435
Cato of Stono, 395
Cavanaugh, R. W., 526
Celts, 234, 290, 360
Census of 1870, 85, 96, 294
Census of 1880, 85, 96
Census of 1890, 204–5, 211, 294–95, 404–5
Central America, 368, 604–5, 609, 613–14. *See also* Mexico
Century, 101, 118
Ceylon (Sri Lanka), 160
Chain gangs, 117, 165, 446, 448, 450, 466
Chamberlain, Daniel H., 80, 84–85, 95
Chambers, Francis, 341–42
Chambers, Morgan, 484
Character qualifications for voting, 406
Charles, Robert, xxviii–xxix, 299–305
Charleston, S.C., 87, 177–78, 211, 337, 395
Charleston Evening Post, 416
Chase, Calvin, 427
Chase, Mat, 483
Chase, Salmon P., 225
Chattahoochee Brick Company, 462
Chattanooga, Tenn., 136, 147
Cheeshire, William, 591
Cherokee County, Kans., 28, 36
Chesapeake, Ohio & Southwestern Railroad Company, xxi–xxii
Chesapeake, Ohio & Southwestern Railroad Co. v. Wells, xxii–xxiii, 257
Chesnutt, Charles W.: "The Disfranchisement of the Negro," 404–23
Chester, Pa., 356
Chestertown, Md., 141
Chicago, Ill., 134, 356, 393, 470; and civil rights, 474–77; race riot in, xxxiv, 589–98, 606, 616–17
Chicago & Northwestern Railway Co. v. Williams, 257
Chicago Conservator, 427

INDEX

Chicago Defender, 488–91, 555–56
Chicago Inter-Ocean, 136, 172
Chicago Tribune, 19–27, 140, 196, 589–98
Chickasaw nation, 468
Chile, 155
China, 160, 280, 346, 434
Chinese Americans, 252, 259, 270, 336, 341, 434
Chivalry, 194–95, 500
Christian Endeavor Society, 332
Christianity, 99, 129, 141, 147, 155–56, 170, 173, 176, 182–83, 190–91, 194, 246, 282, 291, 293–94, 297, 329, 331–32, 347, 349, 358, 362–63, 372, 434, 499, 510–11
Church, B. B., 585
Church of Christ, 399
Cincinnati, Ohio, xx
Cisneros, E., 517
Citizenship, xxii, 79–81, 97–100, 102, 110, 112, 170, 181, 187, 191, 207, 234, 245–46, 278, 311, 338, 353, 356, 404, 406–7, 409, 421, 467, 470, 473, 510, 614–15; under Articles of Confederation, 177; and caste, 220; and Chinese Americans, 270; and Civil Rights Act (1866), 49; and Civil Rights Act (1875), 43–44, 76–77, 236; and Constitution, 48, 269, 509; equality of, 220, 501, 503, 509; and Fifteenth Amendment, 265; and Fourteenth Amendment, 43–44, 49, 52–53, 59–60, 62–66, 68–72, 77, 101, 109, 122, 161, 164, 215–16, 220–21, 223–26, 231–34, 236–40, 253, 264–65, 269, 272, 423, 471, 478, 565; Frederick Douglass on, 154–55, 159, 161; for Native Americans, 49; *Scott v. Sanford*, 47, 50, 224; state, 47, 59–60, 62–65, 70–72, 177, 215–16, 221–24, 226, 232–33, 236, 239–40, 248, 253; and Thirteenth Amendment, 49, 167
Civil equality, 392, 399
Civil freedom, 51–53, 55, 264, 270–71, 474, 500, 538–39
Civil inferiority, 398, 401
Civil rights, xxvii, xxx, 12, 17, 34, 146, 295, 391–92, 397, 399–400, 410, 416–17, 474, 500; and *Civil Rights Cases*, 51–54, 59, 64–66, 70–72, 74, 76–78, 237; and Fifteenth Amendment, 59, 64–65, 72, 265, 269, 272, 408, 418, 421–22, 478; and Fourteenth Amendment, 11, 13, 16, 52–53, 59, 64–66, 70–72, 74, 77, 215, 223–24, 239, 247, 264–65, 269, 272, 408, 422, 478; and *Plessy v. Ferguson*, 215, 222–24, 237, 239, 246–48, 260, 264–65, 268–72; and Thirteenth Amendment, 51–53, 59, 64–65, 72, 215, 237, 246, 264, 269, 273
Civil Rights Act (1866), 49–53, 74
Civil Rights Act (1870), 41
Civil Rights Act (1875), xxi, 43–44, 56–59, 70, 73, 75–76, 78, 101, 109, 139–40, 167, 236, 255, 565
Civil Rights Cases (1883), xxi, 43–79, 167, 235–37, 252, 255, 562
Civil service. *See* Government service
Civil War, 11, 80–81, 85, 95, 102, 106–9, 157, 164, 232, 234, 280, 286, 336, 376, 396, 400, 410, 415–16, 420–22, 466, 473, 518, 523; black soldiers/sailors in, 3, 12, 79, 160–61, 177, 305, 324–25, 499, 524; Confederate Army in, 82, 115, 143, 159, 193, 211, 285, 296, 337, 348, 406; Fort Wagner, battle of, 177; Gettysburg, battle of, 499, 522; Port Hudson, siege of, 177; slaves remaining on plantations during, 82, 131, 159, 193, 195, 211, 369–70
Claghorn, Kate, 171
Clark, Ike, 384
Clark, Sarah, 134
Clarksdale, Miss., 484
Clarksville, Ga., 130, 192
Clef Club, xxx, 492–95
Clement, Edward H., 474
Cleveland, Grover, 321, 323–24, 416; letter to Booker T. Washington, 207
Cleveland, Ohio, 427, 476
Cleveland Gazette, 132–33
Clyatt, Samuel, 446
Clyatt v. United States, 446–48
Coalitions, interracial, xxiv–xxv
Coal mines, 173, 449, 451, 462
Cochran, Ala., 484
Coffee County, Ala., 465

Cole, Mattie, 139
Coleridge, John, 57
Coleridge-Taylor, Samuel, 494
Coles, J. D., 73
Collins, John, xix
Collinsville, Ill., 557
Colonization/migration to Africa, xxix, xxxiii–xxxiv, 11–13, 16, 181, 277–79, 297–98, 373–75, 396, 398–99
Colorado, 514, 516
Colored American Magazine, 427, 428–32
Colored High School (Washington), 438
Color line, xx, 114, 120–21, 184–86, 194, 249, 272, 493, 600, 602
Columbia, S.C., 119, 127, 152, 174, 204, 206
Columbian Law School, 436, 440
Colyar, A. S., 147–48
Comité des Citoyens (New Orleans), xxiii
Commerce, 76, 198, 200, 240, 255, 257, 574
Commercialism, 391–92
Committee of Twelve for the Advancement of the Interests of the Negro Race, 426
Committees of safety, 26
Competition, 293, 336, 378, 398, 401, 412, 478, 578, 599–600
Concordia Parish, La., 20–23, 25–26
Condorcet, marquis de (Jean-Antoine de Caritat), 178
Confederacy, 17, 118, 164, 232, 522
Congo, 84
Congress, U.S., 77, 116, 165, 210, 231, 240, 247, 273, 281, 313, 317, 327, 349, 377, 410, 445; and agriculture, 309–11; Anti-Lynching Bill, 557–67; black members of, xxvi, 18, 124–27, 178, 197; and civil rights, 407, 412, 419; Civil Rights Act (1866), 49–53, 74; Civil Rights Act (1870), 41; Civil Rights Act (1875), 43–44, 56–59, 70, 73, 75–76, 101, 109, 139–40, 167, 236, 255, 565; and colonization, 12–13; and District of Columbia, 254, 259–60, 345–46, 350–51, 433; Elections Bill, 124–27; and Fifteenth Amendment, 422–23, 478; and Fourteenth Amendment, 60–62, 66–73, 75–76, 255–56, 259, 422–23, 478, 561–67; and Freedman's Bank, 321–26; Fugitive Slave Act (1793), 45–47, 50, 69, 225; Fugitive Slave Act (1850), 47, 50, 69, 225, 247; and interstate commerce, 76, 257, 574; and lynching, 320–21, 557–67; and migration from the South, 28–39; and Native American citizenship, 49; and pensions for freedmen, 377–78; Reapportionment Act, 311, 314–17; Reconstruction Acts, 213; speech by Benjamin R. Tillman, 336–79; speech by George H. White, 309–27; speech by Leonidas C. Dyer, 557–67; speech by Thomas E. Miller, 124–27; testimony by Benjamin Singleton, 28–39; testimony by John Pero, 535–46; and Thirteenth Amendment, 448; and voting rights, 418–19, 422; and World War I, xxxi
Connecticut, 166, 184, 474
Constitution, Alabama, 402, 407, 420
Constitution, Louisiana, xxv, 26, 402
Constitution, Mississippi, xxv, 165, 406–7
Constitution, South Carolina, 204–6, 208–13, 347–48, 377
Constitution, U.S., 4, 117, 178, 312, 316, 345, 412, 472, 478, 500, 509, 576, 603; and Anti-Lynching Bill, 562–64; and *Civil Rights Cases*, 43–48, 50, 59, 61–73, 76; and human rights, 419; and *Plessy v. Ferguson*, 214–15, 221–24, 233–34, 240, 248, 257, 259–60, 263–64, 268–69, 271–73; and *Scott v. Sanford*, 47–48, 50, 72, 224, 247, 269; and voting rights, 205, 208–9, 212, 286. *See also* Fifteenth Amendment; Fourteenth Amendment; Thirteenth Amendment
Constitution, Virginia, 365, 367, 406
Constitutional Convention, 416
Contracts, 53, 61; credit system for sharecroppers, 21–27
Conveyances, public, segregation on, xix–xxv, xxxi, 43–44, 54–56, 59, 74–76, 78, 80, 112–17, 140, 149–50, 167–69, 214–20, 229, 235, 237–38, 241–

44, 249–52, 255–59, 262–64, 266–67, 269–72, 319, 333, 408, 434, 440, 470, 473, 477, 551, 570, 574
Convict lease system, xxvi, xxix, 118–19, 165, 169–74, 446–67, 477, 571–73, 575
Cook, John F., 427
Cook, John Francis, 180
Cook, Will Marion, 494
Cooper, Edward E., 427
Cooper, Henry A., 538–39
Cooper Union, 435
Coosa County, Ala., 463–64
Copiah County, Miss., 139, 190
Corbett, James J., 489–90
Corcoran Art School, 435
Corfield v. Coryell, 63
Cormier (Cromier), Charles, 591–92
Cornish, Samuel, 180
Corruption, 418
Cory v. Carter, 254
Cotton, xxxiii, 12–13, 19, 21–24, 34–35, 38, 82, 93, 98–99, 212, 319, 369, 377, 395, 454, 556
Cotton States and International Exposition, xxviii, 197–203, 207, 392, 400
Council Hill, Indian Terr., 468
Councill, W. H.: "The Future of the Negro," 290–98
Covington, Ky., 149
Covington County, Ala., 464
Cowper, William: "God Moves in a Mysterious Way," 374; "The Negro's Complaint," 186
Cox, Mary J., 40
Coy, Edward, 136, 138
Crafus, Richard (Big Dick), 179
Crawford, James, 591
Credit system for sharecroppers, 19–27
Creek nation, 468–69
Creelman, James, 206
Crenshaw County, Ala., 465
Criminals, 170, 350–51, 355–56
Crisis, xxxi–xxxii, 524–25, 544–54, 568, 574, 582–83
Crummell, Alexander, 396
Crumpacker, Edgar D., 317
Crusader, xxxiii, 569
Cuba, 376, 399, 444–45, 451
Cuervo, New Mexico Terr., 482

Cuffe, Paul and John, 395
Cunningham, Thomas W., 381, 383–84
Curtis, A. M., 585
Cutcheon, Byron M., 125
Cuthbert, Ga., 483

Daggett v. Hudson, 259
Dahomey, 160
Dalmatians, 364
Daniel (biblical prophet), 331
Daniels, Rufe, 545–48, 552
Dante Alighieri, 465
Danville, Va., xxiv
Darwin, Charles, 485
Daskin, Roby, 482
Davenport, Sam, 482
David (biblical king), 485
Davidson County, Tenn., 37–39
Davis, Henrietta Vinton, 604, 609, 615
Davis, Jefferson, 374, 392
Davis, Livett, 483
Davis, Melvin, 592, 594
Dawson, John, 21–22
Dawson, Texas, 482
Dawson v. Lee, 254
Day, John T., 300, 303
Day v. Owen, 257
DeBow, James D. B., 175
Debt: national, 3, 376; of sharecroppers, 19–27; state, 212
Decker, P. D., 383–84
Declaration of Independence, 47, 79, 105, 125, 155, 247–48, 376, 403, 421
Delaware, 166, 175, 613
DeLeon, Edwin, 175
Delhi, La., 484
Delta, La., 24
Democracy, 394, 473–74, 541, 568, 580, 582–83, 588, 604–5, 610
Democratic Party, xix, xxii, 10, 33, 176, 318, 611; administration of Woodrow Wilson, 509; benefiting from black suffrage, 17; black voters encouraged to support, 445, 503; election of 1908, 470–71; fear of black suffrage, 6–7; in North Carolina, 284, 311–14; rejected by black voters, 79; in South Carolina, 125–27, 204–6, 337; in Tennessee, 38; white voters as southern power base, 165, 293

Denison, F. A., 595
Denmark/Danes, 363, 395
Denver Daily Tribune, 6–7
Derham, James, 395
DeRosset, William L., 285
Desdunes, Daniel, xxiii
Dewey, George, 334
Dewey, John, 474, 476
Discrimination. *See* Race discrimination
Disenfranchisement, xx, xxv–xxvi, 11, 140, 146, 159, 165–66, 174, 316, 319, 396, 398, 401, 467, 473, 477, 499, 541, 570, 582; in Alabama, 405–8, 419–20; Charles W. Chesnutt on, 404–25; and election of 1908, 470–71; in Georgia, 472; in Louisiana, 405–6; in Mississippi, 405–7; in North Carolina, 405–6; in South Carolina, 204–6, 208–13, 377, 405–6; in Virginia, 365–67, 405–6. *See also* Voting rights
Dismukes, W. C., 169
District of Columbia. *See* Washington, D.C.
Dixon, Thomas: *The Clansman*, 518–23
Domestic servants, xxvi, 93, 98, 198–99, 329, 333, 613
Domestic slaves, 20, 81–82, 98–99, 177, 333, 522
Domestic slave trade, 82, 188
Domingo, W. A.: "If We Must Die," 616–18
Dorr, Ellerton L., 139
Douglass, Frederick, xix, xxviii, 180, 189, 326, 396, 435, 489; letter to Ida B. Wells, 129; speech to Republican National Convention, 3–5; from *The Reason Why the Colored American is not in the World's Columbian Exposition*, 154–63
Dred Scott case, see *Scott v. Sanford*
Dreier, Mary E., 474
Dublin, Ireland, 187
Du Bois, Alexander, 396
Du Bois, W. E. B., xxx–xxxii, 184, 408, 474, 476, 542; appeal to Woodrow Wilson, 498–500; "Close Ranks," 568; letter from William Monroe Trotter, 426–27; "Of Mr. Booker T. Washington and Others," 391–403; "Returning Soldiers," 582–83; "We Should Worry," 524–25
Dudley, Thomas U., 185
Due process of law, 71, 155, 159, 218–20, 253, 257, 265, 561, 565–66
Dugo, Anton, 591
Duke, Jesse, 132
Dunbar, Paul Laurence: "The White Man's Solution," 571
Durham Coal and Coke Company, 462
Dvořák, Antonín, 182
Dwight, H. C., 340–41
Dyer, Leonidas C.: speech in Congress on Anti-Lynching Bill, 557–67

East Brookland Citizens' Association, 440
Eastern Railroad Company, xix
East Louisiana Railroad Company, 257
Easton, Hosea, 179–80
East St. Louis, Ill.: race riot in, xxxii, xxxiv, 526–41, 553, 557, 606
East Tennessee, Virginia & Georgia Railway Company, 114–15
Economic development, 391–93, 397–98, 416, 473
Economic equality, 508
Economic warfare, 577–78
Eden, Miss., 482
Edgefield, S.C., 190, 210–11
Edgefield County, S.C., 371
Edison, Thomas A., 485
Education, 11, 26, 91, 98, 122, 144, 151, 186, 194–95, 200, 280, 283, 297, 303, 318, 343, 352–53, 355, 358, 368–69, 400–401, 411, 413, 418, 425, 431, 468, 473, 582–83; in Georgia, 291–92, 408–9; Hampton Institute, 80, 87, 89, 96; higher, 87, 94, 100, 126, 294, 397–99, 403–4, 417, 435–36, 438, 478; and literacy, 8, 112, 205, 211–12, 294, 311–12, 319, 348, 404, 406; literary, 92, 94, 100, 294, 478; in Louisiana, 9, 121, 409; in Mississippi, 9; segregated, 120–21, 253–54, 259–60, 415–16, 435–36, 438–40, 570; in South Carolina, 9, 125–26, 348; and teachers, 92, 319, 434, 439–40, 499–500; Tuskegee

Institute, 184, 392–93, 398, 402; vocational, 92, 94–95, 99–100, 294, 307, 359, 391, 398–99, 402–3, 414, 417, 478; in Washington, D.C., 9, 350, 438–40. *See also* Schools, public
Educational qualifications for voting, 406
Edward VII, 430
Edwards, Alonzo (army private), 545–48, 552
Edwards, Alonzo (Hartford homeowner), 340–41
Edwards, Mr. (of Hartford), 339–42
Edwards Station, Miss., 25
Egypt, 160, 604; ancient, 245, 290, 295–97, 366
Election of 1876, xxii, 3–5, 396
Election of 1892, 147
Election of 1904, 377
Election of 1908, 445, 470–71
Elections Bill, 124–27
Elkins, W.Va., 482
Ellenton, S.C., 139
Elliott, John L., 474
Elliott, Robert Brown, 396
Ellis, Anderson, 482
El Paso, Texas, 553
Elyria, Ohio, 132
Emancipation, 4, 47–48, 65, 82–84, 101, 105, 109, 143, 154, 156, 158, 161, 164–65, 175, 178, 180, 186, 188, 194, 198, 249, 265, 303, 324, 353, 396, 423, 446, 466–67, 471, 605
Emancipation Day (Juneteenth), 496–97
Emancipation Proclamation, 81, 85, 176, 472, 497, 499
Emerson, Ralph Waldo, 186
Emmett, Robert, 612
Employment, 86, 575, 583, 597; agriculture, 19–27, 93, 198–200, 411, 524, 556; and competition, 293, 336, 378, 398, 401, 412, 478, 578, 599–600; domestic service, 93, 98, 198–99, 329, 333, 613; factories, 524–26, 536, 555; government service, 337–38, 365–66, 371–72, 409, 498–504, 507–13; and labor unions, 181, 319, 327, 440–41, 477, 526, 536, 598–603, 611; mechanical trades, 93–95, 339;

office work, 436; retail stores, 320, 436–38; and strikes, 478, 509; teaching, 92, 319, 434, 439–40, 499–500
Employment qualifications for voting, 406
England. *See* Britain
Enslavers, 4, 20, 45–47, 50–51, 69, 73, 81–82, 91, 99, 105–9, 122, 156–58, 188, 245–46, 370–71, 401, 433, 570
Episcopalians, 178, 185
Epworth League, 332
Equality, xxii, 17, 106, 108, 125, 184, 186, 290, 336, 359, 370, 410, 414–15, 424, 430, 470, 478, 490–91, 514, 519, 561, 568; before the law, 253, 260, 264–66, 268, 270–72, 364–65, 412, 416, 421, 472, 574; of citizenship, 220, 501, 503, 509; civil, 392, 399; economic, 508; legal, 252; political, 10–11, 107, 253, 358, 392, 578; racial, 291; of rights, 44, 57, 64, 69, 74–76, 221, 223–24, 234, 239, 255, 264, 270, 418, 420; social, 120–21, 200, 203, 253, 260, 270, 292, 332, 358, 444
Equal opportunity, 434, 478
Equal protection of the laws, 41, 71, 73, 79, 108, 216, 222, 227, 231, 234–35, 253–54, 559, 562–65
Equity for black people, 101–23, 444
Erie and North-East Railroad Co. v. Casey (Pennsylvania), 55
Esquimaux (Inuit), 160
Essex, Miss., 453
Estes, James, 484
Esther (biblical book), 229
Eufaula, Indian Terr., 469
Europe, James Reese, xxx, 493
Evans, Frank, 304
Exeter, N.H., 343
"Exodusters," xxviii
Ex parte Virginia, 60, 64, 73–74, 265–66, 562–65
Ex parte Yarbrough, 562
Extein Norton University, 170

Faber, Frederick W.: "The Right Must Win," 335
Factory work, 524–26, 536, 555

Family, 89–90, 96–97, 157, 353
Farragut, David, 177
Felton, Rebecca, xxv, 280–84
Felton, W. H., 281
Ferguson, James E., 553
Field, Stephen, 225–26; Opinion in *Pace v. Alabama*, 40–42
Fifteenth Amendment, xxv, 101, 109, 122, 364; and *Civil Rights Cases*, 65; and *Plessy v. Ferguson*, 265–66; and voting rights, 65, 159, 161, 164, 190, 204, 311–12, 346–48, 404–5, 407–9, 418, 420–24, 471, 478
15th New York National Guard Regiment, 579–81, 608
First African Methodist Episcopal Zion Church (Brooklyn), 444
Fitzgerald, Edward, 137, 139
Flanders, 605
Fleet, John, 180
Fleming, J. L., 131
Fletcher, Andrew, 182
Fletcher v. Peck, 44
Flores, Manuel, 517
Florida, 97; convict lease system in, 169; intermarriage prohibited in, 166; juries in, 8; lynching in, 481–84; Minorcan settlement, 93, 100; prisons in, 450–52, 466
Flower Brothers Lumber Company, 462
Foote, Andrew Hull, 177
Foraker, Joseph B., 433
Foreign slave trade, 48–49, 59, 84, 97–99, 101–2, 104, 181–82, 210–11, 269, 316, 372, 454, 522
Forrest, Nathan B., 369
Forten, James, 180, 396
Fort Erie, Ont., xxx
Fort Leavenworth penitentiary, 451
Fortune, Timothy Thomas, 426–27
Fort Wagner, battle of, 177
Forum, 175, 186, 290
Foss, George E., 537
Foster, Charles B., 493
Foster, Martin D., 538–39
Fourteenth Amendment, xxi, xxiii, 40–41, 54–58, 204, 313–15, 346, 408, 422, 561–64, 566–67; and citizenship, 43–44, 49, 52–53, 59–60, 62–66, 68–72, 77, 101, 109, 122, 161, 164, 215–16, 220–21, 223–26, 231–34, 236–40, 253, 264–65, 269, 272, 423, 471, 478, 565; and *Civil Rights Cases*, 43–45, 49, 52–53, 59–74, 77, 235–36, 252, 255; and *Plessy v. Ferguson*, 215–18, 220–21, 223–29, 231–36, 239–40, 247, 249, 251–53, 255–57, 259, 264–66, 269, 272
Fowler, Ebenezer, 137
Fowler, John, 482
France, 105, 435, 527, 607, 609, 612; and Africa, 608; black Americans in, 185; in World War I, xxxiii, 524, 557–58, 579, 582–83, 588, 605
Francis of Assisi, 392
Frank, John, 170
Frankfort, Ky., 483
Franklin, Benjamin, 178
Frazier, James, 173
Freedman's Bank, 12–13, 321–26
Freedmen's Bureau, 324, 378
Freedmen's Schools, 393
Freedom's Journal, 180
Freeman, Henry F., 585
Free persons of color, 106, 178–81, 244, 396
French Americans, 106, 499
French and Indian War, 177
Frost, Ransom, 24
Froude, James A., 353–54
Fugitive Slave Act (1793), 45–47, 50, 69, 225
Fugitive Slave Act (1850), 47, 50, 69, 225, 247
Fugitive slaves, 45–47, 50, 69, 89, 223, 225, 239
Fullerton, Lee, 382, 385–86
Fusionists (North Carolina), xxiv–xxv

Gainesville, Fla., 482
Galena, Mo., 388
Gallagher, Thomas J., 591
Galton, Francis, 182
Garrison, William Lloyd, 179–80, 295, 438
Garrison, William Lloyd, Jr., 474
Garvey, Marcus, xxxiii; speech in New York City, 604–15
Garza, Agustín S., 514, 517
Gates, Horatio, 177
Genesis (biblical book), 315

Geneva, Ill., 356
George Washington University, 436, 440
Georgia, 32, 147, 193, 280–82; black population of, 119; convict lease system in, 169; disenfranchisement in, 472; intermarriage prohibited in, 166; lynching in, 130, 140, 192, 481–84, 574–75, 605; prisons in, 171–73, 446–48, 455–62, 465–66; public schools in, 291–92, 408–9; separate railroad cars in, 167; strikes in, 478; voting rights in, 346, 472
Georgia Prison Commission, 460–62
German Americans, 106, 557
Germany/Germans, xxxi, 106, 178, 360, 363, 527, 558, 568, 579, 582, 607–9
Gettysburg, battle of, 499, 522
Gibson, Joe, 357
Gibson v. Mississippi, 255, 266
Gilbert, Jim, 482
Gilbert, Matthew W., 443–44
Giles, Jackson W., 409
Giles v. Harris, 407, 409–10, 419–20
Gilyard, Thomas, 380–90
Gliddon, George R., 175
Goins, John N., 284–85
Gompers, Samuel, 600
Gonzales, A., 517
Goodman, A., 342
Goodman, James H., 24
Gordon, Joe, 482
Government service, xxvi, 337–38, 365–66, 371 72, 409, 498 504, 507 13
Grady, Henry W., 146, 202
Grant, Ulysses S., 177, 325, 485, 522
Graves, John Temple, 278–79
Gray v. Ohio, 261
"Great Camp-Meeting in the Promised Land" (spiritual), 391
Great Migration, xxxi–xxxiv, 524–26, 538–39, 544, 553–56
Great War. *See* World War I
Greece, 93, 100; ancient, 182, 290–91, 360, 569
Green, Andrew H., 344
Green, Ebitt, 24
Green, Martin, 344–45
Green, Mary R., 343–45
Green, Samuel F., 344

Greene, Nathaniel, 177
Greener, Jacob, 180
Greener, Richard T., 16–17; "The White Problem," 175–87
Greensburg, La., 484
Greenville, Miss., 484
Greenville, Texas, 484
Grégoire, Henri, 175, 178
Gregory, Thomas W., 558
Grice, Hezekiah, 180
Griffin, Phil, 591
Griffin, W. H. and J. H., 459–60
Griggs, Richard, xxxi–xxxii
Grimes County, Texas, xxiv–xxv, 306–8
Grimké, Archibald H., 399, 426–27, 476
Grimké, Francis J., 399, 474
Grizzard, Ephraim, 138
Grout, William W., 350
Groves Plantation (Louisiana), 24
Grubbs, Vincent Woodbury, 307
Gruening, Martha: "Houston: An N.A.A.C.P. Investigation," 544–52
Guardian, 427
Guinea coast, 84
Gum Branch, Ga., 484
Guthrie, Okla. Terr., 139

Hackett, Frances: "Brotherly Love," 518–22
Haiti, 83–85, 155, 370, 395, 398
Hale, Matthew, 58
Halifax, N.C., 312–13
Hall, Prince, 179
Hall, Thomas C., 474
Hall v. De Cuir, 76, 255
Hamburg, S.C., 139, 190
Hamby and Toomer (convict leasers), 462
Hampton, Wade, 10
Hampton Institute, 80, 87, 89, 96
Hancock, Russell, 139
Hanford Daily Journal, 481–84
Hanifin, Pat, 138
Hanna, Mark, 377–78
Hansling, Mr. (of Hartford school committee), 341
Harlan, John Marshall, 236, 562; Dissenting Opinion in *Civil Rights Cases*, 43–77; Dissenting Opinion in *Plessy v. Ferguson*, 262–73

Harlem, xxx, xxxiii, 580, 609, 614
Harris & Lewis (merchants), 25
Harrisburg, Pa., 345
Harris County, Texas, 544
Harrison, Benjamin, 147
Hart, Albert B., 575–76
Hartford, Conn., 339–42
Hartford Daily Courant, 339–42
Harvard, John, 484
Harvard University, 184, 329
Hausner, Edward, 591
Haven, Julia, 33
Hawaii/Hawaiians, 358, 399
Hawkes, Chester P., 493
Hayes, James H., 365–68, 426
Hayes, Rutherford B., 5, 11–12, 17
Haygood, Atticus G., 193
Hayward, William, 579–81
Health, public, 225–29, 237
Heard v. Georgia Railroad Co., 257
Hearn, Texas, 482
Heflin, James T., 440
Helms, Glenny, 573
Hemphill, John J., 124
Hereditary qualifications for voting, 406
Hernando, Miss., 135
Herschel, William, 485
Hershaw, Lafayette M., 426–27, 476
Hewitt, Abraham, 6–7
Hickman, Hester: "The Land That Gives Birth to Freedom," 14–15
Hickory Bill (Ellsworth Fields), 388–89
Hicks, R. W., 285
Higginson, Thomas W., 80, 86–89, 93–94, 97, 100
Higher education, 87, 94, 100, 126, 294, 397–99, 403–4, 417, 435–36, 438, 478
Hill, Charles S., 585
Hill, Henry, 484
Hill, Leslie Pinckney, 476
Hill, Pie, 483
Hilliard, Mr. (lynching victim), 482
Hilliard, Walter, 493
Hinds County, Miss., 25
Hinton, William, 23
Hirsch, Emil G., 474
Hobson, Richard P., 334
Hodges, Jim, 483

Hoffman, Frederick L.: *The Race Traits and Tendencies of the American Negro*, 349–55, 359
Hollandale, Miss., 140
Holman, J. A., 280
Holmes, John Haynes, 474, 476
Holt, Hamilton, 474
Homer, 485
Honey Springs, Indian Terr., 468–69
Hope, Ark., 482
Hopkins, Pauline, 427
Hottentots (Khoikhoi), 492
Houck v. Southern Pacific Railway Co., 257
House of Representatives, U.S. *See* Congress, U.S.
Houston, Miss., 482
Houston, Texas: race riot in, xxx–xxxiii, 544–54
Houston County, Ala., 465
Houston County, Texas, 454
Houston Post, 553
Howard, Mr. (black student), 343
Howard, Oliver O., 325
Howard University, 16, 438
Howe, John T., 284–85
Howell, Clark: letter to *New York World*, 202–3
Howells, William Dean, 179, 474
Hudson, W. T., 482
Huguenots, 105
Hulseman v. Rems, 259
Human rights, 103, 147, 155, 185, 248, 334, 403, 419, 613
Hume, David, 175
Hungary, 365
Hurd, Carlos F., 527–34

Illegitimacy, 351–52, 354–55
Illinois, 58, 166, 257, 356; lynching in, 481–82, 484, 531, 533, 557; race riots in, xxx, xxxii, xxxiv, 526–41, 553, 557, 589–98, 606, 616–17
Illinois National Guard, 526, 529–33, 540, 553, 598
Imlay, William, 175
Immigration/immigrants, xxxiii, 85, 98, 160, 181, 198, 336, 499, 555, 557
Immigration Act (1917), xxxiii
Imperialism, 514, 608, 610
Independent, 107, 328, 417

India, 160, 194, 280, 291, 344, 359–64, 434, 604, 606
Indiana, 37, 64, 166, 254
Indiana v. Gibson, 254
Indianola, Miss., 146, 371
Indian Territory, 336, 468–69
Industrial education. *See* Vocational education
Industrial progress, 197
Industrial slavery, 400
Industrial Workers of the World, 600, 602, 611
Inferiority, alleged, 48, 50, 52, 56, 91, 102, 104, 122, 144, 186, 227, 230, 238, 244, 253–54, 260, 269, 272, 286, 308, 314, 317, 397–98, 401, 415, 417, 488–91, 499, 501, 569–70, 583
Ingersoll, Robert G., 332
Inhabitants of Worcester v. Western Railroad Corp., 54, 264
In re Coy, 562
In re Neagle, 561
Intermarriage, 166–67, 214, 219–20, 292, 365
International Migration Society, xxix
Interstate commerce, 76, 240, 255, 257
Interstate Commerce Commission, 574
Iowa, 166
Ireland, John, 185–86
Ireland/Irish, 84, 178, 181, 186–87, 234, 604, 606–7
Irish Americans, 106, 612
Isaiah (biblical book), 298
Islam, 569
Israelites, ancient, 4, 229, 245, 296–97, 366, 569
Issaquena County, Miss., 137
Italian Americans, 106, 454, 499
Italy/Italians, 84, 86, 93, 100, 608

Jackson, Ala., 484
Jackson, Andrew, 177
Jackson, Peter, 179
Jackson, R. R., 595–96
Jackson, Tenn., 140
Jackson, Thomas ("Stonewall"), 369
Jacksonville, Fla., 150, 452
Jacobs, Frederick M., 444
Jamaica, xxxiii–xxxiv, 83–85, 100, 353–55, 609, 617
James, Will, 484

Jamestown, Va., 164, 210–11
Japan, 160, 280, 434, 577
Japanese Americans, 342, 434, 516
Java, 160
Jazz, 580
Jefferson, Thomas, 125, 156; *Notes on the State of Virginia*, 175
Jeffries, James J., 485, 488–91
Jesus, 291, 293, 520
Jews, 23, 183–84, 186, 229, 297, 360, 437, 448, 499, 577, 612
Jim Crow, origins of, xix–xx
Johnson, Ben, 539–40
Johnson, Carrie, 585, 588
Johnson, Daniel, 482
Johnson, Edward A., 167
Johnson, Fred ("Deacon"), 494
Johnson, George, 484
Johnson, Henry, 608
Johnson, J. Rosamond, 493
Johnson, Jack, 485–91
Johnson, James Weldon, xxxii, xxxiv; "An Army with Banners," 541–42
Johnson, Jeanette, 152
Johnson, Moses, 152
Johnson, Richard L., 152
Johnson, William, 343–45
Johnston, Joseph E., 369
John Worthy School, 356
Joliet, Ill., 356
Jones, Berrell, 152
Jones, Mr. (black student), 343
Jones, Mr. (musician), 493
Jones, Thomas Goode, 420
Jones v. Virginia, 261
Joplin, Mo., 380–90
Joplin Daily Globe, 380–90
Joseph (biblical figure), 296
Joshua (biblical book), 366, 403
Judges (biblical book), 368
Juneteenth (Emancipation Day), xxx, 496–97
Juries, 8, 73, 111–12, 118, 120, 254–55, 265, 271–72, 564–66
Justice Department, U.S., 586

Kansas, 166, 451; black migration to, xxviii, 14–15, 28–39; lynching in, 151
Kansas City, Mo., 14
Kelley, Florence, 474
Kendall, Miles, 210

INDEX

Kennaday, Paul, 476
Kent, James, 247
Kentucky, 32, 82, 149–50, 171, 254; convict lease system in, 169; intermarriage prohibited in, 166; lynching in, 140, 482–84; prisons in, 449–50, 466; separate railroad cars in, 167
Kerns, Mr. (of Hartford), 341–42
King, John M., 307
Kitchin, Claude, 312
Kitchin, William H., 311–13, 317
Knight, Lewis B., 592
Knoxville, Tenn., 451
Koran, 569
Ku Klux Klan, xxxiv, 78, 139, 164, 190, 366, 520, 523

Labor movement, xxxiii–xxxiv, 599–603, 611
Lafayette, Ky., 483
Lafayette Parish, La., 139
Lally, John F., 300, 304
Lamb, Peter J., 300, 303
Lamentations (biblical book), 11–12
Land tenure, 27
Langston, John Mercer, 396
Lapland, 160
Larned, Kans., 151
Latin races, 511, 516, 570
Law, Bonar, 614–15
Lawrence, James, 177
Lawson, Albert, 484
Lawton, Mr. (black student), 343
Lecky, William Edward Hartpole, 77
Leclere, A. V., 304
Lee, Robert E., 296, 365, 369, 522
Legal rights. *See* Civil rights
Lehew v. Brummell, 254
Leighton, Ala., 482
Lend a Hand: A Record of Progress, 175
Leslie, Preston H., 449
Leslie, Theodore, 380, 382, 384, 386–90
Lewis, W. H., 543
Lewis, Will, 140
Lexington, Ky., 150
Lexington, S.C., 482
Liberator, 179–80, 602
Liberia, xxix, 12–13, 180, 520

Lincoln, Abraham, xxx–xxxi, 11, 155, 176, 295, 325, 405, 472–74, 497, 503, 510, 520, 522, 527, 571, 580–81
Lincoln, Fred M., 341–42
Lincolnton, Ga., 483
Lions, George, 304
Lipton, Thomas, 429
Literacy, xxv–xxvii, 8, 112, 205, 211–12, 294, 311–12, 319, 348, 404, 406
Literary education, 92, 94, 100, 294, 478
Littlefield, Charles E., 321
Little Rock, Ark., 130, 192
Liverpool, England, 605–7
Living Way (magazine), xxi
Lloyd George, David, 614
Logan v. United States, 561
Logwood v. Memphis Railroad, 257
London, England, 179, 429–30, 605–6, 614–15
Long, William, 591
Longview, Texas, xxxiv
Lookout Mountain Coal and Coke Company, 462
Los Angeles Times, 485–87
Louis (lynching victim), 484
Louisiana, xxii, 32–33, 76, 115, 225, 240, 301, 417; agriculture in, 20–27; black code in, 106; constitutional convention, xxv, 26, 402; convict lease system in, 169; disenfranchisement in, 405–6; intermarriage in, 166; lynching in, 130, 140, 192, 481–82, 484; prisons in, 171; race riots in, xxviii–xxix, 139, 299–305; separate railroad cars in, xxiii–xxiv, 167, 215, 219–20, 243–44, 250–51, 255, 257, 259, 261–63, 266–67, 269–70, 272; voting rights in, 405–6
Louisville, Ky., xxxiii, 170, 466
Louisville, New Orleans & Texas Railway Co. v. Mississippi, xxiii, 241, 256
Louisville & Nashville Railroad Co. v. Kentucky, 259
Louverture, Toussaint, 398
Love, Dorcas Robertson, 468
Love, June, 468
Lowden, Frank O., 526, 595–96

Lowndes County, Ga., 465, 574
Lowndes County, Miss., 166
Lowell, James Russell, 176, 183–84
Lumber mills, 449, 451–53, 462, 572
Lundy, Benjamin, 179–80
Luther, Martin, 298
Lynch, Charles, 128
Lynch, Frederick, 474
Lynching, xxvi–xxviii, xxx, xxxii, xxxiv, 124, 158–60, 169, 211, 288, 319, 401–2, 408, 471, 477, 499, 525, 541, 553, 570–71, 582, 587, 609, 616–17; in Alabama, 130, 143, 152, 192, 482–84; Anti-Lynching Bill, 557–67; in Arkansas, 130, 140, 143, 192, 482–83; in Florida, 481–84; in Georgia, 130, 140, 192, 481–84, 574–75, 605; Ida B. Wells on, 128–53, 189–93, 196; in Illinois, 481–82, 484, 531, 533, 557; in Kansas, 151; in Kentucky, 140, 482–84; in Louisiana, 130, 140, 192, 481–82, 484; in Mississippi, 140, 152, 190, 482, 484; in Missouri, 380–90, 482, 484; and morality, 141; in New Mexico Territory, 481–82; in Oklahoma, 481–82, 484; Rebecca Felton's defense of, 280–83; in South Carolina, 119, 137, 140, 152, 190, 482–83; in Tennessee, 135, 138, 140, 143–45; in Texas, 481–84
Lyon, Burt W., 390
Lyon, Kans., 28, 37

MacDonald, Ramsay, 615
Macedonians, 364
Mack, Jacob W., 476
MacKenzie, Constance, 429
MacLean, Mrs. M. D., 476
Madison, James, 177
Madison County, Texas, 454
Madison Parish, La., 22–24
Magna Charta, 421
Magyars, 364–65
Maine, 166, 321
Manassas, Va., 476
Manchester, England, 605–7
Mangham, La., 484
Manly, Alexander L., xxv, 284–89
Manly, F. G., 284–85
Manly, L. D., 284–85
Mannes, David, 494
Marion, Francis, 177, 379
Maroons, 395
Marot, Helen, 474
Marshall, John, 67
Marshall, Mr. (black student), 343
Marshall, Mrs. (of Natchez), 136–37
Marshall, Texas, 483
Marthaville, La., 482
Martinique Quartet, 494
Martinsburg, W.Va., 427
Marxism, xxxiv
Maryland, 175, 179, 345; intermarriage prohibited in, 166
Massachusetts, 54, 503, 558; intermarriage in, 166; public schools in, 253–54; separate railroad cars in, xix
Massachusetts Anti-Slavery Society, xix
Mattes, Oliver W., 553
Matthew (biblical book), 617
Maxey, John, 483
Maxwell & Goodman (merchants), 24
May, Ben, 387
Mayersville, Miss., 137
McCall, Samuel W., 558
McCay, R. C., 23
McCleary, James T., 350
McClellan & Calthorp (merchants), 23
McCulloch v. Maryland, 67
McDaniels, Herman, 484
McDonald, Frances, 592–93
McDonald, J. G., 306
McDonald, Mamie, 592–93
McDowell, Calvin, xxvii, 144–46
McDowell, Mary E., 474
McEnery, Samuel D., 417
McGuinn v. Forbes, 257
McIntosh, John, 468
McIntosh, William F., 468
McKay, Claude: "If We Must ", xxxiv, 617–18
McKinley, William, 295, 297
McMahon, John P., 586
McRay, Frank, 460
McRee, E. J., 462
Mechanical trades, 93–95, 200, 339, 391, 398
Meehan, Miss., 484
Melanchthon, Philip, 2

Memphis, Tenn., xxi–xxii, xxvii–xxviii, 128, 130–31, 134–35, 139–40, 142–45, 149, 192, 374
Memphis & Charleston Railroad Co. v. Benson, 257
Memphis Daily Commercial, 130–31, 142, 146
Memphis Evening Scimitar, 131, 142–44
Memphis Free Speech, xxvii, 128, 130–32, 134, 145–46, 149, 192
Memphis Herald, 132
Memphis Ledger, 134–35
Merrill, James G., 474
Messenger, xxxiv, 599–603, 616–18
Methodists, 147
Mexia, Ala., 482
Mexican Americans, xxvi, xxxi–xxxii, 252, 482, 514–17, 558
Mexican-American War, 177
Mexico, 280, 358, 514, 516–17, 524
Michigan, 166, 184, 257, 261
Middle Passage, 316, 372
Migration from the South, 16–18, 26–93, 149, 153, 212, 356, 366, 377; Africa (colonization), xxix, xxxiii–?, 11–13, 16, 181, 277–29, 297–98, '6, 396, 398–99, 520; to Kansas, 14–15, 28–39; to the North Migration), xxxi–xxxiv, 524––39, 544, 553–56
?, John E., 474, 476
?rades, 579–81
?vice qualifications for ?6
?e Frazier, 427, 601–2
?83
?4
?9, 426
? E., 206; speech in Mil?
?lections Bill, 124–27
Milt? La., 23
Mines, 485
462 ?2–73, 449, 451–52,
Ministe?
80, 27?, 100, 114–15, 178–443–4?7, 332, 373–75,
Minneapol?
Minnesota, ?47
Minorcan se?
?3, 100

Minstrelsy, blackface, xix–xx
Miscegenation, 40–42, 104, 132, 134, 136, 166–67, 176, 192, 194, 367–68
Missionaries, 155, 194, 280, 282, 344, 353, 373–74
Mississippi, 32–33, 75, 301, 382, 526; agriculture in, 25–27; banking in, 26–27; constitution, xxv, 165, 406–7; convict lease system in, 169; disenfranchisement in, 405–7; intermarriage prohibited in, 166; lynching in, 140, 152, 190, 482, 484; prisons in, 172, 453, 465; public schools in, 9; race riot in, 139; separate railroad cars in, xxiii, 167, 256–57; slavery in, 27; voting rights in, 165–66, 346, 405–7
Mississippi River, 336, 539
Missouri, 47, 167, 485; intermarriage prohibited in, 166; lynching in, 380–90, 482, 484; prisons in, 451
Mobile, Ala., xxiii, 9, 178, 482
Mollman, Fred, 526, 534
Moltke, Helmuth von, 485
Monroe County, Ala., 152
Monroe v. Collins, 259, 261
Montana, 166
Monteith, Mr. (lawyer), 126
Montgomery, Ala., 132, 152, 407
Montgomery, Howard, 483
Montgomery County, Ala., 407
Moody, William H., 446–47
Mora, August, 303
Morality, 129, 154, 156, 159, 169, 293, 353, 369, 401, 403, 413, 422, 519; in Africa, 84; among black people, 89, 95, 97, 170, 357, 404, 544; crime, 350–51, 355–56; and equity toward freedmen, 101–6, 110–11, 116–17, 120–23; illegitimacy, 351–52, 354–55; and intermarriage, 166; and lynching, 141; of poor white people, 283–84; prostitution, 331, 544; and reputation of southern white women, 130–31, 193–95; and slavery, 48, 101–2, 105, 122, 157; on the stage, 431–32. See also Religion
Morgan, Clement, 426
Morgan, John Tyler, 279, 297, 401
Morgan, Will, 134
Morris, Charles S., 426–27, 445

Morris, Maik, 483
Morris County, Kans., 28, 37
Morrissey, John, 7
Mose, Creole, 483
Moses (biblical prophet), 366, 485
Moskowitz, Henry, 474, 476
Moss, Thomas, xxvii–xxviii, 144–46
Motion pictures, 518–23
Moton, Robert R., 610
Mt. Holyoke College, 475
Mount Olivet Baptist Church (New York City), 443–44
Mulattoes, 84, 87, 96–97, 105, 134, 136, 166, 194, 367, 378, 395, 405, 519
Mullen, J. R., 288
Mullen, Joseph, 590
Müller, Max: "Essay on Caste," 359–63
Munitions plants, 526
Munn v. Illinois, 54, 58
Murdoch, Mr. (merchant), 25
Murphy, Mr. (prison warden), 356
Music, xxx, 182, 391, 429–30, 492–96, 580, 615
Music School Settlement for Colored People, 494–95
Muslims, 527, 569
Myers, Thomas R., 169

Napoléon Bonaparte, 363, 485
Nash, Joe, 468
Nash, Sally Love, 468–69
Nashville, Tenn., xxi, 30, 33, 37–38, 138, 147, 170
Nashville American, 147
Natchez, Miss., 19, 26–27, 136–37
National Association for the Advancement of Colored People, xxxi, xxxiv, 476, 498–500, 544–54, 574
National Association for the Promotion of Labor Unions among Negroes, 601
National Association of Colored Women, xxix
National Baptist Convention, xxix
National Civic Federation Review, 602
National Colored Colonization Society, 11–13
National Negro Committee, 476–78
National Prison Association, 450
National Urban League, xxxi

Native Americans, xxxii, 12, 36–37, 49, 82, 86–88, 98, 121, 176, 182, 336, 358–59, 368, 468–69, 515, 570, 607
Naturalization, 49, 104, 224, 264, 272
Natural rights, 215, 221, 223–24, 227, 231–33, 238–39, 246–48
Navasota Daily Examiner, 306–8
Navy, Union: black sailors in, 177
Navy, U.S.: black sailors in, 177, 375
Navy Department, U.S., 502
Neal v. Delaware, 65, 255, 266, 564
Nebraska, 169
"Negro domination," 17, 159, 190–91, 193, 286–87, 338, 348, 364, 379, 519–20
"Negro problem," 80–100, 175, 183–84, 186, 204, 290–91, 314, 326–35, 402, 424, 571. *See also* Race problem
"Negro question," 8–9, 90, 336, 346. *See also* Race question
Nell, William C., 177, 210, 396
Nelson, Samuel, 54, 263
Netherlands, 164, 181, 210–11
Nevin, Robert P., xx
Newellton, La., 25
New England, 146, 298, 371, 522
New England Anti-Slavery Society, 179
New Freedom, 500, 504
New Hampshire, 166
New Hanover County, N.C., 284–86
New Haven, Conn., 396
New Jersey, 166
New Jersey Steam Navigation Co. v. Merchants' Bank, 54, 263
New Mexico, 514, 516
New Mexico Territory, 481–82
New Negro, xxxiv, 608, 616–17
New Orleans, battle of, 177
New Orleans, La., xxiii, 6, 26, 115, 155, 173, 450; free persons of color in, 178; lynching in, 130, 192; public schools in, 9, 121, 409; race riot in, xxviii–xxix, 299–305
New Orleans Daily Picayune, 299–301
New Orleans Times-Democrat, 356
Newport News, Va., 609
New Republic, 518–21
New South, 146, 197–201
Newton, Isaac, 405
New York, 184, 254, 260, 338, 371, 453–54, 604; black vote in, 443,

445; emancipation in, 180; intermarriage in, 166; labor movement in, 602; and lynching, 147

New York Age, xxvii, 128, 426–27, 492–95, 541–42, 584–86

New York City, xxx–xxxi, xxxiii, 128–29, 131, 146, 184, 334, 358, 395, 427, 470, 498, 518, 604, 608–9, 613; black churches in, 395, 443–45; and civil rights, 474–76; concert in, 492–95; free persons of color in, 178; labor movement in, 601–2, 611; military parade in, 579–81; opportunities for black people in, 435–37; protest parade in, 541–42

New York Evening Post, 472–75, 498–500

New York Globe, 78–79

New York Times, 16–18, 443–45, 526, 611

New York World, 202–6, 601–2

Niagara Movement, xxx

Nicholls, Francis T., 10

Nicodemus, Kans., xxviii

Nineteenth Century and After (magazine), 446

Nordic races, 570

Norfolk, Va., 325

North American Review, 180

North Carolina, 32, 167, 184, 261, 311–13, 317; black population of, 424; black press in, 282, 284–86, 288–898; coalitions in, xxiv–xxv; convict lease system in, 169; disenfranchisement in, 405–6; intermarriage in, 166; prisons in, 172–73, 451, 453–54; voting rights in, 405–6, 424–25

North Carolina Society, 424–25

North Carolina v. Chavers, 261

North Dakota, 166

Northen, William J., 147

Norwood, Charles W., 284

Nott, Josiah C., 175

Noxubee County, Miss., 165–66

O'Brien, John, 589–91, 593
O'Connell, Daniel, 180
O'Connell, John, 591
Octoroons, 361

Offett, William, 132–33
Office work, 436
Ogden, Robert C., 426–27
Ohio, 64, 133, 166, 253, 259, 261, 377
Ohio v. McCann, 253
Ohio River, 481
Oklahoma, 468–69; black migration to, xxviii; lynching in, 481–82, 484
Oklahoma Territory, 166
Olcott v. Supervisors, 54, 263
Oliphant, Robert, 306
Olivet Baptist Church (Chicago), 595
Omaha, Neb., 147
O'Neil, John, 591
Opelousas, La., 484
Orangeburg, S.C., 339
O'Reilly, Leonora, 474, 476
Orman v. Riley, 259
Otey, Peter J., 316–17
Ottoman Empire, 8, 527
Outlook, 522–23
Ovington, Mary W., xxx, 474, 476
Owen, Chandler, xxxiv, 601–2
Owen, Sheriff (of Carthage, Mo.), 389
Oxford University, 429

Pace, Tony, 40
Pace v. Alabama, 40–42
Pacific Islands, 194
Packer, Jim, 152
Packer, John, 152
Paducah, Ky., 150
Page, Thomas Nelson, 401
Paget, Mrs. Arthur, 429
Paine, Thomas, 179
Pan-Africanism, xxxiii
Panama, 425
Pan-American Exposition, 338
Pankhurst, Emmeline, 615
Paris, France, 435
Paris, Ky., 484
Parish, C. H., 170
Parker, Will, 482
Parkhurst, Charles H., 416, 474
Parsons, Major, 543
Paternalism, 17, 518
Patriotism, 6, 337, 346
Paul, Thomas, 179–80
Paul v. Virginia, 63
Payne, Daniel, 396
Payne, Elizabeth, 494

Peik v. Chicago & Northwestern Railway Co., 58
Peirce City, Mo., 388
Pennsylvania, 46, 55, 257, 259; intermarriage in, 166; and lynching, 147; prisons in, 355–56
Pennsylvania Railroad, 554
Pensacola, Fla., 483
Pensions, 377–78
Peonage, xxvi, 408, 446–67, 477, 571–73, 575, 605
People's Advocate, 171
People's Grocery, xxvii, 144–46
People v. Dean, 261
People v. Gallagher, 254, 260
People v. King, 257
Pero, John: testimony before U.S. House of Representatives, 535–46
Perrigo, L., 517
Perry, Fla., 484
Persia (Iran), 160; ancient, 490
Personal rights. *See* Natural rights
Peters, John P., 474
Philadelphia, Pa., 177, 184, 339; black churches in, 395; and civil rights, 474, 476; free persons of color in, 178, 180, 396
Philanthropy, 17, 112, 169–70, 200, 324, 378–79, 418
Philippines/Filipinos, 376, 399, 418, 434, 439
Phillips, Lewis, 592, 594
Phillips, Wendell, 295, 367, 421, 438
Phillips Academy, 343
Phosphate mines, 212, 449, 451
Pickens, William, 488
Pickett, William P.: *The Negro Problem: Abraham Lincoln's Solution*, 571–76
Pike County, Ala., 465
Pillsbury, Albert E., 476
Pine Bluff, Ark., 483
Pioneer Press, 427
Platte City, Mo., 484
Plessy, Homer A., xxiii, 242–43, 251
Plessy v. Ferguson, xxiii–xxiv, 214–73
Pocahontas, 121
Poinciana Quintet, 493–94
Poland, 8
Police brutality, 544
Political equality, 10–11, 107, 253, 358, 392, 578

Political rights, xxx, 8, 10, 12, 17, 34, 140, 156, 293, 367, 391–92, 397–98, 400, 410, 416–17, 474; and Fifteenth Amendment, 101, 418, 421–22, 478; and Fourteenth Amendment, 13, 16, 101, 253, 422; and *Plessy v. Ferguson*, 253, 260; and *United States v. Harris*, 78
Poll taxes, xxiv–xxv, 26, 165, 406
Pontiac, Mich., 356
Poor, Salem, 395
Poor white people, 93, 213, 280–81, 283–84, 303, 330, 477
Pope, Alexander, 368
Poplarville, Miss., 482
Porteous, Gabriel, 300, 304
Port Jervis, N.Y., 151
Porter, David D., 177
Porter, Robert H., 292
Port Hudson, siege of, 177
Portland, Ark., 483
Portugal, 83
Post, Louis F., 474
Post Office Department, U.S., 419, 501–2
Potter, Henry C., 185
Potter, Justice (of Joplin, Mo.), 387
Power, Police Officer, 344
Praeger, Robert P., 557
Prejudice. *See* Race prejudice
Prescriptive qualifications for voting, 406
Press, black, 128, 130–32, 134, 145–46, 149, 151, 153, 180, 282, 284–86, 288–89
Presswood, J. T., 306
Price, Joseph C., 184, 391, 396
Price, Thomas F., 391
Prigg v. Pennsylvania, 45–46, 51, 66, 223, 239
Prisons/convicts, 117–19, 126, 165, 169–74, 355–56, 446–67, 477
Progress, xxviii, 96, 139, 154, 161–62, 197, 199–200, 202–3, 287, 303, 373, 392, 394, 398, 405–6, 430, 432, 473
Property, one's race as, 217–18, 258
Property ownership, 292, 303, 319, 329–30, 339–42, 364, 398, 405, 411, 416
Property qualifications for voting, 406, 419

Property rights, 45–47, 50–51, 53, 69, 73, 157, 245
Prosser, Gabriel, 395, 398
Prostitutes, 331, 544
Protest parades, 541–42
Providence Sunday Journal, 601–2
Provisional Directorate of the Revolutionary Plan, 514–17
Prussians, 527, 579
Public opinion, 183, 419–23
Pulaski County, Ga., 459
Purvis, Robert, 180, 396

Quadroons, 105
Quakers, 178
Qualifications for voting, 406–7, 419

Rabisohn, Herman, 591
Race consciousness, 597
Race determination, 214–15, 219–20, 243, 260–61
Race discrimination, 112, 183, 186, 395, 399–400, 473, 493, 574, 583; and Anti-Lynching Bill, 561, 564; and anti-miscegenation laws, 41–42; black woman's view of, 433–42; in churches, 170, 434; and *Civil Rights Cases*, xxi, 43–44, 51–54, 56–59, 64–66, 68–73, 75–77; in federal government offices, 498–504, 507–13; and Fifteenth Amendment, 65, 265–66, 347–48, 407–8, 420; and *Plessy v. Ferguson*, 214, 224–30, 235, 237–38, 246, 249, 252, 259, 265–66. *See also* Segregation
Race feeling, 101, 121, 397
Race harmony, 513
Race hatred, 155, 175, 201, 269, 291, 303, 327, 364–65, 369, 371, 377, 398, 401, 412, 415, 521, 523, 544, 569–71, 576–77, 596
Race identity, 291–92
Race instinct, 121, 185, 260
Race prejudice, xix, 17, 93, 120, 128, 182, 185, 187, 260, 272, 291, 296–97, 327, 339, 345, 374, 393, 397, 399–400, 402, 409, 413, 415–16, 421, 428, 439, 443–45, 501, 506, 510–11, 541, 571, 596, 600
Race pride, 187, 264, 291, 296, 298, 337, 367, 486–87

Race problem, 183–84, 203, 290–98, 314, 336–37, 397, 402–3, 405, 416, 422, 425, 428, 569–78, 617. *See also* "Negro problem"
Race question, 136, 143, 543. *See also* "Negro question"
Race riots/massacres, xxviii–xxxii, xxxiv, 140, 164–65, 189–90, 193, 408; Chicago, 589–98, 606, 616–17; Copiah County, Miss., 139; East St. Louis, 526–41, 553, 557, 606; Ellenton, S.C., 139; Hamburg, S.C., 139; Houston, 544–54; Lafayette Parish, La., 139; Memphis, 144; New Orleans, 299–305; Washington, D.C., 584–88, 606, 616–17
Race traits/tendencies, 349–55
Rachel, Henry, 484
Radicalism, 392, 514–17, 599–618
Ragtime, 493, 580
Railroad Co. v. Brown, 255
Railroad Co. v. Husen, 259
Railroad Co. v. Mississippi, 257
Railroads: built by Chinese laborers, 336; built by leased convicts, 119, 169, 466; and migration from the South, 554; in the North, xix; segregation on, xix–xxv, 54–56, 74–76, 78, 80, 114–17, 140, 150, 167–69, 214–20, 229, 235, 237–38, 241–44, 249–52, 255–59, 262–64, 266–67, 269–71, 319, 332–33, 470, 473, 574
Rainey, Joseph, 18
Raker, John E., 535–38
Raleigh, Walter, 327
Raleigh News and Observer, 286–89
Ramos, B., Jr., 517
Randall, Samuel J., 6
Randolph, A. Philip, xxxiv; "Our Reason for Being," 599–603
Rape, xxv, 130–33, 135, 137–38, 140–43, 146–47, 150, 159, 191–93, 281–82, 334, 370
Raymond, John T., 179
Raynal, Guillaume-Thomas, 179
Readjuster Party (Virginia), xxiv
Reapportionment Act, 311, 314–17
Reason Why the Colored American is not in the World's Columbian Exposition, the (pamphlet), 154–74

Reconstruction, xxi–xxii, xxx, 17, 82, 107–10, 115, 139, 164, 167, 190, 193, 205, 211, 213, 347, 364, 370, 396, 418, 518–24
Redden, Joe, 482
Redeemers, xxii
Redfield, Isaac F., 56
Red Record, A (pamphlet), xxvii, 188–96
Reed, Isaiah, 206
Reese, Albert, 483
Reese, Maggie, 138
Reese, Michael, 590
Regulators, 190
Religion, 155, 169, 281, 283, 331, 350, 352–53, 355, 610; black ministers, 94, 100, 114–15, 178–80, 277–79, 296–97, 332, 373–75, 443–45, 468; among black people, 89–91, 100, 104, 106, 182–83; establishment of black churches, 179–80, 373, 395; and race problem, 293, 297; segregated churches, 170, 434. *See also* Bible; Christianity; Morality
Remond, Charles Lenox, 396
Reno, Nev., 485–86, 488
Rentie, William, 469
Rentiesville, Indian Terr., 468–69
Republicanism, 63–64, 71, 99, 108, 154, 190, 224, 235, 273, 406, 410, 413, 420
Republican National Convention: Frederick Douglass's speech to, 3–5
Republican Party, xxi–xxii, xxiv, 125, 176, 611; and black voters, 6, 8–9, 16, 78–79, 293, 345, 603; black voters as southern power base, 165; black voters encouraged not to support, 445; election of 1876, 3–5; election of 1892, 147; election of 1904, 377; election of 1908, 470–71; in North Carolina, 284–85, 312–14; radicals during Reconstruction, 522; in South Carolina, 204–6; in Tennessee, 38; and Washington, D.C., 351; and white voters, 316
Restaurants, 434, 438
Revolutionary War, 47, 177, 379, 395, 409, 416, 499, 524
Rex v. Ivens (Britain), 57
Rhode Island, 166, 418–19

Rice, 85, 99, 212
Rice, Thomas Dartmouth "Daddy," xix–xx
Richmond, Va., 9, 365, 419, 558
Richmond Planet, 302–5
Ridgefield Park, N.J., 476
Rights. *See* Civil rights; Human rights; Natural rights; Political rights; Voting rights
Riots. *See* Race riots/massacres
Rittenhouse, David, 178
Robbins, Jane, 474
Roberson, Douglas, 482
Roberts, Needham, 608
Roberts v. City of Boston, 253–54
Robinson, Will, 484
Robinson & Wife v. Memphis & Charleston Railroad Co., 75
Rockwall, Texas, 482
Roger, Charles, 540
Rome, ancient, 290, 296, 485, 529, 569, 579
Rome, Ga., 447
Roosevelt, Theodore, 337–39, 347, 357, 365, 371–72, 377, 393, 443–45, 451
Roosevelt, Theodore, Jr., 444
Rough Riders, 444–45
Royal Albert Hall, 614–15
Runkle, Lieutenant, 593
Rush, Benjamin, 178
Russell, Charles Edward, 474, 476
Russia/Russians, 4, 9, 164, 172, 293, 346, 363, 448, 538, 577, 607, 617
Russian Americans, 499
Russian Revolution, xxxiv
Russwurm, John B., 180

Saenz, A. A., 517
St. Augustine, Fla., 93
St. Bartholomew's Day massacre, 527
St. John, John P., 30, 34–35
Saint Joseph, La., 25
St. Louis, Mo., 452, 539
St. Louis Globe Democrat, 8–10
St. Louis Post-Dispatch, 527–34
St. Philip's Church, 494
Salem, Peter, 395
Salter, William M., 475
Salzner, Henry, 484
Sampson, William T., 334
Samuels, Frank, 483

San Diego, Texas, xxxi–xxxii, 514, 517
Sandoval, Manuel, 482
San Francisco, Calif., 259
San Juan Hill, 444–45
San Pedro Daily News, 470–71
Santo Domingo (Dominican Republic), 155, 370
Santos, Porfirio, 517
Savannah, Ga., 9, 372, 448
Savannah River, 372
Saxons, 360, 363
Saxton, Rufus, 86, 325
Scabs, 599–600
Scandinavians, 570
Scarborough, Charles, 483
Scarborough, William S., 184, 476
Schley, Winfield Scott, 334
Schools, public, 398–99, 401–2, 411, 413, 434, 473, 478; black, number of, 294, 319; in Georgia, 291–92, 408–9; in Indian Territory, 468; in Louisiana, 9, 121, 409; in Massachusetts, 253–54; in Mississippi, 9; segregation in, 120–21, 253–54, 259–60, 415–16, 438–40, 570; in South Carolina, 9, 125–26, 348; in Washington, D.C., 9, 350, 438–40. *See also* Education
Schopenhauer, Arthur, 183
Scotland, 178, 181
Scotland Neck, N.C., 312
Scott, Dred, 47
Scott, Emmett J., 427
Scott, James E.: "Statement on Attack by Rioters in Washington, D.C.," 587
Scott, Walter, 389
Scott, William, 591
Scott, Winfield, 177
Scott v. Sanford, 47–48, 50, 72, 78, 157, 224, 244, 247, 269, 409
Sea Island settlements, 18, 87
Sectionalism, 126
Sedgwick, Theodore, 267
Segregation, 537–38, 541, 571, 573, 583; in federal government departments, 498–504, 507–13; in higher education, 435–36; in public accommodations, 43–44, 54, 56–57, 59, 74, 78, 80, 112–13, 115, 167, 252, 255, 408, 434; in public amusement places, 43–44, 54, 57–59, 74, 78, 112–13, 167, 252, 255, 408, 435, 438–39, 473, 493, 570; on public conveyances, xix–xxv, xxxi, 43–44, 54–56, 59, 74–76, 78, 80, 112–17, 140, 149–50, 167–70, 214–20, 229, 235, 237–38, 241–44, 249–52, 255–59, 262–64, 266–67, 269–72, 319, 333, 408, 434, 440, 470, 473, 477, 551, 570, 574; in public schools, 120–21, 253–54, 259–60, 415–16, 438–40, 570; in restaurants, 434, 438; in Washington, D.C., 433–42. *See also* Race discrimination
Seligman, Edwin R. A., 476
Selma Times, 114–15
Senate, U.S. *See* Congress, U.S.
"Separate but equal," xxii–xxiii, 167–68, 242, 250
Sepoy Rebellion, 363
Serbs, 364, 605
Sermon on the Mount, 99
Sexuality, 88–89, 523
Seymour, Ind., 453
Shadd, Abraham, 396
Shakespeare, William, 90, 405, 431, 485; *Hamlet*, 413; *Macbeth*, 297, 357; *The Merchant of Venice*, 199
Shaler, Nathaniel S.: "The Negro Problem," 80–100
Shannon, Haynes, 306
Sharecroppers, xxvi, 19–27, 34
Shaw, Lemuel, 254
Shaw, Matthew A. N., 614
Shelbyville, Tenn., 148
Sheridan, Philip, 177
Sherman, James S., 471
Sherman, William T., 177
Shreveport, La., 11
Sicily, 84, 86, 93, 100
Silverman, Joseph, 476
Simmons, Quillie, 483
Simms, Martina: "Washington Riot," 588
Sinclair, William, 476
Singleton, Benjamin, 14; testimony before U.S. Senate, 28–39
Sinking Fund Cases, 44
Slaughter-House Cases, 52–53, 60, 63, 70, 225–29, 235, 237, 252–53
Slave auctions, 82
Slave codes, 246

Slave insurrections, 81–82, 369–70, 395, 398

Slavery, xx, xxx, 9, 11, 81, 83–85, 89, 91, 98–99, 101–2, 106–7, 111–12, 131, 139, 143, 153, 164, 188–89, 193, 195, 198, 296, 320–21, 330, 336, 347, 366, 369–71, 373, 395–96, 410–11, 415–17, 421, 470, 496, 514, 522, 569–70, 606–7, 614; abolition of, 158, 185, 353, 414, 423; alleged mildness of, 82; and black women, 333; and caste, 224; and *Civil Rights Cases*, 44–52, 56, 65, 69, 73, 76; enslavement of white persons, 178; Frederick Douglass on, 153–60, 162; industrial, 400; in Mississippi, 27; and morality, 48, 101–2, 105, 122, 157; peonage as, 446, 449–52, 466–67, 477, 605; and race determination, 220; and race prejudice, 17, 402; and *Plessy v. Ferguson*, 215–16, 220, 223–24, 228, 232, 234, 237–38, 244, 251–52, 265, 272; and *Scott v. Sanford*, 47–48, 50, 52, 157, 224, 244, 247; in South Carolina, 372, 376, 378; in Tennessee, 14, 34. *See also* Abolitionism; Emancipation; Thirteenth Amendment

Slaves: agricultural versus domestic, 20, 81–82, 98–99, 176–77, 333, 522; first brought to Virginia, 164, 210–11; fugitive, 45–47, 50, 69, 89, 223, 225, 239

Slave trade: domestic, 82, 188; foreign, 48–49, 59, 84, 97–99, 101–2, 104, 181–82, 210–11, 269, 316, 372, 454, 522

Slavs, 364–65, 511

Sleeman, William H., 362

Smalls, Robert, 18, 206; speech in South Carolina Constitutional Convention, 208–13

Smith, Harry, 427

Smith, John, 483

Smith, Joseph, 475

Smith, Sydney, 179

Smith County, Tenn., 33

Smoaks, S.C., 483

Snow, K. S., 549, 552

Social equality, 120–21, 200, 203, 253, 260, 270, 292, 332, 358, 444

Socialism, xxxiv, 611

Social rights, 74–76

Socrates, 392

Somers, Dick, 33

South America, 368, 376, 604, 613. *See also* Brazil

South Carolina, xxii, 32, 80, 100, 135, 153, 318, 337, 339, 357–58, 361, 373, 520; agriculture in, 212; black code in, 213; black population of, 119, 204–5, 364, 376; constitution, 347–48, 377; constitutional convention, 204–6, 208–13; convict lease system in, 169; disenfranchisement in, 204–6, 208–13, 377, 405–6; intermarriage prohibited in, 166; lynching in, 119, 137, 140, 152, 190, 482–83; prisons in, 171, 174, 451; public schools in, 9, 125–26, 348; race riots in, 139; Sea Island settlements, 18, 87; slave insurrections in, 395; slavery in, 372, 376, 378; taxation in, 211; voting rights in, 124–27, 204–6, 208–13, 347–48, 364, 368, 377, 405–6

South Dakota, 166

Southern Baptist Convention, 170

Southern Horrors (pamphlet), xxvii, 128–53

Spain/Spanish, 83, 368

Spanish Americans, 106

Spanish-American War, 334, 393, 444–45, 451, 499, 524

Sparks, Lee, 545–50

Speech, freedom of, 421

Speer, Emory, 448, 466

Speez, Harry, 592

Spencer, Anna Garlin, 475

Sperry, Anson M., 324–25

Spirituals, 182, 391

Springer, John C., 285

Springer, William McKendree, 6

Springfield, Ill., xxx, 473

Springfield Republican, 474

Stafford, Wendell P., 475, 476

Stampley, W. S., 306

Stanton, Edwin M., 324–25

State citizenship, 47, 59–60, 62–65, 70–72, 177, 215–16, 221–24, 226, 232–33, 236, 239–40, 248, 253

State ex rel. Abbott v. Hicks, Judge, et al., 257

State ex rel. Wood v. Baker, 259
States' rights, 167, 248
Stauber, George, 591–93
Steamships, 279, 613–15
Steffens, Lincoln, 475
Stennien, Sylvester, 483
Stephens, Alexander H., 232
Stevens, Thaddeus, 367, 519, 522–23
Stewart, Will, xxvii, 144–46
Stockbridge tribe, 49
Stockholm (troop ship), 581
Stoermer, Ed, 549
Stokes, Helen, 475
Stokes, J. G. Phelps, 475
Stono Rebellion, 395
Storey, Moorfield, 476; appeal to Woodrow Wilson, 498–500
Story, Joseph, 45–46, 56, 67, 239
Stowe, Harriet Beecher: *Uncle Tom's Cabin*, 369, 452
Strauder v. West Virginia, 50–52, 60, 65–66, 226, 234, 244, 254–55, 265, 562, 564–65
Streetcars, segregation on, xxiv, xxxi, 76, 149, 270, 319, 408, 434, 440, 551
Stricklin, M., 135
Strikes, 478, 599
Strong, William, 263
Submission, 391–92, 395, 397–98, 417, 605, 616
Sudan, 160, 570–71
Suffrage. *See* Voting rights
Sugar, 12–13, 83, 99, 107, 556
Sulphur mines, 452
Sumner, Charles, 254, 295, 326, 419, 438
Sumter, Thomas, 379
Supreme Court, U.S., 101, 212, 374, 412, 419, 470; *Ableman v. Booth*, 47; *Baldwin v. Franks*, 562; *Berea College v. Kentucky*, 473; *Bush v. Kentucky*, 255, 266; *Carter v. Texas*, 562; *Civil Rights Cases*, xxi, 43–79, 167, 235–37, 252, 255, 562; *Clyatt v. United States*, 446–48; *Ex parte Virginia*, 60, 64, 73–74, 265, 562–65; *Ex parte Yarbrough*, 562; *Fletcher v. Peck*, 44; *Gibson v. Mississippi*, 255, 266; *Giles v. Harris*, 407, 409–10, 419–20; *Hall v. De Cuir*, 76, 255; *In re Coy*, 562; *In re Neagle*, 561; and Ku Klux Klan, 78; *Logan v. United States*, 561; *Louisville, New Orleans & Texas Railway Co. v. Mississippi*, xxiii, 241, 256; *Louisville & Nashville Railroad Co. v. Kentucky*, 259; *McCulloch v. Maryland*, 67; *Munn v. Illinois*, 54, 58; *Neal v. Delaware*, 65, 255, 266, 564; *New Jersey Steam Navigation Co. v. Merchants' Bank*, 54, 263; *Olcott v. Supervisors*, 54, 263; *Pace v. Alabama*, 40–42; *Paul v. Virginia*, 63; *Peik v. Chicago & Northwestern Railway Co.*, 58; *Plessy v. Ferguson*, xxiii–xxiv, 214–73; *Prigg v. Pennsylvania*, 45–46, 51, 66, 223, 239; *Railroad Co. v. Brown*, 255; *Railroad Co. v. Husen*, 259; *Robinson & Wife v. Memphis & Charleston Railroad Co.*, 75; *Scott v. Sanford*, 47–48, 50, 72, 78, 157, 224, 244, 247, 269, 409; *Sinking Fund Cases*, 44; *Slaughter-House Cases*, 52–53, 60, 63, 70, 225–29, 235, 237, 252–53; *Strauder v. West Virginia*, 50–52, 60, 65–66, 226, 234, 244, 254–55, 265, 562, 564–65; *Tennessee v. Davis*, 562; *Township of Pine Grove v. Talcott*, 54, 263–64; *Township of Queensbury v. Culver*, 54; *United States v. Caesar*, 238; *United States v. Cruikshank*, 64–65, 232–34, 237–38, 566; *United States v. Davis*, 238; *United States v. Fisher*, 67; *United States v. Harris*, 562; *United States v. Jowers*, 238; *United States v. Reese*, 50, 65–66; *Virginia v. Rives*, 255, 265, 562; and voting rights, 407–10, 472–73; *Ward v. Maryland*, 63; *Yick Wo v. Hopkins*, 259, 562
Supreme Revolutionary Congress, 514
Sutton, Herbert T., 493
Swayne, Noah H., 225
Sweeney, John, 484
Sylvester, Richard H., 350–51
Syncopation, 493
Syphax, Mr. (black student), 343
Syria, 160

Taft, William Howard, 471, 478
Talbotton, Ga., 483

Talladega College, 488
Tallahassee, Fla., 483
Tallapoosa County, Ala., 463–64
Taney, Roger B., 47, 78, 157, 178, 190
Tarrytown, Ga., 484
Tartars, 363
Taxation, 96, 205, 211, 318, 409, 411
Taylor, John D., 282, 284
Taylor, Zachary, 177
Teaching, 92, 319, 434, 439–40, 499–500
Tenant farmers. *See* Sharecroppers
Tennessee, 64, 75, 147–48; agriculture in, 38; black migration from, 14, 28–33, 37–38; black press in, 128, 130–32, 134, 145–46, 149; convict lease system in, 169; elections in, 38–39; intermarriage prohibited in, 166–67; lynching in, 135, 138, 140, 143–45; prisons in, 172–73, 451, 466; race riot in, 144; separate railroad cars in, xx–xxi, xxiii, 167–69, 257; slavery in, 14, 34
Tennessee v. Davis, 562
Tensas Parish, La., 25–26
Terrell, Mary Church, xxix–xxx, 475, 476, 585; "Peonage in the United States," 446–67; "What It Means to Be Colored in the Capital of the United States," 433–42
Terrell, Robert H., 586
Teutons, 90, 106, 178, 360, 363, 570, 582
Texarkana, Texas, 136
Texas, 32, 306–8, 468, 514, 516; coalitions in, xxiv–xxv; intermarriage prohibited in, 167; Juneteenth celebrations in, xxx, 496–97; lynching in, 481–84; prisons in, 172, 454; race riot in, xxxi–xxxii, 544–54; separate railroad cars in, 167
Texas Rangers, xxxii
Thayer, Police Officer, 344
Thirteenth Amendment, 81, 122, 447–48, 455–56, 466; and *Civil Rights Cases*, 43–45, 49–53, 56, 59–60, 64–65, 68, 72, 167, 237, 252; and emancipation, 65, 101, 109, 161, 164, 423, 471; and *Plessy v. Ferguson*, 215–16, 233–34, 237, 244, 246, 251–52, 264, 266, 269, 272

Thomas, Ga., 460
Thomas, John, 483
Thomas, Neval, 585
Thomas, Onesime, 484
Thomas, William I., 475
Thompson, Maurice, 107
Thompson, William H., 595–96
Thomy Lafon Colored School, 299
Thorpe v. Rutland & Burlington Railroad, 228
369th U.S. Infantry Regiment, xxx, 579
Thwing, Charles F., 475–76
Tillman, Benjamin R., 125–26, 137, 141, 174, 204–5, 210–12, 401–2; speech in Congress on the Race Problem, 336–79
Tilton, Theodore, 367
Tompkins, Henry C., 41
Tompkins, John R., 41
Tooley, Smith, 152
Topeka, Kans., 28, 36–37
Tourgée, Albion W., xxiii, 295; Brief for Plaintiff in *Plessy v. Ferguson*, 214–49
Township of Pine Grove v. Talcott, 54, 263–64
Township of Queensbury v. Culver, 54
Travers, Sara, 546–48, 551–52
Treasury Department, U.S., 501–2
Trenholm, George, 321, 324
Trigg, John C., 383
Tripp, Stephen O., 533
Trotter, Geraldine, 426
Trotter, William Monroe, xxx; address to Woodrow Wilson, 501–4; army intelligence memorandum on, 543; exchange with Woodrow Wilson, 505–13; letter to W.E.B. Du Bois, 426–27
Trumbull, John, 177
Tullahoma, Tenn., 140
Tunisia, 160
Turks, 8, 182, 364, 527
Turner, Henry M., xxix, 277–79, 297, 373–75
Turner, Mary, 574–75, 605
Turner, Mr. (convict leaser), 573
Turner, Nat, 395, 398
Turner, Sylvester, 545
Turpentine distilleries, 449, 451–52, 458, 572
Turrentine, John, 285

Tuscumbia, Ala., 136
Tuskegee Institute, xxvii–xxviii, 184, 392–93, 398, 402
24th U.S. Infantry Regiment, xxxi–xxxii, 544–54
25th U.S. Infantry Regiment, 443–45
Tybee, Ga., 280, 282
Tyers, William H., 493
Tyler, Texas, 483
Tyndall, John, 485

Understanding qualifications for voting, 406–7
Underwood, Mrs. J. S., 132–33
Underwood, Oscar W., 313–16
Union League Club, 600, 602
Unions, xxxiv, 181, 319, 327, 440–41, 477, 526, 536, 598–603, 611
United States v. Caesar, 238
United States v. Cruikshank, 64–65, 232–34, 237–38, 566
United States v. Davis, 238
United States v. Fisher, 67
United States v. Harris, 78, 562
United States v. Jowers, 238
United States v. Reese, 50, 65–66
Universal freedom, 50–51, 56
Universal Negro Improvement Association, xxxiii–xxxiv, 604–15
Urban life, xxxi, xxxiii, 93, 96, 333, 418, 437

Vagrancy laws, 165, 466, 573
Valley Forge, encampment at, 177
Vance, Miss., 453
Van Deman, Ralph H.: army intelligence memorandum on William Monroe Trotter, 543
Van Kuren, Andy, 304
Vaudeville, xxx, 428–32
Venice, Italy, 9
Vermont, 166, 184, 228
Vesey, Denmark, 395, 398
Vicksburg, Miss., 152
Vidalia, La., 25
Vikings, 363
Villard, Oswald G., 476, 478; appeal to Woodrow Wilson, 498–500; "Call for a Negro Conference," 472–75
Virginia, 17, 32, 73, 75, 92, 175, 178, 181–82, 261, 317, 434, 609; coalitions in, xxiv; constitution, 365, 367, 406; disenfranchisement in, 365–67, 405–6; first slaves brought to, 164, 210–11; intermarriage prohibited in, 166; slave insurrections in, 395; voting rights in, 405–6
Virginia v. Rives, 255, 265, 562
Virgin Islands, 395
Vocational education, 92, 94–95, 99–100, 294, 307, 359, 391, 398–99, 402–3, 414, 417, 478
Voice of Missions (newspaper), xxix
Voting rights, 4–5, 12–13, 16–17, 34, 38–39, 79–80, 100, 105, 107–8, 139, 178, 191, 270, 281, 286–87, 292–93, 320, 345, 370, 373, 399–400, 524; in Alabama, 405–10, 419–20; and Congress, 418–19, 422; and Fifteenth Amendment, 65, 159, 161, 164, 190, 204, 311–12, 346–48, 404–5, 407–9, 418, 420–24, 471, 478; and Fourteenth Amendment, 204, 313–15, 346, 422–23; in Georgia, 346, 472; and literacy, 8, 205, 211–12, 311–12, 319, 348, 404, 406; in Louisiana, 405–6; in Mississippi, 165–66, 346, 405–7; in North Carolina, 405–6, 424–25; poll taxes, 26, 165, 406; qualifications for voting, 406–7, 419; in South Carolina, 124–27, 204–6, 208–13, 347–48, 364, 368, 377, 405–6; in Virginia, 405–6. *See also* Disenfranchisement

Wads, Jake, 482
Waite, Morrison R., 232
Wald, Lillian D., 475–76
Waldron, J. Milton, 475, 476
Wales, 605–6
Walker, Aida Overton, xxx; "Colored Men and Women on the Stage," 428–32
Walker, David, 180: *An Appeal to the Colored Citizens of the World*, 180–81, 395
Walker, Edward G., 181
Walker, Garfield, 469
Walker, George, 429
Waller, O. M., 427, 476
Walling, William English, 475–76
Walls, Frank, 592

Walsh, David I., 503
Walters, Alexander, 475–76
Walton, Lester A.: "Concert at Carnegie Hall," 493–95
Wanderer (slave ship), 372
Ward, William H., 475
Ward v. Flood, 254
Ward v. Maryland, 63
War Department, U.S., 444, 502
Ware County, Ga., 465–66
War of 1812, 177, 499, 524
Warsaw, Poland, 8
Washington (state), 166, 169
Washington, Booker T., xxx, 184, 202–3, 358–59, 363, 416–17, 426–27, 444, 603, 605–6, 610–11; Atlanta Exposition Address, xxviii, 197–201; letter from Grover Cleveland, 207; W.E.B. Du Bois's critique of, 391–403
Washington, D.C., xxvi, 10, 16–17, 28, 129, 175, 185, 210, 213, 277, 349, 365, 368, 426–27, 452, 481, 582, 611; and civil rights, 474–75, 476; congressional control of, 254, 259–60, 345–46, 350–51, 433; illegitimacy in, 352; Freedman's Bank in, 324–25; free persons of color in, 178, 180; public schools in, 9, 350, 438–40; race riot in, xxxiv, 584–88, 606, 616–17; segregation in, 433–42, 498–99, 501, 509
Washington, George, 177, 405, 434
Washington Bee, 427
Washington Board of Education, 439
Washington Chamber of Commerce, 600
Washington Evening Star, 172–73, 277–79
Washington Post, 339, 365–67
Washington Times, 318
Waterford Plantation, 22
Watkins, William J., 180
Watterson, Henry, 6
Waycross, Ga., 140
Wayne, Anthony, 177
Webb City, Mo., 388
Weems, Frank, 136, 147
Wells, Ida B., xxi–xxiii, xxx, xxxii, 476; from *The Reason Why the Colored American is not in the World's Columbian Exposition*, 164–74; from *A Red Record*, xxvii, 188–96; *Southern Horrors: Lynch Law in All Its Phases*, xxvii, 128–53;
Wellston, Ga., 484
Wesley, John, 156
West, Jesse, 483
West Chester & Philadelphia Railroad Co. v. Miles, 257
Western Reserve University, 475
West Indies, xxxiii–xxxiv, 604–7, 609–10, 613–15. *See also* Cuba; Haiti, Jamaica; Santo Domingo
West Shreveport, La., 484
West Virginia, 167, 254; intermarriage prohibited in, 166; lynching in, 482
Wharton, Mrs. Rodman, 475
Wharton, Susan P., 475, 476
"What Will the Harvest Be?" (hymn), 321
Wheatley, Phillis, 395
Wheeler, William A., 5
White, George H., xxvi; speech in Congress in Defense of the Negro Race, 309–27
White, H. C., 23
White, Horace, 475
White, William F., 574
Whitehead, Benjamin G., 356
White League, 6, 8
White Liners, 139
White Man's Union, xxv, 306–8
White primaries, xxvi
"White problem," 175–87
White superiority, alleged, 122, 238, 244, 268–69, 287, 307–8, 311, 317, 348, 415, 425, 485–87, 569–70, 578, 610
White supremacy, xx, xxii, xxvi–xxvii, xxxiv, 165, 205, 213, 238, 277–78, 307–8, 371
White victims of lynching, 481–84, 557–58, 609
Whittier, John Greenleaf: "Song of Negro Boatmen," 199
Wigg, James E., 206
Wiggins, Joseph, 591
Wight, John B., 350–51
Wilberforce, Ohio, 476
Wilburton, Okla., 483

Wilcox, Henry, 306
Wilhelm II, 608
Wilkes County, Ga., 459
Wilkins, Beriah, 321
Wilkins, John Bird, 427
Williams, Bert, 429
Williams, David, 177
Williams, Frank, 484
Williams, Gladys, 592
Williams, John Skelton, 509
Williams, L. H., 595–96
Williams, Wallace, 550
Williams, Mrs. (of Houston), 546
Williams and Walker Company, 429–30
Willis, Pink, 482
Wilmington, Del., 396
Wilmington, N.C., xxv, 282, 284–89
Wilmington Daily Record, xxv, 282, 284–85, 288–89
Wilmington Morning Star, 280–85
Wilson, Harry, 585, 588
Wilson, J. Finley, 585
Wilson, James, 309
Wilson, Joseph T., 177
Wilson, Muriel, 429
Wilson, Stanyarne, 318–19
Wilson, Woodrow, xxvi, xxxi–xxxii, 498–513, 520, 605, 616
Windom, William, 16, 28–39
Wisconsin, 166, 259
Wise, Stephen S., 475–76
Wolfe, James, 177
Women: black, and the "Negro problem," 328–35; black, and race discrimination, 433–42; black, rights of, 613; black, on the stage, 428–32; in domestic service, xxvi, 93, 98, 198–99, 329, 333, 613; northern, as teachers in the South, 194–95; political power of, xxix–xxx, 6–7; poor white, 280–81, 283–84; and rape, 130–33, 135, 137–38, 140–43, 146–47, 150, 159, 191–93, 281–83, 334, 370
Woman's Christian Temperance Union, 170
Wood, Fernando, 6
Woodson, Carter G., 585
Woolley, Celia Parker, 476
Woolley, Mary E., 475
Worcester, Mass., 343–45
World's Columbian Exposition, 154, 156–57, 160, 163–64
World War I, xxx–xxxiv, 524–25, 527, 543, 554–55, 557–58, 568, 577–83, 588, 597, 604–5, 607–8, 610, 616
Worth, B. G., 285
Wright, R. R., Jr., 476
Wright, Robert F., 447
Wright, Silas P., 288
Wyatt, Rolly, 482
Wyoming, 166

Yazoo City, Miss., 483
Yazoo County, Miss., 165, 190
Yellow fever epidemic, 173
Yellow journalism, 521
Yick Wo v. Hopkins, 259, 562
Yonkers, N.Y., 476
Young Men's Christian Association, 170, 332

Zneblin, Charles, 475
Zwingli, Ulrich, 298

*This book is set in 10 point ITC Galliard, a face designed
for digital composition by Matthew Carter and based
on the sixteenth-century face Granjon. The paper is acid-free
lightweight opaque that will not turn yellow or brittle with age.
The binding is sewn, which allows the book to open easily and lie flat.
The binding board is covered in Brillianta, a woven rayon cloth
made by Van Heek–Scholco Textielfabrieken, Holland.
Composition by Dianna Logan, Clearmont, MO.
Printing by Sheridan, Grand Rapids, MI.
Binding by Dekker Bookbinding, Wyoming, MI.
Designed by Bruce Campbell.*

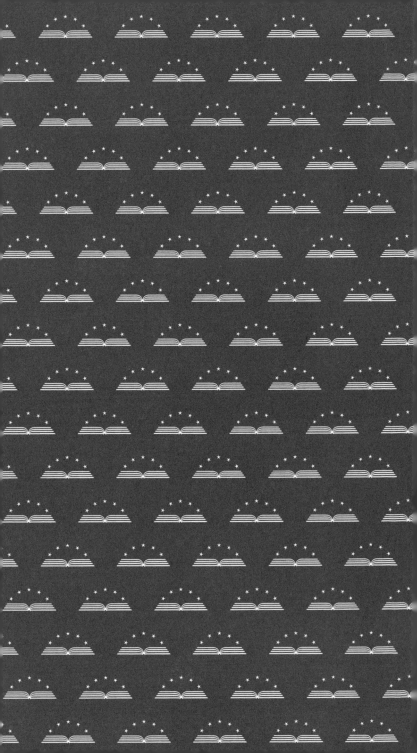